Rick

ROME

Rick Steves & Gene Openshaw

2017

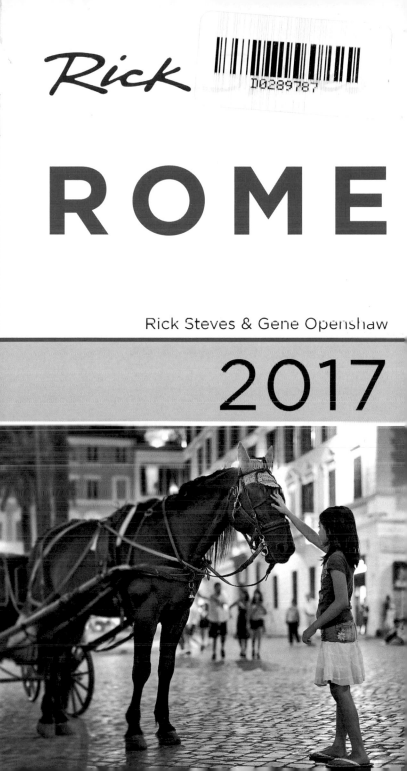

CONTENTS

▶ **Introduction** 1

▶ **Orientation to Rome** 11

▶ **Sights in Rome** 34
   Ancient Rome 35
   Pantheon Neighborhood 58
   Vatican City and Nearby 62
   North Rome. 67
   East Rome 78
   Trastevere and Nearby 91
   South Rome. 96

▶ **Self-Guided Walks & Tours**
   CENTRAL ROME
   Heart of Rome Walk 110
   Pantheon Tour. 125
   Colosseum Tour 142
   Roman Forum Tour 157
   Palatine Hill Tour. 174
   Capitoline Museums Tour. . . .186
   St. Peter-in-Chains Tour 196
   Jewish Ghetto Walk. 201

VATICAN CITY
   St. Peter's Basilica Tour. 211
   Vatican Museums Tour 235

NORTH ROME
   Borghese Gallery Tour 271

EAST ROME
   National Museum of Rome . 286
   Pilgrim's Rome Tour. 301

SOUTH ROME
   Trastevere Walk 319
   Ancient Appian Way Tour . . 332

▶ **Sleeping in Rome**. 343
   Near Termini Station 344
   Near Ancient Rome. 350
   Pantheon Neighborhood . . . 352
   Trastevere. 358
   Near Vatican City 360

▶ **Eating in Rome** 362
  Eating Tips 363
  Trastevere 365
  Jewish Ghetto 368
  Pantheon Neighborhood . . . 369
  North Rome: Near the Spanish
    Steps and Ara Pacis 377
  Ancient Rome: Near the
    Colosseum and Forum 378
  Near Termini Station 382
  Near Vatican City 383
  Testaccio 386

▶ **Rome with Children** 389

▶ **Shopping in Rome** 398

▶ **Nightlife in Rome** 410

▶ **Rome Connections** 417

▶ **Day Trips** 427
  Ostia Antica 429
  Tivoli 441
  Naples & Pompeii 449

▶ **Roman History** 495

▶ **Practicalities** 503
  Tourist Information 503
  Travel Tips 504
  Money 505
  Sightseeing 510
  Sleeping 513
  Eating 521
  Staying Connected 539
  Transportation 545
  Resources from
    Rick Steves 555

▶ **Appendix** 559
  Useful Contacts 559
  Holidays and Festivals 560
  Recommended Books
    and Films 561
  Conversions and Climate . . . 564
  Packing Checklist 567
  Italian Survival Phrases 569

▶ **Index** 571

▶ **Map Index** 586

West Rome

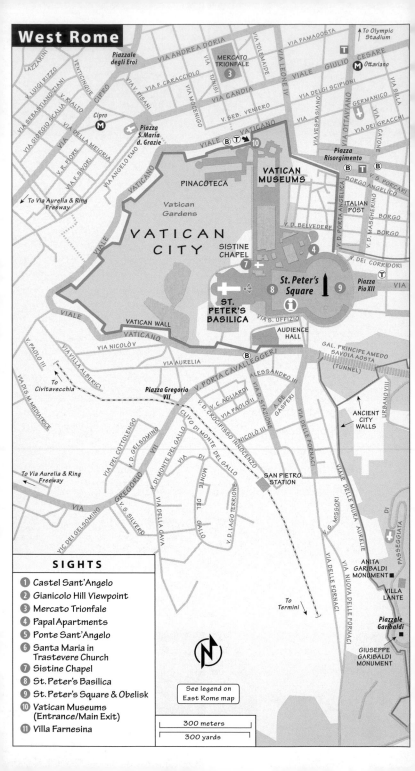

SIGHTS

1. Castel Sant'Angelo
2. Gianicolo Hill Viewpoint
3. Mercato Trionfale
4. Papal Apartments
5. Ponte Sant'Angelo
6. Santa Maria in Trastevere Church
7. Sistine Chapel
8. St. Peter's Basilica
9. St. Peter's Square & Obelisk
10. Vatican Museums (Entrance/Main Exit)
11. Villa Farnesina

See legend on East Rome map

300 meters
300 yards

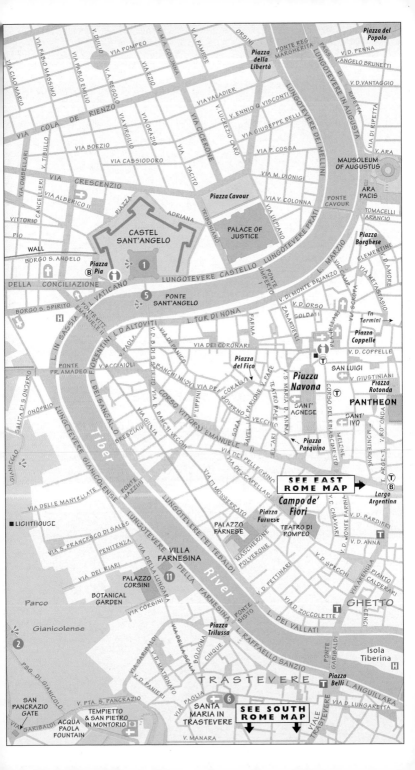

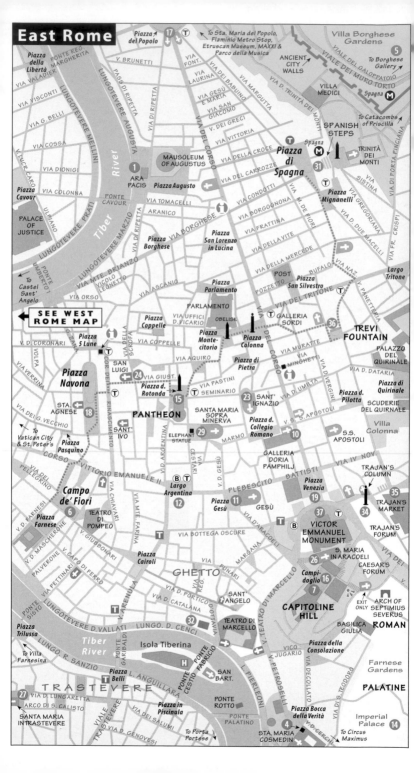

SIGHTS

1. Ara Pacis
2. Arch of Constantine
3. Baths of Diocletian
4. Bocca della Verità
5. To Borghese Gallery
6. Campo de' Fiori
7. Capitoline Museums
8. Capuchin Crypt
9. Colosseum
10. Galleria Doria Pamphilj
11. Gesù Church
12. Largo Argentina
13. Nat'l Museum of Rome
14. Palatine Hill
15. Pantheon
16. Piazza del Campidoglio
17. Piazza del Popolo
18. Piazza Navona
19. Piazza Venezia
20. Roman Forum
21. St. Peter-in-Chains Church
22. San Clemente Church
23. Sant'Ignazio Church
24. San Luigi dei Francesi Church
25. S. Maria della Vittoria Church
26. S. Maria in Aracoeli Church
27. S. Maria in Trastevere Church
28. S. Maria Maggiore Church
29. S. Maria sopra Minerva Church
30. Santa Susanna Church
31. Spanish Steps
32. Synagogue & Jewish Museum
33. Termini Train Station
34. Trajan's Column
35. Trajan's Market & Museum of the Imperial Forums
36. Trevi Fountain
37. Victor Emmanuel Monument

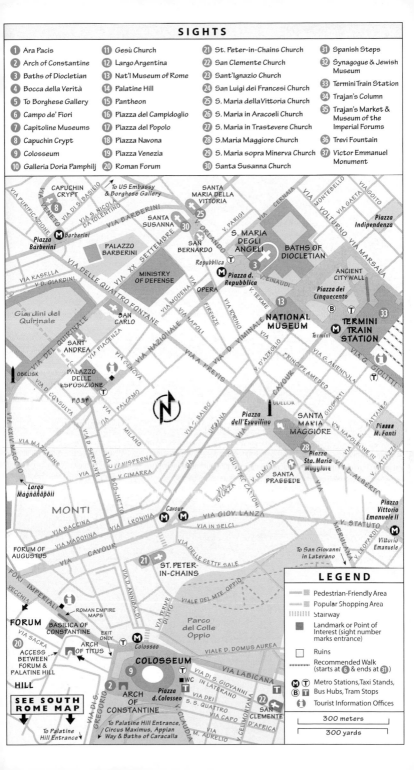

LEGEND

- Pedestrian-Friendly Area
- Popular Shopping Area
- Stairway
- Landmark or Point of Interest (sight number marks entrance)
- Ruins
- Recommended Walk (starts at 6 & ends at 31)
- M T Metro Stations, Taxi Stands,
- B T Bus Hubs, Tram Stops
- Tourist Information Offices

300 meters
300 yards

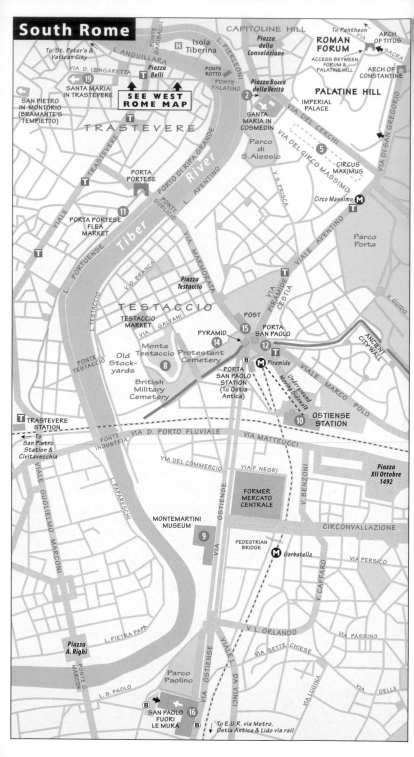

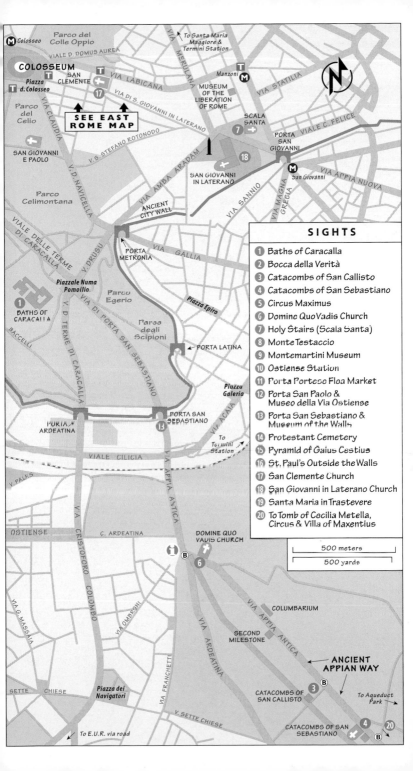

Parco del Colle Oppio

M Colosseo

VIALE D. DOMUS AUREA

COLOSSEUM

T Piazza d. Colosseo

T SAN CLEMENTE

T ⑰

VIA LABICANA

VIA MERULANA

To Santa Maria Maggiore & Termini Station

Manzoni **M**

VIA STATILIA

N

VIA DI S. GIOVANNI IN LATERANO

MUSEUM OF THE LIBERATION OF ROME

Parco del Celio

VIA CLAUDIA

SAN GIOVANNI E PAOLO

SEE EAST ROME MAP

V. S. STEFANO ROTONODO

V. D. NAVICELLA

ANCIENT CITY WALL

SCALA SANTA

⑦

PORTA SAN GIOVANNI

VIALE C. FELICE

⑱

SAN GIOVANNI IN LATERANO

M San Giovanni

VIA APPIA NUOVA

Parco Celimontana

VIA AMBA ARADAM

VIA SANNIO

VIA MAGNA GRECIA

VIALE DELLE TERME DI CARACALLA

V. DRUSU

PORTA METRONIA

VIA GALLIA

Piazza Epiro

BACCELLI

Piazzale Numa Pomilio

① BATHS OF CARACALLA

V. D. TERME DI CARACALLA

Parco Egerio

Parco degli Scipioni

PORTA LATINA

Piazza Galeria

VIA DI PORTA SAN SEBASTIANO

PORTA ARDEATINA

PORTA SAN SEBASTIANO ⑬

VIA ACAIA

To Termini Station

VIALE CILICIA

V. PALES

To Termini Station

APPIA ANTICA

V. CRISTOFORO COLOMBO

OSTIENSE

C. ARDEATINA

V. G. MASSAIA

SETTE CHIESE

Piazza dei Navigatori

VIA FRANCHETTI

VIA ARDEATINA

V. SETTE CHIESE

To E.U.R. via road

DOMINE QUO VADIS CHURCH

ⓘ **B**

✝ ⑥

VIA APPIA ANTICA

COLUMBARIUM

SECOND MILESTONE

ANCIENT APPIAN WAY

CATACOMBS OF SAN CALLISTO

③ **B**

To Aqueduct Park

CATACOMBS OF SAN SEBASTIANO

④ ⑳

B

SIGHTS

① Baths of Caracalla
② Bocca della Verità
③ Catacombs of San Callisto
④ Catacombs of San Sebastiano
⑤ Circus Maximus
⑥ Domine Quo Vadis Church
⑦ Holy Stairs (Scala Santa)
⑧ Monte Testaccio
⑨ Montemartini Museum
⑩ Ostiense Station
⑪ Porta Portese Flea Market
⑫ Porta San Paolo & Museo della Via Ostiense
⑬ Porta San Sebastiano & Museum of the Walls
⑭ Protestant Cemetery
⑮ Pyramid of Gaius Cestius
⑯ St. Paul's Outside the Walls
⑰ San Clemente Church
⑱ San Giovanni in Laterano Church
⑲ Santa Maria in Trastevere
⑳ To Tomb of Cecilia Metella, Circus & Villa of Maxentius

500 meters

500 yards

National Museum of Rome

Roman Forum

Dining near the Pantheon

Rick Steves®

ROME

2017

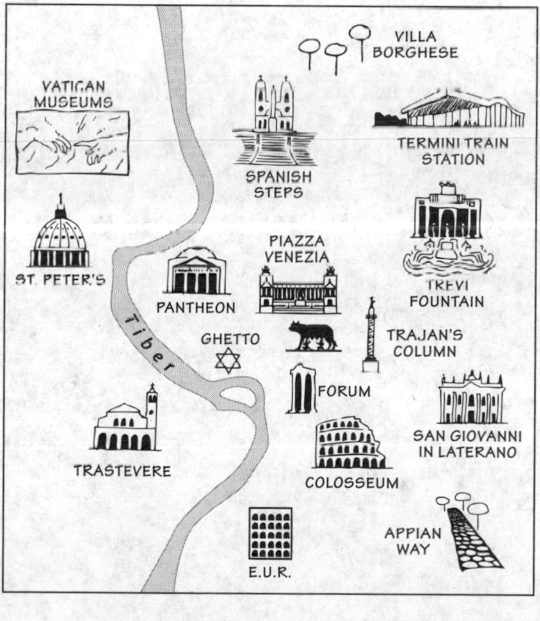

INTRODUCTION

Rome is magnificent and brutal at the same time. It's a showcase of Western civilization, with astonishingly ancient sights and a modern vibrancy. But if you're careless, you'll be run down or pickpocketed. And with the wrong attitude, you'll be frustrated by the kind of chaos that only an Italian can understand. On my last visit, a cabbie struggling with the traffic said, *"Roma chaos."* I responded, *"Bella chaos."* He agreed.

Rome is a magnificent tangled urban forest. If your hotel provides a comfortable refuge; if you pace yourself; if you accept—and even partake in—the siesta plan; if you're well-organized for sightseeing; and if you protect yourself and your valuables with extra caution and discretion, you'll love it. (And Rome is much easier to live with if you can avoid the midsummer heat.)

Over two thousand years ago the word "Rome" meant civilization itself. Everything was either civilized (part of the Roman world) or barbarian. Today, Rome is Italy's political capital, the capital of Catholicism, and the center of its ancient empire, littered with evocative remains. As you peel through its fascinating and jumbled layers, you'll find Rome's buildings, cats, laundry, traffic, and 2.7 million people endlessly entertaining. And then, of course, there are its stupendous sights.

Visit St. Peter's, the greatest church on earth, and scale Michelangelo's 448-foot-tall dome. Learn something about eternity at the huge Vatican Museums, where you'll find the story of creation—bright as the day it was painted—in the restored Sistine Chapel. Do the "Caesar Shuffle" through ancient Rome's Forum and Colosseum. Savor the sumptuous Borghese Gallery, and take an early evening "Dolce Vita Stroll" down Via del Corso with Rome's beautiful people. Dine well at least once. And enjoy an

Map Legend

⅃ Viewpoint	✈ Airport	) ⊂ Tunnel
⬆ Entrance	Ⓣ Taxi Stand	Pedestrian Zone
⊕ Tourist Info	⊤ Tram Stop	------ Railway
WC Restroom	⊕ Bus Stop	············ Ferry/Boat Route
⬛ Castle	Ⓜ Metro Stop	⊢———⊣ Tram
⬆ Church	℗ Parking	⫶⫶⫶⫶⫶ Stairs
▪ Statue/Point of Interest	⬙ Gelato	······ Walk/Tour Route
⊠ Elevator	Park	------- Trail

Use this legend to help you navigate the maps in this book.

after-dark walk from Campo de' Fiori to the Spanish Steps, lacing together Rome's Baroque and bubbly nightspots.

ABOUT THIS BOOK

Rick Steves Rome 2017 is a personal tour guide in your pocket. Better yet, it's actually two tour guides in your pocket: The co-author of this book is Gene Openshaw. Since our first "Europe through the gutter" trip together as high school buddies in the 1970s, Gene and I have been exploring the wonders of the Old World. An inquisitive historian and lover of European culture, Gene wrote most of this book's self-guided museum tours and neighborhood walks. Together, Gene and I keep this book current (though for simplicity, from this point "we" will shed our respective egos and become "I").

In this book, you'll find the following chapters:

Orientation to Rome has specifics on public transportation, helpful hints, local tour options, easy-to-read maps, and tourist information. The "Planning Your Time" section suggests a schedule for how to best use your limited time.

Sights in Rome describes the top attractions and includes their cost and hours.

The **Self-Guided Walks and Tours** lead you through the heart of Rome, connecting the great monuments and atmospheric squares. You'll tour the Pantheon, Colosseum, Roman Forum, Palatine Hill, Capitoline Museums. You'll visit the pilgrimage churches, including the grandest of all—St. Peter's. You'll see the Vatican Museums, Borghese Gallery, National Museum of Rome, and St. Peter-in-Chains Church. You'll explore Trastevere, the crusty, colorful neighborhood across the river; learn about the Jewish ghetto, the city's old Jewish quarter; and take a spin on the ancient Appian Way.

Sleeping in Rome describes my favorite hotels, from good-

Key to This Book

Updates

This book is updated every year—but once you pin down Italy, it wiggles. For the latest, visit www.ricksteves.com/update.

Abbreviations and Times

I use the following symbols and abbreviations in this book:
Sights are rated:

▲▲▲   Don't miss

▲▲   Try hard to see

▲   Worthwhile if you can make it

No rating   Worth knowing about

Tourist information offices are abbreviated as **TI,** and bathrooms are **WCs.** Accommodations are categorized with a **Sleep Code** (described on page 514); eateries are classified with a **Restaurant Price Code** (page 522). To indicate discounts for my readers, I include **RS%** in the listings.

Like Europe, this book uses the **24-hour clock.** It's the same through 12:00 noon, then keeps going: 13:00, 14:00, and so on. For anything over 12, subtract 12 and add p.m. (14:00 is 2:00 p.m.).

When giving **opening times,** I include both peak season and off-season hours if they differ. So, if a museum is listed as "May-Oct daily 9:00-16:00," it should be open from 9 a.m. until 4 p.m. from the first day of May until the last day of October (but expect exceptions).

A ⊞ symbol in a sight listing means that sight is described in greater detail elsewhere—either with its own self-guided tour, or as part of a self-guided walk. A ∩ symbol indicates that a free, downloadable self-guided audio tour is available.

For **transit** or **tour departures,** I first list the frequency, then the duration. So, a train connection listed as "2/hour, 1.5 hours" departs twice each hour and the journey lasts an hour and a half.

value deals to cushy splurges, in several convenient (and for Rome, relatively quiet) neighborhoods near the sights.

Eating in Rome serves up a buffet of options, from inexpensive cafés to fancy restaurants.

Rome with Children includes my top recommendations for keeping your kids (and you) happy.

Shopping in Rome gives you tips for shopping painlessly and enjoyably, without letting it overwhelm your vacation or ruin your budget.

Nightlife in Rome is your guide to fun, including concerts, nightclubs, and my Dolce Vita Stroll.

Rome Connections lays the groundwork for your smooth arrival and departure, covering transportation by train, plane, bus,

INTRODUCTION

car, and cruise ship, with detailed information on Rome's two airports (Fiumicino and Ciampino) and its two train stations (the main Termini Station and smaller Tiburtina).

Day Trips cover nearby sights: Ostia Antica, Tivoli, Naples, and Pompeii.

The **Roman History** chapter takes you on a whirlwind tour through the ages, covering three millennia from ancient Rome to the city today.

The **Practicalities** chapter near the end of this book is a traveler's tool kit, with my best advice about money, sightseeing, sleeping, eating, staying connected, and transportation.

The **appendix** has the nuts-and-bolts: useful phone numbers and websites, a holiday and festival list, recommended books and films, a climate chart, a handy packing checklist, and Italian survival phrases.

Throughout this book, you'll find money- and time-saving tips for sightseeing, transportation, and more. Some businesses—especially hotels and walking tour companies—offer special discounts to my readers, indicated in their listings.

Browse through this book and select your favorite sights. Then have a great trip! Traveling like a temporary local, you'll get the absolute most out of every mile, minute, and dollar. As you visit places I know and love, I'm happy that you'll be meeting my favorite Romans.

Planning

This section will help you get started planning your trip—with advice on trip costs, when to go, and what you should know before you take off.

TRAVEL SMART

Many people travel through Italy thinking it's a chaotic mess. They feel that any attempt at efficient travel is futile. This is dead wrong—and expensive. Rome, which seems as orderly as spilled spaghetti, actually functions quite well. Only those who understand this and travel smart can enjoy Rome on a budget.

This book can save you lots of time and money. But to have an "A" trip, you need to be an "A" student. Read it all before your trip, noting holidays, specific advice on sights, and days when sights are closed. For instance, to see the Borghese Gallery, you must reserve ahead. If you go to the Vatican Museums on a Sunday, you'll run smack into closed doors, or—if it's the last Sunday of the month—huge crowds. You can wait an hour to buy a ticket at the Colosseum, or save time by buying your ticket online or at the nearby Palatine Hill. Day-tripping to Ostia Antica on Monday is bad news. Designing a smart trip is a puzzle—a fun, doable, and worthwhile challenge.

Make your itinerary a mix of intense and relaxed stretches. Every trip—and every traveler—needs slack time (laundry, picnics, people-watching, and so on). Pace yourself. Assume you will return.

Even with the best-planned itinerary, you'll need to be flexible. Update your plans as you travel. Get online or call ahead to learn the latest on sights (special events, tour schedules, and so on), book tickets and tours, make reservations, reconfirm hotels, and research transportation connections.

Enjoy the friendliness of the Roman people. Connect with the culture. Set up your own quest for the best piazza, church facade, or gelato. Slow down and be open to unexpected experiences. Ask questions—most locals are eager to point you in their idea of the right direction. Keep a notepad in your pocket for noting directions, organizing your thoughts, and confirming prices. Wear your money belt, learn the currency, and figure out how to estimate prices in dollars. Those who expect to travel smart, do.

TRIP COSTS

Six components make up your trip costs: airfare to Europe, transportation in Europe, room and board, sightseeing and entertainment, shopping/miscellany, and gelato.

Airfare to Europe: A basic round-trip flight from the US to Rome can cost, on average, about $1,000-2,000 total, depending on where you fly from and when (cheaper in winter). If Rome is part of a longer trip, consider saving time and money in Europe by flying into one city and out of another; for instance, into Rome and out of Paris. Overall, Kayak.com is the best place to start searching for flights on a combination of mainstream and budget carriers.

Transportation in Europe: For a typical one-week visit, allow $60-100 for taxis (which can be shared by up to four people); if you opt for buses and the Metro, figure about $30 per person. The cost of round-trip transportation to day-trip destinations ranges from minimal (a few dollars to get to Tivoli or Ostia Antica) to pricey ($90 for second-class train tickets for a day trip to Naples and Pompeii—book a month in advance for deals). For a one-way trip between Rome's main airport and the city center, allow $15 per person by train or about $55 by taxi (can be shared by up to 4 people). For more on trains and flights, see "Transportation" in Practicalities.

Room and Board: You can manage comfortably in Rome in 2017 on $125 a day per person for room and board. This allows $15 for lunch, $30 for dinner, and $80 for lodging (based on two people splitting the cost of a $160 double room). Students and tightwads

Rome Almanac

Population: Approximately 2.7 million people

Currency: Euro (€)

Nickname: The Eternal City

City Layout: Rome, the capital of Italy, is divided into 22 *rioni* (districts). Of the famous seven hills of Rome, you're most likely to see Palatine Hill (birthplace of the legendary founders of the city, Romulus and Remus), Capitoline Hill (topped by museums and a Michelangelo-designed square), and the Quirinale, one of the highest of the hills and the site of many of my recommended hotels.

Best Viewpoints: From the rooftop of the Victor Emmanuel Monument (you can take the Rome from the Sky elevator to the top); from the top of the dome of St. Peter's Basilica; and from the top of Castel Sant'Angelo. The best view of the Roman Forum is from Capitoline Hill—particularly the Tabularium (underground galleries) that are part of the Capitoline Museums.

Best Strolls: Two major thoroughfares are open to pedestrians and closed to traffic: the northern part of Via del Corso (best for strolling Mon-Sat around 17:00-19:00, earlier afternoon on Sun) and the southern part of Via dei Fori Imperiali (open to buses/taxis Mon-Sat, closed to all vehicles Sun). My two favorite walks in Rome take me through Trastevere, and through the heart of the city at night. The Monti area (near the Roman Forum) is another enjoyable area to wander.

Tourist Tracks: The Colosseum attracts about 5.9 million visitors every year. About €3,000 is collected from the Trevi Fountain daily.

Culture Count: The vast majority of Romans are indigenous Italians; only about 10 percent of the city's residents are immigrants, mostly from Poland, Romania, Ukraine, and Albania. Rome's population is largely Roman Catholic.

Average Roman: The average Roman is 44 years old, has 1.4 children, and will live until the age of 82.

can enjoy Rome for as little as $65 a day ($35 for a hostel bed, $30 for meals and snacks).

Sightseeing and Entertainment: Figure about $15-20 per major sight (Colosseum, Vatican Museums), $2 for minor ones (lights to illuminate art in churches), and $30 for splurge experiences (such as concerts). An overall average of $20 per day works for most people. Don't skimp here. After all, this category is the driving force behind your trip—you came to sightsee, enjoy, and experience Rome.

Shopping and Miscellany: Figure $2 per postcard and $3 per coffee, soft drink, and gelato. Shopping can vary in cost from nearly nothing to a small fortune. Good budget travelers find that this category has little to do with assembling a trip full of lifelong memories.

WHEN TO GO

Rome's best travel months (also busiest and most expensive) are April, May, June, September, October, and early November. These months combine the convenience of peak season with pleasant weather.

The most grueling thing about travel in Rome is the summer heat in July and August, when temperatures can soar to the high 90s and pricier hotels discount their rooms. Fortunately air-conditioning is the norm in all but the cheapest hotels (though it's generally available only from June through September).

Spring and fall can be cool, and many hotels do not turn on their heat. Rome is fine in winter—cool and crisp with temperatures in the 40s and 50s (for more information, see the climate chart in the appendix). Street life stays in full swing all year, restaurants set up heaters to warm the outdoor tables, and nativity scenes grace churches through January. Off-season has none of the sweat and stress of the tourist season, but sights may have shorter hours, lunchtime breaks, and fewer activities. Confirm your sightseeing plans locally, especially when traveling off-season.

KNOW BEFORE YOU GO

Check this list of things to arrange while you're still at home.

You need a **passport**—but no visa or shots—to travel in Italy. You may be denied entry into certain European countries if your passport is due to expire within six months of your ticketed date of return. Get it renewed if you'll be cutting it close. It can take up to six weeks to get or renew a passport (for more on passports and requirements for Italy, see www.travel.state.gov). Pack a photocopy of your passport in your luggage in case the original is lost or stolen.

Book rooms well in advance if you'll be traveling during the peak of the summer season and any major **holidays** (see page 560).

Call your **debit- and credit-card companies** to let them know the countries you'll be visiting, to ask about fees, to request your PIN if you don't already know it, and more. See page 506 for details.

Do your homework if you're considering **travel insurance.** Compare the cost of the insurance to the cost of your potential loss. Also check whether your existing insurance (health, homeowners, or renters) covers you and your possessions overseas. For more information, see www.ricksteves.com/insurance.

If you're taking an **overnight train** (especially between Rome and Vienna or Munich), and need a couchette *(cuccetta)* or sleeper—and you *must* leave on a certain day—consider booking it in

Rick Steves Audio Europe

My free **Rick Steves Audio Europe app** is a great tool for enjoying Europe. This app makes it easy to download my audio tours of top attractions, plus hours of travel interviews, all organized into destination-specific playlists.

My self-guided **audio tours** of major sights and neighborhoods are free, user-friendly, fun, and informative. In this book, these audio tours include the Pantheon, St. Peter's Basilica, Roman Forum, Colosseum, Sistine Chapel, Vatican Museums, Heart of Rome Walk, Trastevere Walk, Jewish Ghetto Walk, Ostia Antica, and Pompeii. Sights covered by my audio tours are marked with this symbol: ∩. These audio tours are hard to beat: Nobody will stand you up, your eyes are free to appreciate the sights, you can take the tour exactly when you like, and the price is right.

The Rick Steves Audio Europe app also offers a far-reaching library of insightful **travel interviews** from my public radio show with experts from around the globe—including many of the places in this book.

This app and all of its content are entirely free. (New content is added about twice a year.) You can download Rick Steves Audio Europe via Apple's App Store, Google Play, or the Amazon Appstore. For more information, see www.ricksteves.com/audioeurope.

advance through a US agent (such as www.ricksteves.com/rail), even though it may cost more than buying it in Italy. Other Italian trains, such as high-speed ES trains, require a seat reservation, but it's usually possible to make these arrangements in Italy just a few days ahead. (For more on train travel, see Practicalities.)

While plenty of the city's sights can be nearly empty, the famous ones come with very long lines. These lines are largely avoidable if you follow the directions in this book to **get tickets or make reservations in advance.** Reservations for the Vatican Museums are smart (see page 236) and may be helpful for the Colosseum and the Roman Forum (see page 143). Reservations are required for the Borghese Gallery (see page 271).

If you plan to hire a **local guide,** reserve ahead by email. Popular guides can get booked up.

If you're bringing a **mobile device,** consider signing up for an international plan for cheaper calls, texts, and data (see page 539). Download any apps you might want to use on the road, such as translators, maps, transit schedules, and **Rick Steves Audio Europe** (see sidebar).

Check for recent updates to this book at www.ricksteves.com/update.

How Was Your Trip?

Were your travels fun, smooth, and meaningful? You can share tips, concerns, and discoveries at www.ricksteves.com/feedback. To check out readers' hotel and restaurant reviews—or leave one yourself—visit my travel forum at www.ricksteves.com/travel-forum. I value your feedback. Thanks in advance.

Traveling as a Temporary Local

We travel all the way to Italy to enjoy differences—to become temporary locals. You'll experience frustrations. Certain truths that we find "God-given" or "self-evident," such as cold beer, ice in drinks, bottomless cups of coffee, "the customer is king," and bigger being better, are suddenly not so true. One of the benefits of travel is the eye-opening realization that there are logical, civil, and even better alternatives. A willingness to go local ensures that you'll enjoy a full dose of Italian hospitality.

Europeans generally like Americans. But if there is a negative aspect to Italians' image of Americans, it's that we are loud, wasteful, ethnocentric, too informal (which can seem disrespectful), and a bit naïve. Think about the rationale behind "crazy" Italian decisions. For instance, many hoteliers turn off the heat in spring and can't turn on air-conditioning until summer. The point is to conserve energy, and it's mandated by the Italian government. You could complain about being cold or hot...or bring a sweater in winter, and in summer, be prepared to sweat a little like everyone else.

While Italians, flabbergasted by our Yankee excesses, say in disbelief, *"Mi sono cadute le braccia!"* ("I throw my arms down!"), they nearly always afford us individual travelers all the warmth we deserve.

Judging from all the happy feedback I receive from travelers who have used this book, it's safe to assume you'll enjoy a great, affordable vacation—with the finesse of an independent, experienced traveler.

Thanks, and *buon viaggio!*

Rick Steves

Back Door Travel Philosophy

From *Rick Steves Europe Through the Back Door*

Travel is intensified living—maximum thrills per minute and one of the last great sources of legal adventure. Travel is freedom. It's recess, and we need it.

Experiencing the real Europe requires catching it by surprise, going casual..."through the Back Door."

Affording travel is a matter of priorities. (Make do with the old car.) You can eat and sleep—simply, safely, and enjoyably—anywhere in Europe for $100 a day plus transportation costs. In many ways, spending more money only builds a thicker wall between you and what you traveled so far to see. Europe is a cultural carnival, and time after time, you'll find that its best acts are free and the best seats are the cheap ones.

A tight budget forces you to travel close to the ground, meeting and communicating with the people. Never sacrifice sleep, nutrition, safety, or cleanliness to save money. Simply enjoy the local-style alternatives to expensive hotels and restaurants.

Connecting with people carbonates your experience. Extroverts have more fun. If your trip is low on magic moments, kick yourself and make things happen. If you don't enjoy a place, maybe you don't know enough about it. Seek the truth. Recognize tourist traps. Give a culture the benefit of your open mind. See things as different, but not better or worse. Any culture has plenty to share. When an opportunity presents itself, make it a habit to say "yes."

Of course, travel, like the world, is a series of hills and valleys. Be fanatically positive and militantly optimistic. If something's not to your liking, change your liking.

Travel can make you a happier American, as well as a citizen of the world. Our Earth is home to seven billion equally precious people. It's humbling to travel and find that other people don't have the "American Dream"—they have their own dreams. Europeans like us, but with all due respect, they wouldn't trade passports.

Thoughtful travel engages us with the world. It reminds us what is truly important. By broadening perspectives, travel teaches new ways to measure quality of life.

Globetrotting destroys ethnocentricity, helping us understand and appreciate other cultures. Rather than fear the diversity on this planet, celebrate it. Among your most prized souvenirs will be the strands of different cultures you choose to knit into your own character. The world is a cultural yarn shop, and Back Door travelers are weaving the ultimate tapestry. Join in!

ORIENTATION
TO ROME

Sprawling Rome actually feels manageable once you get to know it.
The old core, with most of the tourist sights, sits inside a diamond
formed by Termini train station (in the east), the Vatican (west),
Villa Borghese Gardens (north), and the Colosseum (south). The
Tiber River snakes through the diamond from north to south. At
the center of the diamond is Piazza Venezia, a busy square and
traffic hub. It takes about an hour to walk from Termini Station to
the Vatican.

ROME: A VERBAL MAP

Think of Rome as a collection of neighborhoods, huddling around
major landmarks.

Ancient Rome: In ancient times, this was home to the grandest buildings of a city of a million people. Today, the best of the
classical sights stand in a line from the Colosseum to the Forum to
the Pantheon. Just north of this area, between Via Nazionale and
Via Cavour, is the atmospheric and trendy Monti district.

Pantheon Neighborhood: The Pantheon anchors the neighborhood I like to call the "Heart of Rome." It stretches eastward
from the Tiber River through Campo de' Fiori and Piazza Navona,
past the Pantheon to the Trevi Fountain. Between the river and the
Pantheon area is the former Jewish ghetto.

Vatican City: Located west of the Tiber, it's a compact world
of its own, with two great, huge sights: St. Peter's Basilica and the
Vatican Museums.

North Rome: With the Spanish Steps, Villa Borghese Gardens, and trendy shopping streets (Via Veneto and the "shopping
triangle"—the area along Via del Corso and between the Spanish
Steps, Piazza Venezia, and Piazza del Popolo), this is a more modern, classy area.

East Rome: This includes the area around Termini Station and Piazza della Repubblica, with many recommended hotels and public-transportation connections. Just to the south and east is the neighborhood I call "Pilgrim's Rome," with several prominent churches.

Trastevere: South of Vatican City and just west of the Pantheon neighborhood is Trastevere, the colorful, wrong-side-of-the-river neighborhood with a village feel. It's the city at its crustiest—and perhaps most "Roman."

South Rome: Farther south are the postindustrial Testaccio neighborhood, the 1930s suburb of E.U.R., and the Appian Way, home of the catacombs.

Within each of these neighborhoods, you'll find elements from the many layers of Rome's 2,500-year story: the marble ruins of ancient times; tangled streets of the medieval world; early Christian churches; grand Renaissance buildings and statues; Baroque fountains and church facades; 19th-century apartments; and 21st-century boulevards choked with traffic.

Since no one is allowed to build taller than St. Peter's dome, and virtually no buildings have been constructed in the city center since Mussolini got distracted in 1938, central Rome has no modern skyline. The Tiber River is basically ignored—after Italy unified (1870) and Rome became the capital, the banks were built up very high to guard against the frequent floods, and Rome turned its back on its naughty river.

PLANNING YOUR TIME

After considering Rome's major tourist sights, I've covered just my favorites. You won't be able to see all of these, so don't try—assume you'll come back. After several dozen visits, I still have a healthy list of excuses to return.

Rome in a Day

Some people actually "do" Rome in a day. Crazy as that sounds, if all you have is a day, it's one of the most exciting days Europe has to offer. Start at 8:30 at the Colosseum. Then explore the Forum, hike over Capitoline Hill, and cap your "Caesar Shuffle" with a visit to the Pantheon. After a quick lunch, taxi to the Vatican Museums (the lines usually die down midafternoon, or you can reserve a visit online in advance). See the Vatican Museums, then St. Peter's Basilica (open until 19:00 April-Sept). Taxi back to Campo de' Fiori to find dinner. Finish your day lacing together all the famous floodlit spots (see my Heart of Rome Walk chapter). Note: This busy plan is possible only if you ace the line-avoidance tricks.

Overview of Maps

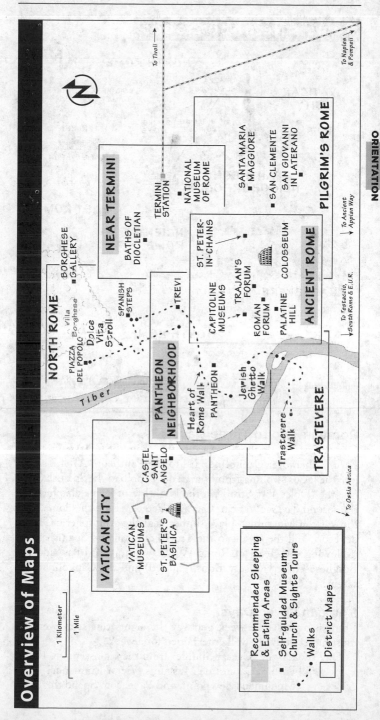

Rome's Neighborhoods

- VATICAN MUSEUMS
- VATICAN CITY
- ST. PETER'S
- NORTH ROME
- PIAZZA DEL POPOLO
- VILLA BORGHESE
- BORGHESE GALLERY
- "SHOPPING TRIANGLE"
- SPANISH STEPS
- TERMINI
- TRAIN STATION
- NATIONAL MUSEUM
- PANTHEON NEIGHBORHOOD
- PIAZZA VENEZIA
- Tiber River
- EAST ROME
- CAPITOLINE HILL
- ANCIENT ROME
- FORUM
- COLOSSEUM
- PILGRIM'S ROME
- SAN GIOVANNI IN LATERANO
- SANTA MARIA
- TRASTEVERE
- TESTACCIO
- SOUTH ROME
- SOUTH OF TESTACCIO
- E.U.R.
- APPIAN WAY
- Not to Scale

Rome in Two to Three Days

On the first day, do the "Caesar Shuffle" from the Colosseum to the Forum, then over Capitoline Hill to the Pantheon. After a siesta, join the locals strolling from Piazza del Popolo to the Spanish Steps (see the "Dolce Vita Stroll" in the Nightlife in Rome chapter). On the second day, see Vatican City (St. Peter's, climb the dome, tour the Vatican Museums). Have dinner near the atmospheric Campo de' Fiori, and then walk to the Trevi Fountain and Spanish Steps (following my Heart of Rome Walk). With a third day, add the Borghese Gallery (reservations required) and the Capitoline Museums.

Rome in Seven Days

Rome is a great one-week getaway. Its sights can keep even the most fidgety traveler well entertained for a week.

Day 1: Do the "Caesar Shuffle" from the Colosseum to the Forum, Capitoline Museums, Victor Emmanuel Monument viewpoint, and Pantheon. Spend the late

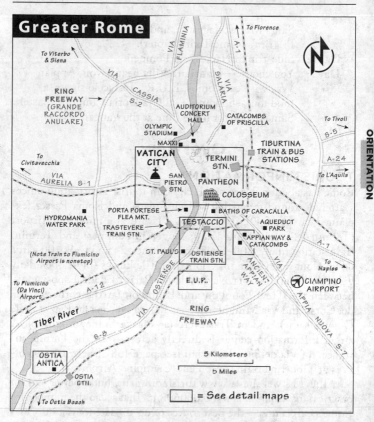

Greater Rome

To Florence

To Viterbo & Siena

VIA FLAMINIA

VIA SALARIA
A-1

VIA CASSIA S-2

RING FREEWAY (GRANDE RACCORDO ANULARE)

AUDITORIUM CONCERT HALL

CATACOMBS OF PRISCILLA

To Tivoli
S-5

OLYMPIC STADIUM

MAXXI

TIBURTINA TRAIN & BUS STATIONS

VATICAN CITY

To Civitavecchia

VIA AURELIA S-1

SAN PIETRO STN.

TERMINI STN.

PANTHEON

COLOSSEUM

A-24

To L'Aquila

PORTA PORTESE FLEA MKT.

BATHS OF CARACALLA

HYDROMANIA WATER PARK

TRASTEVERE TRAIN STN.

TESTACCIO

AQUEDUCT PARK

APPIAN WAY & CATACOMBS

A-7

ST. PAUL'S

OSTIENSE TRAIN STN.

(Note Train to Fiumicino Airport is nonstop)

ANCIENT APPIAN WAY

VIA APPIA NUOVA S-7

To Naples

To Fiumicino (Da Vinci) Airport

A-12

VIA OSTIENSE

E.U.R.

CIAMPINO AIRPORT

Tiber River

RING FREEWAY

S-8

OSTIA ANTICA

OSTIA STN.

5 Kilometers

5 Miles

To Ostia Beach

☐ = See detail maps

ORIENTATION

afternoon doing the Heart of Rome Walk. While it's an exhausting day, you now have your bearings and have seen the essential Rome.

Day 2: Morning—National Museum of Rome and the nearby Baths of Diocletian. In the afternoon do my Jewish Ghetto Walk followed immediately by the Trastevere Walk. Enjoy dinner in Trastevere.

Day 3: Vatican City—St. Peter's Basilica, dome climb, and Vatican Museums. Spend the early evening shopping and enjoying the local *passeggiata* by doing the "Dolce Vita Stroll."

Day 4: Side-trip to Ostia Antica (closed Mon). In the evening, you could repeat my Heart of Rome Walk from Campo de' Fiori to the Spanish Steps to enjoy the after-dark scene.

Day 5: Borghese Gallery (reservation required) and Pilgrim's Rome: the churches of San Giovanni in Laterano,

Santa Maria Maggiore, and San Clemente (see Pilgrim's Rome Tour chapter).

Day 6: Side-trip to Naples and Pompeii.

Day 7: You choose—Hadrian's Villa near Tivoli, Appian Way with catacombs, E.U.R., Testaccio sights, a food tour, shopping, Galleria Doria Pamphilj, Castel Sant'Angelo, or more time at the Vatican.

Overview

TOURIST INFORMATION

Rome has about a dozen small city-run tourist information offices scattered around town that sell city maps and Roma Passes (explained on page 42). The largest TIs are at Fiumicino Airport (Terminal 3, daily 9:00-17:30, longer in summer) and Termini train station (daily 8:00-18:45, exit by track 24 and walk 100 yards down along Via Giovanni Giolitti). Little kiosks (most open daily 9:30-19:00) are on Via Nazionale (at Palazzo delle Esposizioni), between the Trevi Fountain and Pantheon (at the corner of Via del Corso and Via Minghetti), near Piazza Navona (at Piazza delle Cinque Lune), and in Trastevere (at Piazza Sidney Sonnino). A larger information center is directly across from the Forum entrance, on Via dei Fori Imperiali (see page 158). There are also offices at Tiburtina train station and Ciampino Airport.

The TI's website is www.turismoroma.it, but a better site for practical information is www.060608.it. That's also the number for Rome's **call center**—the best source of up-to-date tourist information, with English speakers on staff (answered daily 9:00-21:00, just dial 06-0608, and press 2 for English).

At any TI, ask for a free city map (or pay for a better one). Your hotel will have a freebie map and may also have a booklet with up-to-date listings of the city's sights and hours. To find the city's many small streets and alleys, map apps work better than paper maps. If you do want a paper map, you'll find better quality ones at bookstores than at newsstands. See page 21 for recommended public transport maps.

Several English-language **websites,** oriented to those staying longer in Rome, provide insight into events and daily life in the city: www.inromenow.com (light tourist info on lots of topics), www.wantedinrome.com (events and accommodations), and www.rome.angloinfo.com (on living in and moving to Rome).

ARRIVAL IN ROME

For a rundown of Rome's train stations and airports, see the Rome Connections chapter.

Daily Reminder

Sunday: These sights are closed: the Vatican Museums (except for last Sun of the month, when it's free and even more crowded), Villa Farnesina (except for second Sun of the month), Catacombs of San Sebastiano, and Testaccio Market. In the morning, the Porta Portese flea market opens, and the old center is delightfully quiet. Much of the Appian Way is closed to traffic and fun to stroll. The following sights are free (and very crowded) on the first Sunday of each month, and no reservations are available: Colosseum, Roman Forum, Palatine Hill, Borghese Gallery, National Museum of Rome, Castel Sant'Angelo, Etruscan Museum, and Baths of Caracalla.

Monday: Many sights are closed, including the National Museum of Rome, Borghese Gallery, Catacombs of Priscilla, Montemartini Museum, Etruscan Museum, Museum of the Liberation of Rome, MAXXI, some Appian Way sights (Tomb of Cecilia Metella and the Circus and Villa of Maxentius), Ostia Antica, and Villa d'Este (at Tivoli).

Major sights that are open include the Colosseum, Forum, Vatican Museums, Capitoline Museum, Ara Pacis, and the Museum of the Imperial Forums (includes Trajan's Market and Trajan's Forum), among others. Churches are open as usual. The Baths of Caracalla close early in the afternoon.

Tuesday: All sights are open in Rome. This isn't a good day to side-trip to Naples because its Archaeological Museum is closed.

Wednesday: All sights are open, except the Catacombs of San Callisto. St. Peter's Basilica is typically closed in the morning for a papal audience.

Thursday/Friday: All sights are open.

Saturday: Most sights are open in Rome, except for the Synagogue and Jewish Museum.

HELPFUL HINTS

Exchange Rate: €1 = about $1.10

Country Calling Code: 39 (see page 540 for dialing instructions).

Sightseeing Tips: Those planning at least a couple days of sightseeing can save money by buying the Roma Pass (see page 42), available at TIs and participating sights—buy one before visiting the Colosseum or Forum, and you can shorten the wait in line there. Another way to speed your entry to the Colosseum and Forum is to buy a ticket online in advance (see page 143). If you want to see the Borghese Gallery, remember to reserve ahead (see page 271). To sidestep the long Vatican Museums line, reserve an entry time online (see page 236 for details).

Wi-Fi: All the hotels in this book have Wi-Fi, but if yours doesn't, your hotelier can point you to a café that does.

Useful App: ☊ For free audio versions of some of the self-guided tours in this book (the Heart of Rome, Jewish Ghetto, and Trastevere walks, and tours of the Pantheon, Colosseum, Roman Forum, St. Peter's Basilica, Vatican Museums, Sistine Chapel, and Ostia Antica), get the **Rick Steves Audio Europe** app (for details, see page 8).

Bookstores: It's easy to find stores selling English-language books (all below are open daily except Anglo American and Open Door closed Sun). There are two large chains: **Borri Books** is at Termini Station, while **Feltrinelli International,** with a large English section, is just off Piazza della Repubblica at Via Vittorio Emanuele Orlando 86 (see map on page 80, tel. 06-487-0171). A few small, independent bookstores have a more personal touch: The **Anglo-American Bookshop** has great art and history sections (closed all day Sun and Mon morning, a few blocks south of Spanish Steps at Via della Vite 102—see map on page 415, tel. 06-679-5222). In Trastevere, the **Almost Corner Bookshop** stocks an extensive Italian-interest section (Via del Moro 45—see map on page 357, tel. 06-583-6942, Dermot from Ireland), and the **Open Door Bookshop** carries the only used books in English in town (closed Sun, Via della Lungaretta 23—see map on page 357, tel. 06-589-6478).

Laundry: Coin launderettes are common in Rome; your hotelier can direct you to the closest one. The **Ondablu** chain has a branch near Termini Station (about €8/load, usually open daily 8:00-21:00, Via Principe Amedeo 70b—see map on page 384, tel. 06-474-4647). The Funny Palace Hostel's **Splashnet,** two blocks from Termini, offers full-serve laundry for about the same price (see details on page 349).

Travel Agencies: You can get train tickets and rail-pass-related reservations and supplements at travel agencies (at little or no additional cost), instead of making a trip to a train station or figuring out an online system. Your hotelier will know of a convenient agency.

Updates to This Book: For the latest, see www.ricksteves.com/update.

DEALING WITH (AND AVOIDING) PROBLEMS

Theft Alert: While violent crime is rare in the city center, petty theft is rampant. With sweet-talking con artists meeting you at the station, well-dressed pickpockets on buses, and thieving gangs of children at the ancient sites, Rome is a gauntlet of rip-offs. Pickpockets don't want to hurt you—they usually just want your money—but green or sloppy tourists will be scammed. Thieves strike when you're distracted. Don't trust kind strangers. Keep nothing important in your pockets. If you must carry a backpack, never leave it unattended and try to keep it attached to your body in some way (e.g., when you're seated for a meal). Wear it in front when riding public transportation and whenever you're in a thick crowd. Always use your money belt.

Be particularly on guard wherever there's a crowd (like at the Trevi Fountain or in front of a famous painting in a church). And be vigilant when boarding and leaving buses and subways. Thieves crowd the door, then stop and turn while others crowd and push from behind. You'll find less crowding and commotion—and less risk—waiting for the end cars of a subway rather than the middle cars. The sneakiest thieves pretend to be well-dressed businessmen (generally with something in their hands) or tourists wearing fanny packs and toting cameras. Lately a lot of youths and even pregnant mothers are working as pickpockets. Thieves are particularly thick on the Metro and the crowded and made-for-tourists buses #40 and #64.

If you know what to look out for, fast-fingered moms with babies and gangs of children picking the pockets and handbags of naive tourists are not a threat, but an interesting, albeit sad, spectacle. Pickpockets troll through the tourist crowds around the Colosseum, Forum, Vatican, train and Metro stations. Watch them target tourists who are overloaded with bags or distracted with a camera. The kids look like beggars and hold up newspapers or cardboard signs to confuse their victims. They scram like stray cats if you're on to them.

Scams abound: Always be clear about what paper money you're giving someone, demand clear and itemized bills, and count your change. Don't give your wallet to self-proclaimed "police" who stop you on the street, warn you about counterfeit (or drug) money, and ask to see your cash. If a bank machine eats your ATM card, see if there's a thin plastic insert with a tongue hanging out that thieves use to extract it.

Beggars: Throughout Rome, you'll often encounter downtrodden-looking people asking for money. Many of those you see hunched over are actually able-bodied foreigners from poorer parts of Europe, preying on people's sympathy. You may see them at churches trying to collect money, sometimes for opening church doors. But they are not affiliated, and are lining their own pockets. Know that social services are available to them, so give at your own discretion.

Reporting Losses: To report lost or stolen items, file a police report (at Termini Station, with *polizia* at track 11 or with Carabinieri at track 20; offices are also at Piazza Venezia and at the corner of Via Nazionale and Via Genova). You'll need the report to file an insurance claim for lost gear, and it can help with replacing your passport—first file the police report, then call your embassy to make an appointment (US embassy: tel. 06-46741, http://italy.usembassy.gov, Via Vittorio Veneto 121). For information on how to report lost or stolen credit cards, see page 508.

Emergency Numbers: Police—tel. 113. Ambulance—tel. 118.

Pedestrian Safety: Your main safety concern in Rome is crossing streets without incident. Use extreme caution. Some streets have pedestrian-crossing signals (red means stop—or jaywalk carefully; green means go...also carefully; and yellow means go...extremely carefully, as cars may be whipping around the corner). But just as often, multilane streets have crosswalks with no signals at all. And even when there are traffic lights, they are provisional: Scooters don't need to stop at red lights, and even cars exercise what drivers call the "logical option" of not stopping if they see no oncoming traffic. Each year, as noisy gasoline-powered scooters are replaced by electric ones, the streets get quieter (hooray) but more dangerous for pedestrians.

Follow locals like a shadow when you cross a street (or spend a good part of your visit stranded on curbs). When you do cross alone, don't be a deer in the headlights. Find a gap in the traffic and walk with confidence while making eye contact with approaching drivers—they won't hit you if they can tell where you intend to go.

Staying/Getting Healthy: The siesta is a key to survival in summertime Rome. Lie down and contemplate the extraordinary power of gravity in the Eternal City. I drink lots of cold, refreshing water from Rome's many drinking fountains (the Forum has three).

Every neighborhood has a **pharmacy** (marked by a green cross). The 24-hour Farmacia Piram is several blocks down from Piazza della Repubblica at Via Nazionale 228 (tel. 06-488-4437). Pharmacies stay open late in Termini Station (daily 7:30-22:00, along northeast side of station, enter from Via Marsala), at Piazza dei Cinquecento 51 (Mon-Fri 7:00-23:30, Sat-Sun 8:00-23:00, next to Termini Station on the corner of Via Cavour—see map on page 384, tel. 06-488-0019), and in the Pantheon neighborhood (Farmacia Senato, between Piazza Navona and the Pantheon, Mon-Fri 7:30-24:30, Sat 8:30-24:30, Sun 12:00-23:00, Corso del Rinascimento 50—see map on page 370).

Embassies and hotels can recommend English-speaking doctors. Consider MEDline, a 24-hour private home-medical service; doctors speak English and make calls at hotels for about €150 (tel. 06-808-0995, www.soccorso-medico.com). Another private clinic is International Medical Services, Via Firenze 47, tel. 06-488-2371, www.imc84.com. Anyone is entitled to free emergency treatment at public hospitals. The hospital closest to Termini Station is Policlinico Umberto 1 (entrance for emergency treatment on Via Lancisi, translators available, Metro: Policlinico).

GETTING AROUND ROME

Sightsee on foot, by city bus, by Metro, or by taxi. I've grouped your sightseeing into walkable neighborhoods. Make it a point to visit sights in a logical order. Needless backtracking wastes precious time.

Public Transportation

Rome's public transportation system is cheap and efficient, but also confusing and crowded. Consider it part of your Roman experience, and if you get a seat, think of it as a bonus. The three Metro lines are relatively sane and straightforward, but serve a limited area. Buses are more chaotic—there are no posted timetables or maps, and stop names are announced only in the newest vehicles. But they run frequently and go everywhere. If you're in town for more than a day or two, mastering a couple key bus routes serving your neighborhood is worth the effort and will make you feel like a Rome pro.

The websites www.muovi.roma.it (with a very clean, quick interface), www.agenziamobilita.roma.it, and www.atac.roma.it all have **journey planners** in English that will help you sort through the thicket of routes. The ATAC website has downloadable network maps. If you have a smartphone and an international data plan, consider downloading the free apps "Roma Bus" (by Movenda) or "Muoversi a Roma." There's no official paper map of the system, but Edizioni Lozzi produces a frequently updated "Roma Metro Bus" map for €6 (at bookstores), which includes a booklet with details on all bus routes. For information by phone, call ATAC at 06-57003.

Rome Walks has a good (though now slightly outdated) five-minute orientation video to Rome's transportation system; find it on YouTube by searching for "Understanding Rome's Public Transport."

Buying Tickets

All public transportation uses the same ticket. It costs €1.50 and is valid for one Metro ride—including transfers underground—plus unlimited city buses and trams during a 100-minute period. Passes good on buses and the Metro are sold in increments of 24 hours (€7), 48 hours (€12.50), 72 hours (€18), one week (€24, about the cost of three taxi rides), and one month (€35, plus €3 for the re-chargeable card, valid for a calendar month).

You can purchase tickets and passes from machines at Metro stations and a few major bus stops (cash only), and from some newsstands and tobacco shops (*tabacchi*, marked by a black-and-white *T* sign). Tickets are not sold on board. It's smart to stock up on tickets early, or to buy a pass or a Roma Pass (which includes public transportation—see page 42). That way, you don't have to run around searching for an open tobacco shop when you spot your bus approaching.

Validate your ticket by sticking it in the Metro turnstile (magnetic-strip-side up, arrow-side first) or in the machine when you board the bus (magnetic-strip-side down, arrow-side first)—watch others and imitate. It'll return your ticket with your expiration time printed. To get through a Metro turnstile with a transit pass or Roma Pass, use it just like a ticket; on buses and trams, however, you need to validate your pass only if that's your first time using it.

If you need help from a real person, ATAC runs a small ticket office at Termini Station. Follow signs for *Metro Linea B*, then *ATAC ticket office* (Mon-Sat 7:00-20:00, Sun 8:00-20:00).

By Metro

The Roman subway system (Metropolitana, or "Metro") is simple, clean, cheap, and fast. The two lines you need to know—A and B—intersect at Termini Station. The Metro runs from 5:30 to 23:30 (Fri-Sat until 1:30 in the morning). The subway's first and last compartments are generally the least crowded, and the least likely to harbor pickpockets.

The Metro's new line C is now partly finished but serves only a sub-urb of little interest to tourists. You'll notice a big construction site in the corner of the Roman Forum, where line C will intersect with the Colosseo Metro stop (hopefully by 2021).

By Bus

The Metro is handy, but it won't get you everywhere—you often have to take the bus (or tram). Bus routes are listed at each stop. Route and system maps aren't posted, but with some knowledge of major stops, you can wing it without one. (The ATAC website has

a PDF bus map that you can download, bookstores sell paper transport maps, and the various journey planners are helpful.)

Buses—especially the touristy #40 and #64—are havens for thieves and pickpockets. These two lines in particular can be nose-to-armpit crowded during peak times...and while you're sniffing that guy's pit, his other hand could be busily rifling through your pockets. Assume any commotion is a thief-created distraction. If one bus is packed, there's likely a second one on its tail with far fewer crowds and thieves. Or read the signs posted at stops to see if a different, less crowded bus route can get you to or near your destination.

The tram lines are of limited use for most tourists, but a few lines can save some walking. For all intents and purposes, trams function identically to buses. Once you're comfortable with the bus/tram system, you'll find it's easier than searching for a cab.

On buses, tickets must be inserted in the yellow box with the

digital readout (magnetic-strip-side down, arrow-side first; be sure to retrieve your ticket after it's spit out). Do this as you board, otherwise you're cheating. Inspectors fine even innocent-looking tourists €50. You don't need to validate a transit pass or Roma Pass on the bus, as long as it's been stamped elsewhere in the transit system. Bus etiquette (not always followed) is to board at the front or rear doors and exit at the middle.

Regular bus lines start running at about 5:30, and during the day major routes run every 10-15 minutes. After 23:30 (and sometimes earlier) and on Sundays, buses are less frequent. Night buses are marked with an *N* and an owl symbol on the bus-stop signs. Frustratingly, the exact frequency of various bus routes is difficult to predict (and not printed at bus stops). At major stops, an electronic board shows the number of minutes until the next buses arrive, but at most stops you'll never know how long you have to wait. If your phone has Internet access, you can try checking the journey planners listed above.

These are the most important bus routes for tourists:

Bus #64: This bus cuts across the city, linking Termini Station with the Vatican, stopping at Piazza della Repubblica (sights), Via Nazionale (recommended hotels), Piazza Venezia (near Forum), Largo Argentina (near Pantheon and Campo de' Fiori), St. Peter's

ORIENTATION

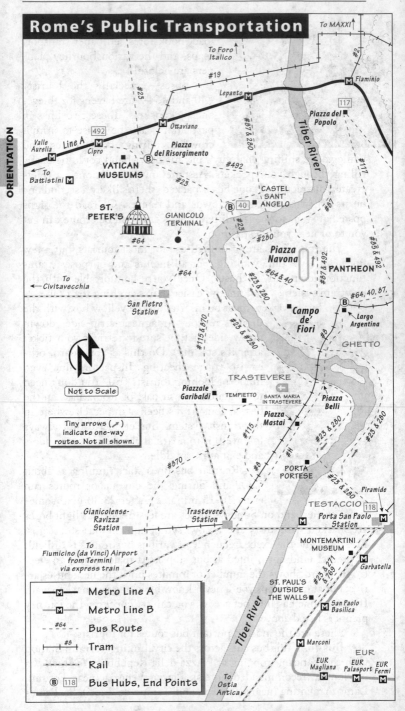

Rome's Public Transportation

To MAXXI

To Foro Italico

#19

#23

Lepanto

Flaminio

117

Piazza del Popolo

Tiber River

#87 & 280

Ottaviano

Line A   492

Valle Aurelia

Cipro

To Battistini

Piazza del Risorgimento

VATICAN MUSEUMS

#492

#23

#117

CASTEL SANT' ANGELO

40

#87

#280

#23

ST. PETER'S

GIANICOLO TERMINAL

#64

Piazza Navona

PANTHEON

#87 & 492

#85 & 492

To Civitavecchia

#64

#64 & 40

#23 & 280

#8

#64, 40, 87,

Largo Argentina

San Pietro Station

#115 & 870

#23 & #280

Campo de' Fiori

GHETTO

N

Not to Scale

TRASTEVERE

Piazzale Garibaldi

TEMPIETTO

SANTA MARIA IN TRASTEVERE

Piazza Belli

Tiny arrows (➚) indicate one-way routes. Not all shown.

Piazza Mastai

#115

#23 & 280

#23 & 280

#870

#8

PORTA PORTESE

#23 & 280

Piramide

Gianicolense-Ravizza Station

Trastevere Station

TESTACCIO

118

Porta San Paolo Station

To Fiumicino (da Vinci) Airport from Termini via express train

MONTEMARTINI MUSEUM

Garbatella

#23 & 271 & 769

ST. PAUL'S OUTSIDE THE WALLS

San Paolo Basilica

Tiber River

Marconi

EUR

EUR Magliana

EUR Palasport

EUR Fermi

To Ostia Antica

Ⓜ——	Metro Line A
Ⓜ······	Metro Line B
#64	Bus Route
#8	Tram
	Rail
Ⓑ 118	Bus Hubs, End Points

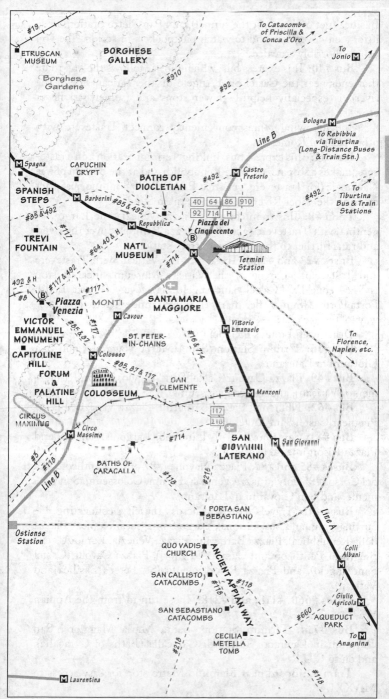

ORIENTATION

Basilica (get off just past the tunnel), and San Pietro Station. Ride it for a city overview and to watch pickpockets in action. The #64 can get horribly crowded.

Bus #40: This express bus, which mostly follows the #64 route (but ends near the Castel Sant'Angelo on the Vatican side of the river), is especially helpful—fewer stops and (somewhat) fewer crowds.

The following routes conveniently connect Trastevere with other parts of Rome:

Bus #H: This express bus, linking Termini Station and Trastevere, makes a stop near Piazza Repubblica and at the bottom of Via Nazionale (for Trastevere, get off at Piazza Belli/Sonnino, just after crossing the Tiber River). It doesn't run on Sundays.

Tram #8: This tram connects Piazza Venezia and Largo Argentina with Trastevere (get off at Piazza Belli, just over the river) and runs further to the Trastevere train station.

Buses #23 and #280: These link the Vatican with Trastevere and Testaccio, stopping at the Vatican Museums (nearest stop is Via Leone IV), Castel Sant'Angelo, Trastevere (Piazza Belli), Porta Portese (Sunday flea market), and Piramide (Metro and gateway to Testaccio).

Other useful routes include:

Bus #16: Termini Station, Santa Maria Maggiore, and San Giovanni in Laterano.

Bus #49: Piazza Cavour/Castel Sant'Angelo, Piazza Risorgimento (Vatican), and Vatican Museums.

Bus #62: Tiburtina, Piazza Barberini, Piazza Venezia, Piazza Pia (near Castel Sant'Angelo).

Bus #81: San Giovanni in Laterano, Largo Argentina, and Piazza Risorgimento (Vatican).

Buses #85 and #87: Piazza Navona (#87 only), Pantheon, Via del Corso (#85 only), Piazza Venezia, Forum, Colosseum, San Clemente, and San Giovanni in Laterano.

Bus #492: Travels east-west across the city, connecting Tiburtina (train and bus stations), Largo Santa Susanna (near Piazza della Repubblica), Piazza Barberini, Piazza Venezia, Largo Argentina (near Pantheon and Campo de' Fiori), Piazza Cavour (Castel Sant'Angelo), and Piazza Risorgimento (St. Peter's Basilica and Vatican).

Buses #660, #118, and #218: These run to/from the Appian Way.

Bus #714: Termini Station, Santa Maria Maggiore, San Giovanni in Laterano, Terme di Caracalla (Baths of Caracalla), and on to E.U.R.

Tram #2: Board near Flaminio Metro stop for easy access to MAXXI.

Bus Bravado

Zip around Rome like a local by learning to read the bus signs.

The sign in the photo shows the three buses (#40, #60, and #64) that stop at the "Nazionale (Torino)" stop. If you're asking yourself the following questions, it's got answers.

❶ Where am I? You're at the bus stop *(fermata)* called Nazionale (Torino). There are several bus stops along Via Nazionale, identified by their cross-streets (in this case, Via Torino).

❷ Which buses stop here? Three do: #40, #60, and #64. Notice the arrow—it shows which direction the bus is headed.

❸ Where is the bus going? Bus #64, for example, starts its journey at "Termini"

(Termini Station), goes to Repubblica, and then serves four stops *(fermate)* along Via Nazionale—including this one. (Find "Nazionale," with the box around it.) From here, the #64 continues to "Pza Venezia" (Piazza Venezia), "Argentina" (Largo Argentina), makes several more stops, and ends its journey at "Pza Stz S. Pietro" (Piazza Stazione San Pietro). Easy.

Scan the list to see if any of these buses stop where you want to go. If you don't see your destination, look for a major stop where you can transfer—such as Largo Argentina, Piazza Venezia, or Termini Station. Note that if your destination is listed *above* your current bus stop, you need to cross the street to catch the bus going in the other direction.

❹ When will my bus come? The bottom of the sign (not shown) lists the first and last departure times from the beginning of the route. "*lun./ven.*" means it runs on weekdays, "*sab.*" means Saturday, and "*fest.*" means Sundays and holidays.

Tram #3: Zips from the Colosseum to San Giovanni in Laterano in one direction, and to Piramide (Testaccio) in the other.

Tram #19: Connects Piazza del Risorgimento and the Ottaviano Metro stop (by the Vatican Museums) to the Etruscan Museum and the Villa Borghese.

***Elettrico* Minibuses:** Cute *elettrico* minibuses that wind through the narrow streets of old and interesting neighborhoods are great for transport or simple joyriding (although they're so small it can be hard to find a seat). ***Elettrico* #117** connects San Giovanni in Laterano, Colosseo, Via dei Serpenti, Trevi Fountain, Piazza di Spagna, and Piazza del Popolo—and vice versa. Where Via del Corso hits Piazza del Popolo, a #117 is usually parked and ready to go. Riding it from here to the end of the line, San Giovanni in Laterano, makes for a fine joyride that leaves you, conveniently, at a great sight.

By Taxi

I use taxis in Rome more often than in other cities. They're reasonable and useful for efficient sightseeing in this big, hot metropolis. Taxis start at €3, then charge about €1.50 per kilometer (surcharges: €1.50 on Sun, €3.50 for nighttime hours of 22:00-6:00, one regular suitcase or bag rides free, tip by rounding up—€1 or so). Sample fares: Termini area to Vatican-€15; Termini area to Colosseum-€7; Termini area to the Borghese Gallery-€9; Colosseum  to Trastevere-€12 (or look up your route at www.worldtaximeter.com). Three or four companions with more money than time should taxi almost everywhere.

Romans don't hail taxis. Find the nearest taxi stand (many are marked on this book's maps) or ask a passerby or a clerk in a shop, *"Dov'è una fermata dei taxi?"* (doh-VEH OO-nah fehr-MAH-tah DEH-ee TAHK-see). Easiest of all, have your hotel or restaurant call a taxi for you. (It's routine for Romans to ask the restaurant to call a taxi when they're ready to go.) The meter starts when the call is received. To call a cab on your own, dial 06-3570, 06-4994, or 06-6645, or use the official city taxi line, 06-0609; they'll likely ask you for an Italian phone number (give them your mobile number or your hotel's).

Beware of corrupt taxis. First, only use official Rome taxis. They're white, with a taxi sign on the roof and a maroon logo on the door that reads *Roma Capitale*. When you get in, make sure the meter *(tassametro)* is turned on (you'll see the meter either on the dashboard or up by the rearview mirror). If the meter isn't on, get out and find another cab. Check that the meter is reset to the basic drop charge (should be around €3, or around €5 if you phoned for the taxi). Some meters show both the fare and the time elapsed during the ride, and some tourists—mistaking the time for the fare—end up paying more than the fair meter rate. Also, keep an eye on the fare on the meter as you near your destination; some cabbies turn the meter off instantly when they stop and tell you a higher price.

By law, every cab must display a multilingual official price chart—usually on the back of the seat in front of you. If the fare doesn't seem right, point to the chart and ask the cabbie to explain it. When you pay the cabbie, have your wits about you. A common cabbie scam is to take your €20 note, drop it, and pick up a €5 note (similar color), claiming that's what you gave him. To avoid this scam, pay in small bills; if you only have a large bill, show it to the cabbie as you state its face value.

At the train station or airport, avoid hustlers conning naive visitors into unmarked, rip-off "express taxis" (for tips on taking a taxi from the airport, including how not to get scammed, see page 422). If you encounter any problems with a taxi, making a show of writing down the taxi number (to file a complaint) can motivate a driver to quickly settle the matter.

By Bike

Riding a bicycle in Rome's traffic is best suited to serious urban bikers—use caution and never assume you have the right of way. The best rides are on small streets in the city center, at the Villa Borghese Gardens, and along the Appian Way. Also, a bike path along the banks of the Tiber River makes a good 20-minute ride (easily accessed from the ramps at Porta Portese and Ponte Regina Margherita near Piazza del Popolo).

Top Bike Rental and Tours is professionally run by Roman bike enthusiasts who want to show off their city. Your rental comes with a helmet, a lock, and a handy map that suggests a route and indicates less-trafficked streets. They also offer English-only guided tours around the city (4 hours) and the Appian Way (6 hours); check their website for itineraries and schedules (rental: €15/day, €25/day for electric bike, 10 percent discount with this book, best to reserve in advance via email, bring ID for deposit; bike tours start at €45, reservations required; daily 10:00-19:00, Via Labicana 49, Metro: Colosseo—exit left and walk 10 minutes past the Colosseum, tel. 06-488-2893, www.topbikerental.com, info@topbikerental.com, ask for Florien from the Netherlands).

Cool Rent, a sidewalk operation, is cheaper but less helpful and has only basic bikes (€4/hour, €10/day, daily April-Oct 9:30-

20:00, Nov-March 9:30-18:00, driver's license or other ID for deposit, 10 yards to the right as you exit the Colosseo Metro stop). A second outlet is just off Via del Corso (on Largo di Lombardi, near corner of Via del Corso and Via della Croce, mobile 328-277-3993).

You can also rent a bike at the Appian Way (see Ancient Appian Way Tour chapter) and in the Villa Borghese Gardens (see page 67).

Tours in Rome

ON FOOT

Local guides are good but pricey. Tour companies are cheaper, but quality and organization are unreliable. If you do hire a private Italian guide and it feels tough on your budget, consider inviting others from your hotel to join you and split the cost (around €180 for a three-hour tour). This ends up costing about the same per person as going on a scheduled tour from one of the walking-tour companies listed below—and you'll likely get a better guide.

∩ To sightsee on your own, download my **free audio tours** that illuminate some of Rome's top sights and neighborhoods, including the Heart of Rome, Jewish Ghetto, and Trastevere walks, and tours of the Pantheon, Colosseum, Roman Forum, St. Peter's Basilica, Vatican Museums, Sistine Chapel, and Ostia Antica (see sidebar on page 8 for details).

Local Guides

I've worked with and enjoyed each of these licensed independent local guides. They're native Italians, speak excellent English, and enjoy tailoring tours to your interests. Their prices (roughly €60/hour) flex with the day, season, and demand. Arrange your date and price by email. **Carla Zaia** (carlaromeguide@gmail.com); **Cristina Giannicchi** (mobile 338-111-4573, www.crisromanguide.com, crisgiannicchi@gmail.com); **Sara Magister** (a.magister@iol.it); **Giovanna Terzulli** (gioterzulli@gmail.com); **Alessandra Mazzoccoli** (www.romeandabout.com, alemazzoccoli@gmail.com); and **Massimiliano Canneto** (a Catholic guide with a Vatican forte, but does all of Rome, massicanneto@gmail.com).

Francesca Caruso, who works almost full time with my tours when in Rome, has contributed generously to this book (www.francescacaruso.com, francescainroma@gmail.com). Popular with my readers, Francesca understandably books up quickly; if she's busy, she'll recommend one of her colleagues. At her website you can listen to the many interviews I've enjoyed with Francesca on my public radio program.

Is the Pope Catholic?

Rome's tour guides, who introduce tourists to the city's great art and Christian history, field a lot of interesting questions and comments from their groups. Here are a few of their favorites:

- Oh, to be here in Rome... where our Lord Jesus walked.
- Is this where Christ fought the lions?
- Who's the guy on the cross?
- This guy who made so many nice things, Rene Sance, who is he?
- Was John Paul II the son of John Paul I?
- What's the Sistine Chapel worth in US dollars?
- How did Michelangelo get Moses to pose for him?
- What's Michelangelo doing now?
- (Upon seeing the arrow-pierced St. Sebastian) Oh, you Italians had problems with the Indians, too.

Walking-Tour Companies

Rome has many highly competitive tour companies, each offering a series of themed walks through various slices of the city. Three-hour guided walks generally cost €25-30 per person. Guides are usually native English speakers, often American expats. Tours are limited to small groups, geared to American tourists, and given in English only. Before your trip, spend some time on these companies' websites to get to know your options, as each company has a particular teaching and guiding personality. Some are highbrow and more expensive. Others are less scholarly. It's sometimes required, and always smart, to book a spot in advance (easy online). Readers report that advertising can be misleading, and scheduling mishaps are common. Make sure you know what you are booking and when.

These companies are each well-established, creative, and competitive, with their various tours explained on their websites. Each offers a 10 percent discount with online bookings for Rick Steves travelers:

Enjoy Rome (tel. 06-445-1843, www.enjoyrome.com, info@enjoyrome.com).

Rome Walks (mobile 347-795-5175, www.romewalks.com, info@romewalks.com, Annie).

Europe Odyssey (tel. 06-8854-2416, mobile 328-912-3720, www.europeodyssey.com, Rahul).

Through Eternity (for discount look for "Group Tours Rome" and enter "RICKSTEVES," tel. 06-700-9336, www. througheternity.com, office@througheternity.com, Rob).

Walks of Italy (for discount enter "10ricksteves," US tel. 888/683-8670, tel. 06-9480-4888, www.walksofitaly.com).

The Roman Guy (enter "ricksteves" for discount, ask about electric-assist bike tours, www.theromanguy.com, Sean Finelli).

Miles & Miles Private Tours, described under "Car & Minibus Tours," below, also offers walking tours (www.milesandmiles. net).

Context Rome's walking tours are more intellectual than most, designed for travelers with longer-than-average attention spans. They are more expensive than others (no discounts) and are led by "docents" rather than guides (tel. 06-9672-7371, US tel. 800-691-6036, www.contexttravel.com).

Sketching Rome Tours, offered by American expat Kelly Medford, draw on your creative side with fun, three-hour **sketching tours** geared to (aspiring) artists of any skill level ($125, www. sketchingrometours.com).

While some of the above also offer **food-oriented walking tours,** I'd favor the food-tour companies listed on page 375.

ON WHEELS
Hop-On, Hop-Off Bus Tours
Several different agencies run hop-on, hop-off tours around Rome.

These tours are constantly evolving and offer varying combinations of sights. You can grab one (and pay as you board; usually around €20) at any stop; Termini Station and Piazza Venezia are handy hubs. Although the city is perfectly walkable and traffic jams can make the bus dreadfully slow, these open-top bus tours remain popular.

Car and Minibus Tours
Autoservizi Monti Concezio, run by gentle, capable, and English-speaking Ezio (pronounced Etz-io), offers private cars or minibuses with driver/guides (car-€40/hour, minibus-€45/hour, 3-hour minimum for city sightseeing, transfers between cities are more expensive, mobile 335-636-5907 or 349-674-5643, www. tourservicemonti.it, info@tourservicemonti.it).

Miles & Miles Private Tours, a family-run company, offers a number of tours, all with good English-speaking Italian driver/ guides (descriptions and pricing on their website, mention Rick Steves when booking direct, then show the book on the day of service to get a discount). They also provide walking tours, shore excursions (from Civitavecchia, Livorno, Naples, Venice, and other ports), and unguided long-distance transportation; if traveling with a small group or a family from Rome to Florence, the Amalfi Coast, or elsewhere, consider paying extra to turn the trip into a memorable day tour with door-to-door service (mobile 331-466-4900, www.milesandmiles.net, info@milesandmiles.net).

TOUR PACKAGES FOR STUDENTS

Andy Steves (Rick's son) runs Weekend Student Adventures (WSA Europe), offering three-day and 10-day budget travel packages across Europe including accommodations, skip-the-line sightseeing, and unique local experiences. Locally guided and DIY unguided options are available for student and budget travelers in 12 of Europe's most popular cities, including Rome (guided trips from €199, see www.wsaeurope.com for details).

ORIENTATION

SIGHTS IN ROME

I've clustered Rome's sights into walkable neighborhoods, some quite close together (see map on page 14). Save transit time by grouping your sightseeing according to location. For example, in one great day you can start at the Colosseum, then go to the Forum, then Capitoline Hill, and from there either to the Pantheon or back to the Colosseum (by way of additional ruins along Via dei Fori Imperiali).

When you see a 📖 in a listing, it means the sight is described in greater detail in one of my self-guided walks or tours. A 🎧 means the walk or tour is also available as a free audio tour (via my Rick Steves Audio Europe app—see page 8). Some walks and tours are available in both formats—take your pick. This is why some of Rome's most important sights get the least coverage in this chapter—we'll explore them in greater depth elsewhere in this book.

For general tips on sightseeing, see page 510. Rome's good city-run information website, www.060608.it, lists current opening hours.

To connect some of the most central sights, follow my Heart of Rome Walk (see the next chapter), which takes you from Campo de' Fiori to the Trevi Fountain and Spanish Steps. This walk is most enjoyable in the evening—after the museums have closed, when the evening air and lit-up fountains show off Rome at its most magical. To join the parade of people strolling down Via del Corso every evening, take my Dolce Vita Stroll (see the end of the Nightlife in Rome chapter).

Price Hike Alert: Many of Rome's sights host a special exhibit and require you to pay extra for your ticket, even if all you want to see is the permanent collection. This means admission fees jump by €3 or more. Expect this practice at the Capitoline Museums, Borghese Gallery, National Museum of Rome, Ara Pacis, and others. Come expecting this higher price...and consider yourself lucky if you happen to visit on the rare occasion when you can get in for less.

Free First Sundays: The state museums in Italy are free to all on the first Sunday of each month (no reservations are available). Among the biggies in Rome, that means the Colosseum, Roman Forum, Palatine Hill, Borghese Gallery, National Museum of Rome, Castel Sant'Angelo, Etruscan Museum, and Baths of Caracalla are free—and packed. It's actually bad news and I'd make a point to avoid the Colosseum and Roman Forum on that day.

Ancient Rome

The core of ancient Rome, where the grandest monuments were built, is between the Colosseum and Capitoline Hill. Among the ancient forums, a few modern sights have popped up. I've listed these sights from south to north, starting with the biggies—the Colosseum and Forum—and continuing up to Capitoline Hill and Piazza Venezia. Then, as a pleasant conclusion to your busy day, consider my relaxing self-guided walk back south along the broad, parklike main drag—Via dei Fori Imperiali—with some enticing detours to nearby sights.

ANCIENT CORE
▲▲▲Colosseum (Colosseo)

This 2,000-year-old building is the classic example of Roman engineering. Used as a venue for entertaining the masses, this colos-

sal, functional stadium is one of Europe's most recognizable landmarks. Whether you're playing gladiator or simply marveling at the remarkable ancient design and construction, the Colosseum gets a unanimous thumbs-up.

Cost and Hours: €12 combo-ticket includes Roman Forum and Palatine Hill (see page 42), free and very crowded first Sun of the month, open daily 8:30 until one hour before sunset (see page 142 for times), last entry one hour before closing, audioguide-€5.50, Metro: Colosseo, tel. 06-3996-7700, www.archeoroma.beniculturali.it/en. For line-avoiding tips, see page 143.

📖 See the Colosseum Tour chapter or 🎧 download my free audio tour.

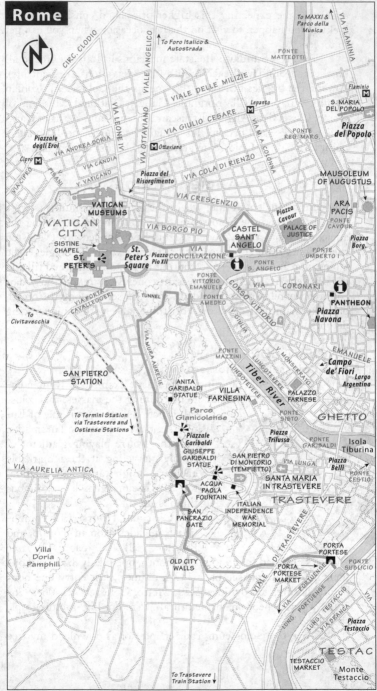

Rome

To MAXXI & Parco della Musica

To Foro Italico & Autostrada

VIA FLAMINIA

PONTE MATTEOTTI

CIRC. CLODIO

VIALE DELLE MILIZIE

VIALE ANGELICO

VIA OTTAVIANO

VIA LEONE IV.

Flaminio

S. MARIA DEL POPOLO

Piazza del Popolo

VIA GIULIO CESARE

Lepanta

VIA M. A. COLONNA

PONTE REG. MARG.

Ottaviano

Piazzale degli Eroi

VIA ANDREA DORIA

MAGIPRO PISANI

Cipro

V. VATICANO

VIA CANDIA

Piazza del Risorgimento

VIA COLA DI RIENZO

VIA CRESCENZIO

MAUSOLEUM OF AUGUSTUS

Piazza Cavour

ARA PACIS

PONTE CAVOUR

VATICAN MUSEUMS

VIA BORGO PIO

CASTEL SANT' ANGELO

PALACE OF JUSTICE

Piazza Borg.

VATICAN CITY

SISTINE CHAPEL

ST. PETER'S

St. Peter's Square

Piazza Pio XII

VIA CONCILIAZIONE

PONTE UMBERTO I

PONTE S. ANGELO

PONTE S. ANGELO

VIA CORONARI

PANTHEON

VIA DI PORTA CAVALLEGGERI

TUNNEL

PONTE VITTORIO EMANUELE

PONTE AMEDEO

CORSO VITTORIO

V. GIULIA

Piazza Navona

To Civitavecchia

VIA MURA AURELIE

PONTE MAZZINI

LUNGOTEVERE

V. MONSERRATO

EMANUELE

Campo de' Fiori

Largo Argentina

SAN PIETRO STATION

ANITA GARIBALDI STATUE

VILLA FARNESINA

Tiber River

PALAZZO FARNESE

GHETTO

To Termini Station via Trastevere and Ostiense Stations

Parco Gianicolense

PONTE SISTO

PONTE GARIBALDI

Isola Tiburina

VIA AURELIA ANTICA

Piazzale Garibaldi

Piazza Trilussa

GIUSEPPE GARIBALDI STATUE

SAN PIETRO DI MONTORIO (TEMPIETTO)

VIA LUNGA

Piazza Belli

PONTE CESTIO

ACQUA PAOLA FOUNTAIN

SANTA MARIA IN TRASTEVERE

TRASTEVERE

Villa Doria Pamphili

SAN PANCRAZIO GATE

ITALIAN INDEPENDENCE WAR MEMORIAL

VIALE DI TRASTEVERE

PORTA PORTESE

PONTE SUBLICIO

OLD CITY WALLS

PORTA PORTESE MARKET

VIA PORTUENSE

LUNG. TESTACCIO

VIA FRANCA

Piazza Testaccio

To Trastevere Train Station

TESTACCIO MARKET

TESTAC

Monte Testaccio

SIGHTS

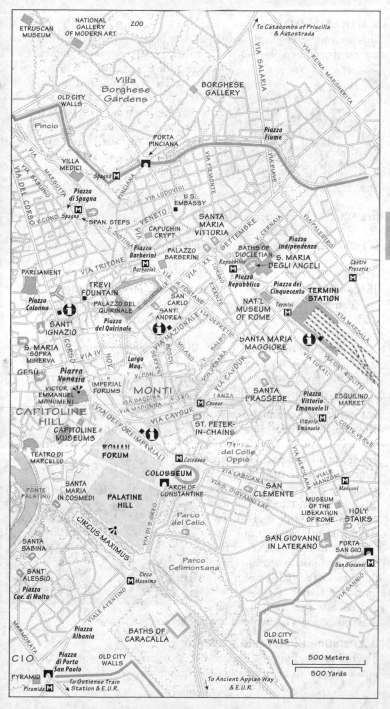

SIGHTS

SIGHTS

▲Arch of Constantine

This well-preserved arch, which stands between the Colosseum and the Forum, commemorates a military coup and, more impor-

tant, the acceptance of Christianity by the Roman Empire. When the ambitious Emperor Constantine (who had a vision that he'd win under the sign of the cross) defeated his rival Maxentius in A.D. 312, Constantine became sole emperor of the Roman Empire and legalized Christianity. The arch is free to see—always open and viewable.

The Arch of Constantine is covered in more detail on page 151 of my 📖 Colosseum Tour chapter, and 🎧 in my free audio tour.

Roman Forum and Palatine Hill

Though I've covered them separately, the Forum and Palatine Hill are organized as a single sight with one admission (ticket also includes Colosseum). You'll need to see both sights in a single visit (see page 157 for details).

Cost and Hours: €12 combo-ticket includes Roman Forum and Colosseum—see page 42, free and very crowded first Sun of the month, open same hours as Colosseum, audioguide-€5, Metro: Colosseo, tel. 06-3996-7700, www.archeoroma.beniculturali.it/en.

▲▲▲Roman Forum (Foro Romano)

This is ancient Rome's birthplace and civic center, and the common ground between Rome's famous seven hills. As just about anything

important that happened in ancient Rome happened here, it's arguably the most important piece of real estate in Western civilization. While only a few fragments of that glorious past remain, history seekers find plenty to ignite their imaginations amid the half-broken columns and arches.

📖 See the Roman Forum Tour chapter or 🎧 download my free audio tour.

▲▲Palatine Hill (Monte Palatino)

The hill overlooking the Forum was the home of the emperors and now contains a museum, scant (but impressive when understood)

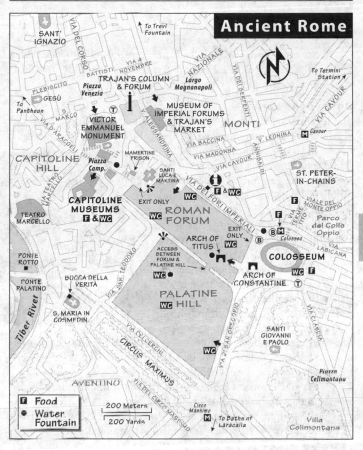

Ancient Rome

(Map labels:)

SANT' IGNAZIO
To Trevi Fountain
VIA DEL CORSO
VIA 4 NOVEMBRE
VIA NAZIONALE
VIA DEI SERPENTI
To Termini Station
PLEBISCITO
BATTISTI
GESÙ
Piazza Venezia
TRAJAN'S COLUMN & FORUM
Largo Magnanapoli
To Pantheon
S. MARCO
VIA D'ARACOELI
VICTOR EMMANUEL MONUMENT
V. ALESSANDRINA
MUSEUM OF IMPERIAL FORUMS & TRAJAN'S MARKET
MONTI
VIA CAVOUR
Cavour
VIA BACCINA
V. LEONINA
CAPITOLINE HILL
Piazza Camp.
Mamertine Prison
VIA MADONNA
VIA CAVOUR
ANNIBALDI
ST. PETER-IN-CHAINS
SANTI LUCA E MARTINA
VIA DEI FORI IMPERIALI
VIALE DEL MONTE OPPIO
CAPITOLINE MUSEUMS
EXIT ONLY
ROMAN FORUM
Parco del Colle Oppio
VIA DELLE TERME DI TITO
TEATRO MARCELLO
VIA DEL TEATRO MARCELLO
EXIT ONLY
Colosseo
VIA LABICANA
PONTE ROTTO
ARCH OF TITUS
ACCESS BETWEEN FORUM & PALATINE HILL
COLOSSEUM
PONTE PALATINO
BOCCA DELLA VERITÀ
VIA SAN TEODORO
PALATINE HILL
ARCH OF CONSTANTINE
Tiber River
S. MARIA IN COSMEDIN
VIA DEI CERCHI
SANTI GIOVANNI E PAOLO
VIA CLAUDIA
CIRCUS MAXIMUS
VIA DI SAN GREGORIO
Piazza Celimontana
AVENTINO
VIA DEL CIRCO MASSIMO
Circo Massimo
To Baths of Caracalla
Villa Colimontana

Legend:
- F Food
- ● Water Fountain

200 Meters
200 Yards

SIGHTS

remains of imperial palaces, and a view of the Circus Maximus (if it's not blocked by ongoing archaeological work).

📖 See the Palatine Hill Tour chapter.

Mamertine Prison (Carcere Mamertino)

This 2,500-year-old cistern-like prison on Capitoline Hill is where, according to Christian tradition, the Romans imprisoned Saints Peter and Paul (it's also known as Carcere di San Pietro). You can walk through and imagine how this dank cistern once housed prisoners of the emperor. Amid fat rats and rotting corpses, unfortunate humans awaited slow deaths. It's said that a miraculous fountain sprang up inside so Peter could convert and baptize his jailers, who were also subsequently martyred. The prison is sometimes closed for repairs.

Cost and Hours: €3; daily June-Sept 9:00-19:00, Oct-May 9:00-17:00, audioguide-€2, Clivo Argentario 1, tel. 06-698-961, www.operaromanapellegrinaggi.org.

Bocca della Verità

The legendary "Mouth of Truth" at the Church of Santa Maria in Cosmedin—a few blocks southwest of the other sights listed here—draws lots of mindless "selfie-stick" travelers. Stick your hand in the mouth of the gaping stone face in the porch wall. As the legend goes (and was popularized by the 1953 film *Roman Holiday,* starring Gregory Peck and Audrey Hepburn), if you're a liar, your hand will be gobbled up. The mouth is only accessible when the church gate is open, but it's always (partially) visible through the gate, even when closed. If the church itself is open, step inside to see one of the

few unaltered medieval church interiors in Rome. Notice the mismatched ancient columns and beautiful cosmatesque floor—a centuries-old example of recycling.

Cost and Hours: €0.50 suggested donation, daily 9:30-17:50, Piazza Bocca della Verità 18, near the north end of Circus Maximus, a 10-minute walk south from Piazza Venezia, bus #81 from Vatican area or #170 from Termini/Via Nazionale, tel. 06-678-7759.

CAPITOLINE HILL

Of Rome's famous seven hills, this is the smallest, tallest, and most famous—home of the ancient Temple of Jupiter and the center of

city government for 2,500 years. There are several ways to get to the top of Capitoline Hill. If you're coming from the north (from Piazza Venezia), take Michelangelo's impressive stairway to the right of the big, white Victor Emmanuel Monument. Coming from the southeast (the Forum), take the steep staircase near the Arch of Septimius Severus. From near Trajan's Forum along Via

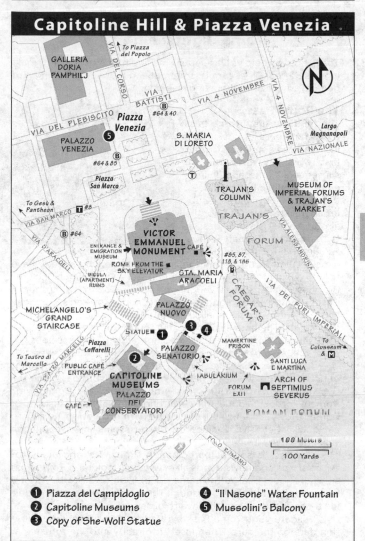

Capitoline Hill & Piazza Venezia

GALLERIA DORIA PAMPHILJ

VIA DEL CORSO

To Piazza del Popolo

VIA BATTISTI

VIA 4 NOVEMBRE

VIA 4 NOVEMBRE

Piazza Venezia #64 & 40 ❺

VIA DEL PLEBISCITO

S. MARIA DI LORETO

Largo Magnanapoli

VIA NAZIONALE

PALAZZO VENEZIA #64 & 85 Ⓑ

Piazza San Marco

Ⓣ

TRAJAN'S COLUMN

MUSEUM OF IMPERIAL FORUMS & TRAJAN'S MARKET

To Gesù & Pantheon Ⓣ #8

VIA SAN MARCO

TRAJAN'S FORUM

Ⓑ #64

VIA D'ARACOELI

ENTRANCE & EMIGRATION MUSEUM

VICTOR EMMANUEL MONUMENT CAFÉ

ROME FROM THE SKY ELEVATOR

#85, 87, 118, & 186 Ⓑ

VIA ALESSANDRINA

CAESAR'S FORUM

INSULA (APARTMENT) RUINS

STA. MARIA ARACOELI

VIA DEI FORI IMPERIALI

MICHELANGELO'S GRAND STAIRCASE

PALAZZO NUOVO

Piazza Caffarelli

STATUE ❶ ❸ ❹

MAMERTINE PRISON

To Colosseum & Ⓜ

To Teatro di Marcello

VIA TEATRO MARCELLO

❷

PUBLIC CAFÉ ENTRANCE

PALAZZO SENATORIO

SANTI LUCA E MARTINA

CAPITOLINE MUSEUMS PALAZZO DEI CONSERVATORI

TABULARIUM

FORUM EXIT

ARCH OF SEPTIMIUS SEVERUS

CAFÉ

FORO ROMANO

ROMAN FORUM

100 Meters

100 Yards

❶ Piazza del Campidoglio
❷ Capitoline Museums
❸ Copy of She-Wolf Statue
❹ "Il Nasone" Water Fountain
❺ Mussolini's Balcony

dei Fori Imperiali, take the winding road. All three converge at the top, in the square called Campidoglio (kahm-pee-DOHL-yoh).

▲Piazza del Campidoglio

This square atop the hill, once the religious and political center of ancient Rome, is still the home of the city's government. In the 1530s, the pope called on Michelangelo to reestablish this square as a grand center. Michelangelo placed the ancient equestrian statue of Marcus Aurelius as its focal point—very effective. (The original statue is now in the adjacent museum.) The twin buildings

Rome Sightseeing Tips

These tips will help you use your time and money efficiently, making the Eternal City seem less eternal and more entertaining. For general advice on sightseeing, see page 510.

The Roma Pass

The full **three-day Roma Pass** (www.romapass.it) costs €36, includes free admission to your first two sights, a discount on subsequent sights, and unlimited use of public transit (buses, trams, and Metro, plus the suburban train to Ostia, but not the airport train). Using the pass at the Colosseum/Roman Forum/ Palatine Hill (considered a single sight) lets you stand in the line for people who already have tickets (which in theory gets you in faster). Other sights include: Borghese Gallery (reservations required), Capitoline Museums, Castel Sant'Angelo, Montemartini Museum, Ara Pacis, Etruscan Museum, Baths of Caracalla, Trajan's Market, and some Appian Way sights. The pass also covers the four branches of the National Museum of Rome (considered a single sight). The pass does not cover the Vatican Museums (which contain the Sistine Chapel).

The Roma Pass saves most visitors a little money and a lot of ticket-buying stress. To get the most out of your pass, visit the two most expensive sights first—for example, the Colosseum/ Roman Forum/Palatine Hill (€12) and the National Museum of Rome (€10). A three-day transit pass normally costs €18, so you can quickly get €40 of value from the pass, plus any discounts on subsequent sights.

The pass is sold at participating sights, TIs, and many tobacco shops and newsstands all over town (look for a *Roma Pass* sign; all should charge the same price). Don't wait to buy it at a crowded sight like the Colosseum. There's no advantage in ordering a pass online—you still have to pick it up in Rome.

Validate your Roma Pass by writing your name and validation date on the card. Then insert it directly into the turnstile at your first two (free) sights. At other sights, show it at the ticket office and you'll get the same reduction as local students (usually about 30 percent).

To use the included transit pass, write your name and birthdate on the pass and validate it on your first bus or Metro ride by passing it over a sensor at a turnstile or validation machine (look for a yellow circle). Now you can take unlimited rides within Rome's city limits (until midnight of the third day). Once the pass is validated you can hop on any bus without showing it, but you'll need to swipe it to get through Metro turnstiles.

The **48-hour Roma Pass** costs €28 and includes free entry

to one sight, the same discounts on additional ones, and unlimited use of public transit (for 48 hours after validation—a €12.50 value). It saves money only if you visit at least one or two sights beyond your free one, but it can save time if you're visiting the Colosseum/Roman Forum/Palatine Hill and don't have a reservation.

For families, only adults will need a Roma Pass. Children under age 18 get into national museums and sights for free and kids under 6 get into city museums, including Museo dell'Ara Pacis, for free; they can skip the lines alongside their pass-holding parents. Note that passports may be required as proof of age (driver's licenses may not be accepted). Kids 10 and over need their own transit tickets or passes; those 9 and under ride free.

Top Tips

Museum Reservations: The marvelous Borghese Gallery requires reservations in advance (for specifics, see page 271). You can reserve online to avoid long lines at the Vatican Museums (see page 237).

Opening Hours: Rome's sights have notoriously variable hours from season to season. It's smart to check each sight's website in advance. On holidays, expect shorter hours or closures.

Forum/Palatine Hill: These two sights share a single admission ticket. If you want to visit Palatine Hill after seeing the Forum, go to the Arch of Titus and climb Palatine Hill from there. (You can't exit the Forum and reenter at Palatine Hill.)

Churches: Many churches, which have divine art and free entry, open early (around 7:00-7:30), close for lunch (roughly 12:00-15:30), and close late (about 19:00). Kamikaze tourists maximize their sightseeing hours by visiting churches before 9:00 or late in the day; during the siesta, they see major sights that stay open all day (St. Peter's, Colosseum, Forum, Capitoline Museums, Pantheon, and National Museum of Rome). Dress modestly for church visits.

Picnic Discreetly: Public drinking and eating is not allowed at major sights, though the ban has proven difficult to enforce. To avoid the risk of being fined, choose an empty piazza for your picnic, or keep a low profile.

Miscellaneous Tips: I carry a water bottle and refill it at Rome's many public drinking spouts. Because public restrooms are scarce, use toilets at museums, restaurants, and bars.

on either side are the Capitoline Museums. Behind the replica of the statue is the mayoral palace (Palazzo Senatorio).

Michelangelo intended that people approach the square from his grand stairway off Piazza Venezia. From the top of the stairway, you see the new Renaissance face of Rome, with its back to the Forum. Michelangelo gave the buildings the "giant order"—huge pilasters make the existing two-story buildings feel one-storied and more harmonious with the new square. Notice how the statues atop these buildings welcome you and then draw you in.

The terraces just downhill (past either side of the mayor's palace) offer grand views of the Forum. To the left of the mayor's palace is a copy of the famous she-wolf statue on a column. Farther down is *il nasone* ("the big nose"), a refreshing water fountain (see photo). Block the spout with your fingers, and water spurts up for drinking. Romans joke that a cheap Roman boy takes his date out for a drink at *il nasone*.

▲▲▲Capitoline Museums (Musei Capitolini)

Some of ancient Rome's most famous statues and art are housed in the two palaces that flank the equestrian statue in the Campidoglio. You'll see the Dying Gaul, the original she-wolf, and the original version of the equestrian statue of Marcus Aurelius. Admission includes access to the underground vacant Tabularium, with its panoramic overlook of the Forum.

Cost and Hours: €15, €11.50 if no special exhibitions, daily 9:30-19:30, last entry one hour before closing, audioguide-€5, tel. 06-0608, www.museicapitolini.org.

📖 See the Capitoline Museums Tour chapter.

Santa Maria in Aracoeli Church

The church atop Capitoline Hill is old and dear to the hearts of Romans. It stands on the site where Emperor Augustus (supposedly) had a premonition of the coming of Mary and Christ standing on an "altar in the sky" *(ara coeli)*.

Cost and Hours: Free, May-Sept daily 9:00-18:30, Oct-April until 17:30, tel. 06-6976-3839.

Visiting the Church: Climb up the long, steep staircase from street level (the right side of Victor Emmanuel Monument as you face it).

The church is Rome in a nutshell, where you can time-travel across 2,000 years by standing in one spot. The building dates from Byzantine times (sixth century) and was expanded in the 1200s. Inside, the mismatched columns (red, yellow, striped, fluted) and marble floor are ancient, plundered from many different monuments. The medieval world is evident in the gravestones beneath your feet. The early Renaissance is featured in beautiful frescoes by Pinturicchio (first chapel on the right from the main entrance), with their 3-D perspective and natural landscapes. The coffered ceiling celebrates the Christian victory over the Ottoman Turks (Battle of Lepanto, 1571), with thanks to Mary (in the center of the ceiling). The chandeliers in the nave hint at the elegance of Baroque. Napoleon's occupying troops used the building as a horse stable. But like Rome itself, it survived and retained its splendor.

The church comes alive at Christmastime. Romans hike up to enjoy a manger scene *(presepio)* assembled every year in the second

chapel on the left. They stop at the many images of the Virgin (e.g., the statue in the marble gazebo to the left of the altar), who made an appearance to the pagan Augustus so long ago. And, most famously, they venerate a wooden statue of the Baby Jesus (Santo Bambino), displayed in a chapel to the left of the altar (go through the low-profile door and down the hall). Though the original statue was stolen in 1994, the copy continues this longtime Roman tradition. A clear box filled with handwritten prayers sits nearby.

The daunting 125-step staircase up Capitoline Hill to the entrance was once climbed—on their knees—by Roman women who wished for a child. Today, they don't...and Italy has Europe's lowest birthrate.

PIAZZA VENEZIA

This vast square, dominated by the big, white Victor Emmanuel Monument, is a major transportation hub and the focal point of modern Rome. With your back to the monument (you'll get the best views from the terrace by the guards and eternal flame), look down Via del Corso, the city's axis, surrounded by Rome's classiest shopping district. In the 1930s, Benito Mussolini whipped up Italy's nationalistic fervor from a balcony above the square (it's the less-grand building on the left). He gave 64 speeches from this balcony, including the declaration of war in 1940. This Early Renaissance building (with hints of medieval showing with its crenellated roof line) was the seat of Mussolini's fascist government. Fascist masses filled the square screaming, "Four more years!"—

Rome at a Glance

▲▲▲**Colosseum** Huge stadium where gladiators fought. **Hours:** Daily 8:30 until one hour before sunset: April-Aug until 19:15, Sept until 19:00, Oct until 18:30, off-season closes as early as 16:30. See page 35.

▲▲▲**Roman Forum** Ancient Rome's main square, with ruins and grand arches. **Hours:** Same hours as Colosseum. See page 38.

▲▲▲**Capitoline Museums** Ancient statues, mosaics, and expansive view of Forum. **Hours:** Daily 9:30-19:30. See page 44.

▲▲▲**Pantheon** The defining domed temple. **Hours:** Mon-Sat 8:30-19:30, Sun 9:00-18:00, holidays 9:00-13:00, closed for Mass Sat at 17:00 and Sun at 10:30. See page 58.

▲▲▲**St. Peter's Basilica** Most impressive church on earth, with Michelangelo's *Pietà* and dome. **Hours:** Church—daily April-Sept 7:00-19:00, Oct-March 7:00-18:00, often closed Wed mornings; dome—daily April-Sept 8:00-18:00, Oct-March 8:00-17:00. See page 62.

▲▲▲**Vatican Museums** Four miles of the finest art of Western civilization, culminating in Michelangelo's glorious Sistine Chapel. **Hours:** Mon-Sat 9:00-18:00. Closed on religious holidays and Sun, except last Sun of the month (open 9:00-14:00). May be open some Fri nights by online reservation only. Hours are subject to change. See page 63.

▲▲▲**Borghese Gallery** Bernini sculptures and paintings by Caravaggio, Raphael, and Titian in a Baroque palazzo. Reservations mandatory. **Hours:** Tue-Sun 9:00-19:00, closed Mon. See page 67.

▲▲▲**National Museum of Rome** Greatest collection of Roman sculpture anywhere. **Hours:** Tue-Sun 9:00-19:45, closed Mon. See page 78.

▲▲**Palatine Hill** Ruins of emperors' palaces, Circus Maximus view, and museum. **Hours:** Same hours as Colosseum. See page 38.

▲▲**Trajan's Column, Market, and Forum** Tall column with narrative relief, forum ruins, and museum with entry to Trajan's Market. **Hours:** Forum and column always viewable; museum open daily 9:30-19:30. See page 50.

SIGHTS

▲▲**Museo dell'Ara Pacis** Shrine marking the beginning of Rome's Golden Age. **Hours:** Daily 9:30-19:30. See page 75.

▲▲**Dolce Vita Stroll** Evening *passeggiata*, where Romans strut their stuff. **Hours:** Roughly Mon-Sat 17:00-19:00 and Sun afternoons. See page 74.

▲▲**Catacombs** Underground tombs, mainly Christian, some outside the city. **Hours:** Generally open 10:00-12:00 & 14:00-17:00. See pages 77, and 109.

▲▲**Church of San Giovanni in Laterano** Grandiose and historic "home church of the popes," with one-of-a-kind Holy Stairs across the street. **Hours:** Daily 7:00-18:30. See page 89.

▲**Arch of Constantine** Honors the emperor who legalized Christianity. **Hours:** Always viewable. See page 38.

▲**St. Peter-in-Chains** Church with Michelangelo's *Moses*. **Hours:** Daily 8:00-12:20 & 15:00-19:00, off-season until 18:00. See page 58.

▲**Piazza del Campidoglio** Square atop Capitoline Hill, designed by Michelangelo, with a museum, grand stairway, and Forum overlooks. **Hours:** Always open. See page 41.

▲**Victor Emmanuel Monument** Gigantic edifice celebrating Italian unity, with Rome from the Sky elevator ride up to 360-degree city view. **Hours:** Monument open daily 9:30-18:30; elevator open Mon-Thu 9:30-18:30, Fri-Sun 9:30-19:30. See page 48.

▲**Trevi Fountain** Baroque hot spot into which tourists throw coins to ensure a return trip to Rome. **Hours:** Always flowing. See page 61.

▲**Castel Sant'Angelo** Hadrian's Tomb turned castle, prison, papal refuge, now museum. **Hours:** Daily 9:00-19:30. See page 63.

▲**Baths of Diocletian/Basilica S. Maria degli Angeli** Once ancient Rome's immense public baths, now a Michelangelo church. **Hours:** Mon-Sat 7:00-18:30, Sun 7:00-19:30. See page 79.

or something like that. Mussolini created the boulevard Via dei Fori Imperiali (to your right, capped by Trajan's Column) to open up views of the Colosseum in the distance. Mussolini lied to his people, mixing fear and patriotism to push his country to the right and embroil the Italians in expensive and regrettable wars. In 1945, they shot Mussolini and hung him from a meat hook in Milan. (Former Prime Minister Silvio Berlusconi's headquarters are still located—thought-provokingly—just behind Mussolini's. That explains all the security on Via del Plebiscito.)

With your back still to the monument, circle around the left side. At the back end of the monument, look down into the ditch on your left to see the ruins of an ancient apartment building from the first century A.D.; part of it was transformed into a tiny church (faded frescoes and bell tower). Rome was built in layers—almost everywhere you go, there's an earlier version beneath your feet.

Continuing on, you reach two staircases leading up Capitoline Hill. One is Michelangelo's grand staircase up to the Campidoglio. The steeper of the two leads to Santa Maria in Aracoeli, a good example of the earliest style of Christian church (described earlier). The contrast between this climb-on-your-knees ramp to God's house and Michelangelo's elegant stairs illustrates the changes Renaissance humanism brought civilization.

From the bottom of Michelangelo's stairs, look right several blocks down the street to see a condominium actually built upon the surviving ancient pillars and arches of Teatro di Marcello.

▲Victor Emmanuel Monument

This oversize monument to Italy's first king, built to celebrate the 50th anniversary of the country's unification in 1861, was part of

Italy's push to overcome the new country's strong regionalism and create a national identity. Today, the monument houses museums (one of them good and free), a café with a great view, and a €7 elevator to an even better view. See the map on page 188.

The scale of the monument is over-the-top: 200 feet high, 500 feet wide. The 43-foot-long statue of the king on his high horse is one of the biggest equestrian statues in the world. The king's moustache forms an arc five feet long, and a person could sit within the horse's hoof. At the base of this statue, Italy's Tomb of the Unknown Soldier (flanked by Italian flags and armed guards) is watched over by the goddess Roma (with the gold mosaic background).

Cost and Hours: Monument—free, daily 9:30-18:30, a few WCs scattered throughout, tel. 06-6920-2049; Rome from the Sky Elevator—€7, Mon-Thu 9:30-18:30, Fri-Sun 9:30-19:30, ticket office closes 45 minutes earlier, WC at entrance, tel. 06-679-3598; follow *ascensori panoramici* signs inside the Victor Emmanuel Monument (no elevator access from street level).

Background: With its gleaming white sheen (from a recent scrubbing) and enormous scale, the monument provides a vivid sense of what Ancient Rome looked like at its peak—imagine the Forum filled with shiny, grandiose buildings like this one. It's also lathered in symbolism meant to connect the modern city and nation with its grand past: The eternal flames are reminiscent of the Vestal Virgins and the ancient flame of Rome. And it's crowned by glorious chariots like those that topped the ancient Arch of Constantine.

Locals have a love/hate relationship with this "Altar of the Nation." Many Romans say it's a "punch in the eye" and regret its unfortunate, clumsy location atop precious antiquities. Others consider it a reminder of the challenge that followed the creation of the modern nation of Italy: actually creating "Italians."

Visiting the Monument: The "Vittoriano" (as locals call it) is free to the public. You can simply climb the front stairs, or go inside from one of several entrances: midway up the monument through doorways flanking the central statue, on either side at street level, and at the base of the colonnade (two-thirds of the way up). Just inside the west entrance (by the stairs to the Capitoline Hill) is an excellent, free **museum of Italian emigration** (same hours as monument, www.museonazionaleemigrazione.it). Deeper into the monument, the little-visited **Museum of the Risorgimento** fills several floors with displays (well-described in English) on the movement and war that led to the unification of Italy. A section on the lower east side hosts temporary exhibits of minor works by major artists (€5 to enter museum, temporary exhibits around €10, tel. 06-322-5380, www.risorgimento.it). A café is at the base of the top colonnade, on the monument's east side.

Best of all, the monument offers a grand, free view of the Eternal City. You can climb the stairs to the midway point for a decent view, keep climbing to the base of the colonnade for a better view, or head up to the café and its terrace (at the back of the monument). For the grandest, 360-degree view—even better than from the top of St. Peter's dome—pay to ride the **Rome from the Sky** (Roma dal Cielo) elevator, which zips you from the café level to the rooftop. Once on top, you stand on a terrace between the monument's two chariots. You can look north up Via del Corso to Piazza del Popolo, west to the dome of St. Peter's, and south to the Roman Forum and Colosseum. Helpful panoramic diagrams describe the skyline, with powerful binoculars available for zooming in on particular sights. It's best in late afternoon, when it's beginning to cool off and Rome glows.

THE IMPERIAL FORUMS

Though the original Roman Forum is the main attraction for today's tourists, there are several more ancient forums nearby.

As Rome grew from a village to an empire, it outgrew the Roman Forum. Several energetic emperors built their own forums complete with temples, shopping malls, government buildings, statues, monuments, and piazzas. These new imperial forums were a form of urban planning, with a cohesive design stamped with the emperor's unique personality. Julius Caesar built the first one (46 B.C.), and over the next 150 years, it was added onto by Augustus (2 B.C.), Vespasian (A.D. 75), Nerva (A.D. 97), and Trajan (A.D. 112).

Today the ruins are out in the open, never crowded, and free to view any time, any day. The forums stretch in a line along Via dei Fori Imperiali, from Piazza Venezia to the Colosseum. The boulevard was built by the dictator Benito Mussolini in the 1930s—supposedly so he could look out his office window on Piazza Venezia and see the Colosseum, creating a visual link between the glories of the imperial past with what he thought would be a glorious imperial future. Today, the once-noisy boulevard is a pleasant walk, since it now is closed to private vehicles—and, on Sundays and holidays, to all traffic.

❍ **Self-Guided Walk:** For an overview of the archaeological area, take this walk from Piazza Venezia down Via dei Fori Imperiali to the end of the Imperial Forums. After a busy day of sightseeing, this stroll offers a relaxing way to wind down (while seeing a few more ancient wonders, but without crowds or turnstiles) on your way to Via Cavour and the nearby Cavour and Colosseo Metro stops.

• *Start at Trajan's Column, the colossal pillar that stands alongside Piazza Venezia.*

Trajan's Column: The world's grandest column from antiquity (rated ▲▲) anchors the first of the forums we'll see—Trajan's Forum. The 140-foot column is decorated with a spiral relief of 2,500 figures trumpeting the emperor's exploits. It has stood for centuries as a symbol of a truly cosmopolitan civilization. At one

The Imperial Forums

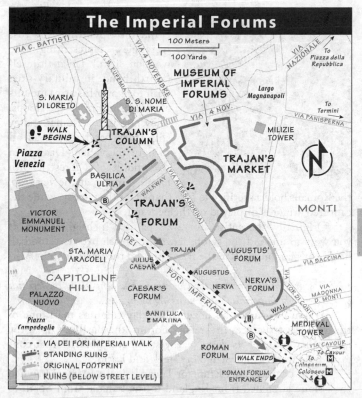

VIA C. BATTISTI

To Piazza della Repubblica

VIA NAZIONALE

100 Meters

100 Yards

S. MARIA DI LORETO

VIA 4 NOVEMBRE

V. S. EUFEMIA

S. S. NOME DI MARIA

MUSEUM OF IMPERIAL FORUMS

Largo Magnanapoli

To Termini

VIA 4 NOV.

VIA PANISPERNA

WALK BEGINS

TRAJAN'S COLUMN

MILIZIE TOWER

Piazza Venezia

TRAJAN'S MARKET

BASILICA ULPIA

WALKWAY

TRAJAN'S FORUM

(VIA ALESSANDRINA)

MONTI

VICTOR EMMANUEL MONUMENT

B

VIA

DEI

TRAJAN

AUGUSTUS' FORUM

VIA BACCINA

STA. MARIA ARACOELI

JULIUS CAESAR

AUGUSTUS

CAPITOLINE HILL

CAESAR'S FORUM

NERVA

NERVA'S FORUM

VIA MADONNA D. MONTI

PALAZZO NUOVO

FORI

VIA TOR DI CONTI

Piazza Campidoglio

SANTI LUCA E MARTINA

IMPERIALI

WALL

B

MEDIEVAL TOWER

VIA CAVOUR

VIA DEI FORI IMPERIALI WALK

STANDING RUINS

ORIGINAL FOOTPRINT

RUINS (BELOW STREET LEVEL)

ROMAN FORUM

B

WALK ENDS

To Cavour M

To Colosseo M Colosseo M

ROMAN FORUM ENTRANCE

SIGHTS

point, the ashes of Trajan and his wife were held in the base, and

the sun glinted off a polished bronze statue of Trajan at the top. (Since the 1500s, St. Peter has been on top.) Built as a stack of 17 marble doughnuts, the column is hollow (note the small window slots) with a spiral staircase inside, leading up to the balcony.

The **relief** unfolds like a scroll, telling the story of Rome's last and greatest foreign conquest, Trajan's defeat of Dacia (modern-day Romania). The staggering haul of gold plundered from the Dacians paid for this forum. The narrative starts at the bottom with a trickle of water that becomes a river and soon picks up boats full of supplies. Then come the soldiers themselves, who spill out from the gates of the city. A river god (bottom band, south side) surfaces to bless the journey. Along the way (second band), they build roads and forts to sustain the vast enterprise, including (third band, south side) Trajan's half-mile-long bridge over the Danube, the

longest for a thousand years. (Find the three tiny crisscross rectangles representing the wooden span.) Trajan himself (fourth band, in military skirt with toga over his arm) mounts a podium to fire up the troops. They hop into a Roman galley ship (fifth band) and head off to fight the valiant Dacians in the middle of a forest (eighth band). Finally, at the very top, the Romans hold a sacrifice to give thanks for the victory, while the captured armor is displayed on the pedestal.

Originally, the entire story was painted in bright colors. If you were to unwind the scroll, it would stretch over two football fields—it's far longer than the frieze around the Parthenon in Athens.

• *Now, start heading toward the Colosseum, walking along the left side of Via dei Fori Imperiali. You're walking alongside...*

Trajan's Forum: The dozen-plus gray columns mark one of the grandest structures in Trajan's Forum, the Basilica Ulpia, the largest law court of its day. Nearby stood two libraries that contained the world's knowledge in Greek and Latin.

Rome peaked under Emperor Trajan (ruled A.D. 98-117), when the empire stretched from England to the Sahara, from Spain to the Fertile Crescent. A triumphant Trajan returned to Rome with his booty and shook it all over the city. Most was spent on this forum, complete with temples, law courts, and the monumental column trumpeting his exploits. To build his forum, Trajan literally moved mountains. He cut away a ridge that once connected the Quirinal and Capitoline hills, creating this valley. This was the largest forum ever, and its opulence astounded even jaded Romans.

• *But most astounding of all was Trajan's Market. That's the big, semicircular brick structure nestled into the cutaway curve of Quirinal Hill. If you want a closer look, there's a pedestrian pathway that leads you up to it.*

Trajan's Market: This structure was part shopping mall, part warehouse, and part administration building and/or government offices. For now the conventional wisdom holds that at ground level, the 13 tall (shallow) arches housed shops selling fresh fruit, vegetables, and flow-

ers to people who passed by on the street. The 26 arched windows (above) lit a covered walkway lined with shops that sold wine and olive oil. On the roof (now lined with a metal railing) ran a street that likely held still more shops, making about 150 in all.

By now, Rome was a booming city of more than a million people. Shoppers could browse through goods from every corner of Rome's vast empire—exotic fruits from Africa, spices from Asia, and fish-and-chips from Londinium.

Above the semicircle, the upper floors of the complex housed bureaucrats in charge of a crucial element of city life: doling out free grain to unemployed citizens, who lived off the wealth plundered from distant lands. Better to pacify them than risk a riot. Above the offices, at the very top, rises a tower added in the Middle Ages.

The market was beautiful and functional, filling the space of the curved hill perfectly and echoing the curved side of the Forum's main courtyard. (The wall of rough volcanic stones on the ground once extended into a semicircle.) Unlike most Roman buildings, the brick facade wasn't covered with plaster or marble. The architect liked the simple contrast between the warm brick and the white stone lining the arches and windows.

If you'd like to walk around the market complex and see some excavated statues, visit the **Museum of the Imperial Forums** (described later; enter just uphill from Trajan's Column).

• *Return to the main street, and continue toward the Colosseum for about 100 more yards.*

You're still walking alongside Trajan's Forum. In Trajan's day, you would have entered the forum at the Colosseum end through a triumphal arch and would have been greeted in the main square by a large statue of the soldier-king on a horse.

But none of those things remain. The ruins you see in this section are actually from the medieval era. These are the foundations of the old neighborhood that was built atop the ancient city. In modern times, that neighborhood was cleared out to build the new boulevard.

You'll soon reach a bronze **statue of Trajan** himself. Though the likeness is ancient, this bronze statue is not. It was erected by the dictator Benito Mussolini when he had the modern boulevard built. Notice the date on the pedestal—Anno XI. That would be "the 11th year of the Fascist Renovation of Italy"— i.e., 1933. Imagine Mussolini strolling proudly down this historic boulevard with his fellow fascist leader, Adolf Hitler, in 1938. Anticipating the chance to host Hitler, he made sure all the props were in place enabling him to share stories of Rome's tradition of powerful rulers.

Across the street is a similar statue of **Julius Caesar.** That marks the first of these imperial forums, built by Julius in 46 B.C., as an extension of the Roman Forum. Near him stand the three remaining columns of his forum's Temple of Venus—the patron goddess of the Julian family.

• *Continue along (down the left side). As Trajan's Forum narrows to an end, you reach a statue of Emperor Augustus that indicates...*

The Forums of Augustus and Nerva: The statue captures **Emperor Augustus** in his famous hailing-a-cab pose (a copy of the original, which you can see at the Vatican Museums). This is actually his "commander talking to his people" pose. Behind him was the Forum of Augustus. Find the four white, fluted, Corinthian columns that were part of the forum's centerpiece, the Temple of Mars. The ugly gray stone wall that borders the forum's back end was built for security. It separated fancy "downtown Rome" from the workaday world beyond (today's characteristic and trendy Monti neighborhood) and protected Augustus' temple from city fires.

Farther along is a statue of **Emperor Nerva,** trying but failing to have the commanding presence of Augustus. (In fact, he seems to be gazing jealously across Via dei Fori Imperiali at the grandeur of the Roman Forum—the Curia and Palatine Hill.) Behind Nerva, you can get a closer look at his forum. Gaze down at an original marble inlaid floor that was once under a grand roof, surrounded by offices and shops within a semicircular mall. As with Augustus' Forum, the big stone wall (composed of volcanic tuff) on the far side was built to protect the "important" part of town from the fire-plagued working-class zone beyond.

Continuing a little farther (toward the Colosseum), find some fine marble reliefs from Nerva's Forum showing women in pleated robes parading in religious rituals.

• *You've reached the end of the Imperial Forums. You're at the intersection of Via dei Fori Imperiali and busy Via Cavour. From here, you have a number of options.*

Nearby: Here at the intersection stands an impressive crenellated tower. This was a medieval noble family's fortified residence—a reminder that the fall of Rome left a power vacuum, and with no central authority, it was every big shot for himself. Behind that (and the firewall) is the colorful neighborhood of Monti (see page 56, and home to a slew of fun little eateries, see page 379).

Two blocks up busy Via Cavour is the Cavour Metro stop. From there, you could turn right to find St. Peter-in-Chains Church (see page 58).

Across Via dei Fori Imperiali is an entrance to the Roman Forum (see page 157); 100 yards farther down Via dei Fori Imperiali (on the left) is a tourist information center with a handy café, info desk, and WC.

• *Our walk is over. Your transportation options include the Cavour and Colosseo Metro stops. Several buses stop along Via dei Fori Imperiali. And it's easy to hail a cab from here.*

NORTH OF VIA DEI FORI IMPERIALI

Several worthwhile sights sit across Via dei Fori Imperiali from the Roman Forum—and offer a break from the crowds.

Museum of the Imperial Forums (Museo dei Fori Imperiali)

The museum, housed in buildings from Trajan's Market, features discoveries from the forums built by the different emperors. Though its collection of statues is not impressive compared to Rome's other museums, it's well displayed. And—most importantly—it allows you to walk outside, atop and amid the ruins, making this the only way you can actually get up close to Trajan's Market and Forum (described earlier). Focus on the big picture to mentally resurrect the fabulous forums.

Cost and Hours: €11.50 when no special exhibitions, daily 9:30-19:30, last entry one hour before closing, tel. 06-0608, www.mercatiditraiano.it. Skip the museum's slow, dry €4 audioguide (you'll find some English descriptions within the museum); enter at Via IV Novembre 94 (up the staircase from Trajan's Column).

Visiting the Museum: Start by simply admiring the main hall—three stories with marble framed entries, fine brickwork, and high windows to allow natural light (Cheapskates can see this much from outside the entrance without paying admission.) A caryatid (a female statue serving as a column) from the Forum of Augustus stands in the museum's entryway, alongside a bearded mask of Giove (Jupiter). Nearby, a bronze foot is all that's left of a larger-than-life *Winged Victory* that adorned Augustus' Temple of Mars the Avenger. Then explore the statues and broken columns that once decorated the sites.

Upstairs, cross over to the other side of the hall (use the outdoor balcony) to find a section on Julius Caesar's Forum, including baby Cupids (the son of Venus and Mars) carved from the pure white marble that would eventually adorn all of Rome.

The rest of the upstairs is dedicated to the Forum of Augustus. A model of the Temple of Mars and some large column fragments give a sense of the enormous scale. You'll see bits and pieces of the hand of the 40-foot statue of Augustus that once stood in his forum.

From here, you can go outside. Walkways let you descend to stroll along the curved top of Trajan's Market. You get a sense of how inviting the market must have been in its heyday. As you walk around, you'll also enjoy expansive views of Trajan's Forum, his

SIGHTS

Rome vs. Milan: A Classic Squabble

In Italy, the North and South bicker about each other, hurling barbs, quips, and generalizations. All the classic North/South traits can be applied to Milan (the business capital) and Rome (the government and religious capital). Italians like to say that people come to Milan to sin, and they go to Rome to ask for forgiveness.

The Milanesi say the Romans are lazy. Government jobs in Rome come with short hours—made even shorter by multiple coffee breaks, three-hour lunches, chats with colleagues, and phone calls to friends and relatives. Milanesi contend that "Roma *ladrona*" (Rome, the big thief) is a parasite that lives off the taxes of people up North. There's still a strong Milan-based movement promoting secession from the South.

Romans, meanwhile, dismiss the Milanesi as uptight workaholics with nothing else to live for—gray like their foggy city. Romans do admit that in Milan, job opportunities are better and based on merit. And the Milanesi grudgingly concede the Romans have a gift for enjoying life.

While Rome is more of a family city, Milan is the place for high-powered singles on the career fast-track. Milanese yuppies

column, other forums in the distance, and the modern Victor Emmanuel Monument.

▲Monti Neighborhood

Tucked behind the imperial forums is a quintessentially Roman district called Monti. One of the oldest corners of Rome, this was the original "suburb" (from "subura"—outside the sacred center). Separated from the Imperial Forums by a tall stone firewall (which stands to this day), this was the rough, fire-prone, working-class zone. And it kept that character until just a few years ago when it became trendy. Now artisans, prostitutes, and colorful misfits have mostly been driven out by higher rents.

Squeezed between Via Nazionale and Via Cavour, this hilly tangle of lanes helps visitors understand why the Romans see their hometown not as a sprawling metropolis, but as a collection of villages. Exploring back lanes you can still find neighbors hanging out on the square and chatting, funky boutiques and fashionable shops sharing narrow streets with hole-in-the-wall hardware shops and *alimentari,* and wisteria-strewn cobbled lanes beckoning photographers. How this charming little bit of village Rome survived, largely undisturbed, just a few steps from some of Italy's

mix with each other...not the city's longtime residents. Milan is seen as wary of foreigners and inward-looking, and Rome as fun-loving, tolerant, and friendly. In Milan, bureaucracy (like social services) works logically and efficiently, while in Rome, accomplishing even small chores can be exasperating. Everything in Rome—from finding a babysitter to buying a car—is done through friends.

Milanesi find Romans vulgar. The Roman dialect is considered one of the coarsest in the country. Much as they try, Milanesi just can't say "Damn your dead relatives" quite as effectively as the Romans. Still, Milanesi enjoy Roman comedians and love to imitate the accent.

The Milanesi feel that Rome is dirty and Roman traffic nerve-wracking. But despite the craziness, Rome maintains a genuine village feel. People share family news with their neighborhood grocer. Milan lacks people-friendly piazzas, and entertainment comes at a high price. But in Rome, *la dolce vita* is as close as the nearest square, and a full moon is enjoyed by all.

most trafficked sights, is a marvel. While well-discovered by now (savvy travelers have been reading about Monti in "hidden Rome" magazine and newspaper articles for years), it's still a great place to peruse.

From the Roman Forum's main entrance, cross Via dei Fori Imperiali and angle up Via Cavour two blocks to Via dei Serpenti. Turn left, and in one block, you hit Monti's main square, **Piazza della Madonna dei Monti.** (The Cavour Metro stop also brings you steps away.) To get oriented, face uphill, with the big fountain to your right. That fountain is the neighborhood's meeting point—and after hours, every square inch is thronged with young Romans socializing and drinking. They either buy bottles of wine or beer to go at the little grocery at the top of the square or at a convenience store on nearby Via Cavour.

From this hub, interesting streets branch off in every direction. The characteristic core of the district can be enjoyed by strolling one long street with three names (Via della Madonna dei Monti, which leads from the ancient firewall to the central Piazza Madonna dei Monti, before continuing uphill as Via Leonina and then Via Urbana).

Monti is an ideal place for a quick lunch or early dinner, or for a memorable meal; for recommendations, see page 379. It's also a fine place to shop (see page 401) or hang out after dark (see page 413).

▲St. Peter-in-Chains Church (San Pietro in Vincoli)

Built in the fifth century to house the chains that held St. Peter, this church is most famous for its Michelangelo statue of Moses, intended for the tomb of Pope Julius II (which was never built). Check out the much-venerated chains under the high altar, then focus on mighty Moses. (Note that this isn't the famous St. Peter's Basilica, which is in Vatican City.)

Cost and Hours: Free, daily April-Sept 8:00-12:20 & 15:00-19:00, Oct-March until 18:00, modest dress required; the church is a 10-minute uphill walk from the Colosseum, or a shorter, simpler walk (but with more steps) from the Cavour Metro stop; tel. 06-9784-4950.

◘ See the St. Peter-in-Chains Tour chapter.

Pantheon Neighborhood

Besides being home to ancient sites and historic churches, the area around the Pantheon is another part of Rome with an urban-village feel. Wander narrow streets, sample the many shops and eateries, and gather with the locals in squares marked by bubbling fountains. Just south of the Pantheon is the Jewish quarter, with remnants of Rome's Jewish history and culture.

PANTHEON AND NEARBY

Exploring this area is especially nice in the evening, when restaurants bustle and streets are jammed with foot traffic. For a self-guided walk in this neighborhood, from Campo de' Fiori to the Trevi Fountain (and ending at the Spanish Steps), ◘ see the Heart of Rome Walk chapter or ∩ download my free audio tour.

▲▲▲Pantheon

For the greatest look at the splendor of Rome, antiquity's best-preserved interior is a must. Built two millennia ago, this influential domed temple served as the model for Michelangelo's dome of St. Peter's and many others.

Cost and Hours: Free, Mon-Sat 8:30-19:30, Sun 9:00-18:00, holidays 9:00-13:00, audioguide-€5, tel. 06-6830-0230.

◘ See the Pantheon Tour chapter or ∩ download my free audio tour.

▲▲Churches near the Pantheon

For more information on the following churches, see the latter half of my Pantheon Tour chapter. Modest dress is recommended.

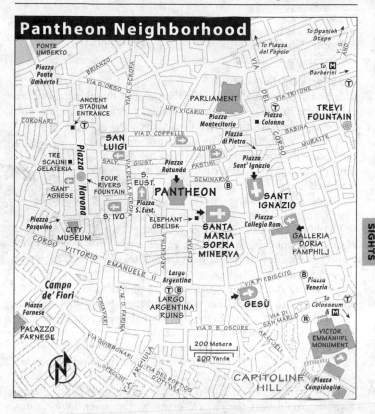

Pantheon Neighborhood

PONTE UMBERTO

Piazza Ponte Umberto I

VIA D'ORSO

BRIANZO

VIA D. SCROFA

To Piazza del Popolo

To Spanish Steps

To M Barberini

VIA TRITONE

VIA DEL CORSO

ANCIENT STADIUM ENTRANCE

CORONARI

UFF. VICARIO

PARLIAMENT

Piazza Montecitorio

Piazza Colonna

TREVI FOUNTAIN

SABINA

MURATTE

TRE SCALINI GELATERIA

Piazza Navona

SAN LUIGI

VIA D. COPPELLE

SALV.

GIUST.

AQUIRO

Piazza di Pietra

Piazza Sant' Ignazio

VIA DELLA SCROFA

PASTINI

FOUR RIVERS FOUNTAIN

SANT' AGNESE

Piazza Rotunda

S. EUST.

SEMINARIO

PANTHEON

SANT' IGNAZIO

Piazza Pasquino

CITY MUSEUM

S. IVO

Piazza S. Eust.

ELEPHANT OBELISK

SANTA MARIA SOPRA MINERVA

Piazza Collegio Rom.

GALLERIA DORIA PAMPHILJ

CORSO

VITTORIO

EMANUELE II

ARGENTINA

CESTARI

Largo Argentina

VIA PLEBISCITO

Piazza Venezia

To Colosseum & M

Campo de' Fiori

VIA D. FARINA

CHIAVARI

LARGO ARGENTINA RUINS

GESÙ

VIA DI SAN MARCO

Piazza Farnese

PALAZZO FARNESE

VIA GIUBBONARI

ARENULA

VIA D. B. OSCURE

200 Meters

200 Yards

VICTOR EMMANUEL MONUMENT

SPECCHI

VIA DEL PORTICO D'OTTAVIA

CAPITOLINE HILL

Piazza Campidoglio

SIGHTS

The **Church of San Luigi dei Francesi** has a magnificent chapel painted by Caravaggio (free, daily 9:30-12:30 & 14:30-18:30 except opens Sun at 10:30, between the Pantheon and the north end of Piazza Navona). The only Gothic church in Rome is the **Church of Santa Maria sopra Minerva,** with a little-known Michelangelo statue, *Christ Bearing the Cross* (free, Mon-Fri 7:30-19:00, Sat-Sun 8:00-12:30 & 15:30-19:00, on a little square behind the Pantheon, to the east). The **Church of Sant'Ignazio,** several blocks east of the Pantheon, is a riot of Baroque illusions with a false dome (free, Mon-Sat 7:30-19:00, Sun 9:00-19:00). A few blocks away, across Corso Vittorio Emanuele, is the rich and Baroque **Gesù Church,** headquarters of the Jesuits in Rome (free, daily 7:00-12:30 & 16:00-19:45, interesting daily ceremony at 17:30—see page 134 for details).

Two blocks down Corso Vittorio Emanuele from the Gesù Church, you'll hit **Largo Argentina,** an excavated square about four blocks south of the Pantheon. Stroll around this square and look into the excavated pit at some of the oldest ruins in Rome. Julius Caesar was assassinated near here. At the far (west) side of the square is a cat refuge where volunteers try to find adoptive families for some 250 felines (visitors welcome daily 12:00-18:00, tel. 06-6880-5611, www.romancats.com).

▲Galleria Doria Pamphilj

This underappreciated gallery, in the heart of the old city, offers a rare chance to wander through a noble family's lavish rooms with the prince who calls this downtown man-  sion home. Well, almost. Through an audioguide, the prince lovingly narrates his family's story as you tour the palace and its world-class art.

Cost and Hours: €12, includes worthwhile 1.5-hour audioguide, daily 9:00-19:00, last entry one hour before closing, elegant café, from Piazza Venezia walk 2 blocks up Via del Corso to #305, tel. 06-679-7323, www.dopart.it/roma.

Visiting the Galleria: The story begins upstairs in the grand entrance hall (Salone del Poussin), wallpapered with French land-scapes. In the adjoining throne room, you'll see a portrait of Pope Innocent X (1574-1655), patriarch of the Pamphilj (pahm-FEEL-yee) family. His wealth and power flowed to his nephew, who built the palace—a cozy relationship that inspired the word "nepotism" (*nepotem* is Latin for "nephew"). The family eventually married into English nobility, which is why today's prince speaks the Queen's English. You'll visit the red velvet room, the green living room, and the mirror-lined ballroom that once hosted music by resident composers Scarlatti and Handel. Along the way, the prince tells charming family secrets, like when he and his sister were scolded for roller-skating through the palace.

Past the bookshop is the painting collection. (Major works have a number to dial up audioguide information.) Don't miss Velázquez's intense, majestic, ultrarealistic portrait of the family founder, Innocent X. It stands alongside an equally impressive bust of the pope by the father of the Baroque art style, Gian Lorenzo Bernini. Stroll through a mini-Versailles-like hall of mirrors to more paintings, including works by Titian and Raphael. Finally, relax along with Mary, Joseph, and Jesus, and let the angel serenade you in Caravaggio's *Rest on the Flight to Egypt*.

Piazza di Pietra (Piazza of Stone)

This square, between the Pantheon and Via del Corso, is worth walking through to admire the remains of the ancient Temple of Hadrian. One huge wall from the temple survives as the facade of a 17th-century building. The temple was dedicated to the deified emperor responsible for building the Pantheon, nearby. To help you imagine the square in A.D. 145, look for a model of the temple in a window across the square at #36. In 1696 the city incorporated the remains of the temple into the building of Rome's central customs house. Today the building houses the chamber of commerce. The holes chipped into the ancient stones could be where the marble facing (which once adorned the temple) was attached. Historians think that Dark Age scavengers dug out the metal pins the Romans used to hold the marble stones in place; or the holes may have been used to anchor beams of medieval buildings built into this ruined structure. Look down over the railing to see ground level—with some original paving stones—from 1,900 years ago. (The piazza is two blocks toward Via del Corso from the Pantheon.)

▲Trevi Fountain

The bubbly Baroque fountain, worth ▲▲ by night, is a minor sight to art scholars...but a major nighttime gathering spot for teens on the make and tourists tossing coins. Those coins are collected daily to feed Rome's poor.

    ⬓ See the Heart of Rome Walk chapter or ⌥ download my free audio tour.

SIGHTS

JEWISH QUARTER

From the 16th through the 19th century, Rome's Jewish population was forced to live in a cramped ghetto at an often-flooded bend of the Tiber River. While the medieval Jewish ghetto is long gone, this area—between Campo de' Fiori and Capitoline Hill—is still home to Rome's synagogue and fragments of its Jewish heritage.

    ⬓ See the Jewish Ghetto Walk chapter or ⌥ download my free audio tour.

Synagogue (Sinagoga) and Jewish Museum (Museo Ebraico)

Rome's modern synagogue stands proudly on the spot where the medieval Jewish community was sequestered for more than 300 years. The site of a historic visit by Pope John Paul II, this synagogue features a fine interior and a museum filled with artifacts of Rome's Jewish community. The only way to visit the synagogue—unless you're here for daily prayer service—is with a tour.

    Cost and Hours: €11 ticket includes museum, audioguide, and guided tour of synagogue; April-Sept Sun-Thu 10:00-18:00, Fri until 16:00; Oct-March Sun-Thu 10:00-17:00, Fri 9:00-14:00, closed Sat year-round; last entry 45 minutes before closing, English tours usually at :15 past the hour, 30 minutes, check schedule at ticket counter, modest dress required, on Lungotevere dei Cenci, tel. 06-6840-0661, www.museoebraico.roma.it. Walking tours of the ghetto are conducted at least once a day except Saturday.

Vatican City and Nearby

Vatican City, the world's smallest country, contains St. Peter's Basilica (with Michelangelo's exquisite *Pietà*) and the Vatican Museums (with Michelangelo's Sistine Chapel). A helpful **TI** is just to the left of St. Peter's Basilica as you're facing it (Mon-Sat 8:30-18:15, closed Sun, tel. 06-6988-1662, www.vaticanstate. va). The entrances to St. Peter's and the Vatican Museums are a 15-minute walk apart (follow the outside of the Vatican wall, which links the two sights). The nearest Metro stop—Ottaviano—still involves a 10-minute walk to either sight. For information on Vatican tours, post offices, and the pope's schedule, see page 212.

Modest dress is required of men, women, and children throughout Vatican City, even outdoors. Cover your shoulders; bring a light jacket or cover-up if you're wearing a tank top. Wear long pants instead of shorts. Skirts or dresses should extend below your knee.

▲▲▲St. Peter's Basilica (Basilica San Pietro)

There is no doubt: This is the richest and grandest church on earth. To call it vast is like calling Einstein smart.

Cost and Hours: Free, daily April-Sept 7:00-19:00, Oct-March 7:00-18:00. The church closes on Wednesday mornings during papal audiences (until roughly 13:00). Masses occur daily throughout the day. Audioguides can be rented near the checkroom (€5 plus ID, for church only, daily 9:00-17:00). The view from the dome is worth the climb (€7 for elevator to roof, then take stairs; €5 to climb stairs all the way, cash only, allow an hour to go up and down, daily April-Sept 8:00-18:00, Oct-March 8:00-17:00, last entry one hour before closing if you take the stairs the whole way). Tel. 06-6988-1662, www.vaticanstate.va.

 See the St. Peter's Basilica Tour chapter or download my free audio tour.

▲▲▲Vatican Museums (Musei Vaticani)

The four miles of displays in this immense museum complex—from ancient statues to Christian frescoes to modern paintings—culminate in the Raphael Rooms and Michelangelo's glorious Sistine Chapel.

Cost and Hours: €16, €4 online reservation fee, Mon-Sat 9:00-18:00, last entry at 16:00 (though the official closing time is 18:00, the staff starts ushering you out at 17:30), closed on religious holidays and Sun except last Sun of the month (when it's free, more crowded, and open 9:00-14:00, last entry at 12:30); may be open Fri nights May-July and Sept-Oct 19:00-23:00 (last entry at 21:30) by online reservation only—check the website. Hours are subject to frequent change and holidays; look online for current times. Lines are extremely long in the morning—go in the late afternoon, or skip the ticket-buying line altogether by reserving an entry time on their website. A €7 audioguide is available (ID required). Tel. 06-6988-3860, http://mv.vatican.va.

📖 See the Vatican Museums Tour chapter. You can also 🎧 download my free Sistine Chapel and Vatican Museums audio tours.

▲Castel Sant'Angelo

Built as a tomb for the emperor, used through the Middle Ages as a castle, prison, and place of last refuge for popes under attack, and today a museum, this giant pile of ancient bricks is packed with history. The structure itself is striking, but the sight feels empty and underexplained—come for the building itself and the views up top, not for the exhibits or artifacts.

Cost and Hours: €10, free and very crowded first Sun of the month, daily 9:00-19:30, last entry one hour before closing, audioguide-€5, near Vatican City, 10-minute walk from St. Peter's Square at Lungotevere Castello 50, Metro: Lepanto or bus #40 or #64, tel. 06-681-9111, www.castelsantangelo.beniculturali.it.

Background: Ancient Rome allowed no tombs—not even the emperor's—within its walls. So Emperor Hadrian grabbed

the most commanding position just outside the walls and across the river and built a towering tomb (c. A.D. 139) well within view of the city. His mausoleum was a huge cylinder (210 by 70 feet) topped by a cypress grove and crowned by a huge statue of Hadrian himself riding a chariot. For nearly a hundred years,

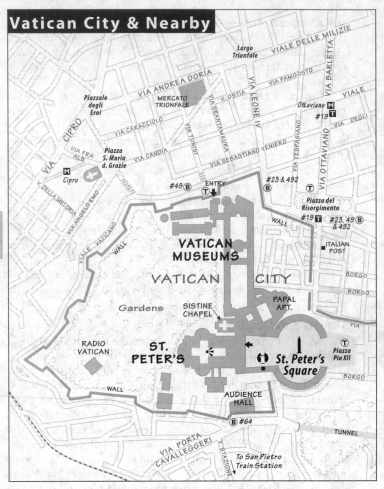

Vatican City & Nearby

Largo Trionfale

VIALE DELLE MILIZIE

VIA ANDREA DORIA

V. OSTIA

VIA LEONE IV

VIA FAMGOSTO

VIA BARLETTA

VIALE

Piazzale degli Eroi

MERCATO TRIONFALE

Ottaviano M #19

VIA DEGLI

VIA CARACCIOLO

VIA TUNISI

VIA BEANTAMAURA

VIA OTTAVIANO

VIA

CIPRO

VIA FRA ALB

Piazza S. Maria d. Grazie

VIA CANDIA

VIA SEBASTIANO VENIERO

VIA YESPASIANO

VIA DELLA MELORIA

M Cipro

VIA ANGELO EMO

#49 B

ENTRY T

#23 & 492 B

T

Piazza del Risorgimento

#19 T

#23, 49 B & 492

WALL

VIALE VATICANO

WALL

VATICAN MUSEUMS

ITALIAN POST

VATICAN   CITY

BORGO

BORGO

Gardens

SISTINE CHAPEL

PAPAL APT.

VIA

RADIO VATICAN

ST. PETER'S

St. Peter's Square

T Piazza Pio XII

Piazza Pio XII

BORGO

WALL

AUDIENCE HALL

B #64

VIA PORTA CAVALLEGGERI

V. STAZIONE

To San Pietro Train Station

TUNNEL

Roman emperors (from Hadrian to Caracalla, in A.D. 217) were buried here.

In the year 590, the archangel Michael appeared above the mausoleum to Pope Gregory the Great. Sheathing his sword, the angel signaled the end of a plague. The fortress that was Hadrian's mausoleum eventually became a fortified palace, renamed for the "holy angel."

Castel Sant'Angelo spent centuries of the Dark Ages as a fortress and prison, but was eventually connected to the Vatican via an elevated corridor at the pope's request (1277). Since Rome was repeatedly plundered by invaders, Castel Sant'Angelo was a handy place of last refuge for threatened popes. In anticipation of long sieges, rooms were decorated with papal splendor (you'll see paintings by Carlo Crivelli, Luca Signorelli, and Andrea Mantegna). In

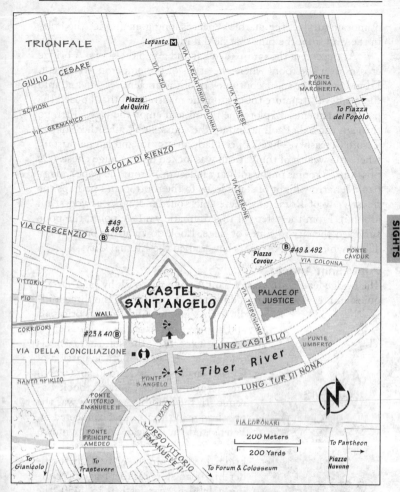

1527, during a sacking of Rome by troops of Charles V of Spain, the pope lived inside the castle for months with his entourage of hundreds (an unimaginable ordeal, considering the food service at the top-floor bar).

Visiting the Castle: Touring the place is a stair-stepping workout. After you walk around the entire base of the castle—buying your ticket en route—take the small staircase down to the original Roman floor (following the route of Hadrian's funeral procession). In the atrium, study the model of the mausoleum as it was in Roman times. Imagine being surrounded by a veneer of marble, and the niche in the wall filled with a towering "welcome to my tomb" statue of Hadrian. From here, a ramp leads to the right, spiraling 400 feet. While some of the fine original brickwork and bits of mosaic survive, the marble veneer is long gone (notice the holes in the wall from the pins that held it in place).

At the end of the ramp, turn left and go up the stairs. A bridge crosses over the room where the ashes of the emperors were kept. From here, more stairs continue out of the ancient section and into the medieval structure (built atop the mausoleum) that housed the papal apartments. Explore the rooms and enjoy the view. Then go through the Sala Paolina and up the stairs; don't miss the Sala del Tesoro (Treasury—likely once Hadrian's tomb, and later a prison), where the wealth of the Vatican was locked up in a huge chest. (*Do* miss the 58 rooms of the military museum.) From the pope's piggy bank, a narrow flight of stairs leads to the rooftop and perhaps the finest view of Rome anywhere (pick out landmarks as you stroll around). From the safety of this dramatic vantage point, the pope surveyed the city in times of siege. Look down at the bend of the Tiber, which for 2,700 years has cradled the Eternal City.

Ponte Sant'Angelo
The bridge leading to Castel Sant'Angelo was built by Hadrian for quick and regal access from downtown to his tomb. The three mid-

dle arches are actually Roman originals and a fine example of the empire's engineering expertise. The statues of angels (each bearing a symbol of the passion of Christ—nail, sponge, shroud, and so on) are Bernini-designed and textbook Baroque. In the Middle Ages, this was the only bridge in the area that connected St. Peter's and the Vatican with downtown Rome. Nearly all pilgrims passed this bridge to and from the church. Its shoulder-high banisters recall a tragedy: During a Jubilee Year festival in 1450, the crowd got so huge that the mob pushed out the original banisters, causing nearly 200 to fall to their deaths.

Today, as through the ages, pilgrims cross the bridge, turn left, and set their sights on the Vatican dome. Around the year 1600, they would have also set their sights on a bunch of heads hanging from the crenellations of the castle. Ponte Sant'Angelo was infamous as a place for beheadings (banditry in the countryside was rife). Locals said,

"There are more heads at Castel Sant'Angelo than there are melons in the market."

North Rome

BORGHESE GARDENS AND NEARBY
▲Villa Borghese Gardens

Rome's semi-scruffy three-square-mile "Central Park" is great for its quiet shaded paths and for people-watching plenty of modern-day Romeos and Juliets. The best entrance is at the head of Via Veneto (Metro: Barberini, then 10-minute walk up Via Veneto and through the old Roman wall at Porta Pinciana, or catch a cab to Via Veneto—Porta Pinciana). There you'll find a cluster of buildings with a café, a kiddie arcade, and bike rental (€4/hour). Rent a bike or, for romantics, a pedaled rickshaw (*riscio*, €12/hour). Bikes come with locks to allow you to make sightseeing stops. Follow signs to discover

the park's cafés, fountains, statues, lake, and prime picnic spots. Some sights require paid admission, including the Borghese Gallery (see Borghese Gallery Tour chapter), Rome's zoo (described on page 395), the National Gallery of Modern Art (which holds 19th-century art; not to be confused with MAXXI, described later), and the Etruscan Museum (described later).

You can also enter the gardens from the top of the Spanish Steps (facing the church, turn left and walk down the road 200 yards beyond Villa Medici, then angle right on the small pathway into the gardens), and from Piazza del Popolo (in the northeast corner of the piazza, stairs lead to the gardens via a terrace with grand views out to St. Peter's Basilica—bikes and Segways can be rented nearby).

▲▲▲Borghese Gallery (Galleria Borghese)

This plush museum, filling a cardinal's mansion in the park, offers one of Europe's most sumptuous art experiences. You'll enjoy a collection of world-class Baroque sculpture, including Bernini's *David* and his excited statue of Apollo chasing Daphne, as well as paintings by Caravaggio, Raphael, Titian, and Rubens. The museum's mandatory reservation system keeps crowds to a manageable size.

Cost and Hours: €11, free and very crowded first Sun of the month, Tue-Sun 9:00-19:00, closed Mon. Reservations are man-

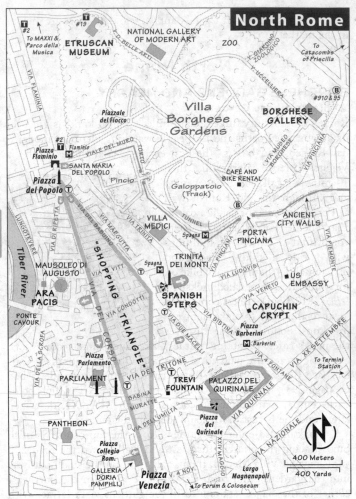

North Rome

To MAXXI & Parco della Musica

ETRUSCAN MUSEUM

NATIONAL GALLERY OF MODERN ART

ZOO

To Catacombs of Priscilla

VIA FLAMINIA

Villa Borghese Gardens

Piazzale del Fiocco

BORGHESE GALLERY

#910 & 95

Piazza Flaminio

Flaminio

SANTA MARIA DEL POPOLO

Piazza del Popolo

Pincio

VIALE DEL MURO

TORTO

Galoppatoio (Track)

CAFÉ AND BIKE RENTAL

VIA RIPETTA

VIA DEL BABUINO

VIA MARGUTTA

VIA TRINITA

VILLA MEDICI

Spagna

TUNNEL

ANCIENT CITY WALLS

PORTA PINCIANA

VIA PINCIANA

VIA PIEMONTE

Tiber River

LUNGOTEVERE

MAUSOLEO DI AUGUSTO

"SHOPPING TRIANGLE"

VIA VITT.

Spagna

TRINITA DEI MONTI

SPANISH STEPS

VIA LUDOVISI

US EMBASSY

VIA VENETO

CAPUCHIN CRYPT

ARA PACIS

PONTE CAVOUR

VIA DELLA SCROFA

VIA DEL CORSO

VIA CONDOTTI

VIA DUE MACELLI

VIA SISTINA

Piazza Barberini

Barberini

VIA 4 FONTANE

VIA XX SETTEMBRE

To Termini Station

Piazza Parlamento

PARLIAMENT

VIA DEL TRITONE

SABINA

MURATTE

TREVI FOUNTAIN

PALAZZO DEL QUIRINALE

VIA QUIRINALE

PANTHEON

VIA DELL'UMILTA

Piazza del Quirinale

VIA NAZIONALE

Piazza Collegio Rom.

GALLERIA DORIA PAMPHLIJ

Piazza Venezia

4 NOV.

XXIV MAGGIO

Largo Magnanapoli

To Forum & Colosseum

400 Meters

400 Yards

SIGHTS

datory and easy to get in English online (€4 per person extra, www.galleriaborghese.it) or by calling 06-32810. The further in advance you reserve, the better—a minimum of several days for a weekday visit, or at least a week ahead for weekends (less in winter). Admission times are strictly enforced (you'll get exactly two hours). The 1.5-hour audioguide (€5) is excellent.

📖 For more on reservations, as well as a self-guided tour, see the Borghese Gallery Tour chapter.

Etruscan Museum
(Museo Nazionale Etrusco di Villa Giulia)

The fascinating Etruscan civilization thrived in Italy around 600 B.C., when Rome was an Etruscan town. The Villa Giulia (a once fine, now down-at-heel Renaissance palace in the Villa Borghese Gardens) hosts a museum that tells the story. The displays are clean and bright, with thorough but stilted English descriptions.

Cost and Hours: €8, free and very crowded first Sun of the month, Tue-Sun 8:30-19:30, closed Mon, last entry one hour before closing, Piazzale di Villa Giulia 9, tel. 06-322-6571, www. villagiulia.beniculturali.it.

Getting There: Take tram #19 from Ottaviano or Lepanto Metro stations to the Museo Etrusco Villa Giulia stop, right next to the museum. You can also walk from Metro: Flaminio (15 minutes) or the Borghese Gallery (20 minutes).

Visiting the Museum: The map in Room 1 shows how the Etruscans held the area from Rome to Florence (modern-day Tuscany and Umbria) before the rise of Rome. Find the key Etruscan cities (Vulci, Tarquinia, Cerveteri) where the museum's treasures were unearthed. Farther along, a painted, room-sized tomb from Tarquinia (Room 8, down the spiral staircase) shows how Etruscans buried

their dead, along with their possessions. Stroll through room after room of cases with vases—pottery painted either red-on-black or black-on-red. The star of the museum's sculptures is the famous "husband and wife sarcophagus" (Il Sarofago degli Sposi, Room 12)—a dead couple seeming to enjoy an everlasting banquet from atop their tomb (sixth century B.C. from Cerveteri).

Room 13b has a treasure: the Pyrgi Tablets, three gold sheets with inscriptions in both Etruscan and Phoenician. Texts like these have helped scholars decipher the Etruscan language. Sadly, most surviving Etruscan texts are gravestone epitaphs with a limited vocabulary—not very interesting reading. Etruscan isn't related to any other known language and its origin is a mystery.

Upstairs on the mezzanine, pass through the long hall of small, mostly bronze objects (statuettes and mirrors). Continuing up to the second floor, ogle gold jewelry that belonged to sophisticated, luxury-loving Etruscans (Room 24). Near the exit, Room 40 displays a well-known terra-cotta statue, the Apollo of Veio, which stood atop Apollo's temple. The smiling god welcomes Hercules, while his mother Latona stands nearby cradling baby Apollo.

MAXXI

Rome's "National Museum of Art of the 21st Century," billed as Italy's "first national museum dedicated to contemporary creativity,"

SIGHTS

is a playful concrete and steel structure filled with bizarre installations. Like many contemporary art museums, it's notable more for the building (designed by Zaha Hadid and costing €150 million) than the art inside. To me, it comes off as a second-rate Pompidou Center. While not to my taste, it's one of the few places in the city where fans of contemporary architecture can see the latest trends.

Since it's away from the center, consider combining it with a walk around fellow "starchitect" Renzo Piano's **Auditorium** to see how the city continues to evolve (15-minute walk to auditorium, from MAXXI follow Via Guido Reni to tram #2 stop and keep going—it's just beyond the elevated road; see page 410).

Cost and Hours: €10, Tue-Sun 11:00-19:00, Sat until 22:00, closed Mon, last entry one hour before closing, café; no permanent collection, several rotating exhibits throughout the year—preview on their website; take tram #2 (direction: Mancini) from the Flaminio Metro station to the Apollodoro tram stop, then walk west 5 minutes to Via Guido Reni 4a; to return (direction: Flaminio), the tram stop is 50 yards closer to MAXXI, tel. 06-320-1954, www.fondazionemaxxi.it.

VIA VENETO

In the 1960s, movie stars from around the world paraded down curvy Via Veneto, one of Rome's glitziest nightspots. Today it's still lined with the city's poshest hotels and the US Embassy, and retains a sort of faded Champs-Elysées elegance—but any hint of local color has turned to bland.

Capuchin Crypt (Cripta dei Frati Cappuccini)

If you want to see artistically arranged bones in Italy, this (while overpriced) is the place. The crypt is below the Church of Santa Maria della Immacolata Concezione on the tree-lined Via Veneto, just up from Piazza Barberini. The bones of about 4,000 friars who died in the 1700s are in the basement, all lined up in a series of six crypts for the delight—or disgust—of the always-wide-eyed visitor.

Cost and Hours: €8.50, daily 9:00-19:00, modest dress required, no photos, Via Veneto 27, Metro: Barberini, tel. 06-8880-3695, www.cappucciniviaveneto.it.

Visiting the Crypt: Before the crypt, a six-room museum covers the history of the Capuchins, a branch of the Franciscan order. You'll see painting after painting of monks with brown robes and tonsure (ring-cut hair). The exhibits, featuring clothing, books, and other religious artifacts used by members of the order, are explained in English, but the only real artistic highlight is a painting of *St. Francis in Meditation,* once attributed to Caravaggio (but now thought to be a contemporary copy).

For most travelers, however, the main attraction remains the morbid crypt. You'll begin with the Crypt of the Three Skeletons (#1). The ceiling is decorated with a skeleton grasping a grim-reaper scythe and scales weighing the "good deeds and the bad deeds so God can judge the soul"—illustrating the Catholic doctrine of earning salvation through good works. The clock with no hands, on the ceiling above the aisle, is a symbol: It means that life goes on forever, once led into the afterlife by Sister Death. The chapel's bony chandelier and the stars and floral motifs made by ribs and vertebrae are particularly inspired. Finally, look down to read the macabre, monastic, thought-provoking message that serves as the moral of the story: "What you are now, we used to be; what we are now, you will be."

In the large Crypt of the Tibia and Fibula (#2), niches are inhabited by Capuchin friars, whose robes gave the name to the brown coffee drink with the frothy white cowl. (Unlike monks, who live apart from society, the Capuchins are friars, who depend on charity and live among the people, and are part of the Franciscan order.) In this chapel we see the Franciscan symbol: the bare arm of Christ and the robed arm of a Franciscan friar embracing the faithful. Above that is a bony crown. And below, in dirt brought from Jerusalem 400 years ago, are 18 graves with simple crosses.

The Crypt of the Hips (#3) is named for the canopy of wavy hipbones with vertebrae bangles over its central altar. Between

crypts #3 and #4, look up to see the jaunty skull with a shoulder-blade bowtie.

In the Crypt of the Skulls (#4), look close on the central wall to find the hourglass with wings. Yes, time on earth flies.

The next room (#5) is the boneless chapel. This is part of a church, and the monks sometimes hold somber services here.

In the last room, the Crypt of the Resurrection (#6), with a painting of Jesus bringing Lazarus back to life, sets the theme of your visit: the Christian faith in resurrection.

As you leave (humming "the foot bone's connected to the..."), pick up a few of Rome's most interesting postcards—the proceeds support Capuchin mission work. Head back outside, where it's not just the bright light that provides contrast with the crypt. Within a few steps are the US Embassy, Hard Rock Café, and fancy Via Veneto cafés, filled with the poor and envious keeping an eye out for the rich and famous.

SIGHTS

BETWEEN PIAZZA DEL POPOLO AND THE PANTHEON

These sights are on or within a short walk of the bustling Via del Corso thoroughfare, which connects Piazza del Popolo to the heart of town.

▲Piazza del Popolo

This vast oval square marks the traditional north entrance to Rome. From ancient times until the advent of trains and airplanes, this was most visitors' first look at Rome. Today the square, known for its symmetrical design and its art-filled churches, is the starting point for the city's evening *passeggiata* (see the Dolce Vita Stroll at the end of the Nightlife in Rome chapter).

In 1480, Pope Sixtus IV recognized that the ramshackle medieval city was making a miserable first impression on pilgrims who walked here from all over Europe (similar to the Muslim pilgrimage to Mecca). He authorized city planners to appropriate property (establishing "eminent domain"), demolish old buildings, and create straight streets to accommodate traffic. This was the first of several papal campaigns to spruce up the square and make it a suitable entrance for the grand city. The German monk, Martin Luther, would have been impressed when, after walking 700 miles from Germany, he entered the city through this gate (in 1510).

Reach the square via the Flaminio Metro stop, pass through the third-century Aurelian Wall via the Porta del Popolo, and look south. The 10-story **obelisk** in the center of the square once graced the temple of Ramses II in Egypt and the Roman Circus Maximus racetrack. The obelisk was brought here in 1589 as one of the square's beautification projects. (The oval shape dates from the early 19th century.) At the south side of the square, twin **domed churches** mark the spot where three main boulevards exit the square and form a trident. The central boulevard (running between the churches) is Via del Corso, which since ancient times has been the main north-south drag through town, running to Capitoline Hill (the governing center) and the Forum. The road to the right led to the Vatican, and the road to the left led to the big pilgrimage churches of San Giovanni in Laterano and Santa Maria Maggiore. With the help of this *tridente,* pilgrims arriving without a good Rome guidebook knew just where to go. The three churches on Piazza del Popolo are all dedicated to Mary, setting the right tone.

Along the north side of the square (flanking the Porta del

Popolo) are two 19th-century buildings that give the square its pleasant symmetry: the Carabinieri station and the Church of Santa Maria del Popolo.

Two large **fountains** grace the sides of the square—Neptune to the west and Roma to the east (marking the base of Pincio Hill; steps lead up to the overlook with fine views to St. Peter's and the rest of the city). Though the name Piazza del Popolo means "Square of the People" (and the square is a popular hangout), it probably derives from the poplar trees that once stood here.

Church of Santa Maria del Popolo

One of Rome's most overlooked churches, this features two chapels with top-notch art by Caravaggio and Bernini, and a facade built of travertine scavenged from the Colosseum. The church is brought to you by the Rovere family, which produced two popes, and you'll see their symbol—the oak tree and acorns—throughout.

Cost and Hours: Free but bring coins to illuminate the art, daily 7:00-12:30 & 16:00-19:00, often partially closed to accommodate its busy schedule of Masses, on north side of Piazza del Popolo—as you face the gate in the old wall from the square, the church entrance is to your right.

Visiting the Church: Go inside and enjoy the big view from the entrance. This Augustianian church is a fine example of Roman Renaissance architecture, exuding harmony, rhythm, and lightness as its arches lope to the front where a few rare Renaissance glass windows shine behind the altar. (Most church windows in Rome are from Baroque times, and are clear.)

Like a mini art-history class, this church exposes you to various periods: art of the 1400s, celebrating realism (in the Della Rovere Chapel); the 1500s, embracing humanism (Chigi Chapel); and the 1600s, getting emotional with Baroque and the Counter-Reformation (Cerasi Chapel).

In the **Della Rovere Chapel** (immediately right of the church entrance), Pinturicchio's *Nativity with St. Jerome* illustrates the groundbreaking mastery of realistic landscape painting typical of the Renaissance. It's a Bible scene but it's set in 1490 Italy, so that parishioners could relate to it. Enjoy the delicate and harmonious scene with a stretch of ancient Rome's brick wall included.

The **Chigi Chapel** (KEE-gee, second on the left from the entrance) was designed by Raphael and inspired (as Raphael was) by the Pantheon. Notice the Pantheon-like dome, pilasters, and capitals. Above in the oculus, God looks in, aided by angels who power the eight known planets. Raphael built the chapel for his wealthy banker friend Agostino Chigi, buried in the pyramid-shaped tomb in the wall to the right of the altar. Later, Chigi's great-grandson hired Bernini to make two of the four statues, and Bernini—in good Baroque style—delivers with theatrics. In one corner, Daniel straddles a lion and raises his praying hands to God for help. Kitty-corner across the chapel, an angel grabs the prophet Habakkuk's hair and tells him to go take some food to poor Daniel in the lion's den.

In the **Cerasi Chapel** (left of the main altar) Carracci's *Assumption of Mary* is pretty, classical, and forgettable. The highlights are the two Caravaggios on either side. Caravaggio's *Conversion of St. Paul* (from 1601) shows the future saint sprawled on his back beside his horse while his servant looks on. The startled Paul is blinded by the harsh light as Jesus' voice asks him, "Why do you persecute me?" In the style of the Counter-Reformation, Paul receives his new faith with open arms. The big butts, dirty feet, harsh foreshortening, and striking angels are all classic, melodramatic Caravaggio.

In the same chapel, Caravaggio's *Crucifixion of St. Peter* is shown as a banal chore; the workers toil like faceless animals. The light and dark are in high contrast. Caravaggio liked to say, "Where light falls, I will paint it."

▲▲Dolce Vita Stroll

All over the Mediterranean world, people are out strolling in the early evening. Rome's *passeggiata* is both elegant (with chic people enjoying fancy window shopping in the grid of streets around the Spanish Steps) and a little crude (with young people on the prowl). Watching the spectacle is a key Rome experience; I recommend following the action on Piazza del Popolo and along Via del Corso (roughly Mon-Sat 17:00-19:00 and Sun afternoons; for more, see the Dolce Vita Stroll in the Nightlife in Rome chapter).

▲Spanish Steps

The wide, curving staircase, culminating with an obelisk between two Baroque church towers, is one of Rome's iconic sights. Beyond that, it's a people-gathering place. By day, the area hosts shoppers looking for high-end fashions; on warm evenings, it attracts young people in love with the city. 📖 For more about the steps, see the Heart of Rome Walk chapter or 🎧 download my free audio tour.

Shopping Triangle

The triangular-shaped area between the Spanish Steps, Piazza Venezia, and Piazza del Popolo (along Via del Corso, see map on page 68) contains Rome's highest concentration of upscale boutiques and fashion stores. For more, see the Shopping in Rome chapter.

▲▲Museo dell'Ara Pacis (Museum of the Altar of Peace)

On January 30, 9 B.C., soon-to-be-emperor Augustus led a procession of priests up the steps and into this newly built "Altar of

Peace." They sacrificed an animal on the altar and poured an offering of wine, thanking the gods for helping Augustus pacify barbarians abroad and rivals at home. This marked the dawn of the Pax Romana (c. A.D. 1-200), a Golden Age of good living, stability, dominance, and peace (pax). The Ara Pacis (AH-rah PAH-chees) hosted annual sacrifices by the emperor until the area was flooded by the Tiber River. For an idea of how high the water could get, find the measure (idrometro) scaling the right side of the church closest to the entrance. Buried under silt, it was abandoned and forgotten until the 16th century, when various parts were discovered and excavated. Mussolini gathered the altar's scattered parts and reconstructed them in a building here in 1938. Today, the Altar of Peace stands in a pavilion designed by American architect Richard Meier (opened 2006). If this modern building seems striking, perhaps that's because it's about the only entirely new structure permitted in the old center of Rome since Mussolini's day.

Cost and Hours: €10.50 when no special exhibits, tightwads can look in through huge windows for free, daily 9:30-19:30, last entry one hour before closing, good audioguide-€4; a long block west of Via del Corso on Via di Ara Pacis, on the east bank of the Tiber near Ponte Cavour, Metro: Spagna plus a 10-minute walk down Via dei Condotti; tel. 06 0608, www.arapacis.it.

◆ Self-Guided Tour: Start with the model in the museum's lobby. The Altar of Peace was originally located east of here, along today's Via del Corso. The model shows where it stood in relation to the Mausoleum of Augustus (now next door) and the Pantheon. (The Ara Pacis originally faced west; now it faces east. Be aware that some art-history books and even the Ara Pacis website may describe it using the original—and opposite—orientation.) Nearby, you'll also see a row of emperors' heads, a good film telling the story of the Ara Pacis and its recovery (press the button for English), and other exhibits.

Entrance Side: Approach the Ara Pacis and look through the doorway to see the raised altar. This simple structure has just the basics of a Roman temple: an altar for sacrifices surrounded by cubicle-like walls that enclose a consecrated space. Its well-preserved reliefs celebrate Rome's success. After a sacrifice, the altar was washed, and the blood flowed out drain holes still visible at the base of the walls. Flanking the doorway are (badly damaged) reliefs of Rome's legendary founders—Romulus and Remus (on the left, being suckled by the she-wolf) and bearded Aeneas (right), the mythical hero of Troy and Rome, who's pouring a wine offering and preparing to sacrifice a sow.

Interior: Climb the 10 steps and go inside. From here, the priest would climb the eight altar steps to make sacrifices. The walls of the enclosure are decorated with the kinds of things offered to the gods: animals (see the cow skulls), garlands of fruit, and ceremonial platters to present the offerings. Circle to the left side of the altar to find a relief showing a sacrifice in action. Priests lead the animals to slaughter. They carry swords to do the job, plates and jugs for offering food and wine, and leafy sprigs to dip into the blood and shake around.

Right (North) Side: Head back out and walk around the right side of the structure. This relief probably depicts the parade of dignitaries who consecrated the altar. Just left of center is Augustus, his body sliced in two, vertically, by a missing stone—he's the one with only half a body. Augustus wears the victor's crown of laurel leaves, having just conquered parts of Spain and Gaul. Augustus is followed by a half-dozen bigwigs and priests (with spiked hats) and the man shouldering the sacrificial ax. Next comes Agrippa (wearing the hood of a priest), Augustus' right-hand man in battles against Mark Antony and Cleopatra. Agrippa married Augustus' daughter, Julia—their little son, Gaius, tugs on his dad's toga while turning to look at Livia, Augustus' wife (a few heads farther back). When Agrippa died, Gaius was adopted and named as successor by Augustus. Gaius also died young, making the next in line Tiberius, Livia's son by a first marriage, shown standing next to his mother. Confused? Find these names and other descendants of Julius Caesar on the genealogical chart and the row of busts in the museum lobby.

Before proceeding farther around the altar, look out the window to see the overgrown Mausoleum of Augustus and his family, once capped with a dome of earth, elegant spruces, and statues of the emperor. To the left is an example of Mussolini's fascist architecture—intended to remind Italians of their imperial Roman roots. Note the travertine, brick, low-relief propaganda, stony inscriptions, Roman numerals, and cold rationality. (Locals don't like it.) This area was the Field of Mars, Rome's only neighborhood continuously inhabited since ancient times.

Back Side: The altar's back door is flanked with reliefs celebrating the two things Augustus brought to Rome: peace (goddess Roma as a conquering Amazon, right side) and prosperity (fertility goddess surrounded by children, plants, and animals, left side). For a closer look at details from the various reliefs, see the model back near the museum entrance.

Left (South) Side: Leading the parade of senators is a *lictor*—a ceremonial bodyguard—carrying the *fasces*. This bundle of sticks symbolized how unity brings strength, and it gave us the modern word "fascism." The reliefs feature the first official portrayal of women and children in a public monument.

Beneath the parade, notice the elaborate floral relief that runs all the way around the Ara Pacis. Acanthus tendrils spiral out, forming decorative garlands, intertwining with ivy, laurel, and more. Swans with outstretched wings hide among the patterns. Some 50 plants are blooming in this display of abundance. Imagine the altar as it once was, standing in an open field, painted in bright colors—a mingling of myth, man, and nature.

BEYOND THE ANCIENT WALLS
▲▲Catacombs of Priscilla (Catacombe di Priscilla)
Of the dozens of catacombs honeycombing the ground just outside the ancient city walls, only five are open to the public. While most tourists and nearly all tour groups go out to the Appian Way to see the famous catacombs of San Sebastiano and San Callisto, the Catacombs of Priscilla (on the other side of town) are less commercialized and less crowded—they just feel more intimate, as catacombs should.

Cost and Hours: €8, Tue-Sun 9:00-12:00 & 14:00-17:00, closed Mon, closed one random month a year—check website or call first, Via Salaria 430, tel. 06-8620-6272, www.catacombepriscilla. com.

Getting There: The catacombs are on the northeast edge of the city but well-served by direct buses (30 minutes from Termini or 40 minutes from Piazza Venezia) or a €15 taxi ride. From Termini, take bus #92 or #310 from Piazza Cinquecento. From Piazza Venezia, along Via del Corso or Via Barberini, take bus #63 or #83. Tell the driver "Piazza Crati" and "kah-tah-KOHM-bay" and he'll let you off near Piazza Crati (at the Nemorense/Crati stop). From there, walk through the little market in Piazza Crati, then down Via di Priscilla (about 5 minutes). The entrance is in the orange building on the left at the top of the hill.

Visiting the Catacombs: The Catacombs of Priscilla likely originated as underground tombs for Christians, who'd meet to worship in the wealthy Christian's home that was on this spot. As poor people couldn't generally afford a nice plot in a cemetery, they would dig graves at a generous person's home...and dig and dig.

At the Catacombs of Priscilla, you enter from a convent and explore the result of 250 years of tunneling that occurred from the second to the fifth centuries.  Visits are by 30-minute guided tour only (English-language tours go whenever a small group gathers—generally every 20 minutes or so). You'll see a few thousand of the 40,000 niches carved here, along with some beautiful frescoes, including what is considered the first depiction of Mary nursing the Baby Jesus.

As in other catacombs, some of the tunnels date from an earlier quarry. Volcanic tuff, the stone ancient Rome was built with, works great for burial niches—it's easy to dig and dries hard when exposed to air.

📖 For more information on catacombs, see the Ancient Appian Way Tour chapter.

East Rome

NEAR TERMINI TRAIN STATION

Most of these sights are within a 10-minute walk of the train station (except for the Baroque Surprises Stroll and art exhibitions, which are a bit farther).

▲▲▲National Museum of Rome (Museo Nazionale Romano Palazzo Massimo alle Terme)

The National Museum's main branch, at Palazzo Massimo, houses the greatest collection of ancient Roman art anywhere, including busts of emperors and a Roman copy of the Greek *Discus Thrower*.

Cost and Hours: €10 combo-ticket covers three other branches—all skippable, free and very crowded first Sun of the month, Tue-Sun 9:00-19:45, closed Mon, last entry one hour before closing, audioguide-€5, about 100 yards from train station, Metro: Repubblica or Termini, tel. 06-3996-7700, www.archeoroma. beniculturali.it/en.

📖 See the National Museum of Rome Tour chapter.

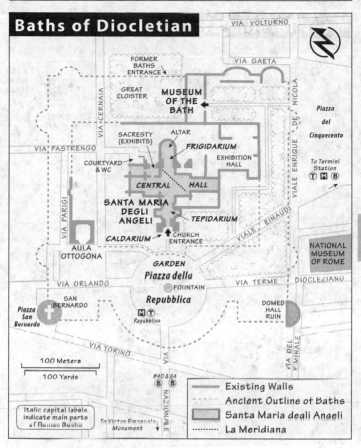

Baths of Diocletian

Existing Walls
- - - - Ancient Outline of Baths
▨ Santa Maria degli Angeli
·········· La Meridiana

Italic capital labels indicate main parts of Roman Baths

SIGHTS

▲**Baths of Diocletian/Church of Santa Maria degli Angeli (Terme di Diocleziano/Basilica S. Maria degli Angeli)**

Of all the marvelous structures built by the Romans, their public baths were arguably the grandest, and the Baths of Diocletian were the granddaddy of them all. Built by Emperor Diocletian around A.D. 300 and sprawling over 30 acres—roughly five times the size of the Colosseum—these baths could cleanse 3,000 Romans at once. Today, tourists can visit one grand section of the baths, the former main hall. This impressive remnant of the ancient complex was later transformed (with help from Michelangelo) into the Church of Santa Maria degli Angeli.

Cost and Hours: Free, Mon-Sat 7:00-18:30, Sun until 19:30, entrance on Piazza della Repubblica (Metro: Repubblica), www.santamariadegliangeliroma.it. Note that the Museum of the Bath, attached to the back (north side) of the complex and entered separately, is not part of the church but rather a branch of the National

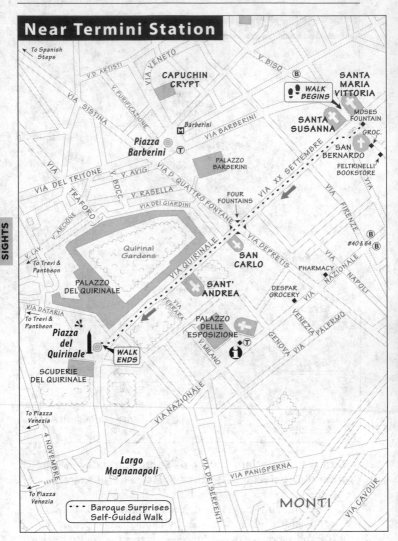

Near Termini Station

To Spanish Steps

V.D. ARTISTI

V. VENETO

V. PURIFICAZIONE

CAPUCHIN CRYPT

V. BISO

VIA SISTINA

Barberini

M Barberini

VIA BARBERINI

Piazza Barberini

T

PALAZZO BARBERINI

WALK BEGINS

SANTA MARIA VITTORIA

MOSES FOUNTAIN

GROC.

SANTA SUSANNA

SAN BERNARDO

FELTRINELLI BOOKSTORE

VIA

VIA XX SETTIMBRE

VIA DEL TRITONE

V. AVIG.

BOCC.

VIA D. QUATTRO FONTANE

FOUR FOUNTAINS

VIA DEL TRAFORO

V. ARCIONE

V. RASELLA

VIA DEI GIARDINI

VIA DEPRETIS

#40 & 64

B

SAN CARLO

Quirinal Gardens

VIA QUIRINALE

SANT' ANDREA

PHARMACY

DESPAR GROCERY

VIA NAZIONALE NAPOLI

V. LAV.

To Trevi & Pantheon

PALAZZO DEL QUIRINALE

VIA FERRARA

PALAZZO DELLE ESPOSIZIONE

VENEZIA VIA PALERMO

GENOVA VIA

VIA DATARIA

To Trevi & Pantheon

Piazza del Quirinale

WALK ENDS

V. MILANO

T

SCUDERIE DEL QUIRINALE

To Piazza Venezia

4 NOVEMBRE

VIA NAZIONALE

Largo Magnanapoli

VIA DEI SERPENTI

VIA PANISPERNA

MONTI

VIA CAVOUR

To Piazza Venezia

- - - Baroque Surprises Self-Guided Walk

SIGHTS

Museum of Rome that houses an exhibit of ancient inscriptions (see page 286).

Background: Large building projects like the baths were political security: They provided employment and fed the masses. Diocletian (ruled A.D. 285-305) struggled to find a system to rule his unwieldy empire. He broke it into zones ruled by four "tetrarchs." During Diocletian's "tetrarchs" period, architecture and art were grandiose, but almost a caricature of greatness—meant to proclaim to Romans that their city was still the power it had once been.

The baths were one of the last great structures built before Rome's 200-year fall. They functioned until A.D. 537, when bar-

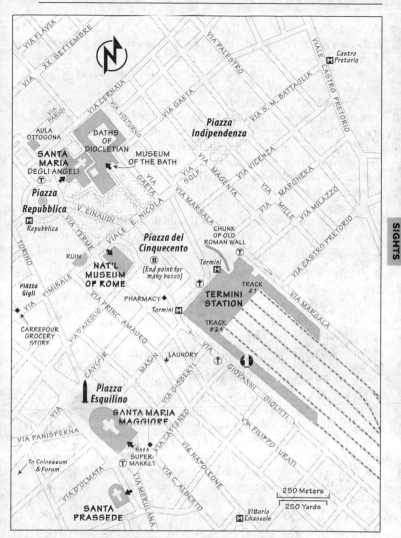

SIGHTS

barians attacked and the city's aqueducts fell into disuse, plunging Rome into a thousand years of poverty, darkness, and BO.

⊙ **Self-Guided Tour:** Start outside the church. The curved brick facade of today's church was once part of the *caldarium*, or steam room, of the ancient baths. Romans loved to sweat out last night's indulgences. After entering the main lobby (located where Piazza della Repubblica is today), they'd strip in the locker rooms, then enter the steam room. The *caldarium* had wood furnaces under the raised floors. Stoked by slaves, these furnaces were used to heat the floors and hot tubs. The low ceiling helped keep the room steamy.

Entry Hall: Step into the vast and cool church. This round-domed room with an oculus (open skylight, now with modern stained glass) was once the ***tepidarium***—the cooling-off room of the baths, where medium, "tepid" temperatures were maintained. This is where masseuses would rub you down and clean you off with a metal scraper called a strigil (Romans mostly used oils, including olive, rather than soap).

Large Transept: Step into the biggest part of the church and stand under the towering vault on the inlaid marble cross. In ancient times, from the *tepidarium*, Romans would have continued on

to this space, the **central hall** of the baths. While the decor around you dates from the 18th century, the structure dates from the fourth century.

This hall retains the grandeur of the ancient baths. It's the size of a football field and seven stories high—once even higher, since the original ancient floor was about 15 feet below its present level. The ceiling's crisscross arches were an architectural feat unmatched for a thousand years. The eight red granite columns are original, from ancient Rome—stand next to one and feel its five-foot girth. (Only the eight in the transept proper are original. The others are made of plastered-over brick.) In Roman times, this hall was covered with mosaics, marble, and gold, and lined with statues.

From here, Romans could continue (through what is now the apse, near the altar) into an open-air courtyard to take a dip in the vast 32,000-square-foot swimming pool (the *frigidarium*) that paralleled this huge hall. Many other rooms, gardens, and courtyards extended beyond what we see here. The huge complex was built in only 10 years (around A.D. 300)—amazing when you think of the centuries it took to build puny medieval cathedrals, such as Notre-Dame in Paris.

Mentally undress your fellow tourists and churchgoers, and imagine hundreds of naked or toga-clad Romans wrestling, doing jumping jacks, singing in the baths, networking, or just milling about.

The baths were more than washrooms. They were health clubs

with exercising areas, equipment, and swimming pools. They had gardens for socializing. Libraries, shops, bars, fast-food vendors, pedicurists, depilatories, and brothels catered to every Roman need. Most important, perhaps, the baths offered a spacious, cool-in-summer/warm-in-winter place for Romans to get out of their stuffy apartments and schmooze or simply hang out.

Admission was virtually free, requiring only the smallest coin. Baths were open to men and women—and during Nero's reign, coed bathing was popular—but generally there were either separate rooms or separate entry times. Most Romans went daily.

Michelangelo's Church: The church we see today was (at least partly) designed by Michelangelo (1561), who used the baths' main hall as the nave. Later, when Piazza della Repubblica became an important Roman intersection, another architect renovated the church. To allow people to enter from the grand new piazza, he spun it 90 degrees, turning Michelangelo's nave into a long transept. The four large paintings flanking the main altar were originally in St. Peter's (they were replaced there with mosaics).

La Meridiana (1702): Embedded in the floor of the right transept (roped off) is a brass rod, pointing due north. It acts as a sundial. As the sun arcs across the southern sky, a ray of light beams into

the church through a tiny hole high in the wall and a cut in the cornice of the right transept. (To find the hole, follow the rod to the right to the wall and look up 65 feet.) The sunbeam sweeps across the church floor, crossing the meridian rod at exactly noon (before modern innovations like Daylight Saving Time).

This celestial clock is also a calendar. In summer, when the sun is high overhead, the sunbeam strikes the southern end of the rod. With each passing day, the sun travels up the rod (toward the apse), passing through the signs of the zodiac (the 28-day months of the moon's phases) marked alongside the rod. Many of the meridian's markings were intended for its other use, charting the movement of the stars. However, the tiny window that once let in light from the North Star (originally above the archway of the entrance to the apse) has been filled in.

La Meridiana was Rome's official city timekeeper until 1846, when it was replaced by the cannon atop Gianicolo Hill (which is still fired every day at exactly noon).

Exhibits: The small room to the left of the main altar, the **Sacrestia,** now houses temporary exhibits, often illuminating the church's rich architectural history. Admire both the immensity and height of the ancient Roman brickwork in this room. Step outside into the courtyard and re-create the grand architecture. Notice the *exedra* (semicircular recess in a wall or building)—a motif Romans used for decoration and as a kind of stage for philosophers and orators. See the niches that once housed statues, the rectangular holes that could be used to hold wood-beam scaffolding, and the small pockmarks where iron pegs once secured the marble paneling.

Nearby: **Piazza della Repubblica,** in front of the baths, was once a garden at the center of the vast, ancient complex. It was called Piazza Esedra until Italian unification (and is still called that by many Romans). The building wrapping around it is a monumental office block, typical of Italian-unification architecture of the late 19th century. The thundering Via Nazionale starts on the far side at what was an ancient door. Look down it (past the erotic nymphs of the Naiad fountain) to the Victor Emmanuel Monument. The Art Nouveau fountain of the four water nymphs created quite a stir when unveiled in the early 1900s. The nymphs were modeled after a set of twins, who kept coming to visit as late as the 1960s to remind themselves of their nubile youth. Here at the site of the ancient Thermae, the statues bathe eternally.

▲Church of Santa Maria della Vittoria

This church houses Bernini's best-known statue, the swooning *St. Teresa in Ecstasy.*

Cost and Hours: Free (anyone collecting money at the door is not affiliated with the church), pay €0.50 for light, Mon-Sat 8:30-12:00 & 15:30-18:00, Sun 15:30-18:00, about 5 blocks northwest of Termini train station at Via XX Settembre 17, Metro: Repubblica.

Visiting the Church: Inside the church, you'll find St. Teresa to the left of the altar. Teresa has just been stabbed with God's arrow of fire. Now, the angel pulls it out and watches her reaction. Teresa swoons, her eyes roll up, her hand goes limp, she parts her lips...and moans. The smiling, cherubic angel understands just how she feels. Teresa, a 16th-century Spanish nun, later talked of the "sweetness" of "this intense pain," describing her oneness with God in ecstatic, even erotic, terms.

Bernini, the master of multimedia, pulls out all the stops to make this mystical vision real. Actual sunlight pours through the alabaster windows, bronze sunbeams shine on a marble angel holding a golden arrow. Teresa leans back on a cloud and her robe ripples from within, charged with her spiritual arousal. Bernini has created a little stage-setting of heaven. And watching from the "theater boxes" on either side are members of the family who commissioned the work.

The church, originally a poor Carmelite church, was slathered with Baroque richness in the 17th century. (It grew popular in modern times for its part in Dan Brown's *Angels and Demons*, something that serious historians scoff at.) At the altar, in the center of the starburst, is an icon of the Virgin Mary, considered miraculous for the military victories attributed to it during the Thirty Years' War (early 1600s). And, as the 17th century was a time when the Roman Catholic Church was threatened by Protestants, the ceiling shows Mary defeating (Protestant) snakes, who grasp scriptures translated from the pope's Latin into the evil vernacular.

Santa Susanna Church

The home of the American Catholic Church in Rome, the Santa Susanna church building may be closed for renovation during your

visit. During the renovations, Mass is held in English daily in nearby churches; check their website for the temporary locations and times. They also arrange papal audience tickets (see page 212), and their excellent website contains tips for travelers and a list of convents that rent out rooms. You'll find a description of the church's facade next, in my Baroque Surprises Stroll.

Hours: Mass usually held Mon-Sat around 18:00, and on Sunday mornings, Via XX Settembre 15, near recommended Via Firenze hotels, Metro: Repubblica, office tel. 06-4201-4554, www.santasusanna.org.

Baroque Surprises Stroll on Via XX Settembre

When Pope Sixtus V developed an ambitious plan to reorganize Rome around key landmarks (c. 1580s), he transformed this formerly sleepy neighborhood near the Baths of Diocletian. Within three generations, it was a major traffic hub and the center of a new city water system. The streets were lined with grand fountains, obelisks, and churches, all decorated in the new style of the 1600s—Baroque.

⊙ Self-Guided Walk: This half-mile walk starts in Piazza di San Bernardo (near the Church of Santa Maria della Vittoria, with Bernini's famous statue of St. Teresa, described earlier), travels down Via XX Settembre, and ends at the Palazzo del Quirinale, where you can see a distant obelisk (see map on page 80 for route). The churches we'll look at are free to enter; the hours are listed for each one, but keep in mind that they close for an early afternoon break (from 12:00 or 13:00 until 15:30 or 16:00).

• *Start at the wide square known as...*

Piazza di San Bernardo: At the end of the square is the imposing **Fountain of Moses.** After a thousand years of living on well water, the citizens of this neighborhood finally got fresh running water with the opening of this public fountain (1585-1588). It was built by Pope Sixtus V as the end point for a newly restored, 15-mile-long ancient aqueduct. From here, water was distributed to dozens of other nearby fountains. The vast undertaking was celebrated with statues by Domenico Fontana, starring Moses—renowned for miraculously bringing forth water in the desert. Take a look at the fountain's four huge columns, recycled from ancient ruins. Besides being decorative, the fountain was functional, designed to quench the thirst of visiting pilgrims and their horses.

Also on the square is the **Church of Santa Susanna.** You're looking at what was considered the first Baroque facade—see the date: MDCIII (1603). It was designed by Carlo Maderno at the same time he was working on the facade of St. Peter's. As this is Baroque rather than Renaissance, the columns are in higher relief. The structure seems to pop out at you from the center with an energy that enlivens the entire building. The architect added a new Baroque element—curves—seen in the scrollwork "shoulders." We'll see curves in spades later in this walk. (This church, home to the American Catholic community in Rome, is currently closed for renovation; daily Mass in English is offsite—see page 85. They can also help you get tickets for a papal audience—see page 212).

Turn 180 degrees. Opposite the Church of Santa Susanna is the circular **Church of San Bernardo** (built 1598). Why is the church round? Because it was incorporated into one of the corner towers of the Baths of Diocletian. Think of how far away the baths' central hall is (see map on page 80), and appreciate how vast that ancient health club was.

• *Now, with the Fountain of Moses at your back, walk down...*

Via XX Settembre: This is an ancient road. Pope Sixtus knew it as Via Pia, but its name now memorializes a modern military victory—the capture of Rome by Italian nationalists on September 20, 1870. As you walk, you'll pass the local "Pentagon" (the Ministry of Defense, on the left, with the stony bottom and pink top) and other governmental buildings marked by uniforms, tight security, barriers against car bombs, and Italian and European flags.

• *Soon you'll reach the very pedestrian-unfriendly intersection with...*

Via delle Quattro Fontane: This intersection, named for its four fountains, was an important waypoint for 16th-century pilgrims. Imagine poor and haggard wayfarers trudging into town with little money and bereft of a Rick Steves guidebook. They navigated by sighting the obelisks and domes that Sixtus' plan had planted around the city. Entering from the north (as most Northern European visitors did), they'd hike up the hill and pause here to drink from their choice of fountains. They could then either continue straight to the famous pilgrimage church of Santa Maria Maggiore—whose spire is visible to the left—or (spotting the obelisk down the road), head for Palazzo del Quirinale, then the residence of the pope. The intersection's fountains depict river gods relaxing in the shade. They were designed by a familiar name—Domenico Fontana, or Signor "Fountain."

• *Just past the fountain on the left side of the street (best viewed from the right side, to take in the full facade) is the...*

Church of San Carlo alle Quattro Fontane: On the facade, the distinct curves of Baroque have now evolved into undulating

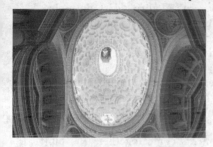

waves, rippling the surface of this watershed church. And the medallion on top introduces another Baroque element—the oval.

The church was designed by Francesco Borromini (c. 1640), who had served his apprenticeship at St. Peter's, carving putti for his cousin Maderno and

building the altar canopy *(baldacchino)* for the famous Bernini. He and Bernini split on bad terms. Now Bernini's competitor, Borromini used this church as a chance to finally go solo and show his stuff.

Step inside (Mon-Fri 10:00-13:00 & 15:00-18:00, Sat 10:00-13:00, Sun 12:00-13:00, www.sancarlino.eu). The tiny interior is oval-shaped, topped with an oval dome, which is itself topped with a tiny oval lantern. The whole upper story is a riot of wavy lines—ovals, arches, circles—that defy classical notions of symmetry. The dome is coffered with a complex mix of polygons and crosses. The dome seems to float, with no visible support, and is lit by no obvious light source.

The church looks rich. But Borromini's patrons—an order of poor monks—had little money. So the church is small and made of simple materials—brick, concrete, and plaster—but manipulated with lots of 3-D tricks. Borromini's design is brilliant: light, soft, and as if in a cloud. Light, a symbol of God, pours in from the holy dove in the cupola above (which seems higher than it is). Borromini designed everything for the tight space—notice the tidy little confessionals. And the cherubs are ever so huggable.

With this church, Borromini shocked the critics. But over the centuries, it's become classically Roman—locals fondly call it San

Carlino. Borromini, who went on to contribute much to Rome's architecture, committed suicide by stabbing himself in the chest.

• *Head one block farther down the street (which is now called Via del Quirinale). On the left is the...*

Church of Sant'Andrea al Quirinale: Often called the "Pearl of the Baroque," this exquisite church sums up the Baroque style (1661). It was designed by the most famous Baroque artist, Gian Lorenzo Bernini, as a chapel for the pope's entourage at the Palazzo del Quirinale. As it was actually used by popes, Bernini had plenty of money for the work—there's lots of marble and gold—but he needed to be pretty conventional. This feels more solid, stable, and classical than the Borromini church.

Inside, the focus is on the altar, dedicated to St. Andrew, or Sant'Andrea (Tue-Sat 8:30-12:00 & 14:30-18:00, Sun 9:00-12:00 & 14:30-18:00, closed Mon, www.gesuitialquirinale.it). Bernini—the master of multimedia—uses every artistic device to tell Andrew's story. The apostle (depicted in the altar painting) is being crucified on his X-shaped cross. He gazes up toward the light. His soul seems to follow the bronze angels above him, up through a light-filled shaft. Then he reappears—now as a marble statue—above the altar. He bursts through the pediment, ascending on a cloud, into the golden light where he joins his fellow saints in the dome of heaven.

Bernini makes all these elements come together. The pink marble columns color-coordinate with the pink frame of the painting. A bronze angel rests his hand on the painting's marble frame. The delightfully backlit cherubs at the base of the shaft playfully look down on the action. And the suffused light filtering in from the dome brings all the colors together. Bernini combines sculpture, painting, and architecture into *"un bel composto"*—a beautiful whole.

• *Continue down Via del Quirinale, walking along the loooong extent of Palazzo del Quirinale (on your right). The building looks somewhat bigger than it is, because the side we're walking along is actually just a long, skinny building enclosing the formal Quirinale Gardens (for a glimpse of them, peek past the guards when you get to the square). Keep walking toward the main entrance on Piazza di Quirinale.*

Palazzo del Quirinale: The building (by Maderno and Signor Fountain) dates from 1583, but this site has housed Rome's ruling elite for 2,000 years. Ancient Roman aristocrats, Baroque-era popes, the kings of

reunited Italy (after XX Settembre, 1870), and today's presidents of Italy have all resided here—it's like a combination of the White House and Versailles. The president is elected by parliament and serves a seven-year term with mostly ceremonial duties; Sergio Mattarella, chosen in 2015, is the current office holder. Notice the three flags above the entrance: Europe, Italy, and—if he's currently at home in the palace—the personal flag of the president. The palace is tourable—in Italian—by advance reservation only (at least 5 days in advance; see www.quirinale.it for details).

Piazza del Quirinale: The square in front of the palace marks the summit of Quirinal Hill, the highest of Rome's fabled seven hills. The fountain in the middle of the square has colossal statues of horses and men (probably Castor and Pollux, third century); as part of his reordering of the city, Pope Sixtus V had the figures moved here around 1585 from a spot near the Baths of Constantine. The obelisk, which formerly stood in front of the Mausoleum of Augustus, was erected here in the late 1700s. Take in the views—there's a fine vista of St. Peter's Basilica in the distance. From here, a set of stairs (in the direction of the dome) leads down to the Trevi Fountain. The big road continues on to Piazza Venezia.

Art Exhibitions

Two temporary exhibition spaces near Palazzo del Quirinale show top-notch art on a rotating basis. Scuderie del Quirinale typically focuses on the great masters (Titian, Vermeer, Caravaggio), while Palazzo delle Esposizioni favors contemporary artworks and photography.

Cost and Hours: Typically €12-15 for each, can be more for some exhibits; both open Sun-Thu 10:00-20:00, Fri-Sat 10:00-22:30 except the Palazzo is closed Mon; both may open—and stay open—much later in summer; last entry one hour before closing; Scuderie—Via XXIV Maggio 16, tel. 06-696-271, www.scuderiequirinale.it; Palazzo—Via Nazionale 194, tel. 06-3996-7500, www.palazzoesposizioni.it.

PILGRIM'S ROME

East of the Colosseum (and south of Termini train station) are several venerable churches that Catholic pilgrims make a point of visiting. Near one of the churches is a small WWII museum.

📖 See the Pilgrim's Rome Tour chapter.

▲▲Church of San Giovanni in Laterano

Built by Constantine, the first Christian emperor, this was Rome's most important church through medieval times. A building alongside the church houses the Holy Stairs (Scala Santa), said to have been walked up by Jesus, which today are ascended by pilgrims on their knees.

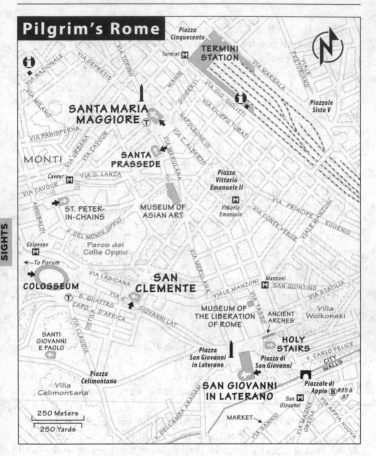

Pilgrim's Rome

Cost and Hours: Church and Holy Stairs-free, cloister-€5, chapel at Holy Stairs-€3.50 (€10 combo-ticket covers cloister, chapel, and audioguide); church open daily 7:00-18:30; Holy Stairs open Mon-Sat 6:30-19:00, Sun 7:00-19:00, Oct-March closes daily at 18:30; Piazza di San Giovanni in Laterano, Metro: San Giovanni, or bus #87; tel. 06-6988-6409, www.scalasantaroma.it.

Museum of the Liberation of Rome
(Museo Storico della Liberazione)

This small memorial museum, near the Church of San Giovanni in Laterano, is housed in what was the prison wing of the Nazi police headquarters while Rome was occupied during World War II. Other than a single pamphlet, there's little in English. Still, for those interested in resistance movements and the Nazi occupation, it's a stirring visit. You'll see a few artifacts, many photos of heroes, and a couple of cells preserved as they were found on June 4, 1944, when the city was liberated.

Cost and Hours: Free but donations accepted, Tue-Sun 9:30-12:30, Tue and Thu-Fri also 15:30-19:30, closed Mon and Aug, just behind the Holy Stairs, look for the flags at Via Tasso 145; tel. 06-700-3866, www.viatasso.eu.

▲Church of Santa Maria Maggiore

Rome's best-surviving mosaics line the nave of this church, built as Rome was falling. The nearby Church of Santa Prassede has still more early mosaics (described on page 309 in the Pilgrim's Rome Tour chapter).

Cost and Hours: Free, daily 7:00-18:45, Piazza di Santa Maria Maggiore, Metro: Termini or Vittorio Emanuele, tel. 06-6988-6800.

▲Church of San Clemente

Besides visiting the church itself, with frescoes by Masolino, you can also descend into the ruins of an earlier church. Descend yet one more level and enter the eerie remains of a pagan temple to Mithras. It's one of the easiest places to fully appreciate the layers of history that lie underfoot in Rome.

Cost and Hours: Upper church-free, lower church-€10, both open Mon-Sat 9:00-12:30 & 15:00-18:00, Sun 12:15-18:00; Via di San Giovanni in Laterano, Metro: Colosseo, or bus #87; tel. 06-774-0021, www.basilicasanclemente.com.

Trastevere and Nearby

Trastevere (trahs-TAY-veh-ray) is a colorful neighborhood with a medieval-village feel across *(tras)* the Tiber *(Tevere)* River. The action unwinds to the chime of the church bells. Go there and wander. This is Rome's Left Bank, the place for poets and artists.

This neighborhood was long a working-class area. Now that it's become trendy, high rents have driven out some of the color. Still, it's a great people scene, especially at night. Stroll the back streets (for restaurant recommendations, see the Eating in Rome chapter).

📖 See the Trastevere Walk chapter or 🎧 download my free audio tour.

▲Church of Santa Maria in Trastevere

One of Rome's oldest church sites, a basilica was erected here in the fourth century, when Christianity was legalized. It is said to have

been the first church in Rome dedicated to the Virgin Mary. The structure you see today dates mainly from the 12th century. Its portico (covered area just outside the door) is decorated with fascinating fragments of stone—many of them lids from catacomb burial niches—and filled with early Christian symbolism. The church is on Piazza di Santa Maria in Trastevere. While today's fountain is from the 17th century, there has been a fountain here since Roman times.

Cost and Hours: Free, daily 7:30-21:00, except Aug 8:00-12:00 & 16:00-21:00.

▲Villa Farnesina

Here's a unique opportunity to see a sumptuous Renaissance villa in Rome decorated with Raphael paintings. It was built in the early

1500s for the richest man in Renaissance Europe, Sienese banker Agostino Chigi. Kings and popes of the day depended on generous loans from Chigi, whose bank had more than 100 branches in places as far-flung as London and Cairo. His villa was the meeting place of aristocrats, artists, beautiful women, and philosophers. It's a quick visit (there are only four main rooms).

Architect Baldassare Peruzzi's design—a U-shaped building with wings enfolding what used to be a vast garden—successfully blended architecture and nature in a way that both ancient and Renaissance Romans loved. Orchards and flower beds flowed down in terraces from the palace to the riverbanks. Later construction of modern embankments and avenues robbed the garden of its grandeur, leaving it with a more melancholy charm. Inside, cavorting gods and goddesses cover the walls and ceilings, most famously Raphael's depiction of the sea nymph Galatea.

Cost and Hours: €6; Mon-Sat 9:00-14:00, closed Sun except open 9:00-17:00 on second Sun of month; across the river from

Campo de' Fiori, a short walk from Ponte Sisto and a block behind the river at Via della Lungara 230; tel. 06-6802-7268, www.villafarnesina.it.

➲ **Self-Guided Tour:** Enjoy the best bits of the villa with this commentary.

• *Begin in Room 1.*

Loggia of Galatea: Note the ceiling painted by Peruzzi, showing the position of the signs of the horoscope at the exact moment of Agostino's birth (21:30, November 29, 1466). The room's claim to fame is Raphael's painting of the nymph Galatea (on the wall by the entrance door). She shuns the doting attention of the ungainly one-eyed giant Polyphemus (in the niche to the left, painted by another artist) and speeds away in the company of her rambunctious entourage on a chariot led by dolphins. She turns back and looks up, amused by the Cyclops' crude love song (which, I believe, was "I Only Have Eye for

SIGHTS

You"). The trigger-happy cupids and lusty, entwined fauns and nymphs announce the pagan spirit revived in Renaissance Rome. All the painting's lines of sight (especially the cupids' arrows) point to the center of the work, Galatea's radiant face. Galatea is considered Raphael's vision of female perfection—not a portrait of an individual woman, but a composite of his many lovers in an idealized vision.

• *Continue into Room 2.*

Loggia of Psyche: This room was painted by Raphael and his assistants. Imagine it without the glass windows, as a continuation of the garden outside, where plays were performed to entertain Agostino's guests. Raphael's two ceiling frescoes were painted to look like tapestries (complete with ruffled edges), suspended from the ceiling by garlands, making the room appear to be an open

bower. View the frescoes from the top, with your back to the garden. The ceiling shows episodes in the myth of a lovely mortal woman, Psyche, who caught the eye of the winged boy-god Cupid (Eros). See the loving couple at the far left end, at the base of the ceiling. The big ceiling fresco on the left depicts the gods of Olympus gathered to plan a series of ordeals to test whether Psyche is worthy to marry a god. (Find Hercules with white beard and club, and Dionysius pouring the wine.) The other shows the happy ending, as Cupid (boy with wings) and Psyche (to his left, in topless robe) stand before Zeus to celebrate their wedding feast, attended by the pantheon of gods.

The whole setting—the room by the gardens, the subject of the frescoes, the fleshy bodies—has an erotic subtext. At the time, Raphael was having a passionate affair with the celebrated Fornarina (the "baker's daughter," who lived down the street). Agostino, noticing that his painter was constantly interrupting his workday to be with her, had the girl kidnapped so that Raphael would finally concentrate. But production slowed even more, as Raphael was depressed. Agostino gave up and had the Fornarina move in with Raphael to keep him company as he happily resumed work in this cheery room. The room's imagery abounds with images both phallic and yonic (the female counterpart of phallic). Next to the ripe and split-open cantaloupe (right end, base of ceiling), find the gourd wearing a condom.

• *Go out the room's main door and upstairs to the...*

Room of the Perspectives: Peruzzi, another trendsetter, painted this room. Walls seem to open onto views and perspectives that actually correspond with what lies outside. The graffiti (for example, on the wall at the far end) dates from 1527, when Protestant mercenaries sent by Charles V sacked the city and wrote some not very nice things about the Catholic Church.

Agostino had his wedding banquet in this room. His parties were the talk of the town. On one occasion, he invited his guests in the (now lost) dining loggia overlooking the Tiber to toss the gold and silver dishes they had just used into the river. (The banker had nets conveniently placed just below the river's surface.)

The small chamber at the end of the Room of the Perspectives was the **bedroom.** The painting on the wall depicts the wedding of Alexander the Great and Rox-anne. Roxanne has the features of Agostino's bride, and the bed is the jewel-encrusted ebony bed that received Agostino and his bride here in this room. On the entrance wall, find the three-arched ruins of the Basilica of Constantine in the Forum. The room was painted by Il Sodoma, a devoted fan of Michelangelo and one of the artists who was canned when Raphael took over the decoration of

the papal apartments at the Vatican. Had that not happened, the Raphael Rooms at the Vatican might have looked like this.

Agostino had famous affairs with the most beautiful courtesans of his day. He eventually settled down, but his wild-living descendants didn't, and—in the space of a couple of generations—the Chigi family lost its fabulous fortune.

Gianicolo Hill Viewpoint Hike

From this park atop a hill, the city views are superb, and the walk to the top holds a treat for architecture buffs. (It's easy to follow the route described below on the map on page 323.) Start at Trastevere's Piazza di Santa Maria and go south (to the left as you face the Church of Santa Maria in Trastevere) a couple of blocks through Piazza di San Calisto to Via Luciano Manara. Go right, and walk until you come to the fountain at the base of the hill (on Via Goffredo Mameli). Go right, following Via Goffredo Mameli until it intersects with Via Garibaldi. Just to the left of the intersection is access to the ramp and stairs that lead to the Church of San Pietro in Montorio. To the right of the church, in a small courtyard, is the **Tempietto** by Donato Bramante. This "small temple," built to commemorate the martyrdom of St. Peter (once believed to have happened at this spot), is considered a jewel of Italian Renaissance architecture and a prototype for the design of St. Peter's dome.

From the church, go right and continue up Via Garibaldi. You'll see immediately across the street on your left the white fascist arches of the **Italian Independence War Memorial,** commemorating the 1849 battle fought here, when Giuseppe Garibaldi's forces valiantly tried to hold back the invading French army. Atop one side is the inscription *Roma o Morte* (Rome or Death), the battle cry of Garibaldi's troops.

Continuing up, as the road curves, you'll see the monumental Baroque **Acqua Paola** fountain, named after Pope Paul V of the Borghese family (if you've been to the Borghese Gallery, you'll recognize the eagle and dragons from their coat of arms). Like the Trevi Fountain, it commemorates the restoration of an aqueduct that brought water to the city and incorporates columns from the original St. Peter's Basilica. Expansive views of the Roman skyline open up on your right. You can't miss the blocky, gleaming white Victor Emmanuel Monument along with assorted domes that rise above the Roman roofscape (look straight out for the rather nondescript, shallow dome of the Pantheon). The green space beyond the roofline is the Villa Borghese Gardens, and looming in the distance are the Alban Hills (home to Frascati, a town known for its wine production, and Castel Gandolfo, summer residence of the popes).

From here, you have two choices. To return to Trastevere, retrace your steps. But a short climb farther is rewarding. If you were to continue up Via Garibaldi you'd reach the cube-shaped **Porta San Pancrazio,** an opening in the Aurelian Walls that were extended up this hill in the third century to protect Rome's strategic water mills.

But by now your quad muscles are reminding you that you are climbing a hill—the Janiculum (Gianicolo in Italian) Hill, named after the two-faced Roman god Janus (who also gives name to the month January—looking back to the previous year and forward to the next). Leaving the fountain, cross the street and take a right through the gate with two urns up the tree-lined Passeggiata del Gianicolo and enter the hill-crowning park. You'll soon reach the large **Piazzale Giuseppe Garibaldi,** dominated by the equestrian statue of the swashbuckling military leader of the Italian unification. He enjoys a *magnifico* view of the Eternal City that you can drink in by standing at the railing on the right. A little farther along, look left to find the baby-carrying, gun-wielding, horse-riding statue of Anita Garibaldi, Giuseppe's Brazilian-born partner in battle (and in life). They had four children before her death from malaria during Garibaldi's retreat from Rome in 1849. The nearby **Manfredi Lighthouse** was built as a gift to Rome from Italian immigrants to Argentina.

From here you can follow the road that snakes its way down to the river. Or if your feet are screaming *"Roma o Morte,"* catch any northbound bus (#115 or #870) down to the river. Consider doing this hike in reverse by taking a bus (or taxi) to the top of the hill and then walking steadily downhill to Trastevere.

South Rome

These second-tier but interesting sights are strung along Metro line B, south of the city. For maximum efficiency, use this spine to quickly hop between these sights, using the following Metro stops: Piramide (Testaccio area and trains to Ostia Antica), Garbatella (Montemartini Museum), Basilica San Paolo (St. Paul's Outside the Walls), and E.U.R. Magliana (Palace of the Civilization of Labor). The color map of South Rome at the beginning of this book gives an overview of this area.

TESTACCIO

In the creative, postindustrial Testaccio neighborhood, you can spend a pleasant hour exploring several fascinating but lesser sights near the Piramide Metro stop, then end with a meal. (This is a quick and easy stop as you return from E.U.R., or when changing trains en route to Ostia Antica.)

In ancient times (when Rome was the first city on earth to reach a population of one million), wharves lined the banks of the

Testaccio

1 Agustarello Ristorante
2 Flavio al Velavevodetto
3 Pizzeria Remo
4 Volpetti Più
5 Perilli
6 L'Oasi della Birra
7 To Eataly

Tiber River here. Back then, 90 percent of the city's food came through this area. More recently, the neighborhood was known for a huge slaughterhouse that opened in the late 19th century. Now the formerly abandoned complex is being redeveloped. Meat hooks and cattle pens have yielded to a branch of Rome's contemporary art museum (MACRO), temporary exhibition space, classrooms from a nearby university, and a weekend farmers and craft market.

Long a working-class neighborhood, Testaccio has gone trendy-bohemian. Visitors wander through an awkward mix of hipster and proletarian worlds, not noticing—but perhaps sensing—the "Keep Testaccio for the Testaccians" graffiti.

Romans come to Testaccio to enjoy its numerous tasty eateries. Thanks to its history as the neighborhood of slaughterhouses, Testaccio (more so than elsewhere in Rome) is home to restaurants that are renowned for their ability to cook up the least palatable parts of the animals...the *quinto quarto* ("fifth quarter"): tripe (stomach), lungs, brains, sweetbreads (organs), tail, and so on. While adventurous foodies (who call this "nose-to-tail" eating) seek out these dishes—and you'll find them at most restaurants here—every place also has plenty of offerings that are anything but offal.

You can pick and choose among the Testaccio sights described here or link them with my walking directions, using the map to follow along. A late morning visit works well, ending with lunch at Testaccio's covered market or nearby restaurants. Note that the neighborhood is quiet, and many restaurants are closed on Sunday.

Testaccio can be reached by taking the Metro to Piramide, or by bus (#23 or #280 from Trastevere or the Vatican area; #83 from Piazza Venezia).

• *From the Metro station exit, look straight across the busy intersection to find the giant pyramid and the adjacent brick fortress. For a closer look at these—carefully cross the several busy lanes of traffic and head for the gap between these two landmarks.*

Pyramid of Gaius Cestius

In the first century B.C., the Roman occupation of Egypt brought exotic Pharaonic styles into vogue. Stoking the fascination with

Egypt even further was the love affair of Mark Antony and Cleopatra; this power couple was the ancient equivalent of Brangelina (Cleopantony?). A rich Roman magistrate, Gaius Cestius, had this pyramid built as his tomb, complete with a burial chamber inside. Made of brick covered in marble, the 90-foot structure was completed in just 330 days (as stated in its Latin inscription). While smaller than actual Egyptian pyramids, its proportions are correct. It was later incorporated into the Aurelian Wall (explained next), and it now stands as a marker to the entrance of Testaccio. The most dramatic views of the pyramid are from inside the Protestant Cemetery (described later), on the other side of the wall.

• *Across the narrow street from the pyramid is the...*

Porta San Paolo and Museo della Via Ostiense

This formidable gate is from the Aurelian Wall, begun in the third century under Emperor Aurelian. The wall, which encircled the city, was 12 miles long and averaged about 26 feet high, with 14 main gates and 380 72-foot-tall towers. Most of what you'll see today is circa A.D. 400, but the barbarians reconstructed the gate later, in the sixth century.

Inside the gate is a tiny free museum, the Museo della Via Ostiense (find entrance near pyramid; Tue-Sun 9:00-13:00, closed Mon, tel. 06-574-3193). The museum offers a chance to explore the gate and a few models of Rome's ancient port, Ostia Antica; its neighbor, Porto, with its famed hexagonal harbor; and the Ostian Way, the straight Roman road that paralleled the curvy Tiber for 15 miles from Rome to the sea.

For more on the Aurelian Wall, visit the Porta San Sebastiano and Museum of the Walls (described in my 📖 Ancient Appian Way Tour chapter). For more on Ostia Antica, see the 📖 Ostia Antica chapter or 🎧 download my free audio tour.

• *Go through the gap between the pyramid and the gate on Via Raffaele Persichetti/Via Marmorata. On your right, notice the beige travertine* **post office** *from 1932. This is textbook Mussolini-era fascist architecture; the huge X theme in the window design celebrates the 10th anniversary of the dictator's reign.*

Take the first left, on sleepy Via Caio Cestio, and walk about 100 yards, looking on the left for the gate of the...

Protestant Cemetery

Lush and lovingly cared for, the Cemetery for the Burial of Non-Catholic Foreigners (Cimitero Acattolico per gli Stranieri al Testaccio) is a tomb-filled "park," running along the wall just beyond the pyramid. The cemetery is also the only English-style landscape (rolling hills, calculated vistas) in Rome, making it a favorite spot for a quiet stroll.

Cost and Hours: €3 suggested donation—leave in box by entrance, Mon-Sat 9:00-17:00, Sun until 13:00, WC inside, staff at info office can help you find specific graves, tel. 06 574 1900, www.cemeteryrome.it.

Visiting the Cemetery: Originally, none of the Protestant epitaphs were allowed to mention heaven. Signs direct visitors to the graves of notable non-Catholics who have died in Rome since 1716. Many of the buried were diplomats. And many, such as the poets Percy Bysshe Shelley (1792-1822) and John Keats (1795-1821), were from the Romantic Age. They came to Italy on the Grand Tour and—"captivated by the fatal charms of Rome," as Shelley wrote—never left.

Shelley's tomb is straight ahead from the entrance, up the hill and a bit to the left, at the base of the stubby tower. It's a big, inscribed, flat slab in the ground. Like so many Romantic age artists and writers, Shelley was enamored with Rome. In 1821 he wrote, "Go thou to Rome,—at once the Paradise, the grave, the city, and the wilderness" (from *Adonais*, his elegy on Keats' death).

Back at the entrance, with your back to the gate, head 90 degrees left to find **Keats' tomb,** near the fence in the far corner of

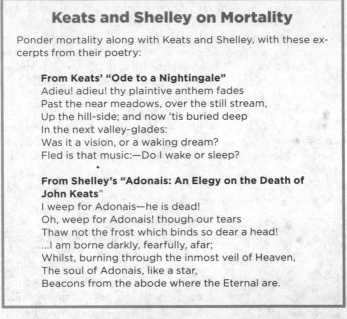

Keats and Shelley on Mortality

Ponder mortality along with Keats and Shelley, with these excerpts from their poetry:

From Keats' "Ode to a Nightingale"
Adieu! adieu! thy plaintive anthem fades
Past the near meadows, over the still stream,
Up the hill-side; and now 'tis buried deep
In the next valley-glades:
Was it a vision, or a waking dream?
Fled is that music:—Do I wake or sleep?

•

From Shelley's "Adonais: An Elegy on the Death of John Keats"
I weep for Adonais—he is dead!
Oh, weep for Adonais! though our tears
Thaw not the frost which binds so dear a head!
...I am borne darkly, fearfully, afar;
Whilst, burning through the inmost veil of Heaven,
The soul of Adonais, like a star,
Beacons from the abode where the Eternal are.

the big park facing the pyramid. Keats died in his twenties, unrecognized. He wanted to be unnamed on a tomb that read, "Young

English Poet, 1821. Here lies one whose name was writ in water." (To see Keats' tomb when the cemetery is closed, look through the tiny peephole on Via Caio Cestio, 10 yards off Via Marmorata.)

There are cats everywhere. At the big park overlooking the pyramid, look down and to the right to find Matilde Talli's cat hospice. Volunteers use donations to care for these "Guardians of the Departed" who "provide loyal companionship to these dead."

• *Exit the cemetery through the main gate and turn left, continuing down Via Caio Cestio. Cross the wide street and head down into the sunken area ringing...*

Monte Testaccio

This "hill," actually a 115-foot-tall ancient trash pile, is made of *testae*—broken shards of earthenware jars mostly used to haul oil 2,000 years ago, when this was a gritty port warehouse district. For 500 years, rancid oil vessels were discarded here. Slowly, Rome's lowly eighth hill was built. Because the caves dug into the hill are naturally air-conditioned, trendy bars, clubs, and restaurants compete with gritty car-repair places for a spot. Testaccio is one of Rome's most popular nightlife spots and, in the summer, the area around here houses Testaccio Village, a festival with concerts and techno raves.

Loop around the left side of the hill until you reach the old slaughterhouse complex. Linger here to pick out the history of this spot—the ornamentation of the building itself, the *frigorifero* (ice house adjacent), and the fine view of the shard mountain.

Within Rome, Testaccio's restaurants are known for serving menus heavy on offal—innards and other "unwanted" parts of the animals that were processed here (tripe, sweetbreads, oxtail, lungs, and so on). While the "nose to tail" foodie aesthetic has become trendy, Testaccio embraced that approach long before it was cool.
• *Circling the rest of the way around Monte Testaccio, you'll run right into main entrance of the former stockyards and, across the street, the very modern-looking...*

Testaccio Market (Mercato di Testaccio)
The covered and colorful market is typically Italian and a focal point of the neighborhood. Locals nurture close relationships with the merchants who sell them their favorite foods. There are several cafés as well as clothing and housewares sections (open Mon-Sat until 14:00, closed Sun, WC on the north side, near the clothing stalls). Find the center (where the sky opens up) and look down at the ancient Roman road littered with the shards of broken amphorae.

For tips on where to eat within the market and the surrounding neighborhood, see page 386. For a better understanding of what Testaccio is all about, consider **Eating Italy Food Tours'** interesting, food-oriented walk (see page 375).

SOUTH OF TESTACCIO
You can ride the Metro to the Montemartini Museum and St. Paul's Outside the Walls, but if you prefer to stay above ground, buses #23 and #769 run along Via Ostiense from the Piramide Metro stop to the museum (stop: Ostiense/Garbatella) and the church (stop: Viale S. Paolo).

▲Montemartini Museum (Musei Capitolini Centrale Montemartini)
This museum houses a dreamy collection of 400 ancient statues, set evocatively in a classic 1932 electric power plant, among generators and *Metropolis*-type cast-iron machinery. While the art is not as famous as the collections you'll see downtown, the effect is fun and memorable—and you won't encounter a single tourist. If you're

SIGHTS

tackling Rome with kids, this museum is ideal: It's uncrowded and cool, immersed in an old power plant, with art placed at kid level.

Cost and Hours: €7.50, Tue-Sun 9:00-19:00, closed Mon, look for red banner marking Via Ostiense 106, a short walk from Metro: Garbatella, tel. 06-0608, www.centralemontemartini.org.

▲St. Paul's Outside the Walls (Basilica San Paolo Fuori le Mura)

According to Christian tradition, the body of St. Paul was buried here, where a small shrine once stood. It was replaced by a

much bigger church in around A.D. 380—in what was the last major construction project of Imperial Rome and the largest church in Christendom until St. Peter's. That church burned in 1823, and the stately, if stark, Neoclassical church you see today was built on its footprint. Pilgrims flock here to venerate the saint, especially since forensic experts concluded in 2009 that the bones interred under the altar date from the first or second century.

Cost and Hours: Free, daily 7:00-18:30, modest dress code enforced, dry audioguide-€5 plus ID, café, Via Ostiense 186, Metro: Basilica San Paolo, exit the Metro station following *via Ostiense* sign, and look for the church's round tower, the entrance is on the far side, tel. 06-6988-0800, www.basilicasanpaolo.org.

Visiting the Church: As the church is part of the Vatican, you'll start your visit by going through security (a metal detector and an X-ray machine for your bags, set up in a tent in the courtyard).

The column-lined courtyard leading up to the church is typical of early Christian churches—the first version of St. Peter's Basilica also had this kind of welcoming zone. The facade, while 19th century, is early Christian in its style—with mosaics picturing Rome and Jerusalem flanking the Lamb of God. In the courtyard's center is a statue of Paul holding his trademark sword, the instrument of his martyrdom. The palm trees, while not native to Rome, remind pilgrims of what they saw in the Holy Land. The central door of bronze and silver, from the 1930s, is dedicated to the patron saints of Rome, Peter (crucified upside-down) and Paul (beheaded).

Step inside and feel as close as you'll get in the 21st century to experiencing a monumental Roman basilica. Marvel at the ceiling, with those massive gilded-wood panels.

The marble-inlaid floor is like that of the Pantheon and typi-

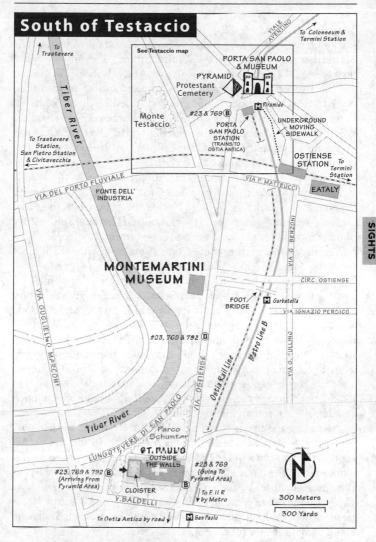

South of Testaccio

To Trastevere

Tiber River

To Colosseum & Termini Station

VIALE AVENTINO

See Testaccio map

PORTA SAN PAOLO & MUSEUM

PYRAMID

Protestant Cemetery

Monte Testaccio

#23 & 769 Ⓑ

PORTA SAN PAOLO STATION (TRAINS TO OSTIA ANTICA)

Ⓜ Piramide

UNDERGROUND MOVING SIDEWALK

To Trastevere Station, San Pietro Station & Civitavecchia

VIA DEL PORTO FLUVIALE

PONTE DELL' INDUSTRIA

OSTIENSE STATION

To Termini Station

VIA P. MATTEUCCI

EATALY

VIA G BENZONI

MONTEMARTINI MUSEUM

CIRC. OSTIENSE

FOOT BRIDGE

Ⓜ Garbatella

VIA IGNAZIO PERSICO

VIA G. SULLINI

VIA GUGLIELMO MARCONI

#23, 769 & 792 Ⓓ

VIA OSTIENSE

Ostia Rail Line

Metro Line B

Tiber River

LUNGOTEVERE DI SAN PAOLO

Parco Schuster

ST. PAUL'S OUTSIDE THE WALLS

#23, 769 & 792 Ⓑ (Arriving From Pyramid Area)

CLOISTER

V. BALDELLI

To Ostia Antica by road ↓

#23 & 769 Ⓑ (Going To Pyramid Area)

To E II R ↓ by Metro

Ⓜ San Paolo

N

300 Meters

300 Yards

SIGHTS

cally Roman. Alabaster windows light the vast interior. It feels sterile, but in a good way—as if you're already in heaven. Along with St. Peter's Basilica, San Giovanni in Laterano, and Santa Maria Maggiore, this church is, legally speaking, part of the Vatican (you can buy Vatican stamps here and send mail).

The triumphal arch leading to the altar has a fifth-century mosaic of Christ raising his hand in blessing. He's flanked by the four evangelists (in symbolic winged-animal guise) and, in white, the mysterious 24 elders of the Apocalypse. At the bottom of the arch are the two early followers of Jesus who, according to tradition, came to Rome to spread the Gospel and ended up dying for it: St. Peter (right) carries the keys to the kingdom of heaven, and St. Paul holds a sword symbolizing the piercing truth. Over the altar is a multicolored marble canopy (13th century). A 20-foot-tall Easter candlestick (c. 1170) stands to the right.

The fine 13th-century mosaic filling the dome in the apse is Byzantine in style; it was likely done by the same craftsmen who decorated St. Mark's in Venice. Notice the tiny, white, bug-like creature washing Jesus' toe. It's Honorius III, the 13th-century pope who paid for the apse renovation—reminding people of his humbleness while getting some credit at the same time (€1 illuminates the dome; machine to the right of the apse).

The church is built upon the supposed grave of St. Paul. According to tradition, Paul was decapitated two miles from this spot. His head was preserved at San Giovanni in Laterano, and his body was buried here under the altar. In 2009, archaeologists unearthed a sarcophagus with early inscriptions identifying it as Paul's, and carbon-dating on the bones inside confirmed their ancient origin. Today, you can descend a few steps in front of the central canopied altar to see the exposed end of Paul's supposed stone coffin, and look down through the glass floor to see the remains of the much smaller original fourth-century church.

Ringing the upper part of the church are round mosaic portraits of 266 popes, from St. Peter (the first one in the right transept) to the present. Find the recent popes to the right of the central altar—not in the nave, but farther to the right, under the arches of the dim right aisle. You'll see globetrotting John Paul II *(Jo Paulus II)* and progressive John XXIII, who oversaw the Vatican II reforms of the 1960s. A portrait of Pope #266, Francis, sits alongside blank medallions for future popes.

The peaceful 13th-century cloister (€4, €6 combo-ticket includes audioguide; enter from the right transept) has elegant Romanesque columns and arches, and fragments of early Christian/Roman sarcophagi, a relic chapel, and a small painting gallery.

E.U.R.

In the late 1930s, Italy's dictator Benito Mussolini planned an international exhibition to show off the wonders of his fascist society. But those wonders helped bring on World War II before Il Duce's celebration could ever happen. The unfinished mega-project was completed in the 1950s, and today it houses apartment blocks,

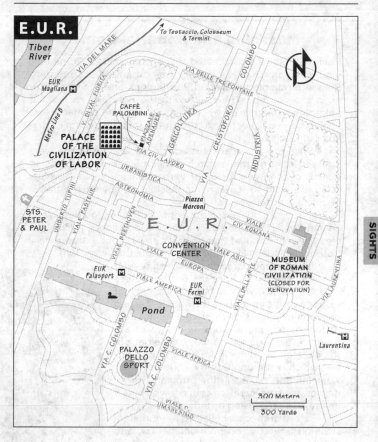

corporate and government offices, and big, obscure museums filled with important, rarely visited relics.

If Hitler and Mussolini had won the war, our world might look like E.U.R. (AY-oor). Hike down E.U.R.'s wide, pedestrian-mean boulevards. Patriotic murals, aren't-you-proud-to-be-an-extreme-right-winger pillars, and stern squares decorate the soulless planned grid and sterile office blocks. Patriotic quotes are chiseled into walls. Boulevards named for Astronomy, Electronics, Social Security, and Beethoven are more exhausting than inspirational. And, not to be outdone by the ancients, Mussolini had a towering fascist-style obelisk erected in the central Piazza Marconi.

Mussolini and Imperial Rome

Benito Mussolini incorporated much from ancient Rome during his dictatorship. His military was organized according to Roman terminology (divided into legions and run by centurions and consuls). The salute with the right arm raised, flat palm down (later used by the Nazis), was also Roman. More hygienic and quicker than a handshake, it fit the dynamic character of fascism.

While the classical values of power and discipline were stressed in the rhythmic march of military parades, convincing Italians of the need for order was a challenge even to Mussolini. He claimed it wasn't impossible to govern the Italian people...just useless.

Mussolini's title, Il Duce, meant "leader" or "guide." When chanted by crowds and carved onto monuments, it likely fueled Mussolini's belief that he was carrying out extraordinary historical missions like Caesar and Augustus before him.

For his symbol, rather than the she-wolf or eagle, Mussolini chose the ancient *fasces lictoriae*—an ax with a bundle (*fasces*) of wooden rods tied around the handle, carried by Roman officers in front of a magistrate (*lictor*) during processions as a sign of authority. (The same symbol was on the back of the old Mercury dime in America.) The symbol, which is the origin of the term "fascist," was aimed at replacing the popular view of Italy as a joyous, carefree country with a new image of austerity and order.

Fascist architects built on a monumental scale (inspired by ancient monuments), with arches, bold statues, and rhetorical inscriptions—resulting in an austere and impersonal feel that Romans today generally dislike.

In spite of his supposed passion for ancient Rome, Mussolini was a dreadful archaeologist. He would isolate a major monument and destroy everything around it. Sections of the imperial forums were sacrificed to build the wide street, Via dei Fori Imperiali, that goes from Piazza Venezia to the Colosseum. A famous fountain by the Colosseum that had survived almost 2,000 years was torn down without a second thought.

Despite its grim past, E.U.R. is now an upscale district with a mix of businessmen and women at work—and young people enjoying its trendy cafés. Because a few landmark buildings of Italian modernism are located here, E.U.R. is an important destination for architecture buffs, and the new futuristic convention center nicknamed "The Cloud" (it's meant to look like a cloud suspended in a glass box) promises to bring even more life to the area.

The Metro skirts E.U.R. with three stops (10 minutes from the Colosseum). Use E.U.R. Magliana for the Palace of the Civilization of Labor. Consider walking 20 minutes from the palace to the museum through the center of E.U.R.

Palace of the Civilization of Labor
(Palazzo della Civiltà del Lavoro)

From the E.U.R. Magliana Metro stop, stairs lead uphill to this epitome of fascist architecture. With its giant no-questions-asked patriotic statues and its stark simplicity, this is E.U.R.'s tallest building and key landmark. It's understandably nicknamed the "Square Colosseum." After many years of standing empty, Fendi, an Italian luxury clothing and fashion company, has leased the building from the government for its headquarters. Though closed to the public, it's still interesting to walk around. Downhill, in front of the building, Caffè Palombini is a popular Roman institution; their buffet line is a hit with local workers for lunch (daily 7:00-22:00; good gelato, pastries, and snacks; Piazzale K. Adenauer 12, tel. 06-591-1700, www.palombini.it).

Museum of Roman Civilization
(Museo della Civiltà Romana)

E.U.R.'s Museum of Roman Civilization, with dozens of fascinating rooms of plaster casts and models illustrating the greatness of classical Rome, is closed for renovation with no indication as to when it will reopen (www.museociviltaromana.it).

ANCIENT APPIAN WAY
AND SOUTHEASTERN ROME

Southeast of the city center lie several ancient sites that make the trek here worthwhile.

Baths of Caracalla (Terme di Caracalla)

Inaugurated by Emperor Caracalla in A.D. 216, this massive bath complex could accommodate 1,600 visitors at a time. Today it's just a shell—a huge shell—with all of its sculptures and most of its mosaics moved to museums. You'll see a two-story roofless brick building surrounded by a garden, bordered by ruined walls. The two large rooms at either end of the building were used for exercise. In between the exercise rooms was a pool flanked by two small mosaic-floored dressing rooms. Niches in the walls once held statues. The baths' statues are displayed elsewhere: For ex-

ample, the immense *Toro Farnese* (a marble sculpture of a bull surrounded by people) snorts in Naples' Archaeological Museum.

In its day, this was a remarkable place to hang out. For ancient Romans, bathing was a social experience. The Baths of Caracalla functioned until Goths severed the aqueducts in the sixth century. In modern times, grand operas are performed here during the summer (www.operaroma.it).

Cost and Hours: €6, includes the Tomb of Cecilia Metella and the Villa dei Quintili on the Appian Way, free and very crowded first Sun of the month, Mon 9:00-14:00, Tue-Sun 9:00 until one hour before sunset: April-Aug until 19:15, Sept until 19:00, Oct until 18:30, off-season closes as early as 16:30; last entry one hour before closing, audioguide-€5, good €8 guidebook; Metro: Circo Massimo, then a 5-minute walk south along Via delle Terme di Caracalla; bus #714 from Termini train station or bus #118 from the Appian Way—see the end of my Ancient Appian Way Tour; tel. 06-3996-7700, www.archeoroma.beniculturali.it.

▲Appian Way

For a taste of the countryside around Rome and more wonders of Roman engineering, take the four-mile trip from the Colosseum out past the wall to a stretch of the ancient Appian Way, where the original pavement stones are lined by several interesting sights. Ancient Rome's first and greatest highway, the Appian Way once ran from Rome to the Adriatic port of Brindisi, the gateway to Greece. Today you can walk (or bike) some stretches

of the road, rattling over original paving stones, past crumbling monuments that once edged the sides. The Tomb of Cecilia Metella and the Circus of Maxentius are the two most impressive pagan sights. Just a few hundred yards away are two major Christian catacombs (briefly described next).

📖 For more on all of these sights, see the Ancient Appian Way Tour chapter.

▲▲Catacombs of San Sebastiano

A guide leads you underground through the tunnels where early Christians were buried. You'll see faded frescoes and graffiti by early-Christian tag artists, as well as some pagan tombs that predate the Christian catacombs. Besides the catacombs themselves, there's a historic fourth-century basilica with the relics of St. Sebastian, the (supposedly) original Quo Vadis footprints of Christ, and an exquisite Bernini statue.

Cost and Hours: €8, includes 35-minute tour, 2/hour, Mon-Sat 10:00-17:00, closed Sun and late-Nov-late-Dec, Via Appia Antica 136, tel. 06-785-0350, www.catacombe.org.

▲▲Catacombs of San Callisto

The larger of the two sets of catacombs, San Callisto also is the more prestigious, having been the burial site for several early popes.

Cost and Hours: €8, includes 30-minute tour, at least 2/hour, Thu-Tue 9:00-12:00 & 14:00-17:00, closed Wed and Feb, Via Appia Antica 110, tel. 06-513-0151, www.catacombe.roma.it.

HEART OF ROME WALK

Rome's most colorful neighborhood features narrow lanes, intimate piazzas, fanciful fountains, and some of Europe's best people-watching. During the day, this walk—worth ▲▲▲—shows off the colorful Campo de' Fiori market and trendy fashion boutiques as it meanders past major monuments such as the Pantheon and the Spanish Steps.

But the sunset brings unexpected magic. A stroll in the cool of the evening is made memorable by the romance of the Eternal City at its best. Sit so close to a bubbling fountain that traffic noise evaporates. Jostle with kids to see the gelato flavors. Watch lovers straddling more than the bench. Jaywalk past *polizia* in flak-proof vests. And marvel at the ramshackle elegance that softens this brutal city for those who were born here and can't imagine living anywhere else. These are the flavors of Rome, best enjoyed after dark.

Orientation

Length of This Walk: Allow anywhere from one to three hours for this mile-long walk, depending on whether you linger and tour the Pantheon.

Getting There: Campo de' Fiori is a few blocks west of Largo Argentina, a major transportation hub. Buses #40, #64, and #492, and tram #8, stop at Largo Argentina and/or along Corso Vittorio Emanuele II (a long block northwest of Campo de' Fiori). A taxi from Termini Station costs about €10.

Pantheon: Free, Mon-Sat 8:30-19:30, Sun 9:00-18:00.

Tours: ∩ Download my free Heart of Rome Walk audio tour.

Other Options: This walk is equally pleasant in reverse order. You could ride the Metro to the Spanish Steps and finish at Campo de' Fiori, near many recommended restaurants. To lengthen this walk, you could continue on from the Spanish Steps to Piazza del Popolo.

The Walk Begins

❶ Campo de' Fiori

Kick off this walk in one of Rome's most colorful spots, Campo de' Fiori. This bohemian piazza hosts a fruit and vegetable **market**

in the morning, cafés in the evening, and crowds of drunks late at night. In ancient times, the "Field of Flowers" was an open meadow. Later, Christian pilgrims passed through on their way to the Vatican, and a thriving market developed.

Lording over the center of the square is a statue of **Giordano Bruno**, an intellectual heretic who was burned on this spot in 1600. The pedestal shows scenes from Bruno's trial and execution, and reads, "And the flames rose up." The statue honoring the heretic faces a Vatican administration building and was erected in 1889, a time when the new state of Italy and the Vatican were feuding. The Vatican protested, but they were overruled by angry neighborhood locals. This district is still known for its free spirit and antiauthoritarian demonstrations.

Campo de' Fiori is the product of centuries of unplanned urban development. At the east end of the square (behind Bruno), ramshackle apartments are built right into the old outer wall of ancient Rome's mammoth Theater of Pompey (you can actually see two white columns and bits of the ancient wall high above street level). This entertainment complex covered several city blocks, stretching from here to Largo Argentina. Julius Caesar was assassinated in the Theater of Pompey, where the Senate was meeting while its main Forum building was being repaired after a fire.

The square is surrounded by fun eateries, and is great for people-watching. Bruno faces the bustling **Forno** (in the left corner of the square), where takeout *pizza bianca* is sold hot out of the oven. On weekend nights, when the Campo is packed with beer-drinking kids, the medieval square is transformed into one vast Roman street party.

• *If Bruno did a hop, step, and jump forward, then turned left, in a block he'd reach...*

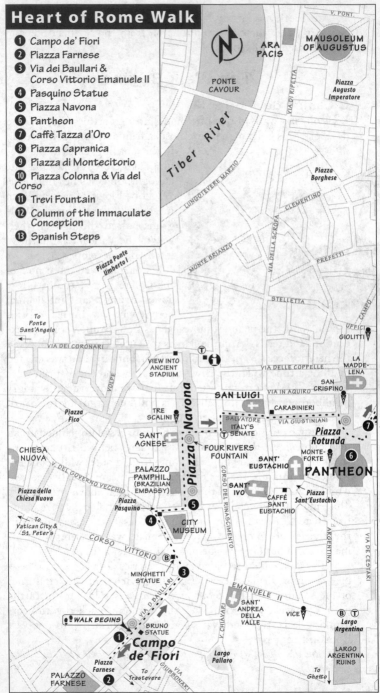

Heart of Rome Walk

1. Campo de' Fiori
2. Piazza Farnese
3. Via dei Baullari & Corso Vittorio Emanuele II
4. Pasquino Statue
5. Piazza Navona
6. Pantheon
7. Caffè Tazza d'Oro
8. Piazza Capranica
9. Piazza di Montecitorio
10. Piazza Colonna & Via del Corso
11. Trevi Fountain
12. Column of the Immaculate Conception
13. Spanish Steps

HEART OF ROME

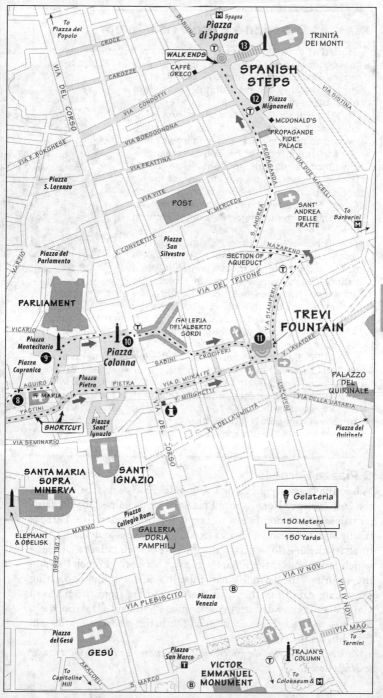

To Piazza del Popolo

Spagna

Piazza di Spagna

13

TRINITÀ DEI MONTI

WALK ENDS

CAFFÈ GRECO

SPANISH STEPS

CROCE

CAROZZE

VIA DEL CORSO

VIA CONDOTTI

VIA BORGOGNONA

VIA FRATTINA

VIA VITE

VIA F. BORGHESE

Piazza S. Lorenzo

12

Piazza Mignanelli

MCDONALD'S

"PROPAGANDE FIDE" PALACE

POST

V. MERCEDE

SANT' ANDREA DELLE FRATTE

To Barberini

PROPAGANDA

VIA DUE MACELLI

VIA SISTINA

V. CONVERTITE

Piazza San Silvestro

S. ANDREA

SECTION OF AQUEDUCT

NAZARENO

Piazza del Parlamento

MARZIO

VIA DEL TRITONE

V. A. STAMPERIA

TREVI FOUNTAIN

PARLIAMENT

VICARIO

Piazza Montecitorio

9

GALLERIA DEL'ALBERTO GORDI

11

V. LEVATORE

PALAZZO DEL QUIRINALE

Piazza Capranica

10

Piazza Colonna

BABINI

CROCIFERI

LUCHESI

VIA DELLA DATARIA

8

AQUIRO

MARIA

FASTINI

Plazza Pietra

PIETRA

VIA D. MURATE

V. MINGHETTI

VIA DELL'UMILTÀ

Piazza del Quirinale

SHORTCUT

Piazza Sant' Ignazio

VIA SEMINARIO

SANTA MARIA SOPRA MINERVA

SANT' IGNAZIO

ELEPHANT & OBELISK

MARMO

Piazza Collegio Rom.

GALLERIA DORIA PAMPHILJ

Gelateria

150 Meters

150 Yards

VIA IV NOV.

Piazza del Gesú

GESÚ

VIA PLEBISCITO

Piazza Venezia

B

VIA MAG.

To Termini

To Capitoline Hill

ARACOELI

Piazza San Marco

S. MARCO

B

VICTOR EMMANUEL MONUMENT

TRAJAN'S COLUMN

To Colosseum &

DEL GESÚ

Giordano Bruno (1548-1600)

Lauded as a martyr to free thought and reviled as an intellectual con man and heretic, the philosopher-priest Bruno has a legacy only a Roman could love. Details of his life are sketchy, and his writings range from the sublime to the ridiculous.

The young Dominican priest was nonconformist and outspoken from the start. He had to flee Italy to avoid a charge of heresy and spent most of his adult life wandering Europe's capitals. In Geneva, he joined the Calvinists, until he was driven out for his unorthodox views. In London, he met with Queen Elizabeth, who found him subversive. In Germany, the Lutherans excommunicated him.

In his writings, Bruno claimed to have discovered the "Clavis Magna" (Great Key) to training the human memory. He published satirical plays tweaking Church morals. He advanced the then-heretical (Copernican) notion that the earth revolved around the sun and speculated about other inhabited planets in the universe. All his works show a vast-ranging mind aware of the scientific trends of the day.

In 1593, Bruno was arrested by the Inquisition and sent to Rome, where he languished in prison for six years. Bruno was sentenced to death by fire. He replied, "Perhaps you who pronounce this sentence are more fearful than I who receive it." On February 17, 1600, the civil authorities led him to the stake on Campo de' Fiori. As they lit the fire, he was offered a crucifix to hold. He pushed it away.

❷ Piazza Farnese

While the higgledy-piggledy Campo de' Fiori feels free and easy, the 16th-century Renaissance Piazza Farnese, named for the family whose palace dominates it, seems to stress order. The Farnese family was nouveau riche and needed to make a statement. They hired Michelangelo to design the top part of their palace's facade—which today houses the French embassy, hence the French flag and the security. The twin Roman tubs in the fountains decorating the square date from the third century and are from the Baths of Caracalla. They ended up here because Pope Paul III, who was a Farnese, ordered the excavation of the baths, and the family had first dibs on the choicest finds.

• *Walk back to Campo de' Fiori, cross the square, and continue a couple of blocks down...*

❸ Via dei Baullari and Corso Vittorio Emanuele II

As you slalom through the crowds, notice the crush of cheap cafés, bars, and restaurants—the center of medieval Rome is morphing into a playground for tourists, students, and locals visiting from the suburbs. High rents are driving families out and changing the character of this district. That's why the Campo de' Fiori market increasingly sells more gifty edibles than basic fruits and vegetables with each passing year.

After a couple of blocks, you reach the busy boulevard, Corso Vittorio Emanuele II. In Rome, any road big enough to have city buses like this is post-unification: constructed after 1870. Look left and right down the street—the facades are mostly 19th century neo-Renaissance, built after this main thoroughfare sliced through the city. Traffic in much of central Rome is limited to city buses, taxis, motorbikes, "dark cars" (limos and town cars of VIPs), delivery vans, residents, and disabled people with permits (a.k.a., friends of politicians). This is one of the increasingly rare streets where anything goes.

• *Cross Corso Vittorio Emanuele II, and enter a square with a statue of Marco Minghetti, an early Italian prime minister. Angle left at the statue, walking along the left side of the Museum of Rome, down Via di San Pantaleo. A block down, at the corner, you'll find a beat-up old statue.*

❹ Pasquino

Pasquino—a third-century B.C. statue that was discovered near here—is one of Rome's "talking statues." For 500 years, this statue has served as a kind of community billboard, allowing people to complain anonymously when it might be dangerous to speak up. And, to this day, you'll see old Pasquino strewn with political posters, strike announcements, and grumbling graffiti. The statue looks literally worn down by centuries of complaining about bad government.

Speaking of government, the road stretching out the far end of this piazza is a typical pre-unification "Papal Road"—as big as roads got before the mid-19th century. It's called the Via del Governo Vecchio—road of the old government.

• *Wrap around Pasquino and head up Via di Pasquino to...*

❺ Piazza Navona

This square has been a center of Roman life since ancient times. It retains the oblong shape of the athletic grounds built here around A.D. 80 by the emperor Domitian. Today's square, while following its ancient foundation, is from the late Renaissance. Coming out of the Middle

Ages, the papacy was putting major scandals behind it. Rome was energized and laying out more efficient street plans, grand palaces, and great public spaces like this.

As you enter the square, the **Palazzo Pamphilj** (now the Brazilian embassy) is the first place on the left. The Pamphilj nobles were big patrons of the arts, and one of them, Giambattista Pamphilj, became Pope Innocent X in 1644. We can thank him for much of what we see on the square today.

Three Baroque fountains decorate the piazza. The first fountain, at the southern end, features a Moor wrestling with a dolphin. In 17th-century Rome, Moors (Africans) represented all that was exotic and mysterious. In the fountain at the northern end, Neptune slays a giant octopus.

The most famous fountain, though, is in the center: the **Four Rivers Fountain** by Gian Lorenzo Bernini, the man who remade

Rome in the Baroque style. As the water of the world gushes everywhere, four burly river gods (representing the four quarters of the world) support an Egyptian-style obelisk that was made in Rome. (The obelisk was popular with Roman emperors because Egyptian society saw its rulers as divine—an idea Rome liked to promote.) Bernini enlivens the fountain with horses plunging through rocks and the exotic flora and fauna of faraway lands.

Stroll around the fountain counterclockwise and admire the gods: The good-looking figure representing the Danube (for Europe) holds the coat of arms of the Pamphilj pope. Next comes the Ganges (for Asia), holding an oar. After an exotic palm tree, you find the Nile (for Africa) with his head covered, since its headwaters were unknown back then. Uruguay's Rio de la Plata, representing the Americas, tumbles backward in shock, wondering how he ever made the top four. (Note that he has the same Moorish features we saw earlier—which for Bernini worked equally well for an American Indian as an African.) The spilled coins represent the easy-to-harvest wealth of the New World.

The Plata river god is gazing upward at the **Church of Sant'Agnese** (St. Agnes), which dominates the square. It's a fine example of Baroque deception: While the facade is mammoth, its interior is only as wide as the middle four columns. It's the work of Francesco Borromini, Bernini's former student-turned-rival. Borromini's concave facade helps reveal the dome and epitomizes the curved symmetry of the Baroque era. An old tradition says that

Bernini designed his river god to look in horror at Borromini's church. Or maybe he's shielding his eyes from St. Agnes' naked-ness, as she was stripped before being martyred. But neither explanation can be true, since the fountain was completed two years before Borromini even started work on the church.

Piazza Navona is Rome's most interesting night scene, with street music, artists, fire-eaters, local Casanovas, ice cream, and outdoor cafés that are worthy of a splurge if you've got time to sit and enjoy Italy's human river.

• *Leave Piazza Navona directly across from* **Tre Scalini** *(famous for its* tartufo, *a rich, chocolate gelato concoction), and go east down Corsia Agonale, past rose peddlers and palm readers. Ahead of you (across the busy street) stands the stately Palazzo Madama, where the Italian Senate meets. (Hence, security is high.) Jog left around this building, and follow the brown sign to the Pantheon, straight down Via del Salvatore.*

After a block, you'll pass (on your left) the **Church of San Luigi dei Francesi**, *with its* très *French decor and precious Caravaggio paintings (church described in detail on page 132 in the Pantheon Tour chapter). If it's open, pop in. Otherwise, continue along, following the crowd, as everyone seems to be heading for the Pantheon.*

As you walk, notice the basalt cobbles underfoot. This is the same stone ancient Romans cobbled their streets with, quarried from volcanic mountains south of here (like Vesuvius). The public debate lately is whether to replace them with modern pavement (more practical and comfortable) or keep them (more character and a part of the heritage). Rounding the next corner, you come to...

❻ The Pantheon

Perhaps the most magnificent building surviving from ancient Rome is this temple to the "pantheon" (literally, all the gods). It faces a piazza, as it has since ancient times, when this was an elegant and shaded gathering place with covered walkways. The ancient Romans introduced the whole piazza culture, and you can see it thrives to this day. In antiquity, the Pantheon was above street level, approached by a staircase (the staircase survives but is buried beneath the square). Notice how the steps of the 18th-century **fountain** in the center of the square disappear into the modern pavement, and how the square slants down toward the street level of 2,000 years ago. The obelisk rising from the fountain originally decorated a temple to the Egyptian goddess Isis (wife of Osiris). Rome had an important connection to Egypt (from where much of its grain came) and was happy to have a temple here for its Egyptian residents.

Sit for a while under the portico of the Pantheon (romantically floodlit and moonlit at night).

The 40-foot, single-piece granite columns of the Pantheon's entrance show the scale the ancient Romans built on. The col-

umns support a triangular Greek-style roof with an inscription that says "M. Agrippa" built it. In fact, it was built *(fecit)* by Emperor Hadrian (A.D. 120), who gave credit to the builder of an earlier structure. This impressive entranceway gives no clue that the greatest wonder of the building is inside—a domed room that inspired later domes, including Michelangelo's St. Peter's and Brunelleschi's Duomo in Florence.

If it's open, pop into the Pantheon for a look around. Also consider detouring to several interesting churches near the Pantheon before continuing on the walk (**Santa Maria sopra Minerva,** with its purely Gothic interior, and **Sant'Ignazio,** with its 3-D Baroque illusions, are just a few steps away). For details on the Pantheon and these other churches, 📖 see the Pantheon Tour chapter or 🎧 download my free Pantheon audio tour.

• *With your back to the Pantheon, veer to the right, uphill toward the yellow sign on Via Orfani that reads* Casa del Caffè—you've reached the...

❼ Caffè Tazza d'Oro

This is one of Rome's top coffee shops, dating back to the days when this area was licensed to roast coffee beans. Locals come here for a shot of espresso or, when it's hot, a refreshing *granita di caffè con panna* (coffee and crushed ice with whipped cream).

Circle through the interior and absorb the aroma and energy of a classic Italian café scene. Coffee to-go is simply wrong here in Rome. Locals pay at the cashier, bring their receipt to the barista, and enjoy an elegant little break. This scene is just as it was in the early 1980s, when Howard Schultz traveled to Italy and was inspired to buy a coffee business in Seattle—and set off to conquer the world. (By the way, the first Starbucks in Italy is planned to open in Milan in early 2017).

• *From here, our walk continues past some interesting landmarks to the Trevi Fountain. But if you'd like to get there a bit more directly, you can take a* **shortcut** *by bearing right at the coffee shop onto Via de' Pastini, which leads through Piazza di Pietra (with some surviving chunks of the Temple of Hadrian—described on page 60), then across busy Via del Corso, where it becomes the touristy, pedestrianized Via delle Muratte and heads straight for the fountain.*

If you'd rather stick with me for the slightly longer version, bear left at the coffee shop and continue up Via degli Orfani to the next square...

❽ Piazza Capranica

This square is home to the big, plain Florentine-Renaissance-style Palazzo Capranica (directly opposite as you enter the square). Its stubby tower was once much taller, but when a stronger government arrived, the nobles were all ordered to shorten their towers. The six-story building to the left was once an apartment building for 17th-century Rome's middle class. Like so many of Rome's churches, Santa Maria in Aquiro, the church on the square, is older than the facade it was given during the Baroque period. Notice the circular little shrine on the street corner (between the palace and the apartment building). For centuries, worshipful spots like this have made pilgrims (and, today, tourists) feel welcome.

• *Leave the piazza to the right of the palace, heading down Via in Aquiro. The street jogs to the left and into a square that's home to Italy's Parliament.*

❾ Piazza di Montecitorio

The square is marked by a sixth-century B.C. **Egyptian obelisk** taken as a trophy by Augustus after his victory in Egypt over Mark

Antony and Cleopatra. The obelisk—the only one in Rome still capped with a pre-Christian ornament—was originally set up as a sundial. Follow the zodiac markings to the well-guarded front door of Italy's **parliament building.** This is where the lower house meets; you may see politicians, political demonstrations, and TV cameras.

The building caps one of ancient Rome's man-made hills, Montecitorio. Before Italy was unified, this was where the high court of the Papal States presided (note the relief of Lady Justice to the right of the door). The facade is mostly a Bernini design—bulging in the middle to make this small and potentially cramped square feel grander. Intentionally jagged and unfinished stones at either end are in keeping with the "back-to-nature" style of the 17th century (as you saw at the Four Rivers Fountain and will see again at the Trevi Fountain).

• *One block to your right is Piazza Colonna, where we're heading next—unless you like gelato...*

A one-block detour to the left (past Albergo Nazionale) brings you to Rome's most famous gelateria. **Giolitti** *is reasonable for takeout or elegant and splurge-worthy for a sit among classy locals (open daily until past midnight, Via Uffici del Vicario 40); get your gelato in a cone* (cono) *or cup* (coppetta).

⑩ Piazza Colonna and Via del Corso

The centerpiece of **Piazza Colonna** is a huge column that's stood on this spot since the second century. The decorative relief wrapped

like a scroll around its length (called a "continuous narration") comes with a propaganda message. It depicts the victories of Emperor Marcus Aurelius over the barbarians. When Marcus died in A.D. 180, the barbarians began to get the upper hand, beginning Rome's long three-century fall. Marcus Aurelius once capped the column, but he was replaced by Paul, one of Rome's patron saints. (Peter, the city's other patron saint, stands atop Trajan's Column nearby.)

The column (which has spiral stairs inside—notice the little windows) was originally painted. Try to imagine the ancient cityscape of Rome as very colorful. While 1,800 years ago, this was a major square surrounded by important classical buildings (such as a temple of Julius Caesar), today the square features Neoclassical facades. The big, important-looking palace (with the flags of Italy and the EU) houses the headquarters for the prime minister's cabinet. Opposite is the office of the right-wing newspaper *Il Tempo* (comfortably situated in what was the headquarters of Mussolini's fascist party).

Beyond Piazza Colonna runs noisy **Via del Corso,** Rome's main north-south boulevard. It's named for the Berber horse races—without riders—that took place here during Carnevale. This wild tradition continued until the late 1800s, when a series of fatal accidents (including, reportedly, one in front of Queen Margherita) led to its cancellation. Historically the street was filled with meat shops. When Via del Corso became one of Rome's first gas-lit streets in 1854, the butcher shops were banned and replaced by classier boutiques, jewelers, and antique dealers. Nowadays the northern part of Via del Corso is closed to traffic, and for a few hours every evening it becomes a wonderful parade of Romans

out for a stroll (see the "Dolce Vita Stroll" in the Nightlife in Rome chapter). Before crossing the street, look left (to the obelisk marking Piazza del Popolo—the ancient north gate of the city) and right (to the Victor Emmanuel Monument).

• *Cross Via del Corso to enter a big palatial building with columns, the* **Galleria Alberto Sordi** *shopping mall. It is typical of the grand galleries built throughout Italy in the late 1800s, powered by the energy of a newly united and proud Italy. To the left are convenient toilets and ahead is Feltri-nelli, the biggest Italian bookstore chain.*

Go to the right and exit out the back, where you'll continue directly to the Trevi Fountain. (If you're here after 21:00, when the mall is closed, circle around the right side of the Galleria on Via dei Sabini.) Once out the back, the tourist kitsch builds as you head up Via de Cro-ciferi to the roar of the water, lights, and people at the...

⓫ Trevi Fountain

This fountain shows how Rome took full advantage of the abundance of water brought into the city by its great aqueducts. It was

built to celebrate the reopening of several of ancient Rome's aqueducts in the Renaissance and Baroque eras. After a thousand years of surviving on poor-quality well water, Romans could once again enjoy pure water brought from the distant hills east of the city. Even in ancient times the water outlet here sat

lower than street level to give it maximal gravitational oomph. The Ionic columns built into the Benetton store facing the fountain are a reminder that long ago this was where the neighborhood gathered, jugs on heads, to fetch their water.

This watery Baroque avalanche by Nicola Salvi was completed in 1762. Salvi used the entire Neoclassical facade of the palace behind the fountain as a theatrical backdrop for the figure of Neptune, who represents water in every form. The statue surfs in his shell-shaped chariot through his wet kingdom—with water gushing from 24 spouts and tumbling over 30 different kinds of plants—while Triton—Neptune's trumpeter—blows his conch shell.

The magic of the square is enhanced by the fact that no

Egyptian Obelisks

Rome has 13 obelisks, more than any other city in the world. In Egypt, they were connected with the sun god Ra (like stone

sun rays) and the power of the pharaohs. The ancient Romans, keen on exotic novelty and sheer size, brought the obelisks here and set them up in key public places as evidence and celebration of their occupation of Egypt. Starting from the 1580s, Rome's new rulers—the popes—relocated the obelisks and topped most of them with Christian crosses. The obelisks came to acquire another significance that guaranteed their survival: the triumph of Christianity over all other religions.

The tallest (105 feet) and the most ancient (16th century B.C.) is the obelisk in Piazza San Giovanni in Laterano. It once stood in the Circus Maximus next to its sister, which now marks the center of Piazza del Popolo.

The obelisks were carved from single blocks of granite. Imagine the work, with only man and horsepower, first to quarry them and set them up in Egypt, then—after the Romans came along—to roll them on logs to the river or the coast, sail (or row) them in special barges across the Mediterranean and up the Tiber, and finally hoist them up.

Rome wasn't above cheap imitations, however: A couple of the obelisks are ancient Roman copies. The one at the top of the Spanish Steps has spelling mistakes in the hieroglyphics.

vehicular streets directly approach it. You can hear the excitement as you draw near, and then—*bam!*—you're there. The scene is always lively, with lucky Romeos clutching dates while unlucky ones clutch beers. Romantics toss a coin over their shoulder, thinking it will give them a wish and assure their return to Rome. That may sound silly, but every year I go through this tourist ritual...and it actually seems to work.

Take some time to people-watch (whisper a few breathy *bellos* or *bellas*) before leaving. There's a peaceful zone at water level on the far right.

• *Facing the Trevi Fountain, walk along its right side up Via della Stamperia. Cross busy Via del Tritone. Continue 100 yards up Via del Nazareno (passing an exposed bit of the ancient aqueduct that for 2,000 years has brought water into Rome). At the T-intersection ahead, veer right on Via Sant'Andrea delle Fratte. The security is protecting the headquarters of Italy's Democratic Party (on the right).*

The street becomes Via di Propaganda, and at the far end (on the right), it's dominated by a palace that, back in the 17th century, housed the Propagande Fide—the university where missionaries learned how to evangelize. This was just one arm of the Catholic Church's Counter-Reformation "propaganda" movement—a priority after the Protestants began stealing converts.

Here the street opens up into a long piazza. You're approaching the Spanish Steps. But first, pause at the...

⑫ Column of the Immaculate Conception

An ancient column, topped with a statue of Mary, is dedicated to the Immaculate Conception of Mary. In Christian belief, everyone is born with the stain of original sin. But for Mary to be a worthy and super-pure vessel for Jesus, the Catholic Church decided she needed to be "immaculately conceived"—born without sin. Pope Pius IX and the Vatican finally settled the long theological debate in 1854 by formally establishing the dogma of Mary's Immaculate Conception. Three years later, officials erected this column honoring Mary, complete with venerable Church prophets—all in total agreement—at its base. Every year on December 8, the feast day of the Immaculate Conception, this spot is the scene of a special celebration. The pope attends, the fire department places flowers on Mary's statue (see remains of the festooning), and the Christmas season is kicked off.

To Mary's immediate left stands the Spanish embassy to the Vatican. Rome has double the embassies of a normal capital because here countries need two: one to Italy and one to the Vatican. And because of this embassy, the square and its famous steps are called "Spanish."

• Just 100 yards past Mary, you reach the...

⑬ Spanish Steps

Piazza di Spagna, with the very popular Spanish Steps, is named for the Spanish embassy to the Vatican, which has been here for 300 years. It's been the hangout of many Romantics over the years (Keats, Wagner, Openshaw, Goethe, and others). In the 1700s, British aristocrats on the Grand Tour of Europe came here to ponder Rome's decay. The British poet John Keats pondered his mortality, then died of tuberculosis at age 25 in the orange building on the right side of the steps. Fellow

Romantic Lord Byron lived across the square at #66. Nearby, Caffè Greco opened in 1760 and was a favored haunt of artists and writers (just down Via dei Condotti at #86, with a historic interior; www.anticocaffegreco.eu).

The wide, curving staircase of the Spanish Steps is one of Rome's iconic sights. Its 138 steps lead sharply up from Piazza di Spagna, forming a butterfly shape as they fan out around a central terrace. The design culminates at the top in an obelisk framed between two Baroque church towers.

The **Sinking Boat Fountain** at the foot of the steps, built by Bernini or his father, Pietro, is powered by an aqueduct. Actually, all of Rome's fountains are aqueduct-powered; their spurts are determined by the water pressure provided by the various aqueducts. This one, for instance, is much weaker than the Trevi's gush.

The piazza is a thriving scene at night. From here you can window-shop along Via Condotti, which stretches away from the steps. This is where Gucci and other big names cater to well-heeled jetsetters. It's clear that the main sight around here is not the famous steps, but the people who sit on them.

• *Our walk is finished. If you'd like to reach the top of the steps sweat-free, take the free elevator just inside the Spagna Metro stop (to the left, as you face the steps; elevator closes at 21:00). A pay WC is underground in the piazza near the Metro entrance, by the middle palm tree (10:00–19:30). The nearby McDonald's (as you face the Spanish Steps, go right one block) is big and lavish, with a salad bar and WC. When you're ready to leave, you can zip home on the Metro (usually open until 23:30, later on Fri–Sat) or grab a taxi at either the north or south side of the piazza.*

PANTHEON TOUR

*The Roman Temple
and Nearby Churches*

If your imagination is fried from trying to reconstruct ancient buildings out of today's rubble, visit the Pantheon, Rome's best-preserved monument. Engineers still admire how the Romans built such a mathematically precise structure without computers, fossil fuel-run machinery, or electricity. (Having unlimited slave power didn't hurt.) Stand under the Pantheon's solemn dome to gain a new appreciation for the sophistication of these ancient people.

The Pantheon is the centerpiece of this tour, and is a must-see on any visit to Rome. The second part of this tour features several interesting churches that cluster near the Pantheon, with art by Michelangelo and Caravaggio, and connections with Galileo, St. Ignatius, and the Jesuit order.

Orientation

Pantheon: Free, Mon-Sat 8:30-19:30, Sun 9:00-18:00, holidays 9:00-13:00, closed for Mass on Sat at 17:00 and Sun at 10:30. Tel. 06-6830-0230.

Church of San Luigi dei Francesi: Free, daily 9:30-12:30 & 14:30-18:30 except opens Sun at 10:30, good €3 booklet, www.saintlouis-rome.net. Bring coins to light the Caravaggios.

Gesù Church: Free, daily 7:00-12:30 & 16:00-19:45 (afternoon visits are easier as there are frequent Masses in the morning), interesting daily ceremony at 17:30, tel. 06-697-001, www.chiesadelgesu.org.

Church of Santa Maria sopra Minerva: Free, Mon-Fri 7:30-19:00, Sat-Sun 8:00-12:30 & 15:30-19:00, www.santamariasopraminerva.it.

Church of Sant'Ignazio: Free, Mon-Sat 7:30-19:00, Sun 9:00-19:00, www.chiesasantignazio.it.

When to Go: Don't go midday, when the Pantheon is packed and two of the churches are closed. Visit the Pantheon before 9:00, and you'll have it all to yourself. Note that the churches have slightly varying hours—plan carefully to avoid getting shut out.

Dress Code: The Pantheon does not allow visitors with skimpy shorts or bare shoulders. Modest dress is recommended for the churches near the Pantheon.

Getting There: Many buses (including #40, #64, #H, #492, #85, and #87, and tram #8) stop on the major boulevards near the Pantheon (Via del Corso, Corso Rinascimento, and Corso Vittorio Emanuele); from any of these it's about a three-block walk. You can also walk from the Spagna or Barberini Metro stops in about 15 minutes.

Tours: The Pantheon has a €5, 25-minute audioguide (€8/2 people).
∩ Download my free Pantheon **audio tour.**

Length of This Tour: Allow a half-hour to see the Pantheon and at least another hour to visit the nearby churches. If you have less time, the essential Pantheon can be seen in a glance. The four nearby churches are far less important.

Services: The nearest WCs are at bars and cafés on the Pantheon's square.

Photography: It's allowed—even with flash—in the Pantheon, but no flash is allowed in the nearby churches.

Eating: Restaurants abound. Several recommended ones are listed in the Eating in Rome chapter (see page 374). You can picnic on the steps of the fountain or along the Pantheon's walls. While picnicking is forbidden under the Pantheon's portico, I enjoy discreetly munching a sandwich at the base of a column. Some of Rome's best gelato is nearby.

Drinks: A drinking fountain spurts near the obelisk in Piazza della Rotonda. For those who prefer their liquids caffeinated, two of Rome's most venerable (and busiest) coffee shops are just steps away: **Tazza d'Oro Casa del Caffè** (their icy *granita di caffè con panna* is heaven on a hot day; Via degli Orfani 84) and **Bar Sant'Eustachio** (they add sugar to their coffee drinks unless you request otherwise; Piazza di Sant'Eustachio 82).

The Tour Begins

• *Start the tour at the top of the square called Piazza della Rotonda, with cafés and restaurants around the edges and an obelisk-topped fountain in the center. You're looking at...*

The Pantheon

Exterior

The Pantheon was a Roman temple dedicated to all *(pan)* of the gods *(theos)*. The original temple was built in 27 B.C. by Emperor Augustus' son-in-law, Marcus Agrippa. In fact, the inscription below the triangular **pediment** proclaims in Latin, "Marcus Agrippa, son of Lucio, three times consul made this." But after a couple of fires, the structure we see today was completely rebuilt by Emperor Hadrian around

A.D. 120. Some say that Hadrian, an amateur architect (and voracious traveler), helped design it.

The Pantheon looks like a pretty typical temple from the outside, but this is perhaps the most influential building in art history. Its dome was the model for the Florence cathedral dome, which launched the Renaissance, and for Michelangelo's dome of St. Peter's, which capped it all off. Even the US Capitol in Washington, DC, was inspired by this dome.

The **portico** is Greek in style, which is logical, because Hadrian was a Grecophile. (He grew a beard to look like a Greek philosopher, bucking the beardless tradition of Rome's 13 previous emperors.) This fine porch is a visual reminder of the great debt Roman culture owed to the Greeks. Fittingly, you cross this Greek space to enter a purely Roman space, the rotunda. The columns are huge and unadorned, made from 40-foot-high single pieces of red-gray granite rather than the standard stacks of cylindrical pieces. They were quarried in Egypt, then shipped down the Nile and across the Mediterranean to Rome. They were then fitted with leafy Corinthian capitals, the Greek order that was most popular among Romans. They are sequoia-huge—it takes the outstretched arms of four large tourists to encircle one column.

The enormous scale of the portico was meant to display power and intimidate common citizens. Sit facing the entry on the corner of a column base (as picnickers have done for 1,800 years). Notice the two huge, empty niches flanking the door—once filled with towering statues of emperors. Look up at the porch roof and imagine the ceiling covered in its original bronze plating. The metal was removed in the 17th century by a scavenging pope from the Barberini family, inspiring the well-known quip, "What the barbarians didn't do, the Barberini did." Melted down, some of the bronze was used to build the huge canopy over the altar at St. Peter's.

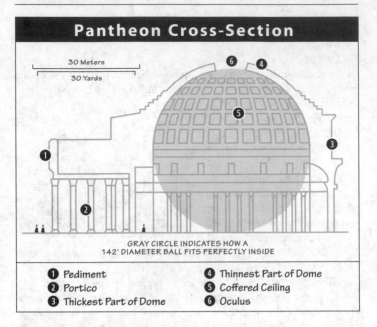

Pantheon Cross-Section

30 Meters
30 Yards

GRAY CIRCLE INDICATES HOW A
142' DIAMETER BALL FITS PERFECTLY INSIDE

1 Pediment
2 Portico
3 Thickest Part of Dome
4 Thinnest Part of Dome
5 Coffered Ceiling
6 Oculus

• *Now pass through the giant **bronze door**—a copy of the original. Take a seat and take it all in.*

Inside the Pantheon

The dome, which was the largest made until the Renaissance, is set on a circular base. The mathematical perfection of this dome-on-a-base design is a testament to Roman engineering. The dome is as high as it is wide—142 feet from floor to rooftop and from side to side. To picture it, imagine a basketball wedged inside a wastebasket so that it just touches bottom.

The dome—clean and feeling loftier than ever—is made from concrete (a Roman invention) that gets lighter and thinner as it reaches the top. The base of the dome is 23 feet thick and made from heavy concrete mixed with travertine, while near the top, it's less than five feet thick and made with a lighter volcanic rock (pumice) mixed in. Note the square indentations in the surface of the dome. This **coffered ceiling** reduces the weight of the dome without compromising strength. The walls are strengthened by brick relieving arches ("blind" arches)—visible in the exposed brickwork in a few of the interior niches and easy to see from outside.

Both Brunelleschi and Michelangelo

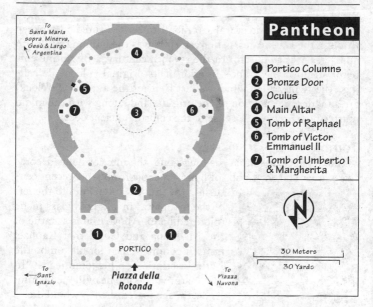

Pantheon

1 Portico Columns
2 Bronze Door
3 Oculus
4 Main Altar
5 Tomb of Raphael
6 Tomb of Victor Emmanuel II
7 Tomb of Umberto I & Margherita

To Santa Maria sopra Minerva, Gesù & Largo Argentina

To Sant' Ignazio

To Piazza Navona

PORTICO

Piazza della Rotonda

30 Meters
30 Yards

studied this dome before building their own (in Florence and the Vatican, respectively). Remember, the grandiose vision for St. Peter's Basilica was to place the dome of the Pantheon atop the Forum's Basilica of Constantine.

At the top, the oculus, or eye-in-the-sky, is the building's only light source. It's completely open and almost 30 feet across. The 1,800-year-old floor—with 80 percent of its original stones surviving—has holes in it and slants toward the edges to let the rainwater drain. Though some of the floor's marble has been replaced, the design—alternating circles and squares—is original.

In ancient times, this was a one-stop-shopping temple where you could worship any of the major gods whose statues decorated the niches. Entering the temple, Romans came face-to-face with a larger-than-life statue of Jupiter, the King of the Gods, where the **altar** stands today. After the fall of Rome, the Pantheon became a Christian church (from "all the gods" to "all the martyrs"), which saved it from architectural cannibalism and ensured its upkeep through the Dark Ages. (The year 2009 was the building's 1,400th anniversary as a church.) In the seventh century, a Byzantine emperor stripped the dome's interior of its original golden-tile ceiling. The twin grilled windows just right of the altar (at 2 o'clock) are a modern re-creation of the original and, along with the inlaid marble floor, give you a sense of the colorful ancient decor.

Tombs

While its ancient statuary is long gone, the interior holds decorative statues and the tombs of famous people from more recent cen-

turies. The artist **Raphael** lies to the left of the main altar in a lighted glass niche (pictured here). Above him is a statue of the Madonna and Child that Raphael himself commissioned for his tomb. The Latin inscription on his tomb reads: "In life, Nature feared to be outdone by him. In death, she feared she too would die."

Facing each other across the base of the dome are the tombs of modern Italy's first two kings. To the right is **Victor Emmanuel II** (*"Padre della Patria,"* father of his country); to the left is **Umberto I** (son of the father). These tombs are a hit with royalists. In fact, a guard often stands by a guestbook in which visitors can register their support for these two kings' now-controversial family, the Savoys (see sidebar on the next page). And finally, under Umberto lies his queen, Margherita...for whom the classic pizza Margherita (mozzarella, tomato sauce, and basil—representing the colors of the Italian flag) was named in 1889.

Think of all the history this place has seen. At Rome's peak it was a temple to pagan gods. As Christianity took over the empire, the pagan priests became persona non grata and the building crumbled along with the empire. When barbarians looted the city, they carried off some exterior marble, but the structure remained intact. In 609 it was saved from architectural cannibalism when it became a Christian church, and the Virgin Mary replaced Jupiter at the altar. It later became the final resting spot of the great Raphael as well as Italian royalty. And these days, visitors from around the world pack the place to remember the greatness of classical Rome.

The Pantheon is the only ancient building in Rome continuously used since its construction. (When you leave, notice that the building is sunken below current street level, showing how the rest of the city has risen on 20 centuries of rubble.) The Pantheon also contains the world's greatest Roman column. There it is, spanning

The Italian Royal Family... in Switzerland

From Italy's unification in 1870 to the end of World War II, the country had four kings, all members of the House of Savoy. Originally from the Alps (along the French border), the Savoy family had long ruled the kingdom of Piedmont (whose capital was Turin, in northern Italy).

In 1946, the Italians voted for a republic and sent the Savoy kings into exile. Until 2002, a law proclaimed that no male Savoy could set foot on Italian soil. That's why only the first two kings are buried in the Pantheon (the last two died abroad).

The Savoia lost favor with their Italian subjects for several good reasons: When Mussolini marched on Rome in 1922, King Victor Emmanuel III actually asked him to form a government. When the Mussolini government issued anti-Semitic laws, the king signed them. And in 1943, instead of standing by his people, the king abandoned Rome to the Germans and fled south to Allied protection.

Today, this would-be royal family of Italy is back in the country but known more for appearances on TV game shows than for any serious political or national relevance.

the entire 142 feet from heaven to earth—the pillar of light from the oculus.

• *Leaving the Pantheon, take a moment to enjoy the square facing it. Piazza della Rotonda has been a gathering place for 2,000 years. Its slope illustrates the literal "rise of Rome." Imagine in past centuries when there was a fish and chicken market in the portico. In an 18th-century urban beautification project, the fountain and obelisk were added. Feel the vibrancy of the piazza culture, which goes back to ancient Rome.*

Churches near the Pantheon

Many visitors just see the Pantheon and leave. But consider visiting one or more of these four unique churches, all less than 10 minutes' walk from the Pantheon (see map for locations). If you're budgeting your energy, here's a quick rundown on what each has to offer: San Luigi houses several stunning Caravaggio paintings. The Gesù is packed with ornate art and Jesuit history. Santa Maria sopra Minerva, Rome's only Gothic church, has a Michelangelo sculpture and St. Catherine's tomb. Finally, Sant'Ignazio is full of Baroque perspective illusions that will leave your head spinning.

Churches near the Pantheon

PANTHEON

CHURCH OF SAN LUIGI DEI FRANCESI

This is the French *(dei francesi)* national church in Rome. You'll find French motifs throughout. Outside, check out the salamander, symbol of François I, the French king who brought Leonardo (and the Renaissance) north, from Italy to France. Step inside and stand on the marble inlaid fleur-de-lis in the center rear of the nave.

This is a Renaissance building with Baroque icing. The stylized fleurs-de-lis—scattered throughout—are emblems of French royalty. On the ceiling of the nave is France's King (a.k.a. Saint) Louis ascending to heaven, and there he is again in a chapel on the left. Joan of Arc stands (posing as usual) over your left shoulder, taking it all in just like you.

The church's highlight is the chapel in the far-left front corner, which was decorated by Caravaggio. This church makes a great little detour between the Pantheon and nearby Piazza Navona.

• In the Caravaggio chapel, pop in a euro coin for light and look first to the left wall.

The Calling of St. Matthew

Matthew (old man with beard) and his well-dressed, tax-collecting cronies sit in a dingy Roman tavern and count the money they've extorted. Suddenly, two men in robes and bare feet enter from the right— Jesus and Peter. Jesus' "Creation-of-Adam" hand emerges from the darkness to point at Matthew. A shaft of light extends the gesture, lighting up the

face of Matthew, who points to himself, *Last Supper*-style, to ask, "You talkin' to me?" Jesus came to convince Matthew to leave his sleazy job and preach Love. Matthew did.

In this, his first large-scale work, 29-year-old Caravaggio (1571-1610) shocked critics and clerics by showing a holy scene in a down-to-earth location. Lower-class people in everyday clothes were his models; his setting was a dive bar (which he knew well). Christ's teeny gold halo is the only hint of the supernatural, as Caravaggio makes a bold proclamation—that miracles are natural events experienced in a profound way.

• Now look to the center wall.

The Inspiration of St. Matthew

Matthew followed Christ's call, traveled with him, and (supposedly) wrote Jesus' life story (the Gospel according to Matthew).

Here, Matthew is hard at work when he's interrupted by an angel with a few suggestions. This sets the scene in motion. Matthew kneels on a stool, which is just about to fall out of the painting and into our zone. Matthew's bald head, wrinkled face, and grizzled beard make him an all-too-human saint. Even the teen angel lacks a holy glow—he just hangs there. Caravaggio paints a dark background, then shines a dramatic spotlight on the few things that tell the story.

• Finally, check out the right wall.

The Martyrdom of St. Matthew

Matthew lies prone, while a truly scary man straddles him and brandishes a sword. The bystanders shrink away from this angry executioner. Caravaggio shines his harsh third-degree spotlight on

Matthew and the killer, who are the focus of the painting. The other figures swirl around them in a circle (with the executioner's arm as the radius). Matthew, who thought he had already given up everything to follow Christ, now gives up his life as well. He is as open as a crucifix,

accepting his fate, and reaching for a palm frond—symbolic of victory over death. The bearded face in the background (to the left of the executioner's shoulder) is a self-portrait of Caravaggio, observing the violence without getting involved.

When the chapel was unveiled in 1600, Caravaggio's ultra-realism shocked Rome. Although he died only 10 years later, his uncompromising details, emotional subjects, odd compositions, and dramatic lighting set the tone for later Baroque painters. (For a bit more on Caravaggio, see page 279.)

GESÙ CHURCH

The center of the Jesuit order (of which Pope Francis is a member) and the best symbol of the Catholic Counter-Reformation, the Gesù (jay-zoo) is packed with overblown art and underappreciated history. Consider seeing this church en route to Capitoline Hill.

Exterior

The facade looks ho-hum, like a thousand no-name Catholic churches scattered from Europe to Southern California... until you realize that this was the first, the model for all of the others.

Its scroll-like shoulders were revolutionary, breaking up the rigid rectangles of Renaissance architecture and signaling the coming of Baroque. The travertine stone facade has been cleaned but—with its sponge-like properties and Rome's pollution— it will be black again soon enough.

The adjacent building, to the right of the church—called Camere of St. Ignatius—is where Ignatius of Loyola, the founder of the Jesuits, lived, worked, and died (free, Mon-Sat 16:00-18:00, Sun 10:00-12:00).

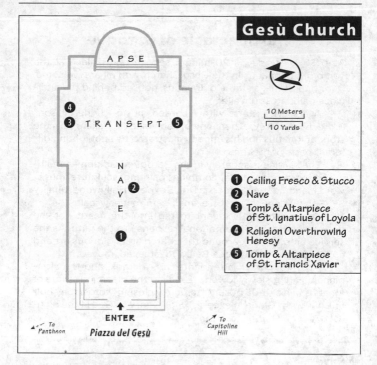

Gesù Church

APSE

10 Meters
10 Yards

TRANSET

N
A
V
E

1. Ceiling Fresco & Stucco
2. Nave
3. Tomb & Altarpiece of St. Ignatius of Loyola
4. Religion Overthrowing Heresy
5. Tomb & Altarpiece of St. Francis Xavier

ENTER
Piazza del Gesù

To Pantheon

To Capitoline Hill

PANTHEON

• *Step inside the Gesù Church, grab a seat, and look up at the huge painting on the ceiling (or take advantage of the neck-saving mirror).*

Inside the Church

❶ Ceiling Fresco—*The Triumph of the Name of Jesus*

The church's sunroof opens, and we can see right up to heaven. A glowing cross with the initials "I.H.S." (from the Latinized Greek, "Jesus Savior of Mankind," adopted as the seal of the Society of Jesus) astounds the faithful and sends the infidels plunging downward. The twisted tangle of bodies—the damned—spills over the edge of the painting's frame on the way to hell. The painted bodies mingle with 3-D stucco bodies and a riot of decoration in a classic example of Baroque multimedia (created by one of Bernini's protégés, Giovanni Battista Gaulli, better known as Il Baciccio, in the 1670s).

During the Counter-Reformation, when Catholics fought Protestants for the hearts and minds of the world's Christians, art was a powerful propaganda weapon. The moral here is clear—hell is the fate of Protestant heretics who dared to pervert the true teachings of Jesus.

> # The Spectacle of Baroque
>
> At 17:30 every day, a 20-minute service takes place at the Tomb of St. Ignatius in the Gesù Church, and all are welcome. During this time, a statue of Ignatius, housed behind the altar-piece painting, is unveiled.
>
> The service starts with recorded music—"Kyrie eleison" (Lord, have mercy). Then a recorded voice (in Italian) tells the story of Ignatius and his impact, illustrated by spotlighting different parts of the tomb.
>
> The service is squarely in the Baroque tradition—a multi-media extravaganza that combines painting, sculpture, music, words, and lighting effects. (Don't expect Hollywood-quality SFX—this is "spectacle" on a small, semi-cheesy scale.)
>
> The ceremony is meant to tap into the heart, not the head, encouraging an emotional response to the faith. As the service unfolds, look around the church at its glorious art and architecture. Don't reflect. Be awed, amazed, moved.
>
> At 17:45, church attendants turn a crank, and the altar-piece painting slowly lowers, revealing the gleaming statue of Ignatius in his ta-da pose. After a few closing words, the choir finishes with "Gloria in excelsis Deo" (Glory to God in the highest). Amen.

PANTHEON

❷ Nave

When the church was originally built (1568), the walls were white and the decor was simple. It was designed for what the Jesuits did best—teaching. The Jesuits wanted to educate Catholics to prepare them for the onslaught of pesky, probing Protestant questions. The church's nave is like one big lecture hall, with no traditional side aisles.

In the 1500s, the best way to keep Protestants from stealing your church members was to reason with them. By the 1600s, it was easier to kill them, and so the Thirty Years' War raged across Europe. The church became crusted over with the colorful, bombastic, jingoistic Baroque we see today.

• *Now look toward the left transept.*

❸ Tomb and Altarpiece of St. Ignatius of Loyola

A big altarpiece with towering columns and topped with statues of the Trinity marks the burial spot of the humble war veteran who founded the Jesuit order.

In the center of this altarpiece, you'll see a painting (by Andrea Pozzo) of Ignatius receiving his call. Behind the painting rests a gleaming statue of the saint, who spreads his arms wide and gazes up, receiving a vision from on high. But you won't be able to see it unless you come after 17:30 (see sidebar).

Ignatius (1491-1556) was a Spanish soldier during the era of conquistadors. Then, at age 30, he was struck down by a cannonball. While convalescing, he was seized by the burning desire to change his life. He wandered Europe and traveled to Jerusalem. He meditated with monks. He lived in a cave. At 33, he enrolled in a school for boys to fill in the knowledge he'd missed. He studied in Paris and Rome. Finally, after almost two decades of learning and seeking, he found a way to combine his military training with his spiritual aspirations.

In 1540, the pope gave approval to Ignatius and his small band of followers—the Society of Jesus (Jesuits). These monks (technically, priests or friars), organized like a military company, vowed complete obedience to their "General" and placed themselves at the service of the pope. Their mission: to be intellectual warriors doing battle with heretics. They were in the right place at the right time— Ignatius and Martin Luther were almost exact contemporaries.

Ignatius' body lies in the small coffin beneath the statue (near ground level). This simple, intense man might have been embarrassed by the lavish memorial to him, with its silver, gold, green marble, and lapis lazuli columns. Above the painting of Ignatius, a statue of God stands near a lapis lazuli globe (under the sunburst, the biggest in the world) and gestures as though to say, "Go and spread the Word to every land"...which the Jesuits tried to do.

• *Look at the marble statue group to the right of Ignatius.*

❹ Religion Overthrowing Heresy

This statue (and a similar one to the left of Ignatius) shows the Church as an angry nun hauling back with a whip and just spank-

ing a bunch of miserable Protestants. The man with the serpent (Luther) is being stepped upon while the angry cherub rips pages out of a heretical book. Not too subtle.

The Jesuits earned a reputation for unfeeling dedication to truth above all else. Their weapons were words, ideas, and critical reasoning. They taught and defended the recently revamped doctrines of the Council of Trent (a reaction against—and a response to—the Reformation, 1545-1563).

• *Now view the right transept.*

PANTHEON

The Jesuit Legacy

The Jesuits produced some great, open-minded thinkers, from the poet Gerard Manley Hopkins to modern mystic Pierre Teilhard de Chardin.

The great sculptor Bernini attended the Gesù Church. He honored the Jesuit Robert Bellarmine (1542-1621) with a bust, which is sometimes on display here. Bellarmine, a theologian at the height of Catholic-Protestant differences, was a voice of reason in the often bitter controversy. He's best known as the man who ordered Galileo to stop teaching the Copernican theory, although he was actually a moderating influence in the debate.

Because of their spiritual fervor, the Jesuits caught flack for being closed-minded. In the 1700s, several countries expelled them, and finally the pope even banned the Society (1773). Chastened, they were brought back (1814), and today they fill the staff of many a Catholic college.

The rehabilitation of this once-suspect order reached its culmination in 2013 with the ascension of Francesco I (Francis)—the first Jesuit pope.

❺ Tomb and Altarpiece of St. Francis Xavier

This was also the Age of Discovery, when Spain and Portugal were colonizing and Christianizing the world, using force if necessary. Francis Xavier joined a Portuguese expedition and headed out to convert the heathens. His right hand, with which he baptized and healed, is encased in a glass reliquary above his tomb. Francis touched down in Africa, India, Indonesia, China, and Japan. Along the way, he learned new languages and customs, trying to communicate a strange, monotheistic religion to puzzled polytheists.

He had been on the road for more than a decade (1552) when he died on an island off the coast of China (see the dim painting over the altar). Thanks largely to the tireless evangelizing of zealous Jesuits such as Francis, Catholicism became a truly worldwide religion.

CHURCH OF SANTA MARIA SOPRA MINERVA

From the outside, survey the many layers of Rome: An Egyptian obelisk sits on a Baroque elephant (by Bernini) in front of a Gothic church built over (sopra) a pre-Christian, pagan Temple of Minerva.

Before stepping in, notice the high-water-

mark plaques *(alluvione)* on the wall to the right of the door. Each time the Tiber River flooded, it left silt, which contributed to the slow and steady geological rise of Rome. Inside, you'll see that the lower parts of some frescoes were lost to floods. After the last great flood, in 1870, Rome built the present embankments along the river, finally breaking the spirit of the mighty Tiber.

Nave

This is the only Gothic church you'll see in Rome. The ceiling has pointed crisscross arches in a starry, luminous blue sky, and the nave is lit by rows of round stained-glass windows. When this Dominican church was built, Gothic was the rage in northern Europe, with large windows to let in the light—though churches in Italy were so colorful there was less emphasis on colored glass. During the Middle Ages, Rome was almost a ghost town, and what little was built during this time was later gussied up in the Baroque style. The lack of Baroque excess in this church (in spite of its over the-top, 19th-century renovation) is a refreshing exception.

Main Altar

The body of St. Catherine of Siena lies under the altar (her head is in Siena). In the 1300s, this Italian nun was renowned for her

righteousness and her visions of a mystical marriage with Jesus. Her impassioned letters convinced the pope to return from France to Rome, thus saving Italy from untold chaos. Behind her, two Medici popes are buried: Leo X, the son of Lorenzo the Magnificent and the man who excommunicated Martin Luther; and his cousin Clement VII. Both men were good friends with Michelangelo, who was raised alongside them in the Medici household.

In 1633, a frail 70-year-old Galileo knelt at this altar on the way to his trial before the Inquisition in the church's monastery. Facing the fierce Dominican lawyers, he renounced his heretical belief that the earth moved around the sun. (Legend has it that as he walked out, he whispered, "But it *does* move.")

• *Left of the altar stands a little-known Michelangelo statue...*

Christ Bearing the Cross, 1519-1520

Note Jesus' athletic body, a striking contrast to the docile Jesus of medieval art. This sculpture shares the same bulging biceps as the Christ in Michelangelo's *The Last Judgment* in the Sistine Chapel.

Christ's pose is slightly twisted, with one leg forward in typical *contrapposto* style, leaning on a large cross along with the symbols of the Crucifixion. Originally, Christ was buck naked, but later prudish Counter-Reformation censors gave him his bronze girdle.

This statue was Michelangelo's second attempt—he was forced to abandon a first effort due to a flaw in the block of Carrara marble. In this version, he left parts—including the face—to be finished by an apprentice, who took the liberty of working on and botching the feet and hands. This ineptitude led him to be replaced by yet another sculptor who finally finished the job. Michelangelo, disturbed that anyone would mess up his work, offered to redo the sculpture, but apparently the patrons were pleased. One contemporary said, "The knees alone are worth more than all of Rome together."

The tomb of the great early Renaissance painter (and Dominican brother) Fra Angelico ("Beato Angelico 1387-1455") is farther to the left, just up the three stairs.

Over in the right (south) transept, pop in a coin for light, and enjoy a Filippino Lippi fresco showing scenes of the life of the great Dominican scholar St. Thomas Aquinas (big man in blue and white). In the central scene, Thomas—seeming to interrupt the Annunciation—presents the chapel's patron to Mary. Above, circling an ascended Mary, is a frolicking carousel of heavenly musicians—notice the delightful instruments. Meanwhile, on the right wall, Thomas displays a book to show everyone the true dogma, causing a heretic to slump defeated at his feet.

• *Exit the church via its rear door (behind the Michelangelo statue), walk down tiny Fra Angelico lane, turn left, and walk to the next square. On your right, you'll find the last church on our tour.*

CHURCH OF SANT'IGNAZIO

This church is a riot of Baroque illusions. Stand in the middle of the nave and look up at the large, colorful ceiling fresco (or use the big mirror). ❶ St. Ignatius, whom we met in the Gesù Church, was the founder of the Jesuits, a disciplined Catholic teaching order charged with spreading the word of God around a world that was rapidly being "discovered." Here you see him (a small figure perched on a cloud in the center) having a ❷ vision of Christ with the Cross. Heavenly light from the vision bounces off his chest, and the rays beam to the four corners of the earth (including ❸ America, to the left, depicted as a bare-breasted Native American maiden spearing naked men). This fresco epitomizes pure Baroque drama, with perspective illusions that fool the eye into thinking the fresco is an extension of the church architecture. Note how the actual columns of the church are extended into the two-dimensional fresco.

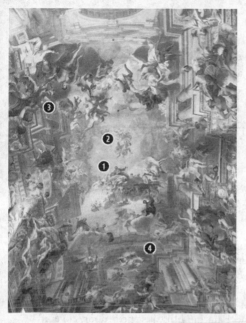

Now fix your eyes on the ❹ arch at the far end of the painting. Walk up the nave, and watch the arch grow and tower over you.

Before you reach the center of the church, stop at the small yellow disc (near the last row of pews) on the floor, and look up into the central (black) dome. Keeping your eye on the dome, walk under and past it. Building project runs out of money? Hire an artist to paint a fake, flat dome.

Now take a moment to survey the art in general, appreciating the tricks of the trade. For example, explore deep inside the right transept, where you'll find an explosive scene. The curtain is pulled back for the theatrical tomb of Pope Gregory XV—textbook bombastic Baroque. With trumpet fanfare and the stony curtain flapping in the spiritual wind, the pope springs with jubilation into eternal life.

Back outside, the church faces a headquarters of the Carabinieri police force (this station deals with art theft—a major problem in a country with so much to protect), forming Piazza Sant'Ignazio, a square with several converging streets that has been compared to a stage set. Sit on the church steps, admire the theatrical yellow backdrop, and watch the "actors" enter one way and exit another, in the human opera that is modern Rome.

• *From here it's a short walk to the left down Via del Seminario back to the Pantheon. Or go right, cross busy Via del Corso, and follow the crowds to the Trevi Fountain.*

COLOSSEUM TOUR

Colosseo

Rome has many layers—modern, Baroque, Renaissance, Christian. But let's face it: "Rome" is Caesars, gladiators, chariots, centurions, *"Et tu, Brute,"* trumpet fanfares, and thumbs-up or thumbs-down. That's the Rome we'll look at. Our "Caesar Shuffle" begins with the most popular relic of ancient Rome, the Colosseum. This was where Romans—whose taste for violence was the equal of modern America's—enjoyed their *Dirty Harry*s and *Terminator*s. Gladiators, criminals, and wild animals fought to the death in every conceivable scenario. It makes sense to see the Colosseum together with the Roman Forum and Palatine Hill, just next door, covered by the same ticket, and described in the following two chapters.

Orientation

Cost: €12 combo-ticket covers both the Colosseum and the Roman Forum/Palatine Hill; also covered by Roma Pass. The combo-ticket is valid for two consecutive days, but once you use your ticket for either the Colosseum or the Forum/Palatine Hill, you can't reenter that sight (even the next day). The Colosseum is free the first Sunday of the month—and mobbed with people.

Hours: The Colosseum and the Roman Forum/Palatine Hill are open daily 8:30 until one hour before sunset: April-Aug until 19:15, Sept until 19:00, Oct until 18:30, Nov-mid-Feb until 16:30, mid-Feb-mid-March until 17:00, mid-March-late March until 17:30; last entry one hour before closing.

Restoration: The arena is being cleaned from top to bottom, given permanent lighting, and outfitted with new shops and services. Plans include building a freestanding ticket booth/visitors center outside the Colosseum. These ongoing renovations, scheduled to last several years, may affect your visit.

Avoiding Lines: Smart travelers buy tickets in advance, and visit when fewer people are trying to get in.

The Colosseum allows a maximum of 3,000 visitors inside at any one time, so you may have to wait in a long line even with an advance ticket. (Only groups get timed-entry tickets that allow them to waltz straight in.) Generally, crowds are thinner (and lines shorter) in the afternoon (especially after 15:00 in summer); this is also true at the Forum. There's usually a huge line at 8:30 when the Colosseum opens.

Ticket-Buying Strategies: You can avoid the slow ticket-buyer lines by buying your combo-ticket in advance online, buying the Roma Pass, buying a ticket at a less-crowded ticket office, booking a guided tour, or renting an audioguide or videoguide. Here are the options:

1. Buy and print a combo-ticket online at www.coopculture.it (€2 booking fee). Make sure to print the ticket, not the voucher. The "free tickets" you'll see listed are valid only for EU citizens with ID.

2. Buy a Roma Pass (see page 42), which you can use to cover your Colosseum and Forum admissions. The pass is sold at TIs, many tobacco shops and newsstands, at the green kiosk in front of the Colosseo Metro station, and at the Roman Forum information center on Via dei Fori Imperiali (see page 158). It should cost the same no matter where you buy it.

3. Buy a combo-ticket at a less-crowded place than the Colosseum. First check the Forum/Palatine Hill entrance facing the Colosseum. If that's also crowded, try the Forum/Palatine Hill entrance 150 yards away, on Via di San Gregorio (facing the Forum, with Colosseum at your back, go left down the street).

4. Pay to join an official guided tour, or rent an audioguide or videoguide (see "Tours," later). If the guard asks, say that you want to sign up for a tour, and they'll let you march right up to the Colosseum's guided visits *(Visite didattiche)* desk. Even if you don't actually do the tour, the extra cost might be worth it just to skip the ticket line.

5. Hire a private walking-tour guide. Guides of varying quality linger outside the Colosseum, offering tours that may

COLOSSEUM

allow you to enter more quickly. Be aware that these private guides may try to mislead you into thinking the Colosseum lines are longer than they really are. Also, the Colosseum administration frowns on these guides and warns visitors against hiring them. For more on this option, see "Tours," later.

Warning: Beware of the crude, modern-day **gladiators.** Though they are officially banned from posing for photos with tour-

ists for money, you may still encounter them, hoping to intimidate easy-to-swindle tourists into paying (too much) for a photo op. Also, look out for **pickpockets** and con artists in this prime tourist spot.

Getting There: The Colosseo Metro stop on line B is just across the street from the monument. Except on Sundays, buses #51, #85, #87, #118, #186, and #810 stop along Via dei Fori Imperiali near the Colosseum entrance, one of the Forum/Palatine Hill entrances, and Piazza Venezia. Tram #3 stops behind the Colosseum.

Getting In: The entrance is divided into two queues: those who need to buy a ticket (the slowest line), and those who are already ticket holders (combo-ticket, online ticket, Roma Pass, or signing up for a tour). There's also a separate entrance for groups, so be sure you follow the signs to get in the right line.

Information: Call center for assistance with tickets and tours: Tel. 06-3996-7700 (Mon-Fri 9:00-13:00 & 14:00-17:00, Sat 9:00-14:00, closed Sun); or www.coopculture.it. General info: www.archeoroma.beniculturali.it/en.

Tours: A fact-filled **audioguide** is available just past the turnstiles (€5.50/2 hours). A handheld **videoguide** senses where you are in the site and plays related clips (€6).

🎧 Download my free Colosseum **audio tour.**

Official **guided tours** in English depart roughly hourly between 10:15 and 17:15, and last 45-60 minutes (€5 plus Colosseum ticket, purchase inside the Colosseum near the ticket booth marked *Visite didattiche;* if you're lost, ask a guard to direct you to the desk).

A longer, 1.5-hour tour takes you through areas that are off-limits to regular visitors, including the top floor and underground passageways. While interesting, this tour certainly isn't essential to appreciating the Colosseum. Although it's possible to sign up for this tour at the Colosseum's guided-tours window, advance reservations are strongly advised, either by phone or online (no same-day reservations). Use the same website as for regular tickets (www.coopculture.it), or contact the call center (see "Information, earlier). After dialing, wait for English instructions to reach a live operator.

Private guides stand outside the Colosseum looking for business (€25-30/2-hour tour of the Colosseum, Forum, and Palatine Hill). If booking a private guide, make sure that your tour will start right away and that the ticket you receive covers all three sights: the Colosseum, Forum, and Palatine Hill.

Length of This Tour: Allow an hour. If you're short on time, you can basically see the entire interior with a single glance. It's not necessary to go upstairs or circle the place.

Baggage: Larger bags and backpacks are not allowed, and there is no bag check. Travel light to avoid being turned away.

Services: A WC (often crowded) is inside the Colosseum, and there's also a water fountain. For more tips on where to eat, drink, and find a WC in the area, see the sidebar on page 152.

The Tour Begins

EXTERIOR

• *View the Colosseum from the Forum fence, across the street from the Colosseo Metro station.*

Built when the Roman Empire was at its peak in A.D. 80, the Colosseum represents Rome at its grandest. The Flavian Amphitheater (the Colosseum's real name) was an arena for gladiator contests and public spectacles. When killing became a spectator sport, the Romans wanted to share the fun with as many people as possible, so they stuck two semicircular theaters together to create a freestanding amphitheater. The outside (where slender cypress trees stand today) was decorated with a 100 foot tall bronze statue of Nero that gleamed in the sunlight. In a later age, the colossal structure was nicknamed a "coloss-eum," the wonder of its age. Towering 150 feet high, it could accommodate 50,000 roaring fans (100,000 thumbs).

The Romans pioneered the use of concrete and the rounded arch, which enabled them to build on this tremendous scale. The exterior is a skeleton of 3.5 million cubic feet of travertine stone. (Each of the pillars flanking the ground level arches weighs five tons.) It took 200 ox-drawn wagons shuttling back and forth every day for four years just to bring the stone here from Tivoli. They stacked stone blocks (without mortar) into the shape of an arch, supported temporarily by wooden scaffolding. Finally, they wedged a keystone into the top of the arch—it not only kept the arch from falling, it could bear even more weight above. Iron pegs held the larger stones together; notice the small holes—the result of medieval peg poachers—that pockmark the sides.

The exterior says a lot about the Romans. They were great engi-

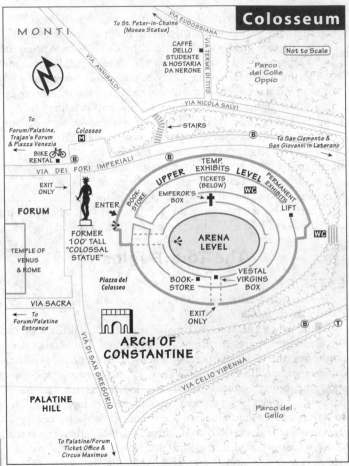

neers, not artists, and the building is more functional than beautiful. (If ancient Romans visited the US today as tourists, they might send home postcards of our greatest works of "art"—freeways.) While the essential structure of the Colosseum is Roman, the four-story façade is decorated with mostly Greek columns—Doric-like Tuscan columns on the ground level, Ionic on the second story, Corinthian on the next level, and at the top, half-columns with a mix of all three. Originally, copies of Greek statues stood in the arches of the middle two stories, giving a veneer of sophistication to this arena of death.

Only a third of the original Colosseum remains. Earthquakes destroyed some of it, but most was carted off as easy precut stones for other buildings during the Middle Ages and Renaissance.

• *To enter, line up in the correct queue. Remember, there's one for ticket buyers, one for ticket holders, and a separate entrance for groups. The visit begins once you show your ticket and pass through the turnstiles.*

INSIDE THE COLOSSEUM

Once past the turnstiles, signs direct you on a suggested (but generally not mandatory) visitors' route: first, you go upstairs, see a small permanent exhibition of artifacts, survey the arena from the upper level, descend to ground level, and exit. It's a fine route, but really, you're free to see the place in almost any order you'd like (though some staircases are one-way). Since the whole arena is visible from everywhere—there wasn't a bad seat in the house—most of this chapter's descriptions can work wherever you may wander.

Entering the Stadium

Imagine being an ancient spectator arriving for the games. Fans could pour in through ground-floor entrances; there were 76 numbered ones in addition to the emperor's private entrance on the north side. Your ticket (likely a piece of pottery) was marked with your entrance, section, row, and seat number. You'd pass by concession stands selling fast food and souvenirs, such as wine glasses with the names of famous gladiators. A hallway leading to the seats was called a *vomitorium*. At exit time, the Colosseum would "vomit" out its contents, giving us the English word. It's estimated that all 50,000 fans could enter and exit in 15 minutes.

• *Wherever you spill out into the arena—upstairs or downstairs, at one side of the arena or the other—just take it all in and get oriented. The tallest side of the Colosseum (with the large Christian cross) is the north side.*

Arena

The games took place in this oval-shaped arena, 280 feet long by 165 feet wide. The ratio of length to width is close to the so-called golden ratio. Since the days of the Greek mathematician Pythagoras, artists considered that proportion (1.6 to 1) to be ideal, with almost mystical properties. The Colosseum's architects may have wanted their structure to embody the perfect mathematical order they thought existed in nature.

When you look down into the arena, you're seeing the underground passages beneath the playing surface (which can only be visited on a private tour). The arena was originally covered with a wooden floor, then sprinkled with sand

The Permanent Exhibition

Upstairs is a display of old artifacts with good English information. You'll see cracked columns and busted busts, plus diagrams and reconstructions showing how the Colosseum once looked.

Especially interesting are the terracotta plates—Romans loved to eat (chicken wings and olives), drink (wine), and play board games while they watched. A fine mosaic depicts a tiger being herded into battle by his handlers. Models illustrate how the wild animals were raised on elevators to arena level. And you'll see the bones of some of the animals used in the games—horses (which some combatants rode), bears, boars, ostriches, and lions.

(*arena* in Latin). The bit of reconstructed floor gives you an accurate sense of the original arena level and the subterranean warren where animals and prisoners were held. As in modern stadiums, the spectators ringed the playing area in bleacher seats that slanted up from the arena floor. Around you are the big brick masses that supported the tiers of seats.

A variety of materials were used to build the stadium. Look around. Big white travertine blocks stacked on top of each other formed the skeleton. The pillars for the bleachers were made with a shell of brick, filled in with concrete. Originally the bare brick was covered with marble columns or ornamental facing, so the interior was a brilliant white (they used white plaster for the upper-floor cheap seats).

The Colosseum's seating was strictly segregated. At ringside, the emperor, senators, Vestal Virgins, and VIPs occupied marble seats with their names carved on them (a few marble seats have been restored, at the east end). The next level upheld those of noble birth. The level tourists now occupy was for ordinary free Roman citizens, called plebeians. Up at the very top (a hundred yards

from the action), there were once wooden bleachers for the poorest people—foreigners, slaves, and women. While no seats survive and

COLOSSEUM

you're likely viewing the arena from what was a passageway that ran under the seats, you can imagine the scene.

The top story of the Colosseum is mostly ruined—only the north side still retains its high wall. This was not part of the original three-story structure but was added around A.D. 230 after a fire necessitated repairs. Picture the awning that could be stretched across the top of the stadium by armies of sailors. Strung along horizontal beams that pointed inward to the center, the awning

covered only about a third of the arena—so those at the top always enjoyed shade, while many nobles down below roasted in the sun.

Looking into the complex web of passageways beneath the arena, you can imagine how busy the backstage action was. Gladiators strolled down the central passageway, from their warm-up yard on the east end to the arena entrance on the west. Some workers tended wild animals. Others prepared stage sets of trees or fake buildings, allowing the arena to be quickly transformed from an African jungle to a Greek temple. Props and sets were hauled up to arena level on 80 different elevator shafts via a system of ropes and pulleys. (You might be able to make out some small rectangular shafts, especially near the center of the arena.) That means there were 80 different spots from which animals, warriors, and stage sets could pop up and magically appear.

The games began with a few warm-up acts—dogs bloodying themselves attacking porcupines, female gladiators fighting each other, or a one-legged man battling a dwarf. Then came the main event—the gladiators.

"Hail, Caesar! *(Ave, Caesar!)* We who are about to die salute you!" The gladiators would enter the arena from the west end, parade around to the sound of trumpets, acknowledge the Vestal Virgins (on the south side), then stop at the emperor's box (supposedly marked today by the cross that stands at the "50-yard line" on the north side—although no one knows for sure where it was). They would then raise their weapons, shout, and salute—and begin

fighting. The fights pitted men against men, men against beasts, and beasts against beasts. Picture 50,000 screaming people around you (did gladiators get stage fright?), and imagine that they want to see you die.

Some gladiators wielded swords, protected only with a shield and a heavy helmet. Others represented fighting fishermen, with

 a net to snare opponents and a trident to spear them. The gladiators were usually slaves, criminals, or poor people who got their chance for freedom, wealth, and fame in the ring. They learned to fight in training schools, then battled their way up the ranks. The best were rewarded like our modern sports stars, with fan clubs, great wealth, and, yes, product endorsements.

The animals came from all over the world: lions, tigers, and bears (oh my!), crocodiles, elephants, and hippos (not to mention exotic human "animals" from the "barbarian" lands). They were kept in cages beneath the arena floor, then lifted up in the elevators. Released at floor level, animals would pop out from behind blinds into the arena—the gladiator didn't know where, when, or by what he'd be attacked. Many a hapless warrior met his death here, and never even knew what hit him. (This sometimes brought howls of laughter from the hardened fans in the cheap upper seats, who had a better view of the action.)

Nets ringed the arena to protect the crowd. The stadium was inaugurated with a 100-day festival in which 2,000 men and 9,000 animals were killed. Colosseum employees squirted perfumes around the stadium to mask the stench of blood.

If a gladiator fell helpless to the ground, his opponent would approach the emperor's box and ask: Should he live or die? Sometimes the emperor left the decision to the crowd, who would judge based on how valiantly the man had fought. They would make their decision: thumbs-up or thumbs-down.

Consider the value of these games in placating and controlling the huge Roman populace. Imagine never having seen an actual lion, and suddenly one jumps out to chase a prisoner in the arena. Seeing the king of beasts slain by a gladiator reminded the masses of man's triumph over nature.

In an age without a hint of a newsreel, it was hard for local Romans to visualize and appreciate the faraway conquests their empire was so dedicated to. The Colosseum spectacles were a way to bring home the environments, animals, and people of these conquered lands, parade them before the public, and make them real. And having the thumbs-up or thumbs-down authority over another person's life gave the spectators a real sense of power. Imagine the psychological boost the otherwise downtrodden masses felt when the emperor granted them this thrilling decision.

Did they throw Christians to the lions as in the movies? Christians were definitely thrown to the lions, made to fight gladiators, crucified, and burned alive...but probably not here in this particular stadium. Maybe, but probably not.

Rome was a nation of warriors that built an empire by conquest. The battles fought against Germans and other barbarians, Egyptians, and strange animals were played out daily here in the Colosseum for the benefit of city-slicker bureaucrats, who got vicarious thrills by watching brutes battle to the death. The contests were always free, sponsored by the government to bribe the people's favor or to keep Rome's growing masses of unemployed rabble off the streets.

• *With these scenes in mind, wander around, then check out the upper level. Stairs are on both the east and west sides, with an elevator at the east end (only accessible to those who really need it). The upper deck offers more colossal views of the arena, plus a bookstore and temporary exhibits. Wherever you may Rome, find a spot at the west end of the upper deck, where you can look out over some of the sights nearby.*

Views from the Upper Level
• *Start your visual tour with the big, white, triumphal arch.*

Arch of Constantine
If you are a Christian, were raised a Christian, or simply belong to a so-called "Christian nation," ponder this arch. It marks one of the great turning points in history: the military coup that made Christianity mainstream. In A.D. 312, Emperor Constantine defeated his rival Maxentius in the crucial Battle of the Milvian Bridge. The night before, he had seen a vision of a cross in the sky.

Constantine—whose mother and sister had already become Christians—became sole emperor and legalized Christianity. With this one battle, a once-obscure Jewish sect with a handful of followers became the state religion of the entire Western world. In A.D. 300, you could be killed for being a Christian; a century later, you could be killed for not being one. Church enrollment boomed.

The restored arch is like an ancient museum. It's decorated entirely with recycled carvings originally made for other buildings.

Modern Amenities in the Ancient World

The area around the Colosseum, Forum, and Palatine Hill is rich in history but pretty barren when it comes to food, shelter, and WCs. Here are a few options:

The Colosseum has a crowded **WC** inside. A WC is behind (east of) the structure (facing ticket entrance, go clockwise; pay WC is under stairway). If you can wait, the best WCs in the area are at Palatine Hill—at the Via di San Gregorio entrance, in the museum, and in the Farnese Gardens. The Forum has WCs at the entrance on Via dei Fori Imperiali, near the Arch of Titus (in the "Soprintendenza" office), and in the middle of the Forum (near #6 on the map on page 161).

Because the area's **eating** options are limited, consider assembling a small picnic. The Colosseo Metro stop has forgettable €5 hot sandwiches. Snack stands on street corners sell overpriced drinks, sandwiches, fruit, and candy. If you prefer to dine in, you'll find a few restaurants behind the Colosseum (with expansive views of the structure but high prices and mediocre food), and several recommended places are within a few blocks (no views but a better value—see page 378). The characteristic Monti neighborhood, with a number of recommended eateries, is just north of the Forum's Via dei Fori Imperiali entrance (see page 379).

To refill your **water** bottle, stop at one of the water fountains in the area. You'll find them along a few city streets, as well as inside the Colosseum, Forum, and Palatine Hill. There's also a high-tech water fountain next to the Colosseo Metro entrance.

A nice oasis is the free **information center** located across from the Forum entrance on Via dei Fori Imperiali and a bit east, toward the Colosseum. It has a small café, a WC, and a few exhibits (daily 9:30-19:00).

If your sightseeing takes you as far as **Capitoline Hill,** you'll find services at the Capitoline Museums, including a nice view café (see page 186).

Several **public buses** (#85, #87, etc.) traverse Via dei Fori Imperiali between the Colosseum and Piazza Venezia, making it easy to hop on for a stop or two. If you need a **taxi,** use the stand near the southeast corner of the Colosseum. The taxis parked

By covering it with exquisite carvings of high Roman art—works that glorified previous emperors—Constantine put himself in their league. Hadrian is featured in the round reliefs, with Marcus Aurelius in the square reliefs higher up. The big statues on top are of Trajan and Augustus. Originally, Augustus drove a chariot similar to the one topping the modern Victor Emmanuel II Monument. Fourth-century Rome may have been in decline, but Constantine clung to its glorious past.

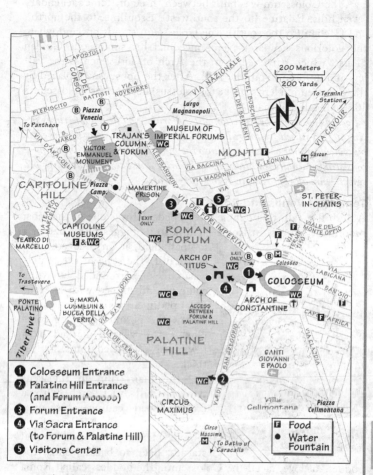

① Colosseum Entrance
② Palatino Hill Entrance (and Forum Access)
③ Forum Entrance
④ Via Sacra Entrance (to Forum & Palatine Hill)
⑤ Visitors Center

🅵 Food
● Water Fountain

near the Colosseo Metro stop (on Via dei Fori Imperiali) have a reputation for being sharks.

Surrounding Hills

Looking southwest, beyond the Arch of Constantine, you see Palatine Hill, dotted with umbrella pines. To the right of the Arch of Constantine is the road called Via Sacra ("Sacred Way"), once Rome's main street. It heads west up an incline toward the Arch of Titus (you can just make out its white top from here). That marks the head of the Forum, the religious, political, and commercial heart of ancient Rome (covered in the next chapter).

COLOSSEUM

The Colosseum was built between three of Rome's legendary seven hills: Palatine (to the southwest), Esquiline (to the north), and Caelian (to the south). The Colosseum stands on land where the notorious Emperor Nero once had his sumptuous Golden House, which stretched from the Arch of Titus, across the valley, and up onto Esquiline Hill. After the house was replaced by the Colosseum, Nero's statue (or colossus) became the Colosseum's 100-foot-tall doorman.

• *Looking west, in the direction of the Forum, you'll see some ruins sitting atop a raised, rectangular-shaped hill. (You can recognize the hill by some door-like openings cut into the hill's support wall.) The ruins—consisting of an arched alcove made of brick and backed by a church bell tower—are all that remain of the once-great...*

Temple of Venus and Rome

At 100 feet tall, this temple atop a pedestal was one of the most prominent temples in Rome—and also its biggest. The size of a

football field, it once covered the entire hill. The style of the temple was Greek—surrounded by white columns and topped with a triangular pediment above the entrance. Today, the perimeter of the complex is still visible, marked by a few massive white columns, six feet thick.

The main ruin in the center—the tall brick arch with a cross-hatched ceiling—was once the *cella*, or sacred chamber of the temple. Here sat two monumental statues, back to back. Venus, the goddess of love, faced the Colosseum. The goddess called Roma Aeterna faced the Forum. The pair of statues symbolized the birth and eternal destiny of the race of people meant to endure forever. The goddesses' Latin names were written in the twin *cella*s. On one side it read "Roma" and on the other, "Amor." Roma and Amor—a perfectly symmetrical palindrome, showing how Rome and Love were meant to go together. In ancient times, newlyweds ascended the staircase from the Colosseum (some parts are still visible) to the temple to ask Venus and Roma Aeterna to bring them good luck. These days, Roman couples get married at the church with the bell tower to ensure themselves love and happiness for eternity.

The temple was designed by Hadrian, the second-century emperor and amateur architect who also designed the Pantheon. Hadrian's design was critiqued by Rome's best-known architect, who complained that the huge statues would be so cramped they'd bump their heads if they stood up. Hadrian listened patiently to the criticism...then had the architect killed.

For a closer-up look at the Temple of Venus and Rome, you can access the ruins from within the Roman Forum.

THE COLOSSEUM'S LEGACY

With the coming of Christianity to Rome, the Colosseum and its deadly games slowly became politically incorrect. However,

some gladiator contests continued here sporadically until they were completely banned in A.D. 435. Animal hunts continued a few decades longer. As the Roman Empire dwindled and the infrastructure crumbled, the stadium itself was neglected. Finally, around A.D. 523—after nearly 500 years of games—the last animal was killed, and the Colosseum shut its doors.

For the next thousand years, the structure was inhabited by various squatters. It was used for makeshift apartments or shops, as a church, a cemetery, and as a refuge during invasions and riots. Over time, the Colosseum was eroded by wind, rain, and the strain of gravity. Earthquakes weakened it, and a powerful quake in 1349 toppled the south side.

More than anything, the Colosseum was dismantled by the Roman citizens themselves, who carted off precut stones to be reused for palaces and churches, including St. Peter's. The marble facing was pulverized into mortar, and 300 tons of iron brackets were pried out and melted down, resulting in the pockmarking you see today.

After centuries of neglect, a series of 16th-century popes took pity on the pagan structure. In memory of the Christians who may (or may not) have been martyred here, they shored up the south and west sides with bricks and placed the big cross on the north side of the arena.

Today, the Colosseum links Rome's glorious past with its vital present. Major political demonstrations begin or end here, providing protesters with an iconic backdrop for the TV cameras. On Good Friday, the pope comes here to lead pilgrims as they follow the Stations of the Cross.

The legend goes that as long as the Colosseum shall stand,

the city of Rome shall also stand. For nearly 2,000 years, the Colosseum has been the enduring symbol of Rome, the Eternal City.

• *The Roman Forum is 100 yards to the right of the arch. You can go in through the entrance across from the Colosseum, the entrance on Via dei Fori Imperiali, or the entrance along Via di San Gregorio—see the map on page 161. If you're ready for a visit, turn to the next chapter.*

ROMAN FORUM TOUR

Foro Romano

The Forum was the political, religious, and commercial center of the city. Rome's most important temples and halls of justice were here. This was the place for religious processions, political demonstrations, elections, important speeches, and parades by conquering generals. As Rome's empire expanded, these few acres of land became the center of the civilized world.

Though I've covered them as two separate tours, the Roman Forum and Palatine Hill are organized as a single sight with one admission—meaning if you want to see both you'll need to do it in a single visit. The passage between the Forum and Palatine Hill is near the Arch of Titus. Don't exit the Forum through the turnstiles, hoping to walk down the street to the Palatine and re-enter; you won't be allowed in.

Orientation

Cost: €12 combo-ticket covers both the Roman Forum/Palatine Hill and the Colosseum; also covered by the Roma Pass. The combo-ticket is valid two consecutive days, but once it's scanned, you can't reenter that sight (even the next day). The Forum is free (and extremely crowded) the first Sunday of the month.

Hours: The Roman Forum/Palatine Hill and the Colosseum are open daily 8:30 until one hour before sunset: April-Aug until 19:15, Sept until 19:00, Oct until 18:30, Nov-mid-Feb until 16:30, mid-Feb-mid-March until 17:00, mid-March-late March until 17:30; last entry one hour before closing.

Avoiding Lines: See "Avoiding Lines" on page 143.

Getting There: The closest Metro stop is Colosseo. Except on Sundays, buses #51, #85, #87, #118, #186, and #810 stop along

Via dei Fori Imperiali near the Colosseum, the Forum, and Piazza Venezia.

Getting In: The Forum and Palatine Hill share three entrances. The handiest (but often most crowded) is directly across from the **Colosseum.** This entrance puts you right by the Arch of Titus, where our tour begins. The **Palatine Hill** entrance (on Via di San Gregorio) is often less crowded. After buying your ticket, reach the Arch of Titus by taking the path to the right; the path to the left goes uphill to the Palatine Hill ruins. A third entrance is along **Via dei Fori Imperiali**, about halfway between the Colosseum and Piazza Venezia, near the intersection with Via Cavour (and through a low-profile building set well back from the street). To reach the Arch of Titus from here, walk down the ramp and turn left.

Information: A free information center, located across from the Via dei Fori Imperiali entrance, can sell you a Roma Pass and has a bookshop, small café, and WCs (daily 9:30-19:00, may stay open later in summer). Vendors outside sell a variety of colorful books with plastic overlays that restore the ruins (official price in bookstore for larger version with DVD is €20 and for smaller version is €10—don't pay more than these prices). Ticket info: Tel. 06-3996-7700, www.coopculture.it. General info: www.archeoroma.beniculturali.it/en.

Tours: An unexciting yet informative **audioguide** helps decipher the rubble (€5/2 hours, €7 version includes Palatine Hill and lasts 3 hours, must leave ID), but you have to return it to where you rented it—meaning you may not be able to exit directly to Capitoline Hill or the Colosseum, for example.

∩ Download my free Roman Forum **audio tour.**

Length of This Tour: Allow 1.5 hours, plus any time you'll spend on Palatine Hill. If you have less time, end the walk at the Arch of Septimius Severus. Don't miss the Basilica of Constantine hiding behind the trees.

Services: WCs are at the Palatine Hill and Via dei Fori Imperiali ticket entrances. Within the Forum itself, there's one near the Arch of Titus (in the "Soprintendenza" office), and another in the middle, near #6 on the map. Others are atop Palatine Hill (see above). For information on food and other WCs in the area, see the sidebar on page 152.

Plan Ahead: The ancient paving at the Forum is uneven; wear sturdy shoes. I carry a water bottle and refill it at the Forum's public drinking fountains.

Improvise: Because of ongoing restoration, paths through the Forum are often rerouted. Use this tour as a starting point, but be prepared for a few detours and backtracking.

Viewpoint: If you (or your kids) rebel against spending an hour and a half walking around in the heat, at least view the Forum from the overlook near the Mamertine Prison (see map on page 153).

The Tour Begins

• *Whichever ticket entrance you use, our tour begins at the Arch of Titus (Arco di Tito). It's the white triumphal arch that rises above the rubble on the east end of the Forum (closest to the Colosseum). Stand at the viewpoint alongside the arch and gaze over the valley known as the Forum.*

View of the Forum

The Forum is a rectangular valley running roughly east (the Colosseum end) to west (Capitoline Hill, with its bell tower). The rocky

path at your feet is the Via Sacra. It leads from the Arch of Titus, through the trees, past the large brick Senate building, through the triumphal arch at the far end, and up Capitoline Hill. The hill to your left (with all the trees) is Palatine Hill.

Picture being here when a conquering general returned to Rome with crates of booty. The valley was full of gleaming white buildings topped with bronze roofs. The Via Sacra—the Forum's Main Street—would be lined with citizens waving branches and carrying torches. The trumpets would sound as the parade began. First came porters, carrying chests full of gold and jewels. Then, a parade of exotic animals from the conquered lands—elephants, giraffes, hippopotamuses—for the crowd to "ooh" and "ahh" at. Next came the prisoners in chains, with the captive king on a wheeled platform so the people could jeer and spit at him. Finally, the conquering hero himself would drive down in his four-horse chariot, with rose petals strewn in his path. The whole procession would run the length of the Forum and up the face of Capitoline Hill to the Temple of Saturn (the eight big columns midway up the hill—#14 on the map in this chapter), where they'd place the booty in Rome's coffers. Then they'd continue up to the summit to the Temple of Jupiter (only ruins of its foundation remain today) to dedicate the victory to the King of the Gods.

❶ **Arch of Titus (Arco di Tito)**

The Arch of Titus commemorated the Roman victory over the province of Judaea (Israel) in A.D. 70. The Romans had a reputation as benevolent conquerors who tolerated local customs and

FORUM

rulers. All they required was allegiance to the empire, shown by worshipping the emperor as a god. No problem for most conquered people, who already had half a dozen gods on their prayer lists anyway. But Israelites believed in only one god, and it wasn't the emperor. Israel revolted. After a short but bitter war, the Romans defeated the rebels, took Jerusalem, destroyed their temple (leaving only a fragment of one wall's foundation—today's revered "Wailing Wall"), and brought home 50,000 Jewish slaves...who were forced to build this arch (and the Colosseum).

Roman propaganda decorates the inside of the arch, where a relief shows the emperor Titus in a chariot being crowned by the

goddess Victory. (Thanks to modern pollution, they both look like they've been through the wars.) The other side shows booty from the sacking of the temple in Jerusalem—soldiers carrying a Jewish menorah and other plunder. The two (unfinished) plaques on poles were to have listed the conquered cities. Look at the top of the ceiling. Constructed after Titus' death, the relief shows him riding an eagle to heaven, where he'll become one of the gods.

The brutal crushing of the A.D. 70 rebellion (and another one 60 years later) devastated the nation of Israel. With no temple as a center for their faith, the Jews scattered throughout the world (the Diaspora). There would be no Jewish political entity again for almost 2,000 years, until modern Israel was created after World War II.

As you begin this Forum tour, here's a hint for seeing things with "period eyes." We imagine the structures in ancient Rome as mostly white, but ornate buildings and monuments like the Arch of Titus were originally more colorful. Through the ages, builders scavenged stone from the Forum, and the finest stone—the colored marble—was cannibalized first. If any was left, it was generally the white stone. Statues that filled the niches were vividly painted, but the organic paint rotted away as statues lay buried for centuries. Lettering was inset bronze and eyes were inset ivory. Even seemingly intact structures, like the Arch of Titus, have been reassembled. Notice the columns are half smooth and half fluted. The

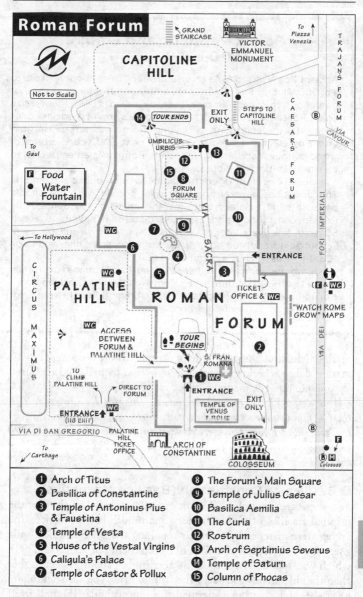

Roman Forum

GRAND STAIRCASE

VICTOR EMMANUEL MONUMENT

To Plazza Venezia

CAPITOLINE HILL

Not to Scale

To Gaul

EXIT ONLY

STEPS TO CAPITOLINE HILL

14 TOUR ENDS

UMBILICUS URBIS

13

12

11

15

8

FORUM SQUARE

10

TRAJANS FORUM

VIA CAVOUR

CAESARS FORUM

B

F Food
● Water Fountain

To Hollywood

WC

7

9

← ENTRANCE

FORI IMPERIALI

"WATCH ROME GROW" MAPS

6

4

3

5

VIA SACRA

CIRCUS MAXIMUS

PALATINE HILL

ROMAN

FORUM

TICKET OFFICE & WC

(**F** & WC)

B

VIA DEI

WC

ACCESS BETWEEN FORUM & PALATINE HILL

TOUR BEGINS

S. FRAN. ROMANA

2

1 WC

ENTRANCE

TO CLIMB PALATINE HILL

DIRECT TO FORUM

EXIT ONLY

ENTRANCE (110 EXIT)

WC

PALATINE HILL TICKET OFFICE

TEMPLE OF VENUS & ROME

B

To Carthage

VIA DI SAN GREGORIO

ARCH OF CONSTANTINE

COLOSSEO

F

B M

Colosseo

1 Arch of Titus
2 Basilica of Constantine
3 Temple of Antoninus Pius & Faustina
4 Temple of Vesta
5 House of the Vestal Virgins
6 Caligula's Palace
7 Temple of Castor & Pollux
8 The Forum's Main Square
9 Temple of Julius Caesar
10 Basilica Aemilia
11 The Curia
12 Rostrum
13 Arch of Septimius Severus
14 Temple of Saturn
15 Column of Phocas

FORUM

fluted halves are original; the smooth parts are reconstructions—intentionally not trying to fake the original.

And speaking of cannibalizing marble, remember that when marble burns it becomes lime, which is used to make cement. In the Middle Ages, before the historic importance of antiquity was appreciated, the Forum was surrounded by kilns used to melt

Rome: Republic and Empire
(500 B.C.-A.D. 500)

Ancient Rome lasted for a thousand years, from about 500 B.C. to A.D. 500. During that time, Rome expanded from a small tribe of barbarians to a vast empire, then dwindled slowly to city size again. For the first 500 years, when Rome's armies made her ruler of the Italian peninsula and beyond, Rome was a republic governed by elected senators. Over the next 500 years, a time of world conquest and eventual decline, Rome was an empire ruled by a military-backed dictator.

Julius Caesar bridged the gap between republic and empire. This ambitious general and politician, popular with the people because of his military victories and charisma, suspended the Roman constitution and assumed dictatorial powers in about 50 B.C. A few years later, he was assassinated by a conspiracy of senators. His adopted son, Augustus, succeeded him, and soon "Caesar" was not just a name but a title.

Emperor Augustus ushered in the Pax Romana, or Roman peace (A.D. 1-200), a time when Rome reached her peak and controlled an empire that stretched even beyond Eurail—from England to Egypt, Turkey to Morocco.

marble. Much of the grandeur of ancient Rome—statues, reliefs, marble slabs—was loaded into these ovens, melted, and repoured as concrete into the medieval city.

• *Walk down Via Sacra into the Forum. Imagine Roman sandals on these original basalt stones—the oldest street you'll ever walk. Many of the stones under your feet were walked on by Caesar Augustus 2,000 years ago. After about 50 yards, turn right and follow a path uphill to the three huge arches of the...*

❷ Basilica of Constantine (Basilica Maxentius)

Yes, these are big arches. But they represent only one-third of the original Basilica of Constantine, a mammoth hall of justice. The arches were matched by a similar set along the Via Sacra side (only a few squat brick piers remain). Between them ran the central hall, which was spanned by a roof 130 feet high—about 55 feet higher than the side arches you see. (The stub of brick you see sticking up began an arch that once spanned the central hall.) The hall itself was as long as a football field, lavishly furnished with colorful inlaid marble, a gilded bronze ceiling, and statues, and filled with strolling Romans. At the far (west) end was an enormous marble statue of Emperor Constantine on a throne. (Pieces of this statue, including a hand the size of a man, are on display in Rome's Capitoline Museums.)

FORUM

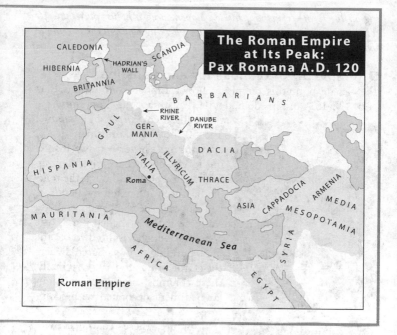

The Roman Empire
at Its Peak:
Pax Romana A.D. 120

CALEDONIA

HADRIAN'S
WALL

HIBERNIA

BRITANNIA

SCANDIA

B A R B A R I A N S

RHINE
RIVER

DANUBE
RIVER

GER-
MANIA

GAUL

ITALIA

ILLYRICUM

DACIA

THRACE

HISPANIA

Roma

ASIA

CAPPADOCIA

ARMENIA

MEDIA

MESOPOTAMIA

MAURITANIA

Mediterranean Sea

SYRIA

AFRICA

EGYPT

Roman Empire

The basilica was begun by the emperor Maxentius, but after he was trounced in battle (see page 151), the victor Constantine completed the massive building. No doubt about it, the Romans built monuments on a more epic scale than any previous Europeans, wowing their "barbarian" neighbors.

For the next few years, you'll see construction in and around the basilica for Rome's new Metro line, currently scheduled to reach here in 2021.

• *Now stroll deeper into the Forum, downhill along Via Sacra, through the trees. Pass by the only original bronze door still swinging on its ancient hinges (the green door at the Tempio di Romolo, the round build-*

ing on the right—if it happens to be open, peek in). Just past that, 10 columns stand in front of a much newer-looking church. The colonnade was part of the...

❸ Temple of Antoninus Pius and Faustina

The Senate built this temple to honor Emperor Antoninus Pius (A.D. 138-161) and his deified wife, Faustina. (The lintel's inscrip-

tion calls them "*divo*" and "*divae*.") The 50-foot-tall Corinthian (leafy) columns must have been awe-inspiring to out-of-towners who grew up in thatched huts. Although the temple has been inhabited by a church, you can still see the basic layout—a staircase led to a shaded porch (the columns), which admitted you to the main building (now a church), where the statue of the god sat. Originally, these columns supported a triangular pediment decorated with sculptures.

Picture these columns, with gilded capitals, supporting brightly painted statues in the pediment, and the whole building capped with a gleaming bronze roof. The stately gray rubble of today's Forum is a faded black-and-white photograph of a 3-D Technicolor era.

The building is a microcosm of many changes that occurred after Rome fell. In medieval times, the temple was pillaged. Note

the diagonal cuts high on the marble columns—a failed attempt by scavengers to cut through the pillars to pull them down for their precious stone. (They used vinegar and rope to cut the marble...but because vinegar also eats through rope, they abandoned the attempt.) In 1550, a church was housed inside the ancient temple. The green door shows the street level at the time of Michelangelo. The long staircase was underground until excavated in the 1800s.

• *With your back to the colonnade, walk straight ahead—jogging a bit to the right to stay on the path—and head for the three short columns, all that's left of the...*

❹ Temple of Vesta

This is perhaps Rome's most sacred spot. Rome considered itself one big family, and this temple represented a circular hut, like the kind that Rome's first families lived in. Inside, a fire burned, just as in a Roman home. And back in the days before lighters and butane, you never wanted your fire to go out. As long as the sacred flame burned, Rome would stand. The flame was tended by priestesses known as Vestal Virgins.

• *Just to the left and up the stairs is a big, enclosed field with two rectangular brick pools (just below the hill). This was the courtyard of the...*

❺ House of the Vestal Virgins

The Vestal Virgins lived in a two story building surrounding a long central courtyard with two pools at one end. Rows of statues depicting leading Vestal Virgins flanked the courtyard. This place was the model—both architecturally and sexually—for medieval convents and monasteries.

Chosen from noble families before they reached the age of 10, the six Vestal Virgins served a 30-year term. Honored and revered by the Romans, the Vestals even had their own box opposite the emperor in the Colosseum. The statues that line the courtyard honor dutiful Vestals.

As the name implies, a Vestal took a vow of chastity. If she served her term faithfully—abstaining for 30 years—she was given a huge dowry and allowed to marry. But if they found any Virgin who wasn't, she was strapped to a funeral car, paraded through the streets of the Forum, taken to a crypt, given a loaf of bread and a lamp...and buried alive. Many women suffered the latter fate.

• *Looming just beyond this field is Palatine Hill—the corner of which may have been...*

❻ Caligula's Palace (Palace of Tiberius)

Emperor Caligula (ruled A.D. 37-41) had a huge palace on Palatine Hill overlooking the Forum. It actually sprawled down the hill into the Forum (some supporting arches remain in the hillside).

Caligula was not a nice person. He tortured enemies, stole senators' wives, and parked his chariot in handicap spaces. But Rome's luxury-loving emperors only added to the glory of the Forum, with each one trying to make his mark on history.

• *Continue downhill, passing the three short columns of the Temple of Vesta, and head for the three taller columns just beyond it.*

❼ Temple of Castor and Pollux

These three columns—all that remain of a once-prestigious temple—have become the most photographed sight in the Forum. The

temple was one of the city's oldest, built in the fifth century B.C. It commemorated the Roman victory over the Tarquin, the notorious Etruscan king who once oppressed them. After the battle, the legendary twin brothers Castor and Pollux watered their horses here, at the Sacred Spring of Juturna (which has been recently excavated nearby).

As a symbol of Rome's self-governing republic, the temple was often used as a meeting place of senators, and its front steps served as a podium for free speech. The three columns are Corinthian style, featuring leafy capitals and fluting. They date from a later incarnation of the temple (first century).

• *You're now standing at the corner of a flat, grassy area.*

❽ The Forum's Main Square

The original Forum, or main square, was this flat patch about the size of a football field, stretching to the foot of Capitoline Hill. Surrounding it were temples, law courts, government buildings, and triumphal arches.

Rome was born right here. According to legend, twin brothers Romulus (Rome) and Remus were orphaned in infancy and raised by a she-wolf on top of Palatine Hill. Growing up, they found it hard to get dates. So they and their cohorts attacked the nearby Sabine tribe and kidnapped their women. After they made peace, this marshy valley became the meeting place and then the trading center for the scattered tribes on the surrounding hillsides.

The square was the busiest and most crowded—and often the seediest—section of town. Besides the senators, politicians, and currency exchangers, there were even sleazier types—souvenir hawkers, pickpockets, fortune-tellers, gamblers, slave marketers, drunks, hookers, lawyers, and tour guides.

Ancient Rome's population exceeded one million, more than any city until London and Paris in the 19th century. All those Roman masses lived in tiny apartments as we would live in tents at a campsite, basically just to sleep. The public space—their Forum, today's piazza—is where they did their living. Consider how, to this day, the piazza is still such an important part of any Italian town. Since Roman times, the piazza has reflected and accommodated the gregarious and outgoing nature of the Italian people.

The Forum is now rubble, but imagine it in its prime: blindingly brilliant marble buildings with 40-foot high columns and shining metal roofs; rows of statues painted in realistic colors; processional chariots rattling down Via Sacra. Mentally replace tourists in T-shirts with tribunes in togas. Imagine the buildings towering and the people buzzing around you while an orator gives a rabble-rousing speech from the Rostrum. If things still look like just a pile of rocks, at least tell yourself, "But Julius Caesar once leaned against these rocks."

• *At the near (east) end of the main square (the Colosseum is to the east) are the foundations of a temple now capped with a peaked wood-and-metal roof.*

❾ Temple of Julius Caesar
(Tempio del Divo Giulio, or Ara di Cesare)
On March 15, in 44 B.C., Julius Caesar was stabbed 23 times by political conspirators. After his assassination, Caesar's body was cremated on this spot (under the metal roof). Afterward, this temple

was built to honor him. Peek behind the wall into the small apse area, where a mound of dirt usually has fresh flowers—given to remember the man who, more than any other, personified the greatness of Rome.

Caesar (100-44 B.C.) changed Rome—and the Forum—dramatically. He cleared out many of the wooden market stalls and began to ring the square with even grander buildings. Caesar's house was located behind the temple, near that clump of trees. He walked right by here on the day he was assassinated ("Beware the Ides of March!" warned a street-corner Etruscan preacher).

Though he was popular with the masses, not everyone liked Caesar's urban design or his politics. When he assumed dictatorial powers, he was ambushed and stabbed to death by a conspiracy of senators, including his adopted son, Brutus *("Et tu, Brute?")*.

The funeral was held here, facing the main square. The citizens gathered, and speeches were made. Mark Antony stood up to say (in Shakespeare's words), "Friends, Romans, countrymen, lend me your ears. I come to bury Caesar, not to praise him." When Caesar's body was burned, his adoring fans threw anything at hand on the fire, requiring the fire department to come put it out. Later, Emperor Augustus dedicated this temple in his name, making Caesar the first Roman to become a god.

• *Continue past the Temple of Julius Caesar, to the open area between the columns of the Temple of Antoninus Pius and Faustina (which we passed earlier) and the boxy brick building (the Curia). You can view these ruins of the Basilica Aemilia from a ramp next to the Temple of Antoninus Pius and Faustina, or find the entrance near the Curia (if it's not closed for archaeological work).*

❿ Basilica Aemilia

The word "basilica" originally meant a covered public forum, often serving as a Roman hall of justice. In a society that was as legal-minded as America is today, you needed a lot of lawyers—and a big place to put them. Citizens came here to work out matters such as inheritances and building permits or to sue somebody.

Notice the layout. It was a long, rectangular building. The stubby columns all in a row form one long, central hall flanked by

Religion in Ancient Rome

Religion in ancient Rome was all about the *pax deorum* (peace, or pact, with the gods) that guaranteed the prosperity of the incredibly superstitious Romans. To appease the fickle gods, they performed elaborate rituals at lavish temples and shrines. Romans had a god for every moment of their days and each important event in their lives. While the Romans adopted the Greek pantheon, they also embraced the gods from many of the people they came into contact with, sometimes using elaborate ceremonies to persuade these new gods to "move" to Rome. Scholars estimate Romans had about 30,000 gods to keep happy. In this high-maintenance religion, there was Cunina, the goddess who protected cradles; Statulinus, to help children stand up; and Fabulina, for their first words. Fornax was the oven god, Pomona the fruit-tree goddess, Sterculinus the manure god, and Venus Cloacina the sewer goddess.

Priests interpreted the will of the gods by studying the internal organs of sacrificed animals, the flight of birds, and prophetic books. A clap of thunder was enough to postpone a battle.

Astrology, magic rites, the cult of deified emperors, house gods, and the near-deification of ancestors permeated Roman life. But all these gods didn't quite do it for the Romans—they were gradually replaced by the rise of monotheistic religions from the East. In A.D. 313, Emperor Constantine legalized and embraced Christianity. By 390, the Christian God was the only legal god in Rome.

two side aisles. Medieval Christians required a larger meeting hall for their worship services than Roman temples provided, so they used the spacious Roman basilica as the model for their churches. Cathedrals from France to Spain to England, from Romanesque to Gothic to Renaissance, all have the same basic floor plan as a Roman basilica.

• *Now head for the big, well-preserved brick building (just beyond the basilica ruins) with the triangular roof—the Curia. (Ongoing archaeological work may restrict access to the Curia, as well as the Arch of Septimius Severus—described later—and the exit to Capitoline Hill.)*

⓫ The Curia (Senate House)

The Curia was the most important political building in the Forum. While the present building dates from A.D. 283, this was the site of Rome's official center of government since the birth of the republic.

FORUM

Three hundred senators, elected by the citizens of Rome, met here to debate and create the laws of the land. Their wooden seats once circled the building in three tiers; the Senate president's podium sat at the far end. The marble floor is from ancient times. Listen to the echoes in this vast room—the acoustics are great.

Rome prided itself on being a republic. Early in the city's history, its people threw out the king and established rule by elected representatives. Each Roman citizen was free to speak his mind and have a say in public policy. Even when emperors became the supreme authority, the Senate was a power to be reckoned with. The Curia building is well preserved, having been used as a church since early Christian times. In the 1930s, it was restored and opened to the public as a historic site. (Note: Although Julius Caesar was assassinated in "the Senate," it wasn't here—the Senate was temporarily meeting across town.)

A statue and two reliefs inside the Curia help build our mental image of the Forum. The statue, made of porphyry marble in about A.D. 100 (with its head, arms, and feet now missing), was a tribute to an emperor, probably Hadrian or Trajan. The two relief panels may have decorated the Rostrum. Those on the left show people (with big stone tablets) standing in line to burn their debt records following a government amnesty. The other shows the distribution of grain (Rome's welfare system), some buildings in the background, and the latest fashion in togas.

• *Go back down the Senate steps and find the 10-foot-high wall just to the left of the big arch, marked...*

⑫ Rostrum

FORUM

Nowhere was Roman freedom more apparent than at this "Speaker's Corner." The Rostrum was a raised platform, 10 feet high and 80 feet long, decorated with statues, columns, and the prows of ships.

On a stage like this, Rome's orators, great and small, tried to draw a crowd and sway public opinion. Mark Antony rose to offer Caesar the laurel-leaf crown of kingship, which Caesar publicly (and hypocritically) refused while privately becoming a dictator. Men such as Cicero railed against the corruption and decadence that came with the city's newfound wealth. In later years, daring citizens even spoke out against the emperors, reminding them that Rome was once free. Picture the backdrop these speakers would

Rome Falls

Remember that Rome lasted 1,000 years—500 years of growth, 200 years of peak power, and 300 years of gradual decay.

The fall had many causes, among them the barbarians who pecked away at Rome's borders. Christians blamed the fall on moral decay. Pagans blamed it on Christians. Socialists blamed it on a shallow economy based on the spoils of war. (Republicans blamed it on Democrats.) Whatever the reasons, the far-flung empire could no longer keep its grip on conquered lands, and it pulled back. Barbarian tribes from Germany and Asia attacked the Italian peninsula and even looted Rome itself in A.D. 410, leveling many of the buildings in the Forum. In 476, when the last emperor checked out and switched off the lights, Europe plunged into centuries of ignorance, poverty, and weak government—the Dark Ages.

But Rome lived on in the Catholic Church. Christianity was the state religion of Rome's last generations. Emperors became popes (both called themselves "Pontifex Maximus"), senators became bishops, orators became priests, and basilicas became churches. The glory of Rome remains eternal.

have had—a mountain of marble buildings piling up on Capitoline Hill.

In front of the Rostrum are trees bearing fruits that were sacred to the ancient Romans: olives (provided food, light, and preservatives), figs (tasty), and wine grapes (made a popular export product).

• *The big arch to the right of the Rostrum is the...*

⓭ Arch of Septimius Severus

In imperial times, the Rostrum's voices of democracy would have been dwarfed by images of the empire, such as the huge six-story-high Arch of Septimius Severus (A.D. 203). The reliefs commemorate the African-born emperor's battles in Mesopotamia. Near ground level, see soldiers marching captured barbarians back to Rome for the victory parade. Despite Severus' efficient rule, Rome's empire was crumbling under the weight of its own corrup-

FORUM

tion, disease, decaying infrastructure, and the constant attacks by foreign "barbarians."

• *Pass beneath the Arch of Septimius Severus and turn left. If the path is blocked, backtrack toward the Temple of Julius Caesar and around the square. On the slope of Capitoline Hill are the eight remaining columns of the...*

⓮ Temple of Saturn

These columns framed the entrance to the Forum's oldest temple (497 B.C.). Inside was a humble, very old wooden statue of the god

Saturn. But the statue's pedestal held the gold bars, coins, and jewels of Rome's state treasury, the booty collected by conquering generals.

Even older than the Temple of Saturn is the Umbilicus Urbis, which stands nearby (next to the Arch of Septimius Severus). A humble brick ruin marks this historic "Navel of the City." The spot was considered the center of the cosmos, and all distances in the empire were measured from here.

• *Standing at the Temple of Saturn, one of the Forum's first buildings, look east at the lone, tall...*

⓯ Column of Phocas

This is the Forum's last monument (A.D. 608), a gift from the powerful Byzantine Empire to a fallen empire—Rome. Given to commemorate the pagan Pantheon's becoming a Christian church, it's like a symbolic last nail in ancient Rome's coffin. After Rome's 1,000-year reign, the city was looted by Vandals, the population of a million-plus shrank to about 10,000, and the once-grand city center—the Forum—was abandoned, slowly covered up by centuries of silt and dirt. In the 1700s, an English historian named Edward Gibbon over-looked this spot from Capitoline Hill. Hearing Christian monks singing at these pagan ruins, he looked out at the few columns poking up

from the ground, pondered the decline and fall of the Roman Empire, and thought, "Hmm, that's a catchy title..."

• *Your tour is over. From the Forum, you have several options:*

1. Your closest exit is right by the Arch of Septimius Severus. From here, you can walk out to Via dei Fori Imperiali, near Trajan's

Column and the Imperial Forums (described on page 50). Or you can climb 50 steps up to Capitoline Hill (described on page 40).

2. To exit near the Colosseum, return to the Arch of Titus and look for the *uscita/exit* signs. You'll pop out facing the Colosseum, near where you entered.

3. The Forum's Via dei Fori Imperiali entrance spills you back out onto Via dei Fori Imperiali near Via Cavour.

• *If you want to see Palatine Hill, don't leave the complex; you won't be allowed back in without a new ticket. Return to the Arch of Titus, from where you can climb Palatine Hill to the top and start the Palatine Hill Tour—see the next chapter.*

PALATINE HILL TOUR

Monte Palatino

While many tourists consider Palatine Hill just extra credit after the Forum, it offers insight into the greatness of Rome that's well worth the effort. (And, if you're visiting the Colosseum or Forum, you've got a ticket whether you like it or not.) Palatine Hill is jam-packed with history—"the huts of Romulus," the huge Imperial Palace, a view of the Circus Maximus—but only the barest skeleton of rubble is left to tell the story. This tour will enable the thoughtful sightseer to bring those remains to life.

Palatine Hill is ideal for those who want to get away from the crowds and feel the romance and the melancholy of Rome's ruins. Become a 19th-century poet or a painter on the Grand Tour, meditating on the destiny of once-great civilizations, and wander through the remains of the palaces that nature has reclaimed for herself.

Though I've covered them as two separate tours, the Forum and Palatine Hill are organized as a single sight with one admission—meaning if you want to see both, you'll need to do it in a single visit (see page 157 for details). The passage between the Forum and Palatine Hill is near the Arch of Titus. Don't exit Palatine Hill through the turnstiles, hoping to walk down the street to the Forum and reenter; you won't be allowed in.

Orientation

Cost: €12 combo-ticket covers both the Roman Forum/Palatine Hill and the Colosseum; also covered by Roma Pass. The combo-ticket is valid two consecutive days, but once it's scanned, you can't reenter that sight (even the next day). Palatine Hill is free and more crowded on the first Sunday of the month.

Hours: The Roman Forum/Palatine Hill and the Colosseum are open daily 8:30 until one hour before sunset: April-Aug until 19:15, Sept until 19:00, Oct until 18:30, Nov-mid-Feb until 16:30, mid-Feb-mid-March until 17:00, mid-March-late March until 17:30; last entry one hour before closing.

Getting There: The closest Metro stop is Colosseo. Except on Sundays, buses #51, #85, #87, #118, #186, and #810 stop along Via dei Fori Imperiali near the Colosseum, the Forum, and Piazza Venezia.

Getting In: To enter Palatine Hill directly, use the entrance on Via di San Gregorio, 150 yards from the Colosseum. You can also enter through the Forum entrances (usually more crowded), see the Forum first if you wish, and then take the path from the Forum over to Palatine Hill.

Just climb to the top of Palatine Hill to the start of our tour. From the Via di San Gregorio entrance, follow the path to the left as it winds to the top. Our tour begins at the one big building still standing—the museum.

Information: Ticket info—tel. 06-3996-7700, www.coopculture. it; general info— www.archeoroma.beniculturali.it/en.

Tours: Audioguides cost €5/2 hours (€7 version includes Roman Forum and lasts 3 hours, must leave ID— so you have to return the audioguide where you rent it).

The **House of Augustus** and the **House of Livia** can be seen only by joining an unguided tour (€4/person) that leaves from inside the Via di San Gregorio entrance daily at 12:45. These are the most intact of Palatine Hill's ruins. The tour gives you about 30 minutes inside each house. Buy your tour ticket as you enter the complex (not available online).

Length of This Tour: Allow 1-1.5 hours. Don't miss the stadium or the view of the Circus Maximus.

Services: WCs are rare in the Colosseum-Roman Forum-Palatine Hill area. Your best (though still meager) options are here at Palatine Hill, where you'll find WCs at the ticket office when you enter, at the museum in the center of the site, and hiding among the orange trees in the Farnese Gardens. For restaurants in the area, see the sidebar on page 152.

Expect Changes: Parts of Palatine Hill have sometimes been closed off in recent years due to ongoing archaeological work. Just see what you can, using this chapter's map to navigate.

The Tour Begins

• *Start on top of the hill at the Palatine Museum (Museo Palatino, #6 on the map; see "Getting In" earlier). Once on top, it's easy to spot the museum: it's the one modern building (big and gray) standing amid the ruins.*

We'll visit the museum later. But for now, grab a stone and sit with your back to the museum to orient yourself, facing in the direction of the Forum (roughly north).

THE IMPERIAL PALACE

You're sitting at the center of what was once a huge palace, the residence of emperors for three centuries. Orgies, royal weddings, assassinations, concerts, intrigues, births, funerals, banquets, and the occasional Tupperware party took place within these walls. What walls? The row of umbrella pines about 200 yards to the east (to your right) now marks one edge of the palace. The reconstructed brick tower (at about 11 o'clock) was the northwest corner. The palace also stretched behind you (the area behind the museum) and beneath you, since parts of it had a lower floor. (Right now, you're standing not on the original palace's ground level but several floors up.)

The area in front was the official wing of the palace; behind were the private quarters. All in all, it made for a cozy little 150,000-square-foot pad.

The palace was built by Emperor Domitian in about A.D. 81. A poet of the day described it as so grand that it "made Jupiter jealous."

• *Now proceed, following the map for this 13-stop tour. With your back to the museum, head left to a big rectangular field with an octagonal brick design in the center—the main courtyard of the palace.*

❶ Main Courtyard (Peristilio) and Octagonal Fountain (Fontana Ottagona)

The brick octagon was a sunken fountain in the middle of an open-air courtyard. Like many fine Roman homes, this palace was built around an oasis of peace where you could enjoy the sun, catch the precious rain, and listen

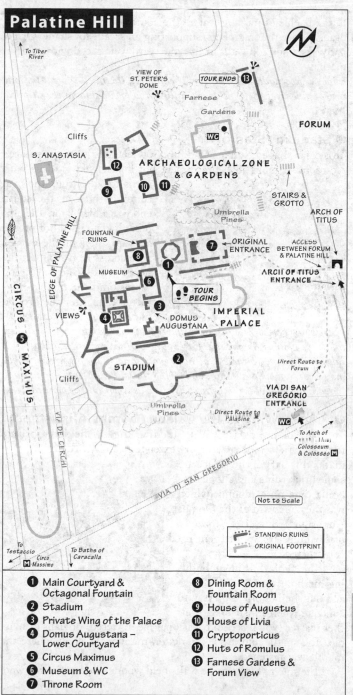

Palatine Hill

To Tiber River

VIEW OF ST. PETER'S DOME

TOUR ENDS · 13

Farnese Gardens

FORUM

Cliffs

WC

S. ANASTASIA

12

ARCHAEOLOGICAL ZONE & GARDENS

9   10   11

STAIRS & GROTTO

Umbrella Pines

ARCH OF TITUS

EDGE OF PALATINE HILL

FOUNTAIN RUINS

8   1   7 · ORIGINAL ENTRANCE

ACCESS BETWEEN FORUM & PALATINE HILL

MUSEUM

6

ARCH OF TITUS ENTRANCE

TOUR BEGINS

CIRCUS MAXIMUS

3

VIEWS

4   DOMUS AUGUSTANA

IMPERIAL PALACE

5

2

Direct Route to Forum

STADIUM

VIA DE CERCHI

Cliffs

VIA DI SAN GREGORIO ENTRANCE

Umbrella Pines

Direct Route to Palatine

WC

To Arch of Constantine, Colosseum & Colosseo M

VIA DI SAN GREGORIO

Not to Scale

To Testaccio M Circo Massimo

To Baths of Caracalla

····· STANDING RUINS
····· ORIGINAL FOOTPRINT

1 Main Courtyard & Octagonal Fountain
2 Stadium
3 Private Wing of the Palace
4 Domus Augustana – Lower Courtyard
5 Circus Maximus
6 Museum & WC
7 Throne Room
8 Dining Room & Fountain Room
9 House of Augustus
10 House of Livia
11 Cryptoporticus
12 Huts of Romulus
13 Farnese Gardens & Forum View

PALATINE HILL

to the babble of moving water. The courtyard was lined with columns (notice the fragments) supporting an arcade for shade. Originally, the floor and walls of the courtyard were faced with colorful marble.

• *The palace's stadium is 100 yards behind you (to the east), near the long row of pine trees. Belly up to the railing and look down on the elliptical track.*

❷ Stadium (Stadio)

This cigar-shaped, sunken stadium (500 feet long) was the palace's rec room. It looks like a racetrack, but it just held gardens with

paths for strolling. The oval running track at the south end was added later. The emperor had a raised box on the 50-yard line, in the curved apse across from you. At the north end were changing rooms, and the marble fragments that litter the ground once held up an arcade.

• *Stretching between the stadium and the museum is a big brick structure called the Domus Augustana. Depending on the progress of archaeological work, you may be able to actually walk through the big arches, or you may have to walk around the end (using the path alongside the stadium) to reach the back of the structure. As much as is possible, explore the...*

❸ Private Wing of the Palace (Domus Augustana)

The part of the palace you're standing in now held the private rooms of the emperor and his extended family. Today, all that

marks this part of the palace are some brick ruins and a lone umbrella pine on a mound (which was the courtyard of the Domus Augustana). Survey the maze of brick rooms (many of them reconstructed).

The typical Roman building method was to build a rectangular shell of brick, fill it with concrete, then finish it with ei-

ther plaster (you'll see an occasional faded fresco) or slabs of marble. The small, round pockmarks on many walls show where the marble was fastened.

The square holes in the walls held wooden beams, which were

used for scaffolding during construction and maintenance, for shelves, and for wooden floors.

Over the doorways, the bricks in the walls form the pattern of an arch. These "blind arches" were structural elements that allowed the walls to be built higher. The iron bar clamps are recent additions and hold the crumbling walls together.

The many niches and apses once held statues. Every family had their own household gods and displayed small images of these guardian spirits, as well as busts of honored ancestors.

The fragments of columns, reliefs, and sculpture scattered about suggest the wealth of this great palace. The floor plan is complex—a fantasyland maze of small, private, sometimes even curved rooms.

• *In the south part of the Domus Augustana (behind the museum), you can look down on the ruins of the lower story.*

❹ Domus Augustana—Lower Courtyard

This open-air courtyard has the concave-convex remains of a large fountain that must have been a marvel. Try to mentally reconstruct the palace that surrounded this

fountain. The emperors could look down on it from the upper story (where you're standing) or view it from the rooms around it on the lower story, where the emperor and his family ate their meals in private.

The lower story was built into the slope of the hill. The southern part of the palace was an extension of the hillside, supported beneath your feet by big arches.

• *Continue to the southern edge of the hill (directly behind the museum), overlooking a long, wide grassy field—what once was the Circus Maximus. Lean over the railing and you might be able to make out the concave shape of the palace's southern facade.*

❺ Circus Maximus

If the gladiator show at the Colosseum was sold out, you could always get a seat at Circus Max. In an early version of today's demolition derby, Ben-Hur and his fellow charioteers once raced recklessly around this oblong course.

The chariots circled the cigar-shaped mound in the center (notice the lone cypress tree that now marks one end of the mound). Bleachers (now grassy banks) originally surrounded the track (see artist's reconstruction in the photo on the next page).

The track was 1,300 feet long, while the whole stadium measured 2,130 feet by 720 feet and seated—get this—250,000 people.

The wooden bleachers once collapsed during a race, killing thousands.

The horses began at a starting gate at the west end (to your
right), while the public entered at
the other end. Races consisted of
seven laps (about 3.5 miles total).
In such a small space, collisions and overturned chariots were common. The charioteers were usually poor, lowborn people who used
this dangerous sport to get rich and famous. Some succeeded. Most
died.

The public was crazy about the races. There were 12 per day,
240 days a year. Four teams dominated the competition—Reds,
Whites, Blues, and Greens—and every citizen was fanatically devoted to one of them. Obviously, the emperors had the best seats
in the house: Built into the palace's curved facade was a box overlooking the track. For their pleasure, emperors occasionally had the
circus floor carpeted with designs in colored powders.

Picture the scene: rowdy crowds, lots of drinking, heroes strut-
ting to the adoration of the masses (and that was just the Rolling
Stones concert held here in 2014). Back in ancient times, imagine
the palace fully intact, with the emperor watching from his balcony. Below, a quarter of a million Romans were cheering, jeering,
and furiously betting. Horses raced here for more than a thousand
years. The track dates from 300 B.C., and the spectacles continued
into the Christian era, until A.D. 549, despite Church disapproval.

From this viewpoint, looking to the left, you can see the ruins
of the Baths of Caracalla (not worth touring if you've seen Palatine)
rising above the trees a half-mile away. About a mile beyond that,
Appian Way led from a grand gate in the ancient wall, past the
catacombs, to Brindisi.

• *Turn around and head back toward the museum.*

❻ Museum (Museo Palatino)

The museum contains statues and frescoes that
help you imagine the luxury of the imperial
Palatine.

Enter on the lower level (note the WCs)
to trace the Palatine's history from the start. In
section 1, find the model of the eighth-century
B.C. Iron Age village of Germalus. Notice the
so-called Huts of Romulus that we'll see later
in the tour. The rest of the lower floor uses au-
diovisual displays to virtually reconstruct the
luxury of the palaces.

Go back outside and climb the stairs to the upper floor. As you enter, turn left and go to the end of the hall to find the statue of "Magna Mater" on her throne. This Great Mother brought life and fertility to the Roman people, who worshipped her at the nearby Temple of Cybele. Her arms and foot were destroyed by time, but there was always a cavity where her head should be—this was a standard Roman device in which interchangeable heads could be inserted. In this case, the Magna Mater's "head" was actually a sacred, black cone-shaped meteorite that caused astonishment when it fell from the sky.

Next comes the "Augustus" room, with frescoes and statues from Augustus' reign and fine decorative terra-cotta panels. (Take an angel selfie at the surviving wings from a Victory statue.) Continuing on, find two torsos—of a tiger and a river god. Next is a room of portrait busts, including the notorious Emperor Nero ("Nerone") and the last great emperor, Trajan. And finally, back near the entrance is a large, headless, topless statue of a Muse (labeled as "muse of Dresden-Zagreb type") that once decorated the Hippodrome.

• *From the museum, begin circling the main courtyard (with its octagonal fountain) counterclockwise. Turn left with the path, then turn right into the first opening, marked by the squat brick pillar with a stubby column on top. You're in the...*

❼ Throne Room (Aula Regia)

The nerve center of an empire that controlled some 50 million people from England to Africa, this was the official seat of power. The curved apse of the largest brick stump (there's now a plaque on it) marks the spot where the emperor sat on his throne for official business.

Imagine being a Roman citizen summoned by the emperor. You'd enter the palace through the main doorway (now a gap) at the far (Forum) end of the room, having climbed up three flights of a monumental staircase. The floor and walls dazzled with green, purple, red, white, and yellow marble. Along the walls were 12 colossal statues of Roman gods. The ceiling towered seven stories overhead. On either side were doorways leading to a basilica and the emperor's private temple.

You'd approach the emperor, who sat on a raised throne in the apse, dressed in royal purple, with a crown of laurel leaves on his head and a scepter cradled in his arm. Big braziers burned on either

Beauty Among Rubble

As you walk through the (mostly brick) ruins, you'll also see colorful marble scraps lying all over Palatine Hill. Flashy building stone was used to boast of the power and vastness of the empire. Citizens knew that the Numidian yellow marble was from Tunisia, the veined Cipollino marble (with swirling designs like an onion) was from the island of Euboea in Greece, and the pink granite was from Aswan in Egypt. This was all sliced and laid out in fine pavement and wall designs, enjoyed by those who could only be thankful they were on the winning team.

side, throwing off a flickering light. As you approached, you'd raise your arm to greet him, saying, *"Ave, Caesar!"* The words would echo through the great hall.

Now imagine yourself as emperor. Stand on the small white stone marking the location of the throne (a few feet in front of the plaque), and look out over your palace. (The ceiling was a barrel vault sitting upon towers as high as the brick tower in the distance to the left.)

• *Continue circling the main courtyard counterclockwise until it dead-ends at a big field filled with pebbles.*

❽ Dining Room (Triclinium) and Fountain Room (Nymphaeum)

The floor of the dining room had a hollow space beneath it (you can see the two-foot gap between the two original floors). Slaves stoked fires from underground stoves to heat the floor with forced air. At the far end of the room, the platform and curved apse mark the spot where the emperor ate while looking down on his subjects. Guests could look into the adjoining room, where an elliptical-shaped fountain (see the brick remains) spurted for their amusement.

Here, the wealthiest Romans enjoyed the spoils that poured into Rome from its vast empire. Reclining on a couch, waited on by slaves, you'd order bowls of larks' tongues or a roast pig stuffed with live birds, then wash it down with wine. If you were full but tempted by yet another delicacy, you could call for a feather, vomit, and start all over. Dancing dark-skinned slaves from Egypt or flute players from Greece entertained. If you fancied one, he or she was yours—the bedrooms were just down the hall.

Or so went the stories. In fact, many emperors were just and simple men, continuing the old Roman traditions of hard work and moderate tastes. But just as many were power-mad scoundrels who used their authority to indulge their every desire.

• *From the dining room, backtrack a few steps and work your way west through openings in the low brick wall to exit the palace.*

ARCHAEOLOGICAL ZONE AND GARDENS

On the far side of Palatine Hill are the two excavated homes (once joined together) of Rome's first power couple—the first emperor, Augustus, and his wife, Livia. Because of their fragility, the homes are not open to unaccompanied visitors—you must pay to join a once-daily unguided tour (see "Tours," earlier). If you join a tour, read #9 and #10 to give meaning to your visit; otherwise, skip ahead to #11.

❾ House of Augustus (Casa di Augusto)

Augustus, a.k.a. Octavian, the first emperor, lived in this house. This relatively modest dwelling, dating from before Octavian became emperor, is a far cry from the later Imperial Palace that was built on top. You'll see several humble rooms (one up a stairway) with finely painted ancient frescoes. Admire the vibrant colors, fake columns and arches, fake windows that once looked out on illusionary landscapes, and the use of perspective centuries before the Renaissance. You'll see that Livia and Augustus had little of the lavish marble found in most homes of the wealthy.

Augustus was a modest man who believed in traditional Roman values. His wife and daughter wove the clothes he wore. He slept in the same small bedroom for 40 years. He burned the midnight oil in his study, where he read and wrote his memoirs. Augustus set a standard for emperors' conduct that would last... until his death.

Augustus wanted to be the new Romulus, building his house adjacent to the home of the mythological founder of Rome.

❿ House of Livia (Casa di Livia)

Scholars think that these ruins were the quarters of Livia, Augustus's wife, because they found her honorific name, "Julia Augusta," inscribed on one of the lead pipes now displayed inside. Your visit includes the former entrance hall—a high-ceilinged room with a few faded frescoes in purple, yellow, blue, and white. The best-preserved ones are in the central alcove, the room known as the *tablinum*, where guests were received. The *tablinum's* right wall depicts the god Mercury (on the right side of the scene), arriving to kill the giant Argus (left) and kidnap the nymph Io (center) so Jupiter can ravish her. Frescoes in the alcove to the right of the *tablinum* show a columned portico draped with garlands. The left alcove has delicate Pompeiian-style designs.

⓫ Cryptoporticus

Around the back side of the House of Livia, find the entrance to this tunnel. At 400 feet long, it allowed the imperial entourage to travel privately through the palace complex. The tunnel was elaborately decorated with frescoes (little remains). The Cryptoporticus may have been built by Emperor Nero to link the Palatine and Forum with his vast mansion, the Domus Aurea, which extended from the edge of the Forum past (what is now) the Colosseum and onto Esquiline Hill. Nero's Cryptoporticus may have been an expansion of an earlier passageway built by Tiberius (Livia's son). Here, the notorious emperor Caligula is said to have been assassinated.

• *Make your way to the nearby section of ruins, protected by a large metal roof. Cozy up to the railing to see ruined walls and foundations.*

⓬ Huts of Romulus (Capanne Romulee)

Looking down into this pit filled with big blocks of stone, you can make out some elliptical and rectangular shapes carved into the stony ground. These are the partial outlines of huts from about 850 B.C. Some have holes that once held the wooden posts of round thatched huts.

This is the village of Germalus, which we saw a model of in the museum, earlier. Picture the village long, long ago: a few dozen people, with their goats, dogs, and crude farm tools, trying to eke out a living.

According to legend, Romulus and Remus (see photo of statue on page 190) were children of the first Vestal Virgin. For complicated family reasons, she was executed and her babies were set adrift on the flooding Tiber River, eventually washing ashore at the foot of Palatine Hill. In a cave just downhill from here, a shepherd discovered them being suckled by a mother wolf. He took them home—maybe right here—and raised them as his own. When Romulus grew up, he killed his brother and built a square wall (Roma Quadrata) on the hilltop, thus founding the city of Rome.

For centuries, the Romans believed this myth. They honored the wolf's cave (called the "Lupercale," where every February 15 men dressed up in animal skins and whipped women), as well as the spot where Romulus was said to have lived. Lo and behold, in the 1940s, these huts were unearthed, and the legend became history. Archaeologists are still at it, and the more they dig, the more they find to confirm the legends. A nearby cave discovered in 2007—ornamented with seashells, colored marble, and a wolf mosaic—may be that original Lupercale. (It's not open to the public, and dissenting archaeologists believe it's a temple to water nymphs.)

Here at Rome's birthplace, reflect on the rise of this great culture—from thatched huts to the modest House of Augustus to the massive Imperial Palace of Domitian, with its stadium and view over the Circus Maximus. It's no wonder that the hill's name gave us our English word "palace."

• *Climb a few steps to the summit of the hill (following signs to* Orti Farnesina*) where there are great views of the city. Start walking through the trees of the Farnese Gardens as you make your way toward the Forum.*

⓭ Farnese Gardens—View of Forum
Fit for an Emperor

Finish your tour with a stroll through the Renaissance gardens of the Farnese family. Walk past the foundations of the House of Tiberius— Livia's son by her first husband—who became emperor after Augustus. Continue on, admiring the exotic plants, fountains, underground grotto, and pavilions. When you see the incredible view of the Forum from the end of the gardens, you'll know why Palatine Hill was Rome's best address.

• *To exit, wind down Palatine Hill into the Forum, ending up at the Arch of Titus.*

CAPITOLINE MUSEUMS TOUR

Musei Capitolini

This enjoyable museum complex claims to be the world's oldest, founded in 1471 when a pope gave ancient statues to the citizens of Rome. Many of the museum's statues have gone on to become instantly recognizable cultural icons. Perched on top of Capitoline Hill, the museum's two buildings (Palazzo dei Conservatori and Palazzo Nuovo) are connected by an underground passage that leads to the Tabularium and panoramic views of the Roman Forum. (For more on Capitoline Hill, see page 40.)

Orientation

Cost: €15, €11.50 if no special exhibitions.

Hours: Daily 9:30-19:30, last entry one hour before closing.

Getting There: The museum (Musei Capitolini in Italian) sits atop Capitoline Hill (Campidoglio), housed in two buildings that flank the square. Buy tickets and enter at the Palazzo dei Conservatori (on your right as you face the equestrian statue).

Information: You'll find some English descriptions within the museum. Tel. 06-0608, www.museicapitolini.org.

Tours: The €5 audioguide is good.

Length of This Tour: Allow two hours.

Baggage Check: Free (mandatory for bags larger than a purse).

Cuisine Art: A great view café, called **Caffè Capitolino** (daily 9:30-19:00, lunch served 12:15-15:30), is upstairs in Palazzo dei Conservatori (enter from inside museum; also has exterior entrance for the public—facing museum entrance, go to your right around the building to Piazzale Caffarelli and through door #4; see map on page 188). The pavilion on the terrace outside offers full service; the tables inside are self-service (pay first, then take receipt to bar; good salads and toasted sandwiches). Piazzale Caffarelli is a fine place for a snooze or a picnic. (Note: While it has great views, it doesn't overlook the Forum.)

Starring: The original she-wolf statue, Marcus Aurelius, the Dying Gaul, the Boy Extracting a Thorn, and Forum views.

OVERVIEW

Capitoline Hill's main square (Piazza del Campidoglio), home to the museum, began in ancient Rome as a religious center, the site

of temples to the gods Jupiter, Juno, and Minerva. In the 16th century, Michelangelo transformed the square from pagan to papal, while adding a harmonious and refined Renaissance touch. (For more on the square, see page 41.)

The museum's layout—with two buildings connected by an underground passage—can be confusing, but this self-guided tour is easy to follow.

You'll enter at the Palazzo dei Conservatori (on your right as you face the equestrian statue), cross underneath the square (beneath the Palazzo Senatorio, the mayoral palace, not open to public), and exit from the Palazzo Nuovo (on your left).

Expect Changes: Because this museum often puts on special exhibits (sometimes an exciting value and sometimes, it seems, just an excuse to raise the price), some items may be in different rooms from those described. Use this chapter's photos or ask a guard to track down highlights.

The Tour Begins

• *Begin at the square on top of Capitoline Hill. After your ticket is checked, enter the courtyard.*

PALAZZO DEI CONSERVATORI

In the courtyard, enjoy the massive chunks of Constantine: his head, hand, feet, bicep, and other bits and pieces. When intact, this giant, 30-foot statue of the emperor sitting on his throne held the place of honor in the Basilica of Con-

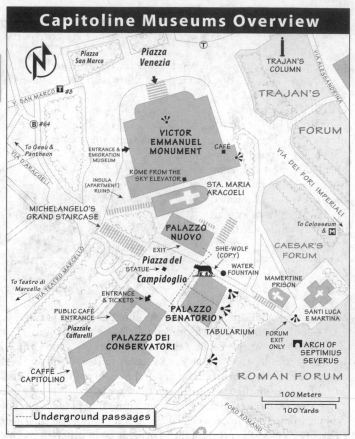

Capitoline Museums Overview

stantine in the Forum. Imagine it's A.D. 330 as you stare up at the emperor, an abstract symbol of power. His face is otherworldly. You can't really connect. You feel like a subject rather than a citizen. You could say the concept of monarchy by divine right starts here.

Only the extremities of the massive statue survive because a statue of this size was not entirely marble. Its core was cheaper and made of more perishable material, like bricks. Appreciate the detail of the vein in his bicep. Notice also the mortise-and-tenon joint and imagine the engineering necessary to construct this Goliath.

Also in the courtyard are reliefs of conquered peoples—not in chains, but new members of an expansive empire. These represent provinces such as Gaul, Britannia, and Thracia, and date from the reign of Hadrian (second century A.D.), whose passion was running the empire not as something to exploit but as a commonwealth.

• Go up the staircase (the one near the entrance, not the one in the courtyard). On the landing, find...

Reliefs of Second-Century Imperial Grandeur

These four fine reliefs show great moments in an emperor's daily grind. Rome was a visual culture and used public art for propaganda purposes. Rather than portray moments unique to a particular emperor, common themes and rituals were illustrated. In this case we see heroics on the battlefield, a triumphal entry into Rome, and the emperor as the top religious authority. Study the three panels, which happen to feature Marcus Aurelius (starting on the left, with him mounted on a horse). The emperor, in an equestrian pose (like the bronze statue in Piazza del Campidoglio), has his hand out, offering clemency to his vanquished foes. The detail, with expressive faces and banners blowing in the wind,

is impressive. In the relief showing Marcus Aurelius in his chariot, someone's missing...it's Commodus, his wicked son (Russell Crowe's nemesis in *Gladiator*). After the assassination of Commodus, his memory was damned, so images of him were erased (or, in this case, chiseled out). And in the religious scene, the emperor oversees preparations to sacrifice a bull (with even the bull looking on curiously).

• *Continue up the stairs to the first floor. Go through two large frescoed rooms (Rooms I and II) and through the doorway on the right of the far wall to find Room III, with the...*

Boy Extracting a Thorn *(Spinario)*

He's just a boy, intent only on picking a thorn out of his foot. As he bends over to reach his foot, his body sticks out at all angles, like a bony chicken wing. He's even scuffed up, the way small boys get. At this moment, nothing matters to him but that splinter. Our lives are filled with these mundane moments (when we'd give anything for tweezers), which are rarely captured in art.

The boy is a bronze cast with eyes once inlaid as in the adjacent bronze cast of Brutus. Take a close look at Brutus (whose descendent took part in the killing of Caesar). This wonderful bust typifies Roman character: determined, thoughtful, no-nonsense, and capable. The ivory eyes are original.

Now, look up, and appreciate the fresco that has lined this

room since it was part of a municipal palace in the 16th century. It's a stirring battle scene that celebrates the power and glory of ancient Rome. Find the wagonload of enemy armor and weapons and sweep 360 degrees as if joining in this triumphal parade. It's another great military victory, and the troops are bringing home precious statues of bronze and marble as plunder. There's the emperor on his four-horse chariot. The enemy prisoners are bound and ready to absorb your disdain. And after the sacrificial bulls is a chorus of trumpets and throngs of your fellow adoring citizens—all thankful to be loyal subjects of the emperor.

• *In the next room (Room IV) is the...*

Capitoline She-Wolf

The original bronze she-wolf suckles the twins Romulus and Remus. This symbol of Rome is ancient, though the wolf statue

itself (long thought to be Etruscan, from the fifth century B.C.) was made in the 13th century, and the boys are an invention of the 15th century. Look into the eyes of the wolf. An animal looks back, with ragged ears, sharp teeth, and staring eyes. This wild animal, teamed with the wildest creatures

of all—hungry babies—makes a powerful symbol for the tenacious city/empire of Rome.

• *Continue to the next room.*

From Michelangelo to Medusa

Along with a bust of Michelangelo made from his death mask, this room contains Bernini's anguished bust of Medusa—with writhing snakes on her head. This goes way beyond

a bad hair day. Enjoy the artistry of Bernini as he fashions a marble lock of hair into a writhing snake.

Then appreciate the room you're in as a piece of art in itself: Murano glass chandelier, fine painted coffered ceiling, fabric walls, inlaid marble floor, medallions celebrating papal donations to the collection, and frescoed panels set in fanciful grotesque-style decor. As a bonus, you've got Rome, including St. Peter's dome, out the window.

• *Pass through three small rooms: Room VI has the* Artemis of Efenina, *with her extremely fertile draping of numerous bull testicles, breasts, or perhaps puka shells (no one knows for sure). Room VII features Greek red-figured vases (and the elevator up to the second-floor café—need a coffee break?). Continue through Room VIII, straight to a set of seven stairs and follow them up to the next room to discover the remarkable bust of...*

Commodus as Hercules

This arrogant emperor brat used to run around the palace in animal skins pretending (or believing) he was Hercules. Here, he wears a

lion's head over his own and drapes the lion's paws over his chest. This lion king made a bad emperor (ruled A.D. 180-192). Commodus earned a reputation as a good athlete and warrior, and a rough character. He hung out with low-class gladiators, and even fought in the arena himself. The fights were staged—no one was allowed to hurt the emperor—which meant that Commodus killed innocent people, some of them beaten to death with his beloved Hercules club. The people hated Commodus. Commodus-the-jock was also at odds with his father, the previous emperor and noted scholar and philosopher, Marcus Aurelius.

This statue dates from the late second century, a period of debauchery and decline. The emperor is self indulgent. The gravitas is gone, and soon the empire will follow. Examine the statue's details—the perfect curls of hair and beard, sheen of the skin, and manicured nails. Notice also the symbols of astrology, fertility, and abundance. While Commodus' memory was damned (remember how he was chiseled out of the panel downstairs), somehow this masterpiece survived.

• *As you are looking at Commodus, directly behind you is his dad, the Emperor...*

Marcus Aurelius (C. A.D. 176)

This is the greatest surviving equestrian statue of antiquity. Marcus Aurelius was a Roman philosopher-emperor (ruled A.D. 161-180) known more for his *Meditations* than his prowess on the battlefield. His gesture is of clemency, pardoning defeated enemies. The patina of time almost drips off him. While he has the same fine hair and features

of his son, Commodus (see earlier), the emperor is still working for the glory of Rome rather than for the glory of himself.

Christians in the Dark Ages thought that the statue's hand was raised in blessing, which probably led to their misidentifying him as Constantine, the first Christian emperor. While most pagan statues were destroyed by Christians, "Constantine" was spared. It graced several prominent locations in medieval Rome, including the papal palace at San Giovanni in Laterano.

In 1538, this gilded bronze statue was placed in the center of the Campidoglio (directly outside the museum), and Michelangelo was hired to design the buildings around it with the statue as the centerpiece. A few years ago, the statue was moved inside and restored, while the copy you see outside today was placed on the square. (Notice that Aurelius doesn't use stirrups—an Asian invention, those newfangled devices wouldn't arrive in Europe for another 500 years.)

Also in the room are more hunks—head, hand, and a globe—of another statue of Constantine. (Or was it the Emperor Sylvestrus Stalloneus?)

• *Descend the ramp to the wall of blocks from the...*

Temple of Jupiter

This is part of the foundation of the ancient Temple of Jupiter (Giove), once the most impressive in Rome. Find the scale model of the temple (1:40) to get a sense of its size and where you stand in relation to the ruins. Imagine you're standing before a wall that has stood here, crowning the capital hill of Rome, for over 2,500 years. It is in situ; this part of the museum is built around this wall.

The King of the Gods resided atop Capitoline Hill in this once-classy 10,000-square-foot temple, which was perched on a podium and lined with Greek-style columns, overlooking downtown Rome. The most important rites were performed here, and victory parades through the Forum ended here. Replicas of this building were erected in every Roman city. The temple was begun by Rome's last king (the Tarquin), and its dedication in 509 B.C. marks the start of the Roman Republic.

All that remains of the temple today are these ruined foundation stones, made of volcanic tuff, an easily carved rock commonly used in Roman construction. Although there are hundreds of these blocks here, they represent only a portion of the immense foundation, which is only a fraction of the temple

itself. In its prime, the temple rose two stories above our heads. Inside stood a statue of the god of thunder wielding a lightning bolt. The temple was refurbished a number of times over the centuries, often after damage by...lightning bolts.

• *By the way, a good WC is behind the wall.*

Here's how to get to the next stop, the Tabularium: With your back to the center of the old wall, climb seven steps and go straight to the end of the hall. Exiting the hall, make a U-turn right and go down the stairs you climbed earlier, all the way to the basement—the piano sotteraneo. Then cross underneath the square through the long passageway filled with ancient inscriptions (well described in English). Near the far end, turn right and climb a set of stairs into the...

TABULARIUM

Built in the first century B.C., these sturdy vacant rooms once held the archives of ancient Rome. The word Tabularium comes from "tablet," on which Romans wrote their laws.

The rooms offer a stunning head-on view over the Forum, giving you a more complete picture of the sprawl of ancient Rome. Belly up to the overlook. Panning left to right, find the following landmarks: Arch of Septimius Severus, Arch of Titus (in the distance), the lone Column of Phocas, the three columns of the Temple of Castor and Pollux, the three columns (closest to you) of the Temple of Vespasiano, and the eight columns of the Temple of Saturn.

Now do an about-face and look up to see a huge white hunk of carved marble, an overhang from the Temple of Vespasiano. Wander around. Appreciate the towering vaulted ceiling and ancient Roman engineering. While some say Rome was built of marble, that's not quite true. The Romans invented concrete. They baked thin bricks to make their giant buildings, then faced them with marble veneer.

• *Leave the Tabularium by going back down the stairs you just climbed. Turn right (passing a low-key WC), and go up three flights of stairs. You're now on the first floor of the...*

PALAZZO NUOVO

• *From the top of the stairs, continue directly into Room VIII—the "Hall of the Gaul"—with one of the museum's most famous pieces.*

Dying Gaul

A first-century B.C. copy of a Greek original, this was sculpted to celebrate the Greeks' victory over the Galatians. Wounded in

battle, the dying Gaul holds himself upright, but barely. Minutes earlier, before he was stabbed in the chest, he'd been in his prime. Now he can only watch helplessly as his life ebbs away. His sword is useless against this last battle. With his messy hair, downcast eyes, and crumpled position, he poignantly reminds us that every victory also means a defeat.

• *The next few rooms are filled with interesting art. As you wander, take a quick look at...*

Ancient Roman Statues and Busts

In the first room, a faun—carved out of red marble—glories in grapes and life, oblivious to the loss of his penis (at least he still has his tail). The statue, found among a couple of dozen pieces in Hadrian's Villa, was skillfully restored. Check out the chandeliered ceilings in this room and elsewhere; this building is truly a *palazzo* (palace).

The next room, the large hall, features more sculpture from Hadrian's Villa (and elsewhere). Notice the Wounded Amazon, near the window, in a classic *contrapposto* pose (weight on one leg), one breast exposed so the fabric wouldn't be in the way of her archery. This is a Roman copy of a fifth-century B.C. Greek original by Polycletus.

Roll through two rooms lined with busts—the Hall of Philosophers (Socrates, Homer, Euripides, Cicero, and many more) and the Hall of Emperors (Con-

stantine's mom Helena sits center stage, resting after her journey to Jerusalem to find Christ's cross). In this 3-D yearbook of ancient history, there are few labels. The only purple-chested bust is Caracalla. Infamous for his fervent brutality, he instructed his portraitists to stress his meanness. Directly across on the lower shelf, the smallest bust—of Emperor Gordiano (ruled A.D. 238-244)—is one of the finest of late antiquity. His expression shows the concern and consternation of a ruler whose empire is in decline. In this room you can find classic expressions of confidence, brutality, and anguish—human drama through the ages. Before leaving, sample the delicate elegance of ancient Roman hairstyles for women.

• *Enter the hallway, turn right, and start down the hall. The small octagonal room on your left contains one of the museum's treasures.*

Capitoline Venus

This is a Roman copy of a fourth-century B.C. Greek original by the master Praxiteles. Venus, leaving the bath, is suddenly aware that someone is watching her. As she turns to look, she reflexively covers up (nearly). Her blank eyes hold no personality or emotion. Her fancy hairstyle is the only complicated thing about her. She is simply beautiful—generically erotic.

• *Head to the last room on the left before the stairs. Displayed on the wall is the...*

Mosaic of Doves

Four doves perch on the rim of a bronze bowl as one drinks water from the bowl. Minute bits make up this small,

exquisite work. Found in the center of a floor in one of the rooms in Hadrian's Villa, this second-century A.D. mosaic was based on an earlier work done, of course, by the Greeks.

We all know that ancient Rome was grand. But the art in this museum tells us that its culture was refined as well. Before leaving, walk slowly around this last room, looking into the eyes of the characters who were the real foundation of ancient Rome.

• *To exit, head down the stairs to the ground floor, and follow signs to the* uscita. *Take a photo with the colossal river-god statue of Marforio. If you checked a bag, cross the courtyard to retrieve it.*

ST. PETER-IN-CHAINS TOUR

San Pietro in Vincoli

Michelangelo—the world's greatest sculptor—died having failed to complete his greatest work, the tomb of Pope Julius II. Today, you can visit the powerful remains of that unfinished masterpiece, including the famous statue of Moses, housed in a historic church that also contains Peter's chains.

Orientation

Cost: Free.

Hours: Daily 8:00-12:20 & 15:00-19:00, Oct-March until 18:00.

Dress Code: Modest dress is required.

Getting There: The church is a 10-minute uphill walk north of the Colosseum. From the Colosseo Metro stop, take the escalator just inside the station exit (following *S. Pietro in Vincoli* signs). When you emerge, cross the pedestrian bridge and head straight up the Via della Polveriera. At the top, turn left to reach the church. There's also a staircase 50 yards east of the station. For a shorter walk (but with steep steps), use the Cavour Metro stop; from that station, go downhill on Via Cavour a half-block, then climb the big pedestrian staircase called Via di San Francesco di Paola, which leads right to the church. If asking for directions, say "San Pietro in Vincoli" (sahn pee-AY-troh een VEEN-koh-lee). From the outside, St. Peter-in-Chains' rounded arches and columns look more like a Renaissance loggia than a church.

Information: Tel. 06-9784-4950.

Length of This Tour: Allow 30 minutes.

Photography: Generally, photos without flash are allowed in Rome's churches. Bring €1 coins to light Moses and the tomb.

Eating: See the recommended eateries for the Monti neighborhood listed on page 379, as well as those closer to the Colosseum on page 382.

The Tour Begins

• *In the far-right corner of the church, you'll find a wall full of marble statues. In the center sits...*

Michelangelo's *Moses* (1515)

Moses has just returned from meeting face-to-face with God. Now he senses trouble back home. Slowly he turns to see his followers worshipping a golden calf. As his anger builds, he glares at them. His physical strength is symbolic of his moral and spiritual fortitude as a leader of his people. His powerful left leg tucks under and tenses, as if he's just about to spring up out of his chair and punish the naughty Children of Israel with the Ten Commandments under his arm. Enjoy the cascading beard, one of the greatest in art history.

And if he did stand up, this statue would be 13 feet tall, nearly the height of Michelangelo's famous *David*. This Charlton

Heston-with-horns is interesting in photographs...and awe-inspiring when confronted in person. His bare, muscular arms exude power. Michelangelo completed the statue after practicing for four years painting the seated prophets on the Sistine ceiling.

Like other Michelangelo statues, *Moses* is both at rest (seated) and in motion (his tensed leg, turning head, and nervous fingers). This restlessness may reflect Michelangelo's Neo-Platonic belief that the soul is the claustrophobic prisoner of the body. Or it's the statue itself fighting to emerge from the stone around it. A fanciful legend says that Michelangelo, frustrated at trying to bring

God's statue into existence, hit *Moses* with his hammer (causing the scar on *Moses*' right knee), imploring, "Now, speak!"

The horns are the crowning touch. In medieval times, the Hebrew word for "rays of light" (halo) was mistranslated as "horns." Michelangelo knew better but wanted to give the statue an air of *terribilità*, a kind of scary charisma possessed by Moses, Pope Julius II...and Michelangelo. This Moses radiates the smoldering *terribilità* of a borderline-abusive father.

The Tomb Today

In 1542, remnants of the tomb project were brought to the

The Tomb of Pope Julius II

Moses sits on the bottom level of a three-story marble wall filled with statues. This is a puny, cobbled-together version of what was to have been a grand tomb for Pope Julius II.

In 1505, Pope Julius II hired young Michelangelo to build his tomb, a huge monument to be placed in St. Peter's Basilica. An excited Michelangelo sketched designs for a three-story wedding-cake mountain of marble studded with 48 statues and bronze reliefs and topped with a huge statue of the egomaniacal pope. *Moses* was to have been placed on an upper level on the right-hand corner, looking away from the monument.

Michelangelo traveled to Carrara, selected 100 tons of marble for the project, and started working. Then Julius changed his mind. He ordered Michelangelo to paint the Sistine Chapel instead. Michelangelo knocked it off in a mere four years so that he could return to his true masterwork. Michelangelo would spend 40 years of his life working in fits and starts on the tomb. But when Julius died (1513), the funding for the project petered out, and Michelangelo eventually moved on to other things. Julius was buried in a simple grave in St. Peter's Basilica at the Vatican.

St. Peter-in-Chains church and pieced together by Michelangelo's assistants. What we see today is a far cry from the original design, which was to have been fully three-dimensional and five times as big. Some of the best statues ended up elsewhere, such as the *Prisoners* in Florence and the *Slaves* in the Louvre. Though the assistants had Michelangelo's original instruction manual, they were trying to assemble the tomb with most of the parts missing.

Moses and the Louvre's *Slaves* are the only statues Michelangelo personally completed for the project. Flanking *Moses* are the Old Testament sister-wives of Jacob, Leah (to our right) and Rachel, both begun by Michelangelo but probably finished by pupils. On the second story, a Madonna and Child stand above a reclining, thoughtful-looking Pope Julius II on a coffin.

The sheer variety of decoration we see here gives us a glimpse of the tomb's original scope—nearly 50 statues laced together with Pompeii-esque garlands and proto-Baroque scrolls.

Michelangelo went to his grave thinking that he'd wasted the best years of his life on the tomb. Today, we can only reconstruct it in our minds, imagining a monument intended to exceed (according to Giorgio Vasari) "every ancient or imperial tomb ever made."

The Church

Founded in 440, it's one of Rome's oldest, built to house Peter's chains. Though the church was greatly changed in 1475, the 20 Doric columns flanking the wide nave are from the original church. The central ceiling painting (c. 1700) shows the chains—with their miraculous curative powers in action—healing someone possessed by demons, on the steps of St. Peter's Basilica at the Vatican. Sculpted skeletons and grim reapers adorn a number of the tombs lining the side naves. These *memento mori* (Latin for "remember you must die") were popular in the 17th century and are graphic reminders of mortality, the fate that awaits rich and poor alike.

• *On the altar is a gold-and-glass case containing what tradition claims to be...*

Peter's Chains

There are actually two different sets of chains, linked together.

One set is said to have held Peter when he and Paul were in the Mamertine Prison in Rome (near the Forum). The other dates from when Herod jailed Peter in Jerusalem (Acts 12; see the scene frescoed on the left wall of the apse). During the night, "Peter was sleeping between two soldiers, bound with chains, while sentries were guarding the doors. And behold, an angel of the Lord appeared and a light shone in the cell. The angel struck Peter on the side and woke him, saying, 'Get up quickly.' And the chains fell off his hands." The angel led Peter, who thought he was dreaming, out of the prison to safety. (Raphael's depiction of this is in the Vatican Museums. A less-famous 1577 version by Jacopo Coppi is behind the altar, on the left wall.)

In the waning days of ancient Rome, the Jerusalem chains ended up here as a gift from the Eastern empress (as depicted in another Coppi fresco on the right wall of the apse).

According to tradition, when the Jerusalem chains arrived and were paired with the Mamertine chains, the two sets—chink!—joined together miraculously.

JEWISH GHETTO WALK

East Bank of the Tiber

For centuries, Rome's Jewish ghetto—even while a site of relentless persecution—has showcased the undying pride and solidarity of a tight-knit community. Built in 1555 on the banks of a frequently flooded bend of the Tiber River, the ghetto was the forced home of the city's Jewish population for more than 300 years, ending only with Italian unification in 1870. Though most of the old ghetto buildings were torn down long ago, the area is still a lively center of Jewish life.

Orientation

Length of This Walk: Allow about 30 minutes, plus an additional hour or more if you tour the synagogue and visit the museum. You might also plan a meal here.

When to Go: Avoid Saturday and late Friday afternoon, when the synagogue, museum, and bakery are closed.

Getting There: The Jewish ghetto is on the east bank of the Tiber River, near the river's island (Isola Tiberina) and the ancient ruins of the Theater of Marcellus (Teatro di Marcello). The walk's starting point is right across the river from Trastevere and is a 10-minute walk from Largo Argentina. Bus #23 stops nearby.

Jewish Museum and Synagogue: €11 ticket covers both, includes one-hour audioguide for museum and guided tour of synagogue; April-Sept Sun-Thu 10:00-18:00, Fri 10:00-16:00, shorter hours off-season, closed Sat year-round; last entry 45 minutes before closing, on Lungotevere dei Cenci, tel. 06-6840-0661, www.museoebraico.roma.it. Modest dress is required. Entry to the synagogue (unless you're attending services) is only by guided **tour** (included in museum admission,

In the Ghetto

The word "ghetto" comes from the Italian *geto* (foundry) and was first used in Venice to describe the part of town where Jews lived near the copper foundry. Initially the term meant only Jewish neighborhoods, but it later came to mean any neighborhood where a single ethnic group is segregated.

English tours usually at :15 past the hour, lasts 30 minutes, confirm times at ticket counter).

Tours: Walking tours of the Jewish ghetto leave from the museum at least once a day Sun-Fri (€8, usually at 13:15, no tours on Sat, www.cinquescole.org). Ask for the schedule at the museum and sign up at least 30 minutes before the tour departure time (minimum of three people required).

Local Guide: Micaela Pavoncello is uniquely equipped to guide visitors through the neighborhood her family has lived in for generations (€130/2 hours, tel. 328-863-8128, www.jewishroma.com, info@jewishroma.com).

 Download my free Jewish Ghetto **audio tour.**

Eateries: Near the end of this tour, you'll find restaurants offering traditional Roman and Jewish fare and several places to pick up snacks, including a Jewish bakery.

Nearby: The Trastevere Walk starts near where this one does—on Ponte Fabricio (see page 319).

BACKGROUND

Today, nearly half of Italy's 35,000 Jews call Rome home. Jews here have a uniquely Roman style of worship and even preserve remnants of their own Judaic-Roman dialect. That's because, unlike most of the world's Jewish people, Roman Jews are neither Sephardic (descended from Spain) nor Ashkenazi (descended from Eastern Europe). Italy's Jews came from the Holy Land before the Diaspora, some directly and some via Greece; after Rome invaded Judaea in the first century A.D., others came as POWs sold into slavery. These first Jews lived, like other foreigners, outside the city—across the river, in Trastevere.

With the fall of the Roman Empire, the status of Jews declined. As Christianity enveloped Rome, the state denied Jews their full rights as citizens, and once the pope became literally the king of Rome, the Church enforced laws that limited the spread of

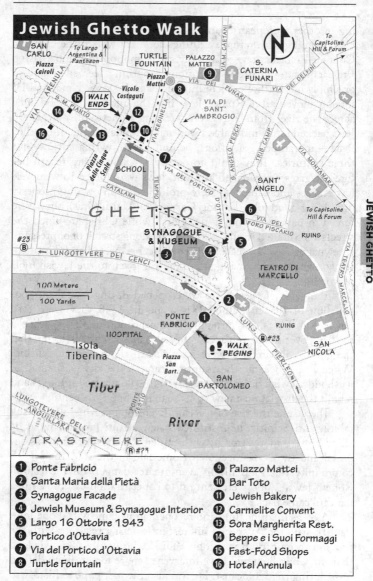

Jewish Ghetto Walk

1. Ponte Fabricio
2. Santa Maria della Pietà
3. Synagogue Facade
4. Jewish Museum & Synagogue Interior
5. Largo 16 Ottobre 1943
6. Portico d'Ottavia
7. Via del Portico d'Ottavia
8. Turtle Fountain
9. Palazzo Mattei
10. Bar Toto
11. Jewish Bakery
12. Carmelite Convent
13. Sora Margherita Rest.
14. Beppe e i Suoi Formaggi
15. Fast-Food Shops
16. Hotel Arenula

the Jewish faith (such as no proselytizing, no new synagogues, no intermarriage). The severity of these laws varied from pope to pope. Despite this, Rome's Jews prospered for the most part and were often held in high regard as physicians, businessmen, and confidants of popes. The community in Trastevere was even allowed to spill across to the opposite bank of the Tiber.

In 1492, Spain expelled its Jews, with similar removals following in other European countries. Rome's Jewish population doubled, swelling with refugees. Things soon got worse. The Catholic Counter-Reformation—originally set in motion to combat rising Protestantism—turned its attention to anything deemed a "heresy" or simply not Catholic, including Judaism. In 1555, Pope Paul IV forcibly moved all of Rome's Jews into the undesirable flood zone across the river from Trastevere, creating a ghetto of some 2,000 Jews packed into a miserable seven acres of mucky land. There they lived—in cramped conditions, behind a wall, with a curfew—for three centuries. They could go out by day, but had to return before the gates were locked at night. Jews were forced to wear yellow scarves and caps, and were prohibited from owning property or holding good jobs. During Carnevale (Mardi Gras), they were forced to parade down Via del Corso while Christians lined the streets and shouted insults. Through this long stretch of oppression, the synagogue was a place Jews could feel respected and dignified. It's no wonder such loving attention was given to the Jewish tools of worship.

The gates of the ghetto were opened during Napoleon's occupation of the city (1805-1814), and in 1848 they were torn down. But it was only after Italian unification in 1870—when a secular government replaced religious rule by the Vatican—that the ghetto's inhabitants were granted full rights and citizenship. When Rome became the country's capital, the city—ashamed of its shoddy Jewish quarter—destroyed the old ghetto buildings and rebuilt the district on a new street plan in a fine 19th-century style.

Then came the rise of fascism. Even though Mussolini wasn't rabidly anti-Semitic, he instituted a slew of anti-Jewish laws as he allied himself more strongly with Hitler. When Mussolini was deposed and the Nazis occupied Rome late in the war, the Jewish community was suddenly in even greater danger. Of the 10,000 Roman Jews, 2,000 were sent off to concentration camps. Only a handful came back.

A measure of healing and reconciliation came with Pope John Paul II, who took a special interest in fostering relations with the Jewish community. It was John Paul II who finally acknowledged that the Church should have intervened more forcefully to defend Jews during the Holocaust. He was also the first pope in history to enter a synagogue (here in this neighborhood in 1986).

Today, Rome's Jewish ghetto is not as evocative as Venice's (where the original buildings remain intact), but its school, shops, restaurants, and synagogue make it more lively.

The Walk Begins

• *Start at the north end of Ponte Fabricio, which connects central Rome with the Isola Tiberina and the neighborhood of Trastevere. You'll see the big synagogue with its square dome. The neighborhood consists of the synagogue and the several blocks behind it.*

❶ Ponte Fabricio

Ponte Fabricio is nicknamed Ponte Quattro Capi ("Bridge of the Four Heads") for its statues of the two-faced pagan god Janus.

In ancient times, it was called Pons Judaeorum ("Jews' Bridge") because foreigners, immigrants, and Jews—who weren't allowed to live in central Rome—would commute across this bridge to get into town. Some 30,000 Jews once lived in Trastevere. Look down at the river. The embankment was only built in the late 19th century. Before then, this was the worst flood zone along the Roman riverbank—just right for a ghetto for the politically powerless.

• *With your back to the river, look left to see the synagogue, with its square-domed roof. But our first stop is the little church just across the busy street from the bridge—the beige building with an oval painting on the facade.*

❷ Santa Maria della Pietà (a.k.a. San Gregorio)

When the ghetto was a walled-in town, Catholics built churches at each gate to try and spread their faith to the Jews. Every time Jews entered or left their home, they got a little sermon from the church's facade. There was the Crucifixion in the oval painting, which reminded all that it was the "Jews" who killed Christ (who, of course, was Jewish himself). And notice the Hebrew script under the crucifix. It quotes the Jewish prophet Isaiah—"All day long, I have stretched out my hands to a disobedient and faithless nation that has lost its way" (Isaiah 65:2)—but misuses the quote to give it an anti-Semitic twist.

• *Turning your back to the church, walk one block along the river and then turn right on Via del Tempio. On your right, find the synagogue's main entrance, reserved for worshippers—this is the best vantage point to admire the...*

❸ Synagogue Facade

Take in the impressive structure. Its warm golden stone glows. The dome on top was made square to distinguish it from a Chris-

tian church. Scan the facade for familiar Jewish iconography: a menorah, the Ten Commandments, a Star of David, palm branches, and a few inscriptions in Hebrew script.

The structure is modern (completed in 1904), but this has been the place of worship for Rome's Jews for half a millennium—since the 16th century, when Pope Paul IV forced the Jews to reside within a walled ghetto. After Rome became the capital of the newly unified

Italy in 1870, Jews gained equal rights and were free to live anywhere in the city. Not long after, the original ghetto buildings were demolished and replaced with the modern blocks you see today. The Jewish community was offered better real estate for its synagogue, but chose instead to build a new "Great Synagogue" here, on the original site.

• *To visit the Jewish Museum, which includes a guided tour of the synagogue, circle around the left side of the synagogue and walk down pedestrian-only Via Catalana to the "Museo Ebraico" entrance at the far end of the building.*

❹ Jewish Museum (Museo Ebraico) and Synagogue Interior

On a single basement level, the worthwhile **museum** tells the story of Roman Jews from ancient times to today, showing off historically significant artifacts. You'll see second-century B.C. reliefs with Jewish symbols, finely worked religious items, and other relics of the past. A reconstructed image shows how the neighborhood looked in the 19th century, with tall buildings not unlike those in Venice's ghetto. The museum also shows a film (subtitled in English) about the Nazi occupation of Rome, along with a display of artifacts and documentation from this dark time.

Your admission includes a guided visit inside the **Great Synagogue.** Gaze up into the dome painted with the colors of the rainbow, symbolizing God's promise to Noah that there would be no more floods. The stars on the ceiling recall God's pledge that Abraham's descendants would flourish and be as many as the stars in the sky. Architects designed the structure in the Art Nouveau style, with a dash of Tiffany. The sandy color tones are a reminder of the community's desert heritage. You'll also get a brief tour of the

older, smaller **Spanish Synagogue**—which once stood on a nearby square but was moved in 1932 to the ground floor of this building.
• *Just outside the museum entrance is a small square (along Via Portico d'Ottavia) dominated by a big Roman ruin. This square is called...*

❺ Largo 16 Ottobre 1943

This square is named for the day when Nazi trucks parked here and threatened to take the Jews to concentration camps unless the community came up with 50 kilos (110 pounds) of gold in 24 hours. Everyone, including many non-Jewish Romans, tossed in their precious gold, and the demand was met. The Nazis took the gold—and later, they took many of the Jews as well. Some 2,000 of the ghetto's residents were sent to concentration camps, most of them never to return.
• *The big ancient ruin is the...*

❻ Portico d'Ottavia

This monumental gateway—with columns supporting a triangular pediment—was built by soon-to-be-emperor Augustus. Once flanked by temples and librar-

ies, the passageway served as a kind of cultural center. After Rome's fall, the portico housed a thriving fish market. In the eighth century, the ruins of the portico were incorporated into the Church of Sant'Angelo in Pescheria. (You can find the entrance to the church behind the portico.) For centuries, this Christian church was packed every Saturday with Jews—forced by decree to listen to Christian sermons. Notice the faded bits of Christian fresco on the arch. Locals love to tell of the poor old woman who lives under the arch; she refused to sell her land and now owns this priceless bit of real estate that includes the ancient ruin. If you like, walk through the archway into the quiet backstreets, then return.

Find the walkway and the small bridge on your right, where you can look down at the level of the street in Roman times. On the right is a fine view of the Teatro di Marcello, which predates and inspired the design of the Colosseum. One of three major theaters in the ancient city, it could hold more than 10,000 spectators. In the Middle Ages, it was converted into a fortress, and today those are luxury apartments on the top level. Beyond it is the tree-capped Capitoline Hill. You can take a short detour down the ramp into the archaeological area and enjoy the hodgepodge of ancient fragments scattered about.

• *Now walk along the ghetto's main street...*

❼ Via del Portico d'Ottavia

This main drag is a fine place to get a taste of yesterday's ghetto and today's Rome. From the start (near the Roman arch), look down

the street. On the left is a new building from 1911. On the right, in the distance, is the only surviving line of old ghetto building-fronts. Imagine today's street as it was then: much narrower (as it is at the far end today). Walking down the street, notice kosher restaurants advertising artichokes *(carciofi)*, either braised *(alla romana)* or deep-fried in the "Jewish" style *(alla giudia)*. You might see posters for community events, a few men wearing yarmulkes, shops selling Judaica, and political graffiti, both pro- and anti-Israel. The Palestine Liberation Organization attacked this area in 1982, and a police presence still lingers.

After a block, you reach the center of the district. Look right, down very narrow **Via di Sant'Ambrogio,** an old surviving street.

Imagine the dense population, flood muck, and squalor of the past. At #7 on the main drag (first door on the right after Via di Sant'Ambrogio), is a mezuzah (prayer capsule)—observant Jews touch it as they come and go as a sign of respect for God.

On the pedestrianized **square** ahead, older folks hang out together and shoot the breeze, sometimes even bringing their favorite chairs from home. This neighborhood has become trendy, and apartment prices are expensive. Though the Jewish community has long since dispersed all over Rome, they still come back here for activities and worship. The big tan building (on the left) houses the Jewish school.

Opposite the big school, take a one-block detour down **Via della Reginella,** where you'll find some fun shops (see page 401 in the Shopping in Rome chapter) as well as some poignant artifacts. In front of #10 (on the right), you'll see several small bronze plaques in the shape of cobbles, memorials to members of the community arrested in these homes during the Nazi occupation. These

Stolperstein ("stumbling stones"), designed by a German artist, commemorate victims of the Holocaust and are found in front of their residences throughout the city (and the rest of Europe). At #28, notice where the six-floor buildings end and more elegant and spacious (but no taller) three-floor buildings begin...marking the end of the ghetto.

In the square (Piazza Mattei) at the end of the lane is a fun ❽ **turtle fountain**—an old Mannerist work, later embellished with turtles by Bernini. It's said that Bernini cared about the Jews and honored them with the symbol of a turtle—an ancient creature that carries all its belongings on its back.

Cross the square and jog right down Via de' Funari ("Street of the Ropemakers") to the big brick ❾ **Palazzo Mattei** (#31, on the left). Step inside to be reminded that very often in Rome, grim, uninviting exteriors contain unexpected treasures, like this building's courtyard. Encrusted with the family's collection of ancient Roman sculpture, it was intended to show off their wealth and refined taste. Today, the palazzo is home to the Italian Center for American Studies.

Returning to the ghetto's main drag (Via del Portico d'Ottavia), continue to ❿ **Bar Toto** (the second café on the right).

Next to the door you'll see a slot in the wall—a ghetto-era charity box for orphans that still accepts donations for worthy causes. The ancient relief below the box marks the home of a big-shot who, at the start of the Renaissance age (before the ghetto's establishment in 1555), plugged this chunk of ancient Rome into his facade for prestige. A few steps farther down (before the kosher gelato shop at #1), another bit of ancient marble depicts a lion attacking a gazelle. Also on the building is a big stone panel with a Latin inscription dated "MMC-CXX." Yes, that's 2220, and no, it's not from the future. It was carved in A.D. 1467—marking the years since the birth of Rome in 753 B.C.

At the next intersection (Piazza Costaguti), stand in the center of the white decorative design and get oriented for your next move. To the left—on the car-filled square called Piazza delle Cinque Scole—is a recommended restaurant, **Sora Margherita** (at #30, described on page 368).

JEWISH GHETTO

Directly ahead of you, the main street leads to more recommended eateries, and eventually to Campo de' Fiori.

Now, let's see our final sights. On your right, at the corner, is a tiny ⓫ **Jewish bakery.** Go inside to check out the braided challah bread (Friday only), cheesecakes, almond paste-filled macaroons, and misleadingly named "Jewish pizzas" *(pizza Ebraica)*—which are actually like little €3 fruitcakes, but better tasting, with a crunchy top.

Around the corner, the curving, white-columned structure is part of a former ⓬ **Carmelite convent.** Consider how Rome's Jews felt when the Church built a convent and a Catholic school here in the ghetto to preach to their children, and forced locals to attend Mass. Finally, pop through the tunnel-like passageway next to the convent, from which you emerge into a tiny courtyard ringed with tall tenements. Imagine the tight conditions of thousands of Jews living in this small seven-acre area. Think of the turbulent history of the ghetto—and the rich heritage of Rome's Jewish community.

• *The tour is over. From here, you're within walking distance of many sights in Rome. For transportation options, get out your map, and you'll see that a major transit hub—Largo Argentina—is just a couple of blocks away. Shalom.*

ST. PETER'S BASILICA TOUR

Basilica San Pietro

St. Peter's is the greatest church in Christendom. It represents the power and splendor of Rome's 2,000-year domination of the Western world. Built on the memory and grave of the first pope, St. Peter, this is where the grandeur of ancient Rome became the grandeur of Christianity.

Orientation

Cost: Free entry to basilica and crypt. Dome climb-€5 if you take the stairs all the way up, or €7 to ride an elevator partway (to the roof), then climb to the top of the dome (cash only; for details, see "Dome Climb," page 215). Treasury Museum-€7 (€3 audioguide).

Hours: The **church** is open daily April-Sept 7:00-19:00, Oct-March 7:00-18:00. It closes on Wednesday mornings during papal audiences (until roughly 13:00).

The **dome** *(cupola)* is open to climbers daily from 8:00; if you're climbing the stairs all the way up, the last entry time is 17:00 (16:00 Oct-March); if you're riding the elevator, you can enter until 18:00 (17:00 Oct-March).

The **Treasury Museum** is open daily 8:00-18:50, Oct-March until 17:50.

The **crypt** *(grotte)* is open daily 9:00-16:00.

Avoiding Lines: There's often a bottleneck at the security check. The checkpoint is typically on the north side of the square, but is sometimes closer to the church or tucked under the south colonnade.

If you're also visiting the Vatican Museums (and going through security there), a shortcut usually—but not always—lets you exit from the Sistine Chapel directly into St. Peter's.

Vatican City

The tiny independent country of Vatican City is contained entirely within Rome. (Its 100 acres could fit eight times over in New York's Central Park.) The Vatican has its own postal system, armed guards, beautiful gardens, a helipad, mini train-station, and radio station (KPOP). It also has two huge sights: St. Peter's Basilica and the Vatican Museums. Politically powerful, the Vatican is the religious capital of 1.2 billion Roman Catholics. If you're not a Catholic, become one for your visit.

The pope is both the religious and secular leader of Vatican City. For centuries, the Vatican was the capital of the Papal States, and locals referred to the pontiff as "King Pope." Because of the Vatican's territorial ambitions, it didn't always have good relations with Italy. Even though modern Italy was created in 1870, the Holy See didn't recognize it as a country until 1929.

Like every European country, Vatican City has its own versions of the euro coin (with a portrait of the pope). You're unlikely to find one in your pocket, though, as they're snatched up by collectors before falling into circulation.

Vatican Gardens: To walk through the manicured Vatican Gardens (with views over Rome and a good look at St. Peter's dome), you must book a guided tour several days in advance at http://biglietteriamusei.vatican.va (€32, 2 hours, daily except Wed and Sun, includes entry to Vatican Museums; tours usually start at 9:30 or 11:00 at Vatican Museums tour desk). On rare occasions, same-day tickets are available at the Vatican TI. A 45-minute open-bus tour through the gardens is offered in good weather (€36 includes audioguide and admission to Vatican Museums).

Post Offices: The Vatican postal service is famous for its stamps, which you can get from offices on St. Peter's Square (one next to the TI, another by the columns just before the security checkpoint), in the Vatican Museums (closed Sun), or from a "post bus" that's often parked on St. Peter's Square (open Sun). To get a Vatican postmark, you must mail your cards from postboxes at the Vatican itself (although the stamps are good throughout Rome).

Seeing the Pope: Your best chances for a sighting are on Sunday or Wednesday. Most Sundays (though not always, especially in July or August), the pope gives a **blessing** at noon from his apartment on St. Peter's Square to the faithful assembled below.

You don't need a ticket—just show up. On most Wednesdays, the pope holds a **general audience** at 10:00. That's when he arrives in his Popemobile and gives a short sermon from a canopied platform on the square. (In winter, it's sometimes held indoors at the big Paolo VI Auditorium, next to St. Peter's Basilica, though Pope Francis prefers the square, even in cold weather.) Note that whenever the pope appears on the square, the basilica closes and crowds are substantial—so avoid these times if you just want to sightsee. To get the pope's schedule for your visit, see www.vatican.va (click on "Prefecture of the Papal Household").

General Audience Tickets: For the Wednesday audience, you need a (free) ticket to get close to the papal action and get a seat. Reserve tickets (available about a month or two in advance) by sending a request by mail or fax (access the form at www.vatican.va, under "Prefecture of the Papal Household"). You'll then pick up the tickets at St. Peter's Square before the audience (available Tue 15:00-19:00 and Wed 7:00-9:00; usually under Bernini's colonnade, to the left of the church).

You can also book tickets online through the American Catholic Church in Rome (details at www.santasusanna.org; free, but donations appreciated). Pick up your reserved tickets or check for last-minute availability at the church office the Tuesday before the audience between 16:30 and 18:15 (Via XX Settembre 15, Metro: Repubblica, tel 06-4201 1554   charming Rosanna speaks English).

Finally, starting the Monday before the audience, Swiss Guards hand out tickets from their station near the basilica exit (see map on page 218). There's no need to go through security—just march up, ask nicely, and say "danke." While this is perhaps the easiest way, I'd reserve in advance to guarantee a ticket.

General Audience Tips: On Wednesday morning, you'll need to be dressed appropriately (shoulders covered, no short shorts or tank tops—long pants or knee-length skirts are safest) and clear security (no big bags; lines tend to move more quickly on the side of the square farthest from the Metro stop). To get a seat (much less a good one), it's smart to be there a couple of hours early—there are far fewer seats than ticketholders. If you just want to see the pope, get a good photo, and don't mind standing, you can show up later (though still at least 30 minutes early) and take your place in the standing-room section in the back half of the square. The service gets underway around 9:30 when the names of attending pilgrim groups are announced. Shortly thereafter, the Popemobile appears, winding through the adoring crowd (the best places—seated or standing—are near the cloth-covered wooden fences that line the Popemobile route). Around 10:00, the Pope's multilingual message begins and lasts for about an hour (you can leave at any time).

This is a great time-saving trick, but unfortunately not a reliable one (for details, see page 238).

Visiting before 10:00 is one way to avoid the worst crowds. Crowds also thin after 16:00, when sunbeams work their magic on the altar, and the 17:00 Mass (Mon-Sat) in the apse fills the place with spiritual music. The downside is that after 16:00, the crypt is closed, and the area around the altar is often roped off to prepare for Mass.

Dress Code: No shorts, above-the-knee skirts, or bare shoulders (this applies to men, women, and children). Attendants enforce this dress code, even in hot weather. Carry a cover-up, if necessary.

Getting There: Take the Metro to Ottaviano, then walk 10 minutes south on Via Ottaviano. The #40 express bus drops off at Piazza Pio, next to Castel Sant'Angelo—a 10-minute walk from St. Peter's. The more crowded bus #64, beloved by pickpockets, stops just outside St. Peter's Square to the south (get off the bus after it crosses the Tiber, at the first stop past the tunnel; backtrack toward the tunnel and turn left when you see the rows of columns; the return bus stop is adjacent to the tunnel). Bus #492 heads through the center of town, stopping at Largo Argentina, and gets you near Piazza Risorgimento (get off when you see the Vatican walls). A few other handy buses (see page 22) get you to the general Vatican area. A taxi from Termini train station to St. Peter's costs about €13.

Information: The Vatican TI, up close to the church on the left (south) side of the square, is excellent (Mon-Sat 8:30-18:15, closed Sun, tel. 06-6988-1662). For the Vatican, see www.vaticanstate.va.

Church Services: Mass, generally in Italian, is said varyingly in the south (left) transept, the Blessed Sacrament Chapel (on right side of nave), or at the main altar. Confirm times on the signboard as you enter. Typical schedule: Mon-Sat at 8:30, 9:00, 10:00, 11:00, 12:00, 16:30, and (in Latin, at the main altar) at 17:00; Sun and holidays at 9:00, 10:30 (in Latin), 11:30, 12:15, 13:00, 16:00, 16:45 (vespers), and 17:30.

Tours: The Vatican TI conducts free 1.5-hour **tours of St. Peter's** (depart from TI Mon-Fri at 14:15, confirm schedule at TI). **Audioguides** can be rented near the baggage check (€5 plus ID, for church only, daily 9:00-17:00).

♪ Download my free St. Peter's Basilica **audio tour.**

To see St. Peter's original grave, you can take a *Scavi* (excavations) tour into the **Necropolis** under the basilica (€13, 1.5 hours, ages 15 and older only, no photos). Book at least two months in advance by email (scavi@fsp.va) or fax (06-6987-3017), following the detailed instructions at www.vatican.va

(search for "Excavations Office"); no response means they're booked.

> **Dome Climb:** You can take the elevator (€7) or stairs (€5) to the roof (231 steps), then climb another 323 steps to the top of the dome. The entry to the elevator is just outside the north side of the basilica—look for signs to the *cupola*. If you're climbing the dome without your travel partner, confirm where you'll exit before you split up (exit sometimes moves). For more on the dome, see the end of this chapter.

Length of This Tour: Allow one hour, plus another hour if you climb the dome (or a half-hour to the roof). With as little as 15 minutes, you could stroll the nave, glance up at the dome, down at St. Peter's resting place, and adore the *Pietà* on your way out.

Baggage Check: The free bag check (mandatory for bags larger than a purse or daypack) is inside security, but outside the basilica (to the right as you face the entrance). Pocketknives are not allowed inside the basilica.

Vatican Museums Tickets: The Vatican TI at St. Peter's often has museum tickets on sale for €20. There may also be a table selling museum tickets in the narthex (portico) of St. Peter's (€16 entry plus €9 service fee). You skip the ticket-buying line at the Vatican Museums and get an entry time, generally for the same day (see page 237 for other Vatican Museums ticketing options)

Services: WCs are on both sides of St. Peter's Square (by the TI and just outside security), near the baggage check down the steps by the church entrance, and on the roof. **Drinking fountains** are near the obelisk and the WCs. **Post offices** are next to the TI and just outside the security checkpoint.

Starring: Michelangelo, Bernini, St. Peter, a heavenly host...and, occasionally, the pope.

BACKGROUND

Nearly 2,000 years ago, St. Peter's oval-shaped "square" was the site of Nero's Circus—a huge, cigar-shaped Roman chariot racecourse. The Romans had no marching bands, so for halftime entertainment they killed Christians. This persecuted minority was forced to fight wild animals and gladiators, or they were simply crucified. Some were tarred up, tied to posts, and burned—human torches to light up the evening races.

One of those killed here, in about A.D. 65, was Peter, Jesus' right-hand man, who had come to Rome to spread the message of love. At his own request, Peter was crucified upside down, because he felt unworthy to die as his master had. His remains were buried

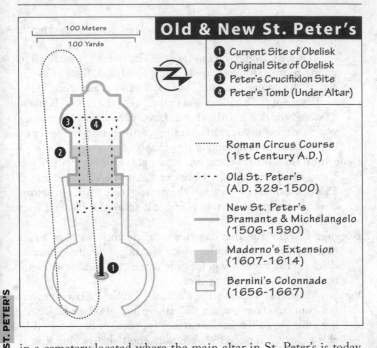

Old & New St. Peter's

100 Meters
100 Yards

1 Current Site of Obelisk
2 Original Site of Obelisk
3 Peter's Crucifixion Site
4 Peter's Tomb (Under Altar)

·········· Roman Circus Course
(1st Century A.D.)

- - - - Old St. Peter's
(A.D. 329-1500)

New St. Peter's
Bramante & Michelangelo
(1506-1590)

Maderno's Extension
(1607-1614)

Bernini's Colonnade
(1656-1667)

ST. PETER'S

in a cemetery located where the main altar in St. Peter's is today. For 250 years, these relics were quietly and secretly revered.

Peter had been recognized as the first "pope," or bishop of Rome, from whom all later popes claimed their authority as head of the Church. When Christianity was finally legalized in 313, the Christian emperor Constantine built a church on the site of Peter's martyrdom. "Old St. Peter's" lasted 1,200 years (A.D. 326-1500).

By the time of the Renaissance, Old St. Peter's was falling apart and was considered unfit to be the center of the Western Church. The new, larger church we see today was begun in 1506 by the architect Donato Bramante. (Bramante was in such a hurry to demolish parts of the original church that he earned the nickname "Master Ruiner.") He was succeeded by Michelangelo and a number of other architects, each with his own designs. Later, Carlo Maderno took Michelangelo's Greek-cross-shaped church and lengthened it, adding a long nave. As the construction proceeded, the new church rose around the old one (see diagram above). The project was finally finished 120 years, 20 popes, and 10 architects later, and Old St. Peter's was dismantled and carried out of the new church. (A few bits survive from the first church: the central door, some columns in the atrium, eight spiral columns around the tomb from the Jerusalem Temple, the venerated statue of Peter, and Michelangelo's *Pietà*.) It took another 200 years to decorate. All told, it took 320 years to build the largest church in the world in what is now the smallest country in the world.

Michelangelo designed the magnificent dome. Unfortunately, although it soars above St. Peter's, it's barely visible from the center of the square because of Maderno's extended nave. To see the entire dome, you'll need to step outside the open end of the square, where in the 1930s Benito Mussolini opened up the broad boulevard, finally letting people see the dome that had been hidden for centuries by the facade. Though I don't make a habit of thanking fascist dictators, in this case I'll make an exception: *"Grazie, Benito."*

The Tour Begins

• Ideally, you should head out to the obelisk at the center of the square and read this. But let me guess—it's 95 degrees outside, right? OK, find a shady spot under one of these stone sequoias. If the pigeons have left a clean spot, sit on it.

ST. PETER'S SQUARE

St. Peter's Square, with its ring of columns, symbolizes the arms of the church welcoming everyone—believers and nonbelievers—in

its motherly embrace. It was designed a century after Michelangelo by the Baroque architect Gian Lorenzo Bernini, who did much of the work that we'll see inside. Numbers first: 284 columns, 56 feet high, in stern Doric style. Topping them are Bernini's 140 favorite saints, each 10 feet tall. The "square" itself is actually el-liptical, 660 by 500 feet (roughly the same dimensions as the Colosseum). Though large, it's designed like a saucer, a little higher around the edges, so that even when full of crowds (as it often is), it allows those on the periphery to see above the throngs.

The **obelisk** in the center is 90 feet of solid granite weighing more than 300 tons. It once stood about 100 yards from its current location, in the center of the circus course (to the left of where St. Peter's is today). Think for a second about how much history this monument has seen. Originally erected in Egypt more than 2,000 years ago, it witnessed the fall of the pharaohs to the Greeks and then to the Romans. Then the emperor Caligula moved it to impe-

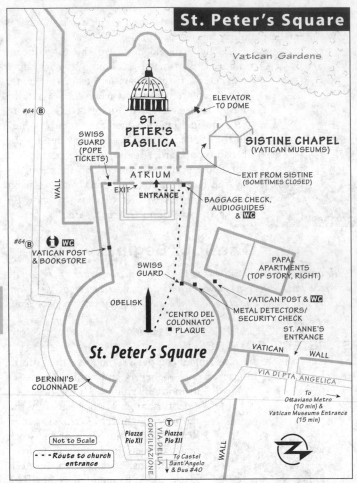

St. Peter's Square

Vatican Gardens

ELEVATOR
TO DOME

ST. PETER'S BASILICA

SISTINE CHAPEL
(VATICAN MUSEUMS)

SWISS GUARD
(POPE TICKETS)

#64 B

WALL

ATRIUM

EXIT FROM SISTINE
(SOMETIMES CLOSED)

EXIT   ENTRANCE

BAGGAGE CHECK,
AUDIOGUIDES
& WC

#64 B   🛈 WC
VATICAN POST
& BOOKSTORE

SWISS GUARD

PAPAL
APARTMENTS
(TOP STORY, RIGHT)

VATICAN POST & WC

OBELISK

"CENTRO DEL
COLONNATO"
■ PLAQUE

METAL DETECTORS/
SECURITY CHECK

ST. ANNE'S
ENTRANCE

St. Peter's Square

VATICAN   WALL

VIA DI PTA. ANGELICA

BERNINI'S
COLONNADE

To
Ottaviano Metro
(10 min) &
Vatican Museums
Entrance
(15 min)

Not to Scale

Piazza
Pio XII   T   Piazza
Pio XII

- - - Route to church
entrance

VIA DELLA CONCILIAZIONE

WALL

To Castel
Sant'Angelo
& Bus #40

rial Rome, where it stood impassively watching the slaughter of Christians at the racecourse and the torture of Protestants by the Inquisition (in the yellow-and-rust building just outside the square, to the left of the church). Today, it watches over the church, a reminder that each civilization builds on the previous ones. The puny cross on top reminds us that Christian culture has cast but a thin veneer over our pagan origins.

• *Now venture out across the burning desert to the obelisk, which provides a narrow sliver of shade.*

As you face the church, the gray building to the right at two o'clock,

rising up behind Bernini's colonnade, is, at least officially, the **pope's abode.** The last window on the right of the top floor is the papal bedroom; to the left of that window is the study window, where popes have often appeared to greet the masses. Pope Francis, however, has shunned the grand papal apartments and lives instead in a modest Vatican guesthouse (upon first seeing the papal suite, he exclaimed, "You could fit 300 people in here!").

On more formal occasions (which you may have seen on TV), the pope appears from the church itself, on the small balcony above the central door.

The Sistine Chapel is just to the right of the facade—the small gray-brown building with the triangular roof, topped by an antenna. The tiny chimney—the pimple along the roofline midway up the left side—is where the famous smoke signals announce the election of each new pope (an extension is added for the occasion). If the smoke is black, a two-thirds majority hasn't been reached. White smoke means a new pope has been selected.

Walk to the right, five pavement plaques from the obelisk, to one marked *Centro del Colonnato*. From here, all of Bernini's columns on the right side line up. The curved Baroque square still pays its respects to Renaissance mathematical symmetry.

• *Now make your way up toward the security checkpoint.*

Notice that there are two entrances into Vatican City: one to the left of the facade, and one to the right, in the crook of Bernini's

"arm." Guarding this small but powerful country's border crossing are the mercenary guards from Switzerland. You have to wonder if they really know how to use those pikes. Their colorful uniforms are said to have been designed by Michelangelo, though he was not known for his sense of humor.

• *After you clear security, continue up, passing the huge statues of St. Paul (with his two-edged sword) and St. Peter (with his bushy hair and keys). Along the way, you'll pass by the dress-code enforcers and a gaggle of ticked-off tourists in shorts. If you need to rent an audioguide or use the baggage check or WCs, do it now (on the right). Then enter the church narthex.*

THE BASILICA
The Narthex
The narthex (portico) is itself bigger than most churches. The huge white columns on the portico date from the first church (fourth century). Five famous bronze doors lead into the church.

Made from the melted-down bronze of the original door of Old St. Peter's, the central door was the first Renaissance work in Rome (c. 1450). It's only opened on special occasions. The panels (from the top down) feature Jesus and Mary, Paul and Peter, and (at the bottom) how each was martyred: Paul decapitated, Peter crucified upside down.

The far-right entrance is the ❶ **Holy Door,** opened only during Holy Years (and special "Jubilee" years designated by the pope). On Christmas Eve every 25 years, the pope knocks three times with a silver hammer and the door opens, welcoming pilgrims to pass through. After Pope John Paul II opened the door on Christmas Eve, 1999, he bricked it up again with a ceremonial trowel a year later to wait another 24 years. Then—surprise!—Pope Francis decided to open it from late 2015 to late 2016 for a special Jubilee Year. On the door itself, note the crucified Jesus and his shiny knees, polished by pious pilgrims who touch them for a blessing.

• *Now for one of Europe's great "wow" experiences: Enter the church. Gape for a while. But don't gape at Michelangelo's famous* Pietà *(on the right). I'll cover it later in the tour. I'll wait for you at the round maroon pavement stone on the floor near the central doorway.*

Overview of the Church

This church is appropriately huge. Size before beauty: The golden window at the far end is two football fields away. The dove in the golden window has the wingspan of a 747 (OK, maybe not quite, but it *is* big). The church covers six acres. The babies at the base of the pillars along the main hall (the nave) are adult-size. The lettering in the gold band along the top of the pillars is seven feet high. Really. The church has a capacity of 60,000 standing worshippers (or 1,200 tour groups).

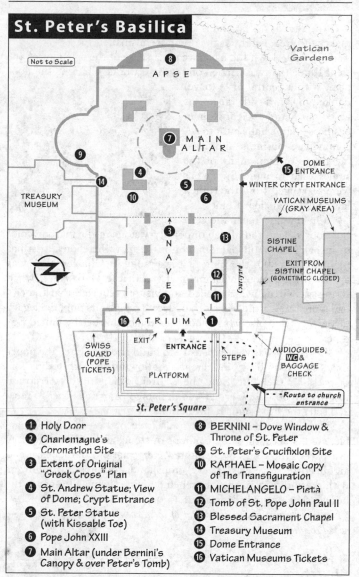

St. Peter's Basilica

Not to Scale

Vatican Gardens

APSE

MAIN ALTAR

DOME ENTRANCE

WINTER CRYPT ENTRANCE

TREASURY MUSEUM

NAVE

ATRIUM

VATICAN MUSEUMS (GRAY AREA)

SISTINE CHAPEL

EXIT FROM SISTINE CHAPEL (SOMETIMES CLOSED)

Courtyard

SWISS GUARD (POPE TICKETS)

EXIT

ENTRANCE

STEPS

PLATFORM

AUDIOGUIDES, **WC** & BAGGAGE CHECK

- - - Route to church entrance

St. Peter's Square

ST. PETER'S

❶ Holy Door
❷ Charlemagne's Coronation Site
❸ Extent of Original "Greek Cross" Plan
❹ St. Andrew Statue; View of Dome; Crypt Entrance
❺ St. Peter Statue (with Kissable Toe)
❻ Pope John XXIII
❼ Main Altar (under Bernini's Canopy & over Peter's Tomb)
❽ BERNINI – Dove Window & Throne of St. Peter
❾ St. Peter's Crucifixion Site
❿ RAPHAEL – Mosaic Copy of The Transfiguration
⓫ MICHELANGELO – Pietà
⓬ Tomb of St. Pope John Paul II
⓭ Blessed Sacrament Chapel
⓮ Treasury Museum
⓯ Dome Entrance
⓰ Vatican Museums Tickets

The church is huge and it feels huge, but everything is designed to make it seem smaller and more intimate than it really is. For example, the statue of St. Teresa near the bottom of the first pillar on the right is 15 feet tall. The statue above her near the top looks the same size, but is actually six feet taller, giving the impression that it's not so far away. Similarly, the fancy bronze canopy over the altar at the far end is as tall as a seven-story building. That makes the great height of the dome seem smaller.

Looking down the nave, we get a sense of the splendor of ancient Rome that was carried on by the Catholic Church. The floor

plan, with a central aisle (nave) flanked by two side aisles, is based on that of ancient Roman basilicas—large halls built to accommodate business and legal meetings. In fact, many of the stones used to build St. Peter's were scavenged from the ruined law courts of ancient Rome.

On the floor near the central doorway is a round slab of porphyry stone in the maroon color of ancient Roman officialdom. This is the spot where, on Christmas night in A.D. 800, the king of the Franks ❷ **Charlemagne was crowned** Holy Roman Emperor. Even in the Dark Ages, when Rome was virtually abandoned and visitors reported that the city had more thieves and wolves than decent people, its imperial legacy made it a fitting place to symbolically establish a briefly united Europe.

St. Peter's was very expensive to build and decorate. The popes financed it by selling "indulgences," allowing the rich to buy forgiveness for their sins from the Church. This kind of corruption inspired an obscure German monk named Martin Luther to rebel and start the Protestant Reformation.

The ornate, Baroque-style interior decoration—a riot of marble, gold, stucco, mosaics, columns of stone, and pillars of light—was part of the Church's "Counter" Reformation. Baroque art and architecture served as cheery propaganda, impressing followers with the authority of the Church and giving them a glimpse of the heaven that awaited the faithful.

• *Now, walk straight up the center of the nave toward the altar.*

❸ Michelangelo's Greek-Cross Church

The plaques on the floor show where other, smaller churches of the world would end if they were placed inside St. Peter's: St. Paul's Cathedral in London (Londinense), Florence's Duomo, and so on.

You'll also walk over circular golden grates. Stop at the second one (at the third pillar from the entrance). Look back at the en-

From Pope to Pope

When a pope dies—or retires—the tiny, peaceful Vatican stirs from its timeless slumber and becomes headline news. Millions of people converge on Vatican City, and hundreds of millions around the world watch raptly on TV.

The deceased pope's body is displayed in state in front of the main altar in St. Peter's Basilica. Thousands of pilgrims line up down Via della Conciliazione, waiting for one last look at their pope. On the day of the funeral, hundreds of thousands of mourners, dignitaries, and security personnel gather in St. Peter's Square. The pope's coffin is carried out to the square, where a eulogy is given.

Most popes are laid to rest in the crypt below St. Peter's Basilica, near the tomb of St. Peter and among shrines to many other popes. Especially popular popes—such as John Paul II or John XXIII—eventually find a place upstairs, inside St. Peter's itself.

While the previous pope is being laid to rest, 100-plus cardinals, representing Catholics around the globe, descend on Rome to elect a new pope. Once they've assembled, the crimson-robed cardinals are stripped of their mobile phones, given a vow of secrecy, and locked inside the Sistine Chapel. This begins the "conclave" (from Latin *cum clave*, with key). As they cast votes, their used paper ballots are burned in a stove inside the chapel. The smoke rises up and out the tiny chimney, visible to the crowds assembled in St. Peter's Square. Black smoke means they haven't yet agreed on a new pope.

Finally, the anxious crowd looks up to see a puff of white smoke emerging from the chapel. The bells in St. Peter's clock towers ring out gloriously, the crowd erupts in cheers, and Romans watching on TV hail taxis to hurry to the square.

On the balcony outside St. Peter's, the newly elected pope steps up and raises his hands, as thousands chant *"Viva il Papa."* A cardinal introduces him to the crowd, announcing his newly chosen name. "Brothers and sisters," the cardinal says in several languages, *"habemus papam."* "We have a pope."

trance and realize that if Michelangelo had had his way, this whole long section of the church wouldn't exist. The nave was extended after his death.

Michelangelo was 71 years old when the pope persuaded him to take over the church project and cap it with a dome. He agreed, intending to put the dome over Donato Bramante's original Greek-Cross floor plan, with four equal arms. In optimistic Renaissance times, this symmetrical arrangement symbolized perfection—the orderliness of the created world and the goodness of man (who was created in God's image). But Michelangelo was a Renaissance Man in Counter-Reformation times. The Church, struggling against Protestants and its own corruption, opted for a plan designed to impress the world with its grandeur—the Latin cross of the Crucifixion, with its nave extended to accommodate the grand religious spectacles of the Baroque period.

• *Continue toward the altar, entering "Michelangelo's church." Park yourself in front of the* ❹ *statue of St. Andrew to the left of the altar, the guy holding an X-shaped cross. (Note that the **entrance to the crypt** is usually here; see map on page 221.)*

Like Andrew, gaze up into the dome, and also like him, gasp. (Never stifle a gasp.)

The Dome

The dome soars higher than a football field on end, 448 feet from the floor of the cathedral to the top of the lantern. It glows with

light from its windows, the blue and gold mosaics creating a cool, solemn atmosphere. In this majestic vision of heaven (not painted by Michelangelo), we see (above the windows) Jesus, Mary, and a ring of saints, rings of more angels above them, and, way up in the ozone, God the Father (a blur of blue and red, unless you have binoculars).

When Michelangelo died (1564), he'd completed only the drum of the dome—the circular base up as far as the windows—but the next architects were guided by his designs.

Listen to the hum of visitors echoing through St. Peter's and reflect on our place in the cosmos: half animal, half angel, stretched between heaven and earth, born to live only a short while, a bubble of foam on a great cresting wave of humanity.

• *But I digress.*

Peter's Remains

The base of the dome is ringed with a gold banner telling us in massive blue letters why this church is so important. According to Catholics, Peter was selected by Jesus to head the church. The banner in Latin quotes

ST. PETER'S

from the Bible where Jesus says to him, "You are Peter *(Tu es Petrus)* and upon this rock I will build my church, and to you I will give the keys of the kingdom of heaven" (Matthew 16:18). (Every quote from Jesus to Peter found in the Bible is written out in seven-foot-tall letters that continue around the entire church.)

Peter was the first bishop of Rome. His prestige and that of the city itself made this bishopric more illustrious than all others, and Peter's authority has supposedly passed in an unbroken chain to each succeeding bishop of Rome—that is, the 260-odd popes that followed.

Under the dome, under the bronze canopy, under the altar, some 23 feet under the marble floor, rest the bones of St. Peter, the "rock" upon which this particular church was built. You can't see the tomb, but go to the railing and look down into the small, lighted niche below the altar to see a box containing bishops' shawls—a symbol of how Peter's authority spread to other churches. Peter's tomb is just below this box.

Are they really the bones of Jesus' apostle? According to a papal pronouncement: definitely maybe. The traditional site of his tomb was sealed when Old St. Peter's was built on it in A.D. 326, and it remained sealed until 1940, when it was opened for archaeological study. Bones were found, dated from the first century, of a robust man who died in old age. His body was wrapped in expensive cloth. A third-century tag artist had graffitied a wall near the tomb with "Peter is here," indicating that early visitors thought this was Peter's tomb. Does that mean it's really Peter? Who am I to disagree with the pope? Definitely maybe.

If you line up the cross on the altar with the dove in the window, you'll notice that the niche below the cross is just off-center compared with the rest of the church. Why? Because Michelangelo built the church around the traditional location of the tomb, not the actual location—about two feet away—discovered by modern archaeology.

Back in the nave sits a bronze **❺ statue of Peter** under a canopy. This is one of a handful of pieces of art that were in the earlier church. In one hand he holds keys, the symbol of the authority given him by Christ, while with the other hand he blesses us. He's wearing the toga of a Roman senator. It may be that the original statue was of a senator and that the bushy head and keys were added later to make it Peter. His big right toe has been worn smooth by the lips of pilgrims and foot fetishists. Stand

Peter, the "Fisher of Men"

According to the Bible, Peter was a fisherman chosen by Christ to catch sinners instead. This "fisher of men" had human weaknesses that have endeared him to Christians. He was the disciple who tried to walk on water—but failed. In another incident, he impetuously cut off a man's ear when soldiers came to arrest Jesus. And he even denied knowing Christ, to save his own skin. But Jesus chose him anyway and gave him his nickname—Rock (in Latin: *Petrus*).

Legends say that Peter came to the wicked city of Rome after Jesus' death to spread the gospel of love. He may have been imprisoned in the Mamertine Prison near the Roman Forum (see page 39), and other stories claim he had a vision of Christ along the Appian Way (described on page 339). Eventually, Peter's preaching offended the Nero administration. Christ's fisherman was arrested, crucified upside down, and buried here, where St. Peter's now stands.

in line and kiss it, or, to avoid foot-and-mouth disease, touch your hand to your lips, then rub the toe. This is simply an act of reverence with no legend attached, though you can make one up if you like.

• *Circle to the right around the statue of Peter to find another stop that's popular among pilgrims: the lighted glass niche with the red-robed body of...*

❻ Pope John XXIII

Pope John XXIII, whose papacy lasted from 1958 to 1963, is nicknamed "the good pope." He is best known for initiating the landmark Vatican II Council (1962-1965) that instituted major reforms, bringing the Church into the modern age. The Council allowed Mass to be conducted in the vernacular rather than in Latin. Lay people were invited to participate more in services, Church leadership underwent some healthy self-criticism, and a spirit of ecumenism flourished. Pope John was a populist, referring to people as "brothers and sisters"...a phrase popular today amongst popes. In 2000, during the beatification process (a stop on the way to sainthood), Church authorities checked his body, and it was surprisingly fresh. So they moved it upstairs, put it behind glass, and now old Catholics who remember him fondly enjoy another stop on their St. Peter's visit. Pope John was canonized in 2014.

We'll visit the tomb of another beloved pope-turned-saint—John Paul II—near the end of this tour.

❼ The Main Altar

The main altar (the white marble slab with cross and candlesticks) beneath the dome and canopy is used only when the pope himself says Mass. He sometimes conducts the Sunday morning service when he's in town, a sight worth seeing. I must admit, though, it's a little strange being frisked for weapons at the door to the holiest place in Christendom.

The tiny altar would be lost in this enormous church if it weren't for Gian Lorenzo Bernini's seven-story bronze canopy (God's "four-poster bed"), which "extends" the altar upward and reduces the perceived distance between floor and ceiling. The corkscrew columns echo the marble ones that surrounded the altar/tomb in Old St. Peter's. Some of the bronze used here was taken and melted down from the ancient Pantheon. On the marble base of the columns are three bees on a shield, the symbol of the Barberini family, who commissioned the work and ordered the raid on the Pantheon.

Starting from the column to the left of the altar, walk clockwise around the canopy. Notice the female faces on the marble

bases, about eye level above the bees. Someone in the Barberini family was pregnant during the making of the canopy, so Bernini put the various stages of childbirth on the bases. Continue clockwise to the last base to see how it came out.

Bernini (1598-1680), the Michelangelo of the Baroque era, is the man most responsible for the interior decoration of the church. The altar area was his masterpiece, a "theater" for holy spectacles. Bernini did: 1) the bronze canopy; 2) the dove window in the apse, surrounded by bronze work and statues; 3) the massive statue of lance-bearing St. Longinus ("The hills are alive..."), which became the model for the other three statues in the niches around the main altar; 4) much of the marble floor decoration; and 5) the balconies above the four statues, incorporating some of the actual corkscrew columns from Old St. Peter's, said to have been looted by the Romans from the Temple of Herod (called "Solomon's Temple") in Jerusalem. Bernini, the father of Baroque, gave an impressive unity to an amazing variety of pillars, windows, statues, chapels, and aisles.

• *Approach the apse, the front area with the golden dove window.*

Pope Francis I

In 2013, Cardinal Jorge Bergoglio of Argentina became Francis I, the Catholic Church's 266th pope. Signaling a new direction for the Church, his election represents three "firsts": As the first pope from the Americas, Francis personifies the 80 percent of Catholics who live outside Europe. As the first Jesuit pope—from the religious order known for education—he stands for spreading the faith through teaching. And as the first Francis—named after St. Francis of Assisi—he calls to mind that medieval friar's efforts to return a corrupt church to simple Christian values of poverty and humility. In addition, Francis is in the unusual position of sharing the world stage with "pope emeritus" Benedict XVI (who decided to retire rather than die in office).

Born in 1936, Francis grew up in Buenos Aires in a family of working-class Italian immigrants. He worked as a chemist and a high-school teacher before entering the priesthood. Ordained a Jesuit in 1969, he eventually rose to become archbishop of Buenos Aires. He first came to the world's attention in 2005, when he was the runner-up in the election of Pope Benedict. While bishop in Argentina, he worked in the worst of slums and denounced (though some say not loudly enough) Argentina's bloody dictatorship during the Dirty War of the 1970s.

PAPA FRANCESCO

Now a resident of Vatican City, Francis lives simply, staying in a Vatican guesthouse rather than the official papal apartments overlooking St. Peter's Square. He reportedly eats leftovers. When people talk about Francis, the word that comes up time and again is "dialogue." He's known for listening to every point of view, whether mediat-

The Apse

Bernini's ❽ **dove window** shines above the smaller front altar used for everyday services. The Holy Spirit, in the form of a six-foot-high dove, pours sunlight onto the faithful through the alabaster windows, turning into artificial rays of gold and reflecting off swirling gold clouds, angels, and winged babies. During a service, real sunlight passes through real clouds of incense, mingling with Bernini's sculpture. This is the epitome of Baroque—an ornate, mixed-media work designed to overwhelm the viewer. (By the way, as the basilica faces west, rather than the standard east, late in the day the light of the setting sun pours through the alabaster window.)

ing between dictators and union leaders, sitting down with the Orthodox Patriarch, celebrating Rosh Hashanah with Jews, visiting a mosque, or speaking well of gays and atheists. In Argentina, he was often seen sharing *mate* (the national tea) with people of every stripe. At the Vatican, his management style stresses the collegiality of the cardinals. He speaks a number of languages, including fluent Italian—the language of his parents and of the Vatican. As Francis himself has pointed out, the original Latin word for pope—"*pontifex*"—literally means "bridge builder."

But Francis is not a liberal. He strongly defends traditional Catholic beliefs. No one expects major shifts under Francis in the Church's positions on abortion, gay marriage, contraception, or the celibate, male-only priesthood. He inherited a Catholic Church with many problems: financial shenanigans, charges that they've protected pedophile priests, and alleged blackmailing of gay priests. And though the Catholic religion is growing worldwide, its home base—Europe—is becoming increasingly secular.

As pope, Francis has made it clear that he wants the Church to focus less on money and power, and more on the poor and the outcast. Francis is skeptical of globalization, worldliness, and unchecked capitalism, with the economic inequality they bring. He's well aware that many of Rome's homeless people camp out right by the basilica. (In fact, Francis—making a point to walk the talk—has opened up a service center just off St. Peter's Square where the local homeless can get a haircut, shower, and use the toilet.) One of his favorite Christian rituals is to literally kneel down before the poor, sick, or imprisoned, and wash their feet. Francis' personal credo, "Miserando atque eligendo," focuses on how God shows "mercy"—*miserando*—and compassion by forgiving sinners and helping the downtrodden.

Beneath the dove is the centerpiece of this structure, the so-called **Throne of St. Peter,** an oak chair built in medieval times for a king. Subsequently, it was encrusted with tradition and encased in bronze by Bernini as a symbol of papal authority. Statues of four early Church Fathers support the chair, a symbol of how bishops should support the pope in troubled times—like the Counter-Reformation.

Remember that St. Peter's is a church, not a museum. In the apse, Mass is said daily for pilgrims, tourists, and Roman citizens alike (for Mass times, see "Church Services" on page 214). Wooden confessional booths are available in the north transept (to the right of the main altar) for Catholics to tell their sins to a listening ear and receive forgiveness and peace of mind (daily, usually mornings and late afternoons). The faithful renew their faith, and the faithless gain inspiration. Look at the light streaming through the windows, turn and gaze up into the dome, and quietly contemplate your deity (or lack thereof).

• *To the left of the main altar is the* **south transept.** *It may be roped off for worship, but anyone can step past the guard if you say you're there "for prayer." At the far end, left side, find the dark "painting" of St. Peter crucified upside down.*

❾ Peter's Crucifixion Site

This marks the exact spot (according to tradition) where Peter was killed 1,900 years ago. Peter had come to the world's greatest city to preach Jesus' message of love to the pagan, often hostile Romans. During the reign of Emperor Nero, he was arrested and brought to Nero's Circus so all of Rome could witness his execution. When the authorities told Peter he was to be crucified just like his Lord, Peter said, essentially, "I'm not worthy" and insisted they nail him on the cross upside down.

The Romans were actually quite tolerant of other religions, but they required their conquered peoples to worship the Roman emperor as a god. For most religions, this was no problem, but monotheistic Christians re-fused to worship the emperor even when they were burned alive, crucified, or thrown to the lions. Their bravery, optimism in suffering, and message of love struck a chord among slaves and members of the lower classes. The religion started by a poor carpenter grew, de-spite the occasional persecution of minorities by fanatical emperors. In three short centuries, Christianity went from a small Jewish sect in Jerusalem to the official religion of the world's greatest empire.

This and all the other "paintings" in the church are actually mosaic copies made from thousands of colored chips the size of your little fingernail. Because smoke and humidity would damage real paintings, since about 1600 church officials have replaced the paintings with mosaics (a.k.a. the "art of eternity") produced by the Vatican Mosaic Studio. Around the corner on the right (head-ing back toward the central nave), pause at the mosaic copy of Ra-phael's epic painting of ❿ *The Transfiguration.* The original is now beautifully displayed in the Pinacoteca of the Vatican Museums.

• *Back near the entrance of the church, in the far corner, behind bullet-proof glass, is the sculpture everyone has come to see, the...*

⓫ *Pietà*

Michelangelo was 24 years old when he completed this *pietà*—a

Bernini Blitz

Nowhere is there such a conglomeration of works by the flamboyant genius who remade this church—and the city—in the Baroque style. Here's your scavenger-hunt list. You have 20 minutes. Go!

1. St. Peter's Square: design and statues
2. Constantine equestrian relief (right end of atrium)
3. Decoration (stucco, gold leaf, marble, etc.) of side aisles (flanking nave)
4. Tabernacle (the temple-like receptacle) inside Blessed Sacrament Chapel
5. Much of the marble floor throughout church
6. Bronze canopy (*baldacchino*) over main altar
7. St. Longinus statue (holding a lance) near main altar
8. Balconies (above each of the four statues ringing main altar) with corkscrew columns
9. Dove window, bronze sunburst, angels, "Throne," and Church Fathers (in apse)
10. Tomb of Pope Urban VIII (far end of apse, right side)
11. Tomb of Pope Alexander VII (between apse and left transept, over a doorway, with the gold skeleton smothered in jasper poured like maple syrup)

Bizarre...Baroque...Bernini.

representation of Mary with the body of Christ taken from the cross. It was Michelangelo's first major commission (by the French ambassador to the Vatican), done for Holy Year 1500.

In Italian, *pietà* means "pity." Michelangelo, with his total mastery of the real world, captures the sadness of the moment. Mary cradles her crucified son in her lap. Christ's lifeless right arm drooping down lets us know how heavy this corpse is. His smooth skin is accented by the rough folds of Mary's robe. Mary tilts her head down, looking at her dead son with sad tenderness. Her left hand turns upward, asking, "How could they do this to you?"

Michelangelo didn't think of sculpting as creating a figure, but as simply freeing the God-made figure from the prison of marble around it. He'd attack a project like this with an inspired passion, chipping away to find what God had placed inside.

The bunched-up shoulder and rigor-mortis legs show that Michelangelo learned well from his studies of cadavers. But realistic as this work is, its true power lies in the subtle "unreal" features. Life-size Christ looks childlike compared with larger-than-life Mary, which accentuates the impression of Mary enfolding Jesus in her maternal love. Mary—the mother of a 33-year-old man—looks like a teenager (she would have been about 50), emphasizing how she was the eternally youthful "handmaiden" of the Lord, always serving him, even at this moment of supreme sacrifice. She accepts God's will, even if it means giving up her son.

The statue is a solid pyramid of maternal tenderness. Yet within this, Christ's body tilts diagonally down to the right and Mary's hem flows with it. Subconsciously, we feel the weight of this dead God sliding from her lap to the ground.

In 1972, a madman with a hammer entered St. Peter's and began hacking away at the *Pietà*. The damage was repaired, but that's why there's now a shield of bulletproof glass in front of the sculpture.

This is Michelangelo's only signed work. The story goes that he overheard some pilgrims praising his finished *Pietà,* but attributing it to a second-rate sculptor from a lesser city. He was so enraged that he grabbed his chisel and chipped "Michelangelo Buonarroti of Florence did this" in the ribbon running down Mary's chest.

On your right (covered in gray concrete with a gold cross) is the back side of the Holy Door. It will next be opened in 2025, the next Jubilee Year. If there's a prayer inside you, ask that St. Peter's will no longer need security checks or bulletproof glass when this door is next opened.

• *In the chapel to the left is the...*

⑫ Tomb of Pope John Paul II

John Paul II (1920-2005) was one of the most beloved popes of recent times. During his papacy (1978-2005), he was the highly visible face of the Catholic Church as it labored to stay relevant in an increasingly secular world. The first non-Italian pope in four centuries, he traveled widely. He was the first pope to visit a mosque and a synagogue. He oversaw the fall of communism in his native Poland. He survived an assassination attempt, and he publicly endured his slow decline from Parkinson's disease with great stoicism.

When John Paul II died in 2005, hundreds of thousands lined up outside the church, waiting up to 24 hours to pay their respects. At his funeral in St. Peter's Square, the crowd began chanting "*Santo subito, santo subito!*" insisting he be made a saint (*santo*) right now (*subito*).

They didn't have to wait long—he was sainted in April 2014, just nine years after his death...lightspeed by Vatican standards.

The tomb has no monument—just a simple stone slab with the inscription *Ioannes Paulus PP. II (1920-2005)*. St. John Paul II lies beneath a painting of the steadfast St. Sebastian—the martyr who calmly suffered the slings and arrows of outrageous Romans. Sebastian was John Paul's favorite saint. There's also a plaque in the floor on the opposite side of the church honoring the man. Of 260-plus popes, two have been given the title "Great." That elite group may soon grow by 50 percent, as there's talk of calling him "John Paul the Great."

⓭ Blessed Sacrament Chapel (Capella di Santissimo Sacramento)

You're welcome to step through the metalwork gates into this oasis of peace reserved for prayer and meditation. Mass is sometimes said here. The chapel is located on the right-hand side of the church, about midway to the altar.

⓮ Treasury Museum (Museo-Tesoro)

The museum, located on the left side of the nave near the altar, contains the room-size tomb of Sixtus IV by Antonio Pollaiuolo, a big pair of Roman pincers used to torture Christians, an original corkscrew column from Old St. Peter's, and assorted jewels, papal robes, and golden reliquaries—a marked contrast to the poverty of early Christians.

OTHER SIGHTS AT THE CHURCH
Crypt (Grotte/Tombe)

Visitors can go down to the foundations of Old St. Peter's, containing tombs of popes and memorial chapels. In summer, the crypt entrance is usually beside the statue of St. Andrew, to the left of the main altar; in winter, it's by the cupola entrance. Stairs lead you down to the floor level of the previous church, where you'll pass the sepulcher of Peter. This lighted niche with an icon is not Peter's actual tomb, but part of a shrine that stands atop Peter's tomb. Nearby is the chapel where Pope John Paul II was buried before being moved upstairs in 2011. Next are the tombs of past popes, including the traditionalist Paul VI (1897-1978), who suffered reluctantly through the church's modernization. Finally, you can see a few column fragments from Old St. Peter's (a.k.a. "Basilica Costantiniana"). Continue your one-way visit until it spills you out, usually near the checkroom.

The walk through the crypt is free and quick (15 minutes)—but you won't see St. Peter's original grave unless you take a *Scavi* (excavations) tour—see "Tours" on page 214.

Up to the Dome (Cupola)

A good way to finish a visit to St. Peter's is to go up to the dome for the best view of Rome anywhere. The ⓯ **entrance to the dome**

is along the right (north) side of the church, but the line begins to form out front, at the church's right door (as you face the church). Look for *cupola* signs.

There are two levels: the rooftop of the church and the very top of the dome. Climb or take an elevator to the first level, on the church roof just above the facade. From the roof, you have a commanding view of St. Peter's Square, the statues on the colonnade, Rome across the Tiber in front of you, and the dome itself—almost terrifying in its nearness—looming behind you. (Depending on the routing when you visit, you might see this view from the roof only after descending from the dome.)

From the roof, you can also go inside the gallery ringing the interior of the dome and look down inside the church. Notice the dusty top of Bernini's seven-story-tall canopy far below. Study the mosaics up close—and those huge letters! It's worth the elevator ride for this view alone.

From this level, if you're energetic, continue all the way up to the top of the dome. The staircase actually winds between the outer shell and the inner one. It's a sweaty, crowded, claustrophobic 15-minute, 323-step climb, but worth it. The view from the summit is great, the fresh air even better. Admire the arms of Bernini's colonnade encircling St. Peter's Square. Find the big, white Victor Emmanuel Monument, with the two statues on top; and the Pantheon, with its large, light, shallow dome. The large rectangular building to the left of the obelisk is the Vatican Museums complex, stuffed with art. Survey the Vatican grounds, with its minitrain system and lush gardens. Look down into the square at the tiny pilgrims buzzing like electrons around the nucleus of Catholicism.

VATICAN
MUSEUMS
TOUR

Musei Vaticani

The glories of the ancient world displayed in a lavish papal palace, decorated by the likes of Michelangelo and Raphael...the Musei Vaticani. A conglomerate of many submuseums, the Vatican Museums hold some of the greatest art anywhere. Unfortunately, many tourists see these collections only as an obstacle between them and the grand finale, the Sistine Chapel. True, this huge, confusing, and crowded megamuseum can be a jungle—but with this book as your vine, you should swing through with ease, enjoying the highlights and getting to the Sistine just before you collapse.

With the Fall of Rome (A.D. 476), the Catholic ("universal") Church became the great preserver of civilization, collecting artifacts from cultures dead and dying. Renaissance popes (15th and 16th centuries) collected most of what we'll see, using it as furniture to decorate their palace (today's museum). Combining the classical and Christian worlds, they found the divine in the creations of man.

We'll concentrate on classical sculpture and Renaissance painting. But along the way (and there's a lot of along-the-way here), we'll stop to leaf through a few yellowed pages from this 5,000-year-old scrapbook of humankind.

The always crowded museum has an online reservation system and a website with up-to-date hours and information. For more on Vatican City, the small, independent country where this museum is located, see page 212.

Orientation

Cost: €16, €4 online reservation fee, free on the last Sun of each month (when it's very crowded).

Hours: Mon-Sat 9:00-18:00, last entry at 16:00 (the staff starts ushering you out at 17:30). Closed Sun, except last Sun of the month, when it's open 9:00-14:00, last entry at 12:30. Open Fri nights May-July and Sept-Oct 19:00-23:00 (last entry at 21:30) by online reservation only; note that during evening visits, parts of the museum—including the Pinacoteca—are often closed.

The museum is closed on many holidays (mainly religious ones), including, for 2017: Jan 1 (New Year's), Jan 6 (Epiphany), Feb 11 (Vatican City established), March 19 (St. Joseph's Day), April 16 and 17 (Easter Sunday/Monday), May 1 (Labor Day), June 29 (Sts. Peter and Paul), Aug 15 (Assumption of the Virgin), Nov 1 (All Saints' Day), Dec 8 (Immaculate Conception), and Dec 25 and 26 (Christmas). Because changes in hours and other holiday closures may occur, always check the current hours and calendar at http://mv.vatican.va.

Individual rooms may close at odd hours, especially in the afternoon. The rooms described here are usually open.

Reservations: The Vatican Museums can be extremely crowded, with waits of up to two hours to buy tickets (figure about a 10-minute wait for every 100 yards in line). Bypass the long ticket lines by reserving an entry time at http://mv.vatican.va for €20 (€16 ticket plus €4 booking fee). It's easy. Just choose your day and time, then check your email for your confirmation and print out

the voucher. At the Vatican Museums, bypass the ticket-buying line and queue up at the "Visitor Entrance with Online Reservations" line (to the right). Show your voucher to the guard and go in. Once inside the museum, present your voucher at a ticket window *(cassa),* either in the lobby or upstairs, and they'll issue your ticket. Even with a reservation, read "When to Go," next.

When to Go: Except in winter, the museum is generally hot and crowded, with long ticket lines and shoulder-to-shoulder sightseeing through much of it. The worst days are Saturdays, the last Sunday of the month (when it's free), Mondays, rainy days, and any day before or after a holiday closure. Mornings are most crowded. The best (or least-worst) time to visit is a weekday after 14:00—the later the better. Another good time is during the papal audience on Wednesday morning, when many tourists are at St. Peter's Square (the only drawback is that St. Peter's Basilica is closed until roughly 13:00, as is the exit to it from the Sistine Chapel—described later, under "Museum Strategies").

More Line-Beating Tips: If you didn't book tickets in advance, you have a few other line-avoiding options. Booking a **guided tour** (described later, under "Tours") gets you right in—just show the guard your voucher.

You can often buy **same-day tickets** without a ticket-buying line at the Vatican TI in St. Peter's Square (€20; to the left, as you face the basilica). If you're going to St. Peter's Basilica first, you can normally buy Vatican Museums tickets in the narthex (€25). The Opera Romana Pellegrinaggi (a.k.a., Roma Cristiana), a private pilgrimage tour company, also sells same-day tickets (€27.50, entrances almost hourly, office in front of St. Peter's Square, Piazza Pio XII 9, tel. 06-6980-6380, www.operaromanapellegrinaggi.org). Hawkers peddling skip-the-line access swarm the Vatican area, offering tours with guides of varying quality—museum staff advise against accepting their offers.

Dress Code: Modest dress is required (no shorts, above-knee skirts, or bare shoulders). This dress code is strictly enforced here, at St. Peter's Basilica, and throughout Vatican City.

Getting There: The Ottaviano Metro stop is a 10-minute walk from the entrance. Bus #49 from Piazza Cavour/Castel Sant'Angelo stops at Piazza Risorgimento and continues right to the entrance. Bus #23 from Trastevere hugs the west bank of the Tiber and stops on Via Leone IV, just downhill from the entrance. Bus #492 heads from the city center past Piazza Risorgimento and the Vatican walls, and also stops on Via Leone IV. Bus #64 stops on the other side of St. Peter's Square, a 15 to 20-minute walk (facing the church from the obelisk, take a right through the colonnade and follow the Vatican Wall). Or take a taxi from the city center—they are reasonable (hop in and say, "moo-ZAY-ee vah-tee-KAH-nee").

Getting In: Make sure you get in the right entry line. Generally, individuals without tickets line up against the Vatican City wall (to the left of the entrance as you face it), and reservation holders (both individuals and groups) enter on the right. All visitors must pass through a metal detector (no pocketknives allowed).

Information: As you enter the main lobby of the museum, an info desk is to your left, and TV screens list which rooms are open or closed. Bookstores are scattered throughout the museum, and many exhibits have English explanations. You can virtually tour the Sistine Chapel ceiling at www.vatican.va (click on "Basilicas and Papal Chapels"). Info tel. 06-6988-3860, http://mv.vatican.va.

Tours: A €7 **audioguide** is available at the top of the spiral ramp/escalator, and can be prepaid when you book tickets online. No ID is required to rent an audioguide, and you can drop it off either where you rented it or after leaving the Sistine Chapel if taking the shortcut to St. Peter's (described later, under "Museum Strategies"). Confirm the drop-off location when renting.

🎧 Download my free Vatican Museums and Sistine Chapel **audio tours.**

The Vatican offers **guided tours** in English that are easy to book on their website (€32, includes admission). As with individual ticket reservations, present your confirmation voucher to a guard to the right of the entrance; then, once inside, go to the Guided Tours desk (in the lobby, up a few stairs).

For a list of **private tour** companies and guides, see page 30.

Length of This Tour: Until you expire, the museum closes, or 2.5 hours pass, whichever comes first. If you're short on time, see the octagonal courtyard *(Laocoön),* then follow the crowd flow directly to the Sistine Chapel, sightseeing along the way. From the Sistine Chapel, head straight to St. Peter's via the shortcut, if open (see "Museum Strategies," below).

Services: The museum's "checkroom" (to the right after security) takes only bigger bags, not day bags. The post office, with stamps that make collectors drool, is upstairs. WCs are mainly at the entrance/exit, plus a few scattered within the collection.

Museum Strategies: The museum has two exits. The **main exit** is near the entrance. Use this one if you're asked to return an audioguide there or if you plan on following this self-guided tour exactly as laid out, visiting the Pinacoteca at the end.

The other exit is a handy (but sometimes closed) **shortcut** that leads from the Sistine Chapel directly to St. Peter's Basilica (spilling out alongside the church; see map on page 240). The shortcut saves you a 30-minute walk backtracking to the basilica's main entrance and lets you avoid the often-long security line there. Officially, this exit is for Vatican guides and their groups only. However, it's often open to anyone (depending on how crowded the chapel is and how the guards feel). It's worth a shot (try blending in with a group that's leaving), but be prepared for the possibility that you won't get through.

Photography: No photos allowed in the Sistine Chapel, but photos without flash are permitted elsewhere.

Cuisine Art: A **$** self-service cafeteria is inside, near the Pinacoteca. Smaller **$$** cafés are in the outdoor Cortile della Pigna and near the Sistine Chapel. All offer mediocre food at inflated prices. Cheaper choices outside the museum include nearby supermarkets and the great Mercato Trionfale produce market on Via Andrea Doria, three blocks north of the entrance (head across the street, down the stairs, and continue straight). Inexpensive *pizza rustica* shops selling pizza by the slice line Viale Giulio Cesare and Via Candia, and good restaurants are nearby (see page 383).

Starring: World history, a pope's palace, Michelangelo, Raphael, *Laocoön,* the Greek masters, and their Roman copyists.

The Tour Begins

This heavyweight museum is shaped like a barbell—two buildings connected by a long hall. The entrance building covers the ancient world (Egypt, Greece, Rome). The one at the far end covers its "rebirth" in the Renaissance (including the Sistine Chapel). The halls there and back are a mix of old and new. Move quickly—don't burn out before the Sistine Chapel, near the end of this tour—and see how each civilization borrows from and builds on the previous one.

• *Leave Italy by entering the doors.*

Once you clear the security checkpoint, exchange your printed voucher (on the ground floor) or buy your ticket (upstairs). Scan your ticket at the turnstiles, then take the long escalator or spiral ramp up, up, up to a glass-covered courtyard.

Pause at the courtyard and get your bearings: The audioguide kiosk is here. To your right are the cafeteria and the Pinacoteca painting gallery. To your left is the beginning of our tour.

• *To start, go left, then take another left up a flight of marble stairs to reach the first-floor Egyptian rooms (Museo Gregoriano Egizio). Enter, and don't stop until you find your mummy.*

Note: *Occasionally, the stairs up to Egypt are closed off, and crowds are routed through a spacious open-air courtyard, the Cortile della Pigna (see map). Just keep following the masses until you reach a much smaller octagonal courtyard with the* Apollo Belvedere *and* Laocoön *figures. Tour the museum from there to the "Sarcophagi," where you'll find the entrance to the Egyptian rooms.*

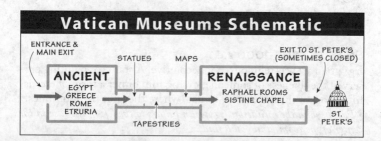

Vatican Museums Schematic

ENTRANCE & MAIN EXIT

STATUES   MAPS

EXIT TO ST. PETER'S (SOMETIMES CLOSED)

ANCIENT
EGYPT
GREECE
ROME
ETRURIA

RENAISSANCE
RAPHAEL ROOMS
SISTINE CHAPEL

TAPESTRIES

ST. PETER'S

VATICAN MUSEUMS

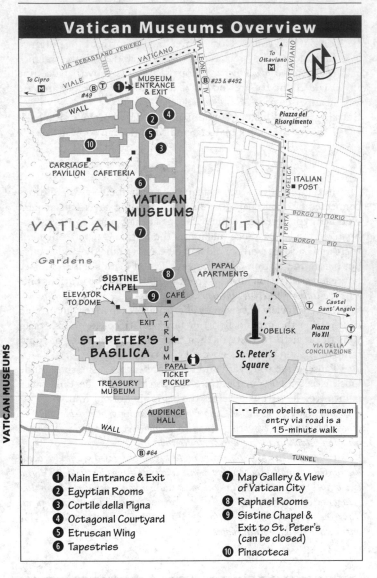

Vatican Museums Overview

1. Main Entrance & Exit
2. Egyptian Rooms
3. Cortile della Pigna
4. Octagonal Courtyard
5. Etruscan Wing
6. Tapestries
7. Map Gallery & View of Vatican City
8. Raphael Rooms
9. Sistine Chapel & Exit to St. Peter's (can be closed)
10. Pinacoteca

Ancient Wing

EGYPT (3000-1000 B.C.)

Egyptian art was religious, not decorative. A statue or painting preserved the likeness of someone, giving him or her a form of eternal life. Most of the art was for tombs, where they put the mummies.

• *Pass beyond the imitation Egyptian pillars to the left of the case in the center of the room, and you'll find...*

Mummies

This woman died three millennia ago. Her corpse was disemboweled, and her organs were placed in a jar like those you see near

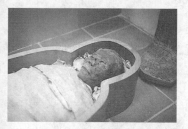

by. Then the body was refilled with pitch, dried with natron (a natural sodium carbonate), wrapped in linen, and placed in a wood coffin, which went inside a stone coffin, which was placed in a tomb. (Remember that the pyramids were just big tombs.) Notice the henna job on her hair—in the next life, your spirit needed a body to be rooted to...and you wanted to look your best.

Painted inside the coffin lid is a list of what the deceased "packed" for the journey to eternity. The coffins were decorated with magical spells to protect the body from evil and to act as crib notes for the confused soul in the netherworld. In nearby cases are *shahtis*, small figurines of the deceased placed inside the tomb.

• *In the next room are...*

Egyptian Statues

Egyptian statues walk awkwardly, as if they're carrying heavy buckets, with arms straight down at their sides. Even these Roman reproductions (made for Hadrian's Villa) are stiff, two-dimensional, and schematic—the art is only realistic enough to get the job done. In Egyptian belief, a statue like this could be a stable refuge for the wandering soul of a dead person. Each was made according to an established set of proportions. Little changed over the centuries—these statues had a function, and they worked.

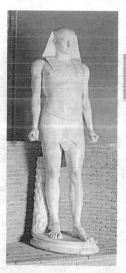

• *Walk through the next small room and into the curved hallway, and look for...*

Various Egyptian Gods as Animals

Before technology made humans top dogs on earth, it was easier to appreciate our fellow creatures. Egyptians saw the superiority of animals and worshipped them as incarnations of the gods. Wander through a pet store of Egyptian animal gods. In the small room, by the big win-

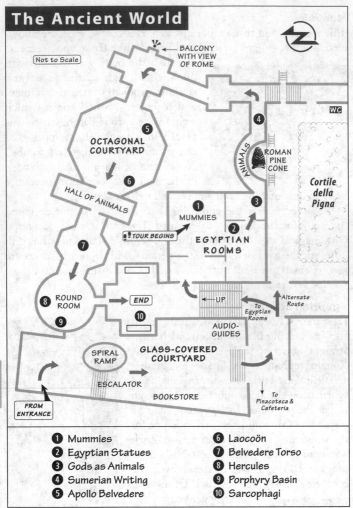

The Ancient World

Not to Scale

BALCONY
WITH VIEW
OF ROME

WC

OCTAGONAL
COURTYARD

ANIMALS

ROMAN
PINE
CONE

Cortile
della
Pigna

HALL OF ANIMALS

❶ MUMMIES

📱 TOUR BEGINS

EGYPTIAN
ROOMS

❷
❸
❹
❺
❻

❼

ROUND
ROOM

❽
❾

END

❿

UP

←
To
Egyptian
Rooms

Alternate
Route

AUDIO-
GUIDES

SPIRAL
RAMP

GLASS-COVERED
COURTYARD

ESCALATOR

BOOKSTORE

FROM
ENTRANCE

To
Pinacoteca &
Cafeteria

VATICAN MUSEUMS

❶ Mummies
❷ Egyptian Statues
❸ Gods as Animals
❹ Sumerian Writing
❺ Apollo Belvedere

❻ Laocoön
❼ Belvedere Torso
❽ Hercules
❾ Porphyry Basin
❿ Sarcophagi

dow, find Anubis, a jackal in a toga. In the curved room, find the lioness, the fierce goddess Sekhmet. The clever baboon is the god of wisdom, Thoth. At the end of the curved hall on your right is Bes (the small white marble statue), the patron of pregnant women (and beer-bellied men).

• *Continue into the darkened wing and proceed to the third room (Room VIII), pausing at the glass case, which contains small, brown clay tablets.*

Sumerian Writing

Even before Egypt, civilizations flourished in the Middle East. The Sumerian culture in Mesopotamia (the ancestors of the ancient Babylonians and of today's Iraqis) invented writing in about

3000 B.C. People wrote on clay tablets by pressing into the wet clay with a wedge-shaped (cuneiform) pen. The Sumerians also rolled cylindrical seals into soft clay to make an impression that authenticated documents and marked property.

• *Pass through the next room, and then turn left, to a balcony with a view of Rome through the window. You're in what was originally the Belvedere Palace—the pope's summer palace, on a hill, with a breeze and fine views.*

GREEK AND ROMAN SCULPTURE
(500 B.C.-A.D. 500)

This palace wouldn't be here, this sculpture wouldn't be here, and our lives would likely be quite different if it weren't for a few thousand Greeks in a small city about 450 years before Christ. Athens set the tone for the rest of the West. Democracy, theater, economics, literature, and art all flourished in Athens during a 50-year "Golden Age." Greek culture was then appropriated by Rome, and revived again 1,500 years later, during the Renaissance. The Renaissance popes built and decorated these papal palaces, re-creating the glory of the classical world.

• *Enter the **Octagonal Courtyard**. In 1506, the Vatican Museums were born here as a place for popes to entertain VIPs and guests with their fine collection of art. The galleries opened to the public around 1800 but then closed in the 1870s feud that followed modern Italy's unification. The museums opened to the public again in 1932.*

Find the statue of Apollo Belvedere, on your left as you enter.

Apollo Belvedere

Apollo, the god of the sun and of music, is hunting. He's been running through the woods, and now he spots his prey. Keeping his

eye on the animal, he slows down and prepares to put a (missing) arrow into his (missing) bow. The optimistic Greeks conceived of their gods in human form...and buck naked.

This Apollo is a Roman copy (2nd century A.D.) of a Hellenistic original that followed the style of the great Greek sculptor Praxiteles. It fully captures the beauty of the human form. The anatomy is perfect, his pose is natural. Instead of standing at attention, face-forward with his arms at his sides (Egyptian-style), Apollo is on the move, coming to rest with his weight on one leg.

The Greeks loved balance. A well-rounded man was both a thinker and an athlete, a poet and a warrior. In art, the *Apollo Belvedere* balances several opposites. He's moving, but not out of control. Apollo eyes his target, but hasn't attacked yet. He's realistic, but with idealized, godlike features. And the smoothness of his muscles is balanced by the rough folds of his cloak. The only sour note: his left hand, added in modern times. Could we try a size smaller?

During the Renaissance, when this Roman copy was discovered, it was considered the most perfect work of art in the world. The handsome face, eternal youth, and body that seems to float just above the pedestal made *Apollo Belvedere* seem superhuman, divine, and godlike, even for devout Christians. Remember this face when you see Jesus in Michelangelo's *Last Judgment* in the Sistine Chapel; clearly this Apollo inspired the artist.

• *In the neighboring niche to the right, a bearded old* **Roman river god** *lounges in the shade. This pose reappears in Michelangelo's* Adam *on the Sistine ceiling. While there are a few fancy bathtubs in this courtyard, most of the carved boxes you see are sarcophagi—Roman coffins and relic holders, carved with the deceased's epitaph in picture form.*

In the next niche is...

Laocoön

Laocoön (lay-AWK-oh-wahn), the high priest of Troy, warned his fellow Trojans: "Beware of Greeks bearing gifts." The attacking

Greeks had brought the Trojan Horse to the gates as a ploy to get inside the city walls, and Laocoön tried to warn his people not to bring it inside. But the gods wanted the Greeks to win, so they sent huge snakes to crush Laocoön and his two sons to death. We see them at the height of their terror, when they realize that, no matter how hard they struggle, they—and their entire race—are doomed. Laocoön's agonized face says it all: "Snakes...why'd it have to be snakes?"

The figures (carved from four blocks of marble pieced together seamlessly) are powerful, not light and graceful. The poses are as twisted as possible, accentuating every rippling muscle and bulging vein. Follow the line of motion from Laocoön's left foot, up his leg, through his body, and out his right arm (which some historians used to think extended straight out—until the elbow was dug up in the early 1900s). Goethe would stand here and blink his eyes rapidly, watching the statue flicker to life.

Laocoön was sculpted some four centuries after the Golden

Age (5th-4th century B.C.), after the scales of "balance" had been tipped. Whereas *Apollo* is a balance between stillness and motion, this is textbook Hellenism...unbridled motion. *Apollo* is serene, graceful, and godlike, while *Laocoön* is powerful, emotional, and gritty.

Laocoön—the most famous Greek statue in ancient Rome and considered "superior to all other sculpture or painting"—was lost for more than a thousand years. Then, in 1506, it was unexpectedly unearthed in the ruins of Nero's Golden House near the Colosseum. The discovery caused a sensation. It was cleaned off and paraded through the streets in front of an awestruck populace (before landing here and becoming the first piece of this collection). No one had ever seen anything like its motion and emotion, having been raised on a white-bread diet of pretty-boy *Apollo*s. One of those who saw it was the young Michelangelo, and it was a revelation to him. Two years later, he started work on the Sistine Chapel, and the Renaissance was about to take another turn.

• *Leave the courtyard to the right of* Laocoön *and pause at the **Hall of Animals** (on the left), a Hellenistic zoo of beasts real and surreal. These animals are all ancient statues restored in the 18th century during the Enlightenment. (Can you find the camel?) Then continue to the limbless torso in the middle of the next large hall.*

Belvedere Torso

My experience with sculpting statues ends with snowmen. But standing face-to-face with this hunk of shaped rock makes you

appreciate the sheer physical labor involved in chipping a figure out of solid stone. It takes great strength but, at the same time, great delicacy.

This is all that remains of an ancient statue of Hercules seated on a lion skin. Michelangelo loved this old rock. He knew that he was the best sculptor of his day. The ancients were his only peers—and his rivals. He'd caress this statue lovingly and tell people, "I am the pupil of the Torso." To him, it contained all the beauty of classical sculpture. But it's not beautiful. Compared with the pure grace of the *Apollo*, it's downright ugly.

But Michelangelo, an ugly man himself, was looking for a new kind of beauty—not the beauty of idealized gods, but the innate beauty of every person, even so-called ugly ones. With its knotty lumps of muscle, the Torso has a brute power and a distinct personality despite—or because of—its rough edges. Remember this Torso, because we'll see it again later on.

• *Enter the next, domed room.*

Round Room

This room, modeled on the Pantheon interior, gives some idea of Roman grandeur. Romans took Greek ideas and made them bigger, like the big bronze statue of Hercules with his club, found near the Theater of Pompey (by modern-day Campo de' Fiori). The mosaic floor you're standing on is 1,700 years old—it once decorated the bottom of a pool in an ancient Roman bath. The enormous Roman basin/hot tub/birdbath/vase decorated Nero's place. (It's so big that the room was built around it in the 18th century.) It was made of a single block of purple porphyry marble stone imported from Egypt. Purple was a rare, royal, expensive, and prestigious color in pre-Crayola days. This particular variety, called "imperial porphyry," came from a single mountain in Egypt and was the stone of emperors...and then of popes. Now that source is quarried out, and the only  "imperial porphyry" available to anyone has been recycled.

• *Enter the next room.*

Sarcophagi

These two large porphyry marble coffins were made (though not used) for the Roman emperor Constantine's mother (Helena, on  left) and daughter (Constanza, on right). Helena's coffin depicts a battle game showing dying victims in their barbarian dress. Constanza's is decorated with a mix of Christian and pagan themes. Helena and Constanza were Christians—and therefore outlaws—until Constantine made Christianity legal in A.D. 313, and they became saints. Both sarcophagi were quarried and worked in Egypt. The technique for working this extremely hard stone (a special tempering of metal was required) was lost after this, and porphyry marble was not chiseled again until Renaissance times in Florence.

• *See how we've come full circle in this building—the Egyptian Rooms are ahead on your left. Go upstairs and prepare for the Long March down the hall lined with statues, toward the Sistine Chapel and Raphael Rooms.*

Overachievers may first choose to pop into the Etruscan wing—labeled Museo Gregoriano Etrusco—*located a few steps up from the Long March level. (Others have permission to save their aesthetic energy for the Sistine.)*

THE ETRUSCANS (800-300 B.C.)

Room I

The chariot is from 550 B.C., when the crude Romans were ruled by their more civilized neighbors to the north—the Etruscans. (The wooden portions are a reconstruction.) Imagine the chariot racing around the dirt track of the Circus Maximus, through the marshy valley of the newly drained Forum, or up Capitoline Hill to the Temple of Jupiter—all originally built by Rome's Etruscan kings.

Room II

The golden breastplate (*Pectoral*, 650 B.C., immediately to the right), decorated with tiny winged figures and animals, shows off the sophistication of the Etruscans. Though unwarlike and politically decentralized, these people were able to "conquer" all of central Italy around 650 B.C. through trade, offering tempting metalwork goods like this.

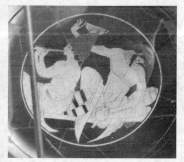

The Etruscan vases done in the Greek style remind us of the other great pre-Roman power—the Greek colonists who settled in southern Italy (Magna Graecia). The Etruscans traded with the Greeks, adopting their fashions. Rome, cradled between the two, grew up learning from both cultures.

A Greek-style bowl (far corner of the room) depicting a man and woman in bed together would have scandalized early Roman farmers. He's peeing in a chamber pot, she's blowing a flute. Etruscan art often showed husbands and wives at ease together, giving them a reputation among the Romans as immoral, flute-playing degenerates.

Room III

This bronze warrior (late 5th century B.C.), whose helmet was sawed off by lightning, has a rare inscription that's readable (on armor below the navel). It probably refers to the statue's former owner: "Aha! Trutitis gave [this] as [a] gift." Archaeologists understand the Etruscans' Greek-style alphabet and some individual words, but they've yet to fully crack the code. As you look around at beautiful bronze pitchers, candlesticks, shields, and urns, ponder yet another of Etruria's unsolved mysteries—no one is sure where these sophisticated people came from.

Room IV

Most of our knowledge of the Etruscans is from sarcophagi and art in Etruscan tombs. Their funeral art is solemn, but hardly morbid—check out the sarcopha-guy with the bulging belly, enjoying a banquet for all eternity.

The Etruscans' origins are obscure, but their legacy is clear. In 509 B.C., the Etruscan king's son raped a Roman noblewoman.

The king was thrown out, the republic was declared, Etruscan cities were conquered by Rome's legions, and their culture was swallowed up in Roman expansion. By Julius Caesar's time, the few remaining ethnic Etruscans were reduced to serving their masters as flute players, goldsmiths, surgeons, and street-corner preachers, like the one that Caesar brushed aside when he called out, "Beware the Ides of March..."

• *Browse the remaining dozen rooms of the Etruscan Wing, or backtrack to the long hall (the Gallery of the Candelabra) leading to the Sistine Chapel and Raphael Rooms.*

THE LONG MARCH—SCULPTURE, TAPESTRIES, MAPS, AND VIEWS

This quarter-mile walk gives you a sense of the scale that Renaissance popes built on. Remember, this building was originally a series of papal palaces. The popes loved beautiful things—statues, urns, marble floors, friezes, stuccoed ceilings—and, as heirs of imperial Rome, they felt they deserved such luxury. The palaces and art represent both the peak and the decline of the Catholic Church in Europe. It was extravagant spending like this that inspired Martin Luther to rebel, starting the Protestant Reformation.

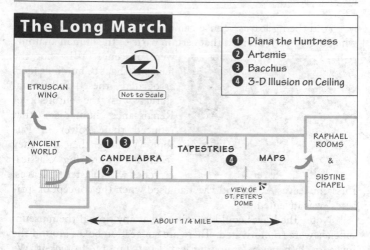

The Long March

Not to Scale

1. Diana the Huntress
2. Artemis
3. Bacchus
4. 3-D Illusion on Ceiling

ETRUSCAN WING

ANCIENT WORLD

1 **3** CANDELABRA
2

TAPESTRIES

4

MAPS

RAPHAEL ROOMS
&
SISTINE CHAPEL

VIEW OF ST. PETER'S DOME

← ABOUT 1/4 MILE →

Gallery of the Candelabra (Galleria dei Candelabri): Classical Sculpture

In the second "room" of the long hall, stop at the statue of **Diana the Huntress** on the left. Here, the virgin goddess goes hunting. Roman hunters would pray and give offerings to statues like this to get divine help in their search for food.

Farmers might pray to another version of the same goddess, in her guise as **Artemis,** on the opposite wall. This billion breasted beauty stood for fertility. "Boobs or bulls' balls?" Some historians say that bulls were sacrificed and castrated, with the testicles draped over the statues as symbols of fertility.

• *Shuffle along to the next "room," remembering that, while the statues seem white and lifeless today, originally they were colorfully painted and had inlaid eyes. On the left is* **Bacchus,** *with a baby on his shoulders.*

Fig Leaves

Why do the statues have fig leaves? Like Bacchus, many of these statues originally looked much different than they do now. First, they were painted, often in gaudy colors. Bacchus may have had brown hair, rosy cheeks, purple grapes, and a leopard-skin sidekick at his feet. Even the *Apollo Belvedere,* whose cool gray tones we now admire as "classic Greek austerity," may have had a paisley pink cloak for all we know. Also, many statues had glass eyes like Bacchus'.

VATICAN MUSEUMS

VATICAN MUSEUMS

And the fig leaves? Those came from the years 1550 to 1800, when the Church decided that certain parts of the human anatomy

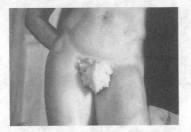

were obscene. (Why not the feet?) Perhaps Church leaders associated these full-frontal statues with the outbreak of Renaissance humanism that reduced their power in Europe. Whatever the cause, they reacted by covering classical crotches with plaster fig leaves, the same leaves Adam and Eve had used when the concept of "privates" was invented.

Note: The leaves could be removed at any time if the museum officials were so motivated. There are suggestion boxes around the museum. Whenever I see a fig leaf, I get the urge to pick-it. We could start an organ-ized campaign...

• *Cover your eyes in case they forgot a fig leaf or two, and continue to the...*

Tapestries

Along the left wall are tapestries designed by Raphael's workshop and made in Brussels (circa 1524). They show scenes from the life of Christ: Baby Jesus in the manger, being adored by shepherds, and presented in the temple. Farther along, the Resurrection tapestry, with Jesus striding out of the tomb, is curiously interactive...as you walk, Jesus' eyes, feet, knee, and even the stone slab follow you across the room. Next to it, *The Supper at Emmaus* (with Jesus sitting at a table) seems equally flexible.

Check out the beautiful sculpted reliefs on the ceiling. Admire the workmanship of this relief, then realize that it's not a relief at all—it's painted on a flat surface! Illusions like this were proof that painters had mastered the 3-D realism of ancient statues.

Map Gallery and View of Vatican City

This gallery still feels like a pope's palace. The crusted ceiling of colorful stucco and paint is pure papal splendor. The maps on the walls show the regions of Italy. Popes could take visitors on a tour of Italy, from the toe (entrance end) to the Alps (far end), with east Italy on the right wall, west on the left. These maps actually functioned as the official maps from 1582 (when they were painted) until the 19th century. Notice how parchments of towns were thumbtacked on. The scenes on the ceiling portray exciting mo-

ments in Church history in
each of those regions.

The windows give you
your best look at the tiny
country of Vatican City, officially established as an independent nation in 1929.
It has its own radio station,
as you see from the tower on
the hill. (Just in front of that radio tower is Pope-Emeritus Benedict XVI's residence—with the three green shutters. On nice afternoons, he can be seen strolling on his rooftop terrace.) What
you see here is pretty much all there is—these gardens, the palaces
you're in, and St. Peter's (for more on Vatican City, see the sidebar
on page 212).

If you have the chance to lean out and
look left, you'll see the dome of St. Peter's the
way Michelangelo would have liked you to see
it—without the bulky Baroque facade.

Near the end of the gallery (on the left) is
a map of Liguria. You can actually see the five
little towns of the Cinque Terre circa 1582 and
a chariot captained by Neptune himself as he
takes Columbus to the New World. The final
maps feature all of Italy in the 16th century
(left) and the Italian peninsula in ancient times
(right).

• *Exit the map room. At the end of the long hall
(or a couple of rooms later), you may have to choose between two routes
to the* Cappella Sistina. *One route makes a beeline to the Sistine. (Most
tired and rushed cruise groups take this one.) But for our tour, turn left,
toward the exquisite Raphael Rooms.*

Renaissance Wing

Papal Wallpaper

We've seen art from the ancient world; now we'll see its rebirth in
the Renaissance. We're entering the living quarters of the great
Renaissance popes—where they slept, worked, and worshiped.
The rooms reflect the grandeur of their position. They hired the
best artists—mostly from Florence—to paint the walls and ceilings, combining classical and Christian motifs.

Entering, you'll immediately see a huge 19th-century painting that depicts the Polish King Jan III Sobieski liberating Vienna
from the Ottomans in 1683, finally tipping the tide in favor of a
Christian Europe. See the Ottoman tents on the left and the spires

of Christian Vienna on the right. This is not by Raphael, but by **Jan Matejko,** a Polish painter who specialized in grand-scale historical epics like this one.

The second room's paintings celebrate the doctrine of the **Immaculate Conception,** establishing that Mary herself was born without sin. This medieval idea wasn't actually made dogma until a century ago. The largest fresco shows how the inspiration came straight from heaven (upper left) in a thin ray of light directly to the pope.

• *Next, you'll pass along an outside walkway that overlooks a courtyard (the parking lot for some of the 4,000 people who commute to work here daily), finally ending up in the first of the Raphael Rooms, the Constantine Room.*

RAPHAEL ROOMS
Constantine Room

These frescoes, painted between 1517 and 1524 (finished after Raphael's death by his assistants, notably Giulio Romano), celebrate the passing of the baton from one culture to the next. Remember, Rome was a pagan empire persecuting a new cult from the East—Christianity.

Then, on the night of October 27, A.D. 312 (left wall), as General Constantine (in gold, with crown) was preparing his troops for a coup d'état, he looked up and saw something strange. A cross appeared in the sky with the words, "You will conquer in this sign."

The next day (long wall), his troops raged victoriously into battle with the Christian cross atop their Roman eagle banners.

There's Constantine in the center with a smile on his face, slashing through the enemy, while God's warrior angels ride shotgun overhead.

Constantine even stripped (right wall) and knelt before the pope to be baptized a Christian (some say). As emperor, he legalized Christianity and worked hand in hand with the pope, although the document in which he supposedly "gave" Rome to the pope (window wall) was later shown to be a forgery. When Rome fell, its glory lived on

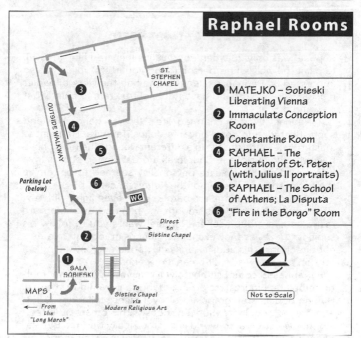

Raphael Rooms

ST. STEPHEN CHAPEL

OUTSIDE WALKWAY

Parking Lot
(below)

WC

Direct
to
Sistine Chapel

SALA SOBIESKI

MAPS

To
Sistine Chapel
via
Modern Religious Art

← From
the
"Long March"

1. MATEJKO – Sobieski Liberating Vienna
2. Immaculate Conception Room
3. Constantine Room
4. RAPHAEL – The Liberation of St. Peter (with Julius II portraits)
5. RAPHAEL – The School of Athens; La Disputa
6. "Fire in the Borgo" Room

Not to Scale

through the Dark Ages in the pomp, pageantry, and learning of the Catholic Church.

Look at the ceiling painting. A classical statue is knocked backward, crumbling before the overpowering force of the cross. Whoa! Christianity triumphs over pagan Rome. (This was painted, I believe, by Raphael's surrealist colleague, Salvadorus Dalio.)

• *Continue on. In the next room you'll reach a room with frescoes arching over the windows (Room of Heliodorus, 1512-1514). Block the sunlight with your hand to see...*

The Liberation of St. Peter

Peter, Jesus' right-hand man, was thrown into prison in Jerusalem for his beliefs. In the middle of the night, an angel appeared and res-cued him from the sleep-ing guards (Acts 12:5-12). The chains miraculously fell away (and were later brought to the St. Peter-in-Chains Church in Rome), and the angel led him to safety (right), while the guards took hell from their captain (left). This

Raphael (1483-1520)

Raphael was only 25 when Pope Julius II invited him, in 1508, to paint the walls of his personal living quarters. Julius was so impressed by Raphael's talent that he had the work of earlier masters scraped off and gave Raphael free rein to paint what he wanted.

Raphael lived a charmed life. He was handsome and sophisticated, and soon became Julius' favorite. He painted masterpieces effortlessly. In a different decade, he might have been thrown out of the Church as a great sinner, but his love affairs and devil-may-care personality seemed to epitomize the optimistic pagan spirit of the Renaissance.

Raphael's paintings are bathed in an even light, with few shadows; his brushwork is smooth and blended, and colors are restrained. In group scenes, Raphael wants you to follow his subjects' gazes as they exchange glances or look off in different directions. This adds a sense of motion and psychological tension to otherwise well-balanced scenes.

Raphael's compositions always have a strong geometric template. Figures are arranged into a pyramid or a circle. Human bodies are composed of oval faces, cylindrical arms, and arched shoulders. Subconsciously, this creates the feeling that God's created world is geometrically perfect. But Raphael always lets a bit of messy reality spill over the lines so his scenes don't appear static. While always graceful, his works are never lightweight or frilly—they're strong, balanced, and harmonious in the best Renaissance tradition. When he died, at just 37 years old, the High Renaissance died with him.

little "play" is neatly divided into three separate acts that make a balanced composition.

Raphael makes the miraculous event even more dramatic with the use of four kinds of light illuminating the dark cell—half-moonlight, the captain's torch, the radiant angel, and the natural light spilling through the museum's window. Raphael's mastery of realism, rich colors, and sense of drama made him understandably famous.

Find portraits of Pope Julius II in several paintings in this room. Julius was the man who commissioned Raphael to paint these rooms, who browbeat Michelangelo into doing the Sistine ceiling, and who started construction of St. Peter's. You can make out gray-bearded Julius in the role of Peter in *The Liberation*, seated on the left in *The Expulsion of Heliodorus* (on the wall to the right), and as the kneeling pope in *The Mass of Bolsena* (opposite the *Liberation*).

• *Enter the next room (Room of the Segnatura, 1508-1511). Here in the pope's private study, Raphael painted...*

The School of Athens

In both style and subject matter, this fresco sums up the spirit of the Renaissance, which was not only the rebirth of classical art, but a rebirth of learning, discovery, and the optimistic spirit that man is a rational creature. Raphael pays respect to the great thinkers and scientists of ancient Greece, gathering them together at one time in a mythical school setting.

In the center are Plato and Aristotle, the two greatest Greeks. Plato points up, indicating his philosophy that mathematics and pure ideas are the source of truth, while Aristotle gestures down,

showing preference for hands-on study of the material world. There's their master, Socrates (midway to the left, in green), ticking off arguments on his fingers. And in the foreground at right, bald Euclid bends over a slate to demonstrate a geometrical formula.

Raphael shows that Renaissance thinkers were as good as the ancients. There's Leonardo da Vinci, whom Raphael worshipped, in the role of Plato. Euclid is the architect Donato Bramante, who designed St. Peter's. Raphael himself (next to last on the far right, with the black beret) looks out at us. And the "school" building is actually an early version of St. Peter's Basilica (under construction at the time).

Raphael balances everything symmetrically—thinkers to the left, scientists to the right, with Plato and Aristotle dead center—showing the geometrical order found in the world. Look at the square floor tiles in the foreground. If you laid a ruler over them and extended the line upward, it would run right to the center of the picture. Similarly, the tops of the columns all point down to the middle. All the lines of sight draw our attention to Plato and Aristotle, and to the small arch over their heads—a halo over these two secular saints in the divine pursuit of knowledge.

While Raphael was painting this room, Michelangelo was at work down the hall in the Sistine Chapel. Raphael had just fin-

ished *The School of Athens* when he got a look at Michelangelo's powerful figures and dramatic scenes. He was astonished. From this point on, Raphael began to beef up his delicate, graceful style to a more heroic level. He returned to *The School of Athens* and added one more figure to the scene—Michelangelo, the brooding, melancholy figure in front, leaning on a block of marble.

• *On the opposite wall is...*

La Disputa

As if to underline the new attitude that pre-Christian philosophy and Church thinking could coexist, Raphael painted *La Disputa* facing *The School of Athens*.

Christ and the saints in heaven are overseeing a discussion of the Eucharist (the communion wafer) by mortals below. The classical-looking character in blue and gold looks out as if to say, "The pagans had their *School of Athens*, but we Christians (pointing up) have the School of Heaven." These rooms were the papal library, so themes featuring learning, knowledge, and debate were appropriate.

In Catholic terms, the communion wafer miraculously becomes the body of Christ when it's consecrated by a priest, bringing a little bit of heaven into the material world. Raphael's painting also connects heaven and earth, with descending circles: Jesus in a halo floats above a circle surrounding the dove of the Holy Spirit, which radiates down toward the round communion wafer on the altar. Balance and symmetry reign, from the angel trios in the upper corners to the books littering the floor. Find Dante wearing his poet's laureate in the lower right. (Hint: He's the guy on your €2 coin, modeled after this detail of *La Disputa*.)

Moving along, the last Raphael Room (called the **"Fire in the**

Borgo" Room, 1514-1517) shows work done mostly by Raphael's students, who were influenced by the bulging muscles and body-builder poses of Michelangelo.

• *Pause here—WCs are nearby. Next stop: the Sistine Chapel, just a five-minute walk away. Exit the final Raphael Room through a passageway, bear right, and go down the stairs.*

At the foot of the stairs you'll find several quiet rooms with benches. Have a seat and read ahead before entering the hectic Sistine Chapel.

When you're ready to tackle the Sistine, stroll through the extensive (and impressive) **Modern Religious Art** *collection, following signs to the chapel. Near the end of the modern collection (Room XXXVII and on), you'll pass religious paintings by modern masters—Chagall, Dalí, Bacon, and others.*

The Sistine Chapel

The Sistine Chapel contains Michelangelo's ceiling and his huge *Last Judgment.* The Sistine is the personal chapel of the pope and the place where new popes are elected. (The small, old-fashioned stove that burns pope-vote ballots—which sends out puffs of tell-tale smoke—is near today's shortcut exit.)

When Pope Julius II asked Michelangelo to take on this important project, he said, "No, *grazie."* Michelangelo insisted he

was a sculptor, not a painter. The Sistine ceiling was a vast undertaking, and he didn't want to do a half-vast job. But the pope pleaded, bribed, and threatened until Michelangelo finally consented, on the condition that he be able to do it all his own way.

Julius had asked for only 12 apostles along the sides of the ceiling, but Michelangelo had a grander vision—the entire history of the world until Jesus. He spent the next four years (1508-1512) craning his neck on scaffolding six stories up, covering the ceiling with frescoes of biblical scenes.

In sheer physical terms, it's an astonishing achievement: 5,900 square feet, with the vast majority done by his own hand. (Raphael

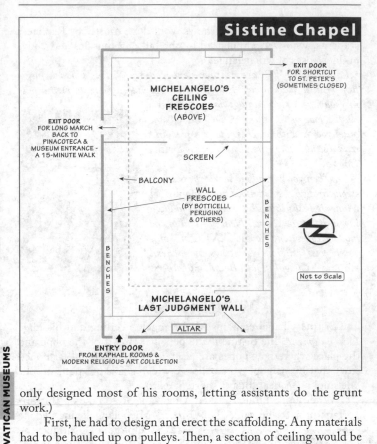

Sistine Chapel

EXIT DOOR
FOR SHORTCUT
TO ST. PETER'S
(SOMETIMES CLOSED)

MICHELANGELO'S
CEILING
FRESCOES
(ABOVE)

EXIT DOOR
FOR LONG MARCH
BACK TO
PINACOTECA &
MUSEUM ENTRANCE –
A 15-MINUTE WALK

SCREEN

BALCONY

WALL
FRESCOES
(BY BOTTICELLI,
PERUGINO
& OTHERS)

BENCHES

BENCHES

Not to Scale

BENCHES

MICHELANGELO'S
LAST JUDGMENT WALL

ALTAR

ENTRY DOOR
FROM RAPHAEL ROOMS &
MODERN RELIGIOUS ART COLLECTION

only designed most of his rooms, letting assistants do the grunt work.)

First, he had to design and erect the scaffolding. Any materials had to be hauled up on pulleys. Then, a section of ceiling would be plastered. With fresco—painting on wet plaster—if you don't get it right the first time, you have to scrape the whole thing off and start over. And if you've ever struggled with a ceiling light fixture or worked under a car for even five minutes, you know how heavy your arms get. The physical effort, the paint dripping in his eyes, the creative drain, and the mental stress from a pushy pope combined to almost kill Michelangelo.

But when the ceiling was finished and revealed to the public, it simply blew 'em away. Like the *Laocoön* statue discovered six years earlier, it was unlike anything seen before. It both caps the Renaissance and turns it in a new direction. In perfect Renaissance spirit, it mixes Old Testament prophets with classical figures. But the style is more dramatic, shocking, and emotional than the balanced Renaissance works before it. This is a very personal work—the Gospel according to Michelangelo—but its themes and subject matter are universal. Many art scholars contend that the Sistine ceiling is the single greatest work of art by any one human being.

The Sistine Schematic

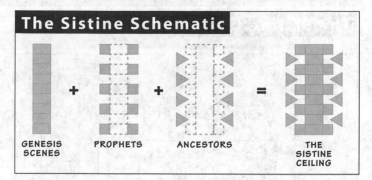

GENESIS SCENES + PROPHETS + ANCESTORS = THE SISTINE CEILING

THE SISTINE CEILING
Understanding What You're Standing Under

The ceiling shows the history of the world before the birth of Jesus. We see God creating the world, creating man and woman, destroying the earth by flood, and so on. God himself, in his purple robe, actually appears in the first five scenes. Along the sides (where the ceiling starts to curve), we see the Old Testament prophets and pagan Greek prophetesses who foretold the coming of Christ. Dividing these scenes and figures are fake niches (a painted 3-D illusion) decorated with nude statue-like figures with symbolic meaning.

The key is to see three simple divisions in the tangle of bodies:
1. The central spine of nine rectangular biblical scenes;
2. The line of prophets on either side; and
3. The triangles between the prophets showing the ancestors of Christ.

• *Ready? Within the chapel, try to find a seat along the side. Face the altar with the big* Last Judgment *on the wall—more on that later. (If you're using this book's diagram of the ceiling on page 260, follow the "how to use this diagram" instructions carefully.) Now look up to the ceiling and find the central panel of...*

The Creation of Adam

God and man take center stage in this Renaissance version of creation. Adam, newly formed in the image of God, lounges dreamily in perfect naked innocence. God, with his entourage, swoops in with a swirl of activity (which—with a little imagination—looks like a cross-section of a human brain...quite a strong humanist statement). Their reaching hands are the center of this work. Adam's is limp and passive; God's is strong and forceful, his finger twitching upward with energy. Here is the very moment of creation, as God passes the spark of life to man, the crowning work of his creation.

This is the spirit of the Renaissance. God is not a terrifying

The Sistine Ceiling

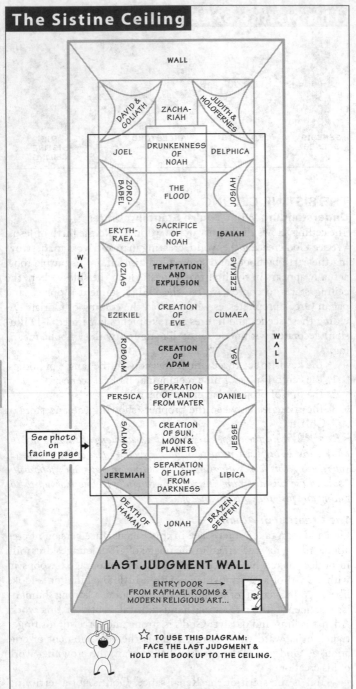

VATICAN MUSEUMS

WALL

DAVID & GOLIATH | ZACHARIAH | JUDITH & HOLOFERNES

JOEL | DRUNKENNESS OF NOAH | DELPHICA

ZORO-BABEL | THE FLOOD | JOSIAH

ERYTH-RAEA | SACRIFICE OF NOAH | ISAIAH

OZIAS | TEMPTATION AND EXPULSION | EZEKIAS

EZEKIEL | CREATION OF EVE | CUMAEA

ROBOAM | CREATION OF ADAM | ASA

PERSICA | SEPARATION OF LAND FROM WATER | DANIEL

SALMON | CREATION OF SUN, MOON & PLANETS | JESSE

JEREMIAH | SEPARATION OF LIGHT FROM DARKNESS | LIBICA

DEATH OF HAMAN | JONAH | BRAZEN SERPENT

WALL

WALL

See photo on facing page →

LAST JUDGMENT WALL

ENTRY DOOR →
FROM RAPHAEL ROOMS &
MODERN RELIGIOUS ART...

☆ TO USE THIS DIAGRAM:
FACE THE LAST JUDGMENT &
HOLD THE BOOK UP TO THE CEILING.

giant reaching down to puny and helpless man from way on high. Here they are on an equal plane, divided only by the diagonal bit of sky. God's billowing robe and the patch of green upon which Adam is lying balance each other. They are like two pieces of a jigsaw puzzle, or two long-separated continents, or like the yin and yang symbols finally coming together—uniting, complementing each other, creating wholeness. God and man work together in the divine process of creation.

• *This celebration of man permeates the ceiling. Notice the Adonises-come-to-life on the pedestals that divide the central panels.*

And then came woman.

The Garden of Eden

In one panel, we see two scenes from the Garden of Eden: *Temptation* and *Expulsion*. On the left is the leafy garden of paradise

where Adam and Eve lie around blissfully. But the devil comes along—a serpent with a woman's torso—and winds around the forbidden Tree of Knowledge. The temptation to gain new knowledge is too great for these Renaissance people. They eat the forbidden fruit.

At right, a sword-wielding angel drives them from Paradise into the barren plains. They're grieving, but they're far from helpless. Adam's body is thick and sturdy, and we know they'll survive in the cruel world. Adam firmly gestures to the angel, like he's saying, "All right, already! We're going!"

The Nine Scenes from Genesis

Take some time with these central scenes to understand the story that the ceiling tells. They run in sequence, starting at the front:

1. God, in purple, divides the light from darkness.
2. God creates the sun (burning orange) and the moon (pale white, to the right). Oops, I guess there's another moon.
3. God bursts toward us to separate the land and water.
4. God creates Adam.
5. God creates Eve, who dives into existence out of Adam's side.
6. Adam and Eve are tempted, then expelled, from the Garden of Eden.

7. Noah kills a ram and stokes the altar fires to make a sacrifice to God.

8. The great flood, sent by God, destroys the wicked, who desperately head for higher ground. In the distance, the ark carries Noah's family to safety. (The blank spot dates to 1793, when a nearby gunpowder depot exploded, shaking the building.)

9. Noah's sons see their drunken father. (Perhaps Michelangelo chose to end his work with this scene as a reminder that even the best of men are fallible.)

Prophets

You'll notice that the figures at the far end of the chapel are a bit smaller than those over *The Last Judgment*.

Michelangelo started at the far end, with the Noah scenes. By 1510, he'd finished the first half of the ceiling. When they took the scaffolding down and could finally see what he'd been working on for two years, everyone was awestruck—except Michelangelo. As powerful as his figures are, from the floor they didn't look dramatic enough for Michelangelo. For the other half, he pulled out all the stops.

Compare the Noah scenes (far end), with their many small figures, to the huge images of God at the other end. Similarly,

Isaiah (near the lattice screen, marked "Esaias") is stately and balanced, while Jeremiah ("Hieremias," in the corner by *The Last Judgment*) is a dark, brooding figure. This prophet who witnessed the destruction of Israel slumps his chin in his hand and ponders the fate of his people. Like the difference between the stately *Apollo Belvedere* and the excited *Laocoön*, Michelangelo added a new emotional dimension to Renaissance painting.

THE LAST JUDGMENT

When Michelangelo returned to paint the altar wall 23 years later (1535), the mood of Europe—and of the artist—was completely different. The Protestant Reformation had forced the Catholic Church to clamp down on free thought, and religious wars raged. Rome had recently been pillaged by roving bands of mercenaries.

The Renaissance spirit of optimism was fading. Michelangelo himself had begun to question the innate goodness of mankind.

It's Judgment Day, and Christ—the powerful figure in the center, raising his arm to spank the wicked—has come to find out who's naughty and who's nice. Beneath him, a band of angels blows its trumpets Dizzy Gillespie-style, giving a wake-up call to the sleeping dead. The dead at lower left leave their graves and prepare to be judged. The righteous, on Christ's right hand (the left side of the picture), are carried up to the glories of heaven. The wicked on the other side are hurled down to hell, where demons wait to torture them. Charon, from the underworld of Greek mythology, waits below to ferry the souls of the damned to hell.

It's a grim picture. No one, but no one, is smiling. Even many of the righteous being resurrected (lower left) are either skeletons or cadavers with ghastly

The Last Judgment

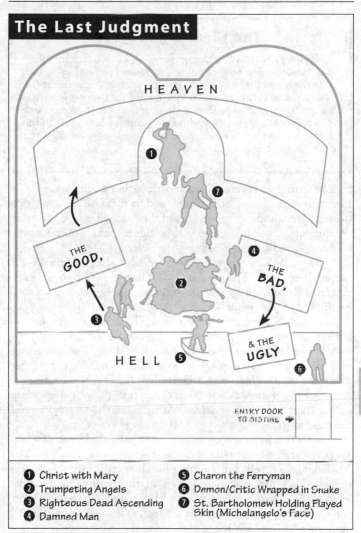

HEAVEN

THE GOOD,

THE BAD,

& THE UGLY

HELL

ENTRY DOOR TO SISTINE →

① Christ with Mary
② Trumpeting Angels
③ Righteous Dead Ascending
④ Damned Man
⑤ Charon the Ferryman
⑥ Demon/Critic Wrapped in Snake
⑦ St. Bartholomew Holding Flayed Skin (Michelangelo's Face)

skin. The angels have to play tug-of-war with subterranean monsters to drag them from their graves.

Over in hell, the wicked are tortured by gleeful demons. One of the damned (to the right of the trumpeting angels) has an utterly lost expression, as if saying, "Why did I cheat on my wife?!" Two demons grab him around the ankles to pull him down to the bowels of hell, condemned to an eternity of constipation.

But it's the terrifying figure of Christ that dominates this scene. He raises his arm to smite the wicked, sending a ripple of fear through everyone. Even the saints around him—even Mary beneath his arm (whose interceding days are clearly over)—shrink

The Cleaning Project

The ceiling and *The Last Judgment* were cleaned in the 1980s and 1990s, removing centuries of preservatives, dirt, and soot from candles, oil lamps, and the annual Papal Barbecue (just kidding). The bright, bright colors that emerged are a bit shocking, and have forced many art experts to reevaluate Michelangelo's style. Notice the very dark patches left in the corner above *The Last Judgment*, and imagine how dreary and dark it was before the cleaning.

back in terror from this uncharacteristic outburst from loving Jesus. His expression is completely closed, and he turns his head, refusing to even listen to the whining alibis of the damned. Look at Christ's twisting upper body. If this muscular figure looks familiar to you, it's because you've seen it before—the *Belvedere Torso*.

When *The Last Judgment* was unveiled to the public in 1541, it caused a sensation. The pope is said to have dropped to his knees and cried, "Lord, charge me not with my sins when thou shalt come on the Day of Judgment."

And it changed the course of art. The complex composition, with more than 300 figures swirling around the figure of Christ, went far beyond traditional Renaissance balance. The twisted figures shown from every imaginable angle challenged other painters to try and top this master of 3-D illusion. And the sheer terror and drama of the scene was a striking contrast to the placid optimism of, say, Raphael's *School of Athens*. Michelangelo had Baroque-en all the rules of the Renaissance, signaling a new era of art.

With the Renaissance fading, the fleshy figures in *The Last Judgment* aroused murmurs of discontent from Church authorities. Michelangelo rebelled by painting his chief critic into the scene—in hell. He's the jackassed demon in the bottom-right corner, wrapped in a snake. Look at how Michelangelo covered his privates. Sweet revenge. (After Michelangelo's death, prudish Church authorities painted the wisps of clothing that we see today.)

Now move in close. Study the details of the lower part of the painting from right to left. Charon, with Dr. Spock ears and a Dalí moustache, paddles the damned in a boat full of human turbulence. Look more closely at the J-Day band. Are they reading music, or is it the Judgment Day tally? Before the piece was cleaned, these details were lost in murk.

The Last Judgment marks the end of Renaissance optimism epitomized in *The Creation of Adam*, with its innocence and exaltation of man. There, he was the wakening man-child of a fatherly God. Here, man cowers in fear and unworthiness before a terrifying, wrathful deity.

Michelangelo himself must have wondered how he would be judged—had he used his God-given talents wisely? Look at St. Bartholomew, the bald, bearded guy at Christ's left foot (our right). In the flayed skin he's holding is a barely recognizable face—the twisted self-portrait of a self-questioning Michelangelo.

• *There are two exits from the Sistine Chapel.*

1. To return to the main entrance/exit, leave the Sistine through the side door next to the screen (on the left, with your back to the altar). You'll soon find yourself facing the **Long March back to the museum's entrance** *(about 15 minutes away) and the Pinacoteca. Along this corridor (located one floor below the long corridor that you walked to get here), you'll see some of the wealth amassed by the popes, mostly gifts from royalty. Find your hometown on the 1529 map of the world: Look in the land labeled "Terra Incognita." The elaborately decorated library that branches off to the right contains rare manuscripts. The corridor eventually spills back outside. Follow signs to the Pinacoteca, where our tour picks up below.*

2. To go **directly to St. Peter's Basilica** *(see "Museum Strategies," page 238), take the shortcut exit at the far-right corner of the chapel (with your back to the altar—once through this door, you've left the Vatican Museums). Though this corner door is likely labeled "Exit for authorized guides and tour groups only," you can probably slide through with the crowds (or protest that your group has left you behind). If this exit is closed (which can happen without notice), hang out in the Sistine Chapel for a few minutes—it'll likely reopen shortly.*

Pinacoteca

Like Lou Gehrig batting behind Babe Ruth, the Pinacoteca (Painting Gallery) has to follow the mighty Sistine & Co. But after the Vatican's artistic feast, this little collection of paintings is a delicious 15-minute after-dinner mint.

See this gallery of paintings as you'd view the time-lapse blossoming of a flower, walking through the evolution of painting from medieval to Baroque with just a few stops.

• *Enter, passing a plaster cast of Michelangelo's Pietà (offering a handy close-up look), and stroll up to Room IV.*

VATICAN MUSEUMS

Melozzo da Forlì, *Musician Angels*, 1470s

Removed from the apse of a Roman church, this playful series of frescoes shows the delicate grace and nobility of Italy during the time known fondly as the Quattrocento (1400s). Notice the detail in the serene faces; the soothing primary colors; the bright and even light; and the classical purity given to these religious figures. Rock on.

• *Walk on to the end room (Room VIII), where precious Raphael-designed tapestries that once hung in the Sistine Chapel now surround the highlight of this collection. They've turned on the dark to let Raphael's* Transfiguration *shine. Take a seat.*

Raphael, *The Transfiguration*, 1516-1520

Christ floats above a stumpy mountaintop, visited in a vision by the prophets Moses and Elijah. Peter, James, and John, who wanted

visual proof that Jesus was Lord, cower in awe under their savior, "transfigured before them, his face shining as the sun, his raiment white as light" (as described by the evangelist Matthew—who can be seen taking notes in the painting's lower left).

Raphael composes the scene in three descending tiers: Christ, the holiest, is on top, then Peter-James-John, and finally, the nine remaining apostles surround a boy possessed by demons. They direct him and his mother to Jesus for healing.

Raphael died in 1520, leaving this final work to be finished by his pupils. The last thing Raphael painted was the beatific face of Jesus, perhaps the most beautiful Christ in existence. When Raphael was buried (in the Pantheon, at age 37), this work accompanied the funeral.

• *Heading back down the parallel corridor, stop in Room IX at the brown, unfinished work by Leonardo.*

Leonardo da Vinci, *St. Jerome*, c. 1482

Jerome squats in the rocky desert. He's spent too much time alone, fasting and meditating on his sins. His soulful face is echoed by his friend, the roaring lion.

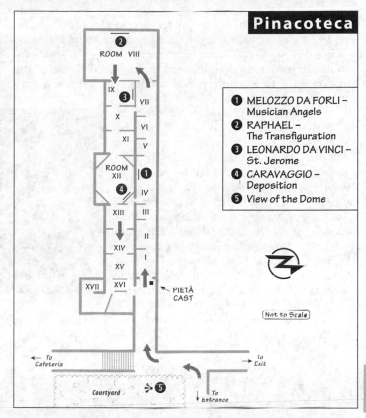

Pinacoteca

❶ MELOZZO DA FORLI –
Musician Angels

❷ RAPHAEL –
The Transfiguration

❸ LEONARDO DA VINCI –
St. Jerome

❹ CARAVAGGIO –
Deposition

❺ View of the Dome

ROOM VIII

IX

VII

X

VI

XI

V

ROOM
XII

IV

XIII

III

II

XIV

I

XV

XVII   XVI

PIETÀ
CAST

Not to Scale

← To
Cafeteria

To
Exit →

Courtyard   ❺

To
Entrance

VATICAN MUSEUMS

This unfinished work gives us a glimpse behind the scenes at Leonardo's technique. Even in the brown undercoating, we see the psychological power of Leonardo's genius. Jerome's emaciated body on the rocks expresses his intense penitence, while his pleading eyes hold a glimmer of hope for divine forgiveness. Leonardo wrote that a good painter must paint two things: "man and the movements of his spirit." (The patchwork effect is due to Jerome's head having been cut out and used as the seat of a stool in a shoemaker's shop.)

• *Roll on through the sappy sweetness of the Mannerist rooms into the gritty realism of Caravaggio (Room XII).*

Caravaggio, *Deposition*, c. 1600-1604

Christ is being buried. In the dark tomb, the faces of his followers emerge, lit by a harsh light. Christ's body has a deathlike color. We see Christ's dirty toes and Nicodemus' wrinkled, sunburned face.

Caravaggio was the first painter to intentionally shock his viewers. By exaggerating the contrast between light and dark, shining a brutal third-degree-interrogation light on his subjects, and using everyday models in sacred scenes, he takes a huge leap away from the Raphael-pretty past and into the "expressive realism" of the modern world.

A tangle of grief looms in the darkness as Christ's heavy, dead body nearly pulls the whole group with him from the cross into the tomb. After this museum, I know how he feels.

• *As you emerge from the Pinacoteca, you're near the museum's entrance/exit (to the left) and the cafeteria (to the right). If interested in a bit more (stress-free) sightseeing, just beyond the cafeteria is a delightful public garden. Beyond that, steps lead into the* **Carriage Pavilion** *(Padiglione delle Carrozze), a peaceful exhibit showing off centuries of papal carriages, cars, and Popemobiles, including the one St. John Paul II was riding in when a would-be assassin shot him in 1981.*

Once you're ready to leave, enjoy one last view of the Vatican grounds and Michelangelo's magnificent dome. Then go in peace.

BORGHESE GALLERY TOUR

Galleria Borghese

More than just a great museum, the Borghese Gallery is a beautiful villa set in the greenery of surrounding gardens. You get to see art commissioned by the luxury-loving Borghese family displayed in the very rooms for which it was created. Frescoes, marble, stucco, and interior design enhance the masterpieces. This is a place where—regardless of whether you learn a darn thing—you can sit back and enjoy the sheer beauty of the palace and its art.

It's hard to believe that a family of cardinals and popes would display so many works with secular and sensual—even erotic—themes. But the Borgheses felt that all forms of human expression, including pagan myths and physical passion, glorified God.

Orientation

Cost: €11; covered by Roma Pass (see "Reservations" below); free and very crowded first Sun of the month.

Hours: Tue-Sun 9:00-19:00, closed Mon.

Reservations: Reservations are mandatory and simple to get. Every two hours, 360 people are allowed to enter the museum. Entry times are 9:00, 11:00, 13:00, 15:00, and 17:00 (and you'll get exactly two hours for your visit). The sooner you reserve, the better—at least several days in advance for a weekday visit, and at least a week ahead for weekends. (In winter, you may be able to get tickets on shorter notice.)

It's easiest to book online at www.tosc.it, though it costs an additional €4 (€15 total). When the site asks what "Dispatch Type" you want, choose "Pick-up at the venue box office." You can also reserve by telephone (with a real person) for no extra fee (tel. 06-32810, press 2 for English, phones answered Mon-Fri 9:00-18:00, Sat 9:00-13:00, closed Sat in Aug and Sun year-round).

After you reserve a day and time, you'll get a claim number. The museum recommends that you arrive at the gallery 30 minutes before your appointed time to pick up your ticket in the lobby on the lower level. After getting your ticket, check your bags (free and mandatory), and then peruse the gift shop or relax in the garden before entering at the designated time. Don't cut it close—arriving late can mean forfeiting your reservation.

You can use a Roma Pass for free or discounted entry, but you're still required to make a reservation (by phone only—not online; specify that you have the Roma Pass).

Getting There: The museum is set idyllically but inconveniently in the vast Villa Borghese Gardens (see page 67). To avoid miss-

ing your appointment, allow yourself plenty of time to find the place. A taxi drops you 100 yards from the museum. Your destination is the Galleria Borghese (gah-leh-REE-ah bor-GAY-zay). Don't tell the cabbie "Villa Borghese," which is the park, not the museum.

The most foolproof approach by public transportation is on bus #910, which goes from Termini train station (and Piazza della Repubblica) to the Via Pinciana stop, 100 yards from the museum. Bus #53 runs to the same stop from the Barberini Metro station.

You can also go by foot (20 minutes) from the Barberini Metro stop: walk 10 minutes up Via Veneto, enter the park, and turn right, following signs another 10 minutes to the Borghese Gallery. (The Spagna Metro stop is equally close, but involves a circuitous walk through underground passageways—a less-than-idyllic approach.)

Information: Piazzale del Museo Borghese 5, tel. 06-32810 (ticket service) or 06-841-3979 (museum), www.galleriaborghese.it.

Tours: Guided English tours are offered for visitors in the 9:00 and 11:00 time slots (€6.50). You can't book a tour when you make your museum reservation—sign up as soon as you arrive. Or consider the excellent 1.5-hour audioguide tour (€5), which covers more than this chapter.

Length of This Tour: Two hours is all you get...and you'll want every minute. But if you have less time, focus on the ground-floor sculptures, especially Bernini.

Museum Strategy: Visits are strictly limited to two hours. Budget most of your time for the more interesting ground floor, but set aside 30 minutes for the paintings of the Pinacoteca upstairs (highlights are marked by the audioguide icons). Though my tour starts on the ground floor, you can avoid the crowds by seeing the Pinacoteca first. The fine bookshop is best visited outside your two-hour entry window (it closes 30 minutes before the gallery).

Services: Baggage check is free, mandatory, and strictly enforced. Even small purses must be checked. The checkroom does not take coats. There's a WC in the staircase between the two floors.

Photography: Allowed without flash.

Cuisine Art: A café is on-site. A picnic-friendly park with benches is just in front of the museum (you can check your picnic with your bags and feast after your visit). The sandwich chain VyTA has a location at Casa del Cinema within the park, a pleasant 10-minute walk directly downhill from the museum, near the bike-rental stand.

Starring: Sculptures by Bernini and Canova; paintings by Caravaggio, Raphael, and Titian; and the elegant villa itself.

OVERVIEW

As you visit this palace-in-a-garden, consider its purpose. Cardinal Scipione Borghese (1576-1633) wanted to create a place just outside the city where he could showcase his fine art while wining and dining the VIPs of his age. He had the villa built, collected ancient works, and hired the best artists of his day. In pursuing the optimistic spirit of the Renaissance, they invented Baroque.

The cardinal was controversial because he was not religious. But as nepotism was routine in the 17th century, just being a nephew of the pope was justification enough to be made a cardinal. And the power of a cardinal could be parlayed into great wealth, still on incredible display here in the gallery.

The Tour Begins

• *Go downstairs (into the basement) to pick up your ticket. Head back outside and up the stairs to begin the tour on the ground floor, in the main entry hall. If you want to start in the Pinacoteca, find the entrance at the far end of the basement and go upstairs to the second floor.*

GROUND FLOOR (SCULPTURE)
Main Entry Hall

The first room that guests saw upon entry was a "theater of the arts"—a multimedia and multi-era extravaganza of art treasures.

BORGHESE GALLERY

Baroque frescoes on the ceiling, Greek statues along the walls, and ancient Roman mosaics on the floor capture the essence of the collection—a gathering of beautiful objects from every age and culture inside a lavish 17th-century villa.

The cardinal was a man of power—gathering all this culture and showing it off added to his prestige. And with men of great culture like him, the glories of ancient Rome and Greece were being surpassed in their own time, and here that could be celebrated. So he made this palace not to live in but as a museum to flaunt his treasures.

Five second- and third-century mosaics from a private Roman villa adorn the floor with colorful, festive scenes of slaughter. Gladiators—as famous in their day as the sports heroes of our age—fight animals and each other with swords, whips, and tridents. The Greek letter Θ marks the dead. Notice some of the gladiators' pro-wrestler nicknames: "Cupid(-o)," "Serpent(-ius)," "Licentious(-us)." On the far left, a scene shows how "Alumnusvic" killed "Mazicinus" and left him lying upside down in a pool of blood.

High up on the wall is a thrilling first-century Greek sculpture of a horse falling. The Renaissance-era rider was added by Pietro Bernini, father of the famous Gian Lorenzo Bernini.

• *We'll tour this floor counterclockwise. From the entrance, turn right and head into...*

Room I
Antonio Canova, *Pauline Borghese as Venus (Paolina Borghese come Venere),* 1808

Napoleon's sister went the full monty for the sculptor Canova, scandalizing Europe. ("How could you have done such a thing?!" she was asked. She replied, "The room wasn't cold.") With the famous nose of her conqueror brother, she strikes the pose of Venus as conqueror of men's hearts. Her relaxed afterglow and slight smirk say she's already had her man. The light dent she puts in the mattress makes this goddess human.

Notice the contrasting textures that Canova (1757-1822) gets out of the pure white marble: the rumpled sheet versus her smooth skin, the satiny-smooth pillows and mattress versus the creases in them, her porcelain skin versus the hint of a love handle. Canova polished and waxed the marble until it looked as soft and pliable as cloth.

The mythological pose, the Roman couch, the ancient hairdo,

Borghese Gallery—Ground Floor

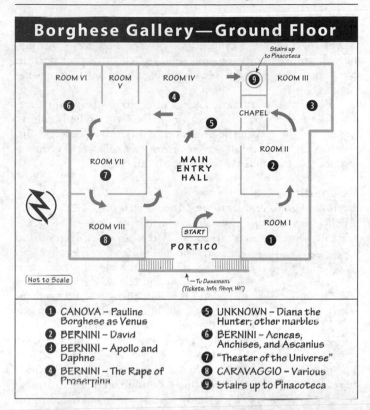

Stairs up
to Pinacoteca

ROOM VI   ROOM V   ROOM IV   **9**   ROOM III

6   **4**   **3**

CHAPEL

5

ROOM II

2

ROOM VII   MAIN ENTRY HALL

7

ROOM VIII   START   ROOM I

8   PORTICO   **1**

Not to Scale

← To Basement
(Tickets, Info, Shop, WC)

1. CANOVA – Pauline Borghese as Venus
2. BERNINI – David
3. BERNINI – Apollo and Daphne
4. BERNINI – The Rape of Proserpina
5. UNKNOWN – Diana the Hunter; other marbles
6. BERNINI – Aeneas, Anchises, and Ascanius
7. "Theater of the Universe"
8. CARAVAGGIO – Various
9. Stairs up to Pinacoteca

and the calm harmony make Pauline the epitome of the Neoclassical style.

Room II
Gian Lorenzo Bernini, *David,* 1624

Duck! David twists around to put a big rock in his sling. He purses his lips, knits his brow, and winds his body like a spring as his eyes lock onto the target: Goliath, who's somewhere behind us, putting us right in the line of fire.

The face of David is a self-portrait of the 25-year-old Bernini (1598-1680). Looking ready to take on the world, David is charged with the same fighting energy that fueled the missionaries and conquistadors of the Counter-Reformation.

Compared with Michelangelo's *David,* this is unvarnished realism—an unbalanced pose, bulging veins, unflattering face, and armpit hair. Michelangelo's *David* thinks, whereas Bernini's acts—with lips pursed, eyes concentrating, and sling stretched. Bernini slays the pretty-boy *David*s of the Renaissance and prepares to invent Baroque.

Flanking David are two ancient sarcophagi carved with scenes from the *Labors of Hercules* (A.D. 160). The twisting bodybuilders' poses were the Hellenistic inspiration for Bernini's Baroque. The painting high on the wall between them, by a follower of Caravaggio, shows a triumphant David with the giant's head.

Room III
Bernini, *Apollo and Daphne (Apollo e Dafne)*, 1625

Apollo—made stupid by Cupid's arrow of love—chases after Daphne, who has been turned off by the "arrow of disgust." Just

as he's about to catch her, she calls to her father to save her. Magically, her fingers begin to sprout leaves, her toes become roots, her skin turns to bark, and she transforms into a tree. Frustrated Apollo will end up with a handful of leaves. (Notice the same scene, colorized, painted on the ceiling above.)

Stand behind the statue to experience it as Bernini originally intended. It's only when you circle around to the front that he reveals the story's surprise ending.

Walk slowly around the statue. Apollo's back leg defies gravity. Bernini chipped away more than half of the block of marble, leaving airy, open spaces. The marble leaves at the top ring like crystal when struck (but don't try it). The statue is now in particularly fine form, having spent two years in restoration (described to me as being similar to dental work). It's virtually flawless—yet Bernini couldn't entirely overcome Nature's imperfections. At the last minute, the sculptor discovered a flaw in the marble that now forms a scar across Daphne's nose.

Bernini carves out some of the chief features of Baroque art. He makes a supernatural event seem realistic. He freezes the scene at its most dramatic, emotional moment. The figures move and twist in unusual poses. He turns the wind machine on, sending Apollo's cape billowing behind him. It's a sculpture group of two, forming a scene, rather than a stand-alone portrait. And the subject is classical. Even in strict Counter-Reformation times, there was always a place for groping, if the subject matter had a moral—this one taught you not to pursue fleeting earthly pleasures. And, besides, Bernini tends to show a lot of skin, but no genitals.

The cardinal's private **chapel** (between Rooms III and IV) is the only even vaguely religious room in the palace. It's relatively humble, a reminder that the cardinal probably didn't stop in here for much longer than tourists do today.

Room IV
Bernini, *The Rape of Proserpina*
(Il Ratto di Proserpina), 1622

Pluto, King of the Underworld, strides into his realm and shows off his catch—the beautiful daughter of the earth goddess Ceres.

His three-headed guard dog, Cerberus (who guards the gates of hell), barks triumphantly. Pluto is squat, thick, and uncouth, with knotted muscles and untrimmed beard. He's trying not to hurt Proserpina, but she pushes her divine molester away and twists to call out for help. Tears roll down her cheeks. She wishes she could turn into a tree.

Bernini was the master of marble. With this work, at the age of 24, he had discovered his Baroque niche. While Renaissance works were designed to be seen from the front, Baroque is theater-in-the-round—full of action, designed to be experienced as you walk around it. Look how Pluto's fingers dig into her frantic body as if it were real flesh. Bernini picked out this Carrara marble, knowing that its relative suppleness and ivory hue would lend itself to a fleshy statue.

• *In a niche over Pluto's right shoulder, find...*

Artist Unknown, *Diana the Hunter (Artemide)*

The goddess has been running through the forest. Now she's spotted her prey and slows down, preparing to string her (missing) bow with an arrow. Or is she smoking a (missing) cigarette? Scholars debate it.

The statues in the niches are classical originals. *Diana the Hunter* is a rare Greek original, with every limb and finger intact, from the second century B.C. The traditional *contrapposto* pose (weight on one leg) and idealized grace were an inspiration for artists such as Canova, who grew tired of Bernini's Baroque bombast.

The Marbles in Room IV

The many ancient Roman statues and portrait busts of Roman emperors in this room were intended as a reminder that the pope was essentially a king, the successor to ancient Roman rulers of the past. (Until around 1800, popes held vast political—and even military—power.)

Appreciate the beauty of the different types of marble in the room: Bernini's ivory Carrara, Diana's translucent white, purple porphyry emperors and the granite-like columns supporting them, wood-grained pilasters on the walls, and the various colors on the floor—green, red, gray, lavender, and yellow, some grainy, some "marbled" like a steak. Some of the world's most beautiful and durable things have been made from the shells of sea creatures layered in sediment, fossilized into limestone, then baked and crystallized by the pressure of the earth—marble.

• *Before leaving this room, notice the staircase in the corner. You'll later return here to reach the Pinacoteca upstairs. But for now, continue through Room V and into...*

Room VI
Bernini, *Aeneas, Anchises, and Ascanius,* 1618-1619

Aeneas' home in Troy is in flames, and he escapes with the three most important things: his family (elderly father Anchises on his shoulder, baby boy Ascanius at his leg), his household gods (the statues in Dad's hands), and the Eternal Flame (carried by his son). They're all in shock, lost in thought, facing an uncertain future. Aeneas isn't even looking where he's going; he just puts one foot in front of the other. Little do they know that eventually they'll wind up in Italy, where—according to legend—Aeneas will house the flame in the Temple of Vesta and found the city of Rome (and the Borghese dynasty).

Bernini was just 20 when he started this, his first major work for Cardinal Borghese. Bernini was probably helped by his dad, who nurtured the child prodigy much like Leopold mentored Mozart, but without the rivalry. Bernini's portrayal of human flesh—from baby fat to middle-aged muscle to sagging decrepitude—is astonishing. Still, the flat-footed statue just stands there—it lacks the Baroque energy of his more mature work. More lively are the reliefs up at the ceiling, with their dancing, light-footed soldiers with do-si-do shields.

Room VII
The "Theater of the Universe"

The room's decor sums up the eclectic nature of the villa. You've got everything here—your Greek statues, your Roman mosaics, even your fake "Egyptian" sphinxes and hieroglyphs (perfectly symmetrical, in good Neoclassical style). Look out the window past the sculpted gardens at the mesh domes of the aviary, once filled with exotic birds. Cardinal Borghese's vision was to make a place where art, history, music, nature, and science from every place and time would come together in "a theater of the universe."

Room VIII
Caravaggio

This room holds the greatest collection of Caravaggio paintings anywhere. Michelangelo Merisi (1571-1610), nicknamed "Cara-

vaggio" after his hometown (near Milan), brought Christian saints down to earth with gritty realism. Caravaggio's straightforwardness can be a refreshing change in a museum full of (sometimes overly) refined beauty.

Trace the course of his brief, dramatic, and sometimes messy life. *Self-Portrait as Bacchus* shows twentysomething Caravaggio as he first arrived in Rome, a poor bohemian enjoying the wild life.

On the facing wall, *Boy with a Fruit Basket* dates from when he eked out a living painting minor figures in other artists' paintings. His specialty? Fruit. Ultrarealistic fruit.

In 1600, Caravaggio completed his first major commission, a painting of St. Matthew for San Luigi dei Francesi, a church across town (see page 132). Overnight, Caravaggio was famous.

In the next 10 years, Caravaggio pioneered Baroque painting, much as Bernini soon would in sculpture. Caravaggio's unique style combined two striking elements: uncompromising realism and strong light-dark contrasts. His saints (e.g., *St. Jerome*) are balding and wrinkled. His models were ordinary people—*St. John the Baptist* is a nude teenager with dirty feet, whose belly fat wrinkles up as he turns. The *Madonna of Palafrenieri* was forbidden to hang in St. Peter's because the boy Jesus was buck naked, and because the Madonna's likeness had been inspired by Rome's best-known prostitute. Caravaggio's figures emerge from a dark background, lit by a harsh, unflattering light, which highlights part of the figure, leaving the rest in deep shadows.

Now rich and famous, Caravaggio led a reckless, rock-star existence—trashing hotel rooms and picking fights. In 1606, he killed a man (the details are sketchy) and had to flee Rome to escape prosecution. In one of Caravaggio's last paintings, David sticks Goliath's severed head right in our face—and "Goliath" is the artist himself. From exile, Caravaggio appealed to Cardinal Borghese (one of his biggest fans) to get him a pardon. But while

Gian Lorenzo Bernini
(1598-1680)

A Renaissance Man in Counter-Reformation times, Bernini almost personally invented the Baroque style, transforming the city of Rome. If you're visiting Rome, you will see Bernini's work, guaranteed.

Bernini was a child prodigy in his father's sculpting studio, growing up among Europe's rich and powerful. His flamboyant personality endeared him to his cultured employers—the popes in Rome, Louis XIV in France, and Charles I in England. He was extremely prolific, working fast and utilizing an army of assistants.

Despite the fleshiness and sensuality of his works, Bernini was a religious man, seeing his creativity as an extension of God's. In stark contrast to the Protestant world's sobriety, Bernini shamelessly embraced pagan myths and nude goddesses, declaring them all part of the "catholic"—that is, universal—church.

Bernini, a master of multimedia, was a...
- Sculptor (Borghese Gallery and *St. Teresa in Ecstasy,* pictured above and described on page 84)
- Architect (elements of St. Peter's—see "Bernini Blitz," page 231, and the Church of Sant'Andrea al Quirinale)
- Painter (Borghese Gallery)
- Interior decorator (the *baldacchino* canopy and other works in St. Peter's)
- Civic engineer (he laid out St. Peter's Square, and he designed and renovated Rome's fountains in Piazza Navona, Piazza Barberini, Piazza di Spagna, and more).

Even works done by other artists a century later (such as the Trevi Fountain) can be traced indirectly to Bernini, the man who invented Baroque, the "look" of Rome for the next two centuries.

returning to Rome, Caravaggio died under mysterious circumstances. Though he lived only to 38, in his short life he'd rocked the world of art.

• *Caravaggio is the perfect transition between the elegant sculpture rooms and the paintings upstairs, in the other half of the museum. To reach the Pinacoteca, head through the main entry hall back to Room IV, find the entry to the staircase in the far-right corner, and spiral up to the...*

PINACOTECA (PAINTING GALLERY)

You must visit the Pinacoteca within the two-hour window of time printed on your Borghese Gallery ticket. Most visitors wait until the last half-hour to see the Pinacoteca, so that's when it's most crowded (and the ground floor is less crowded). If you see the paintings first, remember to save most of your two-hour visit for the ground-floor sculptures.

• *From the top of the stairs or elevator, step into the large Room XIV. This fine room was once a loggia, with open spaces rather than windows. Notice the ceiling and how painted statues literally raise the roof to let in the sun. Along the long wall, you'll find the following statues and paintings by Bernini. First, look for the two identical white busts set on columns.*

Room XIV
Bernini, Busts of Cardinal Borghese, 1632

Say *grazie* to the man who built this villa, assembled the collection, and hired Bernini to sculpt masterpieces. The cardinal is caught

turning as though to greet someone at a party. There's a twinkle in his eye, and he opens his mouth to make a witty comment. This man of the cloth was, in fact, a sophisticated hedonist.

Notice that there are two identical versions of this bust. The first one started cracking along the forehead (visible) just as Bernini was finishing it. *No problema*—Bernini whipped out a replacement in just three days.

• *Between the busts, find these paintings...*

Bernini, Self-Portraits (*Autoritratto Giovanile* and *Autoritratto in età Matura*) 1623, 1630-1635

Bernini was a master of many media, including painting. The younger Bernini (age 25) looks out a bit hesitantly, as if he's still finding his way in high-class society. His jet-black eyes came from his southern Italian mother who, it's said, also gave him his passionate personality.

In his next self-portrait (roughly age 35), with a few masterpieces under his belt, Bernini shows himself with more confidence and facial hair—the dashing, vibrant man who would rebuild Rome in Baroque style, from St. Peter's Square to the fountains that dot the piazzas.

• *On the table below, find the smaller...*

Borghese Gallery—Pinacoteca

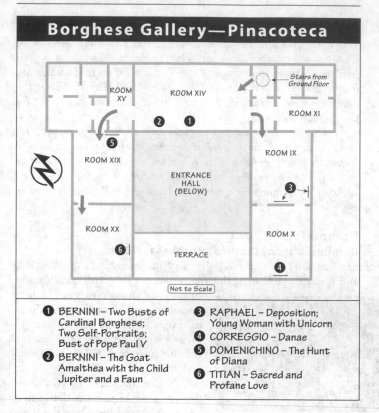

ROOM XV

ROOM XIV

Stairs from
Ground Floor

ROOM XI

❷ ❶

❺

ROOM XIX

ENTRANCE
HALL
(BELOW)

ROOM IX

❸

ROOM XX

ROOM X

❻

TERRACE

❹

Not to Scale

❶ BERNINI – Two Busts of
Cardinal Borghese;
Two Self-Portraits;
Bust of Pope Paul V

❷ BERNINI – The Goat
Amalthea with the Child
Jupiter and a Faun

❸ RAPHAEL – Deposition;
Young Woman with Unicorn

❹ CORREGGIO – Danae

❺ DOMENICHINO – The Hunt
of Diana

❻ TITIAN – Sacred and
Profane Love

Bust of Pope Paul V, 1618

The cardinal's uncle was a more sober man. As pope, Paul V ruled over the artistic era of Caravaggio and Bernini. He reopened an ancient aqueduct, helped steer St. Peter's toward completion, and personally met with Galileo to discuss the heliocentrism controversy.

He was also a patron of the arts with a good eye for talent, who hired Bernini's father. When Paul saw sketches made by little Gian Lorenzo, he announced, "This boy will be the Michelangelo of his age."

• *To the right of the Borghese busts, find a small statue of...*

The Goat Amalthea with the Child Jupiter and a Faun (La Capra Amaltea con Giove Bambino e un Faunetto), 1609/1615

Bernini was barely entering puberty when he made this. (That's about the age when I mastered how to make a Play-Doh snake.)

But already its arrangement takes what would become one of Bernini's trademark forms: the sculptural ensemble. The two kids are milking a goat and drinking it. The kids lean one way, the goat the other, with the whole composition contained neatly in a circle of good fun.

• *Backtrack to the staircase/elevator and turn right to find...*

Room IX
Raphael (Raffaello Sanzio), Deposition (Deposizione), 1507

Jesus is being taken from the cross. The men struggle heroically to support him while the women support Mary (in purple), who has fainted. Mary Magdalene rushes up to take Christ's hand. The woman who commissioned the painting had recently lost her son. She wanted to show the death of a son and the grief of a mother. We see two different faces of grief—mother Mary faints at the horror, while Mary Magdalene still can't quite believe he's gone.

Enjoy the rich colors—solid reds, green, blue, and yellow—that set off Christ's porcelain-skin body. Note Mary's face: She's fainted and is the same deathly gray as her dead son. Notice also the hand of Mary Magdalene holding Jesus' hand—the pink of the living on the gray of the dead. In true Renaissance style, Raphael (1483-1520) orders the scene with geometrical perfection. The curve of Jesus' body is echoed by the swirl of Mary Magdalene's hair, and then by the curve of Calvary Hill, where Christ met his fate.

• *Also in Room IX, to your left as you face the* Deposition, *is...*

Raphael, *Portrait of Young Woman with Unicorn* (*Ritratto di Giovane Donna con un Unicorno*), c. 1506

Raphael's genius as a portrait painter was his ability to simultaneously portray his subjects with masterful photorealism, yet also show them in their best light.

This is likely a wedding portrait. The blonde teenager poses, cradling her little dog (transformed later into a unicorn). Her body faces formally in one direction. Meanwhile, her eyes turn the other way, as if someone had just interrupted the sitting, capturing an unplanned moment. And the colors! Her rich red clothes, accented by the ruby pendant; the pellucid skin; and her delicate face, framed perfectly by the window behind, with its pale blue atmosphere. It's little wonder that Raphael's sweet style dominated painting for a century, until the coming of Caravaggio.

• *Continue into...*

Room X
Correggio, *Danae*, c. 1531

Cupid strips Danae as she spreads her legs, most unladylike, to receive a trickle of gold from the smudgy cloud overhead—this was Zeus' idea of intercourse with a human. The sheets are rumpled, and Danae looks right where the action is with a smile on her face.

• *Backtrack through the room with the two cardinal busts, continue through Room XV, then turn left in the small room to get to...*

Room XIX
Domenichino, *The Hunt of Diana* (*La Caccia di Diana*), 1616-1617

Half-naked Greek nymphs are frolicking under the watchful eye of the goddess of the hunt, Diana (with her crescent-moon diadem).

Notice the archer's fine marksmanship with arrows in the post, the ribbon, and the bird. All eyes turn to see that one of the nymphs has successfully shot the bird. The playful scene is epitomized by the girl sprawled backward with abandon in the pond. No man should look at Diana and her nymphs, but we've been spotted. (Psst—see the two Peeping Toms on the right?)

• *Continue into the next room.*

Room XX
Titian (Tiziano Vecellio), *Sacred and Profane Love* *(Amor Sacro e Amor Profano)*, c. 1515

While you might guess that the naked woman on the right embodies profane love, that's actually represented by the material girl on the left—with her box of treasures, fortified castle, and dark, claustrophobic landscape. Sacred love is represented by the naked woman who has nothing to hide and enjoys open  spaces filled with light, life, a church in the distance, and even a couple of lovers in the field.

The clothed woman at left has recently married, and she cradles a vase filled with jewels representing the riches of earthly love. Her naked twin on the right holds the burning flame of eternal, heavenly love. Baby Cupid, between them, playfully stirs the waters.

Symbolically, the steeple on the right points up to the love of heaven, while on the left, soldiers prepare to "storm the castle" of the new bride. Miss Heavenly Love looks jealous.

This exquisite painting expresses the spirit of the Renaissance—that earth and heaven are two sides of the same coin. And here in the Borghese Gallery, that love of earthly beauty can be spiritually uplifting—as long as you feel it within two hours.

NATIONAL MUSEUM OF ROME

Museo Nazionale Romano •
Palazzo Massimo

Rome lasted a thousand years...and so do most Roman history courses. But if you want a breezy overview of this fascinating society, there's no better place than the National Museum of Rome, which displays the city's best collection of ancient Roman statuary.

Rome took Greek culture and wrote it in capital letters. Thanks to this lack of originality, ancient Greek statues were preserved for our enjoyment today. But the Romans also pioneered a totally new form of art—sculpting painfully realistic portraits of emperors and important citizens.

Think of this museum as a walk back in time. As you gaze at the same statues that the Romans swooned over, the history of Rome comes alive—from Julius Caesar's murder to Caligula's incest to Vespasian's Colosseum to the coming of Christianity.

Orientation

Cost: €10 combo-ticket valid for three days, includes entry into three lesser National Museum branches: the nearby Museum of the Bath (lackluster ancient inscriptions—only for font freaks), Palazzo Altemps (so-so sculptures), and Crypta Balbi (medieval art). The price can drop or rise depending on the number of special exhibits. Free and very crowded the first Sun of the month.

Hours: Tue-Sun 9:00-19:45, closed Mon, last entry one hour before closing.

When to Go: The museum is seldom crowded except the first Sunday of the month. Since it has a convenient and free bag check (even for backpacks and suitcases), consider a visit en route from the train station.

Getting There: The museum is between Piazza della Repubblica and Termini Station, a few minutes' walk from either the Repubblica or Termini Metro stop. As you leave Termini, it's the sandstone-brick building on your left. Enter at the far (west) end, at Largo di Villa Peretti.

Information: Tel. 06-3996-7700, www.archeoroma.beniculturali.it/en.

Tours: Audioguides cost €5 and last two hours.

Length of This Tour: Allow two hours. If you have less time, at least do the ground floor and the first floor as far as the Discus Thrower.

Photography: Photos allowed without flash.

Starring: Roman emperor busts, the Discus Thrower, original Greek statues, and fine Roman copies.

OVERVIEW

The museum is rectangular, with rooms and hallways built around a central courtyard. The ground-floor sculptures follow Rome's history as the city changes from a republic to a dictatorial empire. The first-floor exhibits take Rome from its peak through its slow decline. The second floor houses rare frescoes and fine mosaics, and the basement presents coins and everyday objects. As you tour this museum, note that in Italian, "room" is *sala* and "hall" is *galleria*.

The Tour Begins

GROUND FLOOR—FROM SENATORS TO CAESARS

• *Buy your ticket and pass through the turnstile, where you'll find...*

Minerva

It's big, it's gaudy, it's a weird goddess from a pagan cult. Welcome to the Roman world. The statue is also a good reminder that all the statues in this museum—now missing limbs, scarred by erosion, or weathered down to bare stone—were once whole, and painted to look as lifelike as possible.

• *Continue straight ahead into the courtyard. The first corridor—called Gallery I—is lined with portrait busts.*

Gallery I
Portrait Heads from the Republic, 500–1 B.C.

Stare into the eyes of these stern, hardy, no-nonsense farmer-stock people who founded Rome. The wrinkles and crags of these origi-

National Museum—Ground Floor

```
ROOM                    ROOM II        ROOM I              BAGGAGE
III                                      ❸                 CHECK
                                              STAIRS ELEV.
                GALLERY I                       ❷                    WC
GALLERY II                                                   TICKETS
ROOM                ROOM      Open-air        STEPS              ENTRY
IV          ❻       V         Courtyard                  ❶
            ❼    ❹ ❺
                 ❽          GALLERY III        ❾
            ❿  ROOM   ❽  ROOM              ROOM        STAIRS UP TO
               VI        VII               VIII        FIRST FLOOR

    To                                          To
Termini Train                              Piazza
  Station            [Not to Scale]        Repubblica
```

❶ Minerva	❺ Livia	❾ Socrates
❷ Portrait Heads	❻ Tiberius	❿ Dying Niobid
❸ Julius Caesar (?)	❼ Caligula	⓫ The Boxer at Rest &
❹ Augustus as	❽ Alexander	Hellenistic Prince
Pontifex Maximus	the Great	

nal "ugly republicans" tell the story of Rome's roots as a small agricultural tribe, fighting for survival with neighboring bands.

These faces are brutally realistic, unlike more idealized Greek statues. Romans honored their ancestors and worthy citizens in the "family" *(gens)* of Rome. They wanted lifelike statues to remember them by, and to instruct the young with their air of moral rectitude.

In its first 500 years, Rome was a republic ruled by a Senate of wealthy landowners. But as Rome expanded throughout Italy, and the economy shifted from farming to booty, changes became necessary.

• *Enter Room I (Sala I). Along the left wall, find the portrait bust that may (or may not) be Julius Caesar.*

Room I
Julius Caesar? (labeled *Rilievo con ritratto di uomo anziano*)

Some scholars have identified this bust as representing Rome's most famous citizen. Others point out that it doesn't resemble any of the known images of him. Regardless of who's right, take this as a good moment to reflect on Caesar's life.

NATIONAL MUSEUM

Julius Caesar (c. 100-44 B.C.)—with his prominent brow, high cheekbones, and male-pattern baldness with the forward comb-over—changed Rome forever.

When this charismatic general swept onto the scene, Rome was in chaos. Rich landowners were fighting middle-class plebs, who wanted their slice of the plunder. Slaves such as Spartacus were picking up hoes and hacking up masters. And renegade generals—the new providers of wealth and security in an economy of plunder—were becoming dictators. (Notice the **life-size statue** with a shaved-off head, of an unknown but obviously once-renowned general.)

Caesar was a people's favorite. He conquered Gaul (France), then sacked Egypt, then impregnated Cleopatra. He defeated rivals and made them his allies. He gave great speeches. Chicks dug him.

With the army at his back and the people in awe, he took the reins of government, instituted sweeping changes, made himself the center of power...and antagonized the Senate.

A band of republican assassins surrounded him in a Senate meeting. He called out for help as one by one they stepped up to take turns stabbing him. The senators sat and watched in silence. One of the killers was his adopted son, Brutus, and Caesar—astonished that even he joined in—died saying, *"Et tu, Brute?"*

• *At the end of Gallery I, turn left and enter the large glassed in Room V, with a life-size statue of Augustus.*

Room V
Augustus as Pontifex Maximus
(Augusto Pontefice Massimo)

Julius Caesar died, but his family name, his politics, and his flamboyance lived on—his descendants would rule Rome for a century

after his death, turning the surname "Caesar" into a title. Julius had adopted his grandnephew, Octavian, who united Rome's warring factions and took the name and title "Augustus," meaning "venerable" or "protected by the gods."

Here, Emperor Augustus has taken off his armor and laurel-leaf crown, donning the simple hooded robes of a priest. He's retiring to a desk job after a lifetime of fighting to reunite Rome. He killed Brutus and eliminated his rivals, Mark Antony and Cleopatra. For the first time in almost a century

NATIONAL MUSEUM

of fighting, one general reigned supreme. Augustus became the first of the emperors who would rule Rome for the next 500 years.

In fact, Augustus was a down-to-earth man who lived simply, worked hard, read books, listened to underlings, and tried to restore traditional Roman values after the turbulence of Julius Caesar's time. He outwardly praised the Senate, while actually reducing it to a rubber-stamp body. Augustus' reign marked the start of 200 years of peace and prosperity, the Pax Romana.

See if the statue matches this description of Augustus by a contemporary, the historian Suetonius: "He was unusually handsome. His expression was calm and mild. He had clear, bright eyes, in which was a kind of divine power. His hair was slightly curly and somewhat golden." Any variations were made by sculptors who idealized his features to make him almost godlike.

Augustus proclaimed himself a god—not arrogantly or blasphemously, as Caligula later did, but as the honored "father" of the "family" of Rome. As the empire expanded, the vanquished had to worship statues like this one as a show of loyalty.

• *Here in Room V, in the hallway, and possibly in Room IV, look for busts of other members of his powerful family.*

Rome's First Emperors
(C. 50 B.C.-A.D. 68)
Livia

Augustus' wife, Livia, was a major power behind the throne. Her stern, thin-lipped gaze withered rivals at court. Her hairstyle—bunched up in a peak, braided down the center, and tied in back—became the rage throughout the empire, as her face appeared everywhere, from statues to coins. Notice that by the next generation, a simpler bun was chic (Antonia Minore, Livia's daughter-in-law, often next to Livia). And by the following generation, the trend was tight curls. Empresses dictated fashion the way emperors dictated policy.

Livia bore Augustus no sons. She lobbied hard for Tiberius, her own son by a first marriage, to succeed as emperor. Augustus didn't like him, but Livia was persuasive. He relented, ate some bad figs, and died—the gossip was that Livia poisoned him to seal the bargain. The pattern of succession was established—adopt a son from within the extended family—and Tiberius was proclaimed emperor. (The fine frescoed walls of Livia's Anzio villa are upstairs on the second floor.)

• *Now look in the hallway for the well-worn bust of...*

Tiberius *(Tiberio),* ruled A.D. 14-37

Scholars speculate that acne may have soured Tiberius to the world (but this statue is pocked by erosion). Shy and sullen but diligent, he worked hard to be the easygoing leader that Augustus had been. Early on, he was wise and patient, but he suffered personal setbacks. Politics forced him to divorce his only beloved and marry a tramp. His favorite brother died, then his son. Embittered, he let subordinates run things and retired to Capri, where he built a villa with underground dungeons. There he hosted orgies of sex, drugs, torture, really loud music, and execution. At his side was his young grandnephew, whom he adopted as the next emperor.

• *To your right, in the glass case, is the small bust of...*

Caligula *(Caligola),* ruled A.D. 37-41

This emperor had sex with his sisters, tortured his enemies, made off with friends' wives during dinner parties and then returned to

rate their performance in bed, crucified Christians, took cuts in line at the Vatican Museums, and ordered men to kneel before him as a god. Caligula has become the archetype of a man with enough power to act out his basest fantasies.

Politically, he squandered Rome's money, then taxed and extorted from the citizens. Perhaps he was made mad by illness, perhaps he was the victim of vindictive historians, but still, no one mourned when assassins ambushed him and ran a sword through his privates. Rome was tiring of this family dynasty's dysfunction.

• *Continue down Gallery II and turn left. Busts line Gallery III. Find Alexander the Great ("Alessandro Magno," outside Room VI) and Socrates ("Socrate," farther down the hall, outside Room VIII).*

Gallery III—Rome's Greek Mentors

Rome's legions easily conquered the less-organized but more-cultured Greek civilization that had dominated the Mediterranean for centuries. Romans adopted Greek gods, art styles, and fashions, and sophisticates sprinkled their conversation with Greek phrases.

Alexander the Great *(Alessandro Magno)*

Alexander the Great (356-323 B.C.) single-handedly created a Greek-speaking empire by conquering, in just a few short years, lands from Greece to Egypt to Persia. Later, when the Romans conquered Greece (c. 200 B.C.), they inherited this preexisting collection of cultured Greek cities ringing the Mediterranean.

Alexander's handsome statues set the standard for those of later Roman emperors. His features were chiseled and youthful, and this statue was adorned with pompous decorations, like a golden sunburst aura (fitted into the holes). The greatest man of his day, he ruled the known world by the age of 30.

Alexander's teacher was none other than the philosopher Aristotle. Aristotle's teacher was Plato, whose mentor was...

Socrates *(Socrate)*

This nonconformist critic of complacent thinking is the father of philosophy. The Greeks were an intellectual, introspective, sensitive, and artistic people. The Romans were practical, no-nonsense soldiers, salesmen, and bureaucrats. Many a Greek slave was more cultured than his master, reduced to the role of warning his boss not to wear a plaid toga with a polka-dot robe.

• *Backtrack and enter Room VI.*

Room VI—Greek Beauty in Originals and Copies

Dying Niobid *(Niobide Morente)*, 440 B.C.

The Romans were astonished by the beauty of Greek statues. The smooth skin of this Niobid (the term for any child of the goddess Niobe) contrasts with the rough folds of her clothing. She twists naturally around an axis running straight up and down. This woman looks like a classical goddess awakening from a beautiful dream, but...

Circle around back. The hole bored in her back, right in that itchy place you can't quite reach, once held a golden arrow. The woman has been shot by Artemis, goddess of hunting, because her mother dared to boast to the gods about her kids. The Niobid reaches back in vain, trying to remove the arrow before it drains her of life.

Romans ate this stuff up: the sensual beauty, the underplayed pathos, the very Greekness of it. They crated up centuries-old statues like this and brought them home to their gardens and palaces.

Soon there weren't enough old statues to meet the demand. Crafty Greeks began cranking out knockoffs of Greek originals for mass consumption. Rooms VII and VIII contain both originals (like the Niobid) and copies—some of extremely high quality, others resembling cheesy fake *David*s in a garden store. Appreciate the beauty of the world's rare, surviving Greek originals.

Rome conquered Greece, but culturally the Greeks conquered the Romans.

• *Move next door to see...*

Room VII—Hellenistic and Classical Bronzes

The Boxer at Rest *(Pugilatore),* first century B.C.

An exhausted boxer sits between rounds and gasps for air. Check out the brass knuckles-type Roman boxing gloves. Textbook Hellenistic, this pugilist is realistic and full of emotion. His face is scarred, his back muscles are knotted, and he's got cauliflower ears. He's losing.

Slumped over, he turns with a questioning look ("Why am I losing again?"), and eyes that once held glass now make him look empty indeed. "I coulda been a contender."

Hellenistic Prince *(Principe Elenistico)*

Back then, everyone wanted to be like Alexander the Great. This restored bronze statue—naked and leaning on a spear—shows a prince (probably Attalus II of Pergamon) in the style of a famous statue of his hero from the second century B.C.

• *We've covered Rome's first 500 years. At the end of the hall are the stairs up to the first floor.*

FIRST FLOOR—ROME'S PEAK AND SLOW FALL

As we saw, Augustus' family did not always rule wisely. Under Nero (ruled A.D. 54-68), the debauchery, violence, and paranoia typical of the Julio-Claudians festered to a head. When the city burned in the great fire of 64, the Romans suspected Nero of torching it himself to clear land for his enormous luxury palace.

Enough. Facing a death sentence, Nero committed suicide with the help of a servant. An outsider was brought in to rule—Vespasian, from the Flavian family.

National Museum—First Floor

ROOM VIII

ROOM IX

ROOM X

ROOM XI

ROOM XII

ROOM VI

❽

❾

ROOM VII

❿

WC

ROOM V

❼

Open Courtyard Below

GALLERY II

❶❷❸❹ ROOM I

ROOM II ❺❻

STAIRS FROM GROUND FLOOR

Not to Scale

❶❷ ROOM XIII

❸ ❹ ROOM XIV

❶ Vespasian
❷ Domitian
❸ Domitia
❹ Nerva
❺ Trajan

❻ Hadrian
❼ Aphrodite Crouching
❽ The Discus Thrower
❾ Hermaphrodite Sleeping
❿ Apollo

⓫ Septimius Severus
⓬ Caracalla
⓭ Sarcophagus with Processional Scene
⓮ Christ Teaching

• *At the top of the stairs, enter Room I and then move into the hallway on the left. To your left is the...*

Flavian Family
Vespasian *(Vespasianus)*, ruled A.D. 69-79

Balding and wrinkled, with a big head, a double chin, and a shy smile, Vespasian was a common man. The son of a tax collector, he rose through the military ranks with a reputation as a competent drudge. As emperor, he restored integrity, raised taxes, started the Colosseum, and suppressed the Jewish rebellion in Palestine.

Domitian *(Domitianus)*, ruled A.D. 81-96
Vespasian's son, Domitian, used his father's tax revenues to construct the massive Imperial Palace on Palatine Hill, home to emperors for the next three centuries. Shown with his lips curled in a sneer, he was a moralistic prude who executed several Vestal ex-Virgins, while in private he took one mistress after another. Until...

Domitia

...his stern wife found out and hired a servant to stab him in the groin. Domitia's hairstyle is a far cry from the "Livia" cut, with a high crown of tight curls.

Nerva, ruled A.D. 96-98

Nerva realized that the Flavian dynasty was no better than its predecessors. Old and childless, he made a bold, far-sighted move—he adopted a son from outside of Rome's corrupting influence.

• *Go back to Room I and head straight to Room II, where you'll find Trajan ("Traiano") on the left wall.*

Room II—A Cosmopolitan Culture
Trajan *(Traianus-Hercules)*, ruled A.D. 98-117

Born in Spain, this conquering hero pushed Rome's borders to their greatest extent, creating a truly worldwide empire. The spoils of three continents funneled into a city of a million plus people. As in this statue, Trajan could dress up in a lion's skin, presenting himself as a "new Hercules," and no one found it funny. Romans, in the words of Livy the historian, felt a spirit of Manifest Destiny: "The gods desire that the City of Rome shall be the capital of all the countries of the world"—the Caput Mundi.

• *On the opposite wall (look for "Adriano") is...*

Hadrian *(Hadrianus)*, ruled A.D. 117-138

Hadrian was a fully cosmopolitan man. His trim beard—the first we've seen on an emperor—shows his taste for foreign things; he

poses like the Greek philosopher he imagined himself to be.

Hadrian was a voracious tourist, personally visiting almost every corner of the vast empire, from Britain (where he built Hadrian's Wall) to Egypt (where he sailed the Nile), from Jerusalem (where he suppressed another Jewish revolt) to Athens (where he soaked up classical culture). He scaled Sicily's Mount Etna just to see what made a volcano tick. Back home, he beautified Rome with the Pantheon and his villa at Tivoli, a microcosm of places he'd visited.

Hadrian is flanked here by the two loves of his life. His wife, **Sabina** (right), with modest hairstyle and scarf, kept the home fires burning for her traveling husband. Hadrian was 50 years old when he became captivated by a teenage boy named **Antinous** (left), with his curly hair and full, sensual lips. Together they traveled the Nile, where Antinous drowned. Hadrian wept. Statues of Antinous subsequently went up throughout the Empire, much to the embarrassment of the stoic Romans.

Hadrian spent his last years at his lavish villa outside Rome, surrounded by buildings and souvenirs that reminded him of his traveling days (see Tivoli chapter).

• *Backtrack through Room I and into the gallery, then turn right, down the hall that leads into the large Room V.*

Rooms V and VI—Rome's Grandeur

Pause at Rome's peak to admire the things the Romans found beautiful. Imagine these statues as they originally stood—in the pleasure gardens of the Roman rich, surrounded by greenery with the splashing sound of fountains, all painted in bright, lifelike colors. Though executed by Romans, the themes are mostly Greek, with godlike humans and human-looking gods.

• *At the beginning of Room V is...*

Aphrodite Crouching *(Afrodite al Bagno Accovacciata)*

The goddess of beauty crouches while bathing, then turns to admire herself. This sets her whole body in motion—one thigh goes down, the other up; her head turns clockwise while her body goes in reverse—yet she's perfectly still. The crouch creates a series of symmetrical love handles, molded by the sculptor into the marble-like wax. Hadrian had good taste—he ordered a copy of this Greek classic for his bathroom.

• *At the far end of the room, look for...*

The Discus Thrower *(Discobolo)*

An athlete winds up, about to unleash his pent-up energy and hurl the discus. The sculptor has frozen the moment for us so that we can examine the inner workings of the wonder called Man. The perfect pecs and washboard abs make this human godlike. Geometrically, you could draw a perfect circle around him, with his hipbone at the center. He's natural yet ideal, twisting yet balanced, moving while at rest. For the Greeks, the universe was a rational place, and the human body was the perfect embodiment of the order found in nature.

This statue is the best-preserved Roman copy (not one member is missing—I checked) of the original Greek work by Myron (450 B.C.). (The subtle nubs on his head were aids for a measuring device used when making copies.) Statues of athletes like this commonly stood in the baths, where Romans cultivated healthy bodies, minds, and social skills, hoping to lead well-rounded lives. The Discus Thrower, with his geometrical perfection and godlike air, sums up all that is best in the classical world.

• *Continue into...*

Room VII
Hermaphrodite Sleeping *(Ermafrodito Dormiente)*
Imagine that after leaving the baths, a well-rounded Roman headed off to an orgy, where he saw a reclining nude like this. Titillated, he circled around for a closer look, and said, "Hey! *(Insert your own reaction here)*!"

From the back, this nude, lying on its stomach, possesses the perfect, lithe female form. But as you can see from the front, she/he is equipped with both breasts and a penis. It's the Greek/Roman god Hermaphroditus—the child of Hermes and Aphrodite, and protector of bisexuals.

Apollo *(Apollo del Tevere)*
The god of light appears as a slender youth, not as some burly, powerful, autocratic deity. He stands *contrapposto*—originally he was leaning against the tree—in a relaxed and very human way. His curled hair is tied with a headband, strands tumbling down his neck. His muscles and skin are smooth. (The rusty stains come from the centuries the statue spent submerged in the Tiber.) Apollo is in a reflective mood, and the serenity and intelligence in his face show off classical Greece as a nation of thinkers.

• *Exit Room VII at the far end, cut through Gallery II, and make your way to Room XIII, where you'll find the bust of Septimius Severus.*

Room XIII—Beginning of the End

Septimius Severus, ruled A.D. 193-211

Rome's sprawling empire was starting to unravel, and it took a disciplined emperor-warrior like this African to keep it together. Severus' victories on the frontier earned him a grand triumphal arch in the Forum, but here he seems to be rolling his eyes at the chaos growing around him.

• *Near Severus is his son...*

Caracalla, ruled A.D. 211-217

The stubbly beard, cruel frown, and glaring eyes tell us that Severus' son was bad news. He murdered his little brother to seize power, then proceeded to massacre thousands of loyal citizens on a whim. The army came to distrust rulers whose personal agenda got in their way, and Caracalla was stabbed in the back by a man whose brother had just been executed. Rome's long slide had begun.

• *Move next door into...*

Room XIV—The Fall

There are a lot of serious faces in this room. People who grew up in the lap of luxury and security were witnessing the unthinkable—the disintegration of a thousand years of tradition. Rome never recovered from the chaos of the third century. Disease, corruption, revolts from within, and "barbarians" pecking away at the borders were body blows that sapped Rome's strength.

Sarcophagus with Processional Scene
(Sarcofago con Corteo), A.D. 270

A parade of dignitaries, accompanying a new Roman leader, marches up Capitoline Hill. They huddle together, their backs to

the wall, looking around suspiciously for assassins. Their faces reflect the fear of the age.

By the third century, the Roman army could virtually handpick an emperor to be their front man. At one point, the office of emperor was literally auctioned to the highest bidder. In the space of 40 years, 15 different emperors were saluted, then murdered, at the whims of soldiers of fortune.

Rome would stagger on for another 200 years, but the glory of old Rome was gone. The city was becoming a den of thugs, thieves, prostitutes, barbarians...and Christians.

• *Farther along, on the right-hand wall, find the small...*

Christ Teaching *(Cristo Docente)*, A.D. 350

Christ sits like a Roman senator—in a toga, holding a scroll, dispensing wisdom like the law of the land. The statuette comes from

those delirious days when formerly persecuted Christians could now "come out" and worship in public. Emperor Constantine (ruled A.D. 306-337) legalized Christianity, and within two generations it was Rome's official religion.

Whether Christianity invigorated or ruined Rome is debated, but the fall was inevitable. Rome's once-great legions backpedaled, until even the city itself was raped and plundered by foreigners (410). In 476, the last emperor sold his title for a comfy pension plan, "Rome" became just another dirty city with a big history, and the artistic masterpieces now in this museum were buried under rubble.

THE REST OF THE MUSEUM

• *For extra credit, consider exploring two more parts of the National Museum.*

Second Floor

This floor contains frescoes and mosaics that once decorated the walls and floors of Roman villas. They're remarkably realistic and

unstuffy, featuring everyday people, animals, flowery patterns, and geometrical designs. The **Villa Farnesina frescoes**—in black, red, yellow, and blue—are mostly architectural designs, with fake columns, friezes, and garlands. The **Villa di Livia frescoes,** owned by the

wily wife of Augustus, immerse you in a leafy green garden full of birds and fruit trees, symbolizing the gods.

Basement (Floor -2)

The **"Luxury in Rome"** rooms give a peek into the lives of Rome's well-to-do citizens, featuring fine jewelry and common everyday objects. The mummified body of an eight-year-old girl born in the second century A.D., found in a stone sarcophagus near Rome in 1964, is a highlight; a doll buried with the girl is also on display.

Next, enter the extensive **coin collection.** Find your favorite emperor or empress on the coins: Julius Caesar (case 8, #41-44), Augustus (case 8, #65-69, and case 9, #1-38), Augustus' system of denars (case 10), Tiberius (case 10, #1-16), Caligula (case 10, #17-28), and Nero (case 11, #2-33). Evaluate Roman life by studying how Diocletian tweaked the gold standard (glass case 21). In A.D. 300, one denar bought one egg. The rest of the displays trace Italy's money from denars to euros. Exhibit 59 shows off the early history of a more recent monetary unit, the old Italian lira. And finally, case 62 brings us up to date with the Italian versions of Rome's latest coinage, the euro.

PILGRIM'S ROME TOUR

Pilgrimage Churches

Rome is the "capital" of the world's 1.2 billion Catholics. In Rome, you'll rub elbows with religious pilgrims from around the world— Nigerian nuns, Bulgarian theology novices, students from Notre Dame, extended Mexican families, and everyday Catholics returning to their religious roots.

The pilgrim industry helped shape Rome after the fall of the empire. Ancient Rome's population peaked at about 1.2 million. After Rome fell in A.D. 476, barbarians cut off the water supply by breaking the aqueducts, Romans fled the city, and the mouth of the Tiber River filled with silt and became a swamp.

During the Dark Ages, mosquitoes ruled over a pathetic village of 20,000...bad news for pilgrims, bad news for the papacy. Back then, the Catholic Church was the Christian Church. (Catholic means "universal," and being a Catholic was the only allowable way to be a Christian.) Centuries later, during the Renaissance, popes sought to project an image of prestige and authority. The Church revitalized the city, creating a place fit for pilgrimages. Owners of hotels and restaurants cheered.

In the late 1580s, Pope Sixtus V reconnected aqueducts and built long, straight boulevards connecting the great churches and

pilgrimage sites. Obelisks were moved to serve as markers. As you explore the city, think like a pilgrim. Look down long roads and you'll see either a grand church or an obelisk (from which you'll see a grand church).

Pilgrims to Rome try to visit four great basilicas: St. Peter's Basilica, of course (covered

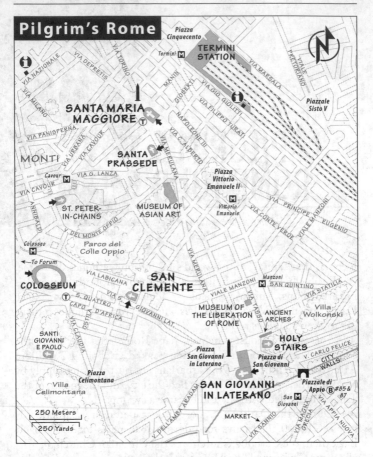

Pilgrim's Rome

in the 📖 St. Peter's Basilica Tour chapter in this book and on my 🎧 free audio tour), St. Paul's Outside the Walls (see page 102), Santa Maria Maggiore, and San Giovanni in Laterano. The last two are covered in this chapter, as well as two other "honorable mentions": The Church of Santa Prassede (Rome's best Byzantine-style mosaics) is near Santa Maria Maggiore, and the fascinating and central San Clemente is between San Giovanni in Laterano and the Colosseum.

Orientation

Planning Your Time: Depending on your time and interest level, you may want to hit every sight described in this chapter— or maybe just visit one or two of the churches. **Santa Maria Maggiore** (and nearby **Santa Prassede**) have mosaics that date back to the first days of Christian Rome. **San Giovanni**

in Laterano is grandiose and historic, and its Holy Stairs are a one-of-a-kind experience. **San Clemente**'s church-beneath-church layout leads you down—layer by mysterious layer—to a pagan Mithraic temple. To link all of this chapter's sights efficiently, check their opening hours (Santa Prassede and San Clemente close for several hours at midday, as does the chapel at the Holy Stairs—the Holy Stairs themselves do not) and decide whether you want to travel on foot, by taxi, or on public transit.

Getting to the Churches: Both Santa Maria Maggiore and San Giovanni in Laterano, this chapter's two biggies, are just a few minutes' walk from Metro stops on line A. Santa Maria Maggiore is on Piazza di Santa Maria Maggiore (Metro: Termini or Vittorio Emanuele), and San Giovanni in Laterano is on Piazza di San Giovanni in Laterano (Metro: San Giovanni).

Santa Maria Maggiore is a block from Santa Prassede (see page 308 for walking directions); from there, it's a 15-minute walk (or €6 taxi ride) to San Clemente, or a 15- to 20-minute walk to San Giovanni in Laterano. If you don't want to walk from Santa Maria Maggiore to San Giovanni in Laterano, catch bus #16 or #714 (along Via Merulana), or hop into a taxi.

San Clemente (Metro: Colosseo) is an easy 15-minute walk from San Giovanni in Laterano, or a quick hop on tram #3 or bus #87. (The useful #87 connects Largo Argentina, Piazza Venezia, the Colosseo Metro stop, San Clemente, and San Giovanni in Laterano.)

Church of Santa Maria Maggiore: Church free, daily 7:00-18:45; museum €3, daily 9:30-18:30; "archaeological zone"—€5; tel. 06-6988 6800, www.vatican.va (search for "Santa Maria Maggiore").

Church of Santa Prassede: Free, bring €0.50 and €1 coins for lights, daily 7:00-12:00 & 15:00-18:30, no visit during Mass (Mon-Sat 7:30 & 18:00; Sun 8:00, 10:00, 11:30, & 18:00).

Church of San Clemente: Upper church—free, lower church—€10, both open Mon-Sat 9:00-12:30 & 15:00-18:00, Sun 12:15-18:00, www.basilicasanclemente.com.

Church of San Giovanni in Laterano: Church—free, daily 7:00-18:30; cloister—€5, daily 9:00-18:00; church audioguide available (donation requested, or pay €10 for combo-ticket that includes audioguide and entry to cloister and Holy Stairs chapel, ID required as deposit; pick up at info desk near the main door, either inside or outside); www.vatican.va (search for "San Giovanni in Laterano").

The **Holy Stairs** (Scala Santa), in a building across the street from the church, are free (Mon-Sat 6:30-19:00, Sun 7:00-19:00, Oct-March until 18:30, www.scala-santa.it). The chapel at the Holy Stairs costs €3.50 (Mon-Sat 9:30-12:40 & 15:00-17:10, closed Sun).

Dress Code: Modest dress is recommended (knees and shoulders covered).

Photography: Generally, photos without flash are allowed in Rome's churches. No photos are allowed in San Clemente, however.

The Tour Begins

Four churches are covered in this tour. You can visit all four or pick and choose the ones that interest you most. See "Getting to the Churches," earlier, for details on linking these sights.

CHURCH OF SANTA MARIA MAGGIORE

The basilica of Santa Maria celebrates Holy Mary, the mother of Jesus. One of Rome's oldest and best-preserved churches, it was built (A.D. 432) while Rome was falling around it. The city had been sacked by Visigoths (410), and the emperors were about to check out (476). Increasingly, popes stepped in to fill the vacuum of leadership. The fifth-century mosaics give the church the feel of the early Christian community. The general ambience of the church really takes you back to ancient times.

Exterior

Start your visit by standing directly in front of the church next to the ornate column in the square. From here you can make out

the earlier medieval church and bell tower (the tower was built in the late 14th century and is the tallest in Rome). The 13th-century mosaics of the medieval church survive behind the newer Rococo facade, which welcomes you like open theater curtains. The wings to the left and right were added for Vatican offices. Like Santa Maria Maggiore, most churches in Rome are much older than their facades. During the Baroque age, many were given facelifts.

Turn around and gape up. Mary's column originally stood in the Forum's Basilica of Constantine. This fifth-century church, built in her honor, proclaims she was indeed the Mother of God—a point disputed by hair-splitting theologians of the day.

When you step inside the church, you'll be entering Vatican property—the church, though on Italian territory, has similar status to an embassy. The "Maggiore" in the church's name indicates

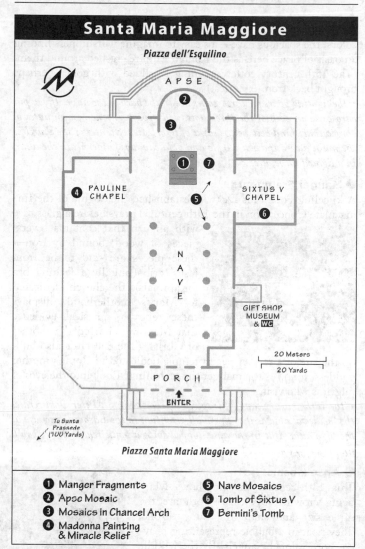

Santa Maria Maggiore

Piazza dell'Esquilino

APSE

② ③

① ⑦

④ PAULINE CHAPEL

⑤

SIXTUS V CHAPEL

⑥

N A V E

GIFT SHOP, MUSEUM & WC

20 Meters
20 Yards

P O R C H
↑ ENTER

To Santa Prassede (100 Yards)

Piazza Santa Maria Maggiore

① Manger Fragments
② Apse Mosaic
③ Mosaics in Chancel Arch
④ Madonna Painting & Miracle Relief
⑤ Nave Mosaics
⑥ Tomb of Sixtus V
⑦ Bernini's Tomb

that it is one of the Catholic Church's four "major basilicas" (all of them in Rome; the others are St. Peter's, San Giovanni in Laterano, and St. Paul Outside the Walls).

Inside the Church

Despite the Renaissance ceiling and Baroque crusting, you still feel like you're walking into an early Christian church. You can feel the joy and lightness typical of early churches that were built before the heavier medieval styles took hold. The stately rows of columns, the simple basilica layout (nave flanked by side aisles), the cheery colors, the spacious nave—it's easy to imagine worshippers finding an oasis of peace here as the Roman Empire crashed around them. (The 15th-century coffered ceiling is gilded with gold—perhaps brought back from America.)

• *The lighting boxes for three zones are in the back of the nave. If you put euro coins in each of the three slots, you give everyone two minutes of gorgeous art (and become the saint of light). In the center of the church is the main altar, under a purple and gold canopy. Underneath the altar, in a lighted niche, are...*

❶ Manger Fragments

A kneeling Pope Pius IX (who established the dogma of the Immaculate Conception in the 19th century) prays before a glass case

with an urn that contains several pieces of wood, bound by iron—these pieces are said to be from Jesus' crib (actually a feeding bin for animals). The church, dedicated to Mary's motherhood, displays these relics as physical evidence that Mary was indeed the mother of Christ. (The church is also built on the site of a former pagan temple dedicated to Rome's mother goddess, Juno.) Is the manger the real thing? Look into the eyes of pilgrims who visit.

• *The 18th-century canopy, inspired by the one in St. Peter's, obliterates the medieval apse as if to draw all attention to the Baroque spectacle at the high altar. But in the apse, topped with a semicircular dome, you'll find beautiful medieval mosaics.*

❷ Apse Mosaic

This 13th-century mosaic shows Mary being crowned by Jesus—both are the same size and share the same throne. They float in a bubble representing heaven, borne aloft by angels. By the Middle Ages, Mary's cult status was secure. Notice how the apostles are smaller and how even they dwarf the puny pope (lower left).

• *Up in the arch that frames the outside of the apse, you'll find some of the church's oldest mosaics.*

❸ Mosaics in Chancel Arch

Colorful panels tell Mary's story in fifth-century Roman terms. Haloed senator-saints in white togas (top panel on left side) attend to Mary, who sits on a throne, dressed in gold and crowned like an empress. The angel Gabriel swoops down to announce to Mary that she'll conceive Jesus, and the Dove of the Holy Spirit follows. Below (the panel in the bottom-left corner) are sheep representing the apostles, entering the city of Jerusalem ("HIERVSALEM").

• *In the separate chapel to your left, over the altar, you'll see a...*

❹ Madonna Painting and Miracle Relief

This chapel is a 17th-century Baroque addition to the church. Its altar, a geologist's delight, is adorned with jasper, agate, amethyst, lapis lazuli, and gold angels. Amid it all is a simple icon of the lady this church is dedicated to: Mary.

Above the painting is a bronze relief panel showing a pope, with amazed bystanders, shoveling snow. One hot August night in the year 358, Mary appeared to Pope Liberius in a dream, telling him: "Build me a church where the snow falls." The next morning, they discovered a small patch of snow here on Esquiline Hill—on August 5—and this church, dedicated to Santa Maria, was begun. The grandiose tombs of two grandiose popes fill the sides of the chapel.

• *Back out in the nave, on the other side of the altar, take a look at the...*

❺ Nave Mosaics

The church contains some of the world's best-preserved mosaics from early Christian Rome. If the floodlights are on, those with good eyesight or binoculars will enjoy watching the story of Moses unfold in a series of surprisingly colorful and realistic scenes—more sophisticated than anything that would be seen for a thousand years.

The small, square mosaic panels are above all the columns, on the right side of the nave. Start at the altar and work back toward the entry.

1. This is a later painting—skip it.
2. Pharaoh's daughter (upper left) and her maids take baby Moses from the Nile.
3. Moses (lower half of panel) sees a burning bush that reconnects him with his Hebrew origins. (Now leap the arch to #4.)
4. A parade of Israelites (left side) flees Egypt through a path in the Red Sea, while Pharaoh's troops drown.
5. Moses leads them across the Sinai desert (upper half), and God provides for them with a flock of quail (lower half).
6. Moses (upper half) sticks his magic rod in a river to desalinate it.
7. The Israelites battle their enemies while Moses commands from a hillside.
8. Skip this one, too.

9. Moses (upper left) brings the Ten Commandments, then goes with Joshua (upper right) to lie down and die.

10. Joshua crosses the (rather puny) Jordan River...

11. ...and attacks Jericho...

12. ...and then the walls come a-tumblin' down.

• *Head back toward the altar to see whether the gate to the right transept is open. If so, enter the late-Renaissance chapel (late 1500s); otherwise, skip ahead to Bernini's Tomb. On the right wall of the chapel is a statue of a praying pope, atop the...*

❻ Tomb of Sixtus V

The Rome we see today is due largely to Pope Sixtus V (or was it Fiftus VI?). This energetic pope (1585-1590) leveled shoddy medieval Rome and erected grand churches connected by long, broad boulevards spiked with obelisks as focal points (such as the obelisk in Piazza dell'Esquilino behind Santa Maria Maggiore). Today the city of Rome has 13 Egyptian obelisks (and the ancient city had many more)—whereas all of Egypt has only five.

The centerpiece of this chapel (called the "Sistine Chapel," but it's not the more famous one) shows four angels carrying a gilded model of the new St. Peter's dome, which was designed by Michelangelo. Finishing this project was a major part of Pope Sixtus' legacy.

The white carved-marble relief panels decorating the pope's tomb celebrate more of his accomplishments in reviving Rome (like the obelisks he raised and the buildings he commissioned).

• *Back in the main nave, on the closest (right) side of the main altar, look down for an inscription on the first step between two white columns. This marks...*

❼ Bernini's Tomb

The plaque reads, *"Ioannes Laurentivs Bernini"*—Gian Lorenzo Bernini (1598-1680)—"who brought honor to art and the city, here humbly rests." Next to it is another plaque to the *"Familia Bernini."* It's certainly humble...a simple memorial for the man who grew up in this neighborhood, then went on to remake Rome in the ornate Baroque style. (For more on Bernini, see page 280.)

• *After looking around Santa Maria Maggiore, fans of mosaics, Byzantines, and the offbeat should consider a visit to the nearby Church of Santa Prassede, about 100 yards away.*

Exiting Santa Maria Maggiore, find the obelisk in the distance (which would have directed medieval pilgrims down Via Merulana to the next big stop on their trail: the Church of San Giovanni in Laterano). Head in that direction just a few steps and follow a lane to the right, leading to a low-key side door where you enter Santa Prassede.

CHURCH OF SANTA PRASSEDE

The mosaics at the Church of Santa Prassede, from A.D. 822, are the best Byzantine-style mosaics in Rome. The Byzantine Empire, with its capital in Constantinople (ancient Istanbul), was the eastern half of the Roman Empire. Unlike the western half, it didn't "fall," and its inhabitants remained Christian, Greek-speaking, and cultured for a thousand years while their distant cousins in Italy were fumbling for the light switch in the Dark Ages. Byzantine craftsmen preserved the techniques of ancient Roman mosaicists (who decorated floors and walls of villas and public buildings), then reinfused this learning into Rome during the city's darkest era. Take the time to let your eyes adjust, and appreciate the Byzantine glory glowing out of the dark church.

Bring €0.50 and €1 coins to buy floodlighting and enjoy the full sparkle of the mosaics. Popping a coin into the box in the Chapel of St. Zeno (described later) saves you a trip to Ravenna.

• *The best mosaics are in the apse (behind the main altar; note another Baroque-era, "look-at-me" canopy over the high altar, like at Santa Maria Maggiore) and in the small Chapel of St. Zeno along the right (north) side of the nave.*

Apse Mosaics

On a blue background is Christ, standing in a rainbow-colored river, flanked by saints. Christ has commanded Peter (to our right of Christ, with white hair and beard) to spread the Good News to all the world. Beneath Christ, 12 symbolic sheep leave Jerusalem's city gates to preach to the world. Peter came here, to what was the world's biggest city, to preach love...and was met with a hostile environment. He turns his palm up in a plea for help. Persecuted Peter was taken in by a hospitable woman named Pudentia (next to him) and her sister, Praxedes (to the left of Christ, between two other saints),  whose house was located on this spot. (The church is named for Praxedes.)

The saint on the far left (with the square halo, indicating he was alive at the time this was made) is Pope Paschal I, who built the church in the 800s in memory of these early sisters, hiring the best craftsmen in the known world to do the mosaics. Pope Paschal was also responsible for evacuating the bones of the early martyrs from the endangered catacombs outside the city walls and building several churches to contain them within the safety of downtown.

Chapel of St. Zeno

The ceiling is gold, representing the Byzantine heaven. An icon-like Christ emerges from the background, supported by winged

angels in white, with lipstick and red cheeks. On the walls are saints walking among patches of flowers. In the altar niche, Mary and the child Jesus are flanked by the sisters Praxedes and Pudentia. On the side wall, the woman with the square blue halo is Theodora, the mom of the pope who built this. And in another niche is a supposed relic of the pillar upon which Christ was whipped on his way to Golgotha.

The chapel, covered completely with mosaics, may be underwhelming to our modern eyes, but in the darkness of Rome's medieval era, it was known as the "Garden of Paradise."

CHURCH OF SAN GIOVANNI IN LATERANO

Imagine the jubilation when this church—the first Christian church in the city of Rome—was opened in about A.D. 318. Christians could finally "come out" and worship openly without fear of reprisal. (Still, most Romans were pagan, so this first great church was tucked away from the center of things, near the city wall.) After that glorious beginning, the church served as the center of Catholicism and the home of the popes until the Renaissance renovation of St. Peter's and the expansion of the Vatican. Until 1870, all popes were "crowned" here. Even today, it's the home church of the Bishop of Rome—the pope. Like Santa Maria Maggiore, it's Vatican property.

• *To reach the church from the San Giovanni Metro station, exit to the right onto Via Magna Grecia, then head toward the old city walls. Before you leave the square, look left to find the* **Via Sannio market,** *which sells clothing and some handicrafts every morning except Sunday. Then pass through the archways, hugging the left side of the street, to approach San Giovanni's white, statue-topped facade.*

Exterior

The massive facade is 18th-century, with Christ triumphant on the top. The blocky peach-colored building adjacent on the right is the Lateran Palace, standing on the site of the old Papal Palace—residence of popes

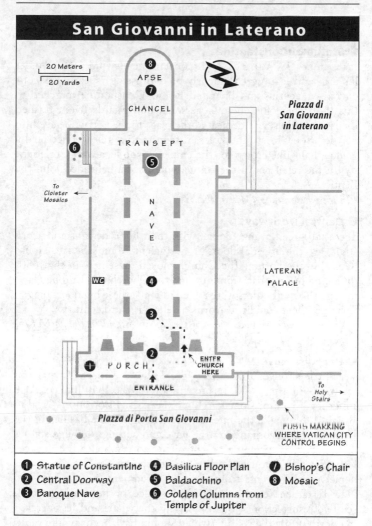

San Giovanni in Laterano

20 Meters
20 Yards

❽ APSE

❼ CHANCEL

Piazza di San Giovanni in Laterano

❻ TRANSEPT

❺

To Cloister Mosaics ←

N A V E

LATERAN PALACE

WC ❹

❸

❷ ENTER CHURCH HERE

❶ PORCH

ENTRANCE

To Holy Stairs →

Piazza di Porta San Giovanni

POSTS MARKING WHERE VATICAN CITY CONTROL BEGINS

❶ Statue of Constantine	❹ Basilica Floor Plan	❼ Bishop's Chair
❷ Central Doorway	❺ Baldacchino	❽ Mosaic
❸ Baroque Nave	❻ Golden Columns from Temple of Jupiter	

until about 1300. Across the street to your right are the pope's private chapel and the Holy Stairs (Scala Santa), popular with pilgrims (we'll see the stairs later). To the left is a well-preserved chunk of the ancient Roman wall. Pass the three-foot-high granite posts surrounding the church to leave Italy and enter the Vatican State—*carabinieri* must leave their guns at the door.

• *Step inside the portico and look left.*

Inside the Portico and Church
❶ Statue of Constantine
It's October 28, A.D. 312, and Constantine—sword tucked under his arm and leaning confidently on a (missing) spear—has conquered Maxentius and liberated Rome. Constantine marched to this spot where his enemy's personal bodyguards lived, trashed their pagan idols, and dedicated the place to the god who gave him his victory—Christ. The holes in Constantine's head once held a golden, halo-like crown for the emperor who legalized Christianity. In the relief above the statue, you'll see a beheaded John the Baptist.

• *In the portico, take a look at the...*

❷ Central Doorway
These tall green bronze doors, with their floral designs and acorn studs, are the original doors from ancient Rome's Senate House (Curia) in the Forum. The Church moved these here in the 1650s to remind people that, from now on, the Church was Europe's lawmaker. The star borders were added to make these big doors bigger. Imagine, those cool little acorns date to the third century.

• *Now go inside the main part of the church. Stand in the back of the nave.*

❸ Baroque Nave
Very little survives from the original church—most of what you see was built after 1600. In preparation for the 1650 Jubilee, Pope Innocent X commissioned architect Francesco Borromini (rival to Bernini) to remake the interior. He redesigned the basilica in the Baroque style, reorganizing the nave and adding the huge statues of the apostles (stepping out of niches to symbolically bring celestial Jerusalem to our world). The relief panels above the statues depict parallel events from the Old Testament (on the left) and New Testament (on the right). For instance, in the very back you'll see two resurrections: Jonah escaping the whale and Jesus escaping death. Only the ceiling (which should have been a white vault) breaks from the Baroque style—it's Renaissance, and the pope wanted it to stay.

❹ Basilica Floor Plan
San Giovanni was the first public church in Rome and the model for all later churches, including St. Peter's. The floor plan—a large central hall (nave) flanked by two side aisles—was based on the ancient Roman basilica floor plan. These buildings, built to hold law courts and meeting halls, were big enough to accommodate the large Christian congregations. Note that Roman basilicas came with two apses. You came in through the main entrance, which was designed to stress the authority of the place by slightly over-

whelming and intimidating those who entered. When the design was adapted for use as a church, a grand and welcoming entry (the west portal) replaced one of the apses. Upon entering, the worshipper could take in the entire space instantly, and the rows of columns welcomed him to proceed to the altar.

• *The canopy over the altar is called the...*

❺ Baldacchino

In the upper cage are two silver statues of Sts. Peter (with keys) and Paul (sword), which contain pieces of their heads. The gossip buzzing among Rome's amateur archaeologists is that the Vatican tested DNA from Peter's head (located here) and from his body (located at St. Peter's)...and they didn't match.

• *Standing in the left transept are the...*

❻ Golden Columns from Temple of Jupiter

Tradition says that these gilded bronze columns once stood in pagan Rome's holiest spot—the Temple of Jupiter, which was dedicated to the king of all gods, on the summit of Capitoline Hill (c. 50 B.C.). Now they support a triangular pediment inhabited by a bearded, Jupiter-like God the Father.

• *In the apse, you'll find the...*

❼ Bishop's Chair

The chair (called a "cathedra") reminds visitors that this is the cathedral of Rome...and the pope himself is the bishop who sits here. Once elected, the new pope must actually sit in this chair to officially become the pope. The ceremonial sitting usually happens within one month of election—Pope Francis took his seat on April 7, 2013.

• *Under the semicircular dome of the apse, take a close look at the...*

❽ Mosaic

The original design dates from about 450 (although it was made in the 13th century and heavily restored in the 19th century). You'll

see a cross, animals, plants, and the River Jordan running along the base. Mosaic, of course, was an ancient Roman specialty adapted by medieval Christians. The head of Christ (above the cross) must have been a glorious sight to early worshippers. It was one of the first legal images of Christ ever seen in formerly pagan Rome.

• *Fans of cosmatesque marble–inlay floor (c. 1100–1300) may want to buy a ticket to visit the cloister (enter near left transept).*

The Holy Stairs are outside the church in a building across the street. To get there, exit the church, turn left, and cross the street to the nondescript building.

Holy Stairs (Scala Santa)

In 326, Emperor Constantine's mother (St. Helena) brought home the 28 marble steps of Pontius Pilate's residence in Jerusalem. Jesus

climbed these steps on the day he was sentenced to death. Each day, hundreds of faithful penitents climb these steps on their knees while reciting a litany of prayers.

Covered with walnut wood spotted with small glass-covered holes showing stains from Jesus' blood, the steps lead to the "Holy of Holies" (Sancta Sanctorum), the private chapel of the popes in the Middle Ages. With its world-class relics, this chapel was considered the holiest place on earth. The relics were moved to the Vatican in 1905.

You can climb the tourist staircases along the sides; look inside the "Holy of Holies" through the grated windows (you can see essentially the entire chapel through the grates, but if you'd like to go inside, you'll have to buy a ticket at the ticket desk downstairs, near the entrance); and buy a souvenir at the gift shop (at the top floor, on the left). Or you're welcome to actually climb the stairs on your knees (pick up the €2 booklet at the gift shop that gives the proper prayer for each of the 28 steps). If you've done a lot of praying in your life, but never accompanied your prayers with a little pain—actually a lot of pain—give this a try.

Nearby: After exiting the steps, look right and notice the broken arch of the **Claudian Aqueduct** (1st century A.D.), which once carried water to the city from more than 40 miles away. The **Museum of the Liberation of Rome** isn't far behind it, just a few blocks down Via Tasso (see page 90). Then head toward the center of Piazza di San Giovanni in Laterano—straight ahead with your back to the Holy Stairs—for a look at the world's tallest obelisk, dating from the 15th century B.C. (This is also the departure point for bus #16, which runs up Via Merulana to the Church of Santa Maria Maggiore.)

CHURCH OF SAN CLEMENTE

Here, like nowhere else, you'll enjoy the layers of Rome—a 12th-century basilica sits atop a fourth-century Christian basilica, which sits atop a second-century Mithraic temple and some even earlier Roman buildings.

Upper Church—12th Century

The church (at today's ground level) is dedicated to the fourth pope, Clement, who shepherded the small Christian community when the religion was, at best, tolerated, and at worst, a capital offense. Clement himself was martyred by drowning in about A.D. 100—tied to an anchor by angry Romans and tossed overboard. You'll see his symbol, the anchor, around the church. The painting on the ceiling shows Clement being carried aloft to heaven.

While today's main entry is on the side, the original entry was through the **courtyard** in back, a kind of defensive atrium common in medieval times. To reach the original entry, enter the church through today's main entrance, walk diagonally toward the right, and exit again into this courtyard. Turn around and face the original entry. (This courtyard is inviting for a cool quiet break, as I imagine it was for a visiting medieval pilgrim.)

Back inside the church, step up to the carved marble **choir**—an enclosure in the middle of the church (Schola Cantorum) where the cantors sat. About 1,200 years ago, it stood in the old church beneath us, before that church was looted and destroyed by invading Normans.

In the apse (behind the altar), study the fine 12th-century mosaics. The delicate Crucifixion—with Christ sharing the cross with a dozen apostles as doves—is engulfed by a Tree of Life richly inhabited by deer, birds, and saints. The message is clear: All life springs from God in Christ. Above it all, a triumphant Christ, one hand on the Bible, blesses the congregation.

St. Catherine Chapel

The chapel in the back corner near the side (tourist) entrance—considered one of the first great Renaissance masterpieces—is dedicated to St. Catherine of Alexandria, a noblewoman martyred for her defense of persecuted Christians. The fresco on the left wall—which shows an early-Renaissance three-dimensional representation of space—is by the Florentine master Masolino (1428), perhaps aided by his young assistant, Masaccio. Studying the left wall, working from left to right, you can follow her story:

1. Catherine (lower-left panel), in black, confronts an assembly of the pagan Emperor Maxentius and his counselors. She bravely ticks off arguments on her fingers why Christianity should be legalized. Her powerful delivery silences the crowd.

2. Under the rotunda of a pagan temple (above, on the upper-left panel), Catherine, in blue, points up at a statue and tells a crowd of pagans, "Your gods are puny compared to mine."

3. Catherine, in blue (upper-right panel, left side), is thrown in prison, where she's visited by the emperor's wife (in green). Catherine converts her.

4. Emperor Maxentius, enraged, orders his own wife killed. The executioner (upper panel, right side), standing next to the empress' decapitated corpse, impassively sheathes his sword.

5. In the best-known scene (the middle panel on the bottom), Maxentius, in black, looks down from a balcony and condemns Catherine (in black) to be torn apart between two large, spiked wheels turned by executioners. But suddenly, an angel swoops in with a sword to cut her loose.

6. Catherine is eventually martyred (lower-right panel). Now dressed in green, she kneels before the executioner, who raises his sword to finish the job.

7. Finally, on the top of holy Mount Sinai (same panel, upper-right corner), two angels bear Catherine's body to its final resting place.

Taking a few steps back, look up at the arch that frames the chapel, topped by the delightful Annunciation fresco (top of the arch) by Masolino. Also notice the big St. Christopher, patron saint of travelers (left pillar), with 500-year-old graffiti scratched in by pilgrims—now covered with glass.

Lower Church—Fourth Century

Buy a €10 ticket in the bookshop, and descend 1,700 years to the time when Christians were razzed on their way to church by pagan neighbors. The first room you enter was the original atrium (entry hall)—the nave extends to the right. (Everything you'll visit from here on was buried until the 19th century.)

• *Most of the way down the atrium, look for the "reversible" stone set into a metal rack that you can rotate.*

Pagan Inscription

This two-sided recycled marble burial slab—one side (with leafy decorations) for a Christian, the other for a pagan—shows how the two Romes lived side by side in the fourth century.

• *Go through the nearby door into the nave, and walk to the far end. Five yards before the altar, on the left wall, look for the...*

Fresco of St. Clement and Sisinnius

Clement (center) holds a secret Mass for early Christians back when it was a capital crime. Theodora, a prominent Roman (in yellow, to the right), is one of the undercover faithful. Her pagan husband, Sisinnius, has come to retrieve and punish her when—zap!—he's struck blind and has to be led away (right side).

But Sisinnius is still unconvinced. When Clement cures his blindness, Sisinnius (very faded, lower panel, far right) orders two servants to drag Clement off to the authorities. But through a miraculous intervention, the servants mistake a column for Clement (see the shadowy black log) and drag that out of the house instead. The inscription (crossword-style on right, waist-high, very faded) is famous among Italians because it's one of the earliest examples of the transition from Latin to Italian. Sisinnius encourages his servants by yelling *"Fili dele pute, traite!"* ("You sons of bitches, pull!")

• *In the far-left corner of the lower church (in the room behind the fresco you just saw), near the staircase leading down, is the...*

Presumed Burial Place of St. Cyril

Cyril, who died in A.D. 869 (see the modern, icon-like mosaic of him), was an inveterate traveler who spread Christianity to the Slavic lands and Russia—today's Russian Orthodox faithful. Along the way, he introduced the Cyrillic alphabet still used by Russians and many other Slavs. Thanks to their tireless missionary work, Cyril and his brother Methodius are considered the most important figures in Slavic Christianity.

• *Now descend farther to the dark, dank Mithraic temple (Mithreum; through a door immediately to the right of the altar and down steps). Nowhere in Rome is there a better place to experience this weird cult.*

Temple of Mithras (Mithreum)—Second Century

• *The barred room to the left is the...*

Worship Hall

Worshippers of Mithras—men only—reclined on the benches on either side of the room. At the far end is a small statue of the god Mithras, in a billowing cape. In the center sits an altar carved with a relief showing Mithras fighting with a bull that contains all life. A scorpion, a dog, and a snake try to stop Mithras, but he wins, run-

ning his sword through the bull. The blood spills out, bringing life to the world.

Mithras' fans gathered here, in this tiny microcosm of the universe (the ceiling was decorated with stars), to celebrate the victory with a ritual meal. Every spring, Mithras brought new life again, and so they ritually kept track of the seasons—the four square shafts in the corners of the ceiling represent the seasons, the seven round ones were the great constellations. Initiates went through hazing rituals representing the darkness of this world, then emerged into the light-filled world brought by Mithras.

Rome's official pagan religion had no real spiritual content and did not offer any concept of salvation. As the empire slowly crumbled, people turned more and more to Eastern  religions (including Christianity), in search of answers and comfort. The cult of Mithras, stressing loyalty and based on the tenuousness of life, was popular among soldiers. Part of its uniqueness and popularity (in this very class-conscious society) was due to its belief that all were equal before God. It dates back to the time of Alexander the Great, who brought it from Persia. In 67 B.C., soldiers who had survived the bloody conquest of Asia Minor returned to Rome swearing by Mithras. When Christians gained power, they banished the worship of Mithras.

Facing the barred room are two rectangular Corinthian columns supporting three arches of the temple's entryway, decorated with a fine stucco coffered ceiling.

At the far end of the hallway, another barred door marks the equivalent of a Mithraic Sunday school room. Peek inside to see a faded fresco of bearded Mithras (right wall) and seven niches carved into the walls representing the seven stages a novice had to go through.

Head back the way you came. On your right, watch for a very narrow ancient alleyway separating Roman walls barely three feet across. If it's open, step in and imagine the first Western city to reach one million residents. Forget the two churches above you, and imagine standing on this exact spot and looking up at the sky 2,000 years ago. Now climb back through the centuries to today's street level.

TRASTEVERE WALK

*From the Tiber to the Church of
Santa Maria in Trastevere*

Trastevere—the colorful neighborhood across the river from down-town—is *the* place to immerse yourself in the crustier side of Rome. This half-mile walk is designed to train your eye to see Rome more intimately. In Trastevere (trahs-TAY-veh-ray), you'll discover a se-cret, hidden city of heroic young martyrs, lovers kissing on Vespas, party-loving Renaissance bankers, and feisty "Trasteverini"—old-timers who pride themselves on never setting foot on the opposite bank of the Tiber River.

Orientation

Length of This Walk: Allow 1.5 hours. To see Trastevere in less time, taxi directly to Santa Maria in Trastevere (the square where this walk ends). You'll still capture plenty of ambience.

When to Go: This walk can work well at any time of day, but start-ing around 10:00 allows you to see the Church of Santa Ce-cilia and the Villa Farnesina (except Sun). Mornings are cool and relatively quiet. Strolling through Trastevere at dusk is especially atmospheric. Consider combining this walk with a meal or as a prelude to my Heart of Rome Walk (see page 110).

Getting There: This walk starts at the island in the Tiber River, just across from Rome's Jewish ghetto and within walking distance of the Capitoline Hill, Piazza Venezia, and Campo de' Fiori. From Piazza Venezia or Largo Argentina, tram #8 can speed your trip—get off at the Belli stop. Except on Sun-day, express bus #H runs to Trastevere from Termini train station and Piazza della Repubblica (on the northeast side of the square, near the entrance to the Baths of Diocletian)—get off at the Sonnino stop. From the Vatican, take bus #23 from Piazza Risorgimento along the river to the Lungotevere Alberteschi stop. From the Colosseum area, take a bus to Piazza Venezia, then tram #8.

Church of Santa Cecilia: Church—free, Mon-Sat 10:00-13:00 & 16:00-19:00, Sun 16:00-19:00; crypt—€2.50, same hours as church; choir loft with frescoes—€2.50, Mon-Sat 10:00-12:30; tel. 06-589-9289.

Church of Santa Maria in Trastevere: Free, daily 7:30-21:00 (except Aug 8:00-12:00 & 16:00-21:00).

Villa Farnesina: €6, Mon-Sat 9:00-14:00, closed Sun (except open 9:00-17:00 on second Sun of the month).

Tours: ∩ Download my free Trastevere Walk audio tour.

Eateries: Several recommended restaurants are on the map and described in the Eating in Rome chapter (see page 365).

The Walk Begins

• *Start halfway across the Ponte Cestio (Cestius Bridge)—called the "Ponte Fabricio" on the east side of the river—which connects Isola Tiberina ("Island in the Tiber") to Trastevere.*

❶ Isola Tiberina and the Tiber River

Rome got its start 3,000 years ago along the Tiber River at this point. This was as far upstream as big boats could sail and the first

place the river could be crossed by bridge. As a center of river trade, Rome connected the interior of the Italian peninsula with the Mediterranean. The area below you would have been bustling in ancient times. Look down and imagine small ports, water mills, ramshackle boats, and platforms for fishing.

The **island** itself was once the site of a temple dedicated to Asclepius, the god of medicine. Ancient Romans who were ill spent the night here and left little statues of their healed body parts (feet, livers, hearts...) as thank-you notes. This tradition survives: Today, throughout Italy, Catholic altars are often encrusted with votive offerings, symbolizing gratitude for answered prayers. During plagues and epidemics, the sick were isolated on the island. These days, the island's largest building is the Fatebenefratelli, the public hospital favored by Roman women for childbirth. The island's reputation for medical care lives on.

The high point of the **bridge** (upon which you're probably leaning) is an ancient stone with a faded inscription dating from about A.D. 370, when this then-400-year-old bridge was rebuilt. The eroding plaque is stapled into the balustrade like a piece of recycled scrap. Run your fingers over the word "Caesar" (top line, just right of center). This part of the Tiber River flooded frequently, which devalued the land on the north bank; in time it would become the site of the Jewish ghetto (started in the 16th century, but now long gone, though Rome's synagogue remains). (For a detailed tour of this area, take my Jewish Ghetto Walk, available 📖 as a chapter in this book and 🎧 as a free audio tour.)

In the 1870s, the Romans removed the threat of flooding by practically walling off the Tiber, building the tall, anonymous embankments that continue to isolate the river from the city today.

• *Head south to leave the bridge. If open, the green riverside Sora Mirella kiosk on the right (run by Mirella's son, Stefano) is the most famous vendor of Rome's summer refresher called a* grattachecca *(pronounced grah-tah-kek-kah, €1), a concoction of shaved ice with fruit-flavored syrup and chopped fruit (similar to a granita). Cross the street and go down the 12 steps into the car-filled piazza.*

❷ Piazza in Piscinula

As you descend and enter the square, look directly ahead. Rising up among the buildings is a cute little church bell tower. Dating from 1069, this is the oldest working bell tower in the city.

• *Facing the tower, turn right and exit the trapezoid-shaped square from the far corner, opposite where you entered, going uphill on Via dell'Arco de' Tolomei. At the top of the small slope, pause and look around.*

❸ Via dell'Arco de' Tolomei

Except for the parking garage, the buildings around you are mostly apartments. The ochre-and-yellow buildings, with green or brown shutters and draped with vines, are characteristic of Trastevere and many Roman neighborhoods. Find the olive trees in planters, and look up at the plant-covered rooftop terraces—the Roman equivalent of a leafy backyard. An *attico con terrazzo* (penthouse with a terrace) is every Roman's dream.

Glancing up, you'll notice an elegantly restored, freshly painted **tower** incorporated into the apartments. In medieval times, the city skyline had 300 of these towers (about 50 survive). Each noble family competed for the tallest one until, in about 1250, city authorities got fed up and had them all lopped off. Later (mainly Baroque) construction incorporated most of the remaining "stumps," and you can still see these remnants of medieval Rome all over the old center. Incorporating old structures into new ones was always considered more economical and practical than demolishing and starting again from scratch. In the Middle Ages, Rome had re-

TRASTEVERE

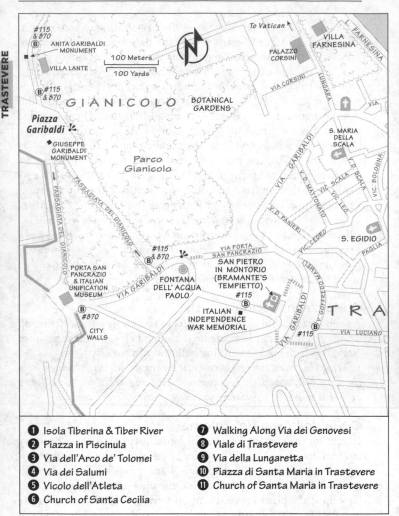

1. Isola Tiberina & Tiber River
2. Piazza in Piscinula
3. Via dell'Arco de' Tolomei
4. Via dei Salumi
5. Vicolo dell'Atleta
6. Church of Santa Cecilia
7. Walking Along Via dei Genovesi
8. Viale di Trastevere
9. Via della Lungaretta
10. Piazza di Santa Maria in Trastevere
11. Church of Santa Maria in Trastevere

gressed to being a big village; any idea of town planning was lost until the Renaissance.

Now look down the lane ahead of you, where there's a low-arched passageway. Lots of aristocratic buildings were connected by these elevated passages. Imagine herds of sheep shuffling through here in medieval times while smoke billowed from the windows and doors of homes that lacked chimneys.

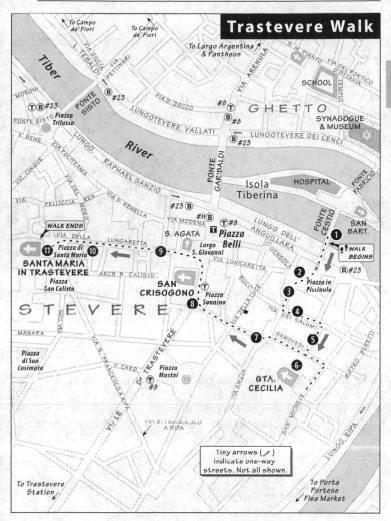

• *Continue on, passing through the arched lane. Turn left immediately, and walk a few steps along...*

❹ Via dei Salumi

This is called "Cold Cuts Street." Here (as elsewhere in Mediterranean countries), many streets were named after the businesses that clustered there. The streets—rarely paved—were clogged by shop stalls.

The red-brown building on your right (pretty ugly unless you're a fascist) is a **school from the Mussolini era.** The fascist leader believed in the classical motto *mens sana in corpore sano* ("a healthy mind in a healthy body"), and loved being seen fencing,

TRASTEVERE

boxing, swimming, and riding. He endowed school buildings with lots of gyms. It's still a school, and you might hear the cheerful noise of kids pouring out the windows.

• *After passing the school, turn right again, heading up...*

❺ Vicolo dell'Atleta ("Alley of the Athlete")

This little alleyway is too narrow for cars—only people and a few scooters. Notice how quiet this makes things. Check out the latest fashions in underwear hanging out to dry. Apartments in Rome tend to be quite small, and electricity is more expensive than in the US, so few have clothes dryers. The small apartments also explain why young people tend to hang around outside in streets like this.

Notice the variety of doorways in this unplanned community. Some structures have ancient fragments recycled ingloriously into medieval buildings. Halfway down the alley on the right (at #14) is a restaurant that, a thousand years ago, was a **synagogue.** Find the Hebrew faintly inscribed on the base of the columns of the exposed brick structure (on the upper floor). A large part of Rome's Jewish community, the most ancient outside Palestine, lived in Trastevere until the popes moved them into the ghetto on the other side of the river in the 1500s.

• *Continue, turning left on Via dei Genovesi, then go right on Via di S. Cecilia to reach Piazza di Santa Cecilia. Here you'll find the Church of Santa Cecilia by passing through the impressive, white, Neoclassical structure that encloses the convent courtyard. Enter the courtyard and take a moment to sit by the fountain.*

❻ Church of Santa Cecilia

The church stands on a spot where Christians have worshipped

as far back as the second and third centuries. Trastevere had early Christian churches like Santa Cecilia because foreigners tended to settle here, including early Christians from Greece and Judaea.

Notice the church's eclectic exterior. Its mismatched columns were recycled from pagan temples. The typical medieval bell tower sports an 18th-century facade.

The church was supposedly built atop what was St. Cecilia's home. Cecilia was a pagan Roman (third century) from a wealthy family, who converted to Christianity in a time when Christians were intensely persecuted. Cecilia revealed her faith to her pagan husband only on their wedding night and told him of her aspiration to remain chaste (uh-oh...). An angel appeared to reason with the frustrated groom. Once converted, he devoted himself to carrying out Christian burials in the catacombs, until he himself was killed. Cecilia was soon condemned as well. The Romans tried unsuccessfully for three days to suffocate her with steam in her bath to make it appear accidental. They finally lost patience and beheaded her.

Before her death, Cecilia had used her lavish house to host Mass, as churches were forbidden. She bequeathed the house to the neighborhood community, and it's been a place of worship since then. A church was built here soon after her death, though the structure we see today dates mostly from the early ninth century and was extensively restored in the 18th century.

Church Interior: If the church is open, head inside and enjoy the cool elegance of the white-and-gold nave.

Cecilia is the patron saint of musicians and singers (notice the fine organ on the left). Legend says she sang at her own wedding. Ever since, the church named for her has been popular for weddings. Of Rome's 40 medieval churches, many have two-year waiting lists for weekend weddings. Most young Roman couples favor the more sober elegance of medieval churches over Baroque, which they dismiss as *troppo pesante*—"too heavy." (On the other hand, there's nothing understated about the typical Italian wedding gown.)

The white-marble **canopy** above the altar (dating from the 1200s) is by Arnolfo di Cambio. Its innovative fusion of Roman styles (realistic statues) and French Gothic architecture (pinnacles and rows of flamboyant "flames") shows that the artist knew his classics and had also been to Paris.

The **mosaic** in the apse dates from the ninth century. It shows Pope Paschal—the man who built the current church—on the left; he holds a little model of it in his hands. His square halo (the "halo of the living") signifies that he was alive when the mosaic was made.

The church's highlight is the evocative **statue of St. Cecilia** by Stefano Maderno (in the case below the altar). In the 1600s, Cecilia's long-buried remains were discovered. When her tomb was opened, Maderno himself was present. He claimed, along with other bystanders, to have seen her body perfectly preserved for an unforgettable instant before it turned to dust. He created this touching statue from his memory of that scene.

It shows Cecilia as she would have appeared just after her martyrdom. She lies with her face turned and hidden, the violence of her death suggested only by the gash in her neck. She died professing her faith. Notice the position of her fingers—showing three fingers on one hand (including the thumb, which Italians today also count with) and one on the other. Three in one—the oneness of the Trinity.

Maderno's statue—though made of hard stone—captures the limpness of Cecilia's lifeless body and the softness of her intricately folded robe and head scarf. It's typical of Counter-Reformation art—charged with great emotional impact to enhance faith.

More Church Sights: The **crypt** contains the so-so remains of a complex of ancient buildings (an *insula* or apartment house) that includes what is thought to have been Cecilia's house (a *domus*). The series of rooms is extensive but pretty bare. You'll see ancient fragments of sarcophagi with inscriptions and early Christian iconography (crosses, shepherds, anchors, doves). You'll walk over patches of original mosaic floors. One room was used for grain storage, and you'll see holes in the floor where the grain was stored (€2.50, entrance at the bookstore located to the left as you enter the church).

The **choir loft** *("Il Coro"),* where cloistered nuns would view the Mass while hidden behind a screen, contains a fragmentary but extraordinary Last Judgment fresco painted by Pietro Cavallini, a contemporary of Giotto (c. 1300). Scholars debate who influenced whom: Giotto or Cavallini. But there's no debate that the art here shows cutting-edge realism in the expressive faces of the apostles who sit believably in their chairs (€2.50, accessed from outside the church through a doorway to the left of the facade; press the buzzer, and the sisters will let you in). If you're here at 18:00 on a Wednesday, you're welcome to read the Lectio Divina with the nuns.

• *Leaving the church, backtrack left, and take the first left onto Via dei Genovesi. From here we'll walk straight along this street several blocks to the busy boulevard of Viale di Trastevere.*

❼ Walking Along Via dei Genovesi

This is one of Trastevere's main streets, yet it's barely wide enough for a single car (as you'll notice whenever you have to step aside to let a car pass). Buildings, people, and cars compete for the precious little available space. Strolling here, you'll understand why the Italian language has no word for "privacy" (they use our word and roll the *r*). Reading a letter on the Metro attracts a crowd. If someone has a fight (or a particularly good orgasm), the entire neighborhood knows. Young lovers with no place to go are adept at riding *moto-rini*...while parked.

As you walk, you'll pass the back side of the Mussolini-era school we saw earlier. Looking to the right, you'll see the low arch we walked under near Via dei Salumi.

After another 100 yards or so, detour right at Via della Luce. Walk a half-block to #21 (on the right) and pop into **Biscottifi-cio Artigiano Innocenti,** a traditional cookie-and-pastry bakery that's been here since the 1940s. In the face of modern efficiency, humble Stefania Innocenti, who was "artisanal" long before it was cool, continues to bake the seasonal cookies that Italians love to eat.

• *Return to Via dei Genovesi, turn right, and continue straight ahead to where it meets a busy street.*

❽ Viale di Trastevere

The wide, modern boulevard called Viale di Trastevere bisects Trastevere, which was otherwise spared most of the demolishing

and rebuilding suffered by other traditional neighborhoods when Rome became the capital of a united Italy in 1870.

Across the street, notice the four big, red columns on the fa-cade of the venerable Basilica di San Crisogono (fifth century). Also notice the convenient #8 tram that passes along Viale di Trastevere. It can take you back to Largo Argentina or Piazza Venezia after our tour is over.

• *Cross to the other side of Viale di Trastevere and turn right, then left into the square called Largo San Giovanni de Matha. Pass by the text-book Baroque facade of the faded yellow church and continue along...*

❾ Via della Lungaretta

Here you'll notice a change in atmosphere—the quiet, mystical charm of the first part of your walk has given way to livelier, more colorful, more touristy (and higher-rent) surroundings.

A small crafts market is often open along here, and street-corner artists display their work. You'll pass lots and lots of res-taurants and boutiques and swim amid a sea of strolling people—tourists and locals alike.

• *Walk several blocks until Via della Lungaretta opens up into the big square. Take a seat on the fountain steps.*

Soccer: The National Obsession

One of Rome's most local "sights" is a soccer match. Winston Churchill said that Italians lose wars as if they were soccer matches and soccer matches as if they were wars. Soccer *(calcio)* is the national obsession: Everyone, regardless of age or social class, is

an expert, quick with an opinion on a coach's lousy decision or a referee's unprofessional conduct. Fans love to insult officials: A favorite is *"arbitro cornuto!"*—the referee is a cuckold (i.e., his wife sleeps around).

Rome has a special passion for soccer. It has two teams, Roma (representing the city) and Lazio (the region), and the rivalry is fanatic. When Romans are introduced,

they ask each other, *"Laziale o romanista?"* The answer can compromise a relationship. Both Roma (jersey: yellow and red; symbol: she-wolf) and Lazio (jersey: light blue and white; symbol: imperial eagle) claim to be truly Roman. Lazio is older (founded in 1900), but Roma has more supporters. Lazio is supposed to be more upper-class, Roma more popular, but the social division is blurred.

The most eagerly awaited sporting event of the year is the derby, when the two teams fight it out at the Olympic Stadium (Stadio Olimpico). All of Italy acknowledges that team spirit is

❿ Piazza di Santa Maria in Trastevere

You're in the heart of the neighborhood. Piazza di Santa Maria in Trastevere—in the shadow of the big brick bell tower of the Church of Santa Maria in Trastevere—is the district's most important meeting place. With its broad and inviting steps, the 17th-century fountain was actually designed to be the "sofa" of the neighborhood. During major soccer games, a large screen is set up here so that everybody can share in the tension and excitement. At other times, children gather here with a ball and improvise matches of their own (one reason for the window grates). For more on soccer, see the sidebar.

• *Dominating the square is the...*

⓫ Church of Santa Maria in Trastevere

One of Rome's oldest church sites, this building stands where early Christians worshipped illegally in a home until the year 313. It was made a basilica—probably the first church in Rome dedicated to the Virgin Mary—in the fourth century, when Christianity was le-

most fervent in Rome. Fans prepare months in advance, and on the day of the match they fill the entire stadium with team colors, flags, banners, and smoke candles.

Witty slogans on banners work like dialogues: A Roma banner proclaimed, "Roma: Only the sky is higher than you." The Lazio banner replied, "In fact, the sky is blue and white" (like its team colors). The exchange revealed that there had been a Lazio informer on the Roma side, which traumatized Roma fans for weeks. Tourists go to a match more for the action in the stands than the action on the field—for some, it's the most Roman of all experiences.

Both teams call the Olympic Stadium home, so you can catch a game most weekends from September to May (Metro line A to Flaminio, then catch tram #2 to the end of the line, Piazza Mancini, and cross the bridge to the stadium). If you're coming from Termini train station, take bus #910; from the Vatican, take bus #32 from Piazza Risorgimento. It's best to buy tickets in advance (which is often the only way to get them) at www.listicket.it or in town at a team store (bring ID).

galized. The tower survives from the 12th century, when the entire church was rebuilt.

Step into the portico (the covered area just outside the door). It's decorated with ancient stone fragments, some from the earlier church. Filled with early Christian symbolism such as the dove and olive branch, many of these stones were lids to burial niches from catacombs. In one fragment at the far-left end of the portico (left of the door, about 10 feet off the ground), notice how early Christians prayed with both hands raised, as evangelical Christians do today.

Now go inside. Make a U-turn left (just around the column), and look up to find a gold-and-white **plaque** on the wall dedicated to "Olea Sancta." This "holy oil" refers to a small petroleum deposit discovered here in

30 B.C. The black liquid was almost magical in its ability to power lamps and was incorporated into the lore of this church.

Grab a pew. Most of what you see dates from around the 12th century, although the granite columns are from ancient Roman buildings. Later architects tried hard to match them, but notice how the capitals are mismatched (some have tiny pagan heads of Egyptian gods), and the shorter columns have taller bases. The ancient basilica floor plan (and ambience) survives. The intricate coffered ceiling has an unusual image of Mary painted on copper at the center.

Approach the main altar for a closer look at the fine **mosaics** in the apse. Pop a coin in the box (to the left) to light them. The central scene is one of the few surviving examples of an early medieval mosaic (8th-10th century) in Rome. It's rich in symbolism. Christ and Mary sit side by side, enthroned in majesty. They wear rich gold robes, and Mary has a crown. Notice the stature Mary is given. Tour guides claim this is the first mosaic to show her at the throne with Jesus in heaven. He has his arm around his mother as if introducing her to us. Christ's almond eyes and the elaborate  folds in the robes show the influence of Byzantine icons. Flanking Christ and Mary are early bishops of Rome, including the first one, St. Peter (in gray). Beneath them, the row of sheep is not just any flock—it represents Jesus in the middle (marked by a halo with a cross in it) and the 12 apostles. Sitting on the ground below all of these mosaics is the throne-like chair of the bishop, giving legitimacy to the Church leadership.

The mosaic panels below the sheep show scenes from the life of Mary. These more "modern" mosaics (from the late 1300s, also by Cavallini, who also did the Last Judgment at Santa Cecilia) are impressively realistic and expressive, yet predate the Renaissance by a hundred years. The first panel (far left, facing out from the curved apse) shows Mary (in the lower corner of the scene) as a baby. A servant prepares to bathe her, but first she checks the temperature of the water with her hand, introducing an element of human tenderness almost unheard of in medieval art. The next panel shows the angel arriving to announce Jesus' coming to Mary (and Mary asking, "Who, me?!"). Next, Mary reclines, having just given birth to Jesus in a stable, while shepherds arrive to admire him. Next comes the Three Kings, who kneel to adore the babe, followed by the presentation of the child Jesus in the temple. The final scene shows Mary's eternal sleep (not "death"). The gold mosaic backgrounds show buildings that, while not fully realistic, are a good step toward accurate 3-D representation.

The incredibly expensive 13th-century **floor** is a fine example of Cosmati mosaic work. The Cosmati family specialized in piecing together different colors of stone (in this case, made with marble scavenged from Roman ruins) to make intricate interlacing patterns of geometric shapes: circles, squares, triangles, and diamonds. The Cosmatis' work set the tone for the pavement in the rest of the church.

As you leave, spend a moment with **St. Anthony** (the statue in the back corner of the nave, opposite the "Olea Sancta" plaque). He was a favorite of the poor and is inundated with prayer requests on scraps of paper. The Community of St. Egidio operates from this church. They feed the local poor and care for young drug addicts. Each Christmas they take out all the pews, move in tables and chairs, and put on a huge dinner for those in need.

• *From here, enjoy exploring Rome's most colorful district. Saunter around the streets to the left of the church as you leave. The farther you venture from the square, the less touristy and more rustic the neighborhood becomes. Wandering the back lanes and pondering the earthy enthusiasm people seem to have for life here, I can imagine that bygone day when proud Trastevere locals would brag that they never crossed the river.*

On the other hand, if you'd like to soak up expansive views of the city and interesting architecture, you can extend this walk from Piazza di Santa Maria up to the Gianicolo Hill park and viewpoint (see page 95). Or, to cap off your Trastevere stroll with one more sight, visit **Villa Farnesina***, a Renaissance villa decorated by Raphael (see page 92 for a self-guided tour). To get there, face the Church of Santa Maria in Trastevere and leave the piazza by walking along the right side of the church, following Via della Paglia to Piazza di S. Egidio. Turn right and exit the piazza near the church—you'll be on Via della Scala. Follow through the Porta Settimiana, where the street changes names to Via della Lungara. On your right, you'll pass John Cabot University. Look for a white arch that reads Accademia dei Lincei (#230). The villa is through this gate.*

Another way to extend this walk is to head to the river, cross the Ponte Sisto pedestrian bridge, and make your way to Campo de' Fiori, where my **Heart of Rome Walk** *begins (see that chapter for details).*

From Piazza di Santa Maria in Trastevere, to get back to downtown Rome by public transportation, backtrack along Via della Lungaretta to Viale di Trastevere to catch tram #8. Or keep going straight down Via della Lungaretta to reach Ponte Cestio and Isola Tiberina, where our Trastevere walk began.

ANCIENT APPIAN WAY TOUR

Via Appia Antica

The wonder of its day, the Appian Way was the largest, widest, fastest road ever, called the "Queen of Roads." Begun in 312 B.C. and named after Appius Claudius Caecus (a Roman official), it connected Rome with Capua (near Naples), running in a straight line for much of the way and ignoring the natural contours of the land. Eventually, this most important of Roman roads stretched 430 miles to the port of Brindisi—the gateway to the East—where boats sailed for Greece and Egypt. Twenty-nine such roads fanned out from Rome. Just as Hitler built the autobahn system in anticipation of empire maintenance, the expansion-minded Roman government realized the military and political value of good roads.

The Hollywood image of the Appian Way as lined with the crucified bodies of Spartacus and his slave rebels is only partially accurate. While Spartacus was killed in battle, not crucified, historians do believe that after his defeat in 71 B.C., 6,000 slaves were crucified on crosses spaced about 30 yards apart along the length of the Appian Way—a distance of more than 100 miles. As a warning to other slaves, their bodies were left to hang for several months. Imagine the eerie welcome this provided visitors arriving in Rome.

After the Christian faith permeated Rome, the Appian Way became a popular underground burial place for Christians. It later falsely entered Romantic lore as a place where Christians hid from persecution. Today the road and the landscape around it are preserved as a cultural park.

For the tourist, the ancient Appian Way offers three attractions: the road itself, with its ruined monuments; the two major Christian catacombs open to visitors; and the peaceful atmosphere, which provides a respite from the city. Be aware, however, that the road today is quite treacherous in spots—very narrow, with almost no shoulder, and busy with traffic. I recommend following this tour's route, which avoids the worst of the traffic, making the area a pleasant place for strolling or biking.

Orientation

Length of This Tour: Budget five hours to get to and from the Appian Way, to walk or bike the stretch of sights, and to visit one of the catacombs.

When to Go: Visit in the morning or midafternoon (note that the Catacombs of San Callisto shut down from 12:00 to 14:00), but don't go too late; the last tours at both catacombs depart at 16:30 (and other sights close as early as 16:00). All the recommended sights are open on Tuesday, Thursday, Friday, and Saturday. On Monday several sights are closed, including the Tomb of Cecilia Matella and the Circus and Villa of Maxentius. On Wednesday, the Catacombs of San Callisto and the pedestrian path through the park are closed. On Sunday, the Catacombs of San Sebastiano are closed, but the Appian Way is closed to most car traffic, making it a great day for walking or biking (see "Bike Rental," later).

Getting There: You can reach the Appian Way by taxi or public transportation. This chapter's map shows bus stops, though locations can change. There are only a few places to buy bus tickets on the Appian Way (including the TI and the shop at the Catacombs of San Sebastiano)—have one in hand for your return trip.

A **taxi** will get you from Rome to the starting point of our tour, the Tomb of Cecilia Metella, for about €20. However, to return by taxi, you'll have to phone for one; there are no taxi stands on the Appian Way.

To ride **public transit** to the Tomb of Cecilia Metella, take Metro line A to the Colli Albani stop, then take bus #660 (2/hour) 15 minutes to the last stop—Cecilia Metella/Via Appia Antica (at the intersection of Via Cecilia Metella and Via Appia Antica). Alternatively, you can take bus #118 from downtown Rome to the Catacombs of San Sebastiano, then walk 500 yards (less than 10 minutes) south to the Tomb of Cecilia Metella. Ask at a TI for the latest information on where to catch the #118, as its route is occasionally diverted.

Returning to downtown Rome is easily done by bus. Bus #118 is the quickest option from the end of our tour. It runs along the Appian Way at the road's north end; catch it at the Domine Quo Vadis Church. It stops at Circo Massimo Metro station, near the Forum and Palatine Hill, as well as other downtown locations. Bus #218 is an alternate way to return to Rome from the end of the tour. It goes from Domine Quo

Sebastiano vs. Callisto

Which of the two catacombs is the best? They're actually quite similar. Both include a half-hour tour that takes you underground to see the niches where early Christians were buried (but no bones). Both have some faded frescoes and graffiti with Christian symbols. Both have small chapels and a few memorial statues. Most people pick one catacomb to visit, and either will fit the bill.

I lean slightly in favor of San Callisto, but only because of its historical importance, not because it's inherently more interesting. San Sebastiano tends to be less crowded, is historic in its own right (as the relics of Sts. Peter and Paul and St. Sebastian were kept here), and—most significantly—offers an experience with a bit more variety, since it also includes several remarkably well-preserved pagan Roman tombs and a Baroque church with a bust by Gian Lorenzo Bernini.

(Note that the **Catacombs of Priscilla**—more intimate and less crowded than these two more famous ones—can be found at the other end of town, northeast of the Villa Borghese Gardens; see page 77.)

Vadis Church to San Giovanni in Laterano, where you can pick up the Metro. It also stops by the west entrance of the Catacombs of San Callisto.

Information: The **Via Appia Antica TI** near Domine Quo Vadis Church is a resource for the entire park, which stretches east and south of the visit outlined here (Mon-Sat 9:30-13:00 & 14:00-17:00, Sun 9:30-17:00, rents bikes, sells good map, Via Appia Antica 58, tel. 06-513-5316, www.parcoappiaantica.it).

The archaeological site of **Capo di Bove** has a small info center that sits deep in a tranquil, inviting garden surrounding active excavations (Mon-Sat 10:00-16:00, Sun 10:00-18:00, closes earlier in winter, good place for discreet picnic, clean WCs, Via Appia Antica 222, tel. 06-3996-7700).

Tomb of Cecilia Metella: €6, includes entry to the Baths of Caracalla and Villa dei Quintili, April-Sept Tue-Sun 9:00-19:00, closes earlier Oct-March, closed Mon year-round, last entry one hour before closing, tel. 06-3996-7700, http://archeoroma.beniculturali.it.

Circus and Villa of Maxentius: Free, Tue-Sun 10:00-16:00, closed Mon, www.villadimassenzio.it.

Catacombs of San Sebastiano: €8, includes 35-minute tour, 2/hour; Mon-Sat 10:00-17:00, closed Sun and late Nov-late Dec, handy café and WCs, tel. 06-785-0350, www.catacombe.org.

Catacombs of San Callisto: €8, includes 30-minute tour, at least

2/hour; Thu-Tue 9:00-12:00 & 14:00-17:00, closed Wed and late Jan-late Feb, tel. 06-513-0151, www.catacombe.roma.it.

Domine Quo Vadis Church: Free, daily 8:00-18:00 (until 19:00 in summer), tel. 06-512-0441.

Bike Rental: Some may find the old paving stones too bumpy for biking. But if you'd like to try it, the best day for biking is Sunday, when the Appian Way is closed to traffic (though a few cars with special permission can still sneak through). Take bus #660 to the last stop (Cecilia Metella/Via Appia Antica), and you'll find **Appia Antica Caffè,** where you can rent a bike (€4/hour, €10/3 hours, Tue-Sun 9:00-sunset, Mon 9:00-13:30, near Tomb of Cecilia Metella at Via Appia Antica 175, on corner with Via Cecilia Metella, tel. 06-8987-9575, www. appiaanticacaffe.it). On Mondays, you could take bus #118 to the **Via Appia Antica TI** (see "Information," earlier), rent a bike there, and cycle down to the beginning of the tour (€3/ hour, €15/day). I don't recommend biking all the way from downtown, it's a long ride with heavy traffic.

Services: Free WCs are at the San Sebastiano and San Callisto catacombs and at Capo di Bove, and WCs for paying customers are at the Tomb of Cecilia Metella and the Appia Antica Caffè. There are several fountains along the way for refilling water bottles.

Eating: Appia Antica Caffè (see "Bike Rental," earlier) makes big salads and abundant sandwiches and has a shaded, restful seating area in back; tucked even farther back in their garden is a fine little *gelateria.* If you've brought your own food, great picnic spots are just a half-mile farther south from here. Several pricey restaurants are along the stretch between the Tomb of Cecilia Metella and the Catacombs of San Sebastiano, and there is normally a sandwich-and-drinks cart by the Catacombs of San Sebastiano.

Starring: An old road, crumbling tombs, and underground Christian cemeteries.

OVERVIEW

Our tour begins near the Tomb of Cecilia Metella, at the far (southern) end of the sightseeing highlights, and works northward for a mile-and-a-half to Domine Quo Vadis Church, toward the center of Rome. Sightseers share the road with speeding drivers talking on mobile phones (except on Sundays, when it's off limits to most cars). We'll avoid the worst stretch—between the Catacombs of San Sebastiano and Domine Quo Vadis Church—by taking a pedestrian path through a quiet park that parallels the busy road (except on Wednesdays, when the path is closed).

The Tour Begins

• *From the Tomb of Cecilia Metella, head south (away from downtown) 200 yards, where you walk (or rattle your bike) over a stretch of the...*

Original Paved Road

Huge basalt stones formed the sturdy base of a road 14 feet across. In its heyday, a central strip accommodated animal-powered vehicles, and elevated sidewalks served pedestrians. The first section (near Rome) was perfectly straight and lined with tombs and funerary monuments.

Return the way you came, and as you near the entrance to the Tomb of Cecilia Metella, look for the original **mile marker III,** one of more than 400 such stones that counted the distance from Rome to Brindisi. Rome's leaders knew that a fine network of roads was key to expanding and administering the republic—and later the empire. This road, from c. 312 B.C., kicks off the expansion period.

• *On the right, you can't miss the...*

Tomb of Cecilia Metella
(Mausoleo di Cecilia Metella)

This massive cylindrical tomb, one of the best preserved of the many tombs of prominent Romans that line the road, was built in the time of Augustus (c. 30 B.C.) for the daughter-in-law of Crassus, Rome's richest man. Faced with white travertine and situated on the crest of a hill, the tomb was an imposing sight. This grand tomb in the suburbs rivaled Augustus' own round mausoleum in the city center (see page 75).

Since no one was allowed to be buried inside the city walls, the Appian Way was a popular place to have a tomb where everyone could see and admire it. Later, Christians were buried here, though not in tombs (they preferred to be buried underground). Picture a funeral procession passing under the pines and cypresses, past a long line of pyramids, private mini temples, altars, and tombs.

In the 1300s, the area was turned into a fortified compound for an aristocratic family. The circular tomb was used as a tower (notice the crenellation on top) and a wall continued across the street, enclosing the newly built church and other structures (since destroyed).

If you pay to go inside, you'll see the tomb's eerily hollow

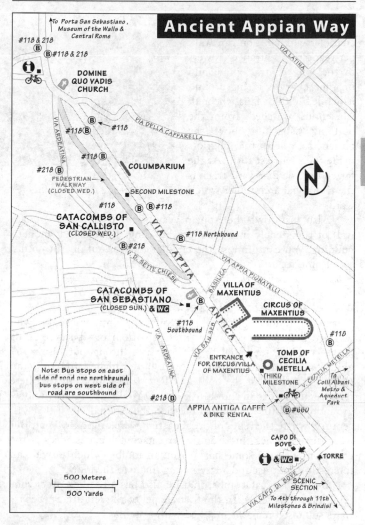

Ancient Appian Way

To Porta San Sebastiano, Museum of the Walls & Central Rome

#118 & 218

Ⓑ Ⓑ #118 & 218

DOMINE QUO VADIS CHURCH

VIA ARDEATINA

VIA DELLA CAFFARELLA

Ⓑ ←#118

#118 Ⓑ

#118 Ⓑ Ⓑ COLUMBARIUM

#218 Ⓑ

PEDESTRIAN WALKWAY (CLOSED WED.)

SECOND MILESTONE

#118 Ⓑ Ⓑ #118

CATACOMBS OF SAN CALLISTO (CLOSED WED.)

VIA APPIA

#118 Northbound

Ⓑ #218

V. D. SETTE CHIESE

VIA APPIA PIGNATELLI

CATACOMBS OF SAN SEBASTIANO (CLOSED SUN.) & WC

Ⓑ #118 Southbound

VILLA OF MAXENTIUS

CIRCUS OF MAXENTIUS

BASILICA

VIA SAN SEB.

VIA APPIA ANTICA

#118 Ⓑ

VIA ARDEATINA

ENTRANCE FOR CIRCUS/VILLA OF MAXENTIUS

TOMB OF CECILIA METELLA

THIRD MILESTONE

V. CECILIA METELLA

To Colli Albani Metro & Aqueduct Park

Note: Bus stops on east side of road are northbound; bus stops on west side of road are southbound.

#218 Ⓑ

APPIA ANTIGA CAFFÈ & BIKE RENTAL

Ⓑ #660

CAPO DI BOVE

ℹ & WC

→TORRE

SCENIC SECTION→

VIA CAPO DI BOVE

To 4th through 11th Milestones & Brindisi↓

500 Meters

500 Yards

N

APPIAN WAY

---

interior *(il sepolcro)*; a few statues of deceased Romans that once adorned tombs; and, in the cellar, a former paving-stone quarry with a preserved wagon-wheel groove.

• *About 200 yards farther along (north) from the tomb, on the right, are the ruins of the...*

Circus and Villa of Maxentius (Circo e Villa di Massenzio)

This was the suburban home of the emperor who was eventually defeated by Constantine in A.D. 312. The main sight to see here is a whole lot of nothing—that is, the expansive stretch of open space

contained by this huge former chariot racetrack. You can walk between the entrance towers to the long central spine, and imagine chariots racing around it while 10,000 fans cheered. Maxentius watched from the building rising up above the bleachers, where the chariots made their hairiest turn. At the far end of the 260-yard track is the triumphal arch under which the winner rode to receive his reward.

Also, just down the Appian Way from this circus is a square wall of ruins enclosing a modern building. Behind that modern building, you can glimpse the circular mausoleum of Maxentius' son, Romulus.

• *About 300 yards farther down the road (on the left) are the...*

▲▲Catacombs of San Sebastiano

This underground cemetery is named for the Christian soldier who was tied to a column and shot through with arrows because of his faith—a subject depicted by many artists throughout history. A guide takes you below ground to see burial niches, frescoes, and graffiti. It's said that the bodies of Peter and Paul were kept here for several decades in the third century. You'll also see the underground chapel (in its original location, but spiffed up in the 17th century) where the relics of St. Sebastian were originally kept. But what distinguishes this from other catacombs experiences is the chance to also see some pagan Roman tombs, which provide an interesting contrast and a fascinating finale to the tour.

Besides the catacombs, the site also has a basilica (free) containing various relics. In the first chapel to the left are St. Sebastian's supposed remains, marked with a statue of an arrow-pierced corpse. On the opposite side of the nave, a chapel displays an arrow he was shot with, a section of the column he was tied to, and the (supposedly) original footprints from the Domine Quo Vadis legend (see next page). Nearby stands a curly-haired bust of *The Savior (Il Salvatore)* by Bernini—his final creation, carved when he was in his eighties.

• *The stretch of the Appian Way beyond the Catacombs of San Sebastiano is the least interesting and most crowded (and dangerous). Avoid it by taking the pedestrian and bike path (open daily except Wed), which begins just past the Catacombs*

of San Sebastiano, at the intersection with Via delle Sette Chiese. To reach the path, go through the arch at #126. The quiet path parallels the Appian Way and takes you directly to the Catacombs of San Callisto. On Wednesdays, when the gate is closed, you'll have to stay straight on Via Appia Antica, being careful of traffic.

▲▲Catacombs of San Callisto

Named for the first caretaker, St. Callixtus, this was the official cemetery for Rome's early Christians and the burial place of nine third-century popes, other bishops of Rome, and various martyrs. The most famous martyr was St. Cecilia, patron saint of music, a Roman noble who was killed for converting to Christianity. Her tomb is marked with a copy of a famous Maderno statue. (For more on Cecilia and the statue, take my Trastevere Walk, available 📖 as a chapter in this book and 🎧 as a free audio tour.)

Buy your ticket and wait for your language to be called. They move lots of people quickly. If one group seems ridiculously large (more than 50 people), wait for the next tour in English.

• *From the catacombs, continue along the pedestrian path another three-quarters of a mile, where you'll spill out at a busy three-way intersection. There you'll find the small...*

Domine Quo Vadis Church

The tiny ninth-century church (redone in the 17th) was built on the spot where Peter, while fleeing the city to escape Nero's persecu-

tion, saw a vision of Christ. Peter asked Jesus, "Lord, where are you going?" (*"Domine quo vadis?"* in Latin), to which Christ replied, "I am going to Rome to be crucified again." This miraculous sign gave Peter faith and courage and caused him to return to Rome. Inside the nave of the church, stumble over the stone marked with the supposed footprints of Jesus. You'll see a fresco of Peter with keys on the left wall and one of Jesus on the right. A bust depicts Nobel Prize-winning Polish author Henryk Sienkiewicz, who wrote a historical novel that was the basis for the 1951 Hollywood movie *Quo Vadis.* The church is also called Santa Maria in Palmis.

• *The tour is over.* "Quo vadis, *pilgrim?*"

If you rented a bike at Appia Antica Caffè, near the beginning of the tour, you'll want to pedal back to the starting point, from where you can return to Rome via bus #660 and the Metro.

Without a bike, catch bus #118 from the bus stop about 75 yards past Domine Quo Vadis Church (beyond the TI and across the street). Bus #118 makes several interesting stops on its way to the center (see "Sights

APPIAN WAY

Catacombs

The catacombs are burial places for (mostly) Christians who died in ancient Roman times. By law, no one was allowed to be buried within the walls of Rome. While pagan Romans were into cremation, Christians preferred to be buried (so that they could be resurrected when the time came). But land was expensive, and most Christians were poor. A few wealthy, landowning Christians allowed their properties to be used as burial places.

The 40 or so known catacombs are scattered outside the ancient walls of Rome. *Catacombe* means, literally, "near the quarry"—as some of these were dug into the exposed walls of existing quarries. From the first through the fifth centuries, Christians dug an estimated 375 miles of tomb-lined tunnels, with networks of galleries as many as five layers deep. The volcanic tuff that Rome sits atop—which is soft and easy to cut, but hardens when exposed to air—was perfect for the job. The Christians burrowed many layers deep for two reasons: to get more mileage out of the donated land, and to be near martyrs and saints already buried there. Bodies were wrapped in linen (like Christ's). Since they figured the Second Coming was imminent, there was no interest in embalming the body. They called this place a *dormitorio*—a "place to sleep" while awaiting the rapture. After each corpse was laid to rest, it was covered with a stone slab—though most of these are now long-gone, shattered by looters and vandals.

When Emperor Constantine legalized Christianity in A.D. 313, Christians had a new, interesting problem: There would be no more recently persecuted martyrs to bind them together and inspire them. Instead, the early martyrs and popes assumed more importance, and Christians began making pilgrimages to their burial places in the catacombs.

In the 800s, when barbarian invaders started ransacking the tombs, Christians moved the relics of saints and martyrs to the safety of churches in the city center. For a thousand years, the catacombs were forgotten. In early modern times, they were

on Bus #118 Route Back to Rome" at the end of this chapter). You could also take bus #218 from here to San Giovanni in Laterano, where you can change to the Metro.

For those with more energy, there's more to see, especially if you're renting a bike and want to just get away from it all.

Other Sights on or near Appian Way
Consider these diversions if you have the time and interest.

More of the Appian Way: Heading south away from downtown Rome and from the Tomb of Cecilia Metella, you'll find the best-preserved part of the Appian Way—quieter, less touristed, and lined with cypresses, pines, and crumbling tombs. It's all downhill

excavated and became part of the Romantic Age's Grand Tour of Europe.

When abandoned plates and utensils from ritual meals were found, 18th- and 19th-century Romantics guessed that persecut-ed Christians hid out in these candlelit galleries. The popularity of this legend grew, even though it was untrue: By the second century, more than a million people lived in Rome, and the 10,000 early Christians didn't need to camp out in the catacombs. They hid in plain view, melting into obscurity within the city itself.

The underground tunnels, while empty of bones, are rich in early Christian symbolism, which functioned as a secret language. The dove represented the soul. You'll see it quenching its thirst (worshipping), with an olive branch (at rest), or happily perched (in paradise). Peacocks, known for their purportedly "incorruptible flesh," embodied immortality. The shepherd with a lamb on his shoulders was the "good shepherd," the first portrayal of Christ as a kindly leader of his flock. The fish was used because the first letters of these words—"Jesus Christ, Son of God, Savior"—spelled "fish" in Greek. The combination of an X and a P was actually a chi and a rho—the first two letters of CHRist's name in the Greek alphabet. And the anchor, a cross in disguise, symbolized how true believers felt anchored by their faith. Some fragments were stamped with the hallmark of the mason who created it. A second-century bishop had written on his tomb, "All who understand these things, pray for me." You'll see pictures of people praying with their hands raised—the custom at the time.

after the first few hundred yards. On a bike, you'll travel over lots of rough paving stones (or dirt sidewalks) for about 30 minutes to reach a big pyramid-shaped ruin on its tiny base, and then five minutes more to the back side of Villa dei Quintili. Usually, you can't enter the villa from here, but you can admire the semicircular nymphaeum, or fake grotto. Enjoy a picnic, then turn around and pedal up that long hill to return your bike. Bus #118 also serves the Villa dei Quintili, stopping at the main entrance (far side) on the Via Appia Nuova.

Aqueduct Park (Parco degli Acquedotti): Rome's mighty aqueducts kept water flowing into the thriving and thirsty ancient city of one million. (They also eventually provided a handy Achilles' heel for invading barbarians: Simply break an arch in the aqueduct, and life becomes very tough within the city walls.) This sprawling, evocative park is a favorite these days with Roman joggers, picnickers, and anyone looking for a break from the big city. From the Appian Way, start at Appia Antica Caffè (near the Tomb of Cecilia

Metella), take bus #660 to the Colli Albani Metro station, and catch the Metro to Giulio Agricola. (If you're coming straight from Rome, take Metro line A to Giulio Agricola.)

As you exit the Giulio Agricola Metro stop, follow signs for *Viale Giulio Agricola*. This street has trees in its median strip and ends at a modern church several blocks away. Head for the church, passing a number of cafés and grocery stores (good for picnic fare). To the right of the church, enter the park and pass through the squat brick arches of the first aqueduct (actually two aqueducts—the 16th-century Acqua Felice piggybacked on top of the Acqua Marcia, which dates from the second century B.C.). Continue across the field and up the small hill where you'll see fragments of the more impressive Acqua Claudia (first century A.D.). Follow the path to the left for about 10 minutes; you'll come to the best-preserved section, which stretches into the distance and makes for an easy walk. Loop back to the church and Metro when you're done. If you're not afraid of traffic, you could bike from the Appian Way to Aqueduct Park (takes about an hour; get directions when you rent your bike).

Sights on Bus #118 Route Back to Rome: On the way back, about a half-mile from Domine Quo Vadis Church, the bus stops alongside Rome's ancient city wall at **Porta San Sebastiano**. Here, the **Museum of the Walls** (Museo delle Mura) offers an interesting look at Roman defenses and a chance to scramble along a stretch of the ramparts (free, Tue-Sun 9:00-14:00, closed Mon, Via di Porta San Sebastiano 18, bus stop: Porta San Sebastiano, www.museodellemuraroma.it). The Aurelian Wall (c. A.D. 270) was built in five years because of the threat of invasions. At 12 miles around, it was the biggest building project ever undertaken within the city of Rome.

A few minutes farther on, bus #118 stops near the **Baths of Caracalla** (described on page 107). Next, it makes a stop at the east end of the **Circus Maximus** (the Circo Massimo Metro stop is nearby). Assuming it is following its usual route, the bus continues on to Piazza Venezia before looping back to the Colosseum.

SLEEPING IN ROME

Near Termini Station. 344
Near Ancient Rome 350
Pantheon Neighborhood. 352
Trastevere 358
Near Vatican City 360

Choosing the right neighborhood in Rome is as important as choosing the right hotel. All of my recommended accommodations are in safe areas convenient to sightseeing. The Termini train station neighborhood is handy for public transit and services, though not particularly charming. Hotels near ancient Rome are close to the Colosseum and Roman Forum. The most romantic ambience is in neighborhoods near the Pantheon, which encompass the Campo de' Fiori and the Jewish Ghetto. Equally pleasant, if a bit rougher, is Trastevere. Finally, hotels near Vatican City put St. Peter's and the Vatican Museums at your doorstep.

Rome also has many convents that rent out rooms. At convents, the beds are twins and English is often in short supply, but the price is right. I've listed four nun-run places in this chapter: the expensive but divine Casa di Santa Brigida (near Campo de' Fiori), Suore di Santa Elisabetta (near Termini Station), Casa Il Rosario (near Piazza Venezia), and Casa per Ferie Santa Maria alle Fornaci (near the Vatican). For a longer list of convents, see the Church of Santa Susanna's website (www.santasusanna.org, select "Resources" and then "Convent Accommodations").

Book your accommodations well in advance if you'll be traveling during peak season (April-June and Sept-early Nov) or if your trip coincides with a major holiday or festival (see page 560). For information and tips on pricing, getting deals, making reserva-

Sleep Code

Hotels are classified based on the average price of a standard double room with breakfast in high season.

$$$$	**Splurge:** Most rooms over €170
$$$	**Pricier:** €130-170
$$	**Moderate:** €90-130
$	**Budget:** €50-90
¢	**Backpacker:** Under €50
RS%	**Rick Steves discount**

Unless otherwise noted, credit cards are accepted, hotel staff speak basic English, and free Wi-Fi is available. Comparison-shop by checking prices at several hotels (on each hotel's own website, on a booking site, or by email). For the best deal, *book directly with the hotel*. Ask for a discount if paying in cash; if the listing includes **RS%**, request a Rick Steves discount.

tions, seasonal differences, and other accommodation options—including apartments and other short-term rentals—see page 513.

NEAR TERMINI STATION

While this neighborhood is not as atmospheric as other areas of Rome, the hotels near Termini train station are less expensive, and the Metro and buses link you easily to the rest of the city. All the listings below are within a 10-minute walk of the station (some are actually closer to the Repubblica Metro stop).

West of the Station

Most of these hotels are on or near Via Firenze, a safe, handy, central, and relatively quiet street that's a 10-minute walk from Termini and the airport train, and two blocks beyond Piazza della Repubblica. The Defense Ministry is nearby, so you've got heavily armed guards watching over you all night.

The neighborhood is served by two Metro stops: Repubblica (line A), and Termini (intersection of lines A and B). Virtually all the city buses that rumble down Via Nazionale (#60, #64, #70, and the #40 express) take you to Piazza Venezia (near the Forum). From Piazza Venezia, bus #64 (jammed with people and thieves) and the #40 express bus continue to Largo Argentina (for the Pantheon and Campo de' Fiori) and the Vatican area. Or, at Piazza Venezia, you can transfer to tram #8 to Trastevere (get off at first stop after crossing the river). Bus #H also runs direct to Trastevere, leaving from Piazza della Repubblica (on the northeast side of the square, near the entrance to Baths of Diocletian; none on Sun). If you're staying near the Santa Susanna and Santa Maria della Vittoria churches, buses from nearby Largo Santa Susanna (#62, #85, and #492) wind through the city center (leaving from the Bissolati stop; returning, the stop name is Largo S. Susanna). It's actually a pleasant downhill walk from these hotels to the Pantheon (about 25 minutes along Via Rasella and past the Trevi Fountain); you can save the bus for the uphill return journey.

Neighborhood **supermarkets** include **Despar** at Via Nazionale 213 (daily 7:30-20:30, at the corner of Via Venezia); **Sma** behind Santa Maria Maggiore Church (Piazza Santa Maria Maggiore 5B, in the basement, daily 8:00-21:00); and **Sapori & Dintori,** downstairs from the inner atrium at Termini Station (daily 7:00-24:00). There are many smaller grocery stores as well.

$$$$ Residenza Cellini feels like the guest wing of a gorgeous Neoclassical palace. It offers 11 rooms, "ortho/anti-allergy beds," four-star comforts and service, and a small, breezy terrace (RS%, air-con, elevator, Via Modena 5, third floor, tel. 06-4782-5204, www.residenzacellini.it, info@residenzacellini.it, Barbara, Gaetano, and Donato).

$$$$ Hotel Modigliani, a delightful 23-room place, is energetically run in a clean, bright, minimalist yet in-love-with-life style that its artist namesake would appreciate. It has a vast and plush lounge, a garden, and a newsletter introducing you to each of the staff (RS%, air-con, elevator; northwest of Via Firenze—from Tritone Fountain on Piazza Barberini, go 2 blocks up Via della Purificazione to #42; tel. 06-4281-5226, www.hotelmodigliani.com, info@hotelmodigliani.com, Giulia and Marco).

$$$$ IQ Hotel, in a modern blue building facing the Opera House, feels almost Scandinavian in its efficiency, without a hint of the Old World. It lacks charm, but more than compensates with modern amenities. Its 88 rooms are fresh and spacious, the roof garden comes with a play area and foosball, and vending machines dispense bottles of wine (family rooms, breakfast extra, air-con, elevator, cheap self-service laundry, gym, Via Firenze 8, tel. 06-488-0465, www.iqhotelroma.it, info@iqhotelroma.it, manager Diego).

$$$ Hotel Oceania is a peaceful slice of air-conditioned heaven. The 24 rooms are spacious, quiet, and tastefully decorated, and the elegant sitting room has a manor-house feel. Stefano runs a fine staff, serves wonderful coffee, provides lots of thoughtful extra touches, and works hard to maintain a caring family atmosphere (RS%—use code "RICKSTEVES," family rooms, elevator, videos in TV lounge, Via Firenze 38, third floor, tel. 06-482-4696, www.hoteloceania.it, info@hoteloceania.it; Anna, Kira, and Roberto round out the staff).

$$$ Hotel Aberdeen, which combines quality and friendliness, is warmly run by Annamaria, with support from sister Laura and cousin Cinzia, and staff members Mariano, Costel, and Matteo. The 37 comfy rooms, on the ground floor and one floor up,

Hotels near Termini Station

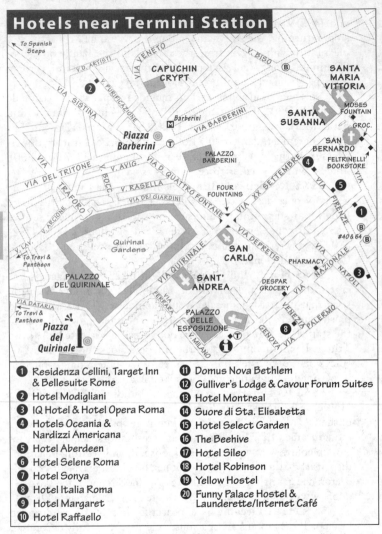

To Spanish Steps

V.D. ARTISTI

VIA VENETO

V. BISO

CAPUCHIN CRYPT

SANTA MARIA VITTORIA

VIA SISTINA

V. PURIFICAZIONE

Barberini

VIA BARBERINI

SANTA SUSANNA

MOSES FOUNTAIN

GROC.

Piazza Barberini

PALAZZO BARBERINI

SAN BERNARDO

FELTRINELLI BOOKSTORE

VIA DEL TRITONE

V. AVIG.

VIA D. QUATTRO FONTANE

VIA XX SETTEMBRE

VIA FIRENZE

TRAFORO

BOCC

V. RASELLA

FOUR FOUNTAINS

VIA DEI GIARDINI

V. ARCIONE

Quirinal Gardens

VIA QUIRINALE

VIA DEPRETIS

#40 & 64

V. LAV.

SAN CARLO

PHARMACY

VIA NAZIONALE

To Trevi & Pantheon

PALAZZO DEL QUIRINALE

SANT' ANDREA

DESPAR GROCERY

NAPOLI

VIA DATARIA

To Trevi & Pantheon

VIA FERRARA

PALAZZO DELLE ESPOSIZIONE

VENEZIA VIA

PALERMO

Piazza del Quirinale

V. MILANO

GENOVA VIA

1. Residenza Cellini, Target Inn & Bellesuite Rome
2. Hotel Modigliani
3. IQ Hotel & Hotel Opera Roma
4. Hotels Oceania & Nardizzi Americana
5. Hotel Aberdeen
6. Hotel Selene Roma
7. Hotel Sonya
8. Hotel Italia Roma
9. Hotel Margaret
10. Hotel Raffaello
11. Domus Nova Bethlem
12. Gulliver's Lodge & Cavour Forum Suites
13. Hotel Montreal
14. Suore di Sta. Elisabetta
15. Hotel Select Garden
16. The Beehive
17. Hotel Sileo
18. Hotel Robinson
19. Yellow Hostel
20. Funny Palace Hostel & Launderette/Internet Café

are a fine value (RS%—use "Rick Steves reader reservations" link, family rooms, air-con, Via Firenze 48, tel. 06-482-3920, www.hotelaberdeen.it, info@hotelaberdeen.it).

$$$ Hotel Opera Roma, with contemporary furnishings and marble accents, boasts 15 spacious, modern, and thoughtfully appointed rooms. It's quiet and just a stone's throw from the Opera House (RS%, air-con, elevator, Via Firenze 11, tel. 06-487-1787, www.hoteloperaroma.com, info@hoteloperaroma.com, Reza, Litu, and Federica).

$$$ Hotel Selene Roma spreads its 40 stylish rooms out on a few floors of a big palazzo. With elegant furnishings and room

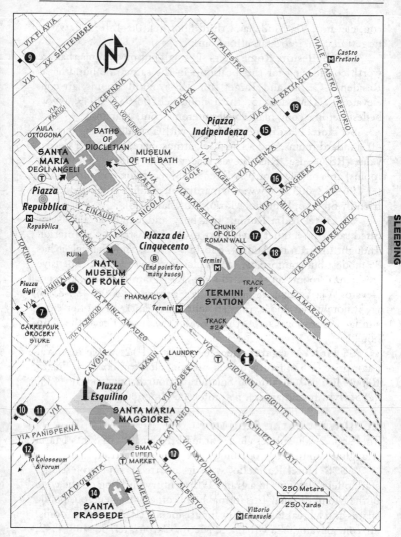

to breathe, it's a good value (RS%, family rooms, air-con, eleva-tor, Via del Viminale 8, tel. 06-474-4781, www.hotelseleneroma.it, reception@hotelseleneroma.it).

$$$ Hotel Sonya offers 40 well-equipped if small rooms, a hearty breakfast, and decent prices (RS%, family rooms, air-con, elevator, faces the Opera House at Via Viminale 58, Metro: Re-pubblica or Termini, tel. 06-481-9911, www.hotelsonya.it, info@hotelsonya.it, Francesca and Ivan).

$$$ Target Inn is a sleek, practical six-room place next to Residenza Cellini (listed earlier). It's owned by the same people who run the recommended Target Restaurant nearby (RS%, air-con, elevator, Via Modena 5, third floor, tel. 06-474-5399, www. targetinn.com, info@targetinn.com).

$$$ Bellesuite Rome offers six small but nice rooms that are worth considering for the location—in the same fine building as Residenza Cellini and Target Inn (RS%, family rooms, air-con, elevator, Via Modena 5, third floor, tel. 06-9521-3049, www. bellesuiterome.com, mail@bellesuiterome.com, Martina).

$$ Hotel Nardizzi Americana, with a small rooftop terrace, 40 standard rooms, and a laid-back atmosphere, is another decent value (RS%—use "Rick Steves readers reservations" link, family rooms, air-con, elevator, Via Firenze 38, reception on fourth floor, tel. 06-488-0035, www.hotelnardizzi.it, info@hotelnardizzi.it; friendly Stefano, Fabrizio, Mario, and Giancarlo).

$$ Hotel Italia Roma, in a busy and handy locale, is located safely on a quiet street next to the Ministry of the Interior. Thoughtfully run by Andrea, Sabrina, Abdul, and Gabriel, it has 35 modest but comfortable rooms plus four newer, more expensive "residenza" rooms on the third floor (RS%, family rooms, air-con, elevator, Via Venezia 18, just off Via Nazionale, tel. 06-482-8355, www.hotelitaliaroma.it, info@hotelitaliaroma.it). They offer eight similar annex rooms across the street for the same price as the main hotel.

$$ Hotel Margaret offers few frills and 12 simple rooms at a fair price (RS%, family rooms, air-con, elevator, north of Piazza Repubblica at Via Antonio Salandra 6, fourth floor, tel. 06-482-4285, www.hotelmargaret.net, info@hotelmargaret.net).

Southwest of the Station

These good-value places cluster around the basilica of Santa Maria Maggiore, on the edge of Rome's international district.

$$$$ Hotel Raffaello, with its courteous and professional staff, offers 41 rooms in a grand 19th-century building on the edge of the Monti district. This formal hotel comes with generous public spaces and a breakfast room fit for aristocrats (RS%, family rooms, air-con, elevator, Via Urbana 3, Metro: Cavour, tel. 06-488-4342, www.hotelraffaello.it, info@hotelraffaello.it).

$$ Domus Nova Bethlem, run by the Oblate Sisters of Baby Jesus, is a spacious, pristine, and institutional-feeling hotel. The 38 high-ceilinged rooms are modest yet classy, and guests have access to a peaceful and leafy courtyard garden (family rooms, air-con, elevator, 1:00 in the morning curfew, Via Cavour 85A, Metro: Cavour, tel. 06-4782-4414, www.domusnovabethlem.it, info@ domusnovabethlem.it).

$$ Gulliver's Lodge has four colorful rooms on the ground floor of a large, secure building. Though it's on a busy street, the rooms are quiet. The public spaces are few, but in-room extras like

DVD players (and DVDs, including my Italy shows) make it a fine home base (RS%, price includes small breakfast at nearby bar, cash only, air-con, Via Cavour 101, Metro: Cavour, tel. 06-9727-3787, www.gulliverslodge.com, info@gulliverslodge.com, Sara and Mary).

$$ Hotel Montreal is a basic, three-star place with 27 small rooms on a big, noisy street a block southeast of Santa Maria Maggiore (RS%, air-con, elevator, small garden terrace, Via Carlo Alberto 4, 1 block from Metro: Vittorio Emanuele, 3 blocks from Termini train station, tel. 06-445-7797, www.hotelmontrealroma.it, info@hotelmontrealroma.it, Pasquale).

$ Suore di Santa Elisabetta is a heavenly Polish-run convent with a serene garden, roof terrace with grand views, and 37 rooms. All doubles have twin beds. Often booked long in advance, with such tranquility it's a super value (family rooms, cheaper rooms with shared bath, fans but no air-con, elevator for top floors, guest kitchen, Wi-Fi in lounge only, 23:00 curfew, a block southwest of Santa Maria Maggiore at Via dell'Olmata 9, Metro: Termini or Vittorio Emanuele, tel. 06-488-8271, www.cssc-roma.com, select "Casa per ferie" for English, ist.it.s.elisabetta@libero.it).

Sleeping Cheaply, Northeast of the Station

The cheapest beds in town are beyond Termini train station, to the northeast: Standing so that the tracks dead-end into your back, this neighborhood is to your right (Metro: Termini). The streets quiet down a block or so away from the station, and these hotels feel plenty safe. The **Splashnet** launderette/Internet café is handy (€8 full serve wash and dry, €2/day luggage storage, daily 8:30-23:00, just off Via Milazzo at Via Varese 33, tel. 06-4470-3523).

$$ Hotel Select Garden, a modern and comfortable 21-room hotel run by the cheery Picca family, boasts lively modern art adorning the walls and a beautiful lemon-tree garden. It's a safe, tranquil, and welcoming refuge just a couple of blocks from the train station (RS%, air-con, Via V. Bachelet 6, tel. 06-445-6383, www.hotelselectgarden.com, info@hotelselectgarden.com, Cristina and Maurizia).

$ The Beehive gives vagabonds—old and young—a cheap, clean, and comfy home in Rome. Thoughtfully and creatively run by friendly Americans Steve and Linda and their hardworking staff, the place offers six great-value artsy-mod double rooms with shared baths and an eight-bed dorm in the main building (no air-con, only fans). Their nearby annexes have similar style and several rooms with private baths (breakfast extra, air-con extra, private garden terrace, dinner sometimes available, 2 blocks from Termini train station at Via Marghera 8, tel. 06-4470-4553, www.the-beehive.com, info@the-beehive.com). They're also a good resource for apartments across the city (www.cross-pollinate.com).

$ Hotel Sileo, with shiny chandeliers in dim rooms, is a homey little place renting 10 basic rooms. It's worn, but run with warmth by friendly Alessandro and Maria Savioli (who don't speak English) and their daughter Anna (who does); their other daughter, Stefania, painted the wall murals (RS%, air-con, elevator, Via Magenta 39, fourth floor, tel. 06-445-0246, www.hotelsileo.com, info@hotelsileo.com).

$ Hotel Robinson is just a few steps from the station, but tucked away from the commotion. Set on an interior courtyard, it has 20 small and simple rooms, handsomely decorated with dark-wood accents, that are a good value (RS%, breakfast extra, air-con extra, Via Milazzo 3, tel. 06-491-423, www.hotelrobinsonrome.com, info@hotelrobinsonrome.com).

¢ Yellow Hostel rents 220 beds to 18- through 45-year-olds only (I'd skip their 16 private rooms, which are basic and over-priced). Hip yet sane, it's well-run with fine facilities, including a café/late-night bar (reserve online—no telephone reservations accepted, breakfast extra, elevator, no curfew, 6 blocks from station, just past Via Vicenza at Via Palestro 44, tel. 06-4938-2682, www.yellowhostel.com, questions@the-yellow.com).

¢ Funny Palace Hostel, adjacent to Splashnet and run by the same entrepreneurial owner, Mabri, rents dorm beds in quiet four-person rooms and 18 stark-but-clean private rooms. It's far less convivial than Yellow Hostel, but suitable for introverts (cash only, includes breakfast in café, elevator, guest kitchen, reception in the launderette—described earlier, Via Varese 33, tel. 06-4470-3523, www.hostelfunny.com, info@hostelfunny.com).

NEAR ANCIENT ROME

This area is central, so you'll find these hotels are a short walk from the Colosseum and Roman Forum, as well as restaurants and shopping in the Monti district (see pages 379 and 401). All except Hotel Lancelot are within a 10-minute walk of the Cavour Metro stop.

$$$$ Hotel Lancelot is a comfortable refuge—a 60-room hotel with an elegant feel at a fair price. Located in a pleasant, low-key residential neighborhood a 10-minute stroll from the Colosseum, it's quiet and safe, with a shady courtyard, restaurant, bar, and tiny communal sixth-floor terrace. It's well-run by the Khan family, who serve a good €25 dinner—a tasty way to connect with your hotel neighbors and the friendly staff. No wonder it's popular with returning guests (RS%, family rooms, some view rooms, air-con, elevator, wheelchair-accessible, cheap parking, 10-minute walk behind Colosseum near San Clemente Church at Via Capo d'Africa 47, tel. 06-7045-0615, www.lancelothotel.com, info@lancelothotel.com). Faris and Lubna speak the Queen's English.

$$$$ Nerva Boutique Hotel is a snazzy slice of tranquility with 20 small, overpriced (but often discounted) rooms. It sits on a quiet, ideally located side street that faces the Roman Forum and backs onto the enjoyable Monti neighborhood (RS%—use code "RICKSTEVES," air-con, elevator, Via Tor de' Conti 3, tel. 06-678-1835, www.hotelnerva.com, info@hotelnerva.com, Antonio and Paolo).

$$$ Nicolas Inn Bed & Breakfast, a delightful little four-room place with thoughtful touches, is spacious and bright, and right on busy Via Cavour. It's run by François and American expat Melissa, who make you feel like you have caring friends in Rome (RS%, cash only, air-con, Via Cavour 295, mobile 328-555-3004, www.nicolasinn.com, info@nicolasinn.com).

$$ Hotel Paba is cozy, chocolate-box-tidy, and lovingly cared for by Alberta Castelli. It's just two blocks from the Forum. You'll take a vintage elevator to reach the seven rooms. Although some overlook busy Via Cavour, it's quiet enough (RS%, email reservations preferred, big beds, breakfast served in room, air-con, elevator, Via Cavour 266, second floor, tel. 06-4782-4902, www.hotelpaba.com, info@hotelpaba.com).

$$ Hotel Antica Locanda is a gem on a small street in the heart of the Monti neighborhood. While there are four floors and no elevator, the 10 rooms—each named for a composer or an artist—come with romantically rustic, stylish furnishings. The rooftop terrace is great for sunbathing or relaxing with a sunset drink (air-con, no elevator, Via del Boschetto 84, tel. 06-487-1164, http://anticalocandaroma.it, anticalocandaroma@gmail.com).

$$ Casa Il Rosario is a peaceful, well-run Dominican convent renting 40 rooms with monastic simplicity to both pilgrims and tourists in a steep but pleasant corner of the Monti neighborhood. Doubles have two single beds which can be pushed together (cheaper single rooms with shared bath, reserve several months in advance, some rooms with air-con and others with fans, elevator, small garden and rooftop terrace, 23:00 curfew, near bottom of Via Nazionale at Via Sant'Agata dei Goti 10, bus #40 or #170 from Termini, tel. 06-679-2346, www.casailrosarioroma.it, irodopre@tin.it).

$ Hotel Rosetta, a homey and family-run *pensione* in the same building as Nicolas Inn, rents 15 simple rooms. It's pretty minimal, with no lounge and no breakfast, but its great location makes it a fine budget option (air-con, up one flight of stairs, Via Cavour 295, tel. 06-4782-3069, www.rosettahotel.com, info@rosettahotel.com, Antonietta and Francesca).

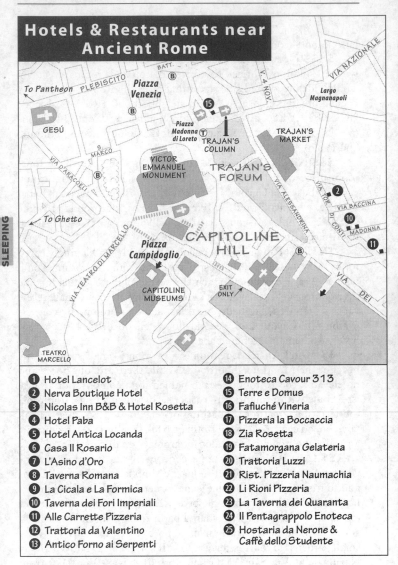

Hotels & Restaurants near Ancient Rome

To Pantheon — PLEBISCITO — BATT.

Piazza Venezia

To Ghetto

GESÚ

S. MARCO

VIA D'ARACOELI

Piazza Madonna di Loreto

VICTOR EMMANUEL MONUMENT

TRAJAN'S COLUMN

Piazza Campidoglio

VIA TEATRO DI MARCELLO

CAPITOLINE HILL

CAPITOLINE MUSEUMS

EXIT ONLY

TEATRO MARCELLO

Largo Magnanapoli

VIA NAZIONALE

VIA 4 NOV.

TRAJAN'S MARKET

TRAJAN'S FORUM

VIA ALESSANDRINA

VIA TOR DE' CONTI

VIA BACCINA

MADONNA

VIA DEI

SLEEPING

- **1** Hotel Lancelot
- **2** Nerva Boutique Hotel
- **3** Nicolas Inn B&B & Hotel Rosetta
- **4** Hotel Paba
- **5** Hotel Antica Locanda
- **6** Casa Il Rosario
- **7** L'Asino d'Oro
- **8** Taverna Romana
- **9** La Cicala e La Formica
- **10** Taverna dei Fori Imperiali
- **11** Alle Carrette Pizzeria
- **12** Trattoria da Valentino
- **13** Antico Forno ai Serpenti
- **14** Enoteca Cavour 313
- **15** Terre e Domus
- **16** Fafiuché Vineria
- **17** Pizzeria la Boccaccia
- **18** Zia Rosetta
- **19** Fatamorgana Gelateria
- **20** Trattoria Luzzi
- **21** Rist. Pizzeria Naumachia
- **22** Li Rioni Pizzeria
- **23** La Taverna dei Quaranta
- **24** Il Pentagrappolo Enoteca
- **25** Hostaria da Nerone & Caffè dello Studente

PANTHEON NEIGHBORHOOD

Winding, narrow lanes filled with foot traffic and lined with small shops and tiny trattorias...this part of Rome still feels like a village. As in a real village, buses and taxis are the only practical way to connect with other destinations. The atmosphere doesn't come cheap, but this is a great place to be—especially at night, when Romans and tourists gather in the floodlit piazzas.

This neighborhood has two main transportation hubs: Piazza delle Cinque Lune (just north of Piazza Navona) has a TI, a taxi

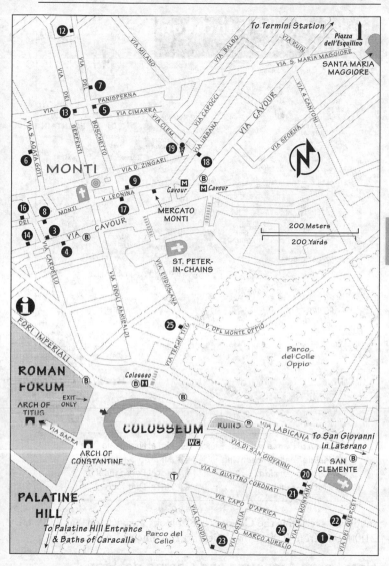

stand, and (just around the corner) handy buses #81 and #87. Largo Argentina has buses to almost everywhere, a taxi stand, and the tram to Trastevere (#8). Peruse my recommended buses on page 22, and you'll likely find a few (#81, #87, #492, and others) that stop near your hotel.

Neighborhood **supermarkets** include **Despar**, half a block from the Pantheon toward Piazza Navona (daily 8:30-22:00, Via Giustiniani 18). A larger supermarket with a good bakery and

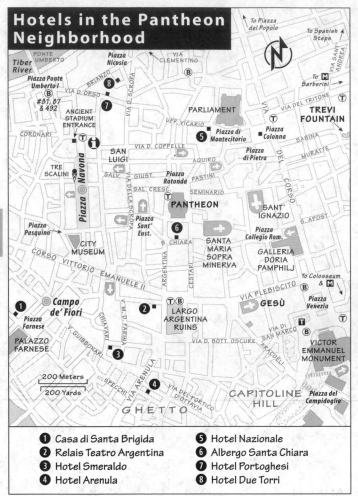

Hotels in the Pantheon Neighborhood

1 Casa di Santa Brigida
2 Relais Teatro Argentina
3 Hotel Smeraldo
4 Hotel Arenula
5 Hotel Nazionale
6 Albergo Santa Chiara
7 Hotel Portoghesi
8 Hotel Due Torri

sandwich section is the **Co-op,** three blocks away (Mon-Sat 8:00-21:00, Sun from 9:00, Corso Vittorio Emanuele II 42).

Near Largo Argentina and Campo de' Fiori

Each of these places is romantically set deep in the tangled back streets near the idyllic Campo de' Fiori and, for many, worth the extra money. This area is connected to Termini Station by bus along Via Nazionale (#40 or #64). From the airport, consider taking the regional train to Trastevere Station and then the #8 tram to Largo Argentina.

$$$$ Casa di Santa Brigida overlooks the elegant Piazza Farnese. With soft-spoken sisters gliding down polished hallways and pearly gates instead of doors, this lavish 20-room convent makes exhaust-stained Roman tourists feel like they've died and gone to heaven. If you don't need a double bed or a TV in your room, it's worth the splurge—especially if you luxuriate in its ample public spaces or on its lovely roof terrace (book well in advance, air-con, elevator, tasty €25 dinners, roof garden, plush library, Via di Monserrato 54, tel. 06-6889-2596, www.brigidine. org, piazzafarnese@brigidine.org, many of the sisters are from India and speak English—pray you get to work with wonderful sister Gertrude).

$$$$ Relais Teatro Argentina, a six-room gem, is steeped in tasteful old-Rome elegance, but has all the modern comforts. It's cozy and quiet like a B&B and couldn't be more centrally located (air-con, 3 flights of stairs, breakfast in room, Via del Sudario 35, tel. 06-9893-1617, mobile 331-198-4708, www.relaisteatroargentina. com, info@relaisteatroargentina.com, Carlotta).

$$$ Hotel Smeraldo, with 66 rooms, is clean and a reasonable deal in a good location. Sixteen of the rooms are in an annex across the street, but everyone has breakfast in the main building (RS%—use code "ricksteves," air-con, elevator, flowery roof terrace, midway between Campo de' Fiori and Largo Argentina at Via dei Chiavari 20, tel. 06-687-5929, www.smeraldoroma.com, info@ smeraldoroma.com; Massimo and Walter).

$$ Hotel Arenula, with 50 decent rooms, is the only hotel in Rome's old Jewish ghetto. Though it has the ambience of a gym and attracts lots of students, it is in the thick of old Rome (RS%, family rooms, air-con, no elevator, down side street from the fountain in the park on Via Arenula, Via Santa Maria de' Calderari 47, tel. 06 687 9454, www.hotelarenula.com, info@hotelarenula.com).

Close to the Pantheon

These places are buried in the pedestrian-friendly heart of ancient Rome, each within about a five-minute walk of the Pantheon. They're an easy walk from many sights, but are a bit distant from the major public transportation arteries (though buses do run nearby). To get close, arrive and depart by taxi.

$$$$ Hotel Nazionale, a four-star landmark, is a 16th-century palace that shares a well-policed square with the Italian Parliament building. Its 101 rooms are accentuated by lush public spaces, fancy bars, a uniformed staff, and a marble-floored restaurant. It's a big, stuffy hotel, but it's a worthy splurge if you want security, comfort, and the heart of Rome at your doorstep (air-con, elevator, Piazza Montecitorio 131, tel. 06-695-001, www.hotelnazionale.it, info@hotelnazionale.it).

$$$$ Albergo Santa Chiara, in the old center, is big, solid, and hotelesque. Flavia, Silvio, and their fine staff offer marbled

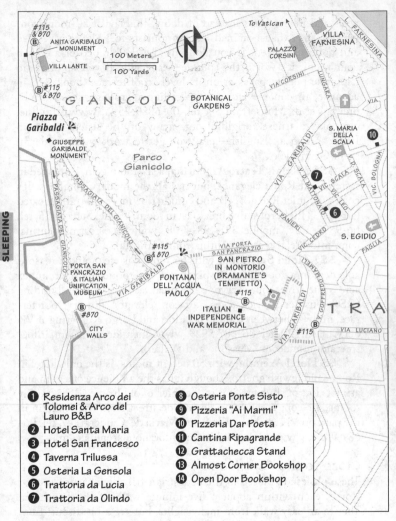

1 Residenza Arco dei Tolomei & Arco del Lauro B&B

2 Hotel Santa Maria

3 Hotel San Francesco

4 Taverna Trilussa

5 Osteria La Gensola

6 Trattoria da Lucia

7 Trattoria da Olindo

8 Osteria Ponte Sisto

9 Pizzeria "Ai Marmi"

10 Pizzeria Dar Poeta

11 Cantina Ripagrande

12 Grattachecca Stand

13 Almost Corner Bookshop

14 Open Door Bookshop

elegance (but basic furniture) and all the hotel services. Its ample public lounges are dressy and professional, and its 97 rooms are quiet and spacious (RS%, elevator, air-con, behind the Pantheon at Via di Santa Chiara 21, tel. 06-687-2979, www.albergosantachiara. com, info@albergosantachiara.com).

$$$$ **Hotel Portoghesi** is a classic hotel with 27 colorful rooms in the medieval heart of Rome. It's peaceful, quiet, and calmly run, and comes with a delightful roof terrace—though you pay for the location (family rooms, breakfast on roof, air-con, elevator, Via dei Portoghesi 1, tel. 06-686-4231, www.hotelportoghesiroma. it, info@hotelportoghesiroma.it).

$$$$ **Hotel Due Torri,** hiding out on a tiny quiet street, is

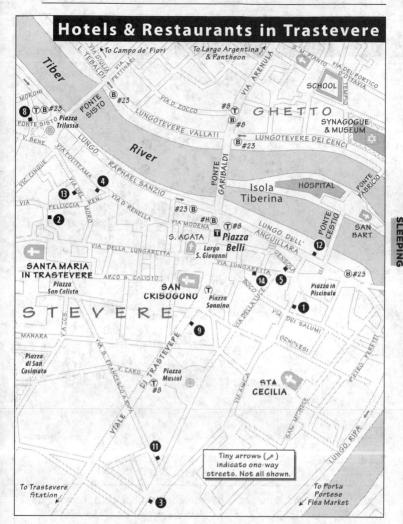

Hotels & Restaurants in Trastevere

beautifully located. It feels professional yet homey, with an accommodating staff, generous public spaces, and 26 rooms (the ones on upper floors are smaller but have views). While the location and lounge are great, the rooms are overpriced unless you score a discount (family rooms, air-con, elevator, a block off Via della Scrofa at Vicolo del Leonetto 23, tel. 06-6880-6956, www. hotelduetorriroma.com, info@hotelduetorriroma.com, Cinzia).

Near the Spanish Steps

$$$$ Hotel San Carlo is buried in the thick of Rome's bustling pedestrian-friendly "shopping triangle" and conveniently close to the Spagna Metro stop. Thoughtfully run by Alberto and his

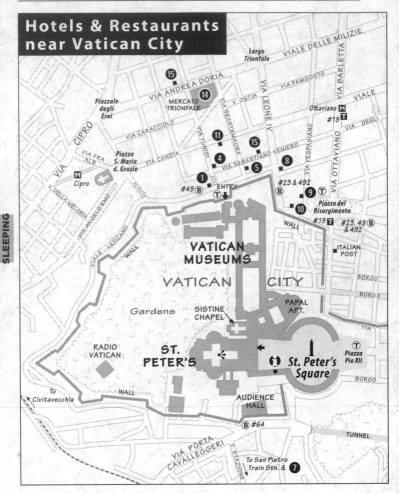

Hotels & Restaurants near Vatican City

staff, its 47 rooms, connected by a treehouse floor plan, provide a tranquil haven (RS%—use code "ricksteves," air-con, elevator, Via delle Carrozze 92—see map on page 415, tel. 06-678-4548, www. hotelsancarloroma.com, info@hotelsancarloroma.com).

TRASTEVERE

Colorful and genuine, with uneven cobbles and remnants of its tumbledown past, Trastevere is a treat for travelers looking for a more residential, bohemian atmosphere. The heart of Rome and its ancient ruins are just across the river, and tram #8 makes getting there and back a snap. Convenient buses #23 and #280 run to the Vatican area and the Piramide Metro stop, and bus #H runs direct to Termini (none on Sun). From the airport, you can reach these

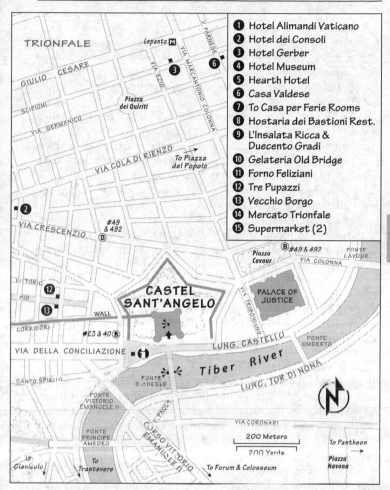

1. Hotel Alimandi Vaticano
2. Hotel dei Consoli
3. Hotel Gerber
4. Hotel Museum
5. Hearth Hotel
6. Casa Valdese
7. To Casa per Ferie Rooms
8. Hostaria dei Bastioni Rest.
9. L'Insalata Ricca & Duecento Gradi
10. Gelateria Old Bridge
11. Forno Feliziani
12. Tre Pupazzi
13. Vecchio Borgo
14. Mercato Trionfale
15. Supermarket (2)

SLEEPING

listings by taking the regional train to Trastevere train station, and the #8 tram downhill from there.

$$$$ Residenza Arco dei Tolomei is your most poetic Trastevere experience imaginable, with six small, unique, antique-filled rooms, some boasting fragrant balconies. In this quiet and elegant setting, you can pretend you're visiting aristocratic relatives (reserve well in advance, from Piazza Piscinula a block up Via dell'Arco de' Tolomei at #27, tel. 06-5832-0819, www.bbarcodeitolomei.com, info@bbarcodeitolomei.com; Marco and Gianna Paola).

$$$$ Hotel Santa Maria sits like a lazy hacienda in the midst of Trastevere. Surrounded by a medieval skyline, you'll feel as if you're on some romantic stage set. Its 20 small but well-equipped, air-conditioned rooms—former cells in a cloister—are mostly on the ground floor, as are a few suites for up to six people. The rooms circle a gravelly courtyard of orange trees and stay-awhile patio furniture (RS%, family rooms, email reservations preferred, free loaner bikes, face church on Piazza Maria Trastevere and go right down Via della Fonte d'Olio 50 yards to Vicolo del Piede 2, tel. 06-589-4626, www.hotelsantamariatrastevere.it, info@ hotelsantamaria.info).

$$$$ Hotel San Francesco, big and blocky yet welcoming, stands practically and efficiently at the far end of all the Trastevere action. It rents 24 trim rooms and comes with an inviting roof terrace. It's fine, but a bit more distant than the others listed here (email reservations preferred, air-con, elevator, Via Jacopa de' Settesoli 7, tel. 06-5830-0051, www.hotelsanfrancesco.net, hotelsanfrancesco@gmail.com).

$$$ Arco del Lauro B&B rents six tight, whitewashed, straightforward rooms around a dim, quiet back courtyard. Consider it the less expensive version of the Residenza Arco dei Tolomei, which is upstairs. The lower prices make up for the lack of public spaces and mostly offsite management (one family room, cash only, includes small breakfast at nearby café, air-con, from Piazza Piscinula a block up Via dell'Arco de' Tolomei at #29, tel. 06-9784-0350, mobile 346-244-3212, www.arcodellauro.it, info@ arcodellauro.it, Lorenza and Daniela).

NEAR VATICAN CITY

Sleeping near the Vatican costs a little more, but some enjoy calling this relaxed, residential neighborhood home. The tree-lined streets are wider than in the historical center, so it feels less claustrophobic. Though it's handy to the Vatican, everything else is a long way away. Fortunately, it's well-served by public transit, especially the Metro (line A).

$$$$ Hotel Alimandi Vaticano, facing the Vatican Museums, is beautifully designed. Run by the Alimandi family (Enrico, Irene, and Germano), it features four stars, 24 spacious rooms, and all the modern comforts you can imagine (air-con, elevator, Viale Vaticano 99, tel. 06-3974-5562, www.alimandi.com, alimandivaticano@alimandi.com).

$$$$ Family-run **Hotel dei Consoli,** with 28 rooms, is a lesser value pleasantly located on a side street. In warm months, breakfast is served on its leafy rooftop terrace, with a view to St. Peter's— a nice way to start the day (air-con, elevator, Via Varrone 2D, tel. 06-6889-2972, www.hoteldeiconsoli.com, info@hoteldeiconsoli. com, friendly Laura and mom Amalia).

$$$ Hotel Gerber, set in a quiet residential area, is family-run with 27 thoughtfully decorated rooms—some chic and modern, others polished and businesslike (RS%, family rooms, air-con, elevator, small leafy terrace; from Lepanto Metro station, go one block down Via M. Colonna and turn right to Via degli Scipioni 241; tel. 06-321-6485, www.hotelgerber.it, info@hotelgerber.it, Piero and Simonetta).

$$$ Hotel Museum is located steps from the Vatican Museums and run by another branch of the entrepreneurial Alimandi family—Paolo, Luigi, Marta, and Barbara. It has 27 modest but comfortable rooms and large public spaces, including a piano lounge, pool table, and rooftop terrace where the grand buffet breakfast is served (elevator, air-con, down the stairs directly in front of Vatican Museums, Via Tunisi 8, Metro: Ottaviano, tel. 06-3972-3941, www.hotelmuseum.it, info@hotelmuseum.it).

$$$ Hearth Hotel, a block from the Vatican wall, has 22 small, modern, efficient, and characterless rooms (RS%—use code "rick steves," air-con, elevator, Via Santamaura 2, tel. 06-3903-8383, www.hearthhotel.com, info@hearthhotel.com).

$$ Casa Valdese is a well-managed, Protestant church-run hotel that's a good value and feels a bit institutional. Its 33 recently renovated—but basic—rooms come with the bonus of two breezy, communal roof terraces with incredible views (RS%, family rooms, air-con, elevator; Via Alessandro Farnese 18, tel. 06-321-5362, www.casavaldeseroma.it, reception@casavaldeseroma.it, Matteo).

$$ Casa per Ferie Santa Maria alle Fornaci is simple and efficient, housing pilgrims and secular tourists just a five-minute walk south of the Vatican in a dull, high-rise residential zone. Its 54 utilitarian rooms are mostly twin-bedded. Reserve at least three months in advance (air-con, elevator; take bus #64 from Termini train station to San Pietro train station, then walk 100 yards north along Via della Stazione di San Pietro to Piazza Santa Maria alle Fornaci 27; or from the airport, take the train to Trastevere Station, then transfer to San Pietro Station; tel. 06-3936-7632, www.santamariafornaci.com, Carmine).

EATING IN ROME

Eating Tips 363
Trastevere 365
Jewish Ghetto 368
Pantheon Neighborhood 369
North Rome: Near the Spanish Steps
    and Ara Pacis 377
Ancient Rome: Near the Colosseum and
    Forum 378
Near Termini Station 382
Near Vatican City 383
Testaccio 386

Romans take great pleasure in dining well. Embrace this passion over a multicourse meal at an outdoor table, watching a parade of passersby while you sip wine with loved ones.

In ancient times, the dinner party was the center of Roman social life. It was a luxurious affair, set in the *triclinium* (formal dining room). Guest lists were small (3-9 people), and the select few reclined on couches during the exotic multicourse meal. Today the couches are gone, and the fare may not include jellyfish, boiled tree fungi, or flamingo, but the *cucina Romana* influence remains. It's fair to say that while French cuisine makes an art of the preparation, Italian (and Roman) cuisine is simpler and all about the ingredients.

Roman meals are still lengthy social occasions. Simple, fresh, seasonal ingredients dominate the dishes. The *cucina* is robust, strongly flavored, and unpretentious—much like the people who've created it over the centuries. It is said that Roman cooking didn't come out of emperors' or popes' kitchens, but from the *cucina po-*

vera—the home cooking of the common people. This may explain the Romans' fondness for meats known as the *quinto quarto* ("fifth quarter"), such as tripe, tail, brain, and pigs' feet, as well as their interest in natural preservatives like chili peppers and garlic.

Rome belongs to the warm, southern region of Lazio, which produces a rich variety of flavorful vegetables and fruit that are the envy of American supermarkets. Rome's proximity to the Mediterranean also allows for a great variety of seafood (especially on Fridays), which can be pricey if you're dining out.

EATING TIPS

For general advice on eating in Italy, including details on ordering, dining, and tipping in restaurants, where to find budget meals, picnicking help, and Italian cuisine and beverages—including wine, see page 521.

Kitchens close at most restaurants between lunch and dinner; if it's a quality restaurant, it won't reopen before 19:00. If a smaller restaurant is booked up later in the evening (from 20:30 or so), they may accommodate walk-ins if you're willing to eat quickly (no lingering).

Choosing Restaurants: I've listed restaurants that I enjoy. Many are in quaint and therefore pricey and touristy areas such as Trastevere, Piazza Navona, and Campo de' Fiori. Others are tucked away from the tourist crush.

I'm impressed by how small the price difference can be between a mediocre Roman restaurant and a fine one. You can pay about 20 percent more for double the quality. If I had $100 for three meals in Rome, I'd spend $50 for one and $25 each for the other two, rather than $33 on all three. For splurge meals, I'd consider Gabriello, Fortunato, and Taverna Trilussa (in that order; all described later).

Rome's fabled squares (most notably Piazza Navona, near the Pantheon, and Campo de' Fiori) are lined with the outdoor tables of touristy restaurants with enticing menus and formal-vested waiters. The atmosphere is super romantic. I, too, like the idea of dining under floodlit monuments, amid a constantly flowing parade of people. But you'll likely be surrounded by tourists and hawkers, and awkward interactions can kill the ambience...leaving you with just a forgettable and overpriced meal. Restaurants in these areas are notorious for surprise charges, forgettable food, microwaved ravioli, and bad service.

I enjoy the view by savoring just a drink or dessert on a famous square, but I dine with locals on nearby low-rent streets, where the proprietor needs to serve a good-value meal and nurture a local following to stay in business. If you're set on eating—or just drinking and snacking—on a famous piazza, you don't need a guide-

> # Restaurant Price Code
>
> I've assigned each eatery a price category, based on the aver-
> age cost of a typical main course (pasta or *secondi*). Drinks,
> desserts, and splurge items (steak and seafood) can raise the
> price considerably.
>
> | | | |
> |---|---|---|
> | **$$$$** | **Splurge:** | Most main courses over €20 |
> | **$$$** | **Pricier:** | €15-20 |
> | **$$** | **Moderate:** | €10-15 |
> | **$** | **Budget:** | Under €10 |
>
> In Italy, pizza by the slice and other takeaway food is **$**; a basic
> trattoria or sit-down pizzeria is **$$**; a casual but more upscale
> restaurant is **$$$**; and a swanky splurge is **$$$$**.

book listing to choose a spot; enjoy the ritual of slowly circling the
square, observing both the food and the people eating it, and sit
where the view and menu appeal to you. (And pizza is probably
your best value and least risky bet.)

The *Aperitivo* **Tradition:** For a budget,
light meal, consider partaking in an *aperitivo*
buffet. Milan and northern Italian cities have
long enjoyed this tradition, in which bars serve
up an enticing buffet of small dishes, and anyone buying a drink (at an inflated price) gets
to eat "for free." Now, competition for customers in the early evening hours has driven
bars in Rome to embrace the same practice.
All over town, bars—from humble to chic-
and-trendy—are offering a light meal with a
cocktail during happy hour. Drinks generally

cost around €8-12, and the food's out anywhere from about 18:00
to 21:00. Some places limit you to one plate; others allow refills.
Either way, if you want a quick, light dinner with a drink, it's a
great deal.

Picnicking: Another cheap way to eat is to assemble a picnic
and dine with Rome as your backdrop. Buy ingredients for your
picnic at one of Rome's open-air produce markets (mornings only;
see page 408), an *alimentari* (corner grocery store), a *rosticcerie*
(cheap food to go), or a *supermercato*, such as Conad, Despar, or
Coop. You'll find handy late-night supermarkets near the Pantheon (Via Giustiniani), Spanish Steps (Via Vittoria), Trevi Fountain
(Via del Bufalo), and Campo de' Fiori (Via di Monte della Farina).
Note that Rome discourages people from picnicking or drinking
at historic monuments (such as on the Spanish Steps) in the old
center. Technically violators can be fined, though it rarely happens.
You'll be OK if you eat *with* a view rather than *on* the view.

TRASTEVERE

Restaurants line the streets of colorful Trastevere. It's a favorite dining neighborhood for both Romans and tourists—more rustic than the downtown zone, but just a short walk across the river. Go beyond the central square, Piazza di Santa Maria in Trastevere, into the back streets and you'll find places which serve with the most sincerity and charm. For locations, see the map on page 357.

$$$$ Taverna Trilussa is your best bet for dining well in Trastevere. Brothers Massimo and Maurizio offer quality without pretense. With a proud 100-year-old tradition, this place has the right mix of style and informality. The service is fun-loving (they're happy to let you split plates into smaller portions to enjoy a family-style meal), yet professional. The menu celebrates local classics and seasonal specials—as well as their award-winning *pasta amatriciana*—and comes with a big wine selection. The spacious dining hall is strewn with eclectic Roman souvenirs. Outdoors, Trilussa has an actual hedged-in terrace rather than just tables jumbled together on the sidewalk (dinner only—Mon-Sat from 19:30, closed Sun, reservations smart, Via del Politeama 23, tel. 06-581-8918, www.tavernatrilussa.it).

$$$ Osteria La Gensola, a seafood restaurant, is a good place to indulge (they also have Roman classics on the menu). The interior (no outside seating), which feels like a rustic yet sophisticated living room, is pleasantly homey (daily 13:00-15:00 & 19:30-23:00, Piazza della Gensola 15, tel. 06 581 6312, www.osterialagensola.it).

$$ Trattoria da Lucia is your basic old-school Trastevere dining experience, and has been family-run since before World War II. The specialty is *spaghetti alla Gricia*, with pancetta (Tue-Sun 12:30-15:00 & 19:30-23:00, closed Mon and much of Aug, cash only, evocative outdoor or comfy indoor seating—but avoid back room, just off Via del Mattonato at Vicolo del Mattonato 2, tel. 06-580-3601).

$$ Trattoria da Olindo takes homey to extremes. You really feel like you dropped in on a family that cooks for the neighborhood. The menu is short, with a choice of about five €8 pastas and five €10 *secondi* (Mon-Sat 19:30-22:30, closed Sun, cash only, indoor and funky outdoor seating, Vicolo della Scala 8 at the corner of Via del Mattonato, tel. 06-581-8835).

$$ Osteria Ponte Sisto, by the river, has a more touristy, old-school feel with nice place settings, white tablecloths, and traditional Roman and Neapolitan cuisine (Thu-Tue 12:30-15:00 & 19:00-23:30, closed Wed, reservations smart, 100 yards in front of the bridge at Via di Ponte Sisto 80, tel. 06-588-3411, www.osteriapontesisto.com, Oliviero).

EATING

Roman Cuisine

Here are some of the specialties you may find on the menu. For more on Italian food, including *salumi*, cheeses, pizza, and pasta, see page 530.

Antipasti (Appetizers)

Antipasto misto: A plate of marinated or grilled vegetables (eggplant, artichokes, peppers, mushrooms), cured meats, cheeses, or seafood (anchovies, octopus).

Bruschetta: Toasted bread brushed with olive oil and garlic, topped with chopped tomatoes, mushrooms, or other tidbits.

Fritti: Fried snacks that have been either battered or breaded—often olives stuffed with meat, potato croquettes, and mozzarella cheese. Other classic *fritti* are *supplí* (rice balls with tomato sauce and mozzarella) and *fiori di zucca* (squash blossoms filled with mozzarella and anchovies).

Prosciutto e melone: Cantaloupe wrapped in thin-sliced ham.

Primo Piatto (First Course)

Bucatini all'amatriciana: Thin pasta tubes with a sauce of tomatoes, onion, pancetta, and pecorino cheese.

Gnocchi alla romana: Small, flattened dumplings made from semolina (not potatoes) and baked with butter and cheese.

Penne all'arrabbiata: Spicy tomato sauce with chili peppers (*pepperoncini*) and garlic over penne.

Rigatoni con la pajata: Pasta topped with a stew of calf intestines.

Spaghetti alla carbonara: Eggs, pancetta or *guanciale* (cured pork cheek), cheese (*pecorino romano* or *parmigiano reggiano*), and black pepper over pasta.

Spaghetti alle vongole veraci: Pasta served with small clams in the shell sautéed with white wine and herbs.

Stracciatella alla romana: Meat broth with whipped eggs, topped with parmesan.

Secondo Piatto (Second Course)

Abbacchio alla scottadito: Baby lamb chops grilled and eaten as finger food.

Anguillette in umido: Stewed baby eels from Lake Bracciano.

Coda alla vaccinara: Oxtail braised with garlic, wine, tomato, and celery.

Filetti di baccalà: Fried salt cod (like fish-and-chips minus the chips).

Involtini di vitello al sugo: Veal cutlets rolled with prosciutto, celery, and cheese in a tomato sauce.

Saltimbocca alla romana: "Jump-in-the-mouth"—thinly sliced veal layered with prosciutto and sage, then lightly fried.

Trippa alla romana: Tripe braised with onions, carrots, and mint.

Contorni (Side Dishes)

You may want to order a side dish if your second course is not served with a vegetable. Note that if you order a salad, olive oil and wine vinegar are the only dressings.

Carciofi: Artichokes served either *alla romana* (simmered with garlic and mint) or *alla giudia* (flattened and fried).

Fave al guanciale: Fava beans simmered with cured pork cheek and onion.

Misticanza: Mixed green salad of arugula *(rucola)* and curly endive *(puntarelle)* with anchovies.

Dolci (Desserts)

Dessert can be a seasonal fruit, such as *fragole* (strawberries) or *pesche* (peaches), or even cheese, such as *pecorino romano* (made from ewe's milk) or *caciotta romana* (combination of ewe's and cow's milk).

Bignè: Cream puff-like pastries filled with *zabaione* (egg yolks, sugar, and Marsala wine).

Crostata di ricotta: A cheesecake-like dessert with ricotta, sweet Marsala wine, cinnamon, and bits of chocolate.

Grattachecca: Sweetened shaved ice. Vendors at little booths scrape shavings off ice blocks, then flavor them with syrups, such as *limoncocco* (lemon and coconut with fresh chunks of coconut).

Tartufo: Rich dark-chocolate gelato ball with a cherry inside, sometimes served *con panna* (with whipped cream).

Roman Pizza

Roman-style pizza is made with a very thin and crispy dough called *scrocchiarella* (thinner and less chewy than Neapolitan-style pizza). In Rome, *pizza bianco* (white pizza) can mean a pizza

made without tomato sauce, but can also simply mean a chunk of flat, crispy bread, or a sandwich made with that bread (similar to what's called a *panino* in other parts of Italy).

Local Wines

Rome is located in the region of Lazio, which produces several pleasant white wines and a few reds. Frascati, probably the best-known wine of the region, is an inexpensive dry white made from trebbiano (from the hills just south of Rome) and malvasia grapes. Castelli Romani, light and fairly dry, is made from trebbiano grapes and is similar to Marino, Colli Albani, and Velletri wines. Torre Ercolana is a dense, balanced, medium-bodied red made from the regional cesanese grape, as well as cabernet and merlot (known as Lazio's best-quality red, aged at least five years).

$$ Pizzeria "Ai Marmi" is a noisy festival of pizza. Tight marble-slab tables (hence the nickname "the Morgue") fill the seating area in front of the oven and pizza-assembly line. It's a classic Roman scene, whether you enjoy the chaos inside, sit at a sidewalk table, or take the famously good, thin, and crispy €8-9 pizza home. They also serve fried cod, rice balls with mozzarella, and bean dishes. Expect brusque service and a long line between 20:00 and 22:00 (Thu-Tue 18:30 until late, closed Wed, cash only, tram #8 from Piazza Venezia to first stop over bridge, just beyond Piazza Sonnino at Viale di Trastevere 53, tel. 06-580-0919).

$$ Pizzeria Dar Poeta, tucked in a back alley and a hit with local students, cranks out €9 wood-fired pizzas and €8 calzones. These pizzas are easily splittable and, if you're extra hungry, pay an extra euro for *pizza alta* (thicker crust). Choose between their sloppy, cramped interior or the lively tables outside on the cobblestones (daily 12:00-24:00, call to reserve or expect a wait, 50 yards directly in front of Santa Maria della Scala Church at Vicolo del Bologna 45, tel. 06-588-0516).

$$ Cantina Ripagrande, a block over Viale di Trastevere from the touristy action, has a funky romantic charm and a small but creative menu for lunch (13:00-15:30) and dinner (19:30-22:30). Drinks are served the rest of the day and during happy hour from 18:00 to 20:30, when a €7 drink comes with a well-made little buffet that can turn into a cheap, light dinner (daily 11:30-late, Via San Francesco a Ripa 73, tel. 06-4547-6237).

JEWISH GHETTO

The Jewish Ghetto sits just across the river from Trastevere (see map on page 203). It's tempting to grab a table (or picnic on a bench) along the main drag to watch the street action. Eating here goes well with my self-guided tour of the neighborhood (see page 205).

$$ Sora Margherita, hiding on a cluttered square, has been a rustic neighborhood favorite since 1927. Amid picturesque commotion, guests chow down on basic old-time Roman and Jewish dishes. Eat here for the experience rather than fine food. The menu's crude term for the fettuccini gives you some idea of the mood of this place: *nazzica culo* ("shaky ass"—what happens while it's made). Reservations are strongly advised. While lunch (12:30-15:00) is open, for dinner there are two seatings: 20:00 and 21:30 (closed Sun and second half of Aug; just south of Via del Portico d'Ottavia at Piazza delle Cinque Scole 30—look for the red curtain, tel. 06-687-4216).

$$$ Beppe e i Suoi Formaggi is entirely dedicated to the fine wines, cold cuts, pastas—and above all the cheeses—of the Piedmont region of northern Italy. Its sleek, woody wine-crate ambiance is designed for foodies with money who are interested in the best of that region's organic cuisine (€28 cheese plate for two, €20 daily specials, wine by the glass, Mon-Sat 12:00-22:30, closed Sun, Santa Maria del Pianto 11, tel. 06-6819-2210, www. beppeeisuoiformaggi.it).

$ *A Fast Lunch in the Ghetto:* The ghetto's main drags—Via del Portico d'Ottavia and Via di Santa Maria del Pianto—are both ideal for a quick lunch. You'll find a falafel counter; a good kosher burger joint (**Fonzie the Burger's House,** with a few tables); **Yesh,** a kebab shop; **Pizzeria Franco e Cristina,** which sells slices and simple pasta dishes by weight and has casual outdoor tables; and the neighborhood Jewish bakery. The kebab shop and the pizzeria sell fried artichokes *(carciofi alla giudia)* for €4. Fonzie's, Yesh, and the pizzeria have casual tables, and there are benches along the street.

PANTHEON NEIGHBORHOOD

I've listed the restaurants in this central area based on which land- mark they're closest to: Campo de' Fiori, Piazza Navona, the Trevi Fountain, or the Pantheon itself.

On and near Campo de' Fiori

By day, Campo de' Fiori hosts a colorful fruit-and-veggies market (with an increasing number of tourist knickknacks; Mon-Sat closes around 13:30, closed Sun). Combined with a sandwich and a sweet from the **Forno** (bakery) in the west corner of the square (behind the fountain), you can assemble a nice picnic.

In the evening, Campo de' Fiori offers a characteristic set- ting—once romantic, but now overrun with students and tourists out drinking. The square is lined with popular and interesting bars, pizzerias, and small restaurants—all great for people-watching over a glass of wine. Later at night any charm is smothered by a younger clubbing crowd, but romance lives on the nearby streets.

$$ Enoteca L'Angolo Divino is an inviting little wine bar run by Massimo Crippa, a sommelier who beautifully describes a fine array of wines along with the best accompanying meats, cheeses, and pastas. With tiny tables, a tiny menu, intriguing walls of wine bottles, smart advice, and more locals than tourists, this place can leave you with a lifelong memory (lots of wines by the glass, daily 11:00-15:00 & 17:00-24:00, no afternoon closure Sun-Mon, a block off Campo de' Fiori at Via dei Balestrari 12, tel. 06-686- 4413).

$$$ Salumeria e Vineria Roscioli is an elegant *enoteca* that's a hit with local foodies, so reservations are a must. While it's just a salami toss away from touristy Campo de' Fiori, you'll dine with classy locals, and feel like you're sitting in a romantic (and expen- sive) deli after hours. While a bit pretentious, they have a good selection of fine cheeses, meats, local dishes, and top-end wines

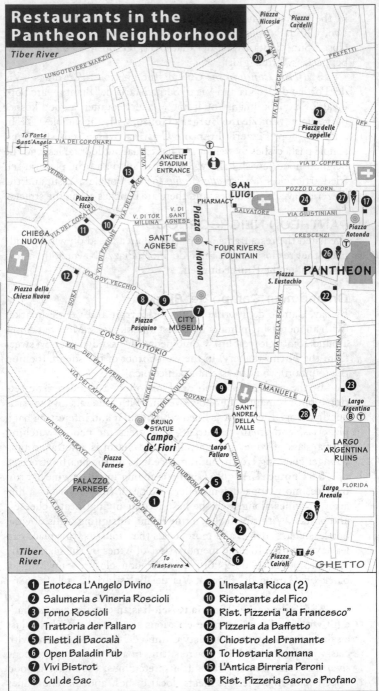

Restaurants in the Pantheon Neighborhood

Tiber River

Piazza Nicosia

Piazza Cardelli

20

21

Piazza delle Coppelle

To Ponte Sant'Angelo

VIA DEI CORONARI

ANCIENT STADIUM ENTRANCE

SAN LUIGI

PHARMACY

SALVATORE

VIA GIUSTINIANI

POZZO D. CORN.

VIA D. COPPELLE

24

27

17

Piazza Rotonda

13

Piazza Fico

V. DI TOR MILLINA

V. DI SANT' AGNESE

Piazza Navona

SANT' AGNESE

FOUR RIVERS FOUNTAIN

CRESCENZI

26

PANTHEON

CHIESA NUOVA

11

10

Piazza della Chiesa Nuova

12

VIA GOV. VECCHIO

SORA

8

9

Piazza Pasquino

7

CITY MUSEUM

Piazza S. Eustachio

22

CORSO VITTORIO

VIA DEL PELLEGRINO

VIA DEI CAPPELLARI

VIA MONSERRATO

CANCELLERIA

VIA DEL BAULLARI

BOVARI

9

EMANUELE II

SANT' ANDREA DELLA VALLE

28

23

Largo Argentina

LARGO ARGENTINA RUINS

BRUNO STATUE

Campo de' Fiori

4

Largo Pallaro

Piazza Farnese

PALAZZO FARNESE

VIA GIULIA

CAPO DE FERRO

VIA GIUBBONARI

CHIAVARI

5

3

FLORIDA

Largo Arenula

29

Tiber River

To Trastevere

VIA SPECCHI

6

Piazza Cairoli

T #8

GHETTO

1 Enoteca L'Angelo Divino	9 L'Insalata Ricca (2)
2 Salumeria e Vineria Roscioli	10 Ristorante del Fico
3 Forno Roscioli	11 Rist. Pizzeria "da Francesco"
4 Trattoria der Pallaro	12 Pizzeria da Baffetto
5 Filetti di Baccalà	13 Chiostro del Bramante
6 Open Baladin Pub	14 To Hostaria Romana
7 Vivi Bistrot	15 L'Antica Birreria Peroni
8 Cul de Sac	16 Rist. Pizzeria Sacro e Profano

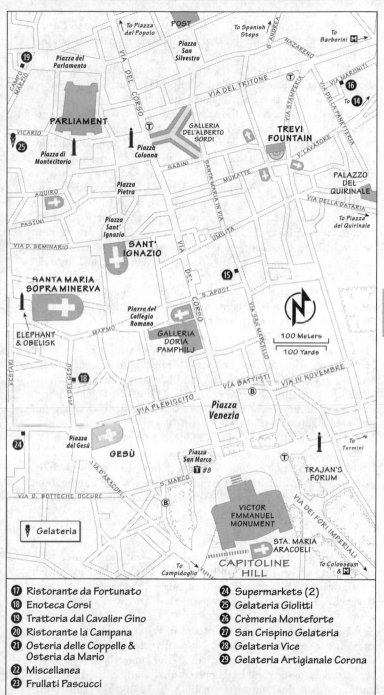

⑰ Ristorante da Fortunato
⑱ Enoteca Corsi
⑲ Trattoria dal Cavalier Gino
⑳ Ristorante la Campana
㉑ Osteria delle Coppelle &
   Osteria da Mario
㉒ Miscellanea
㉓ Frullati Pascucci

㉔ Supermarkets (2)
㉕ Gelateria Giolitti
㉖ Crèmeria Monteforte
㉗ San Crispino Gelateria
㉘ Gelateria Vice
㉙ Gelateria Artigianale Corona

by the glass (Mon-Sat 12:30-16:00 & 19:00-24:00, closed Sun, 3 blocks east of Campo de' Fiori at Via dei Giubbonari 21, tel. 06-687-5287, www.salumeriaroscioli.com).

$ Forno Roscioli, their attractive upscale bakery just down the street, will sell you a quick slice of pizza or pastry to go (Mon-Sat 6:00-20:00, closed Sun, Via dei Chiavari 34).

$$$ Trattoria der Pallaro, an eccentric and well-worn eatery that has no menu, has a slogan: "Here, you'll eat what we want to feed you." Paola Fazi—with a towel wrapped around her head turban-style—and her gang dish up a five-course meal of homey Roman food. You have three menu choices: €25 for the works; €20 for appetizers, *secondi*, and dessert; or €16 for appetizers and pasta. Any option is filling and includes wine. While the service can be odd and the food is, let's say... rustic, the experience is fun (daily 12:00-16:00 & 19:00-24:00, reserve if dining after 20:00, cash only, indoor/outdoor seating on quiet square, a block south of Corso Vittorio Emanuele, down Largo del Chiavari to Largo del Pallaro 15, tel. 06-6880-1488).

$$ Filetti di Baccalà is a cheap and basic Roman classic, where nostalgic regulars cram in at wooden tables and savor €5 fried cod finger-food fillets and raw, slightly bitter *puntarelle* greens (slathered with anchovy sauce, available in spring and winter). Study what others are eating, and order from your grease-stained server by pointing at what you want. Sit in the fluorescently lit interior or try to grab a seat out on the little square, a quiet haven a block east of Campo de' Fiori (Mon-Sat 17:00-23:00, closed Sun, cash only, Largo dei Librari 88, tel. 06-686-4018). If you're not into greasy spoons, avoid this place.

$$ Open Baladin is a busy, modern brewpub featuring a few dozen Italian craft beers on tap and menu of burgers, salads, and freshly cooked potato chips. As burger bars are trendy in Italy, prices are somewhat high. It's a nice break if you're parched and ready for pub grub (daily 12:00-very late, Via degli Specchi 5, tel. 06-683-8989).

Near Piazza Navona

Piazza Navona and the streets just to the west are jammed with an amazing array of restaurants. The places lining the piazza itself are traditional and touristy. Instead, survey the scene on the two streets heading west from the square. Here are my favorites in that zone:

$$ Vivi Bistrot, in the Museum of Rome building, is a good value at the south end of Piazza Navona, with two delightful window tables overlooking the square. This smart little restaurant serves salads, pastas, and burger plates all day and a €10 drink-and-antipasto-plate deal nightly from 19:00 to 22:00 (Tue-Sun 10:00-

24:00, closed Mon, Piazza Navona 2, tel. 06-683-3779, www.vivibistrot.com).

$$ Cul de Sac, a corridor-wide trattoria lined with wine bottles, is packed with an enthusiastic crowd enjoying a wide-ranging menu, from pasta to homemade pâté. They have fun sampler plates of *salumi* and cheese, good wines by the glass, and fine outdoor seating. It's small, and they don't take reservations—come early to avoid a wait (daily 12:00-24:00, a block off Piazza Navona on Piazza Pasquino 73, tel. 06-6880-1094).

$ L'Insalata Ricca, a popular local chain, specializes in filling salads and also serves pasta and €10-12 meal deals (available all day) that include a drink. A small branch is at Piazza Pasquino 72 (tel. 06-6830-7881) and a more spacious and enjoyable location is a couple blocks toward Largo Argentina, just across busy Corso Vittorio Emanuele (Largo dei Chiavari 85, tel. 06-6880-3656). Both are open daily 12:00-24:00.

$$ Ristorante del Fico is a sprawling, rustic-chic place that feels like a huge Italian saloon filled with young, in-the-know locals. It has both a fun energy and an easy-to-enjoy, traditional Italian menu (nightly from 19:30, 3 blocks west of Piazza Navona at Via della Pace 34, tel. 06-688-91373).

$$ Ristorante Pizzeria "da Francesco," bustling and authentic, has a 50-year-old tradition, a hardworking young waitstaff, great indoor seating, and a few tables on the quiet street. Their blackboard explains the daily specials (daily 12:00-15:30 & 19:00-24:00, Piazza del Fico 29, tel. 06-686-4009).

$$ Pizzeria da Baffetto is famous among visiting Italians and therefore generally comes with a ridiculous line— get there very early or late. The pizzas are great, the service is surly, and the tables are tightly arranged amid the mishmash of sketches littering the walls. The pizza-assembly kitchen keeps things energetic, and the pizza oven keeps the main room warm. Take out or eat in: Streetside tables are less congested and sweaty, but also less memorable (daily 12:00-15:30 & 18:30 until late, cash only; order "P," "M," or "D"— small, medium, or large; Via del Governo Vecchio 114, tel. 06-686-1617).

$$ Chiostro del Bramante is a museum café serving light lunches of sandwiches, salads, and pastas in a unique setting—overlooking the tranquil open-air *chiostro* (cloister) of the San Bramante church. Find the stairs just to the left of the church entrance and tell the ticket-window staff that you're just going to the café. Though portions are small, the setting is memorable, peaceful, and relaxing—this is the place to sit and get some writing done (café open daily 10:00-20:00, meals served 12:00-15:00, Arco della Pace 5, tel. 06-6880-9035).

Near the Trevi Fountain

The streets surrounding the Trevi Fountain are littered with mediocre restaurants catering exclusively to tourists. Skip them and walk a few blocks away to one of these.

$$ Hostaria Romana is a busy bistro with a hustling and fun-loving gang of waiters. The upstairs is a tight, tidy, glassed-in terrace, while the cellar has noisy walls graffitied by happy eaters. As its menu specializes in traditional Roman dishes, it's a good place to try *saltimbocca alla romana* or *bucatini all'amatriciana*. Their €12 *antipasti della casa* plate, with a variety of vegetables and cheeses, makes a hearty start to your meal (Mon-Sat 12:30-15:00 & 19:15-23:00, closed Sun and Aug, reservations smart, Via del Boccaccio 1—see map on page 384, walk along Via Rasella to reach restaurant, tel. 06-474-5284, www.hostariaromana.it).

$ L'Antica Birreria Peroni is Rome's answer to a German beer hall. Serving hearty mugs of the local Peroni beer and lots of just plain fun beer-hall food and Italian classics, the place is a hit with Romans for a cheap night out (Mon-Sat 12:00-24:00, closed Sun, midway between Trevi Fountain and Capitoline Hill, a block off Via del Corso at Via di San Marcello 19, tel. 06-679-5310).

$$ Ristorante Pizzeria Sacro e Profano, filling an old church, serves spicy southern Italian (Calabrian) cuisine just far enough away from the Trevi mobs. Their pizza oven is wood-fired, and their hearty €15 *golosità calabresi* appetizer plate is a filling montage of Calabrian taste treats (Tue-Sun 12:00-15:00 & 18:00-23:00, closed Mon, a block off Via del Tritone and Via della Panetteria at Via dei Maroniti 29, tel. 06-679-1836).

Close to the Pantheon

Eating on the square facing the Pantheon is a temptation, and I'd consider it just to relax and enjoy the Roman scene. But if you walk a block or two away, you'll get less view and better value. Here are some suggestions.

$$$$ Ristorante da Fortunato is an Italian classic, with fresh flowers on the tables and white-coated, black-tie career waiters politely serving good meat and fish to politicians, foreign dignitaries, and well-heeled tourists with good taste. Peruse the photos of their famous visitors—everyone from Muammar Gaddafi and Prince Charles to Bill Clinton are pictured with Signore Fortunato, who started this restaurant in 1975 and was a master of simple edible elegance. (His son Jason now runs the show.) The outdoor seating is fine for people-watching, but the elegance is inside. For a dressy night out, this is a reliable and surprisingly reasonable choice—reserve ahead (figure €50/person, daily 12:30-23:30, a block in front of the Pantheon at Via del Pantheon 55, tel. 06-679-2788, www.ristorantefortunato.it).

Resources for Foodies

For those looking to take their Roman culinary endeavors seriously, there's no shortage of in-depth advice. Books and blogs on Roman cuisine abound, and several local companies run food- and wine-themed tours. Here is a sampling:

Katieparla.com, food author Katie Parla's website, has all the latest on the Roman food scene. She also offers private food-oriented tours and tastings.

Katie Parla's Rome, Parla's app, transfers her highly selective, top-notch recommendations into an easy-to-use, searchable format (and once on your device, it doesn't require an Internet connection).

Eat Italy, an excellent iPhone-only app covering many cities—including Rome—by food writer Elizabeth Minchilli, lists a wider range of good eateries and food-oriented shops (works without Internet connection). Her website also features recipes and private food tours (www.elizabethminchilliinrome. com).

Eating Italy Food Tours leads fun and insightful walks almost daily through Rome's colorful Testaccio and Trastevere neighborhoods, interspersing history, tradition, and local food culture while giving you a glimpse into daily life in less-seen parts of the city. Each group of about a dozen people makes about 10 tasty stops. The Testaccio tour is better (€75-88, 4 hours, several morning and evening departures Mon-Sat, www.eatingitalyfoodtours.com). They also offer cooking classes. Rick Steves readers get a 10 percent discount (use promo code "ricksteves").

Vino Roma is a small wine "school" run by several sommeliers who offer evening tasting classes (€50/person), designed to help you understand and enjoy Italian wine. They also offer several neighborhood walks (www.vinoroma.com).

Buon appetito, e salute!

$$ Enoteca Corsi, a wine shop that grew into a thriving restaurant, is a charming local scene with the family table in back, where the kids do their homework. The Paiella family serves straightforward, traditional cuisine to an appreciative crowd of office workers. The board lists daily specials (gnocchi on Thursday, fish on Friday, and so on). Friendly Manuela and her staff welcome eaters with €9 pastas, €13 main dishes, and fine wine at a third of the price you'd pay in normal restaurants—buy from their shop and pay a corking fee; this can be a good value. Show this book for a free glass of homemade *limoncello* for dessert (Mon-Sat 12:00-15:30, Thu-Fri also 19:00-22:30, closed Sun, no reservations, a block toward the Pantheon from the Gesù Church at Via del Gesù 87, tel. 06-679-0821).

$$ Trattoria dal Cavalier Gino, tucked away on a tiny street behind the Parliament, has been a favorite since 1963. Photos on the wall recall the days when it was the haunt of big-time politicians. English-speaking siblings Carla and Fabrizio serve up traditional Roman favorites. Reserve ahead, even for lunch, as you'll be packed in with savvy locals (cash only, Mon-Sat 13:00-14:45 & 20:00-22:30, closed Sun, behind Piazza del Parlamento and just off Via di Campo Marzio at Vicolo Rosini 4, tel. 06-687-3434).

$$ Ristorante la Campana is a classic—an authentic slice of old Rome appreciated by well-dressed locals. Claiming a history dating to 1518, this place feels unchanged over the years. It serves typical Roman dishes and €10 daily specials, plus it has a good self-service *antipasti* buffet (Tue-Sun 12:30-15:00 & 19:30-23:00, closed Mon, inside seating only, reserve for dinner, just off Via della Scrofa and Piazza Nicosia at Vicolo della Campana 18, tel. 06-687-5273, www.ristorantelacampana.com).

$$ Osteria delle Coppelle, a slapdash, trendy place, serves traditional dishes to a local crowd. It has a rustic interior and jumbled exterior seating, and a fun selection of €3 *cicchetti* that lets you enjoy a variety of Roman dishes as tapas (daily 12:30-16:00 & 19:00 until late, Piazza delle Coppelle 54, tel. 06-4550-2826). On the same charming square, the more old-school **Osteria da Mario** is also worth considering.

$$ Miscellanea is run by much-loved Mikki, who's on a mission to keep foreign students well-fed. He offers hearty €4 sandwiches, pizza-like bruschetta, and a long list of €7-8 salads, along with pasta and other staples—it's a good value for a cheap and hearty dinner in a convenient location. Mikki (and his son Romeo) often tosses in a fun little extra (like their "sexy wine") if you have this book on the table (daily 9:00-24:00, indoor/outdoor seating, facing the rear of the Pantheon at Via della Palombella 34, tel. 06-6813-5318).

Picnicking Close to the Pantheon

It's fun to picnic with a view of the Pantheon. (Remember to be discreet.) Here are some options.

$ Frullati Pascucci, a hole-in-the-wall convenient for take-away, has been making refreshing €3-4 fruit *frullati* and frappés (like smoothies and shakes), plus fruit salads, for more than 75 years. Add a €4 sandwich to make a healthy light meal (Mon-Sat 6:00-23:00, closed Sun, north of Largo Argentina at Via di Torre Argentina 20, tel. 06-686-4816).

Supermarkets: For picnic goodies, try **Despar,** half a block from the Pantheon (daily 8:30-22:00, Via Giustiniani 18) or **Co-op,** three blocks away (Mon-Sat 8:00-21:00, Sun 9:00-21:00, Corso Vittorio Emanuele II 42).

Gelato Close to the Pantheon

Several fine *gelaterie* are within three or four blocks of the Pantheon.

Giolitti is Rome's most famous and venerable ice-cream joint (although few would say it has the best gelato). Takeaway prices are reasonable, and it has elegant Old World seating (just off Piazza Colonna and Piazza Montecitorio at Via Uffici del Vicario 40).

Crèmeria Monteforte is known for its traditional gelato and super-creamy sorbets *(cremolati)*. The fruit flavors are especially refreshing—think gourmet slushies (closed Mon, faces the west side of the Pantheon at Via della Rotonda 22).

San Crispino serves small portions of tasty gourmet gelato. Because of their commitment to natural ingredients, the colors are muted; ice cream purists know that bright colors are artificial and used to attract children (a block in front of the Pantheon at Piazza della Maddalena 3).

Gelateria Vice might be the best of all. They use top-quality ingredients in innovative ways, and the flavors change with the seasons (around the northwest corner of Largo Argentina at Corso Vittorio Emanuele II 96).

Gelateria Artigianale Corona feels like a time warp and is nothing fancy, but it's got some of the finest homemade gelato in town, with an array of creative flavors (just south of Largo Argentina at Largo Arenula 27).

NORTH ROME: NEAR THE SPANISH STEPS AND ARA PACIS

To locate these restaurants, see the "Dolce Vita Stroll" map on page 415.

$$$ Ristorante il Gabriello is inviting and small—modern under medieval arches—and provides a peaceful and local-feeling respite from all the top-end fashion shops in the area. Claudio serves with charisma, while his brother Gabriello cooks creative Roman cuisine using fresh, organic products from his wife's farm. Italians normally just trust their waiter and say, "Bring it on." Tourists are understandably more cautious, but you can be trusting here. Invest €45—not including wine—in "Claudio's Extravaganza," created especially for my readers (not on the menu). Specify whether you'd prefer fish, meat, or both. (Romans think raw shellfish is the ultimate in fine dining. If you differ, make that clear.) When finished, I stand up, hold my belly, and say, *"Ahhh, la vita è bella."* While you're likely to dine surrounded by my readers here (especially if eating before 21:00), the atmosphere is fun and convivial (dinner only, Mon-Sat 19:00-23:00, closed Sun, reservations smart, air-con, dress respectfully—no shorts, 3 blocks from Spanish Steps at Via Vittoria 51, tel. 06-6994-0810, www.ilgabriello.it).

EATING

$$ Antica Enoteca, an upbeat, atmospheric 200-plus-year-old *enoteca,* has around 60 Italian-only wines by the glass. For a light and memorable lunch, enjoy a glass of their best wine at the bar (listed on a big blackboard) and split a €14 *antipasti* plate of veggies, *salumi,* and cheese. There's a full menu of eating options, including daily *piatto unico* specials, and the food comes with wonderful ambience both inside and out (daily 12:00-24:00, best to reserve for outdoor seating, Via della Croce 76B, tel. 06-679-0896).

$$ Palatium is a crisp, modern restaurant funded by the government of Lazio (the region around Rome) to show off its finest agricultural fare. Surrounded by locals, you'll enjoy generous, €12-14 shareable plates of cheeses and *salumi*, a limited menu of pasta and meat, and a huge selection of local wine (daily 9:00-22:30, closed three weeks in Aug, 5 blocks in front of the Spanish Steps at Via Frattina 94, tel. 06-6920-2132).

$$$ Caffè Ciampini is delightfully set on a fine traffic-free square. The food is quite pricey and won't win any awards—and you pay for the location—so I'd only stop here for a drink or dessert. Sit outside and people-watch amidst a professional Roman crowd. The cocktails come with a little tray of finger sandwiches and nuts; for some it's a light and inexpensive meal (€20-35 fixed-price dinners; daily 7:30-20:30, later in summer, Piazza San Lorenzo in Lucina 29, tel. 06-687-6606, www.ciampini.com).

Stand-Up Food Crawl down Via della Croce: Two blocks north of the Spanish Steps, Via della Croce is a fun street to shop for a light meal or snack. As you walk down this street from Via del Corso, you'll first pass several takeout shops for pizza and sandwiches, including the pretty but overpriced **$ Grano Frutta e Farina** (#49A). Next, the **Co-op** minisupermarket at #48 fits the bill for budget picnickers, or you can try a sandwich-on-request from the **Foccaci** deli (at #43) with a long, enticing counter of meats and cheeses. Farther down is the more formal, sit-down **Antica Enoteca** (#76b, described earlier). Then comes another classic *alimentari* (corner grocery/deli), **Salsamenteria F.lli Fabbi** at #28. They'll make a sandwich to your specs and price it by weight. **Venchi** (#25-26) has chocolate in every form. **Pompi** (#82), the self-proclaimed "kingdom of tiramisu," features several flavors (classic, strawberry, pistachio) in €4 portions. And finally, **$ Pastificio** (#8) serves up two fresh €4 pasta dishes each day; a cup of water or wine is included if you eat at the stools along the wall (daily 13:00-21:30).

ANCIENT ROME: NEAR THE COLOSSEUM AND FORUM

Within a block of the Colosseum and Forum, you'll find convenient eateries catering to weary sightseers, most offering neither memorable food nor good value. To get your money's worth, stick with one of my recommendations, even if it means a 10-15 minute walk from the ruins. For locations, see the map on page 352.

Monti

Tucked behind Trajan's Forum, in the tight and cobbled lanes between Via Nazionale and Via Cavour, is the characteristic Monti neighborhood. It's just a few steps farther from the ancient sites than the battery of forgettable touristy restaurants, but that extra effort opens up a world of inexpensive and characteristic dining experiences. From the Forum, head up Via Cavour and then left on Via dei Serpenti; the action centers on Piazza della Madonna dei Monti and nearby lanes. For more on this area, see page 56.

$$$ L'Asino d'Oro ("The Golden Donkey") is a top choice for foodies in this neighborhood (so reserve ahead). Chef Lucio Sforza serves Umbrian cuisine with a creative twist—and mingles savory and sweet flavors to create a memorable meal. The service is crisp, the pasta is homemade, and the simple, modern space is filled with savvy diners (Tue-Sat 19:30-23:00, closed Sun-Mon, Via del Boschetto 73, tel. 06-4891-3832).

$$ Taverna Romana is small, simple, and a bit chaotic—with an open kitchen and hams and garlic hanging from the ceiling. This family-run eatery's *cacio e pepe* (cheese and pepper pasta) is a favorite. Arrive early or call to reserve (Mon-Sat 12:30-15:00 & 19:00-23:00, closed Sun, Via della Madonna dei Monti 79, tel. 06-474-5325).

$$ La Cicala e La Formica ("The Cicada and the Ant") has its own little nook on Via Leonina. The terrace dining is good for people-watching, while the homey interior is livelier. The cuisine is Mediterranean and Italian, and their weekday lunch specials are good values (daily 12:00-15:30 & 18:30-23:00, Via Leonina 17, tel. 06-481-7490).

$$ Taverna dei Fori Imperiali serves typical, slightly higher-priced Roman cuisine in a snug interior that bustles with energy (Wed-Mon 12:30-15:00 & 19:30-22:30, closed Tue, Via della Madonna dei Monti 9, reserve for dinner, tel. 06-679-8643, www.latavernadeiforiimperiali.com).

$$ Alle Carrette Pizzeria, simple and rustic, serves great wood-fired pizza just 200 yards from the Forum's side entrance, hidden off a tiny square (daily 12:00-15:30 & 19:00-24:00, Vicolo delle Carrette 14, tel. 06-679-2770).

$ Trattoria da Valentino is a classic time warp hiding under its historic (and therefore protected) Birra Peroni sign. They specialize in €9 *scamorza* (grilled cheese with various toppings), list the day's pastas on a chalkboard, and serve a variety of meat dishes (Mon-Sat 13:00-15:00 & 19:00-23:00, closed Sun, Via del Boschetto 37, tel. 06-488-0643).

EATING

$ Antico Forno ai Serpenti, a hip bakery, puts out a small buffet of pastas and vegetables at lunch and dinner for €10, which includes a drink—a fine value. They also bake good bread and pastries and do breakfasts. With only a few tables, it can fill up (Mon-Sat 8:00-23:00, Sun 9:00-22:00, Via dei Serpenti 122, tel. 06-4542-7920).

$$ Enoteca Cavour 313, a wine bar with a slightly unconventional menu, ranging from couscous and salads to high-quality *affettati* (cold cuts) and cheese, makes a nice alternative to the usual pasta/pizza choices. You'll be served with a mellow ambience under lofts of wine bottles (daily 12:30-14:45 & 18:30-24:00, 100 yards off Via dei Fori Imperiali at Via Cavour 313, tel. 06-678-5496).

At Trajan's Column: **$$ Terre e Domus** is one of the few options around the otherwise unwelcoming Piazza Venezia. Immediately below Trajan's Column, it's a modern little place with a cool, peaceful, and well-lit dining room. Run by the city of Rome, its mission is to showcase local ingredients and cuisine, and to help out-of-work residents return to the job market (daily 9:00-23:30, Foro Traiano 82, tel. 06-6994-0273).

The Monti Four-Course Food Crawl

The streets of Monti are crowded with fun and creative places offering inexpensive quality snacks and light meals to eat on tiny informal tables or to take away. For a fun, four-course movable feast, essentially on one street cutting right through the heart of Monti, drop into each of these places for a little bite. Be open to whatever appeals along the way. Here's your mobile menu:

Course 1, Wine with *Aperitivo* (dinner only): $$ Fafiuché is an intimate yet vibrant family-run wine bar with a fun-loving vibe and no pretense. They serve a broad selection of wines and beers inside or at tables on the cobblestones outside. Each evening from 18:30 to 21:00 Andrea and Maria offer a popular *aperitivo* special: €8 covers a glass of wine and one trip to the buffet—making it a cheap, light meal. Or, for more money, you can order serious regional specialties from Apulia and Piedmont (Mon-Sat 17:30 until late, closed Sun, Via della Madonna dei Monti 28).

Course 2, Pizza by the Slice on the Square: $ Pizzeria la Boccaccia, a hole-in-the-wall, is good for a takeaway pizza slice. Point at what you like and mime how big of a rectangle you want (daily 9:00-24:00, Via Leonina 73). Take it a block away to eat while making the scene at the neighborhood gathering point, Piazza Santa Maria del Monti, where you can buy a to-go bottle of beer at the top of the square.

Course 3, Gourmet Sandwich and Veggie Juice: $ Zia Rosetta specializes in gourmet *rosette*, sandwiches on rose-shaped buns. At €2-3 for the tiny ones or €5-6 for the standard size, they're perfect for a light bite—either to take away or eat in. Their fun, healthy, and creative menu includes salads and €4 *centrifughe*— fresh-squeezed, vitamin-bomb fruit and veggie juices (Tue-Sun 11:00-22:00, closed Mon, Via Urbana 54).

Course 4, Gelato: Fatamorgana, hiding on the welcoming little square just above Zia Rosetta, features some of the most creative gelato flavor combinations I've seen in Italy—along with more conventional ones. Portions are small but good quality—everything is organic and gluten-free (Piazza degli Zingari 5).

Behind the Colosseum

A pleasant little residential zone just up the street from the back of the Colosseum (the opposite direction from the Forum) features a real neighborhood feel and a variety of restaurants that capably serve tired and hungry sightseers.

$ Trattoria Luzzi is a well-worn, no-frills eatery serving simple food in a high-energy—sometimes chaotic—environment (as they've done since 1945). With good prices, big portions, and proximity to the Colosseum, it draws a crowd—reserve or expect a short wait at lunch and after 19:30 (Thu-Tue 12:00-24:00, closed Wed, Via San Giovanni in Laterano 88, tel. 06-709-6332).

$$ Ristorante Pizzeria Naumachia is a good second bet if Trattoria Luzzi next door is jammed up. It's a bit more upscale and serves good-quality pizza and pastas at decent prices (Via Celimontana 7, tel. 06 700 2764).

$$ Li Rioni, a pizzeria, is open only for dinner, when its over-the-rooftops interior and terrace out front are jammed with Romans watching the busy chef plunge dough into its wood-fired oven, then pull out crispy-crust Roman-style pizzas (Wed-Mon 19:30-24:00, closed Tue, Via dei S.S. Quattro 24, tel. 06-7045-0605).

$$ La Taverna dei Quaranta, a casual neighborhood favorite, has a humble, red-checkered tablecloth ambience. They fire up the wood oven for pizza, to go along with a basic menu of Roman classics and seasonal specialties. As the place caters mostly to locals, service can be a bit slow and straightforward (daily 12:00-16:00 & 18:00-23:30, Via Claudia 24, tel. 06-700-0550).

$$ Il Pentagrappolo is an intimate *enoteca*, serving light meals (proudly, no pasta) to go with their selection of quality wines, many organic. Their €10 lunches include water and are convenient to the Forum and Colosseum (food served Mon-Fri 12:00-15:00, Tue-Sun 18:00-24:00, best to reserve on weekends, three blocks east of the Colosseum at Via Celimontana 21, www.ilpentagrappolo.com, tel. 06-709-6301).

Between the Colosseum and
St. Peter-in-Chains Church

You'll find these places across the street and up the hill from the Colosseum. They're more convenient than high cuisine, though they work fine in a pinch.

$$ Hostaria da Nerone is a traditional place serving hearty classics, including tasty homemade pasta dishes. Their *antipasti* plate—with a variety of veggies, fish, and meat—is a good value for a quick lunch. While the *antipasti* menu indicates specifics, you can have a plate of whatever's out—just direct the waiter to assemble the €10 *antipasti* plate of your lunchtime dreams (Mon-Sat 12:00-15:00 & 19:00-23:00, closed Sun, indoor/outdoor seating, Via delle Terme di Tito 96, tel. 06-481-7952).

$ Caffè dello Studente, a normal neighborhood bar popular with tourists and students attending the nearby University, is run by Pina, her perky daughter Simona, and son-in-law Emiliano. I'd skip the microwaved pasta and stick to toasted sandwiches and salad. If it's not busy, show this book when you order at the bar and sit at a table without paying extra (daily 7:30-20:00, closed Sun Nov-March, Via delle Terme di Tito 95, mobile 320-854-0333).

NEAR TERMINI STATION

These restaurants work well for those staying at my recommended hotels around Via Nazionale, Via Firenze, and Termini Station. The station itself has a lot of eateries, and there are many Asian restaurants along nearby streets.

Around Via Flavia

Though a few minutes out of the way, these places are in a quieter neighborhood with less traffic.

$$ Ristorante da Giovanni is an old-fashioned, basement-level neighborhood restaurant where hardworking cooks and waiters serve standard dishes at great prices to a committed clientele (daily specials, Mon-Sat 12:00-15:00 & 19:00-22:00, closed Sun and Aug, corner of Via XX Settembre at Via Antonio Salandra 1, tel. 06-485-950).

$$$ Ristorante la Pentolaccia, more upscale and romantic than the nearby Da Giovanni, is a dressy but still tourist-friendly place with tight seating and traditional Roman cooking—consider their daily specials. This is a local hangout, and reservations are smart (daily 12:00-15:00 & 17:30-23:00, a block off Via XX Settembre at Via Flavia 38, tel. 06-483-477, www.lapentolaccia.eu). To start things off with a free bruschetta, leave this book on the table.

$$ Pizzeria Annicinquanta, big and modern, serves Neapolitan-style pizzas in a calm ambience with outdoor seating (daily

12:30-15:30 & 19:30-24:00 except no lunch on Sat, Via Flavia 3, tel. 06-4201-0460).

$$$ I Colori del Vino Enoteca is a modern wine bar that feels like a laboratory of wine appreciation. It has woody walls of bottles, a creative menu of *affettati* (cold cuts) and cheeses with different regional themes, and a great list of fine wines by the glass. Helpful, English-speaking Marco carries on a long family tradition of celebrating the fundamentals of good nutrition: fine wine, cheese, meat, and bread (Mon-Fri 12:00-15:00 & 19:00-23:00, closed Sat-Sun—except open Sat evenings April-June and Sept-Nov, Via Aureliana 15 at corner of Via Flavia, tel. 06-474-1745).

Around Via Firenze

$$$ Target Restaurant seems to be the favorite recommendation of every hotel receptionist on Via Firenze. It has a sleek and dressy ambience, capable service, and food that's reliably good, but pricey (free *aperitivo* with this book, daily 12:00-15:30 & 19:00-24:00, reserve to specify seating outside or inside—avoid getting seated in basement, Via Torino 33, tel. 06-474-0066, www.targetrestaurant.it).

$ Caffè Torino is a workers' favorite for a quick, cheap lunch. They have good, fresh, hot dishes ready to go for a fine price. Head back past the bar to peruse their enticing display, point at what you want, then grab a seat and the young waitstaff will serve you (Mon-Fri 6:00-17:00, closed Sat-Sun, Via Torino 40A, tel. 06-474-2767).

$ Bar Firenze puts out a lunchtime display of inexpensive pastas and colorful sandwiches, which you can get to take out or eat at casual tables (daily 6:30-24:00, under the "Snack Bar" sign at Via Firenze 33, tel. 06-488-3862).

$ Bufala e Pachino Pizza, across the street, is a convenient place for pizza by the slice and priced by weight—just point and tell them how much you'd like (daily 8:00-23:00, Via Firenze 54, tel. 06-474-3668).

NEAR VATICAN CITY

As in the Colosseum area, some eateries near the Vatican prey on exhausted tourists. Avoid the restaurant pushers handing out fliers: They're usually hawking places with bad food and expensive menu tricks. Instead, tide yourself over with a slice of pizza or at any of these eateries (see map on page 358), and save your euros for a better meal elsewhere.

Handy Lunch Places near Piazza Risorgimento

These listings are a stone's throw from the Vatican wall. They're mostly fast and cheap, with a good *gelateria* nearby.

$$ Hostaria dei Bastioni, run by Antonio while Emilio

EATING

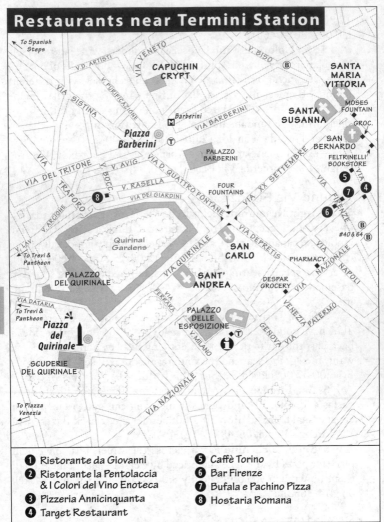

Restaurants near Termini Station

To Spanish Steps

V.D. ARTISTI
VIA VENETO
V. BISO
CAPUCHIN CRYPT
SANTA MARIA VITTORIA
VIA SISTINA
V. PURIFICAZIONE
B
MOSES FOUNTAIN
SANTA SUSANNA
GROC.
Barberini
Piazza Barberini
VIA BARBERINI
SAN BERNARDO
FELTRINELLI BOOKSTORE
VIA DEL TRITONE
V. AVIG.
PALAZZO BARBERINI
VIA D. QUATTRO FONTANE
VIA XX SETTEMBRE
VIA FIRENZE
5
7 4
VIA DEL TRAFORO
BOCC.
V. RASELLA
VIA DEI GIARDINI
FOUR FOUNTAINS
6
8
V. ARCIONE
VIA DEPRETIS
B
#40 & 64
V. LAV.
Quirinal Gardens
VIA QUIRINALE
SAN CARLO
PHARMACY
VIA NAZIONALE NAPOLI
To Trevi & Pantheon
PALAZZO DEL QUIRINALE
SANT' ANDREA
DESPAR GROCERY
VIA VENEZIA PALERMO
VIA DATARIA
To Trevi & Pantheon
VIA FERRARA
PALAZZO DELLE ESPOSIZIONE
GENOVA VIA
Piazza del Quirinale
V. MILANO
i T
SCUDERIE DEL QUIRINALE
VIA NAZIONALE
To Piazza Venezia

1 Ristorante da Giovanni
2 Ristorante la Pentolaccia & I Colori del Vino Enoteca
3 Pizzeria Annicinquanta
4 Target Restaurant

5 Caffè Torino
6 Bar Firenze
7 Bufala e Pachino Pizza
8 Hostaria Romana

cooks, has noisy streetside seating and a quiet interior (Mon-Sat 12:00-15:00 & 18:00-23:00, closed Sun, at corner of Vatican wall at Via Leone IV 29, tel. 06-3972-3034).

$ L'Insalata Ricca is another branch of the popular chain that serves hearty salads and pastas (daily 12:00-23:30, across from Vatican walls at Piazza Risorgimento 5, tel. 06-3973-0387, www.insalataricca.it).

$ Duecento Gradi is a good bet for fresh and creative sandwiches—though at €5-8 they're expensive by Roman standards. Munch your lunch sitting down (€1 extra) or take it away (daily 10:30-24:00, Piazza Risorgimento 3, tel. 06-3975-4239).

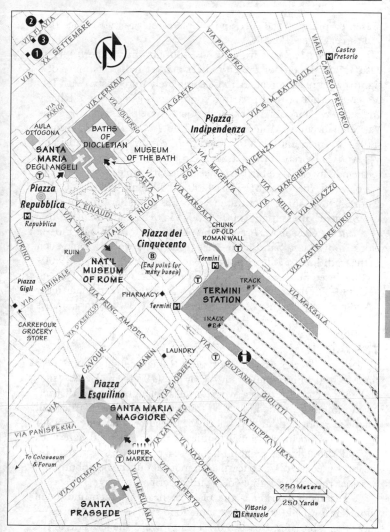

Gelato: **Gelateria Old Bridge** scoops up hearty portions of fresh gelato for tourists and nuns alike—join the line (just off Piazza Risorgimento across from Vatican walls at Viale dei Bastioni di Michelangelo 3).

Other Options in the Vatican Area

Most of these listings are near the Vatican Museums and Cipro Metro stop. The Borgo Pio eateries are near St. Peter's Basilica.

Viale Giulio Cesare and *Via Candia:* These streets are lined with cheap *pizza rustica* shops and self-serve places. **$ Forno Feliziani** (closed Sun, Via Candia 61) is a fancy version with nicely presented pizza by the slice and simple cafeteria-style dishes that you can eat in or take out.

Covered Market: Turn your nose loose in the wonderful **Mercato Trionfale,** one of the city's best market halls. It's more of a sight than a place to eat. Almost completely untouristy (with lots of vendors, but no real prepared-food stands aside from a bakery and a sandwich counter), it's located just three blocks north of the Vatican Museums (Mon-Sat roughly 7:00-14:00, Tue and Fri some stalls stay open until 19:00, closed Sun, corner of Via Tunisi and Via Andrea Doria). If the market is closed, the **Co-op** supermarket to the northwest has a big bakery section with tables where you can eat pizza by the slice (Mon-Sat 8:00-20:30, Sun 9:00-20:00, Via Andrea Doria 46). Closer to the Vatican is a smaller grocery store, **Carrefour Express** (daily 8:00-20:30, Via Sebastiano Veniero 16).

Eating Close to St. Peter's: The pedestrian-only Borgo Pio—a block from Piazza San Pietro—has restaurants worth a look, such as the traditional **$$ Tre Pupazzi** (Mon-Sat 12:00-15:00 & 19:00-23:00, closed Sun, at corner of Via Tre Pupazzi and Borgo Pio, tel. 06-6880-3220). At **$ Vecchio Borgo,** across the street, you can get pasta, pizza by weight, and veggies to go or to eat at simple tables (daily 9:30-22:30, Borgo Pio 27a).

TESTACCIO

To eat far from the crowds in a typical Roman neighborhood, take the Metro (to Piramide), tram #3, or bus (#83 from Piazza Venezia) to Testaccio. Once a working-class slaughterhouse district, Testaccio has gentrified, but isn't touristy. Its bustling market hall has been renovated, and Testaccio has become a favorite spot for local chefs and international foodies. Combine a meal here with a stroll through the neighborhood (see page 96); for restaurant locations, see page 97. To learn even more about the neighborhood, consider the Eating Italy Food Tour (described on page 375).

Testaccio Market is the place to head at lunchtime (open Mon-Sat until 14:00—though some food stalls—called "boxes"—stay open a bit later, closed Sun). Head toward the left side of the market (closest to Via Beniamino Franklin) to search out a few favorites for a light lunch. At **Mordi & Vai** (#15), Sergio makes tasty €3-4 sandwiches; locals love the *trippa* (tripe), but I prefer the *panino con allesso* (boiled beef with the bread dipped in broth) and *picchiapò* (stewed beef in a mildly spicy tomato sauce). As this is a popular place, you'll need to take a number. Nearby, several bakery stalls will satisfy your sweet tooth with their creative pastries. For olives, cheese, and cold cuts, try **Ferraro's** (#2-3, around the corner from Mordi & Vai). They're also a good bet for edible souvenirs—dried porcini mushrooms and sun-dried tomatoes, as well as other specialties, many from Calabria (think spicy).

$$ Agustarello has been serving Roman cuisine since 1957, but their restaurant feels up-to-date and without pretense—the emphasis is on the food. As this family-run place is quite small and very lively, reservations are smart (Mon-Sat 12:30-15:00 & 19:30-24:00, closed Sun, Via Giovanni Branca 98, tel. 06-574-6585).

$$ Flavio al Velavevodetto, partially set inside Monte Testaccio (windows reveal the ancient stacked pottery shards), is a good place to try nose-to-tail classics like *coda alla vaccinara* (oxtail) as well as less adventurous options (daily 12:30-15:00 & 19:45-23:00, reservations smart for dinner, Via di Monte Testaccio 97, tel. 06-574-4194, www.ristorantevelavevodetto.it).

$$ Pizzeria Remo—the humble pizza joint with the huge mob of locals out front late into the evening—is a favorite for Roman-style (thin, crispy-crust) pizza and deep-fried appetizers. It's inexpensive, busy, and crowded. If people are jamming the entrance, muscle your way inside and put your name on the list; there's ample seating, and table turnover is brisk (Mon-Sat 19:00-24:00, closed Sun, Piazza Santa Maria Liberatrice 44, tel. 06-574-6270).

$ Volpetti Più is a much nicer-than-usual version of the typical Italian *tavola calda* (self serve restaurant). Pick up a tray, point to what you want reheated, and find a table. Come for the interesting pizzas, beautiful presentation, and comfortable dining area (Mon-Sat 10:30-16:00 & 17:30-22:00, closed Sun, just off Via Marmorata at Via Alessandro Volta 8, tel. 06-574-2352). Their deli (similar hours) around the corner at Via Marmorata 47 is a cheese-and-meat sensory extravaganza and sells the same pizza, calzones, and bakery items.

$$ Perilli is the neighborhood's classic, old-school eating house—rollicking with tight tables of local families since 1911 (indoor seating only, Thu-Tue 12:30-15:00 & 19:30-23:15, closed Wed, Via Marmorata 39, tel. 06-575-5100).

$$ L'Oasi della Birra ("Beer Oasis") is well-known among Roman beer lovers, as it stocks more than 500 Italian and international brews. The main floor is a bottle shop and classy grocery, while the nondescript cellar and the terrace out front serve as a popular bar for locals to hang out and dine on pub grub. This is not a place for a fine meal or special ambience, but rather, to enjoy a beer and the lively local scene (daily specials; during happy hour from 17:30 to 20:30—except on Sun—€10 buys you a beer and access to their light dinner spread; daily 8:00-13:30 & 16:00-24:00, Piazza Testaccio 38, tel. 06-574-6122).

Upscale Supermarket: **Eataly,** an international gourmet chain, has a huge outlet at the back of the Ostiense train station, a 10-minute walk from Testaccio. The three long, sunny floors of attractive Italian products are fun to browse through. Prepared-food counters and cafés, mixed in amidst the grocery shelves, are a bit pricey but not outrageously so (daily 10:00-24:00, Piazzale XII Ottobre 1492, tel. 06-9027-9292).

To reach Eataly, follow the signs from the Piramide Metro station. An underground walkway takes you from there to the Ostiense train station: Walk under all the platforms and out the back exit (for Via Matteucci) by track 15a—see the map on page 97. Eataly also has a small outlet at Piazza della Repubblica, but only the main branch is worth a trip.

EATING

ROME WITH CHILDREN

Sorry, but Rome is not a great place for little kids. Parks are rare. Kid-friendly parks are rarer. Most museums are low-tech and lack hands-on fun.

But there is some good news. Rome's many squares are traffic-free, with plenty of space to run and pigeons to feed while Mom and Dad enjoy coffee at an outdoor table. Italians are openly fond of kids, so you'll probably get lots of friendly attention. Rome's huge ancient sites (I'm thinking the Colosseum and Pantheon) instill awe in travelers of any age—especially if they can conceive of just how old these structures are. And you won't get many complaints about the cuisine: pizza and gelato. *Buona fortuna!*

Trip Tips

EATING

Rome offers plenty of food options for children. Try these tips to keep your kids content throughout the day.

- For a refreshing respite from the midday heat, take a gelato break or go to a casual, air-conditioned place for lunch.
- Kid-friendly foods found everywhere include fresh bread *(pane)* and pasta (plain is *"pasta bianca"* and pasta with butter is *"pasta al burro"*; grated cheese will be served on the side). Pizza is another popular favorite—kids like *margherita* (tomato, basil, and cheese) and the slightly spicy Italian version of pepperoni

(diavola, salsiccia piccante, or *salame piccante).* Popular drinks are *granitas* (slushies), *frullati* (smoothies), frappés (shakes), Orangina (orange soda), *limonata* (lemonade), *spremuta d'arancia* (fresh-squeezed orange juice), and *cioccolata calda* (hot chocolate).

- Eat dinner early (at about 19:00) to dodge the romantic crowd. Restaurants are less kid-friendly after 21:00. Skip the famous places. Look instead for self-service cafeterias, bars (children are welcome), or fast-food restaurants where kids can move around without bothering others.

- Eating *al fresco* is fun; try places on squares where kids can run free while you dine, but avoid historical monuments in the city center. Picnic lunches and dinners work well—stop by the market and bakery at Campo de' Fiori, get your fixings at the *alimentari* and *frullati* shop near the Pantheon, or try the sandwich shops on Via della Croce. *Pizza rustica* shops sell cheap takeout pizza, and of course gelato provides some of the best high-calorie memories in town. See the Eating in Rome chapter for these and other ideas.

SIGHTSEEING

The key to a successful Roman family vacation is to slow down and incorporate your child's interests into each day's plans.

- Buy your child a trip journal, and encourage him or her to write down observations, thoughts, and favorite sights and memories. This journal could end up being your child's favorite souvenir.

- Let your kids make some decisions, such as choosing lunch spots or deciding which stores or museums to visit. Deputize your child to lead you on my self-guided walks and museum tours.

- Ask at Rome's TIs about kid-friendly activities. TIs sometimes have a helpful "kid's pack."

- Don't overdo it. Tackle only one or two key sights a day (Vatican Museums, or Colosseum and Forum), and mix in a healthy dose of fun activities, like exploring Rome's great public spaces (Piazza Navona, Trevi Fountain, and Villa Borghese Gardens). If you're visiting art museums with younger children, you could hit the gift shop first so you can buy postcards, then hold a scavenger hunt to find the pictured artwork. Museum audioguides are great for older children.

- Italy's national museums generally offer free admission to children under 18—always ask before buying tickets for your kids.

- Follow this book's crowd-beating tips. Kids don't want to stand in a long line for a museum (which they might not even want to see). Consider getting a Roma Pass for yourself, as

Books and Films for Kids

Get your kids into the spirit of the Eternal City with these books and movies:

Classic Myths to Read Aloud: The Great Stories of Greek and Roman Mythology (William F. Russell, 1988). This thoughtful introduction to the tales of the ancient past is sure to captivate children five and up.

Julius Caesar (1953). Portraying the dramatic story of Julius Caesar's assassination and its aftermath, this classic film brings history to life.

The Last Legion (2007). In this adventure film, brave 12-year-old Romulus Augustus takes bold action to save the Roman Empire from rebels in A.D. 470.

The Lizzie McGuire Movie (2003). A middle-school class trip to Rome is an adventure filled with comedy, drama, and romance.

The Pink Panther 2 (2009). Bumbling Inspector Jacques Clouseau heads to Rome with detectives from around the globe in a case of stolen world treasures.

Rome: Panorama Pops (Kristyna Litten, 2013). This accordion style pop-up book takes you through sites like St. Peter's Basilica and Villa Borghese.

The Thieves of Ostia (Caroline Lawrence, 2001). In ancient Rome, a young ship captain's daughter joins three friends to solve a mystery. This is the first book in Lawrence's *The Roman Mysteries* series.

This is Rome (Miroslav Sasek, 1960). History comes alive in this charming picture book of Rome through the ages. The 2007 edition includes a section about the modern-day city.

kids get to skip the line with parents who have the pass (see page 42 for details on the pass).

- Give your child a money belt and an expanded allowance; you are on vacation, after all. Let your children budget their funds by comparing and contrasting the dollar and euro.
- It's good to have a "what if" procedure in place in case something goes wrong. Give your kids your hotel's business card, your phone number (if you brought a mobile phone), and emergency taxi fare. Let them know to ask to use the phone at a hotel if they are lost. And if they have mobile phones, show them how to make calls in Italy.
- If you allow kids to explore a museum or neighborhood on their own, be sure to establish a clear meeting time and place.
- Public WCs are hard to find: Try museums, bars, gelato shops, and fast-food restaurants.
- Rome's hotels often give price breaks for kids. Your kids will

thank you for avoiding the few remaining hotels without air conditioning.

TRANSPORTATION

- Children under age 10 travel free on Rome's public transit system when accompanied by an adult.
- If you're taking the train to another city, check for family discounts; see page 546.

Sights and Activities

ANCIENT SITES, CHURCHES, AND MUSEUMS

While some ancient sites, such as the **Colosseum,** are naturally captivating for kids, others, like the Roman Forum, may be a snooze. To keep them engaged, consider picking up a copy of *Rome: Past and Present,* a book with plastic overlays showing how the ruins used to look. It's available online and at stalls near the entrance of ancient sites (prices are soft, so negotiate).

Catacombs of Priscilla

These spooky tunnels just outside the walls of the ancient city are goblin-pleasers. Kids will get a thrill out of descending into this underground tomb and seeing some of the 40,000 burial niches carved for Christians from the second to the fifth centuries. Visits are by 30-minute guided English-language tours. See listing on page 77.

Cost and Hours: €4 for kids 7-15, free for kids 6 and under, €8 for adults; Tue-Sun 9:00-12:00 & 14:00-17:00, closed Mon, closed one random month a year—check ahead, Via Salaria 430, tel. 06-8620-6272, www.catacombepriscilla.com.

Capuchin Crypt

The most macabre place in Rome is decorated with bones; it's fascinating for children and adults alike. In the basement below the Church of Santa Maria della Immacolata Concezione, bones of about 4,000 friars who died in the 1700s decorate a series of six crypts. Your introduction to the place is the Crypt of the Three Skeletons, where the ceiling is decorated with a scythe-wielding skeleton, a bony chandelier, and floral motifs made of ribs and vertebrae. Other chambers are named for the type of bones that line them: Crypt of the Tibia and Fibia, Crypt of the Hips, and Crypt of the Skulls are a few that'll keep you awake at night. For more information, see page 70.

Cost and Hours: €5 for kids 17 and under, €8.50 for adults, daily 9:00-19:00, modest dress required, no photos, Via Veneto 27, Metro: Barberini, tel. 06-8880-3695, www.cappucciniviaveneto.it.

St. Peter's Basilica Dome

In Vatican City, the climb to the top of St. Peter's is great for its dizzy railing view into the church from halfway up the dome—plus the hike will tire out young adventurers. For details, see page 234.

Cost and Hours: €7 for elevator to roof then take stairs, €5 to climb stairs all the way, cash only, allow an hour to go up and down; daily April-Sept 8:00-18:00, Oct-March 8:00-17:00, last entry one hour before closing if you take the stairs the whole way; no shorts, above-the-knee skirts, or bare shoulders—even for children; tel. 06-6988-1662, www.vaticanstate.va.

Vatican Museums

These extensive museums feature mummies, sarcophagi, ancient statues and armor, old maps, and the bedrooms of Renaissance popes. There's an audioguide designed for families. ◻ See the Vatican Museums Tour chapter for detailed information.

Cost and Hours: €8 for kids 6-18, free for kids 5 and under, €16 for adults, €4 online reservation fee; Mon-Sat 9:00-18:00, last entry at 16:00, closed on religious holidays and Sun except last Sun of the month, check online for current hours; audioguide-€7; no shorts, above-the-knee skirts, or bare shoulders—even for children; tel. 06-6988 3860 or 06-6988-1662, http://mv.vatican.va.

Castel Sant'Angelo

This emperor's tomb-turned-castle has one of the best views of Rome from the rooftop—including striking vistas of the Vatican. The weapon displays will appeal to young knights. See listing on page 63.

Cost and Hours: €10, daily 9:00-19:30, last entry one hour before closing, audioguide-€5, near Vatican City, 10-minute walk from St. Peter's Square at Lungotevere Castello 50, Metro: Lepanto or bus #40 or #64, tel. 06-681-9111, www.castelsantangelo.beniculturali.it.

Church of Sant'Ignazio

This church's riot of Baroque illusions will intrigue kids. The colorful ceiling fresco fools the eye into thinking you're looking up at a dome—including false two-dimensional columns that look like extensions of the real columns below. Kids might also get a kick out of seeing the headquarters of the Carabinieri police force, across the street. Sant'Ignazio is included in the Pantheon Tour chapter; see page 140.

Cost and Hours: Free, Mon-Sat 7:30-19:00, Sun 9:00-19:00, Via del Caravita 8.

Pyramid of Gaius Cestius

Your children can get a whiff of Egypt by visiting Rome's funky little pyramid. Also check out the cat hospice in the adjacent park and climb on the chunk of old Roman wall across the street. See page 98.

Cost and Hours: Free and always viewable, Via Raffaele Persichetti, Metro: Piramide.

Bocca della Verità

The legendary "Mouth of Truth" at the Church of Santa Maria in Cosmedin is fun for kids and parents with cameras. Little ones can test their truthfulness—and bravery—by sticking their hands in the mouth of the stone face in the church's porch wall. Liars will have their hands gobbled up.

Cost and Hours: €0.50 suggested donation, daily 9:30-17:50, Piazza Bocca della Verità 18, near the north end of Circus Maximus, a 10-minute walk south from Piazza Venezia, bus #81 from Vatican area or #170 from Termini/Via Nazionale, tel. 06-678-7759.

Montemartini Museum

Its location in an old power plant may be even more interesting to young visitors than the ancient statuary featured in this unusual museum. Kids can inspect the defunct centrifuges, boilers, and steam turbines that mingle with the statues of muses and satyrs. An added plus: no crowds. For details, see page 101.

Cost and Hours: €6.50 for kids 6-25, free for kids 5 and under, €7.50 for adults; Tue-Sun 9:00-19:00, closed Mon; look for red banner marking Via Ostiense 106, a short walk from Metro: Garbatella, tel. 06-0608, www.centralemontemartini.org.

Explora

This children's museum is a hands-on wonderland for kids 12 and under. The interactive exhibits will have your little ones doing the shopping, pulling toy carrots in the garden, puttering in the kitchen, creating cartoons, and experimenting with weights and measures, among many other fun activities. Descriptions are in Italian (with some English), but kids probably won't care.

Cost and Hours: €5 for kids 1-2, €8 for kids 3-99, parent must accompany child; visit limited to two hours with entry Tue-Sun at 10:00, 12:00, 15:00, and 17:00, closed Mon; confirm times in advance by checking website or calling, reservations required on weekends, helpful English-speaking staff; 10-minute

walk north of Piazza del Popolo at Via Flaminia 82, Metro: Flaminio, tel. 06-361-3776, www.mdbr.it).

OUTDOOR FUN

Rome feels safe at night, and you can easily take your kids on the
walks suggested in this book, such as the "Dolce Vita Stroll" on
page 414. On the Heart of Rome Walk, children like slurping
up chocolate gelato at the Tre Scalini *gelateria* on Piazza Navona
and tossing coins in the Trevi Fountain. Consider letting your
child act as tour guide for an hour by leading one of the walks.

These other outdoor activities will also amuse your young
and active travel companions.

Villa Borghese Gardens

These sprawling gardens are Rome's version of New York City's
Central Park. The best kids' zones are near Porta Pinciana, where
you'll find rental bikes, pony rides, and other amusements. Summer weekends at the gardens, sure to be a hit with kids, include
classic Roman puppet shows at Teatro dei Burattini. Rome's **zoo,**
Bioparco, in the northern section of the park, houses about 900
animals including the endangered black lemur, pygmy hippopot-
amus, and Gila monster.

Cost and Hours: Free for kids "under 1 meter tall," €13
for kids over 1 meter and under age 12, €16 for adults; daily
April-Oct 9:30-18:00, Nov-March 9:30-17:00, last entry one
hour before closing; cafe and picnic areas; Piazzale del Giardino
Zoologico 1—take bus #910 from Termini to Pinciana stop, or
tram #19 from Metro: Ottaviano to Bioparco stop; tel. 06-360-
8211, www.bioparco.it.

Biking the Appian Way

Older children may want to rent a bike to cruise the Appian Way.
The route will take young explorers by the Catacombs of San Sebastiano and San Callisto—great spooky sights for kids—and
the huge, ancient chariot racetrack at the Villa of Maxentius. The
best day for biking is Sunday, when the Appian Way is closed to
cars, though on other days (except Wed) you can use the bike/
pedestrian path to avoid the worst of the traffic. ⌑ See Ancient
Appian Way Tour chapter for details.

Cost and Hours: Rental from Appia Antica Caffè: €4/
hour, €10/3 hours, 10 percent discount off bikes with this book,
Tue-Sun 9:00-sunset, Mon 9:00-13:30, Via Appia Antica 175,
tel. 06-8987-9575, www.appiaanticacaffe.it. Rental from the
Via Appia Antica TI: €3/hour, €15/day, Mon-Sat 9:30-13:00 &
14:00-17:00, Sun 9:30-17:00, Via Appia Antica 58, tel. 06-513-
5316, www.parcoappiaantica.it.

Beaches

Beyond the ruins of Ostia Antica, the sandy beaches of modern Ostia are easily accessible via a combination Metro and suburban train ride. As elsewhere in Italy, most of the shoreline is occupied by private "clubs" *(stabilimenti balneare)* that charge a fee to use their facilities. Clubs lay out rows of beach chairs and umbrellas, and most have cafés, WCs, changing rooms, lockers, and lifeguards on duty. Some even have full-service restaurants and swimming pools. Bring your own towel and picnic, and expect to be surrounded by a thoroughly local scene.

Any club will work. **Belsito** (on Facebook as "Stabilimento Belsito") and its neighbor to the north, **Il Capanno** (www.ilcapanno.net) are nice and unpretentious choices. They are a 15-minute walk south from the public pier (or 5-minute walk from the Stella Polare train station described below—head straight for the water and turn right). Next to Il Capanno, there's a small, free public beach that's usually packed, especially on weekends. Other public beaches are few and far between.

Cost and Hours: Expect to pay around €5 for entry, €10 for each chair, and another €10 for an umbrella. Swimming pools usually cost extra. Beach clubs are open roughly May-Sept. Beach-club areas are free and uncrowded off-season, and public beaches are free year-round.

Getting There: The journey is covered by a normal Metro ticket (passes valid) and takes about an hour from central Rome. Take Metro line B to the Piramide stop, which is linked to the Roma Porta San Paolo train station. Follow signs to *Lido:* Go up the escalator, turn left, and go down the steps to reach the Roma-Lido train line. From here, it's easy since all trains depart in the direction of Lido, leaving every 15 minutes. Look for the information board that reads something like, *"Prossima partenza alle ore 13.25, bin 3,"* meaning, "Next departure at 13:25 from track 3." Hop on and ride for about 45 minutes (no need to validate your Metro ticket again).

You can get off at either of two stations a half-mile apart: Lido Centro or Stella Polare. Stella Polare is a five-minute walk from the beach clubs mentioned above. The Lido Centro station is near downtown Ostia; it's about a 15-minute walk through town (past stores selling food and beach gear), to the public pier (Pontile di Ostia) and surrounding clubs. The way is not well marked; don't hesitate to ask for directions.

Hydromania Water Park

Just outside Rome, cool off at this big water park with looping slides, several swimming pools, terraces of chaise lounges with umbrellas, and a snack bar. A great change of pace from museums and churches, this alternative activity is perfect for a hot Italian summer day.

Cost and Hours: €20, cheaper for kids 12 and under and anyone arriving after 14:00; open daily June-early Sept 9:30-18:30 or 19:00, closed early Sept-May; Vicolo del Casale Lumbroso 200, exit 33 off ring freeway west of the city, tel. 06-6618-3183, www.hydromania.it.

SHOPPING IN ROME

Rome is a wonderful city to shop in. Even if you're not aiming to buy anything, exploring popular shopping areas provides a break from stressful, clogged tourist sights and an excuse to lose yourself on a charming street. Sometimes window shopping, rather than museum going, is the best way to connect with the contemporary life of a city. And that's certainly true in Rome.

Traditionally, shops are open from roughly 9:00 to 13:00 and from 15:30 or 16:00 to 19:00 or 19:30. They're often closed on Sundays, summer Saturday afternoons, and winter Monday mornings. But in the city center, you'll find that many are now staying open through lunch (generally 10:00-19:00). Shop early if you intend to hit Rome's produce or flea markets (described at the end of this chapter)—with the exception of the weekend MercatoMonti market in the Monti neighborhood, they typically close by 13:30.

For information on VAT refunds and customs regulations, see page 509.

Shopping Neighborhoods

I've described four of Rome's most engaging and easy-to-reach shopping zones: the heart of Rome near Piazza Navona and Campo de' Fiori; the Jewish Ghetto; the Monti district, convenient to the ancient sites; and Rome's most famous (and, arguably, least characteristic) shopping zone, the "shopping triangle" along Via del Corso and near the Spanish Steps. For each one, I've outlined a route to help you find the highest concentration of interesting shops, highlighting a few that caught my eye (though turnover is rampant, so some places I mention may have changed hands by the time you visit). Be sure to venture off this framework to make discoveries of your own.

A few other areas are worth exploring. **Via Nazionale** features a range of reasonably priced shops, especially for clothes and shoes. The back lanes of **Trastevere** have a similar feel to Monti, with offbeat boutiques. **Via Cola di Rienzo,** near the Vatican, is good for midrange clothes. Cheapskates scrounge through the junky but dirt-cheap shops in the gritty area around **Piazza Vittorio Emanuele II,** just south of Termini Station.

HEART OF ROME

Although right in the tourist-clogged center, the streets near Piazza Navona and Campo de' Fiori are surprisingly less crowded—and the shops less tacky—than along the main thoroughfares connecting Rome's top squares (outlined in my 📖 Heart of Rome Walk). Heavy on antiques and home furnishings, this area may be better for window shopping than buying, but I've noted some shops with take-home souvenirs as well. Everything mentioned here is within about a 15-minute walk of each other.

Near Piazza Navona

The tangle of lanes just west of Piazza Navona can be fun to explore. But the main shopping street here—and one of the most charming streets in all of Rome, with cobblestones, leafy planters, and little to no traffic—is the straight-shot **Via dei Coronari,** between Piazza Navona and the bend in the river. To find it, pop out the north end of Piazza Navona and turn left. This is the place to browse antiques and daydream about furnishing a Roman apartment. Stampe Antiche "Trincia" Restauro (#15) is a fascinating shop that specializes in painstaking restoration of works of art, with antique prints that will fit in your suitcase. This street also boasts several fine clothing and shoe stores, such as Superga (#18), the classic Italian athletic shoe brand (which also makes designer heels). Made (#25) is a "creative bakery" with bagel sandwiches and delicate cupcakes.

After Piazzetta di San Simeone, there are fewer antiques and more clothes—stylish yet accessible. For example, tucked in the little square on the left, Spazio IF (#44a) features eye-catching Sicilian style—mostly women's fashion, including handbags and scarves. Dimorae Design (#57) sells trendy Italian home furnishings. If you need a snack, Gelateria del Teatro (#66) is a good choice. At Pastori Antichi (#110), an army of military miniatures from around the world stands watch. Lisa Corti Home Textile Emporium (#197, part of a small Italian chain) fills its showroom with colorful fabrics, while Le Tele di Carlotta (#228) is a charming spot with hand-embroidered towels and handkerchiefs.

At the end of Via dei Coronari, you could angle right one block to Castel Sant'Angelo (described on page 63). Or, to make your walk a loop, hook left at the big square and Alimentari Coronari (gourmet sandwiches) onto **Via di Panico.** You'll pass a few more shops along here—including Kromatika Lab (#14), with striking design.

From here, turn right on Via degli Orsini; one block later, turn left onto **Via del Governo Vecchio,** another top shopping street. Passing the Penny Lane shop (#4, with youthful vintage wear), you'll be greeted by a street with fashion, home decor, textiles, and plenty of cute boutiques (casual wear and accessories—mostly women's, but some men's as well). The closer you get to Piazza Navona, the more crowded the street becomes, with souvenir stands and tourist-trap restaurants mixed in with boutiques. When the street opens up into a square, bear left up the narrow Via di Pasquino to reach Piazza Navona.

Near Campo de' Fiori

Two worthwhile parallel shopping streets run northwest (toward the river) from Piazza Farnese, just a block south of Campo de' Fiori: Via Monserrato/Via dei Banchi Vecchi and Via Giulia. (Streets in the opposite direction—to the southeast—are sleepier, with fewer shops.) While I've arranged these as a loop, you can pick and choose as you go.

Heading away from Piazza Farnese on low-key **Via Monserrato,** you'll see several antique, furniture, and home-decorating shops. But there are also some interesting clothing boutiques, as well as some unique shops. Hollywood (#107) is a treat for cinephiles, with movie posters and rare DVDs; their sister store, at #110, sells movie-themed embroidered T-shirts. Between these two, at #108, is a fascinating old-time cobbler, with a crowded workbench crammed into a tiny shop. Estremi (#101) has some inspiring retro furniture, while Antichi Kimono (#43b) features Asian-themed dresses and fabrics.

Farther along, Via Monserrato becomes **Via dei Banchi Vecchi,** with even more antiques of varying aesthetics—from mothballed grannies to hipster vintage. At #138 is a small and tasteful kids' clothing store. Banchievecchi Pellami (#40) is an old-school leather shop, with belts and wallets. And Restore (#51) is packed with housewares, home furnishings, and kitchen gadgets.

When Via dei Banchi Vecchi dead-ends at the big cross street, loop left around the block to stroll more atmospheric **Via Giulia**—narrower, cobbled, and mostly traffic-free. Here you'll find fewer shops and more real-estate offices and architecture firms. House Kitchen & Design, near the start of the street at #101, is a cramped hole-in-the-wall with cooking gadgets; farther down, Magie di Casa (#140c) has a nice selection of linens, from tea towels to aprons.

One more street near Campo de' Fiori may be worth exploring: **Via Giubbonari,** which stretches southeast from the square. More heavily trafficked (and more touristy), it has dozens of stores selling affordable apparel aimed mainly at a younger crowd.

JEWISH GHETTO

In addition to its gorgeous synagogue, evocative history, and bustling restaurants, Rome's Jewish ghetto is also a great place to browse. My 📖 Jewish Ghetto Walk provides a natural spine for shopping explorations.

Near the start of that walk, just around the corner from the synagogue, the Leone Limentani housewares and dishware shop feels like a well-stocked mini warehouse—this is where Roman couples register for wedding gifts (walk away from the river, and turn left at the ruins onto Via del Portico d'Ottavia; it's at the corner on the left at #47).

Farther along Via del Portico d'Ottavia, Mondo di Laura (#6) sells artisan cookies. Just beyond, turn right up **Via della Reginella,** lined with cute boutiques: Giuseppe Casetti's funky shop (#8a), with vintage black-and-white photos, stacks of antique, yellowing books, and other artsy objects; L'Officinaturale (at #3), a natural-products shop with oils, soaps, perfumes, and health foods; takeawaygallery, which is a mod art boutique (#10); and, at the end of the street (#30), Peperita, run by sisters—one of whom makes olive oil, and the other, all manner of hot peppers. Their products—powders, pastes, and infused oils—are ranked on a spiciness scale of 1 to 16; generous samples let you test your limits.

Back on the main drag is a long row of food stands, kosher butchers, and a few Judaica shops. Less than a 10-minute walk straight ahead is the Campo de' Fiori shopping zone described earlier.

MONTI, NEAR THE ROMAN FORUM

Located between Via Cavour and Via Nazionale, across the street from the Roman Forum, the Monti neighborhood is a delight for exploring, dining, and shopping. Rather than designer fashions, Monti has Rome's closest thing to a hipster aesthetic: gourmet foodie shops and funky boutiques alongside very traditional neighborhood stores. Get oriented from the main square, Piazza della Madonna dei Monti (see page 56 for an orientation to this neighborhood). Then take off, strolling each of these areas.

Via del Boschetto and Via dei Serpenti

This little loop takes you up and down the parallel main drags of Monti. First, from the top of the square, head left down **Via del Boschetto.** You'll pass several little boutiques and jewelry shops. Along the way, watch for the fragrant Il Giardino di Tè teahouse

Shopping in Rome

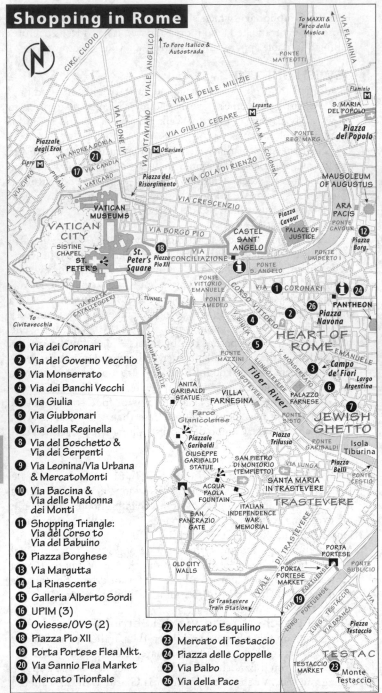

SHOPPING

1. Via dei Coronari
2. Via del Governo Vecchio
3. Via Monserrato
4. Via dei Banchi Vecchi
5. Via Giulia
6. Via Giubbonari
7. Via della Reginella
8. Via del Boschetto & Via dei Serpenti
9. Via Leonina/Via Urbana & MercatoMonti
10. Via Baccina & Via delle Madonna dei Monti
11. Shopping Triangle: Via del Corso to Via del Babuino
12. Piazza Borghese
13. Via Margutta
14. La Rinascente
15. Galleria Alberto Sordi
16. UPIM (3)
17. Oviesse/OVS (2)
18. Piazza Pio XII
19. Porta Portese Flea Mkt.
20. Via Sannio Flea Market
21. Mercato Trionfale
22. Mercato Esquilino
23. Mercato di Testaccio
24. Piazza delle Coppelle
25. Via Balbo
26. Via della Pace

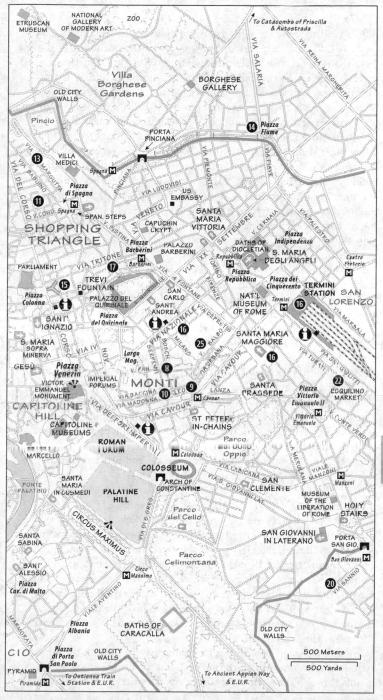

(#107); King Size vintage shop (#94); a cute kids' clothing store (#96); Gallina Smilza, selling colorful plastic dishes and housewares (#129); and Pulp, featuring women's casual fashion (#140).

Soon you'll reach the intersection with **Via Panisperna;** several pioneers in the early study of radiation, including Enrico Fermi, lived or worked along here, earning them the nickname "the Panisperna boys." From this intersection, you can turn right up Panisperna for more shopping (boutiques, antiques, and the Monti Bio organic shop at #225), or continue straight ahead for a few more shops. Otherwise, loop left (downhill on Panisperna), noticing—on the corner—Macelleria Stecchiotti, a classic Roman butcher (where, reportedly, VIPs from the president to the pope get their meat). Continuing downhill on Panisperna, you'll spot the neighborhood's favorite hangout—Ai Tre Scalini bar—and (at the corner) the recommended Antico Forno ai Serpenti bakery (see page 380).

Turning left on **Via dei Serpenti,** on the left just past the bakery entrance, peek in the window to see the bakers at work. Continuing down Serpenti, watch for a funky collection of shops, including Podere Vecciano (at #33)—"a farm in the city" selling enticing Tuscan (not Roman) goods, including wines, olive oils, other gifty edibles, and wood-carved items. Then you'll reach the Officine Gioielli jewelry store (#25); a tempting *alimentari* (grocery); Faces, a boutique selling T-shirts with...faces (#138); the Pifebo vintage shop next door (#141); and on the right, at #4, a neighborhood fixture dating from the days when vintage wasn't yet vintage: the aptly named Di Tutto di Più ("Everything and More"), a general store stuffed to the gills with everything you could possibly need. Near the end of the street is American Apparel—which incited minor outrage in this extremely provincial and proud corner of Rome when it opened a few years back. And just beyond that, you've circled back to the main square.

Via Leonina/Via Urbana

To survey another set of streets with similar shops, leave the top of the main square and jog right (on Via dell'Angeletto, passing some fun little galleries), then left at the T-intersection (where you'll find a local chocolatier, La Bottega del Cioccolato). This puts you on **Via Leonina,** the first few blocks of which are a bit more crowded and urban, with lots of little hole-in-the-wall eateries. The big garage on the right opens its doors on weekends to host the lively MercatoMonti (see "Department Stores, Souvenirs, and Markets" near the end of this chapter).

After passing the entrance to Cavour Metro station, the street swings left, becomes **Via Urbana,** and gets a bit more charming, as it runs through the bottom of a narrow valley between Via Cavour and Santa Maria Maggiore. At the gap with the parking lot, look high on the left to spot the recommended Fatamorgana *gelateria* (see map on page 352). Farther along, watch on the left for the Studio Cassio mosaics workshop (#98), then a fascinating *orologiaio* (clock shop, #103a). Continuing along Via Urbana, window shop local designers' boutiques. Aromaticus, at #134, sells nothing but fresh herbs, as if to emphasize the Italian obsession with seasonal cooking. As the street climbs uphill, you can either go back the way you came, or turn left at Via Panisperna to return to Via del Boschetto, Via dei Serpenti, and the heart of Monti.

Via Baccina and Via della Madonna dei Monti

Via Baccina and Via della Madonna dei Monti have a lower concentration of shops, but they're even more atmospheric than the main drags. From the main square, head down **Via Baccina**, noticing Sotto Bosco at #40, selling colorful, minimalist jewelry and hats. Farther along, this street has a range of art galleries, boutiques, and jewelry shops. Better yet, turn left down vine-strewn Via dei Neofiti (across from Sotto Bosco), then right on **Via della Madonna dei Monti.** While there are more bars and restaurants than shops along here, it's worth a browse.

THE SHOPPING TRIANGLE, NEAR VIA DEL CORSO AND THE SPANISH STEPS

Via del Corso runs south, from Piazza del Popolo to the heart of Rome, and the little streets that poke east off the main drag—toward the Spanish Steps—form an area nicknamed the "shopping triangle." This zone has big international chains to suit every budget—from Dolce & Gabbana to the Gap—along with some very famous designers...all of which makes it less funky and colorful than the neighborhoods described previously. Nevertheless, a few quirky shops hide out here as well.

Streets Between Via del Corso and Via del Babuino

I've described the streets branching off of Via del Corso from north to south, starting at Piazza del Popolo. These are to the left as you walk; the streets to the right have fewer shops. Also note that **Via del Babuino** angles off parallel to Via del Corso, with mostly pricey international chains (Tiffany, Chanel, Dolce & Gabbana, and so on). See the "Dolce Vita Stroll" map in the Nightlife in Rome chapter for specific locations of these streets.

Via Fontanella isn't interesting in its own right, but it does lead to the very chichi Via Margutta—described later.

Via Laurina has some funkier shops, including several with youth fashions; halfway down at #10 is the recommended Fatamorgana *gelateria,* and classier galleries and antiques sit at the far end.

Via di Gesù e Maria, running along its namesake church, has fewer stores. Discount dell'Alta Moda (at #16a, literally "Discount on High Fashion," where last year's big-name designer duds are marked down by half) is a hit with bargain shoppers, while sports fans peruse the store with merchandise promoting the local Lazio soccer team. **Via di San Giacomo,** on the other side of the church, is also fairly sleepy—though it's fun to peek in the windows of the art school to see the artisans and craftspeople of the 21st century hard at work.

Via del Greci has a sheet music store, antiques, fashion boutiques, and a fragrant flower stall.

Via Vittoria and **Via della Croce** are major thoroughfares for reaching the Spanish Steps, so they have less interesting shops and more touristy crowds; however, Via della Croce is a great place to browse for a meal (see suggestions on page 377). The recommended Pastificio (near the end of the street, at #8) is, true to its name, a pasta factory, where you can buy dry pasta as an edible souvenir.

Some of the streets that run parallel to Via del Corso along here are also fun to wander. For example, **Via Mario de' Fiori** is crammed with upscale boutiques, but tucked amidst the glitz is the appealing c.u.c.i.n.a. shop (at #65), where you can stock up on Italian-style kitchen gadgets, utensils, and crockery.

Via delle Carrozze is fun to browse, with shops carrying specialties from other parts of Italy (handy if Rome is your only destination): The Santa Maria Novella perfume shop (#87) stocks scents from that famous church-run perfume works in Florence; Il Cerichio dei Goloso (#19) serves delicate pastries—and sells colorful plates—from Sicily; and La Peonia (#85) specializes in products from Sardinia. Also along this stretch, look in the window of the old-time tailor, Attilio Roncaccia (#12), and pick up some stylish fashions for Junior at Gocco (#18).

From **Via dei Condotti,** you can see the Spanish Steps hovering in the distance. This busy, glamorous strip has the same type of high-roller international shops found on Via del Babuino.

For one more taste of a simpler side of this area, find your way a few blocks west (on Via dei Condotti *away* from the Spanish Steps—toward the river, just south of Ara Pacis) to **Piazza Borghese.** This sleepy little square is filled with green kiosks selling prints, antique books, and curios. Shops in the surrounding streets have a similar flavor.

Via Margutta

Hiding parallel to Via del Corso and Via del Babuino is one of the most chic addresses in town, **Via Margutta.** (To find it, go down

Via della Fontanella, near the top of Via del Corso; or head up from the Spanish Steps.) Here you'll find exclusive-feeling designer boutiques, big-ticket antique shops, home-decorating galleries, day spas, fashion eyewear shops, jewelers, wedding planners, and other places where you have to ring the bell to be let inside (assuming your hem meets their standards). One shop—called Flair—sums up this whole street. Lelli (at #5) has colorful home furnishings and textiles; Saddlers Union (#11) has very expensive leather goods; and Grossi Maurizio (across the street at #109) has marble sculptures and mosaics. Artemide (#107) is one of this street's many intriguing suppliers of mod, upscale home furnishings. Tucked along here, however, is one holdover from simpler times: La Bottega del Marmoraro (#153), where Sandro busily carves marble in a cramped hole-in-the-wall slathered with carved marble signs.

Department Stores, Souvenirs, and Markets

If all you need are souvenirs, a surgical strike at any gift shop will do. Otherwise, stop at a department store, scout near the Vatican or in the Jewish Ghetto for religious items, hit the flea market and produce markets, or—if you're in a pinch—pick up some mementos at the airport on your way out of town.

DEPARTMENT STORES
The shopping complex under Termini train station is a convenient place to peruse clothes, bags, shoes, and perfume at several major Italian chain stores (most open daily 8:00-22:00).

Large department stores offer relatively painless one-stop shopping. A good upscale department store is **La Rinascente** (like Nordstrom or Macy's). Its main branch is on Piazza Fiume (east of Borghese Gallery near the old city walls), and a smaller store is on Via del Corso in the **Galleria Alberto Sordi,** an elegant 19th-century "mall" (across from Piazza Colonna). **UPIM** is a popular midrange department store (many branches, including inside Termini train station, Via Nazionale 111, and Piazza Santa Maria Maggiore). **Oviesse/OVS,** a cheap clothing outlet, is near the Vatican Museums (on the corner of Via Candia and Via Mocenigo, Metro: Cipro) and also near Piazza Barberini (Via del Tritone 172, Metro: Barberini).

RELIGIOUS SOUVENIRS
Rome is a magnet for pilgrims, who find no shortage of shops near the Vatican—in the area directly in front of St. Peter's Square (on and around **Piazza Pio XII**), or along nearby Via Borgo Pio. Sev-

eral shops in the Jewish Ghetto sell Judaica, Jewish-themed art, and other souvenirs.

FLEA MARKETS

For antiques and fleas, the granddaddy of markets is the **Porta Portese** *mercato delle pulci* (flea market). This Sunday-morning market is long and spindly, running be-tween the actual Porta Portese (a gate in the old town wall) and the Trastevere train station. Starting at Porta Portese, walk through the long, tacky parade of stalls selling cheap bras and shoes. Along the way, check out the con artists with the shell games. Each has shills in the crowd "winning big money" to get suckers involved. Hang on to your wallet—literally, in your front pocket, or better yet, use a money belt and make sure it's safely tucked under your clothes. This is a den of thieves. The heart of the market for real flea-market junk (hiding a few little antique treasures) is the square in the center near Via Cesare Pascarella. I find that a slow stroll through the entire market and back to the Porta Portese takes about an hour and a half. While the shopping gets old (and the vendor food shouldn't be consumed), the people-watching is endlessly entertaining (6:30-13:00 Sun only, on Via Portuense and Via Ippolito Nievo; to get to the market, catch bus #75 from Termini train station or tram #8 from Piazza Venezia, get off the bus or tram on Viale di Trastevere, and walk toward the river—and the noise).

At the **Via Sannio** market, you'll find new and used clothing and leather goods, some handicrafts, and random items that were probably stolen. You won't find antiques (Mon-Sat 9:00-13:30, closed Sun, behind Coin department store, just outside the walls of San Giovanni in Laterano, Metro: San Giovanni).

For something a bit hipper, don't miss the weekend **Merca-toMonti** in the Monti district. This flea market has an emphasis on vintage clothes and housewares and up-and-coming designers (Sat-Sun 10:00-20:00, closed July-Aug, Hotel Palatino, Via Leonina 46, Metro: Cavour).

OPEN-AIR PRODUCE MARKETS

Rome's outdoor markets provide a fun and colorful dimension of the city that even the most avid museumgoer should not miss. Wander through the easygoing neighborhood produce markets that clog certain streets and squares every morning (7:00-13:30) except Sunday. Consider the huge **Mercato Trionfale** (three blocks north of Vatican Museums at Via Andrea Doria). Another great food market is the **Mercato Esquilino** (Via Filippo Turati, Metro: Vittorio Emanuele). The covered **Mercato di Testaccio** sells produce and housewares and is a hit with photographers and people-watchers (Metro: Piramide; for more on the market, see page 101). Smaller but equally charming slices of everyday Roman life are at markets on these streets and squares: **Piazza delle Coppelle** (near the Pantheon), **Via Balbo** (near Termini train station and recommended hotels off Via Nazionale), and **Via della Pace** (near Piazza Navona). And **Campo de' Fiori,** despite having become quite touristy, is still a fun scene.

SHOPPING AT FIUMICINO AIRPORT

Rome's main airport (a.k.a. Leonardo da Vinci Airport) sells Italian specialty foods vacuum-packed to clear US customs. Most shops are near the departure gates (after you check your bags and pass through security). Try *parmigiano reggiano* cheese, dried porcini mushrooms or peppers, and better olive oil than you can buy at home. Don't bother buying any salami or prosciutto unless it's canned; you're not allowed to bring fresh meat into the US (and even canned beef products are prohibited). Remember, if you're flying to the US and transferring before your final destination, you'll likely be required to pack purchased liquids in your checked luggage after clearing customs (a potential recipe for disaster). You'll have better odds of carrying it onto a connecting flight if the vendor seals it in a "STEB"—a secure, tamper-evident bag.

NIGHTLIFE IN ROME

Romans get dressed up and eat out in casual surroundings for their evening entertainment. For most visitors, the best after-dark activity is simply to grab a gelato and stroll the medieval lanes that connect the romantic, floodlit squares and fountains. Head for Piazza Navona, the Pantheon, Campo de' Fiori, Trevi Fountain, the Spanish Steps, Via del Corso, Trastevere (around the Santa Maria in Trastevere Church), or Monte Testaccio.

For a great evening stroll, 🕮 see my Heart of Rome Walk chapter or my "Dolce Vita Stroll" (at the end of this chapter).

PERFORMANCES AND FILM

Check out the current listings of concerts, operas, dance, and films. Posters around town also advertise upcoming events. For the most up-to-date events calendar, check these English-language websites: www.inromenow.com, www.wantedinrome.com, and www.rome.angloinfo.com.

Music

Music lovers will seek out the mega-music complex of the Rome **Auditorium** (Auditorium Parco della Musica), designed by contemporary architect Renzo Piano (€20-60 tickets, check availability in advance—concerts often sell out, Viale Pietro de Coubertin 30, take Metro to Flaminio and then catch tram #2 to Apollodoro, from there it's a 5-minute walk east, just beyond the elevated road, tram/metro runs until 23:30, box office toll tel. 892-101, www.auditorium.com). Also called the "Park of Music," it's a place where many Romans go just for the scene—music store, restaurants, cafés, and fresh modern architecture with three state-of-the-art auditoriums (known as "the beetles" for their appearance). If you want to

The *Passeggiata*

Throughout Italy, early evening is time to stroll. While elsewhere in Italy this is called the *passeggiata*, in Rome it's a cruder, big-city version called the *struscio* (meaning "to rub").

Unemployment among Italy's youth is very high; many stay with their parents even into their 30s. They spend a lot of time being trendy and hanging out. Like American kids gathering at the mall, working-class suburban youth *(coatto)* converge on the old center, as there's little to keep them occupied in Rome's dreary outskirts (which lack public spaces). The hot *vroom-vroom* motor scooter is their symbol; haircuts and fashion are follow-the-leader.

In a more genteel small town, the *passeggiata* comes with sweet whispers of *"bella"* and *"bello"* ("pretty" and "handsome"). In Rome, the admiration is stronger, oriented toward consumption—they say *"buona"* and *"buono"*— roughly meaning "tasty." But despite how lusty this all sounds, you'll see just as many chunky, middle-aged Italians out and about as hormone-charged youth.

see today's Romans enjoying the modern culture of their city, an evening here is the best you'll do.

Classical Music and Opera

The **Teatro dell'Opera** has an active schedule of opera and classical concerts. In the summer, the productions move to the Baths of Caracalla, where ancient ruins make an evocative backdrop. You'll see locals in all their finery, so pull your fanciest outfit from your backpack (tickets from €25, online reservations encouraged, box office takes phone reservations beginning 5 days prior at tel. 06 4816-0255; Via Firenze 72, a block off Via Nazionale, Metro: Repubblica; www.operaroma.it).

More tourist-oriented musical events take place at the Episcopal **Church of St. Paul's Within the Walls.** The music ranges from orchestral concerts (usually Tue and Fri at 20:30) to full operatic performances (usually Sat at 20:30). Some Sunday evenings at 18:30, the church hosts hour-long candlelit "Luminaria" concerts. Check the church website (under "Music") to see what's on (€10-30, same-day tickets usually available, arrive 30-45 minutes early for best seat, Via Napoli 58 at corner of Via Nazionale, Metro: Repubblica, tel. 06-482-6296, www.stpaulsrome.it).

Jazz

Rome has a small but vibrant jazz scene. **Alexanderplatz** is the venerable club in town, with performances most evenings (Sun-Thu concerts at 21:45, Fri-Sat at 22:30, closed in summer, Via Ostia 9,

Metro: Ottaviano, tel. 06-3972-1867, www.alexanderplatzjazzclub.it).

Il Pentagrappolo is an *enoteca* that hosts live music (usually jazz) many Thursday, Friday, and Saturday evenings starting at 22:00 from September to June—check under "Eventi musicali" on their website to confirm (Tue-Sun 18:00-24:00, best to reserve on weekends, three blocks east of the Colosseum at Via Celimontana 21—see map on page 352, www.ilpentagrappolo.com, tel. 06-709-6301).

TramJazz, a creative venture by the public transit company, combines dinner, music, and a journey through the city in a vintage cable car for a mostly local crowd (€65, daily at 21:00, 3 hours, leaves from Piazza di Porta Maggiore—reached by tram #5 or #14 from Termini station, book at least a week in advance, www.tramjazz.com).

Movies

Movies in their original language are a bit scarce in Rome, but not impossible to come by (look for v.o.—*versione originale*). For a list of what's showing in English, check www.inromenow.com and www.romereview.com. The most reliable theater for English-language films is the **Nuovo Olimpia** (3 blocks north of Piazza Colonna, just off Via del Corso at Via in Lucina 16, tel. 06-686-1068). **Multisala Barberini** occasionally has v.o. screenings as well (Piazza Barberini, http://barberini.18tickets.it).

EVENING SIGHTSEEING

Some **museums** have later opening hours (especially on Sat in summer), offering a good chance to see art in a cooler, less-crowded environment. See the "Rome at a Glance" sidebar on page 46, and ask the TI if any museums are currently open late.

Both the **Scuderie del Quirinale** and the nearby **Palazzo delle Esposizioni** stay open late when they're hosting major art exhibitions (typically €10-12 each; both open Sun-Thu 10:00-20:00, Fri-Sat 10:00-22:30 except the Palazzo is closed Mon; may open—and stay open—much later in summer; last entry one hour before closing; tel. for both 06-3996-7500; Scuderie—Via XXIV Maggio 16, www.scuderiequirinale.it; Palazzo—Via Nazionale 194, www.palazzoesposizioni.it).

BARS AND NIGHTSPOTS

I've listed some fun neighborhoods worth exploring after dark, along with a few bars and *enoteche* (wine bars) in each. All of these places are recommended in the Eating in Rome chapter, where you'll find more details on each.

Heart of Rome, near the Pantheon

The scene here is touristy but delightful. The monuments—especially the Pantheon and Trevi Fountain—are magically floodlit at night. Not far from the Trevi Fountain, **L'Antica Birreria Peroni** is a big, boisterous beer hall. Farther south, Campo de' Fiori and the surrounding streets become one big, rude street party around 22:00. One good place to sample the youthful energy, as well as some craft beers, is the rollicking **Open Baladin** pub. (For more on these places, see their listings under "Pantheon Neighborhood," on page 369 of the Eating in Rome chapter.)

North Rome, near the Spanish Steps and Via del Corso

A babel of international tourists, this glitzy zone is bustling after dark. For many, just hanging out on and around the Spanish Steps is enough to fill an evening. For nearby dining options, see page 377.

Near the Colosseum and Forum, in Monti

The best plan in this lively village-Rome zone is to pop the top off a brew and hang out at the fountain on Piazza della Madonna dei Monti. To join the after-dark scene, buy a drink at the shop on the uphill side of the square (cheap bottles of wine with plastic glasses, beer, fruit, and munchies) and be part of what becomes the hottest bar in the area. There are plenty of makeshift benches around the fountain (this scene is described on page 56). For something a bit less casual, try **Enoteca Cavour 313** or **Fafiuché.**

For more details, see the "Monti" section of the Eating in Rome chapter (page 379)

Trastevere

After hours in this youthful district, students and younger tourists drink beer, eat late-night pizza-by-the-slice, and lick cones of gelato as they prowl the cobbles. For a more upscale atmosphere, head for **Cantina Ripagrande** (see listing on page 368).

Near Termini Station

This is a pretty sleepy area at night, though there's often some activity around Piazza della Repubblica. To sip wine in a sophisticated setting, stroll over to **I Colori del Vino Enoteca** on Via Flavia (see page 382).

Testaccio

Some find this district a bit seedy after dark, but young Romans don't seem to mind. Beer pilgrims flock to **L'Oasi della Birra,** with hundreds of microbrews (listing on page 387). **Monte Testaccio,** once an ancient trash heap, is now a small hill whose cool caves house funky restaurants and trendy clubs. And the area around Monte Testaccio is a hotspot for club-hopping—after 21:00, just follow the noise.

Pub Crawls

Offered year-round by several companies, these attract a boisterous crowd. I tried one and had never seen 50 young, drunk people having so much fun (or seen so many locals roll their eyes). Look for fliers locally. Late on Friday and Saturday evenings, entire quarters of old Rome seem to be overtaken by young beer-drinking revelers.

▲▲DOLCE VITA STROLL

This is Romans' favorite place for an chic evening stroll (a Mediterranean institution; see the sidebar on page 411). You'll walk from Piazza del Popolo (Metro: Flaminio) down a wonderfully traffic-free section of Via del Corso, and up Via Condotti to the Spanish Steps. Although busy at any hour, this area really attracts crowds from around 17:00 to 19:00 each evening (Fri and Sat are best), except on Sunday, when it occurs earlier in the afternoon. Leave before 18:00 if you plan to visit the Ara Pacis (Altar of Peace), which closes at 19:30 (last entry at 18:30).

As you stroll, you'll see shoppers, people watchers, and flirts on the prowl filling this neighborhood of some of Rome's most fashionable stores (some open after siesta, roughly 16:00-19:30). The most elegance survives in the grid of streets between Via del Corso and the Spanish Steps. For a detailed description of shops in this area, see page 405. If you get hungry during your stroll, see page 377 for listings of neighborhood wine bars and restaurants.

To reach **Piazza del Popolo,** where the stroll starts, take Metro line A to Flaminio and walk south to the square. Delightfully car-free, Piazza del Popolo is marked by an obelisk that was brought to Rome by Augustus after he conquered Egypt. (It used to stand in the Circus Maximus.) In medieval times, this area was just inside Rome's main entry (for more background on the square, see page 72).

If starting your stroll early enough, the Baroque church of **Santa Maria del Popolo** is worth popping into (Mon-Sat until 19:00, Sun until 19:30, next to gate in old wall on north side of square). Inside, look for Raphael's Chigi Chapel (second on left as you face the main altar) and two paintings by Caravaggio (in the Cerasi Chapel, left of altar; see church listing on page 73).

From Piazza del Popolo, shop your way down **Via del Corso.** Though many Italians shop online or at the mall these days, this remains a fine place to feel the pulse of Rome at twilight.

History buffs can side-trip right down Via Pontefici past the fascist architecture to see the massive, round-brick **Mausoleum of Augustus,** topped with overgrown cypress trees. This long-

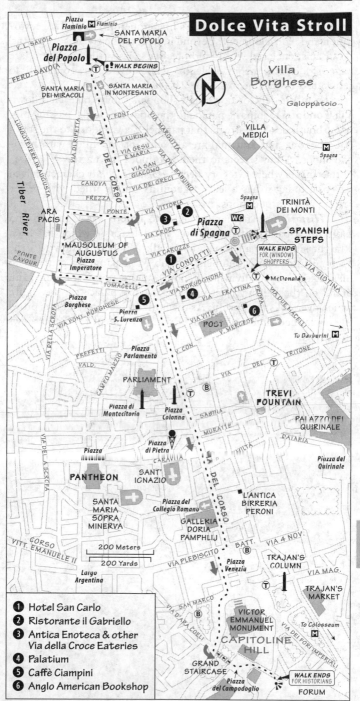

Dolce Vita Stroll

Piazza Flaminio — Flaminio
SANTA MARIA DEL POPOLO
V. L. SAVOIA
Piazza del Popolo
FERD. SAVOIA
WALK BEGINS
SANTA MARIA DEI MIRACOLI
SANTA MARIA IN MONTESANTO

Villa Borghese
Galoppatoio

VILLA MEDICI

Spagna

VIA DI RIPETTA
V. FONT.
V. LAURINA
VIA MARGUTTA
VIA DEL BABUINO
VIA GESU E MARIA
VIA SAN GIACOMO
VIA DEI GRECI
CANOVA
FREZZA
PONTE

Tiber River

LUNGOTEVERE IN AUGUSTA

ARA PACIS

PONTE CAVOUR

MAUSOLEUM OF AUGUSTUS
Piazza Imperatore

VIA VITTORIA
VIA CROCE
VIA CAROZZE
VIA CONDOTTI
VIA BORGOGNONA
TOMACELLI

Piazza di Spagna
Spagna — M
WC
TRINITÀ DEI MONTI
SPANISH STEPS
WALK ENDS FOR (WINDOW) SHOPPERS
VIA SISTINA
McDonald's
VIA DUE MACELLI
PROPAGANDA

Piazza Borghese
Piazza S. Lorenza
VIA DELLA SCROFA
VIA DI PONTE BORGHESE
VIA FRATTINA
VIA VITE
POST
V. MERCEDE
V. CON.
TRITONE

To Barberini — M

PREFETTI
VALD.
CAPO DI MARZIO
Piazza Parlamento
PARLIAMENT
Piazza di Montecitoria
Piazza Colonna
VIA DEL TRITONE
SABINA
MURATTE

TREVI FOUNTAIN
PALAZZO DEI QUIRINALE
DATARIA

Piazza di Pietra
CARAVIA
Piazza del Quirinale

VIA DELLA SCROFA
PANTHEON
SANTA MARIA SOPRA MINERVA
SANT IGNAZIO
Piazza del Collegio Romano
GALLERIA DORIA PAMPHILIJ
VIA DEL CORSO
L'ANTICA BIRRERIA PERONI

CORSO VITT. EMANUELE II
Largo Argentina

200 Meters
200 Yards

VIA PLEBISCITO
Piazza Venezia
BATT.
VIA 4 NOV.
TRAJAN'S COLUMN
VIA MAG.
TRAJAN'S MARKET

VIA SAN MARCO
VIA D'ARACOELI
VICTOR EMMANUEL MONUMENT
CAPITOLINE HILL
VIA DEI FORI IMPERIALI
To Colosseum — M

GRAND STAIRCASE
Piazza del Campodoglio
WALK ENDS FOR HISTORIANS
FORUM

1 Hotel San Carlo
2 Ristorante il Gabriello
3 Antica Enoteca & other Via della Croce Eateries
4 Palatium
5 Caffè Ciampini
6 Anglo American Bookshop

NIGHTLIFE

neglected sight, honoring Rome's first emperor, is slated for restoration and redevelopment. Beyond it, next to the river, is Augustus' **Ara Pacis,** enclosed within a protective glass-walled museum (see page 75). From the mausoleum, walk down Via Tomacelli to return to Via del Corso and the 21st century.

From Via del Corso, window shoppers should take a left down **Via Condotti** to join the parade to the **Spanish Steps,** passing big-name boutiques. The streets that parallel Via Condotti to the south (Borgognona and Frattina) are also elegant and filled with high-end shops. A few streets to the north hides the narrow Via Margutta. This is where Gregory Peck's *Roman Holiday* character lived (at #51); today it has a leafy tranquility and is filled with pricey artisan and antique shops.

Historians: Another option is to ignore Via Condotti and forget the Spanish Steps. Stay on Via del Corso, which has been straight since Roman times, and walk a half-mile down to the Victor Emmanuel Monument. Climb Michelangelo's stairway to his glorious (especially when floodlit) square atop Capitoline Hill. Stand on the balcony (just past the mayor's palace on the right), which overlooks the Forum. As the horizon reddens and cats prowl the unclaimed rubble of ancient Rome, it's one of the finest views in the city.

NIGHTLIFE

ROME CONNECTIONS

Rome is well-connected with the rest of the planet: by train, plane, bus, car, and cruise ship. This chapter explains the various options for your arrival and departure from the city.

By Train

Rome's primary train station, centrally located **Termini**, has high-speed connections to other Italian cities and fast trains to the airport. Rome's other major station is called **Tiburtina**. The most convenient connections for travelers nearly all depart from Termini. But it's always smart to confirm whether your train departs from Termini or Tiburtina (or one of Rome's even smaller stations).

Minimize your time in a station by using the banks of user-friendly ticket machines. Machines for the state-run Trenitalia (marked *Trenitalia/Biglietti*) are handy but cover Italian destinations only. They take euros and credit cards, display schedules, issue tickets, and even make reservations for rail pass holders (found under the "Global Pass" ticket type). If you're not near a station—or for international tickets—it's quickest to get tickets and train info online, or from travel agencies in town. For general information on train travel in Italy—including ticket-buying options—see page 545.

TERMINI TRAIN STATION

Termini, Rome's main train station (www.romatermini.com), is indeed a bustling terminus but gets its name from the nearby Baths *(terme)* of Diocletian. Like much of modern Rome, the station sits atop ancient Roman ruins. The biggest surviving chunk of the impressive 2,300-year-old Servian Wall is just outside (look right as you exit). There are even wall remnants in the McDonald's on the basement level.

The station is a buffet of tourist services. At the head of the tracks are two atriums. The inner atrium, open at both ends, houses shops and eateries. The outer atrium, with glass walls, houses ticket windows and ticket machines plus a good-sized bookstore. Outside the station is a large square where city buses depart. A basement shopping area extends beneath both atriums. Various services (outlined below) are located in halls along the sides of the tracks.

For security, entry to the train platforms themselves is restricted to ticketholders. Entrances are from the inner atrium and from the halls to the sides of the tracks. On my last visit, you needed to show your ticket, but there were no metal detectors and lines were short.

Services: The customer service and ticket windows (in the outer, glassed-in atrium) can be jammed with travelers—find the small red kiosk, take a number, and wait. Whenever possible, use the ticket machines. Though most trains departing from Termini are operated by Italy's state rail company, Trenitalia (www. trenitalia.com), some are run by a private company, Italo (www. italotreno.it), with its own ticket machines and windows in the outer atrium.

In the hall along Via Giovanni Giolitti, on the southwest side of the station (near track 24), you'll find the TI (daily 8:00-18:45), a hotel booking office, and car-rental desks. The baggage storage *(deposito bagagli)* is in the basement (use the elevator, daily 6:00-23:00). The Leonardo Express train to Fiumicino Airport runs from track 23 or 24 on this side of the station (see "By Plane," later).

In general, the best places in the station to sit are in its eateries. A snack bar and a good self-service cafeteria (Ciao) are perched one floor above the ticket windows in the outer atrium, accessible from the side closest to track 24 (daily 11:00-22:30). For good-quality sandwiches to go, try VyTA in the inner atrium across from track 1.

In the hall along Via Marsala, on the northeast side of the station (near track 1), you'll find a pharmacy and an often cramped waiting room. On the basement shopping level, below the inner atrium (go down the escalators on the Via Marsala side) is the large Sapori & Dintori supermarket (daily 7:00-24:00). Pay WCs are also down the escalators from the inner atrium.

The station has some sleazy sharks with official-looking business cards; avoid anybody selling anything unless they're in a legitimate shop at the station. Other shady characters linger around the ticket machines—offers to help usually come with the expectation of a "tip." There are no official porters; if someone wants to carry your bags or help you find your platform, they are simply angling for some cash.

Getting Between Termini and Rome Hotels: From Termini, many of my recommended hotels are easily accessible by foot or by Metro (for those in the Colosseum and Vatican neighborhoods). The Termini Metro station, where Metro lines A and B intersect, is beneath the station. City buses leave from the square directly in front of the outer atrium. Buses to the airport leave from the streets on both sides of the station. Taxis queue in front and outside exits on both the north and south sides; if there's a long taxi line in front, try a side exit instead. Avoid con men hawking "express taxi" services in unmarked cars (only use official white taxis with the maroon *Roma Capitale* logo).

From Rome's Termini Station by Train: Note that unless otherwise specified, the following connections are for Trenitalia. **Fiumicino Airport** (Leonardo Express; 2/hour, 32 minutes—see details under "By Plane," later), **Venice** (Trenitalia: hourly, 4 hours, 1 direct night train, 7 hours; Italo: 4/day, 3-3.5 hours), **Florence** (Trenitalia: 2-3/hour, 1.5 hours; Italo: 2/hour, 1.5 hours), **Siena** (1-2/hour, 1 change, 3-4 hours), **Orvieto** (11/day, 1-1.5 hours; regional trains are half the price and only slightly slower than Intercity trains), **Assisi** (4/day direct, 2 hours; more with change in Foligno), **Pisa** (1-2/hour, 3 hours, some change in Florence), **La Spezia** (7/day direct, 3-4 hours), **Milan** (Trenitalia: 1-3/hour, 3-3.5 hours; Italo: 11/day nonstop, 3 hours, more with stops), **Naples** (Trenitalia: 1-4/hour, 1 hour on Frecciarossa, 2 hours on Intercity, 2.5 hours and much cheaper on regional trains; Italo: hourly, 70 minutes), **Civitavecchia** cruise-ship port (regional trains roughly hourly, 80 minutes; faster but pricier trains every 2 hours, 40-50 minutes), **Brindisi** (3/day, 5 hours), **Bern** (3/day, 6.5 hours, change in Milan), **Munich** (4/day, 10 hours, change in Verona or Padua; 1 direct night train, 11.5 hours), **Nice** (2/day, 8-9 hours, change in Milan), **Paris** (2/day, 11.5 hours, change in Turin; 1 night train, 14.5 hours, change in Milan), **Vienna** (3/day, 12 hours, 1-2 changes; 1 direct night train, 15 hours).

TIBURTINA TRAIN STATION

Tiburtina, Rome's second-largest train station (www.stazioneromatiburtina.it), is next to the Tiburtina Metro station in the city's northeast corner, and across the road from Rome's bus station. It's a pass-through station: Fast trains along the Milan-Naples line stop here and continue on quickly. A few of these fast trains now stop only at Tiburtina, but most stop at both Tiburtina and Termini. Use the station that's most convenient for you.

Getting Between Tiburtina and Downtown Rome: Tiburtina is on Metro line B, four stops from Termini. Note that when going to Tiburtina, Metro line B splits—you want a train signed *Rebibbia*, not *Jonio*. Bus #492 runs conveniently between Tiburtina, several city-center stops (including Piazza Barberini, Piazza Venezia, and Piazza Navona), and the Vatican neighborhood (as you emerge from the train station's front door, the city bus stop is just to the left).

SMALLER STATIONS

Rome has about a dozen small train stations which are usually only useful if you're staying nearby. These stations are served mostly by slow regional trains (for example, from coastal destinations like Civitavecchia, where cruise ships dock), and slow trains from the airport. The ones you're most likely to encounter are **San Pietro** (south of the Vatican City; bus #64 connects it to Piazza Venezia and Termini; if you're staying near the Vatican and taking a regional train, get off here); **Trastevere** (a few minutes' ride on tram #8 from Trastevere and Piazza Venezia); and **Ostiense** (5 minutes from the Piramide Metro stop via an underground walkway). **Porta San Paolo Station,** directly at the Piramide Metro stop, is part of the Metro rather than the national rail system; suburban trains (Metro tickets valid) to Ostia Antica and Rome's Lido (beach) leave from here.

By Bus

ROME'S BUS STATION: AUTOSTAZIONE TIBURTINA

Long-distance buses use Autostazione Tiburtina, 200 yards from the Tiburtina train and Metro station. Buses are slower than trains, but fares are cheap (as little as €5 to Naples or Florence). Buses are also handy for destinations poorly served by rail. To reach the bus station from either Tiburtina station, don't follow the *Bus* signs, which lead to the city bus stop. Instead, exit the station, cross the street under the elevated freeway, and look for the fenced-in area with bus platforms. The station is chaotic and crowded, with nowhere to sit. Ticket-window lines can be slow, so buy your ticket online in advance if possible. If your bus departure platform isn't listed on the digital board, ask one of the drivers for help.

From Rome by Bus to: Siena (9/day, 2.5-3 hours, www.baltour.it), **Sorrento** (1-2/day, 4 hours; this is a cheap and easy way to go straight to Sorrento, buy tickets at www.marozzivt.it—in Italian only, at the Tiburtina ticket office, travel agencies, or on board for a €3.50 surcharge; tel. 080-579-0111), **Naples** (every 1-2 hours, 3 hours, www.baltour.it or www.megabus.com), **Florence** (every 1-2 hours, 4 hours, www.baltour.it or www.megabus.

com), **Assisi** (2/day, 3 hours, www.sulga.it—the train makes much more sense).

By Plane

Rome's two airports—**Fiumicino** (a.k.a. Leonardo da Vinci, airport code: FCO) and the small **Ciampino** (airport code: CIA)—share the same website (www.adr.it).

FIUMICINO AIRPORT

Rome's major airport is manageable. Terminals T1, T2, and T3 are all under one roof—walkable end to end in 20 minutes. T5 is a separate building requiring a short shuttle trip. (T4 is still being built.) The T1-2-3 complex has ground transport, a TI (in T3, daily 9:00-17:30, longer in summer), ATMs, banks, luggage storage, shops, and bars. For airport information, call 06-65951.

Getting Between Fiumicino Airport and Downtown Rome

In either direction, give yourself lots of time to allow for traffic delays, travel between your hotel and the train/bus station, finding your train or bus, and walking to the terminal.

By Train: Trenitalia's slick, direct, first-class-only Leonardo Express train connects the airport train station (called Fiumicino Aeroporto) and Rome's central Termini Station in 32 minutes for €14. Trains run at least twice hourly in both directions from roughly 6:00 to 23:00 (leaving the airport usually at :23 and :53).

From the airport's arrival gate, follow signs to the train icon or *Stazione/Railway Station*. Buy your ticket from a Trenitalia machine, the ticket office *(biglietteria)*, or a newsstand near the platform; then validate it in a green or yellow machine near the track. Machines sell open tickets that can be used on any train. (You know you're in Italy when the machine makes you choose a departure time—even though you're allowed to take any train.) Make sure the train you board is going to the central "Roma Termini" station, as trains from the airport serve other destinations too.

Returning from Termini train station to the airport, trains depart at about :05 and :35 past each hour, usually from track 23 or 24. Check the departure boards for "Fiumicino Aeroporto" and confirm with an official or a local on the platform that the train is indeed going to the airport (€14, buy ticket from Trenitalia machines or any train station tobacco shop or newsstand). Read your ticket: If it requires validation, stamp it in the green or yellow machines near the platform before boarding.

You can access most of the airport's terminals from the airport train station. If your flight leaves from terminal T5 (where most

American air carriers flying direct to the US depart), catch the T5 shuttle bus *(navetta)* on the sidewalk in front of T3—it's too far to walk with luggage.

Cheaper (€8) local trains also run from the airport to some of Rome's smaller train stations (including Trastevere, Ostiense, and Tiburtina). If you're staying in Trastevere or the Pantheon area, it can be simpler and cheaper to take the local train to Trastevere station, then walk out to the street and take the #8 tram downhill to your hotel. The train to Tiburtina is useful if you have a long-distance bus to catch.

Only a couple of long-distance trains per day serve the airport. To connect to other Italian cities, you'll usually have to change at Termini or Tiburtina.

By Bus: Four bus companies—Terravision (www.terravision. eu), SIT (www.sitbusshuttle.com), T.A.M. (www.tambus.it), and Schiaffini (www.romeairportbus.com)—connect Fiumicino and Termini train station. The SIT bus also stops near the Vatican. I'd just hop on whichever one is departing first (every 10-15 minutes at peak times). While much cheaper than the train (about €5 one-way), buses take twice as long (about an hour, depending on traffic) and can potentially fill up (allow plenty of extra time). At the airport, the bus station is at the far end of terminal T3. At Termini, T.A.M. and Schiaffini depart from the south side of the station; Terravision and SIT from the north side.

By Airport Shuttle: Shared shuttle van services run to and from the airport and can be economical for one or two people. Consider Rome Airport Shuttle (€25/1 person, extra people-€6 each, by reservation only, tel. 06-4201-4507 or 06-4201-3469, www.airportshuttle.it).

By Taxi: A taxi between Fiumicino and downtown Rome takes 45 minutes in normal traffic (for tips on taxis, see page 28) and costs exactly €48. (You could add a €2-5 tip for good service.) From the airport, be sure to catch an official taxi at the taxi stand. Avoid unmarked, unmetered taxis; these guys will try to tempt you away from the taxi-stand lineup by offering an immediate (rip-off) ride. Rome's official taxis are white, with a "taxi" sign on the roof and a maroon *Roma Capitale* logo on the door. By law, taxi drivers can only charge €48 for the ride to anywhere in the historic center (within the old city walls, where all of my recommended hotels are located). The fare covers up to four people with normal-size bags (to save money, try teaming up with any tourist also just arriving—most are heading for hotels near yours in the center). An official taxi will have that €48 fare clearly posted on its door.

Less frequent cabs based in Fiumicino (the town near the airport) are allowed to charge €60 for the ride. Signs stating the Rome and Fiumicino price caps are posted next to the taxi stand.

It's best to use the Rome city cabs and establish the price before you get in. If your driver tries to point to the price for Fiumicino-based cabs or otherwise charge you more than €48 from the airport into town, say, *"Quarant'otto euro—è la legge"* (kwah-RAHNTOH-toe AY-oo-roh—ay lah LEJ-jay; which means, "Forty-eight euros—it's the law"), and they should back off.

When departing Rome, your hotel can arrange a taxi to the airport at any hour. Alternatively, they sometimes work with comparably priced private car services, which are usually just fine (if not nicer than a regular cab).

CIAMPINO AIRPORT

Rome's smaller airport (tel. 06-6595-9515) handles charter flights and some budget airlines (including most Ryanair flights).

Getting Between Ciampino Airport and Downtown Rome: Various bus companies—including Cotral, Terravision, Schiaffini, and SIT—will take you to Rome's Termini train station (about €5 and 2/hour, 45 minutes). Cotral also runs a quicker route (25 minutes) to the Anagnina Metro stop, where you can connect by Metro to the stop nearest your hotel (departs every 40 minutes).

The fixed price for any official taxi (with the maroon *Roma Capitale* logo on the door) is €30 to downtown (within the old city walls, including most of my recommended hotels).

Rome Airport Shuttle also offers shared van rides to and from Ciampino (€25/1 person, listed earlier).

By Car

DRIVING AND PARKING IN ROME

Consider this: Your car is a worthless headache in Rome. Avoid a pile of stress and save money by parking at the huge, easy, free, and relatively safe lot behind the train station in the hill town of Orvieto (follow *P* signs from the autostrada) and catching an €8 *regionale* train to Rome (every 1-2 hours, 1.5 hours).

Alternatively, use one of the more than two dozen park-and-ride lots at Rome's outlying Metro stations (€5/24 hours). These vary in size and convenience; one of the largest is at the Anagnina Metro station, just inside Rome's ring expressway along the Via Tuscolana (southeast of downtown). For details, search for "park and ride" *(parcheggi di scambio)* at www.atac.roma.it.

If you must park closer in, there's a large underground garage at the Villa Borghese Gardens near the Spagna Metro station, just outside the restricted downtown zone (€18/day, Viale del Galoppatoio 33, www.sabait.it). Hotel Lancelot (see page 350), though not cheap, is a rare hotel with private parking.

During most of the week, you need a special permit to drive in the old center of Rome. The restricted zone is roughly bounded by Piazza del Popolo, Termini Station, the Colosseum, and the river, plus Trastevere, and on Friday and Saturday nights. Testaccio is off-limits too (for details, go to www.agenziamobilita.roma.it and search for "LTZ" in English or "ZTL" in Italian). Without a permit, you'll be photographed and fined. Your hotel can help you get one if you absolutely must drive or park downtown.

If you do need to drive into Rome, it helps to time your journey for Friday evening or the weekend. A ring-shaped expressway (the Grande Raccordo Anulare) circles greater Rome. This ring road has spokes that lead you into the center. Take the Settebagni exit, then follow the ancient Via Salaria, then *Centro* signs to enter the city from the north. Avoid rush hour and drive defensively: Roman cars stay in their lanes like rocks in an avalanche.

By Cruise Ship

ROME'S CRUISE PORT: CIVITAVECCHIA

Hundreds of cruise ships dock each year at the small, manageable port city of Civitavecchia (chee-vee-tah-VEH-kyah), about 45 miles northwest of Rome. For more details, see my *Rick Steves Mediterranean Cruise Ports* guidebook.

Getting to Rome: As road traffic between Civitavecchia and Rome is terrible, generally the fastest (and most economical) way to day-trip into Rome is to take the **train.** Trains connect Civitavecchia with several stations in Rome, including Ostiense (two Metro stops from the Colosseum), San Pietro (a short walk from Vatican City), or Termini (the main transit hub, but farther from key sights). Trains depart frequently for Rome and take 40-80 minutes. You can buy train tickets at Civitavecchia's station, or the Agenzie 365/Freccia Viaggi travel agency, just outside the station, which also sells transportation tickets of all types, including expensive but time-saving "skip the line" tickets for the Vatican and Colosseum. To reach Civitavecchia's train station, take a free shuttle bus from your ship to the main port gate and then walk (about 25 minutes) or ride an orange city bus (€2, 3/hour, often no buses 12:00-14:30, catch from main port gate). I'd avoid the expensive taxi ride from the cruise port to the station.

Other options for getting into Rome include a cruise-ship excursion package, a taxi, or organized tours run by private tour companies. A **taxi** into Rome takes about 1.5 hours and costs around €110-150 one-way, though many cabbies will inflate their prices (avoid the unlicensed taxis offering a huge price break; you can be fined for taking one). **Organized tours** into Rome are offered by Can't Be Missed Tours (mobile 329-129-8182, www.cantbemissedtours.com, ask about Rick Steves discount) and Miles & Miles Private Tours (see page 32).

DAY TRIPS

Ostia Antica • Tivoli • Naples & Pompeii

There's so much to see and do in Rome that you could easily fill a vacation without ever leaving the city limits. But here are several nearby sights that might match your particular interests.

Ostia Antica is similar to Pompeii, but without the crowds. This excavated ancient Roman city is located an easy 30 minutes by suburban train from Rome's Piramide Metro station. Or stay on the train another 15 minutes and enjoy Ostia's beaches.

Tivoli is less accessible by public transportation (consider see-

ing it via private tour, or hire your own driver for the day), but you're rewarded with the evocative ruins of Hadrian's Villa and with the lush gardens and restored fountains of a Renaissance mansion, the Villa d'Este.

Thanks to Italy's excellent train system, it's around 70 minutes to **Naples** on a direct high-speed train that lands you right in the middle of town (or 2.5 hours on cheaper trains). In Naples, see ancient statues and mosaics at the wonderful Archaeological Museum, stroll colorful Spaccanapoli street, and have lunch in the city where pizza was born, sampling the exotic chaos of southern Italy.

History hounds can venture another 40 minutes south of Naples by train to see the ultimate in ruined Roman cities—**Pompeii**—frozen in time by the eruption of Mt. Vesuvius.

Arrive back in Rome for a late dinner at a sidewalk café to recount your busy day over a glass of wine.

Italy's fast trains put other cities within day-trip range, including **Orvieto** (1-1.5 hours by inexpensive regional train), **Assisi** (4/day direct, 2 hours; more with a change in Foligno), and **Florence** (1.5 hours on fast but expensive trains). For in-depth information on Orvieto and Assisi, see *Rick Steves Italy*, and for Florence, see *Rick Steves Florence & Tuscany*.

OSTIA ANTICA

For an exciting day trip, pop down to the Roman port of Ostia, which is similar to Pompeii but a lot closer and, in some ways, more interesting. Because Ostia was a working port town, it offers a more complete and gritty look at Roman life than wealthier Pompeii. Wandering around today, you'll see warehouses, apartment flats, mansions, shopping arcades, and baths that served a once-thriving port of 60,000 people. With over 70 peaceful park-like acres to explore and relatively few crowds, it's a welcome break from the bustle of Rome.

GETTING TO OSTIA ANTICA

Getting to Ostia Antica from downtown Rome is a snap—it's a 45-minute combination Metro/train ride. (Since the train is part of the Metro system, it only costs one Metro ticket each way—€3 total round-trip.)

From Rome, take Metro line B to the Piramide stop, which is attached to the Roma Porta San Paolo train station. The train tracks are just a few steps from the Metro tracks: Follow signs to *Lido* (beach)—go up the escalator, turn left, and go down the steps to reach the Roma-Lido train line. All trains depart in the direction of Lido, leave every 15 minutes, and stop at Ostia Antica along the way. The lighted schedule will read something like *"Prossima partenza alle ore 13.25, bin 3,"* meaning, "Next departure at 13:25 from track 3." Look for the next train, hop on, ride for about 30 minutes (no need to stamp your Metro ticket again, but keep it handy in case they decide to check), and get off at the Ostia Antica stop.

Leaving the train station in Ostia Antica, cross the road via the blue skybridge and walk straight down Via della Stazione di Ostia Antica, continuing straight (through a small parking lot) until you reach the larger parking lot for the site. The entrance is to your left.

ORIENTATION TO OSTIA ANTICA

Cost: €8 for the site and museum, €11 during special exhibits. Free and crowded on first Sun of the month.

Hours: April-Aug Tue-Sun 8:30-19:15, Sept until 19:00, most of Oct until 18:30, late Oct-mid-Feb until 16:30, shorter hours mid-Feb-March, closed Mon year-round, last entry one hour before closing.

Information: A map of the site with suggested itineraries is available for €2 from the ticket office. Tel. 06-5635-0215. The official website is www.ostiaantica.beniculturali.it; a helpful website run by friends of the ruins is www.ostia-antica.org.

Tours: Although you'll see little audioguide markers throughout the site, there may not be audioguides for rent.

  ∩ Download my free Ostia Antica **audio tour.**

Length of This Tour: Allow two hours inside the site. Add in the round-trip train ride, and it's at least a four-hour excursion from Rome.

Services: There are WCs at the entrance, near the cafeteria, and (often the cleanest of all) in the modern building behind the marble chunks, east of the cafeteria.

Eating: The only option is a small $ cafeteria with sandwiches and a few hot dishes next to Ostia's museum. Ostia is a great place for a discreet picnic among the ruins.

Sightseeing Tip: Maximize sightseeing efficiency by visiting south Rome sights on your return. The Piramide Metro stop—where you'll catch the suburban train—really *is* next to a pyramid, and also near the colorful Testaccio neighborhood. Farther south are St. Paul's Outside the Walls, E.U.R., and the Montemartini Museum (for more on all of these, see page 101).

Beach Time: The train line that leads to Ostia also connects Romans to their beaches. To combine some beach time with your sightseeing, see page 396.

BACKGROUND

Located at (and named for) the mouth *(ostium)* of the Tiber, Ostia was founded in the fourth century B.C. Gobbled up early by Rome, its main industry was salt gleaned from nearby salt flats (salt was a precious preserver of meat in ancient times). Often called Rome's first colony, Ostia served as a naval base, protecting Rome from any invasion by river. By 150 B.C., when Rome controlled the Mediterranean, Ostia's importance became commercial rather than military. At its peak, Ostia was vital to the Roman Empire. Most of

Ostia Antica

1. Necropolis
2. Porta Romana
3. Republican Warehouses
4. Baths of Neptune
5. Theater
6. Square of the Guilds
7. Mill
8. Via Casa di Diana
9. Forum
10. Forum Baths
11. Ostia Museum

what the city of Rome consumed—and that was a lot by historical standards—came in through this port.

Rome eventually outgrew Ostia, and a vast new port was dug a little farther north (where Rome's airport now stands). But Ostia remained a key administrative and warehousing center, busy with the big business of keeping more than a million Romans fed and in sandals.

Eventually things really soured for Ostia. Rome fell. The river changed course. The port was abandoned, silted up, became a malaria-infested swamp, and was eventually forgotten. The mud that buried Ostia actually protected it from the ravages of time—and from stone-scavenging medieval peasants.

SELF-GUIDED TOUR

Consider your visit a three-part affair:

1. Follow this tour (with this chapter or my 🎧 free audio tour). You'll go straight down Decumanus Maximus (the town's main drag), with a couple of slight detours, finishing at the forum (the main square).

2. Pop into the museum, and consider getting a bite to eat at the cafeteria.

3. Explore the back lanes—going on a visual scavenger hunt—as you wander your way back to the entry point.

• *Find the map (30 yards inside the gate, on the right) for an orientation: We're entering at the far right and heading down the main street, labeled* Decumano Massimo, *to the forum, labeled* Foro. *The blue Tiber River borders the top. The pale green shows the former course of the river—which eventually abandoned its city. Notice how the core of Ostia is a rectangular Roman military camp, with two major roads crossing at the forum. One of four city gates lies ahead, and on your left is the...*

❶ Necropolis

As you pass by row after row of brick foundations, you might think that these ruins are former homes in a great city. Oh, this *was* a city—but a city of the dead. These are not homes, but tombs.

Ancient Romans buried their dead outside the city walls. Ostia was a famously pagan town, slow to become Christian. To a pagan, the closest thing to an afterlife was to be remembered. If their families could afford it, they'd place the tomb on the roadside with a thumbnail bio carved into the stone that all could read as they came and went (for example, "My name was Caius. I was a baker."). This area was called a necropolis (city of the dead); Christians preferred the term cemetery (from the Greek for resting place).

Also lining the road, you'll see a few sarcophagi (small stone "coffins" where remains were placed) and statues, which honored the dead.

Burial practices changed over the years. In B.C. times, the remains were placed in these room-like tombs. After the first century A.D., cremation became popular, so this necropolis also has some family sepulchers (marked by arches) lined with niches for ash-filled urns. In the second and third centuries A.D., the Romans here buried their dead in marble and terra-cotta sarcophagi, placed in the tombs.

• *Ahead (where the road narrows), you enter the ancient city of Ostia through the scant remains of the gate called...*

❷ Porta Romana

Just as Rome's Porta San Paolo faced Ostia, Ostia's Porta Romana faced Rome. This gate, which was locked at night, was part of a wall that surrounded the city on three sides. The fourth "wall" of defense was the river.

Pass through the gate and imagine entering the city. On the grand piazza, a statue of Victory greeted visitors (there's a copy up ahead). You could water your animals at the huge water basin on the left (the low, rectangular brickwork structure near the statue), and store your goods in the warehouse on the right (the maze of brick foundations a few steps ahead). Immediately to the left (under an umbrella

pine), find a low wall with marble panels. The Latin inscription proclaimed to all who entered: "The Senate ("...[SE]NATUS...") and the people of the colony of Ostia constructed the walls." The "colony" reference is a reminder that Ostia was the first acquisition of the Roman Empire.

From the gate, Decumanus Maximus leads straight to the forum, where this walk ends. Note that this road was elevated above some buildings' foundations. Over the centuries, Ostia's ground level rose. You can actually identify buildings from the republic (centuries before Christ) and the empire (centuries after Christ) by their level. Anything you walk down into is from the earlier period.

• *Just inside the gate and to the right are the...*

❸ Republican Warehouses (Magazzini Repubblicani)

In the first century B.C., this city bustled in its role as a river port. Walking along the main street, you pass vast warehouses on the

right. The goods of the port, such as grain from Sicily, Egypt, and all of North Africa, were processed and stored in warehouses here (which had elevated floors to keep things dry) before being consumed by Rome.

Ahead, a series of stubby brick columns are the remains of a roofed portico that once provided a shaded walkway into town. Notice the bricks—generally, rough bricks are original, while smooth bricks are part of the reconstruction. Ostia has been picked clean since ancient times. The port's treasures ended up gracing buildings as far away as Constantinople.

• *Continue straight ahead about 100 yards. The little well in the road is medieval—a remnant from Middle Age squatters who found shelter in these ruins. From here, you'll see a viewpoint (with railings), above on the right. Climb up for a view of the...*

❹ Baths of Neptune (Terme di Nettuno)

Examine the fine mosaic depicting Neptune riding four horses through the sea. He's surrounded by a menagerie of sea creatures: fish, crustaceans, and serpents with the heads of horses, goats, and rams. At the top, Triton blows his long horn. Apart from the cupid riding the dolphin, the sea looks frightening—which it was.

The complex of ruins stretching below was a bath house. Romans came here to clean, swim, exercise, and socialize. They'd work up a sweat in the steam room, move to the next room (with another mosaic) to take a cold plunge, then cool down in a medium-temperature room. The large open-air square to the left of the mosaic would have been busy with people wrestling, stretching, doing jumping jacks, and getting rubdowns. The niches that ring the square housed small businesses. A row of umbrella pines in the distance marks the original channel of the river before it changed course, abandoning the town.

• *Climb back down to the main drag, and continue to the right until you reach the theater on your right. Enter the theater through its main central gate.*

❺ Theater (Teatro)

As you pass through the entry tunnel, glance up at the scant remains of the stucco-rosette decor on the ceiling, which hints at the elegance of this place 2,000 years ago. At the end of the tunnel, men would bid farewell to their women (before the women went to sit in the higher seats— typical of the gender division in public Rome).

Take a seat. Before you is a typically Roman complex mixing religion, business, and entertainment: a grand theater facing a temple surrounded by a commercial square. Up to 4,000 residents could gather in this theater.

The musicians (and some actors) performed on the semicircular floor, called the orchestra. Romans also used a wooden stage—the five-foot-tall brick wall formed its lip. A wall once rose behind the stage, where scenery could be hung. Some plays featured actors in masks—notice the carved stone masks on display to the left of the stage. Each face shows a particular emotion, and the mouths are oversized so actors could speak clearly through them.

Plays were rowdy daytime events—like going to a day game at the ballpark—with lots of audience participation. And heaven help a bad actor. The three rows of marble steps near the orchestra were reserved for the chairs of big shots. Even today, this place—one of the oldest brick theaters anywhere—is used for concerts. Climb to the top of the theater for a fine view.

• *From the theater, continue (farther away from the main street) behind the stage into the big square. Head to the right and walk counterclockwise around the square, ending up back at the theater.*

❻ Square of the Guilds (Piazzale delle Corporazioni)

This grand square evolved from a simple place where businessmen would stroll and powwow together to a monumental square lined with more than 60 offices of ship owners and traders. This was the bustling center of Rome's import-export industry.

As you walk along the sidewalk (circling the square counterclockwise), admire the second-century A.D. mosaics advertising the services offered by the businesses inside. Some are in Latin, but most use pictures for illiterate sailors or non-Latin-reading foreigners.

Walking along the right side of the square, you'll pass signs for tanners, grain importers (shipped in decorative barrels), and fish wholesalers. The elephant marks the office of Libyan traders who dealt in ivory or perhaps in exotic animals (great for parties, private spectacles, and Colosseum events). You'll see plenty of mosaics showing Roman ships, with their elaborate sails and rudders. Roman ingenuity enabled boats to tack and sail against the wind. Commerce moved more readily, making the Mediterranean a thriving Roman free-trade zone.

Reaching the end of the right side, continue working clockwise to find the chess-board-like mosaic. In the lower right, this mosaic has one of the most common symbols of all: the lighthouse.

(It's the squat tower with flames coming out the top. Fueled by an oven below, it directed ships into Ostia's port.) The lighthouse became the sign of the port of Ostia.

Continuing on, notice the many statues of notable local guild members and business leaders that decorated the courtyard. The temple in the center was likely related to Ceres, the goddess of harvest and abundance (prosperity from good business).

Turning the corner again, find another lighthouse mosaic. Next comes an amphora (pointed jug) between palm trees—likely marking an importer of palm oil.

At the end of the square, as you leave, notice the small white altar on the right. This would have been used to sacrifice animals—such as the rams carved into the corners—to ask for favor from the gods. The entrails would be read to divine the future and to determine whether the gods were for or against a particular business venture. This altar is a copy; the original is in Rome. (Consider the burden on Italy of protecting and preserving what is actually the cultural heritage of all of Europe against illegal digging, exportation, vandalism, weather, and pollution. There's a special branch of the Carabinieri dedicated to art theft.)

• *Continue down the main street. About two blocks down, you reach the intersection with Via dei Molini. This street marks the wall of the original military* castrum, *or rectangular-shaped camp (described in more detail later, under "Forum"). Turn right and walk about a block and a half down Via dei Molini, keeping a sharp eye out for our next sight (look for the* Molino del Silvano *sign on the left among the ruins). Step inside.*

❼ Mill (Molino)

This mill and bakery building *(panificio)* dates from A.D. 120. The lava millstones in front of you were used to grind grain. Study the workings: The grain was ground between two stones. At bottom is a bowl-like stone. On top of that rests a cylindrical upper section with holes through which wood poles would be inserted. Grain would be sprinkled in from a sack hanging from the ceiling. Then mules or workers would power the grinding by walking in circles, pushing on the wood poles to turn the cylindrical crushing stone. Even-  tually, powdery flour (with not much grit) would tumble out the bottom. They'd walk it next door to make bread.

• *If you need a break before we continue, notice that we're not far from the museum, cafeteria, and WC. Now, backtrack half a block down Via dei Molini in the direction of the main street. At the big tree, take the first right onto Via Casa di Diana. The street is unmarked, but it's distinctive—lined with taller-than-usual buildings.*

❽ Via Casa di Diana

About 75 yards down the street (on the left), stop into the **Insula of the Thermopolium** *(Termopolio)*—an ancient tavern. Step past the

grooved threshold—which once held a sliding wooden door—and make yourself at home. You'll see a couple of display shelves where they stacked food and drinks for sale, and a small sink. A cute fresco on the wall advertised the tavern's offerings: food (the dish), drink (the cup), and music (the castanets). Too smoky and noisy? Step

out back and enjoy the quiet courtyard with the fountain.

Next, cross the street to the **Insula of the Paintings.** Find the staircase (a few steps down the road) and climb all the way to the open rooftop for a good view.

Imagine life as an apartment dweller in ancient Rome. An *insula* was a multistoried apartment complex where the lower-middle class lived. These held miserable, cramped units crammed into buildings up to 10 floors high (the average was 5 floors). To reach their rooms on the higher floors, people climbed treehouse-type stairs. Plumbing didn't exist. It was stinky. "Windows" covered with shutters or cloth curtains dipped in grease did little to cut the street din.

Buildings were made cheaply of wood, with weak foundations, so many burned or collapsed. The apartments had no heat and no kitchen, so residents cooked or purchased food elsewhere. They tossed garbage out the windows. Because chariot and cart traffic was allowed only after dark, there was lots of night noise.

The wealthier classes, on the other hand, lived in sprawling and luxurious homes. These were generally built on one floor, with a series of rooms facing a central open courtyard. Decorative pools collected rainwater. Statues, mosaics, and frescoes were everywhere. Rome's wealthy were as comfortable as the poor were wretched.

From this rooftop perch, find the museum (the modern building). Behind the museum, see modern pleasure boats parked alongside where today's Tiber leaves Ostia. The temporary arched roofing you see is there to protect ancient bits and pieces (worth a look).

• *Now, walk (on street level, of course) to the end of the street, toward the high brick wall and then left into Ostia's forum. For the best view, head for the center of the forum, where there's a round (well-like) brick monument dedicated to the emperor's guardian angels. From here, take in the sights.*

❾ Forum

As in Italian cities today, Ostia's main gathering place was a central piazza. This forum had a large rectangular open space surrounded by columns supporting arcades and buildings.

At one end of the square is the grandest structure—the temple called the **Capitolium** (from A.D. 120), with its grand staircase. The marble veneer was scavenged in the Middle Ages, leaving only the core brickwork. Note the reinforcement arches in the brick. The Capitolium (named after the original atop Capitoline Hill in Rome) was dedicated to the pagan trinity of Jupiter, Juno, and Minerva. A forum dominated by a Capitolium temple was a standard feature of colonies throughout the empire. The purpose: to transport the Roman cult of Jupiter, Juno, and Minerva to the newly conquered population.

On the opposite side of the square, distinguished by its lone sawed-off column, is the Temple of Roma and Augustus. Its position is powerfully symbolic. The power of the emperor stands equal, facing the power of the Capitolium Triad.

The town's **basilica** was also on the forum square. As you face the Capitolium temple, it's to your left and consists of little more than the footprint of the building. Dating from about A.D. 100, this was where legal activities and commercial business took place. Its central nave and two side aisles lead to the "high altar," where the judge sat.

Under your feet runs Decumanus Maximus, one of the town's two main streets that intersect at the forum. Whenever possible, Rome imposed a grid road plan on its conquered cities. After Rome conquered Ostia in about 400 B.C., it built a military camp, or *castrum*—a rectangular fort with east, west, north, and south gates and two main roads converging on the forum. Throughout the empire, Romans found comfort in this familiar city plan. While people found it no fun to be conquered, the empire brought order and stability to their lives through laws and the creation of grid-planned cities and grand squares such as this one.

Standing at the center of the forum, plan your next move after our tour ends. You could visit the **museum**—it's the pink-and-white building behind the Capitolium temple. For more sightseeing, the Decumanus Maximus continues west into a vast urban expanse, great for simply wandering (see "Archaeological Scavenger Hunt" at the end of this chapter). Or the Decumanus can take you east directly back to the entrance/exit—a 15-minute walk away.

• *But first, make one more stop. Walk to the Temple of Roma and Augustus. As you're facing it, look left and find a brick arch over a street. Near that arch is our final sight.*

⑩ Forum Baths (Terme del Foro) and Latrine (Forica)

Try to imagine this huge complex (which may be closed for preservation) peopled, steaming, and busy. Government-subsidized baths were a popular social and business meeting place in any Roman city. Roman engineers were experts at radiant heat. A huge furnace heated both the water and air that flowed through pipes under the floors and in the walls (you can see the hollow bricks in the walls). Notice the fine marble steps—great for lounging—that led into the pools. Bathers used olive oil rather than soap to wash, so the water needed to be periodically skimmed by servants. Like a high-end spa, there was a *laconicum* (sweating room), two *tepidariae* (where Romans were rubbed down by masseuses), and the once-steamy *caldarium* with three pools.

From the baths, walk a few steps farther up the street to find the 20-hole latrine (on the left). You can still see the pivot hole in

the floor that once supported its revolving door. The cutout below each seat was to accommodate the washable sponge on a stick, which was used rather than toilet paper. Rushing water below each seat (brought in by aqueduct) did the flushing. So much for privacy—even today, there's no word in Italian for it.

⑪ Ostia Museum

This small museum offers a delightful look at some of Ostia's finest statuary. Without worrying too much about exactly what's what, just wander and imagine these fine figures—tangled wrestlers, kissing cupids, playful gods— adorning the courtyards of wealthy Ostian families. Most of the statues are second- and third-century A.D. Roman pieces inspired by rare and famous Greek originals. The portrait busts are of real people—the kind you'd sit next to in the baths (or on the toilets).

Roman sculptors excelled at realistic busts. Roman religion revered the man of the house (and his father and grandfather). Statues of daddy and grandpa were common in the corner of any proper house. And with the emperor considered a god, you'd find his bust in classrooms, at the post office, and so on. The sarcophagi (marble coffins) generally show mythological scenes.

The grandest statue is the one that greets you as you go in—the Minerva as Victory that once stood by the Porta Romana, where we entered Ostia. Perhaps the most interesting room (to the left as you enter, just before the steps) features statuary from religions of foreign lands. Being a port town, Ostia accommodated people (and their worship needs) from all over the known world. The large statue of a man sacrificing a bull is a Mithraic altarpiece (see page 317).

The **cafeteria, WC,** and **shop** are in a modern building just behind the museum.

Archaeological Scavenger Hunt

As you return to the entry gate, get off the main drag and explore Ostia's back streets. Wandering beyond the forum and then taking the back lanes as you return to the entry, see if you can find:

- Tarp- and sand-protected mosaic flooring.
- White cornerstones put into buildings to fend off wild carts and reflect corners in the dark.
- Fast-food fish joint (on Decumanus Maximus, just beyond the forum).
- Hidden bits of fresco (clue: under hot tin roofs).
- Republican buildings and buildings dating from the empire.
- Stucco roughed up for fresco work (before applying the wet plaster of a fresco, the surface needs to be systematically gouged so the plaster can grip the wall).
- Millstones for grinding grain (Ostia's big industry).
- Floor patterns made colorful with inlaid marble.
- A *domus*—a single-family dwelling facing a fancy, central, open-air courtyard.

TIVOLI

At the edge of the Sabine Hills, 18 miles east of Rome, sits the medieval hill town of Tivoli, a popular retreat since ancient times. Today, it's famous for two very different villas: Hadrian's Villa (the ruins of a Versailles-like seat of government—outside but still near the capital—from which the emperor ruled), and the restored Villa d'Este (the lush and watery 16th-century residence of a cardinal in exile). These two sights complement each other well: While Hadrian's Villa ("Villa Adriana" in Italian) is about evocative ruins that ache with an untold history, Villa d'Este is simply beautiful, carefree, and relaxing—a pure confection.

Getting to Tivoli, you'll likely travel along the Via Tiburtina. The road was initially built by the ancient Romans; today it takes you through areas of ugly concrete sprawl. Famous for its thermal baths (smell the sulfur?), the area also contains the travertine quarries that supplied Rome with material for many of its buildings, including the Colosseum. While you're in the countryside, keep an eye out for the many olive groves (this area bottles up the prized Sabina olive oil), as well as flocks of sheep that produce the local *pecorino romano* cheese.

PLANNING YOUR TIME

Because public transportation connections are a bit complicated and time-consuming, consider a tour or driver (see next page) and give yourself the better part of a day for the trip to Tivoli, especially if you plan to see both of the villas. Note that Hadrian's Villa is open daily, Villa d'Este is closed on Monday, and buses are limited on Sunday.

If visiting both villas, see Villa d'Este first, then Hadrian's Villa. Those with limited time should focus on Hadrian's Villa.

GETTING TO TIVOLI

With a Tour or Driver: Several Rome tour companies—including Context Rome, Rome Walks, and Through Eternity—offer private tours of the villas (see their respective websites for specifics; tour companies listed on page 31). You can also hire a driver for the day to make the trip there and back faster and easier (drivers are recommended on page 32).

On Your Own: Reaching the town of Tivoli and Villa d'Este is easy. Getting to Hadrian's Villa is more of a challenge and requires patience, but many find it well worth the trouble. The directions given here rely on local buses; Tivoli is also connected to Rome via train, but the Tivoli train station isn't convenient to either sight. The bus is better.

From Rome, take a Metro/bus combination. Ride Metro line B to Ponte Mammolo (20 minutes from Termini Station; make sure to take a train going to Rebibbia, not Jonio). At Ponte Mammolo, catch the local blue Cotral bus to Tivoli (€2.20, 2/hour; check the monitor for departure schedule, then buy bus tickets at the bar or newsstand downstairs, easiest to buy return ticket at the same time; buses leave upstairs and can be crowded, be prepared to stand, validate ticket on board, direction: Tivoli, www.cotralspa. it, select "Pianifica viaggio" for English-language journey planner).

To go straight to **Hadrian's Villa**, ride the Cotral bus roughly 45 minutes to the stop for Villa Adriana (ask the driver or fellow passengers which stop you need). You'll hop off shortly after passing the quarries and walk approximately 20 minutes through a residential area. The way is not well-signed, so don't be shy about asking locals for directions.

For **Villa d'Este,** stay on the bus another 10 minutes to reach downtown Tivoli. Get off near the central square and the big park with the playground (start paying attention as the bus winds up the hill—your stop is shortly after it levels out; ask the driver, "Villa d'Este?"). The round TI kiosk is just uphill to the right. The entrance to the villa is across the square, past the modern-art arch—follow the signs (for about a block downhill).

From Tivoli, to backtrack to **Hadrian's Villa**, catch orange "CAT" city bus #4 or #4X at the bus stop near the playground. Buy your ticket at a tobacco shop—there's one right where you got off the Cotral bus—or newsstand (€1, about 2/hour Mon-Sat, hourly Sun morning, no buses Sun after 12:00, 10-minute ride, drops you near the villa entrance—tell driver "Villa Adriana," schedules at TI or www.catbustivoli.com). A taxi is €10-15 (look for one near the arch in the main square under the pine trees; confirm price before getting in).

From Hadrian's Villa, to return to **Rome**, either walk 20 minutes back to the main road (Via Tiburtina) or catch bus #4 or

#4X (direction: Tivoli) and get off at the main road (buy tickets in advance; schedules and tickets may be available at the entrance to the ruins). At the main road, change to a Cotral bus to Rome (confirm destination with bus driver—ask *"per Roma?"*).

Orientation to Tivoli

The town of Tivoli, with Villa d'Este in its center, is about 2.5 miles from Hadrian's Villa.

Modern Tivoli was heavily reconstructed after being bombed during World War II, when it was a Nazi stronghold. While most of Tivoli blankets the hilltop in less-than-charming concrete, a more rustic and picturesque quarter clings to the cliffs above a gorge on the back side of town. This area, anchored by the sleepy Piazza Rivarola, has a few evocative ancient ruins of its own and the steep Villa Gregoriana park. Strolling the main pedestrian drag gives you a glimpse of a small, unembellished Italian town.

Tourist Information: The TI is on Largo Garibaldi, near the bus stop, and has bus schedules (Tue-Sun 9:30-17:30, shorter hours off-season, closed Mon year-round, tel. 0774-313-536).

Sights In Tivoli

▲Villa d'Este

Clinging to a steep hillside just below Tivoli's main square, this Renaissance-era palace has a dull interior but a spectacularly en-

tertaining garden, divinely landscaped and punctuated by pools, streams, waterfalls, and thundering fountains that harness the natural hydro power of the Aniene River. If you can handle the many stairs (it's more vertical than horizontal), exploring these gardens is a peaceful and picturesque experience.

Cost and Hours: €8, €11 with special exhibits; May-Sept Tue-Sun 8:30-about 19:30, closes as early as 17:00 off-season, closed Mon year-round, last entry one hour before closing; audioguide-€4, tel. 0774-335-850 or 0774-332-920, www.villadestetivoli.info.

Background: Ippolito d'Este's grandfather, Alexander VI, was the

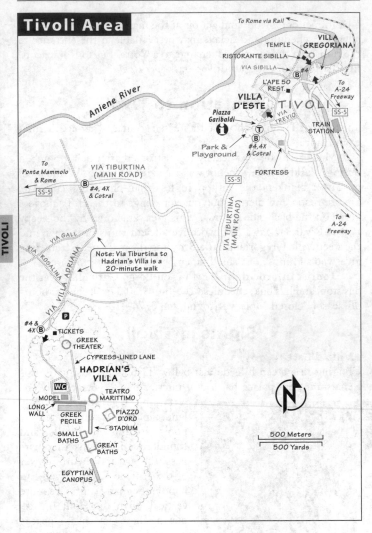

Tivoli Area

pope. Ippolito was fast-tracked for church service from birth and became a cardinal. His claim to fame: his pleasure palace at Tivoli. In the 1550s, he destroyed a Benedictine monastery to build this fanciful late-Renaissance palace. Like Hadrian's Villa, the Villa d'Este is a large residential estate. But this one features hundreds of Baroque fountains, all gravity-powered. The Aniene River, frazzled into countless threads, weaves its way entertainingly through the villa. At the bottom of the garden, the exhausted little streams once again team up to make a sizable river. Pirro Ligorio, Tivoli's architect, was also the archaeologist in charge of excavating Hadrian's Villa, and that site provided much in both inspiration and raw material for the fancy fountains of Villa d'Este. Ligorio could basically use Hadrian's Villa as a quarry to provide statuary and decorative stonework for his vision here.

The cardinal had a political falling-out with Rome, and he was exiled. With this watery wonderland on a cool hillside with fine views, he made sure Romans would come to visit. It's symbolic of the luxurious tastes and secular interests of the cardinal.

After years of neglect, the villa has been completely restored. All the most eye-popping fountains have been put back in operation, and—with the exception of the two highest jets of the central fountain, which are electric-powered—everything still operates on natural hydraulics. The terrace restaurant on the highest level of the garden is opportunely placed to catch cool afternoon sea breezes coming in across the plain of Rome.

Visiting the Villa and Gardens: Pick up the small map as you enter, and follow its suggested counterclockwise route down, then back up, through the garden. Also at the entry, note the posted schedule listing when the water organ *(la fontana dell'organa)* will play—a cute five-minute performance every two hours.

Your ticket also includes the **interior** of the villa itself, but you can make short work of that—the main floor is essentially an empty shell, aside from temporary exhibits, while the lower floor has some vivid frescoes that pale in comparison to similar palace decor in Rome (each room is described by posted English descriptions).

Rather than linger in the rooms, follow the signs for *giardino* until you pop out at the terrace overlooking the gardens. Descending toward the right, you'll first come to the grotto-like **Oval Fountain** *(fontana dell'ovato),* with its soothing cascades. From here, the **Hundred Fountains** *(cento fontane)* scamper all the way across the length of the terrace. But stick to this side of the garden for now, and continue down to the overlook above the **Neptune Fountain** *(fontana di Nettuno),* where you'll also find the water organ. Head back across to the middle of the garden, descending for a good look at the **Fountain of the Dragons** *(fontana dei draghi).* Then descend to the row of fish ponds that stretches scenically in one direction to the bottom of the Neptune Fountain, and in the other to a viewpoint overlooking the countryside. The lowest level of the park has a few smaller fountains (including the many-breasted Artemis, along the bottom wall). When you're ready, huff your way back up to the top...and the exit.

▲Hadrian's Villa

Built at the peak of the Roman Empire by Hadrian (ruled A.D. 117-138), this was a retreat from the political complexity of court life. The Spanish-born Hadrian—an architect, lover of Greek culture (nicknamed "The Little Greek"), and great traveler—envisioned the site as a microcosm of the lands he ruled as emperor, which at that point stretched from England to the Euphrates and encompassed countless diverse cultures. In the spirit of Legoland, Epcot, and Las Vegas, he re-created famous structures from around the world, producing a kind of diorama of his empire in the form of the largest

and richest Roman villa anywhere. Just as Louis XIV governed France from Versailles rather than Paris, Hadrian ruled Rome from this villa of more than 300 evocative acres. He basically spent his last decade here. Regrettably, this "Versailles of Ancient Rome" was plundered by barbarians and Renaissance big shots who all wanted something classical in their courtyards. They even burned the marble to make lime for cement. The scavenged art wound up in the Vatican Museums, the Louvre, and other museums throughout Europe. Today, Hadrian's Villa is a harmonious blend of nature and ruins—ideal for wandering while pondering the legacy of a great civilization.

Cost and Hours: €8, €11 with special exhibits; daily May-Aug 9:00-19:30, April and Sept until 19:00, closes as early as 17:00 off-season, last entry 1.5 hours before closing; audioguide-€5, tel. 0774-382-733, www.villaadriana.beniculturali.it.

Visiting the Ruins: Information at the site is sparse, but occasional posted maps and English descriptions do help keep you on track.

From the ticket booth, hike about 10 minutes up the main path through olive groves. You'll reach a field with a WC (hidden underground); beyond that, inside the modern beige building, is a **model** of the reconstructed site that's helpful for getting oriented.

Just beyond that, go through the high brick wall to pop out at the Athenian-style **Greek Pecile,** a long, enclosed courtyard with a tranquil, fish-stocked pond. This wall—and the pond—are all that remain of the original structure.

Beyond the left end of the pond is a cluster of other ruins, including the long stadium and the **Teatro Marittimo** (a circular palace, Hadrian's favorite retreat on an island, where he did his serious thinking). Continuing up through the ruins and to the left, you'll reach what's left of the palace itself; at the far corner is the vast **Piazza d'Oro,** which was once filled with fountains and flowing water.

Looping back around, you'll come to a dramatic overview of the gigantic (and aptly named) **Great Baths** complex. Descending to explore this area, continue to the left to find the villa's highlight, the **Egyptian Canopus** (sanctuary of the god Serapi), a canal lined with statues.

Backtrack a bit to complete your loop, passing the **Small Baths** on your way to the Pecile. When you get back to the long wall, walk through it and continue straight ahead, down the cypress-lined lane, to reach the circular temple; stairs on the left lead down to the **Greek Theater,** and then back to the entrance.

Villa Gregoriana Park

The steep park called Villa Gregoriana incorporates a landscape enjoyed from antiquity to the Romantic Age and today. Over a 1.5-mile network of trails, you'll descend into the Aniene River valley, passing views of waterfalls, trees, and raw wilderness. For those with more interest in nature than antiquity—although bits of the ancient villa remain—it offers a convenient alternative to Hadrian's Villa.

Cost and Hours: €6, April-mid-Oct daily 10:00-18:30; March and mid-Oct-Dec Tue-Sun 10:00-16:00, closed Mon; closed Jan-Feb, last entry one hour before closing, several hundred feet of elevation change over uneven steps—good shoes and knees helpful, tel. 0774-332-650, www.visitfai.it/parcovillagregoriana.

Getting There: It's handy to access the park through its back entrance, adjacent to the recommended Ristorante Sibilla. From the exit/main entrance (on the other side of the ravine from where you entered), it's a 15-minute walk back to the center of town. Alternatively, bus #4 leaves sporadically from the piazza out front (Largo Sant'Angelo) and goes through the center of town on its way to Hadrian's Villa and beyond (best to have purchased tickets in advance; otherwise try the green newspaper kiosk or Flo's Bar).

Eating in Tivoli

($$$$ = Splurge, $$$ = Pricey, $$ = Moderate, $ = Budget)

Eateries catering to tourists cluster around the main square, Largo Garibaldi—but for more choices and a better look at this tidy, no-frills town, head up Via del Trevio (which eventually curves and becomes Via Palatina then Via Ponte Gregoriano). This also takes you to the more scenic, older part of Tivoli—well worth exploring.

About a 10-minute walk from Largo Garibaldi, you'll arrive at **$$ l'Ape 50** (on the left), a classy but unpretentious place serving big gourmet sandwiches and other foods at a reasonable price (Tue-Sun 12:00-15:00 & 18:00-24:00, closed Mon, shorter hours in winter, seating inside or out, Via di Ponte Gregoriano 5, tel. 0774-556-471).

Farther on, angling left at Piazza Rivarola, you'll find the gourmet's choice for a splurge, **$$$ Ristorante Sibilla.** It's been open since 1720 but boasts a trendy, modern ambience. The restaurant neighbors two ancient temples, provides a glimpse of the waterfalls from its spectacularly set terrace, and offers pricey but tasty traditional cuisine (Tue-Sun 12:30-15:30 & 19:30-22:30, closed Mon, reserve for outdoor seating, Via della Sibilla 50, tel. 0774-335-281, www.ristorantesibilla.com). The restaurant is adjacent to the back entrance to Villa Gregoriana Park.

NAPLES & POMPEII

Napoli · Pompeii

While the Eternal City can keep you busy for ages, here are two excuses to leave Rome for a day. The trip south to Naples and Pompeii is demanding (four to five hours of train travel round-trip). But you'll be rewarded for your time with a chance to wander ancient Rome's most evocative ruins and go on an urban safari in what is perhaps Europe's most intense city.

If you have a week in Rome and are interested in maximum travel thrills, take a day trip to Naples and Pompeii. (See map on page 427.) Note that Naples' Archaeological Museum is closed on Tuesday. Pompeii is open daily.

Naples (Napoll)

If you like Italy as far south as Rome, go farther south—it gets better. If Italy is getting on your nerves stop at Rome. Italy intensifies as you plunge deeper. Naples is Italy in the extreme—its best (birthplace of pizza and Sophia Loren) and its worst (home of the Camorra, Naples' "family" of organized crime).

Neapolis ("new city") was a thriving Greek commercial center 2,500 years ago. Today, it remains southern Italy's leading city. Naples impresses visitors with one of Europe's top archaeological museums (showcasing the artistic treasures of Pompeii), fascinating churches that convey the city's unique personality and powerful devotion, an underground warren of Greek and Roman ruins, fine works of art (including pieces by Caravaggio, who lived here for a time), and evocative Nativity scenes (called *presepi*). Of course, Neapolitans make great pizza and tasty pastries (try the crispy, ricotta-stuffed *sfogliatella*). But more than anything, Naples has a brash and vibrant street life—"Italy in your face" in ways both good and bad. Walking through its colorful old town is one of my favorite experiences anywhere in Europe.

Naples is Italy's third-largest city and Europe's most densely populated, with more than one million people and few open spaces or parks. Watching the police try to enforce traffic sanity is almost comical in this gritty, crowded, and crime-ridden metropolis. Yet Naples surprises the observant traveler with its impressive knack for living, eating, and raising children with good humor and decency. Overcome your fear of being run down or ripped off long enough to talk with people.

Enjoy a few smiles and jokes with the man running the neighborhood tripe shop, or the woman taking her daycare class on a walk through the traffic.

The pulse of Italy throbs in Naples. Like Cairo or Mumbai, it's appalling and captivating at the same time, the closest thing to "reality travel" that you'll find in Western Europe. But this tangled mess still somehow manages to breathe, laugh, and sing—with a joyful Italian accent. Thanks to its reputation as a dangerous place, Naples doesn't get nearly as many tourists as it deserves. While the city has its problems, it has improved a lot in recent years. And even though it's a bit edgy, I feel comfortable here. Naples richly rewards those who venture in.

PLANNING YOUR TIME

A blitz visit to Naples and Pompeii looks something like this:

7:35	Catch the express train from Rome to Naples Centrale train station, where you'll head downstairs to transfer to the commuter train to Pompeii.
10:00	Tour Pompeii, grab a quick lunch (it's best to bring a picnic), then catch the commuter train back to Naples.
14:30	Visit Naples' Archaeological Museum during the heat of the day (closed Tue).
15:30	Take my self-guided "Naples Walk."
18:30	Finish with a pizza dinner as the city comes to life in the early evening.
20:30	Hop on the train back to Rome.
22:30	Arrive in Rome.

NAPLES

Orientation to Naples

Naples is set deep inside the large, curving Bay of Naples, with Mount Vesuvius looming just five miles away. Although Naples is a sprawling city, its fairly compact core contains the most interesting sights. The tourist's Naples is a triangle, with its points at the Centrale train station in the east, the Archaeological Museum to the west, and Piazza del Plebiscito (with the Royal Palace) and the port to the south. Steep hills rise above this historic core, including San Martino, capped with a mighty fortress.

TOURIST INFORMATION

Central Naples has multiple, small TIs, none of them particularly helpful—just grab a map and browse the brochures. The handiest one is in **Centrale train station** (daily 9:00-18:00, near track 23, tel. 081-268-779). Two others are by the entrance to the **Galleria Umberto I** shopping mall, across from Teatro di San Carlo (Mon-Sat 9:00-17:00, Sun 9:00-13:00, tel. 081-402-394); and on Spaccanapoli, across from the **Church of Gesù Nuovo** (Mon-Sat 9:00-17:00, Sun 9:00-13:00, tel. 081-551-2701). For information online, the best overall website is www.inaples.it.

ARRIVAL IN NAPLES

Express **trains** from Rome arrive at the slick, modern main station, **Napoli Centrale**. It has a small TI (near track 23), an ATM (at Banco di Napoli near track 24), a bookstore (La Feltrinelli, near track 24—beyond the pharmacy), and baggage check (*deposito bagagli*, near track 5). Pay WCs are down the stairs across from track 13. Shops and eateries are concentrated in the underground level. A good supermarket (Sapori & Dintorni) is out the front door and to the left. Immediately downstairs is the **Garibaldi** train station, which you'll use if you ride to Pompeii (see page 454).

Getting Downtown from the Station: Choose either Metro or taxi. In the lower-level corridor (below the main Centrale hall), look for signs to **Metro** lines 1 and 2. Line 1 is handy for city-center stops, including the cruise port (Municipio), the main shopping drag (Toledo and Dante), and the Archaeological Museum (Museo). Line 2 is slightly quicker for reaching the Archaeological Museum (ride it to the Cavour stop and walk 5 minutes). For tips on navigating the Metro, see "Getting Around Naples," later.

A long row of white **taxis** line up out front. Ask the driver to charge you the fixed rate *(tariffa predeterminata)*, which should be around €7 for the old center. The TI in the station can tell you the going rate.

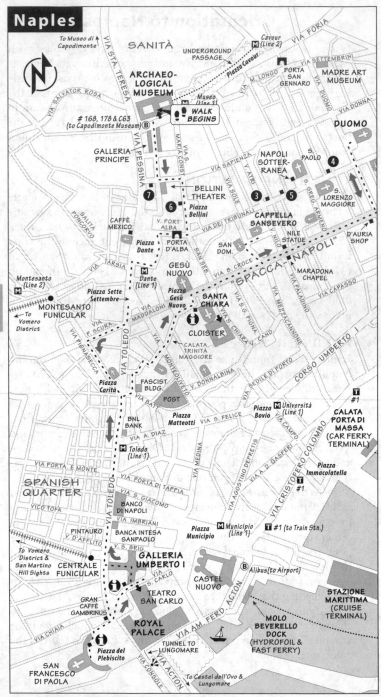

Naples

SANITÀ

To Museo di
Capodimonte

Cavour
(Line 2)

UNDERGROUND
PASSAGE

Piazza Cavour

PORTA
SAN
GENNARO

MADRE ART
MUSEUM

ARCHAEO-
LOGICAL
MUSEUM

Museo
(Line 1)

**WALK
BEGINS**

DUOMO

168, 178 & C63
(to Capodimonte Museum)

GALLERIA
PRINCIPE

S.
PAOLO

4

NAPOLI
SOTTER-
RANEA

S.
GREG. ARMENO

S.
LORENZO
MAGGIORE

BELLINI
THEATER

7

6

3

5

Piazza
Bellini

CAPPELLA
SANSEVERO

D'AURIA
SHOP

CAFFÈ
MEXICO

Piazza
Dante

PORTA
D'ALBA

NILE
STATUE

"SPACCA-NAPOLI"

MARADONA
CHAPEL

SAN
DOM.

Montesanto
(Line 2)

GESÙ
NUOVO

Piazza
Dante
(Line 1)

Piazza Sette
Settembre

MONTESANTO
FUNICULAR

To
Vomero
District

Piazza
Gesù
Nuovo

SANTA
CHIARA

CLOISTER

CALATA
TRINITÀ
MAGGIORE

Piazza
Carità

FASCIST
BLDG.

POST

Piazza
Matteotti

BNL BANK

Piazza
Bovio

Università
(Line 1)

CALATA
PORTA DI
MASSA
(CAR FERRY
TERMINAL)

#1

Piazza
Immacolatella

#1

Toleda
(Line 1)

SPANISH
QUARTER

VICO TOFA

BANCO
DI NAPOLI

BANCA INTESA
SANPAOLO

Piazza
Municipio

Municipio
(Line 1)

#1 (to Train Stn.)

PINTAURO

CENTRALE
FUNICULAR

To Vomero
District &
San Martino
Hill Sights

GALLERIA
UMBERTO I

Alibus (to Airport)

STAZIONE
MARITTIMA
(CRUISE
TERMINAL)

GRAN
CAFFÈ
GAMBRINUS

TEATRO
SAN CARLO

CASTEL
NUOVO

ROYAL
PALACE

TUNNEL TO
LUNGOMARE

MOLO
BEVERELLO
DOCK
(HYDROFOIL &
FAST FERRY)

SAN
FRANCESCO
DI PAOLA

Piazza del
Plebiscito

To Castel dell'Ovo &
Lungomare

NAPLES

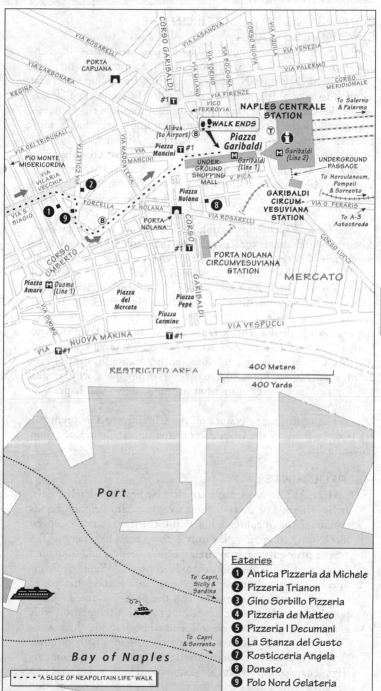

Eateries
1. Antica Pizzeria da Michele
2. Pizzeria Trianon
3. Gino Sorbillo Pizzeria
4. Pizzeria de Matteo
5. Pizzeria I Decumani
6. La Stanza del Gusto
7. Rosticceria Angela
8. Donato
9. Polo Nord Gelateria

- - - - "A SLICE OF NEAPOLITAN LIFE" WALK

CONTINUING TO POMPEII ON THE CIRCUMVESUVIANA

Naples and Pompeii are connected by a **commuter train**—the Fer-rovia Circumvesuviana—handy for tourists, commuters...and pick-pockets (www.eavsrl.it). Note: When coming from Rome, don't be tempted to take a Trenitalia connection to the stop called "Pom-pei," which leaves you at a station in the ugly, modern city center—a long walk to the actual site. It's better to simply get off at Naples' Centrale Station and transfer to the Circumvesuviana.

There are two trains per hour to Pompeii—just take any train marked for Sorrento, and get off at the stop called Pompei Scavi-Villa dei Misteri (about 40 minutes, €2.60 one-way, not covered by rail passes, skip the day pass except on weekends when it's half-price).

At Naples' Centrale Station, follow Circumvesuviana signs downstairs and down the corridor to the Circumvesuviana tick-et windows and turnstiles (no self-service ticket machines—line up). When you buy your ticket, ask which platform your train will depart from *("Quale binario?";* KWAH-lay bee-NAH-ree-oh)—trains marked Sorrento usually depart from platform 3. Insert your ticket at the turnstiles and find your platform (down another level). As you board, double-check with a local that the train goes to Pompeii, as the Circumvesuviana has several lines that branch out.

The Circumvesuviana also has another station in central Na-ples (called Napoli Porta Nolana, across from the Porta Nolana fish market), but there's no reason to use it unless you happen to be nearby.

When returning to Naples on the Circumvesuviana, remem-ber that the name of the Circumvesuviana stop at Centrale Station is "Garibaldi."

HELPFUL HINTS

Theft Alert: While most travelers visit Naples completely safely, err on the side of caution. Don't venture into neighborhoods that make you uncomfortable. While the train station has been nicely spruced up, its glow only extends for a block or so. The areas a little further away are especially seedy, and frequented by some of Italy's most downtrodden people. Walk with con-fidence, as if you know where you're going and what you're doing. Touristy Spaccanapoli and the posh Via Toledo shop-ping boulevard are more upscale, but you'll still see rowdy kids and panhandlers. Assume able-bodied beggars are thieves.

Stick to busy streets and beware of gangs of hoodlums. A third of the city is unemployed, and past local governments have set an example that the Mafia would be proud of. Assume con artists are more clever than you. Any jostle or commotion is probably a thief-team smokescreen. To keep bags safe, it's probably best to leave them back in Rome or at the left-luggage office in Centrale Station.

Always walk on the sidewalk (even if the locals don't) and carry your bag on the side away from the street—thieves on scooters have been known to snatch bags as they swoop by. The less you have dangling from you (including cameras and necklaces), the better. Keep valuables buttoned up.

Perhaps your biggest risk of theft is while catching or riding the Circumvesuviana commuter train. At the train station, carry your own bags—there are no official porters. If you're connecting from a long-distance express, you'll be going from a relatively secure compartment into an often crowded and dingy train, where disoriented tourists with luggage delicately mix with the residents of Naples' most down-and-out districts. It's prime hunting ground for thieves. While I ride the Circumvesuviana comfortably and safely, each year I hear of many travelers who get ripped off on this ride. You won't be mugged—but you may be conned or pickpocketed. Be ready for this very common trick: A team of thieves blocks the door at a stop, pretending it's stuck. While everyone rushes to try to open it, an accomplice picks their pockets. Especially late at night, the Circumvesuviana train is plagued by intimidating ruffians. For maximum safety and peace of mind, sit in the front car, where the driver will double as your protector, and avoid riding it after dark.

Traffic Safety: In Naples, red lights are discretionary, and pedestrians need to be wary, particularly of motor scooters. Even on "pedestrian" streets, stay alert to avoid being sideswiped by scooters that nudge their way through the crowds. Keep children close. Smart tourists jaywalk in the shadow of bold locals, who generally ignore crosswalks. Wait for a break in traffic, cross with confidence, and make eye contact with approaching drivers. The traffic will stop.

GETTING AROUND NAPLES

Naples' entire public transportation system—Metro, buses, funicular railways, and the single tram line—uses the same tickets, which must be stamped as you enter (in the yellow machines). A €1 single ticket *(corsa singola)* covers any ride on most modes of transportation (bus, tram, funicular, or Metro line 1), with no transfers; for Metro line 2 you need the €1.20 version (it's considered a "suburban" line). If you need to transfer, buy the €1.50 *90 minuti* ticket. Tickets are sold at *tabacchi* stores, some newsstands, clunky machines at Metro stations (coins and small bills only), and occasionally at station windows. A *giornaliero* day pass costs €3.50 (or €4.50

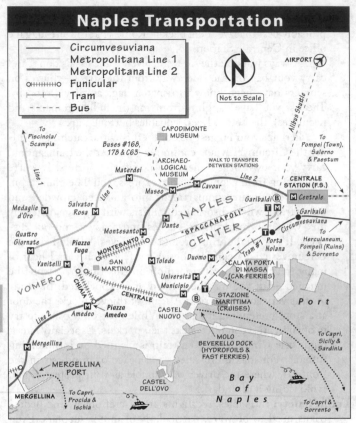

Naples Transportation

Legend:
- ——— Circumvesuviana
- ——— Metropolitana Line 1
- ——— Metropolitana Line 2
- o⊢⊢⊢⊢o Funicular
- ⊢|—|—|—⊣ Tram
- – – – Bus

N — Not to Scale

AIRPORT

To Piscinola/Scampia

Line 1

CAPODIMONTE MUSEUM

Buses #168, 178 & C63

ARCHAEO-LOGICAL MUSEUM

WALK TO TRANSFER BETWEEN STATIONS

Alibus Shuttle

To Pompei (Town), Salerno & Paestum

CENTRALE STATION (F.S.)

Materdei

Museo   Cavour   Line 2

Centrale

NAPLES

Garibaldi

Medaglie d'Oro   Salvator Rosa

Line 1

CENTER

Garibaldi

Circumvesuviana

Quattro Giornate

Montesanto   Dante

"SPACCANAPOLI"

Piazza Fuga

MONTESANTO

Porta Nolana

To Herculaneum, Pompei (Ruins) & Sorrento

Vanvitelli

SAN MARTINO

Toledo   Duomo

Tram #1

Università Municipio

CALATA PORTA DI MASSA (CAR-FERRIES)

VOMERO

CHIAIA

CENTRALE

CASTEL NUOVO

STAZIONE MARITTIMA (CRUISES)

Port

Amedeo   Piazza Amedeo

MOLO BEVERELLO DOCK (HYDROFOILS & FAST FERRIES)

To Capri, Sicily & Sardinia

Mergellina

Line 2

CASTEL DELL'OVO

Bay of Naples

MERGELLINA PORT

MERGELLINA   To Capri, Procida & Ischia

To Capri & Sorrento

NAPLES

including Metro line 2), and pays for itself quickly, but can be hard to find; many *tabacchi* stores don't sell them. For general information, maps, and fares in English, visit www.unicocampania.it. The TI hands out a good free map showing bus, Metro, and funicular routes. For schedules, your only option is the Italian-only site www.anm.it. For journey planning, use http://maps.google.com.

By Metro: Naples' subway, the *Metropolitana*, has three main lines *(linea)*. Station entrances and signs to the Metro are marked by a red square with a white *M*.

Line 1 is very useful for tourists. Starting from the train station (stop name: Garibaldi), it heads to Università (the university), Municipio (at Piazza Municipio, just above the harbor and cruise terminal), Toledo (south end of Via Toledo, near Piazza del Plebiscito), Dante (Piazza Dante), and Museo (Archaeological Museum). Four stops beyond Museo is the Vanvitelli stop, near the hilltop San Martino sights.

Line 2 (part of the Italian national rail system) is most useful for getting quickly from the train station to Piazza Cavour (a 5-minute walk from the Archaeological Museum) or Montesanto (the top of the Spanish Quarter and Spaccanapoli Street, and base of one funicular up to San Martino).

The new **line 6** may not yet be completed by the time of your visit; it will begin at Municipio and head west—unlikely to be of much use to tourists.

By Funicular: Central Naples' three funiculars *(funicolare)* carry commuters and sightseers into the hilly San Martino neighborhood just west of downtown. All three converge near Piazza Fuga, a short walk from the hilltop fortress and monastery/museum. The Centrale line runs from the Spanish Quarter, just near Piazza del Plebiscito and the Toledo Metro stop; the Montesanto line from the Montesanto Metro stop and Via Pignasecca market zone; and the Chiaia line from near the Piazza Amadeo Metro stop.

By Bus: Buses are crowded and poorly signed—not a user-friendly option for uninitiated newcomers.

By Tram: Tram line #1 runs along Corso Garibaldi (at the other end of the big square from Centrale Station) and down to the waterfront, terminating by the ferry and cruise terminals (direction: *Stazione Marittima*).

By Taxi: A short ride in town should cost €10-12. Ask for the *tariffa predeterminata* (a fixed rate). A TI can tell you the going rate for a given ride. You can also ask the driver to use the meter—for metered rides there are some legitimate extra charges (baggage fees, €2.50 supplement after 22:00 or all day Sun and holidays). Radio Taxi 8888 is one reputable company (tel. 081-8888).

Tours in Naples

Local Guides

Pina Esposito has a Ph.D. in ancient archaeology and art and does fine private walking and driving tours of Naples and the region (Pompeii, Capri, the Amalfi Coast, etc.), including Naples' Archaeological Museum (€60/hour, 2-hour minimum, 10 percent off with this book, mobile 338-763-4224, annamariaesposito1@virgilio.it).

The team at **Mondo Guide** offers private tours of the Archaeological Museum (€120/2 hours) and city (€240/4 hours), and can provide guides or drivers throughout the region (tel. 081-751-3290, www.mondoguide.com, info@mondoguide.com).

Walking Tours

Mondo Guide offers my readers special shared tours of Naples and of Pompeii, as well as other trips in the region. For details, see the sidebar.

Mondo Guide's Tours of Pompeii, Naples, the Amalfi Coast, and Capri for My Readers

Mondo Guide, a big Naples-based company, offers "shared tours" for Rick Steves readers. These include a private, professional guide at a fraction of the usual cost (because you'll be sharing the expense with other travelers using this book). A schedule of offerings is on their website, www.mondoguide. com (look for the "Shared Tours for Rick Steves" tab; use your credit card to reserve a spot, then pay cash to the guide). Pre-registration is required, and tours depart only if at least six people sign up. You'll be sent an email confirmation as soon as it's sure your tour will run. If there's not enough demand to justify the trip, they'll notify you three days before the departure date. Confirmed departures are continually updated on the website (tel. 081-751-3290, mobile 340-460-5254, info@mondoguide.com). Note that you'll have to make your own way to the starting point for each tour. Tours run April-October and include **Pompeii** (€15, doesn't include €12 Pompeii entry, daily at 11:00, 2 hours, meet in Pompeii at Hotel/Ristorante Suisse) and a walking tour of **Naples** (€25, daily at 15:00, 3 hours, meet at the steps of the Archaeological Museum—not included in the walk). They also offer an Amalfi Coast minibus tour and a Capri boat trip, both departing from Sorrento (see website for details).

Hop-On, Hop-Off Bus Tours

CitySightseeing Napoli tour buses make three different hop-on, hop-off loops through the city. Only one of these—the red line, which loops around the historical center and stops at the Archaeological Museum—is particularly helpful. The bus route will give you a sense of greater Naples that this chapter largely ignores (€22, ticket valid 24 hours, infrequent departures, buy from driver or from kiosk at Piazza Municipio in front of Castel Nuovo near the port, scant recorded narration; for details, see brochure at TI, tel. 081-551-7279, www.napoli.city-sightseeing.it). The same company offers a shorter, more frequent route around the old center in an open-top minibus (€7, €25 combo-ticket with the main route, 40-minute loop, departs in front of the Church of Gesù Nuovo).

Naples' Archaeological Museum Tour

Naples' Archaeological Museum (Museo Archeologico), worth ▲▲▲, offers the best possible peek at the art and decorations of Pompeii and Herculaneum, the two ancient burgs that were buried in ash by the eruption of Mount Vesuvius in A.D. 79. For lovers of

antiquity, this museum alone makes Naples a worthwhile stop. When Pompeii was excavated in the late 1700s, Naples' Bourbon king bellowed, "Bring me the best of what you find!" The finest art and artifacts ended up here, and today, the ancient sites themselves are impressive but barren. This self-guided tour covers the highlights.

ORIENTATION

Cost and Hours: €8, sometimes more for temporary exhibits, free first Sun of the month, Wed-Mon 9:00-19:30, closed Tue. Early and temporary closures are noted on a board near the ticket office. In July and August, expect some rooms to be closed due to lack of staff.

Getting There: To take the **Metro** *(Metropolitana)* from Centrale Station, first buy a single €1.20 transit ticket at a newsstand or tobacco shop, then follow the signs for *Metro Linea* 2 (down the stairs in front of track 13). Validate your ticket in the small yellow boxes near the escalator going down to the tracks. You're looking for line 2 trains heading in the direction of Pozzuoli (generally departing from track 4). Ride one stop to Piazza Cavour, and take the underground passage following the *Museo* signs. Or exit and walk five minutes uphill through the park along the busy street. Look for a grand old red building located up a flight of stairs at the top of the block.

You can also take the Metro's cheaper line 1 five stops from Centrale Station to Museo—it's only a little slower.

Figure on €11 for a **taxi** from the train station to the museum.

Information: The shop sells a worthwhile *National Archaeological Museum of Naples* guidebook for €12. Tel. 081-442-2149.

Tours: My self-guided tour (below) covers all the basics. For more detail, the decent audioguide costs €5 (at ticket desk). For a guided tour, book Pina Esposito (see "Tours in Naples," earlier).

Baggage Check: Bag check is obligatory and free.

Photography: Photos are allowed without a flash.

Eating: The museum has no café, but vending machines sell drinks and snacks. There are several good places to grab a meal within a few blocks; see page 479.

SELF-GUIDED TOUR

Entering the museum, stand at the base of the grand staircase. To your right, on the ground floor, are the larger-than-life statues of the Farnese Collection, starring the *Toro Farnese* and the *Farnese Hercules*. Up the stairs on the mezzanine level are mosaics and frescoes from Pompeii, including the Secret Room of erotic art. On the top floor are more frescoes, a scale model of Pompeii, and bronze statues from Herculaneum. WCs are behind the staircase.

• *From the base of the grand staircase, turn right through the door marked* Collezione Farnese *and wind to the far end—walking through a rich collection of idealistic and realistic ancient portrait busts. Stop in the farthest room (Sala XIII).*

Ground Floor: The Farnese Collection

The museum's ground floor alone has enough Greek and Roman art to put it on the map. This floor has nothing from Pompeii; its highlight is the Farnese Collection, a grand hall of huge, bright, and wonderfully restored statues excavated from Rome's Baths of Caracalla. Peruse the larger-than-life statues filling the hall. They were dug up in the 1540s at the behest of Alessandro Farnese (by then Pope Paul III) while he was building the family palace on the Campo de' Fiori in Rome. His main purpose in excavating the baths was to scavenge quality building stone. The sculptures were a nice extra and helped the palace come in under budget on decorations. In the 1700s, the collection ended up in the hands of Charles, the Bourbon king of Naples (whose mother was a Farnese). His son, the next king, had it brought to Naples.

• *Quick—look down to the left end of the hall. There's a woman being tied to a snorting bull.*

The tangled ***Toro Farnese*** tells a thrilling Greek myth. At 13 feet, it's the tallest ancient marble group ever found, and the largest intact statue from antiquity. A third-century A.D. copy of a lost bronze Hellenistic original, it was carved out of one piece of marble. Michelangelo and others "restored" it at the pope's request—meaning that they integrated surviving bits into a new work. Panels on the wall show which pieces were actually carved by Michelangelo (in blue on the chart): the head of the woman in back, the torso of the aunt under the bull, and the dog. (Imagine how the statue would stand out if it were thoughtfully lit and not surrounded by white walls.)

Here's the tragic story behind the statue: Once upon an ancient Greek time, King Lycus was bewitched by Dirce. He abandoned his pregnant wife, Antiope (standing regally in the background). The single mom gave birth to twin boys. When they grew up, they killed their deadbeat dad and tied Dirce to the horns of a bull to be bashed against a mountain. Captured in marble, the action is thrilling: cape flailing, dog snarling, hooves in the air. You can almost hear the bull snorting. And in the back, Antiope oversees this harsh ancient justice with satisfaction.

At the opposite end of the hall stands the ***Farnese Hercules***. The great Greek hero is exhausted. He leans wearily on his club (draped with his lion skin) and bows his head. He's just finished the daunting Eleventh Labor, having traveled the world, fought men and gods, freed Prometheus from his rock, and carried Atlas' weight of the world on his shoulders. Now he's returned with the prize: the golden apples of the gods, which he cups behind his back. But, after all that, he's just been told he has to return the apples and do one final labor: descend into hell itself. Oh, man.

The 10-foot colossus is a third-century A.D. Roman marble copy (signed by "Glykon") of a fourth-century B.C. Greek bronze original (probably by Lysippos). The statue was enormously famous in its day. Dozens of copies—some marble, some bronze—have been found in Roman villas and baths. This version was unearthed in Rome's Baths of Caracalla in 1546, along with the *Toro Farnese*.

The *Farnese Hercules* was equally famous in the 16th-18th centuries. Tourists flocked to Rome to admire it, art students studied it from afar in prints, Louis XIV made a copy for Versailles, and petty nobles everywhere put small-scale knock-offs in their gardens. This curly-haired version of Hercules became the modern world's image of the Greek hero.

• *Backtrack to the main entry hall, then head up to the mezzanine level (turn left at the lion and go under the* Mosaici *sign).*

Mezzanine: Pompeiian Mosaics and the Secret Room

Most of these mosaics—of animals, musicians, and geometric designs—were taken from Pompeii's House of the Faun (see page 491). Walk into the third room and look for the 20-inch-high statue in a freestanding glass case: the house's delightful centerpiece, the ***Dancing Faun***. This rare surviving Greek bronze statue (from the fourth century B.C.) is surrounded by some of the best mosaics of that age.

A museum highlight, just beyond the statue, is the grand

Battle of Alexander, a second-century B.C. copy of the original Greek fresco, done a century earlier. It decorated a floor in the House of the Faun and was found intact; the damage you see occurred as this treasure was moved from Pompeii to the king's collection here. Alexander (left side of the scene, with curly hair and sideburns)

is about to defeat the Persians under Darius (central figure, in chariot with turban and beard). This pivotal victory allowed Alexander to quickly overrun much of Asia (331 B.C.). Alexander is the only one without a helmet...a confident master of the battlefield while

everyone else is fighting for their lives, eyes bulging with fear. Notice how the horses, already in retreat, add to the scene's propaganda value. Notice also the shading and perspective, which Renaissance artists would later work so hard to accomplish. (A modern reproduction of the mosaic is now back in Pompeii, at the House of the Faun.)

Farther on, the **Secret Room (Gabinetto Segreto)** contains a sizable assortment of erotic frescoes, well-hung pottery, and perky statues that once decorated bedrooms, meeting rooms, brothels, and even shops at Pompeii and Herculaneum. These bawdy statues and frescoes—many of them once displayed in Pompeii's grandest houses—were entertainment for guests. (By the time they made it to this museum, in 1819, the frescoes could be viewed only with permission from the king—see the letters in the glass case just outside the door.) The Roman nobles commissioned the wildest scenes imaginable. Think of them as ancient dirty jokes.

At the entrance, you're enthusiastically greeted by big stone penises that once projected over Pompeii's doorways. A massive phallus was not necessarily a sexual symbol, but a magical amulet used against the "evil eye." It symbolized fertility, happiness, good luck, riches, straight A's, and general well-being.

Circulating counterclockwise through this section, look for the following: a faun playfully pulling the sheet off a beautiful woman, only to be grossed out by a hermaphrodite's plumbing (perhaps the original *"Mamma mia!";* #12); horny pygmies from Africa in action (#27); a toga with an embarrassing bulge (#34); a particularly high-quality statue of a goat and a satyr engaging in a lewd act

(#36); and, watching over it all with remarkable aplomb, Venus, the patron goddess of Pompeii (#39).

The back room is furnished and decorated the way an ancient brothel might have been. The 10 frescoes on the wall functioned as both a menu of services offered and as a kind of *Kama Sutra* of sex positions. The glass cases contain more phallic art.

• *So, now that your travel buddy is finally showing a little interest in art...finish up your visit by climbing the stairs to the top floor.*

Top Floor: Frescoes, Statues, Artifacts, and a Model of Pompeii

At the top of the stairs, go through the center door to enter a grand, empty hall. (If the doors are locked, circle around through the side wing.) This was the **great hall** of the university (17th and 18th centuries) until the building became the royal museum in 1777. Walk to the center. The sundial (from 1791) still works. Look up to the far-right corner of the hall and find the tiny pinhole. At noon (13:00 in summer), a ray of sun enters the hall and strikes the sundial, showing the time of the year...if you know your zodiac.

To your left, you'll see a door marked *affreschi*. This leads to eight rooms showing off the museum's impressive and well-described collection of (nonerotic) **frescoes** taken from the walls of Pompeii villas. Pompeiians loved to decorate their homes with scenes from mythology (Hercules' labors, Venus and Mars in love), landscapes, everyday market scenes, and faux architecture. Continue around this wing counterclockwise (with the courtyard on your left) through rooms of artifacts found at Pompeii. Look for the famous portrait of baker Terentius Neo and his wife in Room LXXVIII. At the far end is a scale model of Pompeii as excavated in 1879 *(plastic di Pompell)*. Another model (on the wall) shows the site in 2004, after more excavations.

• *Eventually you'll end up back in the great hall.*

Step out to the top landing of the staircase you climbed earlier. Turn left and go down, then up, 16 steps and into the wing labeled *La Villa dei Papiri*. This exhibition shows off artifacts (particularly bronze statues) from the Herculaneum holiday home of Julius Caesar's father-in-law. In the second room (numbered CXVI), look into the lifelike blue eyes of the intense *Corridore* (athletes), bent

on doing their best. The *Five Dancers*, with their inlaid-ivory eyes and graceful poses, decorated a portico. The next room (CXVII) has more fine works: *Resting Hermes* (with his tired little heel wings) is taking a break. Nearby, the *Drunken Faun* (singing and snapping his fingers to the beat, a wineskin at his side) is clearly living for today—true to the *carpe diem* preaching of the Epicurean philosophy. Caesar's father-in-law was a fan of Epicurean philosophy, and his library—containing 2,000 papyrus scrolls—supported his outlook. Back by the entrance, check out the plans of the villa, and in the side room, see how the half-burned scrolls were unrolled and (with luck) read after excavation in the 1750s.

• *Return to the ground floor. The exit hall (right) leads around the museum courtyard and to the gift shop.*

Doriforo

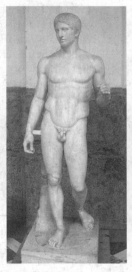

For extra credit on your way out, find *Doriforo*. He was last spotted on the right as you walk down the exit hall. (If he's been moved, ask a guard, *"Dov'è il Doriforo?"*) This seven-foot-tall "spear-carrier" (the literal translation of *doriforo*) just stands there, as if holding a spear. What's the big deal about this statue, which looks like so many others? It's a marble replica made by the Romans of one of the most-copied statues of antiquity, a fifth-century B.C. bronze Greek original by Polyclitus. This copy once stood in a Pompeii gym, where it inspired ancient athletes by showing the ideal proportions of Greek beauty. So full of motion, and so realistic in its *contrapposto* pose (weight on one foot), the *Doriforo* would later inspire Donatello and Michelangelo, helping to trigger the Renaissance. And so the glories of ancient Pompeii, once buried and forgotten, live on today.

Naples Walk

This self-guided walk, worth ▲▲▲, takes you from the Archaeological Museum through the heart of town and back to Centrale Station. Allow at least three hours, plus time for pizza and sightseeing stops. If you're in a rush, do it in half the time by walking briskly and skipping Part 2. To trace the route, see the map on page 452.

Naples, a living medieval city, is its own best sight. Couples artfully make love on Vespas surrounded by more fights and smiles per cobblestone than anywhere else in Italy. Rather than seeing Naples as a list of sights, visit its one great museum and then capture its essence by taking this walk through the core of the city.

Part 1: From the Archaeological Museum to Piazza Bellini and Piazza Dante

The first two parts of this walk are a mostly straight one-mile ramble down a fine boulevard (with a few colorful detours) to the waterfront at Piazza del Plebiscito. Your starting point is the Archaeological Museum (at the top of Piazza Cavour, Metro: Cavour or Museo; for a self-guided tour of the museum, see earlier). As you stroll, remember that here in Naples, red traffic lights are considered "decorations." When crossing a street, try to draft behind a native.

• *From the door of the Archaeological Museum, cross the street, veer right, and enter the fancy mall. (If the mall is closed for renovation, simply loop around the block to its back door.)*

Galleria Principe di Napoli: This was named for the first male child of the royal Savoy family, the Prince of Naples. Walk

directly through it, enjoying this fine shopping gallery from the late 19th century, similar to those popular in Paris and London. In the US, we call this style Art Nouveau; in Italy it's "Liberty Style," named for a British department store that was in vogue at a time when Naples was nicknamed the "Paris of the South." Parisian artist Edgar Degas left Paris to adopt Naples—which he actually considered more cosmopolitan and sophisticated—as his hometown.

• *Leaving the gallery through the opposite end, walk one block downhill. At Via Conte di Ruvo, head left, passing the fine Bellini Theater (also in the Liberty Style). After one block, turn right on Via Costantinopoli, continuing directly downhill to Piazza Bellini. As you walk, look up to enjoy architecture built in the late 19th century, when Naples was the last stop on Romantic Age travelers' Grand Tour of Europe. (From a tourism perspective, Sorrento only rose with the cultural and economic fall of Naples in the decades following Italian independence, around the early 20th century.)*

Soon you'll run into the ragtag urban park called...

Piazza Bellini: Walking between columns of two grand churches, suddenly you're in neighborhood Napoli. A statue of Sicilian opera composer Vincenzo Bellini, who worked in Naples in the early 1800s, marks the center of the park. Survey the many balconies—and the people who use them as a "backyard" in this densely packed city. The apartment blocks were originally the palaces of noble families, as indicated by the stately family crests above grand doorways. At the downhill end of the square, peer down into the sunken area to see the ruined Greek walls: tuff blocks without mortar. This was the wall, and you're standing on land that was outside of the town. You can see the street level from the fifth century B.C., when Neapolis—literally, "the new city"—was founded. For 2,500 years, laundry has blown in the breeze right here.

• *Walk 30 yards downhill. Stop at the horseshoe-shaped Port'Alba gate (on the right). Spin slowly 360 degrees and take in the scene. The proud tile across the street (upstairs, between the two balconies) shows Piazza Bellini circa 1890. Learn to ignore graffiti (as the locals do). Pass through the gate, and stroll past the book stalls down Via Port'Alba to the next big square...*

Piazza Dante: This square is marked by a statue of Dante, the medieval poet. Fittingly, half the square is devoted to bookstores. Old Dante looks out over an urban area that was once grand, then chaotic, and is now slowly becoming grand again.

Originally, a statue of a Spanish Bourbon king stood in the square. (The grand orange-and-gray building is typical of Bourbon structures from that period.) But with the unification of Italy, the king, symbolic of Naples' colonial subjugation, was replaced by Dante, the father of the unified Italian language—a strong symbol of nationalism.

The Neapolitan people are survivors. A long history of corrupt and greedy colonial overlords (German, Norman, French, Austrian, and Spanish) has taught Neapolitans to deal creatively with authority. Many credit this aspect of Naples' past for the strength of organized crime here.

Across the street, **Caffè Mexico** (at #86) is an institution known for its espresso, which is served already sweetened—ask for *senza zucchero* if you don't want sugar (pay first, then take receipt to the counter and hand it over). Most Italians agree that Neapolitan coffee is the best anywhere.

• *Walk downhill on...*

Via Toledo: The long, straight street heading downhill from Piazza Dante is Naples' principal shopping drag. It originated as a military road built under Spanish rule (hence the name) in the 16th century. Via Toledo skirted the old town wall to connect the Spanish military headquarters (now the museum where you started this walk) with the Royal Palace (down by the bay, where you're heading). As you stroll, peek into the many lovely atriums, which provide a break from the big street.

After a couple of hundred yards, you'll reach **Piazza Sette Settembre.** In 1860, from the white marble balcony of the Neoclassical building overlooking the square, the famous revolutionary Giuseppe Garibaldi declared Italy united and Victor Emmanuel II its first king. Only in 1870, a decade later, was the dream of Italian unity fully realized when Rome fell to unification forces.

• *Continue straight on Via Toledo. About three blocks below Piazza Dante and a block past Piazza Sette Settembre, you'll come to Via Maddaloni, which marks the start of the long, straight, narrow street nicknamed...*

Spaccanapoli: Before crossing the street—whose name translates as "split Naples"—look left (toward the train station).

Then look right (to see San Martino hill rising steeply above the center). Since ancient times, this thin street has bisected the city. It changes names several times: Via Maddaloni (as it's called here), Via B. Croce, Via S. Biagio dei Librai, and Via Vicaria Vecchia. We'll return to this intersection later.

• *If you want to abbreviate this walk, turn left here and skip ahead to Part 3. Part 2, described next, is a bit of a detour, and requires backtracking uphill (or a short taxi ride) later. But if you have time, it's worth the effort.*

Part 2: Monumental Naples (Via Toledo, the Spanish Quarter, and Piazza del Plebiscito)

• *We'll detour off of Via Toledo for just a couple of blocks (rejoining it later). At the Spaccanapoli intersection, go right (toward the church facade on the hill, up Via Pasquale Scura). After about 100 yards, you hit a busy intersection. Stop. You're on one of Naples' most colorful open-air market streets...*

Via Pignasecca Market: Snoop around from here if you are so inclined. Then, turn left down Via Pignasecca and stroll this colorful strip. You'll pass meat and fish stalls, produce stands, street-food vendors, and much more. This is a taste of Naples' famous Spanish Quarter, which we'll experience more of later in this walk.

• *Via Pignasecca meets back up with Via Toledo at the square called...*

Piazza Carità: This square, built for an official visit by Hitler to Mussolini in 1938, is full of stern, straight, obedient lines. The big building belonged to an insurance company. (For the best example of fascist architecture in town, take a slight detour from here: With your back to Via Toledo, leave Piazza Carità downhill on the right-hand corner and walk a block to the Poste e Telegrafi building. There you'll see several government buildings with stirring reliefs singing the praises of lobotomized workers and a totalitarian society.)

In Naples—long a poor and rough city—rather than being heroic, people learn from the cradle the art of survival. The modern memorial statue in the center of the square celebrates **Salvo d'Acquisto,** a rare hometown hero. In 1943, he was executed after falsely confessing to sabotage...in order to save 22 fellow Italian soldiers from a Nazi revenge massacre.

• *From Piazza Carità, continue south down Via Toledo for a few blocks, looking to your left for more...*

Fascist Architecture (Banks): You can't miss the two big, blocky bank buildings. First comes the chalky-white BNL Bank.

A bit farther down, past the Metro, imagine trying to rob the even more imposing Banco di Napoli (Via Toledo 178). Step across the street and check out its architecture: typical fascist arches and reliefs, built to celebrate the bank's 400th anniversary (est. 1539—how old is *your* bank?).

The street here was pedestrianized after the Toledo Metro stop opened in 2012. Now the street is even more popular for strolling, property values have risen, and international brands have moved in.

• *On the next block (at #184) is the...*

Banca Intesa Sanpaolo: This fills an older palace—take a free peek at the opulent atrium. In the entry hall, you can buy a ticket for the **Galleria d'Italia Palazzo Zevallos Stigliano,** a small collection located in the upper two floors. The gallery's only piece worth seeing—on the second floor—is a great late Caravaggio painting. *The Martyrdom of Saint Ursula* shows a terrible scene: His marriage proposal rejected, the king of the Huns shoots an arrow into Ursula's chest. Blood spurts, Ursula is stunned but accepts her destiny sweetly, and Caravaggio himself—far right, his last self-portrait—screams to symbolize the rejection of evil. The rest of the second floor holds opulent chandeliered apartments, a few Neapolitan landscapes, and little else. The first floor has temporary exhibits (€5, closed Mon; entry includes audioguide, a look at old Naples paintings, and a fine WC).

• *Feeling bold? From here, side-trip uphill a couple of blocks into the...*

Spanish Quarter: This is a classic world of *basso* (low) living. The streets—which were laid out in the 16th century for the Spanish military barracks outside the city walls—are unbelievably narrow

(and cool in summer), and the buildings rise five stories high. In such tight quarters, life—flirting, fighting, playing, and loving—happens in the road. This is *the* cliché of life in Naples, as shown in so many movies. The Spanish Quarter is Naples at its most characteristic. The shopkeepers are friendly, and the mopeds are bold (watch out). Concerned locals will tug on their lower eyelids, warning you to be wary. Hungry? Pop into a grocery shop and ask the clerk to make you his best prosciutto-and-mozzarella sandwich (the price should be about €4).

• *Return to Via Toledo and work your way down. Near the bottom of the street, on the right at #275, is* **Pintauro,** *a takeaway bakery famous for its* sfogliatelle. *These classic, ricotta-filled Neapolitan pastries are often served warm from the oven and make a tasty €2 treat.*

Just beyond, on the right, notice the station for the **Centrale funicular.** *If you have extra time and enjoy city views, this can take you sweat-free up to the top of San Martino, the hill with a fortress and a monastery/museum looming over town. Across the street is the impressive Galleria Umberto I—but don't go in now, as you'll see it in a minute from the other side.*

For now, just keep heading down the main drag and through the smaller Piazza Trieste e Trento to the immense...

Piazza del Plebiscito: This square celebrates the 1861 vote (*plebiscito*, plebiscite) in which Naples chose to join Italy. Dominating the top of the square is the Church of San Francesco di Paola, with its Pantheon-inspired dome and broad, arcing colonnades. If it's open, step inside to ogle the vast interior—a Neo-

classical re-creation of one of ancient Rome's finest buildings (free, daily 8:30-12:00 & 16:00-19:00).

• *Opposite is the...*

Royal Palace (Palazzo Reale): Having housed Spanish, French, and even Italian royalty, this building displays statues of all those who stayed here. Look for eight kings in the niches, each from a different dynasty (left to right): Norman, German, French, Spanish, Spanish, Spanish,

French (Napoleon's brother-in-law), and, finally, Italian—Victor Emmanuel II, King of Savoy. The statues were done at the request of V. E. II's son, so his dad is the most dashing of the group.

• *Continue 50 yards past the Royal Palace (toward the trees) to enjoy a...*

Fine Harbor View: While boats busily serve Capri and Sorrento, Mount Vesuvius smolders ominously in the distance. Look

back to see the vast "Bourbon red" palace—its color inspired by Pompeii. The hilltop above Piazza del Plebiscito is San Martino, with its Carthusian monastery-turned-museum and Castle of St. Elmo. The promenade you're on continues to Naples' romantic harborfront—the fishermen's quarter (Borgo Marinaro)—a fortified island connected to the mainland by a stout causeway, with its fanciful, ancient Castel dell'Ovo (Egg Castle) and trendy harborside restaurants. Farther along the harborfront stretches the Lungomare promenade and Santa Lucia district.

• *Head back through the piazza and pop into...*

Gran Caffè Gambrinus: This coffee house, facing the piazza, takes you back to the elegance of 1860. It's a classic place to sample a crispy *sfogliatella* pastry, or perhaps the mushroom-shaped, rum-soaked bread-like cakes called *babà*, which come in a huge variety. Stand at the bar *(banco)*, pay double to sit *(tavola)*, or just wander around as you imagine the café buzzing with the ritzy intellectuals, journalists, and artsy bohemian types who munched on *babà* here during Naples' 19th-century heyday.

• *A block away, tucked behind the palace, you can peek inside the Neoclassical...*

Teatro di San Carlo: Built in 1737, 41 years before Milan's La Scala, this is Europe's oldest opera house and Italy's second-most-respected (after La Scala). The theater burned down in 1816, and was rebuilt within the year.

Beyond Teatro di San Carlo and the Royal Palace is the huge, harborfront **Castel Nuovo,** which houses government bureaucrats and the **Civic Museum.** It feels like a mostly empty shell, with a couple of dusty halls of Neapolitan art, but the views over the bay from the upper terraces are impressive (€6, Mon-Sat 8:30-19:00, closed Sun).

Cross the street from Teatro di San Carlo and go through the tall yellow arch into the Victorian iron and glass of the 100-year-old shopping mall, **Galleria Umberto I.** It was built in 1892 to reinvigorate the district after a devastating cholera epidemic occurred here. Gawk up, then walk left to bring you back out on Via Toledo.

• *For Part 3 of this walk, double back up Via Toledo to Piazza Carità, veering right (just above the first big fascist-style building we saw earlier) on Via Morgantini through Piazza Monteoliveto. Cross the busy street, then angle up Calata Trinità Maggiore to the fancy column at the top of the hill. (To avoid the backtracking and uphill walk, catch a €10 taxi to the Church of Gesù Nuovo—JAY-zoo noo-OH-voh.)*

Part 3: Spaccanapoli Back to the Station

You're back at the straight-as-a-Greek-arrow Spaccanapoli, formerly the main thoroughfare of the Greek city of Neapolis.

• *Stop at...*

Piazza Gesù Nuovo: This square is marked by a towering 18th-century Baroque monument to the Counter-Reformation.

Although the Jesuit order was powerful in Naples because of its Spanish heritage, locals never attacked Protestants here with the full fury of the Spanish Inquisition.

If you'd like, you can visit two bulky old churches, starting with the dark, fortress-like, 17th-century **Church of Gesù Nuovo,** followed by the simpler **Church of Santa Chiara** (in the courtyard across the street). Both are described in more detail later, under "Sights in Naples."

• *After touring the churches, continue along the main drag. Since this is a university district, you'll see lots of students and bookstores. This neighborhood is also famously superstitious. Look for incense-burning women with carts full of good-luck charms for sale.*

Farther down Spaccanapoli—passing Palazzo Venezia, the embassy of Venice to Naples when both were independent powers—you'll see the next square...

Piazza San Domenico Maggiore: This square is marked by an ornate 17th-century monument built to thank God for ending the plague. From this square, detour left along the right side of the castle-like church, then follow yellow signs, taking the first right and walking one block to the remarkable **Cappella Sansevero.** This Baroque chapel is well worth visiting (described later, under "Sights in Naples").

• *After touring the chapel, return to Via B. Croce (a.k.a. Spaccanapoli), turn left, and continue your cultural scavenger hunt. At the intersection of Via Nilo, find the...*

Statue of the Nile (on the left): A reminder of the multiethnic makeup of Greek Neapolis, this statue is in what was once the Egyptian quarter. Locals like to call this statue *The Body of Naples*, with the overflowing cornucopia symbolizing the abundance of their fine city. (I once asked a Neapolitan man to describe the local women, who are famous for their beauty, in one word. He replied simply, "Abundant.") This intersection is considered the center of old Naples.

• *Directly opposite the statue, inside of Bar Nilo, is the...*

"Chapel of Maradona": The small "chapel" on the right wall is dedicated to Diego Maradona, a soccer star who played for Naples in the 1980s. Locals consider soccer almost a religion, and this guy was practically a deity. You can even see a "hair of Diego" and a teardrop from the city when he went to another team for more money. Unfortunately, his reputation has since been sullied by problems he's had with organized crime, drugs, and police. Perhaps inspired by Maradona's example, the coffee bar has posted a quadrilingual sign (though, strangely, not in English) threatening that those who take a picture without buying a cup of coffee may find their camera damaged...*Capisce?*

• *As you continue, you'll begin to see shops selling...*

Presepi* (Nativity Scenes) and *Corno*:** Just as many Americans keep an eye out year-round for Christmas-tree ornaments, Italians regularly add pieces to the family ***presepe, the centerpiece of their holiday decorations. Stop after a few blocks at the tiny square, where Via San Gregorio Armeno leads left into a colorful district with the highest concentration of shops selling fantastic *presepi* and their tiny components, including figurines caricaturing local politicians and celebrities. Some even move around.

Another popular Naples souvenir that you'll see sold here—and all over the city—is the ***corno***, a skinny, twisted, red horn that resembles a chili pepper. The *corno* comes with a double symbolism for fertility: It's a horn of plenty, and it's also a phallic symbol turned upside-down. Neapolitans explain that fertility isn't sexual; it provides the greatest gift a person can give—life—and it ensures that one's soul will live on through the next generation. Interestingly, in today's Naples just as in yesterday's Pompeii (where bulging erections greeted visitors at the entrance to a home), fertility is equated with good luck.

Back on Spaccanapoli and a bit farther along, on the right at #87, the **D'Auria** shop sells some of the best-quality *presepi* in town, many of them the classy *campane* version, under a glass bell.

• *As Via B. Croce becomes Via S. Biagio dei Librai, notice the...*

Gold and Silver Shops: Some say stolen jewelry ends up here, is melted down immediately, and gets resold in some other form as soon as it cools. Look for *compro oro* ("I buy gold") signs (for example, in the window of the shop at #95)—a sign of Italy's economic tough times.

• *Cross busy Via Duomo. If you have time and aren't already churched out, consider detouring five minutes north (left) up Via Duomo to visit Naples' **Duomo**; just around the corner is the **Pio Monte della Misericordia Church**, with a fine Caravaggio painting (both described later, under "Sights in Naples"). Afterward, continue straight along Via Vicaria Vecchia. As you stroll, ponder Naples' vibrant...*

Street Life, Past and Present: Here along Via Vicaria Vecchia, the street and side-street scenes intensify. The area is said to be a center of the Camorra (organized crime), but as a tourist, you won't notice. Paint a picture with these thoughts: Naples has the most intact street plan of any surviving ancient Greek or Roman city. Imagine this city during those times (and retain these images as you visit Pompeii), with streetside shop fronts that close up after dark, and private homes on upper floors. What you see today is just one more page in a 2,000-year-old story of a city: all kinds of meetings, beatings, and cheatings; kisses, near misses, and little-boy pisses.

You name it, it occurs right on the streets today, as it has since ancient times. People ooze from crusty corners. Black-and-

white death announcements add to the clutter on the walls. Widows sell cigarettes from buckets. For a peek behind the scenes in the shade of wet laundry, venture down a few side streets. Buy two carrots as a gift for the woman on the fifth floor, if she'll lower her bucket to pick them up. The neighborhood action seems best at about 18:00.

A few blocks on, at the tiny fenced-in triangle of greenery, hang out for a few minutes to just observe the crazy motorbike action and teen scene.

• *From here, veer right onto Via Forcella (which leads to the busy boulevard that takes you to Centrale Station). A block down, a tiny, fenced-in traffic island protects a chunk of the ancient Greek wall of Neapolis. Turn right here on Via Pietro Colletta, walk 40 yards, and step into the North Pole, at the...*

Polo Nord Gelateria: The oldest *gelateria* in Naples has had four generations of family working here since 1931. Before you order, sample a few flavors, including their *bacio* or "kiss" flavor (chocolate and hazelnut)—all are made fresh daily (Via Pietro Colletta 41). Via Pietro Colletta leads past two of Napoli's most competitive **pizzerias** (see "Eating in Naples," later) to Corso Umberto I.

• *Turn left on the grand boulevard-like Corso Umberto I. From here to Centrale Station, it's at least a 10-minute walk (if you're tired, hop on a bus; they all go to the station). To finish the walk, continue on Corso Umberto I—past a gauntlet of purse/CD/sunglasses salesmen and shady characters hawking stolen mobile phones—to the vast* **Piazza Garibaldi,** *with a shiny new modern canopy in the middle. On the far side is the station. You made it.*

Sights in Naples

The following churches are linked—in this order—on Part 3 of my self-guided walk, earlier. The fish market is located near the end of the walk.

▲Church of Gesù Nuovo

This church's unique pyramid-grill facade survives from a fortified 15th-century noble palace. Step inside for a brilliant Neapolitan Baroque interior. The second chapel on the right features a much-adored **statue of St. Giuseppe Moscati** (1880-1927), a Christian doctor famous for helping the poor. In 1987, Moscati became the first modern doctor to be canonized. Sit and watch a steady stream of Neapolitans taking turns to kiss and touch the altar, then hold the good doctor's highly polished hand.

Continue on to the third chapel and enter the **Sale Moscati.** Look high on the walls of this long room to see hundreds of "Ex Votos"—tiny red-and-silver plaques of thanksgiving for prayers answered with the help of St. Moscati (each has a symbol of the ailment cured). Naples' practice of using Ex Votos, while incorporated into its Catholic rituals, goes back to its pagan Greek roots. Rooms from Moscati's nearby apartment are on display, and a glass case shows possessions and photos of the great doctor. As you leave the Sale Moscati, notice the big bomb casing that hangs high in the left corner. It fell through the church's dome in 1943, but caused almost no damage...yet another miracle.

Cost and Hours: Free, daily 6:45-13:00 & 16:00-19:30, Piazza del Gesù Nuovo, www.gesunuovo.it.

Church of Santa Chiara

Dating from the 14th century, this church is from a period of French royal rule under the Angevin dynasty. Consider the stark contrast between this church (Gothic) and the Gesù Nuovo (Baroque), across the street. Inside, look for the faded Trinity on the back wall (on the right as you face the door, under the stone canopy), which shows a dove representing the Holy Spirit between the heads of God the Father and Christ (c. 1414). This is an example of the fine frescoes that once covered the walls. Most were stuccoed over during Baroque times or destroyed in 1943 by Allied bombs. Continuing down the main aisle, you'll step over a huge inlaid-marble Angevin coat of arms on the floor. The altar is adorned with four finely carved Gothic tombs of Angevin kings. A chapel stacked with Bourbon royalty is just to the right.

Cost and Hours: Free, daily 7:30-13:00 & 16:30-20:00, Piazza del Gesù Nuovo, www.monasterodisantachiara.com. Its tranquil cloistered courtyard, around back, is not worth its €6 entry fee.

▲▲Cappella Sansevero

This small chapel is a Baroque explosion mourning the body of Christ, who lies on a soft pillow under an incredibly realistic veil (by Giuseppe "Howdeedoodat" Sammartino, 1753). It's also the personal chapel of Raimondo de Sangro, an eccentric Freemason, containing his tomb and the tombs of his family. Raimondo's mom and dad are buried on either side of the main altar, and Raimondo himself lies buried in a side altar (on the right). Like other 18th-century Enlightenment figures, Raimondo was a wealthy man of letters, scientist and inventor, and patron of the arts—and he was also a grand master of the Freemasons of the Kingdom of Naples.

His chapel—filled with Masonic symbolism—is a complex ensemble, with statues representing virtues such as self-control, religious zeal, and the Masonic philosophy of freedom through enlightenment. Among Raimondo's inventions was the deep-green pigment used on the ceiling fresco. The inlaid M. C. Escher-esque maze on the floor around de Sangro's tomb is a Freemason reminder of how the quest for knowledge gets you out of the maze of life. This tilework once covered the floor of the entire chapel. Downstairs, see two mysterious skeletons Raimondo created to illustrate how the circulatory system works. Though it's a pricey private enterprise, the chapel is worth a visit.

Cost and Hours: €7, buy tickets at office at the corner, Wed-Mon 9:30-18:30, closed Tue, no photos, Via de Sanctis 19, tel. 081-551-8470, www.museosansevero.it. Pick up the free floor plan, which identifies each of the statues lining the nave.

▲Duomo

Naples' historic cathedral, built by imported French Anjou kings in the 14th century, boasts a breathtaking Neo-Gothic facade.

Step into the vast interior to see the mix of styles along the side chapels—from pointy Gothic arches to rounded Renaissance ones to gilded Baroque decor. Explore the two largest side chapels—each is practically a church in its own right. On the left, the **Chapel of St. Restituta** stands on the site of the original, early-Christian church that predated the cathedral. On the right is the **Chapel of San Gennaro**—dedicated to the beloved patron saint of Naples—decorated with silver busts of centuries of bishops, and seven paintings done on bronze. The stairs beneath the altar take you to a **crypt** with the relics of St. Gennaro and (across the room) a statue of the bishop who rescued the relics from a rival town and returned them to Naples.

Cost and Hours: Free, Mon-Sat 8:30-13:30 & 14:30-20:00, Sun 8:30-13:30 & 16:30-19:30, Via Duomo.

Pio Monte della Misericordia

This small church (near the Duomo, and run by a charitable foundation) displays one of the best works by Caravaggio, *The Seven Works of Mercy*, which hangs over the main altar in a humble gray chapel. It's well lit, allowing Caravaggio's characteristically dark canvas to really pop. In one crowded canvas, the great early-Baroque artist illustrates seven virtues: burying the dead (the man carrying a corpse by the ankles); visiting the imprisoned and feeding the hungry (Pero breastfeeding her starving father—a scene from a famous Roman story); sheltering the homeless (a pilgrim on the Camino de Santiago, with his floppy hat, negotiates with an innkeeper); caring for the sick and clothing the naked (St. Martin offers part of his cloak to the injured man in the foreground); and giving drink to the thirsty (Samson chugs from a jawbone in the background)—all of them set in a dark Neapolitan alley and watched over by Mary, Jesus, and a pair of angels.

Cost and Hours: €7, includes audioguide, Thu-Tue 9:00-14:30, closed Wed, Via dei Tribunali 253, tel. 081-446-944, www.piomontedellamisericordia.it.

Porta Nolana Open-Air Fish Market

Naples' fish market squirts and stinks as it has for centuries under the Porta Nolana (gate in the city wall), immediately in front of the

Napoli Porta Nolana Circumvesuviana station and four long blocks from Centrale Station. Of the town's many boisterous outdoor markets, this will net you the most photos and memories. From Piazza Nolana, wander under the medieval gate and take your first left down Vico Sopramuro, enjoying this wild and entirely edible cultural scavenger hunt (Tue-Sun 8:00-14:00, closed Mon).

Eating in Naples

NAPLES

CHEAP AND FAMOUS PIZZA

Naples is the birthplace of pizza. Its pizzerias bake just the right combination of fresh dough (soft and chewy, as opposed to Roman-style, which is thin and crispy), mozzarella, and tomatoes in traditional wood-burning ovens. You can head for the famous, venerable places (I've listed five below), but these can have long lines stretching out the door, and half-hour waits for a table. If you want to skip

the hassle, just ask a local for directions to the neighborhood pizzeria. An average one-person pie (usually the only size available) costs €4-8; most places offer both takeout and eat-in, and pizza is often the only thing on the menu.

Near the Station

These two pizzerias—the most famous—are both a few long blocks from the train station, and at the end of my self-guided "Naples Walk."

$ Antica Pizzeria da Michele is for pizza purists. Filled with locals (and tourists), it serves just two varieties: *margherita* (tomato sauce and mozzarella) and *marinara* (tomato sauce, oregano, and

Restaurant Price Code

I've assigned each eatery a price category, based on the average cost of a typical main course (pasta or *secondi*). Drinks, desserts, and splurge items (steak and seafood) can raise the price considerably.

$$$$ **Splurge:** Most main courses over €20
$$$ **Pricier:** €15-20
$$ **Moderate:** €10-15
$ **Budget:** Under €10

In Italy, pizza by the slice and other takeout food is **$**; a basic trattoria or sit-down pizzeria is **$$**; a casual but more upscale restaurant is **$$$**; and a swanky splurge is **$$$$**.

garlic, no cheese). Come early to sit and watch the pizza artists in action. A pizza with beer costs around €7. As this place is often jammed with a long line, arrive early or late to get a seat. If there's a mob, head inside to get a number. If it's just too crowded to wait, the less-exceptional Pizzeria Trianon (described next) generally has room (Mon-Sat 10:30-24:00, closed Sun; look for the vertical red *Antica Pizzeria* sign at the intersection of Via Pietro Colletta and Via Cesare Sersale at #1; tel. 081-553-9204).

$ Pizzeria Trianon, across the street and left a few doors, has been da Michele's archrival since 1923. It offers more choices, higher prices (€5-8, plus a 15 percent service charge), air-conditioning, and a cozier atmosphere. For less chaos, head upstairs. While waiting for your meal, you can survey the transformation of a humble wad of dough into a smoldering bubbly feast in their entryway pizza kitchen (daily 11:00-15:30 & 19:00-23:00, Via Pietro Colletta 42, tel. 081-553-9426).

On Via dei Tribunali

This street, which runs a couple of blocks north of Spaccanapoli, is home to several pizzerias that are more convenient to sightseeing. Three in particular are on all the "best pizza in Naples" lists...as you'll learn the hard way if you show up at peak mealtimes, when huge mobs of locals crowd outside the front door waiting for a table.

$$ Gino Sorbillo is a local favorite (Mon-Sat 12:00-15:30 & 19:00-24:00, closed Sun, Via dei Tribunali 32—don't confuse this with his relatives' similarly named places at #35 and #37 on the same street, tel. 081-446-643).

At **$$ Pizzeria di Matteo,** people waiting out front line up at the little window to snack on deep-fried goodies—*arancini* (with rice, gooey cheese, peas, and sausage), *frittatine* (balls of mac and cheese plus sausage), and *crocché* (croquettes)—for €1 apiece (sometimes closed Sun, Via dei Tribunali 94, tel. 081-455-262).

$$ Pizzeria I Decumani has a bit nicer seating and is perhaps less chaotic (closed Mon, on Piazza San Gaetano at Via dei Tribunali 61, takeout window at #58, tel. 081-557-1309).

EATING NEAR THE ARCHAEOLOGICAL MUSEUM

$$ La Stanza del Gusto, two blocks downhill from the museum, tackles food creatively and injects crusty Naples with a little modern color and irreverence. The downstairs is casual, trendy, and playful, while the upstairs is more refined yet still polka-dotted (weekday lunch specials, Tue-Sat 12:00-15:30 & 19:30-23:30, closed Sun-Mon, Via Santa Maria di Constantinopoli 100, tel. 081-401-578).

$ Rosticceria Angela is a *tavola calda* with hot ready-to-eat dishes (€3-5) and a coffee bar, run by a team of older gentlemen. Pricing is honest and there's simple, peaceful, air-conditioned indoor seating. Next door (same name, different management) is a tiny meat, cheese, and bread shop with all you need for a cheap meal to go (*rosticceria* open Mon-Sat 7:00-21:00, closed Sun, 3 blocks below museum at Via Conte di Ruvo 21, between Via Pessina and Via Bellini, tel. 081-033-2928).

EATING NEAR THE STATION

$$ Da Donato, an excellent, traditional, family-run trattoria on a glum street near the station, serves delicious food in an unpretentious atmosphere. The best approach is for two people to share the astonishing antipasti sampler—*degustazione "fantasia" della Casa Terra e Mare*—for €25. You'll get more than a dozen small portions, each more delicious than the last. A version without seafood is €15 (Tue-Sun 12:30-14:30 & 19:30-22:00, closed Mon, two blocks from Piazza Garibaldi—turn down Via Silvio Spaventa to #39, tel. 081-287-828).

Pompeii

Stopped in its tracks by the eruption of Mount Vesuvius in A.D. 79, Pompeii offers the best look anywhere at what life in Rome must have been like around 2,000 years ago.

A once-thriving commercial port of 20,000, Pompeii (worth ▲▲▲) grew from Greek and Etruscan roots to become an important Roman city. Then, on August 24, A.D. 79, everything changed. Vesuvius erupted and began to bury the city under 30 feet of hot volcanic ash. For the archaeologists who excavated it centuries later, this was a shake-and-bake windfall, teaching them volumes about daily Roman life. Pompeii was accidentally redis-covered in 1599; excavations began in 1748.

GETTING THERE

By Train: Pompeii is roughly midway between Naples and Sor-rento on the Circumvesuviana train line (2/hour, 40 minutes from Naples, trip costs about €2.60 one-way, not covered by rail passes; for details see page 454). Get off at the Pompei Scavi-Villa dei Misteri stop; from Naples, it's the stop after Torre Annunziata. From the Pompei Scavi train station, it's just a two-minute walk to the Porta Marina entrance: Turn right and walk down the road about a block to the entrance (on your left).

Pompei vs. Pompei Scavi: Make sure you're taking the Cir-cumvesuviana commuter train to Pompei Scavi (*scavi* means "ex-cavations"), the station right next to the ancient site. Pompei is the name of a separate train station on the main national rail line that's a long, dull walk from the ruins. It serves the ugly modern city of Pompei (always with one "i"). When coming from Rome, it's bet-ter to transfer at Naples' Centrale Station to the Circumvesuviana for Pompei Scavi than to take the train straight to the Pompei city station and walk from there.

By Car: Parking is available at Camping Zeus, next to the Pompei Scavi train station (€2.50/hour, €10/12 hours, 10 percent discount with this book); several other campgrounds/parking lots are nearby.

ORIENTATION

Cost: €12, possibly more during special exhibits, free first Sun of each month. If you plan to eat or sightsee outside of the ar-chaeological site, ask for an entrance/exit bracelet that allows you reenter the site up to three times on the same day.

Hours: Daily April-Oct 9:00-19:30, Nov-March 8:30-17:00, last entry 1.5 hours before closing.

Closures: Some buildings and streets are bound to be closed for restoration when you visit. Pompeii's best-preserved home—the House of the Vettii—has been completely blocked off for years; unfortunately, it's unlikely to reopen in time for your visit. If you get totally derailed, just use the map and numbers to find your way.

Crowd-Beating Tip: Up to 15,000 visitors are allowed on the first Sun of the month when it's free—and packed. I'd make a point to avoid Pompeii on that day.

Information: Ignore the "info point" kiosk at the station, which

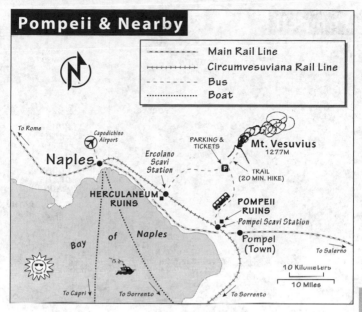

Pompeii & Nearby

Main Rail Line
Circumvesuviana Rail Line
Bus
Boat

To Rome

Capodichino
Airport

Naples

PARKING &
TICKETS

Mt. Vesuvius
1277M

Ercolano
Scavi
Station

P

TRAIL
(20 MIN. HIKE)

HERCULANEUM
RUINS

POMPEII
RUINS

Pompei Scavi Station

Bay   of   Naples

Pompei
(Town)

To Salerno

10 Kilometers
10 Miles

To Capri   To Sorrento   To Sorrento

NAPLES

is a private agency selling tours. Once at the site, pick up the
free, helpful map and booklet at the entrance (ask for it when
you buy your ticket, or check at the info window to the left of
the WCs—the maps aren't available within the walls of Pompeii). Tel. 081-857-5347, www.pompeiisites.org.

The bookshop sells a couple of books with plastic overlays
that allow you to re-create Pompeii from the ruins (€16; if you
buy from a street vendor, pay no more than that).

Tours. My **self-guided tour** in this chapter covers the basics and
provides a good framework for exploring the site on your own,
as does my ∩ free Pompeii **audio tour.**

For a **guided tour,** your best bet is to join the Mondo
Guide tours for Rick Steves readers (€15, doesn't include €12
Pompeii entry, daily at 11:00, reservations required; meet at
Hotel/Ristorante Suisse, just down the hill from the Porta
Marina entrance; see page 458). Stepping off the train, you'll
be accosted by touts for the "info point" kiosk, which sells €12
tours that depart whenever enough people sign up.

Private guides (around €110/2 hours) of varying quality
cluster near the ticket booth at the site and may try to herd
you into a group with other travelers, which is fine as long as it
makes the price more reasonable for you. For a better experience, reserve one of the following guides in advance and mention this book: **Antonio Somma** mainly specializes in Pompeii and gives good, straightforward tours (€120/2 hours for

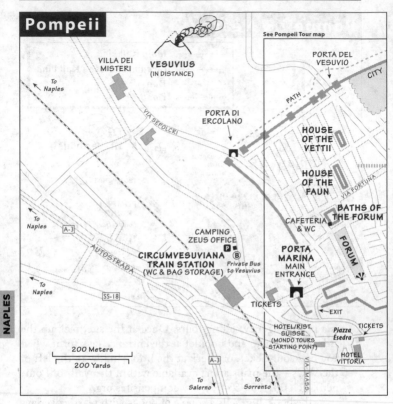

up to 6 people, also offers regional transport, mobile 393-406-3824, tel. 081-850-1992, www.tourspompeiiguide.com, info@pompeitour.com). **Gaetano Manfredi** is pricey but brings energy and theatricality to his tours (€170/2 hours for up to 4 people, www.pompeiitourguide.com, gaetanoguide@hotmail.it). **Silvia Braggio** (mobile 347-643-2307, www.silviaguide.it, silvia@silviaguide.it) and the Naples-based guides recommended on page 457 can also guide you at Pompeii. Parents, note that the ancient brothel and its sexually explicit frescoes are included on tours; let your guide know if you'd rather skip that stop.

    Audioguides are available from a kiosk near the ticket booth at the Porta Marina entrance (€6.50, €10 for 2, ID required), but they offer basically the same info as your free booklet.

Length of This Tour: Allow two hours, or three if you visit the theater and amphitheater. With less time, focus on the Forum, Baths of the Forum, House of the Faun, and brothel.

Baggage Check: Use the free baggage check near the turnstiles at

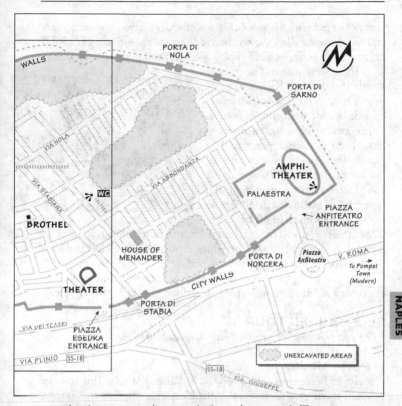

the site entrance (just yards from the station). The train station also offers pay luggage storage (downstairs, by the WC).

Services: A pay WC is at the train station. The Pompeii site has three WCs—one near the entrance, one in the cafeteria, and another near the end of this tour, uphill from the theaters.

Eating: The **$ Ciao** cafeteria within the site serves good sandwiches, pizza, and pasta. **$ Bar Sgambati,** the café/restaurant in the train station, has air-conditioning, Wi-Fi, and reasonably priced pastas and pizzas (tel. 081-861-0966). Your cheapest bet may be to bring your own food for a discreet picnic.

Starring: Roofless (collapsed) but otherwise intact Roman buildings, plaster casts of hapless victims, a few erotic frescoes, and the dawning realization that these ancient people were not that different from us.

BACKGROUND

Pompeii, founded in 600 b.c., eventually became a booming Roman trading city. Not rich, not poor, it was middle class—a perfect example of typical Roman life. Most streets would have been lined with stalls and jammed with customers from sunup to sundown.

Chariots vied with shoppers for street space. Two thousand years ago, Rome controlled the entire Mediterranean—making it a kind of free-trade zone—and Pompeii was a central and bustling port.

There were no posh neighborhoods in Pompeii. Rich and poor mixed it up as elegant houses existed side by side with simple homes. While nearby Herculaneum would have been a classier place to live (traffic-free streets, fancier houses, far better drainage), Pompeii was the place for action and shopping. It served an estimated 20,000 residents with more than 40 bakeries, 30 brothels, and 130 bars, restaurants, and hotels. With most of its buildings covered by brilliant white ground-marble stucco, Pompeii in A.D. 79 was an impressive town.

As you tour Pompeii, remember that its best art is in the Archaeological Museum in Naples (described earlier in this chapter).

SELF-GUIDED TOUR
• *Just past the ticket-taker, start your approach up to the...*

❶ Porta Marina
The city of Pompeii was born on the hill ahead of you. This was the original town gate. Before Vesuvius blew and filled in the harbor,

the sea came nearly to here. Notice the two openings in the gate (ahead, up the ramp). Both were left open by day to admit major traffic. At night, the larger one was closed for better security.

• *Pass through the Porta Marina and continue up to the top of the street, pausing at the three large stepping-stones in the middle.*

❷ Pompeii's Streets
Every day, Pompeiians flooded the streets with gushing water to clean them. These stepping-stones let pedestrians cross without getting their sandals wet. Chariots traveling in either direction could straddle the stones (all had standard-size

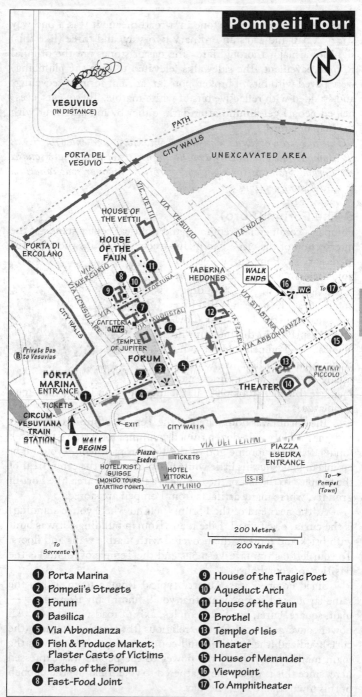

Pompeii Tour

VESUVIUS
(IN DISTANCE)

PATH

CITY WALLS

PORTA DEL
VESUVIO →

UNEXCAVATED AREA

VIA VETTII

VIA VESUVIO

VIA NOLA

HOUSE OF
THE VETTII

PORTA DI
ERCOLANO

**HOUSE
OF THE
FAUN**

VIA MERCURIO

VIA CONSOLARE

CITY WALLS

❽

❾

❿

⓫

VIA FORTUNA

TABERNA
HEDONES

**WALK
ENDS**

⓰

WC

To ⓱

NAPLES

VIA STABIANA

❼

VIA AUGUSTALI

CAFETERIA
& WC

VIA DELLA FORTUNA

❻

⓬

VIA TEATRI

VIA ABBONDANZA

⓯

TEMPLE
OF JUPITER

FORUM

❷

❸

❺

⓭

TEATRO
PICCOLO

Private Bus
Ⓑ to Vesuvius

**PORTA
MARINA
ENTRANCE**

❶

❹

THEATER

⓮

TICKETS

**CIRCUM-
VESUVIANA
TRAIN
STATION**

**WALK
BEGINS**

← EXIT

CITY WALLS

VIA DEI TEATRI

**PIAZZA
ESEDRA
ENTRANCE**

Piazza
Esedra

TICKETS

HOTEL/RIST.
SUISSE
(MONDO TOURS
STARTING POINT)

HOTEL
VITTORIA

SS-18

To →
Pompei
(Town)

VIA PLINIO

To
Sorrento ↓

200 Meters

200 Yards

❶ Porta Marina	❾ House of the Tragic Poet
❷ Pompeii's Streets	❿ Aqueduct Arch
❸ Forum	⓫ House of the Faun
❹ Basilica	⓬ Brothel
❺ Via Abbondanza	⓭ Temple of Isis
❻ Fish & Produce Market; Plaster Casts of Victims	⓮ Theater
❼ Baths of the Forum	⓯ House of Menander
❽ Fast-Food Joint	⓰ Viewpoint
	⓱ To Amphitheater

axles). A single stepping-stone in a road means it was a one-way street, a pair indicates an ordinary two-way, and three (like this) signifies a major thoroughfare. The basalt stones are the original Roman pavement. The sidewalks (elevated to hide the plumbing) were paved with bits of broken pots (an ancient form of recycling) and studded with reflective bits of white marble. These "cats' eyes" helped people get around after dark, either by moonlight or with the help of lamps.

• *Continue straight ahead, don your mental toga, and enter the city as the Romans once did. The road opens up into the spacious main square: the Forum. Stand at the right end of this rectangular space and look toward Mount Vesuvius.*

❸ The Forum (Foro)

Pompeii's commercial, religious, and political center stands at the intersection of the city's two main streets. While it's the most ru-

ined part of Pompeii, it's grand nonetheless. Picture the piazza surrounded by two-story buildings on all sides. The pedestals that line the square once held statues (now safely displayed in the museum in Naples). In Pompeii's heyday, its citizens gathered here in the main square to shop, talk politics, and

socialize. Business took place in the important buildings that lined the piazza.

The Forum was dominated by the **Temple of Jupiter,** at the far end (marked by a half-dozen ruined columns atop a stair-step base). Jupiter was the supreme god of the Roman pantheon—you might be able to make out his little white marble head at the center-rear of the temple. To the left of the temple is a fenced-off area, the **Forum granary,** where many artifacts from Pompeii are stored.

At the near end of the Forum (behind where you're standing) is the **curia,** or city hall. Like many Roman buildings, it was built with brick and mortar, then covered with marble walls and floors. To your left (as you face Vesuvius and the Temple of Jupiter) is the **basilica,** or courthouse.

Since Pompeii was a pretty typical Roman town, it has the same layout and components that you'll find in any Roman city—main square, curia, basilica, temples, axis of roads, and so on. All power converged at the Forum: religious (the temple), political (the curia), judicial (the basilica), and commercial (this piazza was the main marketplace). Even the power of the people was expressed here, since this is where they gathered to vote. Imagine the hubbub of this town square in its heyday.

Look beyond the Temple of Jupiter. Five miles to the north looms the ominous backstory to this site: **Mount Vesuvius.** Mentally draw a triangle up from the two remaining peaks to reconstruct the mountain before the eruption. When it blew, Pompeiians had no idea that they were living under a volcano, as Vesuvius hadn't erupted for 1,200 years. Imagine the wonder—then the horror—as a column of pulverized rock roared upward, and then ash began to fall. The weight of the ash and small rocks collapsed Pompeii's roofs later that day, crushing people who had taken refuge inside buildings instead of fleeing the city.

• *As you face Vesuvius, the basilica is to your left, lined with stumps of columns. Backtrack to the three stepping stones we saw earlier to go inside. (If it's fenced off, peer through the gate.)*

❹ Basilica

Pompeii's basilica was a first-century palace of justice. This ancient law court has the same floor plan later adopted by many Christian churches (which are also called basilicas). The big central hall (or nave) is flanked by rows of columns marking off narrower side aisles. Along the side walls are traces of the original marble.

The columns—now stumps all about the same height—were not ruined by the volcano. Rather, they were left unfinished when

Vesuvius blew. Pompeii had been devastated by an earthquake in A.D. 62, and was just in the process of rebuilding the basilica when Vesuvius erupted, 17 years later. The half-built columns show off the technology of the day. Uniform bricks were stacked around a cylindrical core. Once finished, they would have been coated with marble dust stucco to simulate marble columns—an economical construction method found throughout Pompeii (and the Roman Empire).

Besides the earthquake and the eruption, Pompeii's buildings have suffered other ravages over the years, including Spanish plunderers (c. 1800), 19th-century souvenir hunters, WWII bombs, wild vegetation, another earthquake in 1980, and modern neglect. The fact that the entire city was covered by the eruption of A.D. 79 actually helped preserve it, saving it from the sixth-century barbarians who plundered many other towns into oblivion.

• *Exit the basilica and cross the short side of the square, to where the city's main street hits the Forum. Stop at the three white stones that stick up from the cobbles.*

❺ Via Abbondanza

Glance down Via Abbondanza, Pompeii's main street. Lined with shops, bars, and restaurants, it was a lively, pedestrian-only zone. The three "beaver-teeth" stones are traffic barriers that kept chariots out. On the corner at the start of the street (just to the left), take a close look at the dark travertine column standing next to the white one. Notice that the marble drums of the white column are not chiseled entirely round—another construction project left unfinished when Vesuvius erupted.

• *Head toward Vesuvius, walking along the right side of the Forum. Immediately across from the Temple of Jupiter is a building with four round arches. Go in the door just to the right, and find two glass cases.*

❻ Fish and Produce Market
Plaster Casts of Victims

As the frescoes on the wall (just inside on the left) indicate, this is where Pompeiians came to buy their food—fish, bread, chickens, and so on. These fine examples of Roman art—with their glimpses of everyday life and their mastery of depth and illusion—would not be matched until the Renaissance, a thousand years after the fall of Rome.

The glass cases hold casts of Pompeiians, eerily captured in their last moments. They were quickly suffocated by a superheated avalanche of gas and ash, and their bodies were encased in volcanic debris. While excavating, modern archaeologists detected hollow spaces underfoot, created when the victims' bodies decomposed. By gently filling the holes with plaster, the archaeologists were able to create molds of the Pompeiians who were caught in the disaster.

• *Exit the market, turn right, and go under the arch. On the pillar to the right, look for the pedestrian-only road sign (two guys carrying an amphora, or ancient jug; it's above the REG VII INS IV sign). In the road are more "beaver-teeth" traffic blocks. The modern cafeteria is the only eatery inside the archaeological site (with a coffee bar and WC upstairs).*

Twenty yards past the cafeteria, on the left-hand side at #24, is the entrance to the...

❼ Baths of the Forum (Terme del Foro)

Pompeii had six public baths, each with a men's and a women's sec-

The Eruption of Vesuvius

At about 1:00 in the afternoon on August 24, A.D. 79, Mount Vesuvius erupted, sending a mushroom cloud of ash, dust, and rocks 12 miles into the air. It spewed for 18 hours straight, as winds blew the cloud southward. The white-gray ash settled like a heavy snow on Pompeii, its weight eventually collapsing roofs and floors, but leaving the walls intact. And though most of Pompeii's 20,000 residents fled that day, about 2,000 stayed behind. At around 7:30 the next morning, a pyroclastic flow headed south and struck Pompeii, dealing a fatal blow to those who'd remained.

tion. You're in the men's zone. The leafy courtyard at the entrance was the gymnasium. After working out, clients could relax with a hot bath *(caldarium)*, warm bath *(tepidarium)*, or cold plunge *(frigidarium)*.

The first big, plain room you enter served as the **dressing room.** Holes on the walls were for pegs to hang clothing. High up, the window (with a faded Neptune underneath) was originally covered with a less translucent Roman glass. Walk over the nonslip mosaics into the next room.

The *tepidarium* is ringed by mini statues or *telamones* (male caryatids, figures used as supporting pillars), which divided the lockers. Clients would undress and warm up here, perhaps stretching out on one of the bronze benches near the bronze heater for a massage. Look at the ceiling—half crushed by the eruption and half intact, with its fine blue-and-white stucco work.

Next, admire the engineering in the steam-bath room, or *caldarium.* The double floor was heated from below—so nice with

bare feet (look into the grate across from where you entered to see the brick support towers). The double walls with brown terra-cotta tiles held the heat. Romans soaked in the big tub, which was filled with hot water. Opposite the big tub is a fountain, which spouted water onto the hot floor, creating steam. The lettering on the fountain reminded those enjoying the room which two politicians paid for it...and how much it cost them (5,250 *sestertii*). To keep condensation from dripping annoyingly from the ceiling, fluting (ribbing) was added to carry water down the walls.

• *Today's visitors exit the baths through the original entry (at the far end of the dressing room). Hungry? Immediately across the street is an ancient...*

❽ Fast-Food Joint

After a bath, it was only natural to want a little snack. So, just across the street is a fast-food joint, marked by a series of rectangular marble counters. Most ancient Romans didn't cook for themselves in their tiny apartments, so to-go places like this were commonplace. The holes in the counters held the pots for food. Each container was like a thermos, with a wooden lid to keep the soup hot, the wine cool, and so on. Notice the groove in the front doorstep and the holes out on the curb.

The holes likely accommodated cords for stretching awnings over the sidewalk to shield the clientele from the hot sun, while the grooves were for the shop's folding accordion doors. Look at the wheel grooves in the pavement, worn down through centuries of use. Nearby are more stepping-stones for pedestrians to cross the flooded streets.

• *Just a few steps uphill from the fast-food joint, at #5 (with a locked gate), is the...*

❾ House of the Tragic Poet
(Casa del Poeta Tragico)

This house is typical Roman style. The entry is flanked by two family-owned shops (each with a track for a collapsing accordion door). The home is like a train running straight away from the street: atrium (with skylight and pool to catch the rain), den (where deals were made by the shopkeeper), and garden (with rooms facing it and a shrine to remember both the gods and family ancestors). In the entryway is the famous "Beware of Dog" *(Cave Canem)* mosaic.

Today's visitors enter the home by the back door (circle around to the left). On your way there, look for the modern exposed pipe on the left side of the lane; this is the same as ones used in the ancient plumbing system, hidden beneath the raised sidewalk. Inside the house, the grooves on the marble well-head in the entry hall (possibly closed) were formed by generations of inhabitants dragging the bucket up by rope. The richly frescoed dining room is off the garden. Diners lounged on their couches (the Roman custom) and enjoyed frescoes with fake "windows," giving the illusion of a bigger and airier room. Next to the dining room is a humble BBQ-style kitchen with a little closet for the toilet (the kitchen and bathroom shared the same plumbing).

• Return to the fast-food place and continue about 10 yards downhill to the big intersection. From the center of the intersection, look left to see a giant arch, framing a nice view of Mount Vesuvius.

❿ Aqueduct Arch—Running Water

Water was critical for this city of 20,000 people, and this arch was part of Pompeii's water-delivery system. A 100-mile-long aque-

duct carried fresh water down from the hillsides to a big reservoir perched at the highest point of the city wall. Since overall water pressure was disappointing, Pompeiians built arches like the brick one you see here (originally covered in marble) with hidden water tanks at the top. Located just below the altitude of the main tank, these smaller tanks were filled by gravity and provided each neighborhood with reliable pressure. Look closely at the arch and you'll see 2,000-year-old pipes (made of lead imported from Britannia) embedded in the brick.

If there was a water shortage, democratic priorities prevailed: First the baths were cut off, then the private homes. The last to go were the public fountains, where all citizens could get drinking and cooking water.

• If you're thirsty, fill your water bottle from the modern fountain. Then continue straight downhill one block (50 yards) to #2 on the left.

⓫ House of the Faun (Casa del Fauno)

Stand across the street and marvel at the grand entry with *"HAVE"*

(hail to you) as a welcome mat. Go in. Notice the two shrines above the entryway—one dedicated to the gods, the other to this wealthy family's ancestors. (Contemporary Neapolitans still carry on this practice; you'll notice little shrines embedded in walls all over Naples.)

You are standing in Pompeii's largest home, where you're greeted by the delightful small bronze statue of the *Dancing Faun*, famed for its realistic movement and fine proportion. (The original, described on page 461, is in Naples' Archaeological Museum.) With 40 rooms and 27,000 square feet, the House of the Faun covers an entire city block. The next floor mosaic, with an intricate diamond-like design, decorates the homeowner's office. Beyond that, at the far end of the first garden, is the famous floor mosaic of the *Battle of Alexander*. (The original is also at the museum in Naples.) In 333 B.C., Alexander the Great beat Darius and the Persians. Romans had great respect for Alexander, the first great emperor before Rome's. While most of Pompeii's nouveau riche had notoriously bad taste and stuffed their palaces with over-the-top, mismatched decor, this guy had class. Both the faun (an ancient copy of a famous Greek statue) and the Alexander mosaic show an appreciation for history.

The house's back courtyard is lined with pillars rebuilt after the A.D. 62 earthquake. Take a close look at the brick, mortar, and fake-marble stucco veneer.

• *Now retrace your steps to the Forum. At the Forum's far end, find Via Abbondanza (where you saw the three "beaver-teeth" stones a few minutes ago). Follow this, passing the water fountain on the left with the cornucopia (horn of plenty) that gives the street its name. Turn left up the street after the second fountain (marked* REG VII INS I, *with a small* Vicolo del Lupanare *sign). This leads to the entrance of the...*

⑫ Brothel (Lupanare)

You'll find the biggest crowds in Pompeii at a place that was likely popular 2,000 ago, too—the brothel. Prostitutes were nicknamed *lupe* (she-wolves), alluding to the call they made when trying to attract business. The brothel was a simple place, with beds and pillows made of stone and then covered with mattresses. The ancient graffiti includes tallies and exotic names of the women, indicating the prostitutes came from all corners of the Mediterranean (it also served as feedback from satisfied customers). The faded frescoes above the cells may have been a kind of menu for services offered. Note the idealized women (white, which was considered beautiful; one wears an early bra) and the rougher men (dark, considered horny). The bed legs came with little disk-like barriers to keep critters from crawling up.

• *Leaving the brothel, go right, then take the first left, and continue going downhill two blocks to return to Via Abbondanza. The Forum—and exit—are now to the right, but you should go left.*

Continue for 60 yards, then turn right just beyond the fountain, and walk down Via dei Teatri (labeled REG VIII INS IV*). Turn left before the columns, and head downhill another 60 yards to #28, which marks the...*

⑬ Temple of Isis

This temple served Pompeii's Egyptian community. The little white stucco shrine with the modern plastic roof housed holy water from the Nile. Isis, from Egyptian myth, was one of many foreign gods adopted by the eclectic Romans. Pompeii must have had a synagogue, too, but it has yet to be excavated.

• *Now your goal is the large theater just behind the temple. Try getting there this way: Exit the temple where you entered, and go left, then left again (following the* Foro Triangolare *sign) along the columns, and then left into the theater's upper stands. (If this is closed off, try circling around the other way). There's also a similar but smaller-sized theater next to the large one.*

⓮ Theater

Originally a Greek theater (Greeks built theirs with the help of a hillside), this was the birthplace of the Greek port here in 470

B.C. During Roman times, the theater sat 5,000 people in three sets of seats, all with different prices: the five marble terraces up close (filled with romantic wooden seats for two), the main section, and the cheap nosebleed section (surviving only on the high end, near the trees). The square stones above the cheap seats once supported a canvas rooftop. Take note of the high-profile boxes, flanking the stage, for guests of honor. From this perch, you can see the gladiator barracks—the colonnaded courtyard beyond the theater. They lived in tiny rooms, trained in the courtyard, and fought in the nearby amphitheater.

• *From the theater, return to the street where you entered the Temple of Isis, and turn right (away from the Forum). In a block and a half, on the right you'll see the...*

⓯ House of Menander (Casa di Menandro)

Once owned by a wealthy Pompeiian, this house takes its current name from a fresco of the Greek playwright Menander on one of the walls. Admire the grand atrium (with an altar to the family gods in the corner), the wall frescoes, and the mosaics. The cloister-like back courtyard leads to a room with skeletons (not plaster casts) of eruption victims from this house. Farther back, a passage leads to the servants' quarters.

• *When you're ready to leave, backtrack to the main road and find the sign for the (modern) toilets. Climb up the stairs and find the viewpoint over the ruins.*

⓰ Viewpoint

You're at ground level—post-eruption. To the right (inland), the farmland shows how locals lived on top of the ruins for centuries without knowing what was underneath. To the left, you can see the entire city of Pompeii spread out in front of you and appreciate the magnitude of the excavations.

• *To leave the site, head back down the stairs, turn right on Via Abbondanza, and go uphill to the Forum, where you'll find the main exit. For a shortcut back to the entrance area (with the bookstore, luggage storage, and quickest access to the train station), when you are halfway down the exit ramp, take the eight steps on the right and follow the signs. Otherwise, you'll end up on the main road—where you'll head right and loop around.*

  However, there's much more to see—three-quarters of Pompeii's 164 acres have been excavated, but this tour has covered only a third of the site. If you still have energy to see more, continue along Via Abbondanza toward the eastern part of the site, where the crowds thin out. Go straight for about 10 minutes, likely jogging right after a bit (just follow the posted maps). You'll wind up passing through a pretty, forested area. At the far end is the...

⑰ Amphitheater

If you can, climb to the upper level of the amphitheater (though the stairs are often blocked). With Vesuvius looming in the back-

ground, mentally replace the tourists below with gladiators and wild animals locked in combat. Walk along the top of the amphitheater and look down into the grassy rectangular area surrounded by columns. This is the **Palaestra,** an area once used for athletic training. (If you can't get to the top of the amphitheater, you can see the Palaestra from outside—in fact, you can't miss it, as it's right next door.) Facing the other way, look for the bell tower that tops the roofline of the modern city of Pompei, where locals go about their daily lives in the shadow of the volcano, just as their ancestors did 2,000 years ago.

• *If it's too crowded to bear hiking back along uneven lanes to the entrance, you can slip out the site's "back door," which is next to the amphitheater. Exiting, turn right and follow the site's wall all the way back to the entrance.*

ROMAN HISTORY

Three Millennia in Eight Pages

HISTORY IN A HURRY

Ancient Rome lasted a thousand years (500 B.C.-A.D. 500), half as an expanding republic, half as a dominating empire. When Rome

fell to invaders, all of Europe suffered a thousand years of poverty and ignorance (A.D. 500-1500), though Rome's influence could still be felt through the Catholic Church. Popes rebuilt Rome for pilgrims—in Renaissance, then Baroque and Neoclassical styles (1500-1800). As capital of a newly united Italy, Rome followed fascist Mussolini into World War II (and lost), but rebounded in Italy's postwar economic boom.

Want more?

LEGENDARY BIRTH (1200-500 B.C.)

Aeneas flees burning Troy (1200 B.C.), wanders like Odysseus, and finally finds a home along the Tiber. His descendants, Romulus and Remus—orphaned at birth, suckled by a she-wolf, and raised by shepherds—grow up to steal wives and build a wall, thus founding Rome (753 B.C.).

Closer to fact, the local, Latin-speaking agrarian tribes were dominated by more sophisticated neighbors to the north (Etruscans) and south (Greek colonists). But their convenient location on the Tiber was perfect for a rise to power.

Sights
- Romulus' "huts" and wall (Palatine Hill)
- She-Wolf statue (Capitoline Museums)
- Frescoes of Aeneas and Romulus (National Museum of Rome)
- Bernini's Aeneas statue (Borghese Gallery)
- Etruscan wing (Vatican Museums)
- Etruscan Museum (in Villa Borghese Gardens)
- Etruscan legacy (the original Circus Maximus, the drained Forum)

THE REPUBLIC
(509-27 B.C.)

The city expands throughout the Italian peninsula (500-300 B.C.), then defeats Hannibal's North African Carthaginians (the Punic Wars, 264-146 B.C.) and Greece (168 B.C.). Rome is master of the Mediterranean, and booty and captured slaves pour in. Romans bicker among themselves over their slice of the pie, pitting the wealthy landowners (the ruling Senate) against the working class (plebs) and the rebellious slaves (Spartacus' revolt, 73 B.C.). In the chaos, charismatic generals like Julius Caesar, who can provide wealth and security, become dictators. Change is necessary...and coming.

Sights
- Forum's Curia, Temple of Saturn, Temple of Castor and Pollux, Rostrum, Basilica Aemilia, Temple of Julius Caesar, and Basilica Julia (all rebuilt later)
- Appian Way built, lined with tombs
- Aqueducts, which carry water to a growing city
- Portrait busts of citizens (National Museum of Rome)

- The republic's "S.P.Q.R." monogram and motto, seen today on statues, buildings, and even manhole covers: *Senatus Populusque Romanus,* or the "Senate and People of Rome." (Some northern Italians, who feel the South is dragging them down, translate S.P.Q.R. as *Sono Porci Questi Romani*—"These Romans Are Pigs.")

THE EMPIRE—THE "ROMAN PEACE," OR PAX ROMANA
(A.D. 1-200)

After Julius Caesar is killed by disgruntled republicans, his adopted son Augustus takes undisputed control, ends the civil wars, declares himself emperor, and adopts a family member to succeed him, setting the pattern of rule for the next 500 years.

Rome rules an empire of 54 million people, stretching from England to Africa, from Spain to Turkey. The city, with more than a million inhabitants, is decorated with Greek-style statues and monumental, marble-faced buildings...it is the marvel of the known world. The empire prospers on a (false) economy of booty, slaves, and trade, surviving the often turbulent and naughty behavior of emperors such as Caligula and Nero. You can see Roman history in the faces of the emperors by reading the 📖 National Museum of Rome Tour chapter.

Sights
- Colosseum
- Forum
- Palatine Hill palaces
- Ara Pacis ("Altar of Peace")
- Augustus' house (House of Livia and Augustus) on Palatine Hill
- Pantheon
- Trajan's Column and Forum
- Greek and Greek-style statues and emperors' busts (National Museum of Rome, Vatican Museums, Capitoline Museums)
- Piazza Navona (former stadium)
- Hadrian's Villa (Tivoli) and tomb (now Castel Sant'Angelo)

ROME FALLS
(200-476)

Corruption, disease, and the constant pressure of barbarians pecking away at the borders slowly drain the unwieldy empire. Despite Diocletian's division of the empire and Constantine's legalization of Christianity (313), the city is sacked (410), and the last emperor checks out (476). Rome falls like a huge column, kicking up dust that will plunge Europe into a thousand years of darkness.

Sights
- Arch of Constantine
- The Forum's Basilica of Constantine
- Baths of Diocletian
- Old Roman Wall (gates at Via Veneto or Piramide)

MEDIEVAL ROME
(500-1500)
The once-great city of a million people dwindles to a rough village of 20,000, with a corrupt pope, forgotten ruins, and malaria-carrying mosquitoes. Cows graze in the ruined Forum, and wolves prowl the Vatican at night. During the 1300s, even the popes leave Rome to live in France. What little glory Rome retains is in the pomp, knowledge, and wealth of the Catholic Church.

Sights
- The damage done to ancient Roman monuments, caused by disuse, barbarian looting, and pillaging for precut stones
- Early Christian churches built before Rome fell (Santa Maria Maggiore, San Giovanni in Laterano, and San Clemente)
- Churches of Santa Maria sopra Minerva and Santa Maria in Trastevere
- Castel Sant'Angelo

RENAISSANCE AND BAROQUE ROME
(1500-1800)

As Europe's economy recovers, energetic popes rebuild Rome to attract pilgrims. The best artists decorate palaces and churches, carve statues, and build fountains. The city is not a great political force, but as the center of Catholicism during the struggle against Protestants (c. 1520-1648), it is an influential religious and cultural capital.

Renaissance Sights

- Michelangelo: Sistine Chapel (Vatican Museums), dome of St. Peter's, *Pietà* (St. Peter's), *Moses* (St. Peter-in-Chains Church), Christ statue (Santa Maria sopra Minerva), Piazza del Campidoglio (Capitoline Hill Square), Santa Maria degli Angeli church (in former Baths of Diocletian)

Church Architecture

History comes to life when you visit a centuries-old church. Even if you wouldn't know your apse from a hole in the ground, learning a few simple terms will enrich your experience. Note that not every church has every feature, and that a "cathedral" isn't a type of church architecture, but rather a designation for a church that's a governing center for a local bishop.

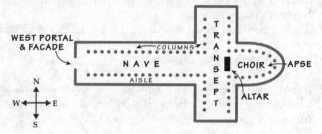

Aisles: The long, generally low-ceilinged arcades that flank the nave.

Altar: The raised area with a ceremonial table (often adorned with candles or a crucifix), where the priest prepares and serves the bread and wine for Communion.

Apse: The space beyond the altar, generally bordered with small chapels.

Barrel Vault: A continuous round-arched ceiling that resembles an extended upside-down U.

Choir: A cozy area, often screened off, located within the church nave and near the high altar, where services are sung in a more intimate setting.

Cloister: A square-shaped series of hallways surrounding an open-air courtyard, traditionally where monks and nuns got fresh air.

Facade: The outer wall of the church's main (west) entrance, viewable from outside and generally highly decorated.

Groin Vault: An arched ceiling formed where two equal barrel vaults meet at right angles. Less common usage: term for a medieval jock strap.

Narthex: The area (portico or foyer) between the main entry and the nave.

Nave: The long, central section of the church (running west to east, from the entrance to the altar) where the congregation stood through the service.

Transept: The north-south part of the church, which crosses (perpendicularly) the east-west nave. In a traditional Latin cross-shaped floor plan, the transept forms the "arms" of the cross.

West Portal: The main entry to the church (on the west end, opposite the main altar).

- Raphael's School of Athens and Transfiguration (Vatican Museums)
- Paintings by Raphael, Titian, and others (Borghese Gallery)

Baroque Sights
- St. Peter's Square and interior (largely by Bernini)
- Bernini statues (at Borghese Gallery; also *St. Teresa in Ecstasy* at Santa Maria della Vittoria church) and fountains (Piazza Navona, Piazza Barberini)
- Ancient obelisks erected in squares (Piazza del Popolo, Piazza Navona)
- Trevi Fountain and Spanish Steps
- Gesù and Sant'Ignazio churches
- Caravaggio's *Calling of St. Matthew* (San Luigi dei Francesi Church) and other paintings (Borghese Gallery and Vatican Museums)
- Baroque paintings (Borghese Gallery)
- Borromini's facade of Sant'Agnese Church (Piazza Navona)

MODERN ROME
(1800-PRESENT)

Rome becomes the capital of a newly reunited Italy (1871) under King Victor Emmanuel II, is modernized by fascist Mussolini, and survives the destruction of World War II to become a republic. Italy's postwar "economic miracle" makes Rome a world-class city of cinema, banking, and tourism.

Sights
- Victor Emmanuel II Monument, which honors modern Italy's first (democratic) king
- Mussolini: the balcony he spoke from (at Palazzo Venezia, on Piazza Venezia), his planned city (E.U.R.), grand boulevards (Via dei Fori Imperiali, Via della Conciliazione), his home (Villa Torlonia), and Olympic Stadium
- Cinecittà film studios and Via Veneto nightlife, which have faint echoes of Fellini's *La Dolce Vita*
- Subway system, broad boulevards, smog

ROME TODAY
After surviving the government-a-year turbulence and Mafia-tainted corruption of the postwar years, Rome is stabilizing. The

Rome in World War II

By 1943, as bombs began falling just outside the walls of Rome, it was clear to all that Italy's alliance with Nazi Germany was a huge mistake, leading the country to ruin. The fascist Grand Council dismissed Mussolini, and the king ordered his arrest. The ex-dictator fled north, and fascism collapsed without violence. Rome was declared an "open city" (meaning a city with no military bases). Italy surrendered to the Allies. The king fled to Allied-occupied southern Italy, abandoning Rome to Nazi forces, which occupied it for nine terrible months. The Roman people and the Vatican joined forces to save some citizens from the Nazis.

The Gestapo demanded 50 kilos of gold from the Roman Jews, who, with great difficulty and help from non-Jews, succeeded in providing it. Regardless, more than 2,000 Jews were deported to concentration camps. After Italian partisans planted a bomb near the Trevi Fountain, killing 32 Germans, more than 300 people randomly chosen from Rome's prison were executed in retaliation. This tragic event—called the Fosse Ardeatine massacre, for the caves near the Appian Way where it took place—remains an important milestone in the Italian consciousness. As the Allies marched closer, they bombed Rome and its surroundings, but avoided striking the center.

Thankfully, Hitler granted the occupying Nazi troops permission to leave the city, which he declared a "place of culture" that should not be "the scene of combat operations." Pope Pius XII agreed, declaring, "Whoever raises a hand against Rome will be guilty of matricide to the whole civilized world and in the eternal judgment of God." Finally, the Germans marched out, the Americans marched in (through the gate of San Giovanni) on June 4, 1944, and the exhausted city welcomed them with joy and relief.

city is less polluted and more organized. And the 21st century has seen a flurry of activity.

In celebration of the year 2000, the Eternal City gave its monuments a facelift, and Christian pilgrims poured in for a Great Jubilee Year to kick off the third millennium of their faith. Bold new architecture was added: the Auditorium Parco della Musica (by Renzo Piano, 2002), the Ara Pacis museum (by Richard Meier, 2006), and MAXXI, a state-of-the-architecture museum of modern art (by Zaha Hadid, 2010).

The Vatican is buzzing, too. In 2013, Pope Benedict XVI shockingly took an early retirement and handed the keys to the kingdom over to a free-wheeling successor, the first Jesuit pope, Francis I. A recent pope, John Paul II, was made a saint. In 2014, the classical world met classic rock when the Rolling Stones entertained the masses at the Circus Maximus. Hail, Caesar!

Today's Rome is ready for pilgrims, travelers, and you to come and make more history.

For more on Roman history, consider *Europe 101: History and Art for the Traveler,* written by Rick Steves and Gene Openshaw (available at www.ricksteves.com).

PRACTICALITIES

Tourist Information 503
Travel Tips 504
Money 505
Sightseeing 510
Sleeping 513
Eating 521
Staying Connected 539
Transportation 545
Resources from Rick Steves 555

This chapter covers the practical skills of European travel: how to get tourist information, pay for things, sightsee efficiently, find good-value accommodations, eat affordably but well, use technology wisely, and get between destinations smoothly. To study ahead and round out your knowledge and skills, check out "Resources from Rick Steves."

Tourist Information

The Italian national tourist offices **in the US** offer many brochures and a free, general Italy guide. Before your trip, scan their website (www.italia.it) for downloadable materials or contact the nearest branch to request information. If you have a specific problem, they're a good source of sympathy (New York: Tel. 212/245-5618, newyork@enit.it; Chicago: Tel. 312/644-0996, chicago@enit.it; Los Angeles: Tel. 310/820-1898, losangeles@enit.it).

In **Rome,** you'll find about a dozen small tourist information kiosks and offices scattered through town. They have maps and sell sightseeing passes but are usually not worth a special trip. It's more helpful to visit their good website (www.060608.it) or utilize their call center (tel. 06-0608, answered daily 9:00-21:00, press 2 for English), which can answer many practical questions. For more details on Rome's tourist information offices (abbreviated **TI** in this book), see page 16.

Travel Tips

Emergency and Medical Help: In Italy, dial 113 for English-speaking police help. To summon an ambulance, call 118. If you get sick, do as the locals do and go to a pharmacist for advice. Or ask at your hotel for help—they'll know the nearest medical and emergency services.

Theft or Loss: To replace a passport, you'll need to go in person to an embassy (see page 559). If your credit and debit cards disappear, cancel and replace them (see "Damage Control for Lost Cards" on page 508). File a police report, either on the spot or within a day or two; you'll need it to submit an insurance claim for lost or stolen rail passes or travel gear, and it can help with replacing your passport or credit and debit cards. For more information, see www.ricksteves.com/help.

Time Zones: Italy, like most of continental Europe, is generally six/nine hours ahead of the East/West Coasts of the US. The exceptions are the beginning and end of Daylight Saving Time: Europe "springs forward" the last Sunday in March (two weeks after most of North America), and "falls back" the last Sunday in October (one week before North America). For a handy online time converter, see www.timeanddate.com/worldclock.

Business Hours: Traditionally, Italy has used the siesta plan, with people generally working from about 9:00 to 13:00 and from 15:30 or 16:00 to 19:00 or 19:30, Monday through Saturday (though in tourist areas, larger shops may be open through lunch). In Rome, stores are usually closed on Sundays, summer Saturday afternoons, and winter Monday mornings. Banking hours are generally Monday through Friday 8:30 to 13:30 and 15:30 to 16:30, but can vary wildly.

Saturdays are virtually weekdays, with earlier closing hours. Sundays have the same pros and cons as they do for travelers in the US: Sightseeing attractions are generally open, while shops and banks are closed, public transportation options are fewer (for example, no bus service to or from the smaller towns), and there's no rush hour. Friday and Saturday evenings are lively; Sunday evenings are quiet.

Watt's Up? Europe's electrical system is 220 volts, instead of North America's 110 volts. Most newer electronics (such as laptops, battery chargers, and hair dryers) convert automatically, so

---

Exchange Rate

1 euro (€) = about $1.10

To convert prices in euros to dollars, add about 10 percent: €20=about $22, €50=about $55. (Check www.oanda.com for the latest exchange rates.) Just like the dollar, one euro is broken down into 100 cents. Coins range from €0.01 to €2, and bills from €5 to €200 (bills over €50 are rarely used; €500 bills are being phased out).

---

you won't need a converter, but you will need an adapter plug with two round prongs, sold inexpensively at travel stores in the US. However, sockets in Italy (and Switzerland) only accept plugs with slimmer prongs, so don't buy an adapter with the thicker ("Schuko" style) prongs—it won't work. Avoid bringing older appliances that don't automatically convert voltage; instead, buy a cheap replacement in Europe.

Discounts: Discounts for sights are generally not listed in this book. However, many sights offer discounts or free admission for youths (up to age 18), students (with proper identification cards, www.isic.org), families, seniors (loosely defined as retirees or those willing to call themselves a senior), and groups of 10 or more. Always ask. Italy's national museums generally offer free admission to children under 18, but some discounts are available only for citizens of the European Union (EU).

Online Translation Tips: Google's Chrome browser instantly translates websites. You can also paste text or the URL of a foreign website into the translation window at http://translate.google.com. The Google Translate app converts spoken English into most European languages (and vice versa) and can also translate text it "reads" with your mobile device's camera.

Money

This section offers advice on how to pay for purchases on your trip (including getting cash from ATMs and paying with plastic), dealing with lost or stolen cards, VAT (sales tax) refunds, and tipping.

WHAT TO BRING

Bring both a credit card and a debit card. You'll use the debit card at cash machines (ATMs) to withdraw local cash for most purchases, and the credit card to pay for larger items. Some travelers carry a third card, in case one gets demagnetized or eaten by a temperamental machine.

For an emergency stash, bring $100-200 in hard cash. Although banks in some countries don't exchange dollars, in a pinch you can always find exchange desks at major train stations or airports—convenient but with crummy rates.

CASH

Although credit cards are widely accepted in Europe, day-to-day spending is generally more cash-based. I find cash is the easiest—and sometimes only—way to pay for cheap food, bus fare, taxis, and local guides. Some vendors will charge you extra for using a credit card, some won't accept foreign credit cards, and some won't take credit cards at all. Having cash on hand can help you avoid a stressful predicament if you find yourself in a place that won't accept your card.

Throughout Europe, ATMs are the easiest and smartest way for travelers to get cash. They work just like they do at home. To withdraw money from an ATM (known as a *bancomat* in Italy), you'll need a debit card (ideally with a Visa or MasterCard logo), plus a PIN code (numeric and four digits). For increased security, shield the keypad when entering your PIN code, and don't use an ATM if anything on the front of the machine looks loose or damaged (a sign that someone may have attached a "skimming" device to capture account information). Try to withdraw large sums of money to reduce the number of per-transaction bank fees you'll pay.

When possible, use ATMs located outside banks—a thief is less likely to target a cash machine near surveillance cameras, and if your card is munched by a machine during banking hours, you can go inside for help. Stay away from "independent" ATMs such as Travelex, Euronet, YourCash, Cardpoint, and Cashzone, which charge huge commissions, have terrible exchange rates, and may try to trick users with "dynamic currency conversion" (described later). Although you can use a credit card to withdraw cash at an ATM, this comes with high bank fees and only makes sense in an emergency.

While traveling, if you want to access your accounts online, be sure to use a secure connection (see page 543).

Pickpockets target tourists. To safeguard your cash, wear a money belt—a pouch with a strap that you buckle around your waist like a belt and tuck under your clothes. Keep your cash, credit cards, and passport secure in your money belt, and carry only a day's spending money in your front pocket or wallet.

CREDIT AND DEBIT CARDS

For purchases, Visa and MasterCard are more commonly accepted than American Express. Just like at home, credit or debit cards work easily at larger hotels, restaurants, and shops. I typically use my debit card to withdraw cash to pay for most purchases. I use my credit card sparingly: to book hotel reservations, to buy advance tickets for events or sights, to cover major expenses (such as car rentals or plane tickets), and to pay for things online or near the end of my trip (to avoid another visit to the ATM). While you could instead use a debit card for these purchases, a credit card offers a greater degree of fraud protection.

Ask Your Credit- or Debit-Card Company: Before your trip, contact the company that issued your debit or credit cards.

Confirm your **card will work overseas,** and alert them that you'll be using it in Europe; otherwise, they may deny transactions if they perceive unusual spending patterns.

Ask for the specifics on transaction **fees.** When you use your credit or debit card—either for purchases or ATM withdrawals—you'll typically be charged additional "international transaction" fees of up to 3 percent (1 percent is normal). If your card's fees seem high, consider getting a card just for your trip: Capital One (www.capitalone.com) and most credit unions have low-to-no international fees.

Verify your daily ATM **withdrawal limit,** and if necessary, ask your bank to adjust it. I prefer a high limit that allows me to take out more cash at each ATM stop and save on bank fees; some travelers prefer to set a lower limit in case their card is stolen. Note that foreign banks also set maximum withdrawal amounts for their ATMs.

Get your bank's **emergency phone number** in the US (but not its 800 number, which isn't accessible from overseas) to call collect if you have a problem.

Ask for your credit card's **PIN** in case you need to make an emergency cash withdrawal or encounter payment machines using the chip-and-PIN system; the bank won't tell you your PIN over the phone, so allow time for it to be mailed to you.

Chip and PIN: While much of Europe is shifting to a chip-and-PIN security system for credit cards, Italy still uses the old magnetic-stripe technology. (European chip and PIN cards are embedded with an electronic security chip and require a four-digit PIN to make a purchase.) If you happen to encounter chip and PIN, it will probably be at payment machines, such as those at toll roads or unattended gas pumps. On the outside chance that a machine won't take your card, find a cashier who can make your card work (they can print a receipt for you to sign), or find a machine that takes cash. Most American travelers don't run into problems. Still, it pays to carry euros; remember, you can always use an ATM to withdraw cash with your magnetic-stripe debit card.

If you're concerned, ask if your bank offers a chip-and-PIN card. Andrews Federal Credit Union (www.andrewsfcu.org) and the State Department Federal Credit Union (www.sdfcu.org) offer these cards and are open to all US residents.

Dynamic Currency Conversion: If merchants or hoteliers offer to convert your purchase price into dollars (called dynamic currency conversion, or DCC), refuse this "service." You'll pay extra for the expensive convenience of seeing your charge in dollars. Some ATMs and retailers try to confuse customers by presenting DCC in misleading terms. If an ATM offers to "lock in" or "guarantee" your conversion rate, choose "proceed without conversion." Other prompts might state, "You can be charged in dollars: Press YES for dollars, NO for euros." Always choose the local currency.

Damage Control for Lost Cards

If you lose your credit or debit card, you can stop people from using your card by reporting the loss immediately to the respective global customer-assistance centers. Call these 24-hour US numbers collect: Visa (tel. 303/967-1096), MasterCard (tel. 636/722-7111), and American Express (tel. 336/393-1111). In Italy, to make a collect call to the US, dial 800-172-444. Press zero or stay on the line for an English-speaking operator. European toll-free numbers (listed by country) can also be found at the websites for Visa and MasterCard.

If you are the secondary cardholder, you'll need to provide the primary cardholder's identification-verification details (such as birth date, mother's maiden name, or Social Security number). You can generally receive a temporary card within two or three business days in Europe (see www.ricksteves.com/help for more).

If you report your loss within two days, you typically won't be responsible for any unauthorized transactions on your account, although many banks charge a liability fee of $50.

TIPPING

Tipping in Italy isn't as automatic and generous as it is in the US. For special service, tips are appreciated, but not expected. As in the US, the proper amount depends on your resources, tipping philosophy, and the circumstances, but some general guidelines apply.

Restaurants: In Italy, a service charge *(servizio)* is usually built into your bill, so the total you pay already includes a basic tip. It's up to you whether to tip beyond this. For more details on restaurant tipping, see page 523.

Taxis: To tip the cabbie, round up your fare a bit (for instance, if the fare is €4.50 fare, pay €5). If the cabbie hauls your bags and zips you to the airport to help you catch your flight, you might want to toss in a little more. But if you feel like you're being driven in circles or otherwise ripped off, skip the tip.

Services: In general, if someone in the tourism or service industry does a super job for you, a small tip of a euro or two is appropriate...but not required. If you're not sure whether (or how much) to tip, ask a local for advice.

GETTING A VAT REFUND

Wrapped into the purchase price of your Italian souvenirs is a Value-Added Tax (VAT) of about 22 percent. You're entitled to get most of that tax back if you purchase more than €155 (about $170) worth of goods at a store that participates in the VAT-refund scheme. Typically, you must ring up the minimum at a single retailer—you can't add up your purchases from various shops to reach the required amount.

Getting your refund is usually straightforward and, if you buy a substantial amount of souvenirs, well worth the hassle. If you're lucky, the merchant will subtract the tax when you make your purchase. (This is more likely to occur if the store ships the goods to your home.) Otherwise, you'll need to:

Get the paperwork. Have the merchant completely fill out the necessary refund document. You'll have to present your passport. Get the paperwork done before you leave the store to ensure you'll have everything you need (including your original sales receipt).

Get your stamp at the border or airport. Process your VAT document at your last stop in the European Union (such as at the airport) with the customs agent who deals with VAT refunds. Arrive an additional hour early before you need to check in for your flight to allow time to find the local customs office—and to stand in line. It's best to keep your purchases in your carry-on. If they're too large or dangerous to carry on (such as knives), pack them in your checked bags and alert the check-in agent. You'll be sent (with your tagged bag) to a customs desk outside security; someone will examine your bag, stamp your paperwork, and put your bag on the belt. You're not supposed to use your purchased goods before you leave. If you show up at customs wearing your new Italian leather shoes, officials might look the other way—or deny you a refund.

Collect your refund. You'll need to return your stamped document to the retailer or its representative. Many merchants work with services—such as Global Blue or Premier Tax Free—that have offices at major airports, ports, or border crossings (either before or after security, probably strategically located near a duty-free shop). These services, which extract a 4 percent fee, can refund your money immediately in cash or credit your card (within two billing cycles). Other refund services may require you to mail the documents from home, or more quickly, from your point of departure (using an envelope you've prepared in advance or one that's been provided by the merchant). You'll then have to wait—it can take months.

CUSTOMS FOR AMERICAN SHOPPERS

You are allowed to take home $800 worth of items per person duty-free, once every 31 days. You can also bring in a liter of alcohol duty-free. As for food, you can take home many processed and packaged foods: vacuum-packed cheeses, dried herbs, jams, baked goods, candy, chocolate, oil, vinegar, mustard, and honey. Fresh fruits and vegetables and most meats are not allowed, with exceptions for some canned items. As for alcohol, you can bring in one liter duty-free (it can be packed securely in your checked luggage, along with any other liquid-containing items).

To bring alcohol (or liquid-packed foods) in your carry-on bag on your flight home, buy it at a duty-free shop at the airport. You'll increase your odds of getting it onto a connecting flight if it's packaged in a "STEB"—a secure, tamper-evident bag. But stay away from liquids in opaque, ceramic, or metallic containers, which usually cannot be successfully screened (STEB or no STEB).

For details on allowable goods, customs rules, and duty rates, visit http://help.cbp.gov.

Sightseeing

Sightseeing can be hard work. Use these tips to make your visits to Rome's finest sights meaningful, fun, efficient, and painless.

MAPS AND NAVIGATION TOOLS

A good map is essential for efficient navigation while sightseeing. The black-and-white maps in this book are concise and simple, designed to help you locate recommended destinations, sights, and local TIs, where you can pick up more in-depth maps. Maps with even more detail are sold at newsstands and bookstores.

You can also use a mapping app on your mobile device. Be aware that pulling up maps or looking up turn-by-turn walking directions on the fly requires an Internet connection: To use this feature, it's smart to get an international data plan (see page 539) or only connect using Wi-Fi. With Google Maps or Apple Maps, it's possible to download a map while online, then go offline and navigate without incurring data-roaming charges, though you can't search for an address or get real-time walking directions. A handful of other apps—including City Maps 2Go, OffMaps, and Navfree—also allow you to use maps offline.

PLAN AHEAD

Set up an itinerary that allows you to fit in all your must-see sights. For a one-stop look at opening hours, see "Rome at a Glance" (page 46; also see the "Daily Reminder" on page 17). Most sights keep stable hours, but you can easily confirm the latest by checking with the TI or visiting museum websites.

For Rome, if you want to see the Borghese Gallery, you must make reservations in advance (see page 271). It's smart to reserve for the Vatican Museums (see page 235) as well. And you can buy tickets in advance for the Colosseum and the Roman Forum (see page 142)—although there are also other ways to skip the line at those ancient sites.

Don't put off visiting a must-see sight—you never know when a place will close unexpectedly for a holiday, strike, or restoration. Many museums are closed or have reduced hours at least a few days a year, especially on holidays such as Labor Day (May 1), Christmas, and New Year's. A list of holidays is on page 560; check online for possible museum closures during your trip. In summer, some sights may stay open late. Off-season, many museums have shorter hours.

Going at the right time helps avoid crowds. This book offers tips on specific sights. Try visiting popular sights very early or very late. Evening visits are usually peaceful, with fewer crowds.

Study up. To get the most out of the self-guided tours and sight descriptions in this book, read them before you visit.

AT SIGHTS

Here's what you can typically expect:

Entering: Be warned that you may not be allowed to enter if you arrive less than 30 to 60 minutes before closing time. And guards start ushering people out well before the actual closing time, so don't save the best for last.

Some important sights have a security check, where you must open your bag or send it through a metal detector. Some sights require you to check daypacks and coats. (If you'd rather not check your daypack, try carrying it tucked under your arm like a purse as you enter.)

Photography: If the museum's photo policy isn't clearly posted, ask a guard. Generally, taking photos without a flash or tripod is allowed. Some sights ban photos altogether; others ban selfie sticks.

Temporary Exhibits: Museums may show special exhibits in addition to their permanent collection. Some exhibits are included in the entry price, while others come at an extra cost (which you may have to pay even if you don't want to see the exhibit).

Expect Changes: Artwork can be on tour, on loan, out sick, or shifted at the whim of the curator. Pick up a floor plan as you enter, and ask the museum staff if you can't find a particular item. Say the title or artist's name, or point to the photograph in this book and ask, *"Dov'è?"* (doh-VEH, meaning "Where is?").

Audioguides and Apps: Many sights rent audioguides, which

PRACTICALITIES

generally offer excellent recorded descriptions in English. If you bring your own earbuds, you can enjoy better sound and avoid holding the device to your ear. To save money, bring a Y-jack and share one audioguide with your travel partner. Museums and sights often offer free apps that you can download to your mobile device (check their websites). And, I've produced free, downloadable audio tours for my Heart of Rome, Trastevere, and Jewish Ghetto walks, and my tours of the Pantheon, St. Peter's Basilica, Roman Forum, Colosseum, Sistine Chapel, Vatican Museums, Ostia Antica, and Pompeii; look for the ∩ in this book. For more on my audio tours, see page 8.

Dates for Artwork: In museums, art is dated with *sec* (for *secolo*—century, often indicated with Roman numerals), A.C. (for *Avanti Cristo*, i.e., before Christ), and D.C. (for *Dopo Cristo*, a.k.a. A.D.). OK?

Services: Important sights may have an on-site café or cafeteria (usually a handy place to rejuvenate during a long visit). The WCs at sights are free and generally clean.

Before Leaving: At the gift shop, scan the postcard rack or thumb through a guidebook to be sure you haven't overlooked something that you'd like to see.

Every sight or museum offers more than what is covered in this book. Use the information in this book as an introduction—not the final word.

FIND RELIGION

Churches offer some amazing art (usually free), a cool respite from heat, and a welcome seat.

A modest dress code—no bare shoulders or shorts for anyone, even kids—is enforced at the Vatican City (St. Peter's Basilica and Vatican Museums) and at Rome's major churches, such as St. Paul's Outside the Walls, but is often overlooked elsewhere. If you're caught by surprise, you can improvise, using maps to cover your shoulders and a jacket for your knees. (I wear a super-lightweight pair of long pants rather than shorts for my hot and muggy big-city Italian sightseeing.)

Some churches have coin-operated audioboxes that describe the art and history; just set the dial on English, put in your coins, and listen. Coin boxes near a piece of art illuminate the art (and present a better photo opportunity). I pop in a coin whenever I can. It improves my experience, is a favor to other visitors trying to appreciate a great piece of art in the dark, and is a little contribution to that church and its work. Whenever possible, let there be light.

Sleeping

I favor hotels and restaurants that are handy to your sightseeing activities. Rather than list hotels scattered throughout Rome, I choose hotels in my favorite neighborhoods. My recommendations run the gamut, from hotels with all of the comforts to less-expensive hostels and convents.

A major feature of this book is its extensive and opinionated listing of good-value rooms—especially in Rome, where hotels are generally pricey, the cheaper hotels can be depressing, and the TI isn't allowed to give opinions on quality. I like places that are clean, central, relatively quiet at night, reasonably priced, friendly, small enough to have a hands-on owner and stable staff, and run with a respect for Italian traditions. I'm more impressed by a convenient location and a fun-loving philosophy than flat-screen TVs and a fancy gym. Most places I recommend fall short of perfection. But if I can find a place with most of these features, it's a keeper.

Book your accommodations well in advance, especially if you want to stay at one of my top listings or if you'll be traveling during busy times. See page 560 for a list of major holidays and festivals in Rome; for tips on making reservations, see page 515.

RATES AND DEALS

I've categorized my recommended accommodations based on price, indicated with a dollar-sign rating (see sidebar). The price ranges suggest an estimated cost for a one-night stay in a standard double room with a private toilet and shower in high season, include breakfast, and assume you're booking directly with the hotel (not through a booking site, which extracts a commission and logically closes the door on special deals). Room prices can fluctuate significantly with demand and amenities (size, views, room class, and so on), but these relative price categories remain constant.

Rome charges a hotel tax of €3-6 per person, per night, which must be paid in cash and is typically not included in the prices in this book. The only exemptions are for hostelers and children under age 10.

Room rates are especially volatile at larger hotels that use "dynamic pricing" to predict demand. Rates can skyrocket during festivals and conventions, while business hotels can have deep discounts on weekends when demand plummets. For this reason, of the many hotels I recommend, it's difficult to say which will be the best value on a given day—until you do your homework.

Once your dates are set, check the specific price for your preferred stay at several hotels. You can do this either by comparing prices online on the hotels' own websites, or by emailing several hotels directly and asking for their best rate. Even if you start your

Sleep Code

Hotels are classified based on the average price of a standard double room with breakfast in high season.

$$$$	**Splurge:** Most rooms over €170
$$$	**Pricier:** €130-170
$$	**Moderate:** €90-130
$	**Budget:** €50-90
¢	**Backpacker:** Under €50
RS%	**Rick Steves discount**

Unless otherwise noted, credit cards are accepted, hotel staff speak basic English, and free Wi-Fi is available. Comparison-shop by checking prices at several hotels (on each hotel's own website, on a booking site, or by email). For the best deal, *book directly with the hotel*. Ask for a discount if paying in cash; if the listing includes **RS%**, request a Rick Steves discount.

search on a booking site such as TripAdvisor or Booking.com, you'll usually find the lowest rates through a hotel's own website.

Many hotels offer a discount to those who pay cash or stay longer than three nights. To cut costs further, try asking for a cheaper room (for example, with a shared bathroom or no window) or offer to skip breakfast.

Additionally, some accommodations offer a special discount for Rick Steves readers, indicated in this guidebook by the abbreviation "**RS%**." Discounts vary: Ask for details when you book. Generally, to qualify you must book direct (that is, not through a booking site), mention this book when you reserve, show the book upon arrival, and sometimes pay cash or stay a certain number of nights. In some cases, you may need to enter a discount code (which I've provided in the listing) in the booking form on the hotel's website. Rick Steves discounts apply to readers with ebooks as well as printed books. Understandably, discounts do not apply to promotional rates.

Haggle if you arrive late in the day during off-season (roughly mid-July through August and November through mid-March). It's common for hotels in Rome to lower their prices 10-50 percent in the off-season, although prices at hostels and the cheaper hotels won't fluctuate much. Room rates are lowest in sweltering August.

TYPES OF ACCOMMODATIONS
Hotels

Double rooms with private bathrooms listed in this book range from about €85 to €350-plus (maximum plumbing and more), with most clustering around €150. I've favored these pricier options, be-

Making Hotel Reservations

Reserve your rooms several weeks or even months in advance—or as soon as you've pinned down your travel dates. Note that some national holidays merit your making reservations far in advance (see page 560).

Requesting a Reservation: It's easiest to book your room through the hotel's website. (For the best rates, always use the hotel's official site and not a booking agency's site.) If there's no reservation form, or for complicated requests, send an email. Most recommended hotels take reservations in English.

The hotelier wants to know:

- the size of your party and type of rooms you need
- your arrival and departure dates, written European-style—day followed by month and year (for example, 18/06/17 or 18 June 2017); include the total number of nights
- special requests (such as en suite bathroom vs. down the hall, cheapest room, twin beds vs. double bed, quiet room)
- applicable discounts (such as a Rick Steves reader discount, cash discount, or promotional rate)

Confirming a Reservation: Most places will request a credit-card number to hold your room. If they don't have a secure online reservation form—look for the *https*—you can email it (I do), but it's safer to share that confidential info via a phone call or fax.

Canceling a Reservation: If you must cancel, it's courteous—and smart—to do so with as much notice as possible, especially for smaller family-run places. Cancellation policies can be strict; read the fine print or ask about these before you book. Many discount deals require prepayment, with no cancellation refunds.

Reconfirming a Reservation: Always call or email to reconfirm your room reservation a few days in advance. For B&Bs or very small hotels, I call again on my day of arrival to tell my host what time I expect to get there (especially important if arriving late—after 17:00).

Phoning: For tips on calling hotels overseas, see page 540.

From:	rick@ricksteves.com
Sent:	Today
To:	info@hotelcentral.com
Subject:	Reservation request for 19-22 July

Dear Hotel Central,
I would like to stay at your hotel. Please let me know if you have a room available and the price for:
- 2 people
- Double bed and en suite bathroom in a quiet room
- Arriving 19 July, departing 22 July (3 nights)

Thank you!
Rick Steves

> ## Keep Cool
>
> If you're visiting Italy in the summer, the extra expense of an air-conditioned room can be money well spent, particularly in the south. Most hotel rooms with air-conditioners come with a control stick (like a TV remote; the hotel may require a deposit) that generally has similar symbols and features: fan icon (click to toggle through wind power, from light to gale); louver icon (choose steady airflow or waves); snowflake and sunshine icons (cold air or heat); clock ("O" setting: run X hours before turning off; "I" setting: wait X hours to start); and the temperature control (20 degrees Celsius is comfortable; also see the thermometer diagram on page 566). When you leave your room for the day, turning off the air-conditioning is good form.

cause intense Rome is easier to enjoy with a welcoming oasis to call home.

Most hotels also offer single rooms, and some offer larger rooms for four or more people (I call these "family rooms" in the listings). Some hotels can add an extra bed to a double room to make a triple for a small charge. Solo travelers find that the cost of a *camera singola* is often only 25 percent less than a *camera doppia*. Three or four people can save money by requesting one big room. (If a Db is €110, a Qb would be about €150.) Most listed hotels have rooms for anywhere from one to five people. If there's room for an extra cot, they'll cram it in for you.

Traffic in Rome roars. Thanks to double-paned windows and air-conditioning, night noise is not the problem it once was. Even so, light sleepers who ask for a *tranquillo* room will likely get a room in the back...and sleep better. Once you actually see your room, consider the potential problem of night noise. Don't hesitate to ask for a quieter room.

Nearly all places offer private bathrooms. Generally rooms with a bath or shower also have a toilet and a bidet (which Italians use for quick sponge baths). The cord over the tub or shower is not a clothesline. You pull it when you've fallen and can't get up.

Double beds are called *matrimoniale*, even though hotels aren't interested in your marital status. Twins are *due letti singoli*. Convents offer cheap accommodation but have more *letti singoli* than *matrimoniali*.

When you check in, the receptionist will normally ask for your passport and keep it for anywhere from a couple of minutes to a couple of hours. Hotels are legally required to register each guest with the police. Relax. Americans are notorious for making this chore more difficult than it needs to be.

Hotels and B&Bs are sometimes located on the higher floors

of a multipurpose building with a secured door. In that case, look for your hotel's name on the buttons by the main entrance. When you ring the bell, you'll be buzzed in. Hotel elevators are becoming more common, though some older buildings still lack an elevator, or you may have to climb a flight of stairs to reach it (if so, you can ask the front desk for help carrying your bags up). Also, elevators are often very small—pack light, or you may need to send your bags up one at a time.

Italian hotels typically include breakfast in their room prices. If breakfast is optional, you may want to skip it. While convenient, it's usually pricey for what you get: a simple continental buffet with (at its most generous) bread, ham, cheese, yogurt, and unlimited *caffè latte*. A picnic in your room followed by a coffee at the corner café can be lots cheaper.

More pillows and blankets are usually in the closet or available on request. Towels and linens aren't always replaced every day. Hang your towel up to dry. Some hotels use lightweight "waffle," or very thin, tablecloth-type towels; these take less water and electricity to launder and are preferred by many Italians.

Most hotel rooms have a TV, telephone, and free Wi-Fi (although in old buildings with thick walls, the Wi-Fi signal doesn't always make it to the rooms; sometimes it's only available in the lobby). Sometimes there's a guest computer with Internet access in the lobby. Simpler places rarely have a room phone, but often have free Wi-Fi. Pricier hotels usually come with a small fridge stocked with beverages called a *frigo bar* (FREE-goh bar; pay for what you use).

Almost no hotels have parking, but nearly all have a line on spots in a nearby garage (typically about €25/day).

If you're arriving in the morning, your room probably won't be ready. Check your bag safely at the hotel and dive right into sightseeing.

Hoteliers can be a great help and source of advice. Most know their city well, and can assist you with everything from public transit and airport connections to finding a good restaurant, the nearest launderette, or a late-night pharmacy.

Some hotels occupy one floor of a building with a finicky vintage elevator or slightly dingy entryway. The hotelier doesn't control the building's common areas, so try not to let the entryway atmosphere color your opinion of the hotel. Even at the best places, mechanical breakdowns occur: Sinks leak, hot water turns cold, toilets may gurgle or smell, the Wi-Fi goes out, or the air-conditioning dies when you need it most. Report your concerns clearly and calmly at the front desk. For more complicated problems, don't expect instant results.

To guard against theft in your room, keep valuables out of

sight. Some rooms come with a safe, and other hotels have safes at the front desk. I've never bothered using one.

While it's customary to pay for your room upon departure, it can be a good idea to settle your bill the day before, when you're not in a hurry and while the manager's in. That way you'll have time to discuss and address any points of contention.

Above all, keep a positive attitude. Remember, you're on vacation. If your hotel is a disappointment, spend more time out enjoying the place you came to see.

Bed-and-Breakfasts (B&Bs)

B&Bs offer double the cultural intimacy for a good deal less than most hotel rooms. Roman B&Bs are small—most have no more than three rooms, and the owner generally lives on-site. (Be aware that small hotels sometimes erroneously use the term "B&B.") You'll pay in cash rather than by credit card. Expect few services and no amenities such as public lounges, in-room phones, private bathrooms, and daily bed-sheet changes (though the basics, such as sheets and towels, are provided). After picking up your keys, you can come and go as you wish. When reserving, confirm what kind of breakfast is included—some less-expensive B&Bs simply give you a voucher for a pastry and coffee at a nearby bar.

Doubles with breakfast start at around €70, with prices increasing along with the number of amenities. Because of my large volume of readers and the small size of Roman B&Bs, it isn't practical to include many B&B listings here. To find a B&B in Rome, start your search with a website such as www.bedandbreakfast.com or www.b-b.rm.it. You'll get better prices, however, by booking directly with the B&B. Some websites connect you directly with the B&B owner, including www.gulliverslodge.com (see listing on page 348).

Many B&Bs come with thin walls and doors that can make for a noisy night. If you're a light sleeper, bring earplugs. And please be quiet in the halls and in your rooms at night (talk softly, and keep the TV volume low)...those of us getting up early will thank you for it.

Short-Term Rentals

A short-term rental—whether an apartment, house, or room in a local's home—is an increasingly popular alternative to a B&B or hotel, especially if you plan to settle in one location for several nights. For stays longer than a few days, you can usually find a rental that's comparable to—or even cheaper than—a hotel room with similar amenities. Plus, you'll get a behind-the-scenes peek into how locals live.

The rental route isn't for everyone. Many places require a minimum night stay, and compared to hotels, rentals usually have less-flexible cancellation policies. Also you're generally on your own: There's no hotel reception desk, breakfast, or daily cleaning service.

Finding Accommodations: Websites such as www.airbnb.com, www.roomorama.com, and www.vrbo.com let you browse properties and correspond directly with European property owners or managers. For more guidance, consider using a rental agency such as www.interhomeusa.com or www.rentavilla.com. Agency-represented apartments may cost more, but this route often offers more help and safeguards than booking direct. Or try Steve and Linda of **Cross-Pollinate,** a booking service for private rooms and apartments in the old centers of Rome, Florence, and Venice; rates start at €30 per person, www.cross-pollinate.com). They also run **The Beehive,** a budget hotel in Rome (see listing on page 349). You can also browse through www.wantedinrome.com.

Before you commit to a rental, be clear on the details, location, and amenities. I like to virtually "explore" the neighborhood using the Street View feature on Google Maps. Also consider the proximity to public transportation, and how well-connected it is with the rest of the city. Ask about amenities that are important to you (elevator, laundry, coffee maker, Wi-Fi, parking, etc.). Reading reviews from previous guests can help identify trouble spots that are glossed over in the official description.

Apartments: If you're staying somewhere for four nights or longer, it's worth considering an apartment (anything less than that isn't worth the extra effort involved, such as arranging key pickup, buying groceries, etc.). Apartment rentals can be especially cost-effective for groups and families. European apartments, like hotel rooms, tend to be small by US standards. But they often come with laundry machines and small, equipped kitchens *(cucinetta),* making it easier and cheaper to dine in. If you make good use of the kitchen (and Europe's great produce markets), you'll save on your meal budget.

Private and Shared Rooms: Renting a room in someone's home is a good option for those traveling alone, as you're more likely to find true single rooms—with just one single bed, and a price to match. Beds range from air-mattress-in-living-room basic to plush-B&B-suite posh. Some places allow you to book for a single night; if staying for several nights, you can buy groceries just as you would in a rental house. While you can't expect your host to also be your tour guide—or even to provide you with much info—some may be interested in getting to know the travelers who come through their home.

Other Options: Swapping homes with a local works for people with an appealing place to offer, and who can live with the idea of having strangers in their home (don't assume where you live is

PRACTICALITIES

The Good and Bad of Online Reviews

User-generated review sites and apps such as Yelp, Booking. com, and TripAdvisor are changing the travel industry. These sites can give you a consensus of opinions about everything from hotels and restaurants to sights and nightlife. If you scan reviews of a hotel and see several complaints about noise or a rotten location, it tells you something important that you'd never learn from the hotel's own website.

But review sites are only as good as the judgment of their reviewers. And while these sites work hard to weed out bogus users, my hunch is that a significant percentage of user reviews are posted by friends or enemies of the business being reviewed.

As a guidebook writer, my sense is that there is a big difference between this uncurated information and a guidebook. A user-generated review is based on the experience of one person, who likely stayed at one hotel and ate at a few restaurants, and doesn't have much of a basis for comparison. A guidebook is the work of a trained researcher who visited many alternatives to assess their relative value. I recently checked out some top-rated user-reviewed hotel and restaurant listings in various towns; when stacked up against their competitors, some were gems, while just as many were duds. Both types of information have their place, and in many ways, they're complementary. If something is well-reviewed in a guidebook, and also gets good ratings on one of these sites, it's likely a winner.

not interesting to Europeans). A good place to start is HomeExchange (www.homeexchange.com).

To sleep for free, Couchsurfing.com is a vagabond's alternative to Airbnb. It lists millions of outgoing members, who host fellow "surfers" in their homes.

Hostels

A hostel provides cheap beds in dorms where you sleep alongside strangers for about €20-30 per night. Travelers of any age are welcome if they don't mind dorm-style accommodations and meeting other travelers. Most hostels offer kitchen facilities, guest computers, Wi-Fi, and self-service laundry. Hostels almost always provide bedding, but the towel's up to you (though you can usually rent one for a small fee). Family and private rooms are often available on request.

Independent hostels tend to be easygoing, colorful, and informal (no membership required; www.hostelworld.com). You may pay slightly less by booking direct with the hostel. **Official hostels** are part of Hostelling International (HI) and share a booking site (www.hihostels.com). HI hostels typically require that you be a member or pay extra per night. If going the hostel route, consider the ones I list in the Sleeping in Rome chapter (within a 10-minute walk of Termini train station).

Convents

Nun-run places are common in Rome, offering cheap twin beds, little English, and an interesting experience. See the Sleeping in Rome chapter for listings.

Eating

The Italians are masters of the art of fine living. That means eating long and well. Lengthy, multicourse meals and endless hours sitting in outdoor cafés are the norm. Americans eat on their way to an evening event and complain if the check is slow in coming. For Italians, the meal is an end in itself, and only rude waiters rush you.

A highlight of your Italian adventure will be this country's cafés, cuisine, and wines. Trust me: This is sightseeing for your palate. Even if you liked dorm food and are sleeping in cheap hotels, your taste buds will relish an occasional first-class splurge. You can eat well without going broke. But be careful: You're just as likely to blow a small fortune on a disappointing meal as you are to dine wonderfully for €25. Rely on my recommendations in the Eating in Rome chapter.

In general, Italians eat meals a bit later than we do. Eating like a Roman means stopping at the neighborhood bar each morning for a light breakfast (coffee—usually cappuccino or espresso—and a pastry, often standing up at a café). Lunch (between 13:00 and 15:00) is traditionally the largest meal of the day, eaten at home, although work habits have changed this for many people who don't want to spend time commuting. Instead, they grab a quick meal in a *tavola calda* bar (cafeteria) or buy a *panino* or *tramezzino* (sandwich). They eat a late, light dinner (around 20:00-21:30, or maybe earlier in winter). To bridge the gap, people drop into a bar in the late afternoon for a *spuntino* (snack) and aperitif.

RESTAURANT PRICING

I've categorized my recommended eateries based on price, indicated with a dollar-sign rating (see sidebar). The price ranges suggest the average price of a typical main course—but not necessarily a complete meal. Sticking to pastas will save you plenty over ordering meat-and-fish *secondi*. Obviously, expensive items (steak, seafood, truffles), fine wine, appetizers, and dessert can significantly increase your final bill.

Restaurant Price Code

I've assigned each eatery a price category, based on the average cost of a typical main course (pasta or *secondi*). Drinks, desserts, and splurge items (steak and seafood) can raise the price considerably.

$$$$	**Splurge:** Most main courses over €20
$$$	**Pricier:** €15-20
$$	**Moderate:** €10-15
$	**Budget:** Under €10

In Italy, pizza by the slice and other takeaway food is **$**; a basic trattoria or sit-down pizzeria is **$$**; a casual but more upscale restaurant is **$$$**; and a swanky splurge is **$$$$**.

The dollar-sign categories also indicate the overall personality and "feel" of a place:

$ Budget eateries include street food, takeaway, order-at-the-counter shops, basic cafeterias, and bakeries selling sandwiches.

$$ Moderate eateries are typically nice (but not fancy) sit-down restaurants, ideal for a straightforward, fill-the-tank meal. Most of my listings fall in this category—great for getting a good taste of the local cuisine on a budget.

$$$ Pricier eateries are a notch up, with more attention paid to the setting, service, and cuisine. These are ideal for a memorable meal that's relatively casual and doesn't break the bank. This category often includes affordable "destination" or "foodie" restaurants.

$$$$ Splurge eateries are dress-up-for-a-special-occasion-swanky—Michelin star-type restaurants, typically with an elegant setting, polished service, pricey and intricate cuisine, and an expansive (and expensive) wine list.

To assign price ranges for restaurants in Italy, these price points were my rule of thumb: **$$$$**—most pastas over €13, *secondi* over €20; **$$$**—most pizzas/pastas €11-12, *secondi* €15-20; **$$**—most pizzas/pastas under €11, *secondi* under €15; **$**—meals under €10. I haven't categorized places where you might assemble a picnic, snack, or graze: supermarkets, delis, ice cream stands, cafés or bars specializing in drinks, chocolate shops, and so on.

BREAKFAST

Italian breakfasts, like Italian bath towels, are small: The basic, traditional version is coffee and a roll with butter and marmalade. These days, most places also have yogurt and juice (the delicious red orange juice—*spremuta d'arancia rossa*—is made from Sicilian blood oranges), and possibly also cereal, cold cuts and sliced cheese, and eggs (typically hard-boiled; scrambled or fried eggs are rare).

Small budget hotels may leave a basic breakfast in your room (stale croissant, roll, jam, yogurt, coffee).

If you want to skip your hotel breakfast, consider browsing for a morning picnic at a local open-air market. Or do as the Italians do: Stop into a bar or café to drink a cappuccino and munch a *cornetto* (croissant) while standing at the bar. While the *cornetto* is the most common pastry, you'll find a range of *pasticcini* (pastries, sometimes called *dolci*—sweets). Look for *otto* (an 8-shaped pastry, often filled with custard, jam, or chocolate), *sfoglia* (can be fruit-filled, like a turnover), or *ciambella* (doughnut filled with custard or chocolate)—or ask about local specialties.

ITALIAN RESTAURANTS

While *ristorante* is self-explanatory, you'll also see other types of Italian eateries. A trattoria and an *osteria* (which can be more ca-

sual) are both generally family-owned places serving home-cooked meals, often at moderate prices. A *locanda* is an inn, a *cantina* is a wine cellar, and a *birreria* is a brewpub. *Pizzerie*, *rosticcerie* (delis), *tavola calda* ("hot table") bars, *enoteche* (wine bars), and other alternatives are explained later.

When restaurant-hunting, choose a spot filled with locals, not the place with the big neon signs boasting, "We speak English and accept credit cards." Restaurants parked on famous squares generally serve bad food at high prices to tourists. Venturing even a block or two off the main drag leads to higher-quality food for less than half the price of the tourist-oriented places. Locals eat better at lower-rent locales. Family-run places operate without hired help and can offer cheaper meals.

Most restaurant kitchens close between their lunch and dinner service. Good restaurants don't reopen for dinner before 19:00. Small restaurants with a full slate of reservations for 20:30 or 21:00 often will accommodate walk-in diners willing to eat a quick, early meal, but you aren't expected to linger.

When you want the bill, mime-scribble on your raised palm or request it: *"Il conto, per favore."* You may have to ask for it more than once. If you're in a hurry, request the check when you receive the last item you order.

Cover and Tipping

Before you sit down, look at a menu to see what extra charges a restaurant tacks on. Two different items are routinely factored into your bill: the *coperto* and the *servizio*.

PRACTICALITIES

The **coperto** (cover charge), sometimes called *pane e coperto* (bread and cover), is the fee for your table setting (including the typical basket of bread). It's not negotiable, even if you don't eat the bread. Think of it as covering the cost of using the table for as long as you like. (Italians like to linger.) Most restaurants add the *coperto* onto your bill as a flat fee (€1-3.50 per person; the amount should be clearly noted on the menu). Technically, cover charges are forbidden by law in Rome, although you may occasionally still see them.

The **servizio** (service charge) of about 10 percent is similar to the mandatory gratuity that American restaurants often add for groups of six or more. Most legitimate eateries don't have a service charge: The words *servizio incluso* on the menu and/or the receipt indicate that you're not required to pay anything beyond the listed prices (the *servizio* is built in). You can add an additional tip, if you choose, by including €1-2 for each person in your party. While Italians don't think about tips in terms of percentages—and many don't tip at all—this extra amount usually comes out to about 5 percent (10 percent is excessive for all but the very best service).

Some trendy restaurants don't include the service in the menu prices—instead they tack a *servizio* charge onto your bill. In these cases you'll see something like *"servizio 10%"* on the menu, and the fee will be added onto your bill (so you don't need to calculate it yourself and pay it separately). Rarely, you'll see the words *servizio non incluso* on the menu or bill; here you are expected to add a tip of about 10 percent.

Most Italian restaurants have a cover charge and include service in the menu prices. A few have just a service charge (especially in Rome, where cover charges are banned). Places with *both* a cover and a tacked-on service charge are best avoided—that's a clue that a restaurant is counting on a nonlocal clientele who can't gauge value. Self-service restaurants never have a cover or service charge, and in recent years some (especially less formal) cafés and restaurants with table service have stopped charging these fees as well.

Courses: Antipasto, *Primo*, and *Secondo*

For a list of Italian cuisine staples, including some of the most common dishes, see page 530. A full Italian meal consists of several courses:

Antipasto: An appetizer such as bruschetta, grilled veggies, deep-fried tasties, thin-sliced meat (such as prosciutto or carpaccio), or a plate of olives, cold cuts, and cheeses. To get a sampler plate of cold cuts and cheeses in a restaurant, ask for *affettato misto* (mixed cold cuts) or *antipasto misto* (cold cuts, cheeses, and marinated vegetables). This could make a light meal in itself.

Primo piatto: A "first dish" generally consisting of pasta, rice, or soup. If you think of pasta when you think of Italy, you can dine well here without ever going beyond the *primo.*

Secondo piatto: A "second dish," equivalent to our main course, of meat or fish/seafood. Italians freely admit the *secondo* is the least interesting part of their cuisine. A vegetable side dish *(contorno)* may come with the *secondo* but more often must be ordered separately.

For most travelers, a meal with all three courses (plus *contorni,* dessert, and wine) is simply too much food—and euros can add up in a hurry. To avoid overeating (and to stretch your budget), share dishes. A good rule of thumb is for each person to order any two courses. For example, a couple can order and share one antipasto, one *primo,* one *secondo,* and one dessert; or two *antipasti* and two *primi;* or whatever combination appeals.

Another good option is sharing an array of *antipasti*—either by ordering several specific dishes or, at restaurants that offer self-serve buffets, by choosing a variety of cold and cooked appetizers from an *antipasti* buffet spread out like a salad bar. At buffets, you pay per plate; a typical serving costs about €8 (generally Italians don't treat buffets as all-you-can-eat, but take a one-time moderate serving; watch others and imitate).

To maximize the experience and flavors, small groups can mix *antipasti* and *primi* family-style (skipping *secondi*). If you do this right, you can eat well in better places for less than the cost of a tourist *menù* in a cheap place.

A few restaurants serve a *piatto unico,* with smaller portions of each course on one dish (for instance, a meat, starch, and vegetable).

Ordering Tips

Seafood and steak may be sold by weight (priced by the kilo—1,000 grams, or just over two pounds; or by the *etto*—100 grams). The abbreviation *s.q. (secondo quantità)* means an item is priced "according to quantity." Unless the menu indicates a fillet *(filetto),* fish is usually served whole with the head and tail. However, you can always ask your waiter to select a small fish for you. Sometimes, especially for steak, restaurants require a minimum order of four or five *etti* (which diners can share). Make sure you're clear on the price before ordering.

Some special dishes come in larger quantities meant to be shared by two people. The shorthand way of showing this on a menu is "X2" (for two), but the price listed generally indicates the cost per person.

In a traditional restaurant, if you order a pasta dish and a side salad—but no main course—the waiter will bring the salad after the pasta (Italians prefer it this way, believing that it enhances digestion). If you want the salad with your pasta, specify *insieme* (een-see-YEH-meh; together). At eateries more accustomed to tourists, you may be asked when you want the salad.

Because pasta and bread are both starches, Italians consider them redundant. If you order only a pasta dish, bread may not come with it; you can request it, but you may be charged extra. On the other hand, if you order a vegetable antipasto or a meat *secondo*, bread is often provided to balance the ingredients.

At places with counter service—such as at a bar or a freeway rest-stop diner—you'll order and pay at the *cassa* (cashier). Take your receipt over to the counter to claim your food.

Fixed-Price Meals and Ordering à la Carte

You can save by getting a fixed-priced meal, which is frequently exempt from cover and service charges. Avoid the cheapest ones (often called a *menù turistico*), which tend to be bland and heavy, pairing a very basic pasta with reheated schnitzel and roast meats. Look instead for a genuine *menù del giorno* (menu of the day), which offers diners a choice of appetizer, main course, and dessert. It's worth paying a little more for an inventive fixed-price meal that shows off the chef's creativity.

While fixed-price meals can be easy and convenient, galloping gourmets prefer to order à la carte with the help of a menu translator (see "Italian Cuisine Staples," later). When going to an especially good restaurant with an approachable staff, I like to find out what they're eager to serve. Sometimes I'll simply say, *"Mi faccia felice"* (Make me happy) and set a price limit.

BUDGET EATING

Italy offers many budget options for hungry travelers, but beware of cheap eateries that sport big color photos of pizza and piles of different pastas. They often have no kitchens and simply microwave disgusting prepackaged food.

Self-service cafeterias offer the basics without add-on charges. Travelers on a hard-core budget equip their room with a pantry stocked at the market (fruits and veggies are remarkably cheap), or pick up a sandwich or *döner kebab*, then dine in at picnic prices. Bars and cafés are also good places to grab a meal on the go.

Pizzerias

Pizza is cheap and readily available. Stop by a pizza shop for stand-up or takeout (*pizza al taglio* means "by the slice"). Supermarkets

usually have a pizza counter too. Some shops sell individual slices of round, Naples-style pizza, while others feature *pizza rustica*—thick pizza baked in a large rectangular pan and sold by weight. If you simply ask for a piece, you may wind up with a gigantic slab and be charged top euro. Instead, clearly indicate how much you want: 100 grams, or *un etto*, is a hot and cheap snack; 200 grams, or *due etti*, makes a light meal. Or show the size with your hands—*tanto così* (TAHN-toh koh-ZEE; this much). They'll often helpfully cut it up into smaller pieces. If you want your pizza warm, say *"si"* when they ask if you want it heated up (*scaldare;* skahl-DAH-ray). For a rundown of common types of pizza, see page 530.

Bars/Cafés

Italian "bars" are not taverns, but inexpensive cafés. These neighborhood hangouts serve coffee, minipizzas, sandwiches, and drinks from the cooler. Many dish up plates of fried cheese and vegetables from under the glass counter, ready to reheat. This budget choice is the Italian equivalent of English pub grub.

Many bars are small—if you can't find a table, you'll need to stand or find a ledge to sit on outside. Most charge extra for table service. To get food to go, say, *"da portar via"* (for the road). All bars have a WC (*toilette, bagno*) in the back, and customers—and the discreet public—can use it.

Food: For quick meals, bars usually have trays of cheap, premade sandwiches (*panini,* on a baguette; *piadini,* on flatbread, or *tramezzini,* on crustless white bread)—some are delightful grilled. (Others have too much mayo.) To save time for sightseeing and room for dinner, stop by a bar for a light lunch, such as a ham-and-cheese sandwich (called *toast*); have it grilled twice if you want it really hot.

Prices and Paying: You'll notice a two- or three-tiered pricing system. Drinking a cup of coffee while standing at the bar is cheaper than drinking it at an indoor table (you'll pay still more at an outdoor table). Many places have a *lista dei prezzi* (price list) with two columns—*al bar* and *al tavolo* (table)—posted somewhere by the bar or cash register. If you're on a budget, don't sit down without first checking out the financial consequences. Ask, "Same price if I sit or stand?" by saying, *"Costa uguale al tavolo o al banco?"* (KOH-stah oo-GWAH-lay ahl TAH-voh-loh oh ahl BAHN-koh). Throughout Italy, you can get cheap coffee at the bar of any establishment, no matter how fancy, and pay the same low, government-regulated price (generally less than a euro if you stand).

If the bar isn't busy, you can probably just order and pay when you leave. Otherwise: 1) Decide what you want; 2) find out the price by checking the price list on the wall, the prices posted near the food, or by asking the barista; 3) pay the cashier; and 4) give the receipt to the barista (whose clean fingers handle no dirty euros) and tell him or her what you want.

For more on drinking, see "Beverages," later.

Ethnic Food

A good bet for a cheap, hot meal is a *döner kebab* (Middle Eastern-style rotisserie meat wrapped in pita bread). Look for little hole-in-the-wall kebab shops (especially around Termini Station and Santa Maria Maggiore), where you can get a hearty takeaway dinner wrapped in pita bread for €3.50. Pay an extra euro to supersize it, and it'll feed two. Asian restaurants, although not as common as in northern Europe, usually serve only Chinese dishes and can also be a good value.

Tavola Calda Bars and *Rosticcerie*

For a fast and cheap lunch, find an Italian variation on the corner deli: a *rosticceria* (specializing in roasted meats and accompanying *antipasti*) or a *tavola calda* bar (a "hot table" point-and-shoot cafeteria with a buffet spread of meat and vegetables). For a healthy light meal, ask for a mixed plate of vegetables with a hunk of mozzarella (*piatto misto di verdure con mozzarella;* pee-AH-toh MEE-stoh dee vehr-DOO-ray). Don't be limited by what's displayed. If you'd like a salad with a slice of cantaloupe and a hunk of cheese, they'll whip that up for you in a snap. Belly up to the bar; with a pointing finger, you can assemble a fine meal. If something's a mystery, ask for *un assaggio* (oon ah-SAH-joh) to get a little taste. To have your choices warmed up, ask for them to be heated (*scaldare;* skahl-DAH-ray).

Wine Bars

Wine bars *(enoteche)* are a popular, fast, and inexpensive option for lunch. Surrounded by the office crowd, you can get a salad, a plate of meats (cold cuts) and cheeses, and a glass of good wine (see blackboards for the day's selection and price per glass). A good *enoteca* aims to impress visitors with its wine, and will generally feature excellent-quality ingredients for the simple dishes it offers with the wine (though the prices add up—be careful with your ordering to keep this a budget choice). The area around the Pantheon and Piazza del Parlamento (popular with politicians and bureaucrats) has plenty of *enoteche* handy for a sightseeing lunch break or evening destination. For more on Italian cocktails and wines, see page 536.

Aperitivo Buffets

The Italian term *aperitivo* means a pre-dinner drink, but it's also used to describe their version of what we might call happy hour: a light buffet that many bars serve to customers during the pre-dinner hours (typically around 18:00 or 19:00 until 21:00). The drink itself may not be cheap (typically around €8-12), but bars lay out an enticing array of meats, cheeses, grilled vegetables, and other *antipasti*-type dishes, and you're welcome to nibble to your heart's content while you nurse your drink. While it's intended as an appetizer course before heading out for a full dinner, light eaters could discreetly turn this into a small meal. Drop by a few bars around this time to scope out their buffets before choosing.

Groceries and Delis

Another budget option is to visit a supermarket, *alimentari* (neighborhood grocery), or *salumeria* (delicatessen) to pick up some cold cuts, cheeses, and other supplies for a picnic. Some *salumerie*, and any *paninoteca* or *focacceria* (sandwich shop), can make you a sandwich to order. Just point to what you want, and they'll stuff it into a *panino;* if you want it heated, remember the word *scaldare*. If ordering an assortment of cold cuts and cheeses, some unscrupulous shops may try to pad the bill by pushing their most expensive ingredients. Be clear on what you want: *"antipasto misto da __ euro, per favore."* For more on *salumi* and cheeses, see page 533.

Picnics

Picnicking saves lots of euros and is a great way to sample regional specialties. A typical picnic for two might be fresh rolls,

100 grams or about a quarter pound—of cheese (*un etto*, EH-toh, plural *etti*, EH-tee), and 100 grams of meat, sometimes ordered by the slice (*fetta*) or piece (*pezzi*). For two people, I might get *cinque pezzi* (five pieces) of prosciutto. Add two tomatoes, three carrots, two apples, yogurt, and a liter box of juice. Total cost: about €10.

In the process of assembling your meal, you get to deal with Italians in the market scene. For a colorful experience, gather your ingredients in the morning at a produce market; you'll probably need to hit several market stalls to put together a complete meal (note that many stalls close in the early afternoon).

While it's fun to visit small specialty shops, an *alimentari* is your one-stop corner grocery store (most will slice and stuff your sandwich for you if you buy the ingredients there). A rare *supermercato* (look for the Conad, Despar, and Co-op chains) gives you more efficiency with less color for less cost. At busier supermarkets, you'll need to take a number for deli service. And *rosticcerie* sell cheap food to go—you'll find options such as lasagna, rotisserie chicken, and sides like roasted potatoes and spinach.

Picnics can be an adventure in high cuisine. Be daring. Try the fresh mozzarella, *presto* pesto, shriveled olives, and any re-

gional specialties the locals are excited about. If ordering *antipasti* (such as grilled or marinated veggies) at a deli counter, you can ask for *una porzione* in a takeaway container *(contenitore).* Use gestures to show exactly how much you want. The word *basta* (BAH-stah; enough) works as a question or as a statement.

Shopkeepers are happy to sell small quantities of produce, but it's customary to let the merchant choose for you. Say *"per oggi"* (pehr OH-jee; for today) and he or she will grab you something ready to eat. To avoid being overcharged, know the cost per kilo, study the weighing procedure, and do the arithmetic.

ITALIAN CUISINE STAPLES

Much of your Italian eating experience will likely center around the big five: pizza, pasta, *salumi,* cheese, and gelato. For a look at cuisine you'll likely find in Rome, see the sidebar on page 366. For more food help, try a menu translator, such as the *Rick Steves' Italian Phrase Book & Dictionary,* which has a menu decoder and plenty of useful phrases for navigating the culinary scene.

Pizza

Here are some of the pizzas you might see at restaurants or at a pizzeria. Note that if you ask for pepperoni on your pizza, you'll get *peperoni* (green or red peppers, not sausage); request *diavola, salsiccia piccante,* or *salame piccante* instead (the closest thing in Italy to American pepperoni).

Bianca: White pizza with no tomatoes (also called *ciaccina*).

Capricciosa: Prosciutto, mushrooms, olives, and artichokes— literally the chef's "caprice."

Funghi: Mushrooms.

Margherita: Tomato sauce, mozzarella, and basil—the red, white, and green of the Italian flag.

Marinara: Tomato sauce, oregano, garlic, no cheese.

Eating with the Seasons

Italian cooks love to serve you fresh produce and seafood at its tastiest. If you must have porcini mushrooms outside of fall, they'll be dried. Each region in Italy has its specialties, which you'll see displayed in open-air markets. To get a plate of the freshest veggies at a fine restaurant, request *"Un piatto di verdure della stagione, per favore"* (A plate of seasonal vegetables, please). Italians take fresh, seasonal ingredients so seriously that a restaurant cooking with frozen ingredients must note it on the menu—look for *congelato*.

Here are a few examples of what's fresh when:

April-May: Romanesco (similar to cauliflower) and fava beans, green beans, and artichokes

April-May and Sept-Oct: Black truffles

April-June: Asparagus, zucchini flowers, and zucchini

May-June: Mussels, cantaloupe, loquats, and strawberries

May-Aug: Eggplant, clams

July-Sept: Figs

Oct-Nov: Mushrooms, white truffles, persimmons, and chestnuts

Nov-Feb: Cardoon (wild artichoke), puntarelle (chicory shoots)

Fresh year-round: Meats and cheese

Napoletana: Mozzarella, anchovies, and tomato sauce.

Ortolana: "Greengrocer-style," with vegetables (also called *vegetariana*).

Quattro formaggi: Four different cheeses.

Quattro stagioni: Different toppings on each of the four quarters.

Pasta

While we think of pasta as a main dish, in Italy it's considered a *primo piatto*—first course. There are more than 600 varieties of Italian pasta, and each is specifically used to highlight a certain sauce, meat, or regional ingredient. Italian pasta falls into two broad categories: *pasta lunga* (long pasta) and *pasta corta* (short pasta).

Pasta lunga can be round, such as *capellini* (thin "little hairs"), *vermicelli* (slightly thicker "little worms"), and *bucatini* (long and hollow), or it can be flat, such as *linguine* (narrow "little tongues"), *fettuccine* (wider "small ribbons"), *tagliatelle* (even wider), and *pappardelle* (very wide, best with meat sauces).

The most common *pasta corta* are tubes, such as *penne, rigatoni, ziti, manicotti,* and *cannelloni;* they come either *lisce* (smooth) or *rigate* (grooved—better to catch and cling to sauce). Many short pastas are named for their shapes, such as *conchiglie* (shells), *farfalle* (butterflies), *cavatappi* (corkscrews), *ditali* (thimbles), *gomiti* ("elbow" macaroni), *lumache* (snails), *marziani* (spirals resembling "Martian" antennae), and even *strozzapreti* (priest stranglers). Some are filled *(ripieni),* including *tortelli* (C-shaped, stuffed ravioli) and *angolotti* or *mezzelune* (shaped like "priest's hats" or "half-moons").

Most types of pasta come in slightly different variations: If it's a bit thicker, *-one* is added to the end; if it's a bit thinner, *-ine, -ette,* or *-elle* is added. For example, *tortellini* are smaller *tortelli,* while *tortelloni* are bigger. Most pastas in Italy are made fresh.

Here's a list of common pasta toppings and sauces. On a menu, these terms are usually preceded by *alla* (in the style of) or *in* (in):

Aglio e olio: Garlic and olive oil.

Alfredo: Butter, cream, and parmesan.

Amatriciana: Pork cheek, *pecorino* cheese, and tomato.

Arrabbiata: "Angry," spicy tomato sauce with chili peppers.

Bolognese: Meat and tomato sauce.

Boscaiola: Mushrooms and sausage.

Burro e salvia: Butter and sage.

Cacio e pepe: *Parmigiano* cheese and ground pepper.

Carbonara: Bacon, egg, cheese, and pepper.

Carrettiera: Spicy and garlicky, with olive oil and little tomatoes.

Diavola: "Devil-style," spicy hot.

Frutti di mare: Seafood.

Genovese: Basil ground with *parmigiano* cheese, garlic, pine nuts, and olive oil; a.k.a. pesto.

Gricia: Cured pork and *pecorino romano* cheese.

Marinara: Usually tomato, often with garlic and onions, but can also be a seafood sauce ("sailor's style").

Norma: Tomato, eggplant, and ricotta cheese.

Pajata: Calf intestines (also called *pagliata).*

Pescatora: Seafood ("fisherman style").

Pomodoro: Tomato only.

Puttanesca: "Harlot-style" tomato sauce with anchovies, olives, and capers.

Ragù: Meaty tomato sauce.

Scoglio: Mussels, clams, and tomatoes.
Sorrentina: "Sorrento-style," with tomatoes, basil, and mozzarella (usually over gnocchi).
Sugo di lepre: Rich sauce made of wild hare.
Tartufi: Truffles (also called *tartufate).*
Umbria: Sauce of anchovies, garlic, tomatoes, and truffles.
Vongole: Clams and spices.

Salumi

Salumi ("salted" meats), also called *affettati* ("cut" meats), are an Italian staple. While most American cold cuts are cooked, in Italy they're far more commonly cured by air-drying, salting, and smoking. (Don't worry; these so-called "raw" meats are safe to eat, and you can really taste the difference.)

The two most familiar types of *salumi* are *salame* and *prosciutto.* *Salame* is an air-dried, sometimes spicy sausage that comes in many varieties. When Italians say *"prosciutto,"* they usually mean *prosciutto crudo*—the raw ham that air-cures on the hock and is then thinly sliced. Produced mainly in the north of Italy, *prosciutto* can be either *dolce* (sweet) or *salato* (salty). Purists say the best is *prosciutto di Parma.*

Other *salumi* may be less familiar:
Bresaola: Air-cured beef.
Capocollo: Peppery pork shoulder (also called *coppa).*
Culatello: Prosciutto made with only the finest cuts of meat.
Finocchiona: *Salame* with fennel seeds.
Lonzino: Cured pork loin.
Mortadella: A finely ground pork loaf, similar to our bologna.
Pancetta: Salt-cured, peppery pork belly meat, similar to bacon; can be eaten raw or added to cooked dishes.
Guanciale: Tender pork cheek.
Salame di Sant'Olcese: What we'd call "Genoa salami."
Salame piccante: Spicy hot, similar to pepperoni.
Speck: Smoked pork shoulder.

If you've got a weak stomach, avoid *testa in cassetta* (head-cheese—organs in aspic) and *lampredotto*—cow stomach that resembles a lamprey (eel).

Cheese

When it comes to cheese *(formaggio),* you're probably already familiar with most of these Italian favorites:
Asiago: Hard cow cheese that comes either *mezzano* (young, firm, and creamy) or *stravecchio* (aged, pungent, and granular).
Burrata: A creamy mozzarella.
Fontina: Semihard, nutty, Gruyère-style mountain cheese.

PRACTICALITIES

Gorgonzola: Pungent, blue-veined cheese, either *dolce* (creamy) or *stagionato* (aged and hard).

Mascarpone: Sweet, buttery, spreadable dessert cheese.

Mozzarella di bufala: Made from the milk of water buffaloes.

Parmigiano-reggiano: Hard, crumbly, sharp, aged cow cheese with more nuanced flavor than American parmesan; *grana padano* is a less expensive variation.

Pecorino: Either *fresco* (fresh, soft, and mild) or *stagionato* (aged and sharp, sometimes called *pecorino romano*).

Provolone: Rich, firm, aged cow cheese.

Ricotta: Soft, airy cheese made by "recooking" leftover whey.

Scamorza: Similar to mozzarella, but often smoked.

Gelato

While American ice cream is made with cream and has a high butterfat content, Italian gelato is made with milk. It's also churned more slowly, making it denser. Connoisseurs believe that because gelato has less air and less fat (which coats the mouth and blocks the taste buds), it's more flavorful than American-style ice cream.

A key to gelato appreciation is sampling liberally and choosing flavors that go well together. At a *gelateria,* ask, as Italians do, for a taste: *"Un assaggio, per favore?"* (oon ah-SAH-joh pehr fah-VOH-ray). You can also ask what flavors go well together: *"Quali gusti stanno bene insieme?"* (KWAH-lee GOO-stee STAH-noh BEH-nay een-see-EH-may).

Most *gelaterie* clearly display prices and sizes. But in the textbook *gelateria* scam, the tourist orders two or three flavors—and the clerk selects a fancy, expensive chocolate-coated waffle cone, piles it high with huge scoops, and cheerfully charges the tourist €10. To avoid rip-offs, point to the price or say what you want—for instance, a €3 cup: *"Una coppetta da tre euro"* (OO-nah koh-PEH-tah dah tray eh-OO-roh).

The best *gelaterie* display signs reading *artiginale, nostra produzione,* or *produzione propia,* indicating that the gelato is made on the premises. Seasonal flavors are also a good sign, as are mellow hues (avoid colors that don't appear in nature). Gelato stored in covered metal tins (rather than white plastic) is more likely to be homemade. Gourmet gelato shops are popping up all over Italy, selling exotic flavors. A chain called Grom is comparable to Ben & Jerry's in the US.

Classic gelato flavors include:

After Eight: Chocolate and mint.

Bacio: Chocolate hazelnut, named for Italy's popular "kiss" candies.

Cassata: With dried fruits.

Cioccolato: Chocolate.

Crema: Vanilla.

Croccantino: "Crunchy," with toasted peanut bits.
Fior di latte: Sweet milk.
Fragola: Strawberry.
Macedonia: Mixed fruits.
Malaga: Similar to rum raisin.
Riso: With actual bits of rice mixed in.
Stracciatella: Vanilla with chocolate shreds.
Tartufo: Super chocolate.
Zabaione: Named for the egg yolk and Marsala wine dessert.
Zuppa inglese: Sponge cake, custard, chocolate, and cream.

Gelato variations or alternatives include *sorbetto* (sorbet—made with fruit, but no milk or eggs); *granita* or *grattachecca* (a cup of slushy ice with flavored syrup); and *cremolata* (a gelato-*granita* float).

BEVERAGES

Italian bars serve great drinks—hot, cold, sweet, caffeinated, or alcoholic.

Water, Juice, and Cold Drinks

Italians are notorious water snobs. At restaurants, your server just can't understand why you wouldn't want good water to go with your good food. It's customary and never expensive to order a *litro* or *mezzo litro* (half-liter) of bottled water. *Acqua leggermente effervescente* (lightly carbonated water) is a meal-time favorite. Or simply ask for *con gas* if you want fizzy water and *senza gas* if you prefer still water. You can ask for *acqua del rubinetto* (tap water) in restaurants, but your server may give you a funny look. Chilled bottled water—still *(naturale)* or carbonated *(frizzante)*—is sold cheap in stores. Half-liter mineral water bottles are available everywhere for about €1. (I refill my water bottle with tap water.)

Juice is *succo*, and *spremuta* means freshly squeezed. Order *una spremuta* (don't confuse it with *spumante*, sparkling wine)—it's usually orange juice *(arancia)*, and from February through April it's almost always made from blood oranges *(arance rosse)*.

In grocery stores, you can get a liter of O.J. for the price of a Coke or coffee. Look for *100% succo* or *senza zucchero* (without sugar) on the label—or be surprised by something diluted and sugary sweet. Hang on to your water bottles. Buy juice in cheap liter boxes, then drink some and store the extra in your water bottle.

Tè freddo (iced tea) is usually from a can—sweetened and flavored with lemon or peach. Lemonade is *limonata*.

Coffee and Other Hot Drinks

The espresso-based style of coffee so popular in the US was born in Italy. If you ask for *"un caffè,"* you'll get a shot of espresso in a little cup—the closest thing to American-style drip coffee is a *caffè americano*. Most Italian coffee drinks begin with espresso, to which they add varying amounts of hot water and/or steamed or foamed milk. Milky drinks, like cappuccino or *caffè latte*, are served to locals before noon and to tourists any time of day (to an Italian, cappuccino is a morning drink; they believe having milk after a big meal or anything with tomato sauce impairs digestion). If they add any milk after lunch, it's just a splash, in a *caffè macchiato*. Italians like their coffee only warm—to get it very hot, request *"Molto caldo, per favore"* (MOHL-toh KAHL-doh pehr fah-VOH-ray). Any coffee drink is available decaffeinated—ask for it *decaffeinato* (deh-kah-feh-NAH-toh). *Cioccolato* is hot chocolate. *Tè* is hot tea.

Experiment with a few of the options:

Cappuccino: Espresso with foamed milk on top (*cappuccino freddo* is iced cappuccino).

Caffè latte: Espresso mixed with hot milk, no foam, in a tall glass (ordering just a "latte" gets you only milk).

Caffè macchiato: Espresso "marked" with a splash of milk, in a small cup.

Latte macchiato: Layers of hot milk and foam, "marked" by an espresso shot, in a tall glass. Note that if you order simply a *"macchiato,"* you'll probably get a *caffè macchiato*.

Caffè corto/lungo: Concentrated espresso diluted with a tiny bit of hot water, in a small cup.

Caffè americano: Espresso diluted with even more hot water, in a larger cup.

Caffè corretto: Espresso "corrected" with a shot of liqueur (normally *grappa*, *amaro*, or *sambuca*).

Marocchino: "Moroccan" coffee with espresso, foamed milk, and cocoa powder; the similar *mocaccino* has chocolate instead of cocoa.

Caffè freddo: Sweet and iced espresso.

Caffè hag: Instant decaf.

Alcoholic Beverages

Beer: While Italy is traditionally considered wine country, in recent years there's been a huge and passionate growth in the production of craft beer *(birra artigianale)*. Even in small towns, you'll see microbreweries slinging their own brews. You'll also find local brews (Peroni and Moretti), as well as imports such as Heineken. Italians drink mainly lager beers. Beer on tap is *alla spina*. Get it *piccola* (33 cl, 11 oz), *media* (50 cl, about a pint), or *grande* (a liter). A *lattina* (lah-TEE-nah) is a can and a *bottiglia* (boh-TEEL-yah) is a bottle.

Cocktails and Spirits: Italians appreciate both *aperitivi* (palate-stimulating cocktails) and *digestivi* (after-dinner drinks designed to aid digestion). Popular *aperitivo* options include Campari (dark-colored bitters with herbs and orange peel), Americano (vermouth with bitters, brandy, and lemon peel), Cynar (bitters flavored with artichoke), and Punt e Mes (sweet red vermouth and red wine). Widely used vermouth brands include Cinzano and Martini.

Digestivo choices are usually either a strong herbal bitters or something sweet. Many restaurants have their own secret recipe for a bittersweet herbal brew called *amaro;* popular commercial brands are Fernet Branca and Montenegro. If your tastes run sweeter, try *amaretto* (almond-flavored liqueur), Frangelico (hazelnut liqueur), *limoncello* (lemon liqueur), *nocino* (dark, sweet walnut liqueur), and *sambuca* (syrupy, anise-flavored liqueur; *con moscha* adds "flies"—three coffee beans). *Grappa* is a brandy distilled from grape skins and stems; *stravecchio* is an aged, mellower variation.

Wine: The ancient Greeks who colonized Italy more than 2,000 years ago called it Oenotria—land of the grape. Centuries later, Galileo wrote, "Wine is light held together by water." Wine *(vino)* is certainly a part of the Italian culinary trinity—grape, olive, and wheat. (I'd add gelato.) Ideal conditions for grapes (warm climate, well-draining soil, and an abundance of hillsides) make the Italian peninsula a paradise for grape growers, winemakers, and wine drinkers.

Even if you're clueless about wine, the information on an Italian wine label can help you choose something decent. Terms you may see on the bottle include *classico* (from a defined, select area), *annata* (year of harvest), *vendemmia* (harvest), and *imbottigliato dal produttore all'origine* (bottled by producers). To figure out what you like—and what suits your pocketbook—visit an *enoteca* (wine bar) and sample wines side by side. For tips on ordering wine, see the sidebar.

In general, Italy designates its wines by one of four official categories:

Vino da Tavola (VDT) is table wine, the lowest grade, made from grapes grown anywhere in Italy. It's inexpensive, but Italy's wines are so good that, for many people, a basic *vino da tavola* is just fine with a meal. Many restaurants, even modest ones, take pride in their house wine *(vino della casa)*, bottling their own or working with wineries.

Denominazione di Origine Controllata (DOC) meets national standards for high-quality wine. Made from grapes grown in a

Ordering Wine

To order a glass of red or white wine, say, "*Un bicchiere di vino rosso/bianco.*" House wine comes in a carafe; choose from a quarter-liter pitcher (8.5 oz, *un quarto*), half-liter pitcher (17 oz, *un mezzo*), or one-liter pitcher (34 oz, *un litro*). When ordering, have some fun, gesture like a local, and you'll have no problems speaking the language of the *enoteca. Salute!*

English	Italian
wine	*vino* (VEE-noh)
house wine	*vino della casa* (VEE-noh DEH-lah KAH-zah)
glass	*bicchiere* (bee-kee-EH-ree)
bottle	*bottiglia* (boh-TEEL-yah)
carafe	*caraffa* (kah-RAH-fah)
red	*rosso* (ROH-soh)
white	*bianco* (bee-AHN-koh)
rosé	*rosato* (roh-ZAH-toh)
sparkling	*spumante/frizzante* (spoo-MAHN-tay/freed-ZAHN-tay)
dry	*secco* (SEH-koh)
earthy	*terroso* (teh-ROH-zoh)
elegant	*elegante* (eh-leh-GAHN-tay)
fruity	*fruttato* (froo-TAH-toh)
full-bodied	*corposo/pieno* (kor-POH-zoh/pee-EH-noh)
mature	*maturo* (mah-TOO-roh)
sweet	*dolce* (DOHL-chay)
tannic	*tannico* (TAH-nee-koh)
young	*giovane* (JOH-vah-nay)

PRACTICALITIES

defined area, it's usually quite affordable and can be surprisingly good. Hundreds of wines have earned the DOC designation. In Tuscany, for example, many such wines come from the Chianti region, located between Florence and Siena.

Denominazione di Origine Controllata e Guarantita (DOCG), the highest grade, meets national standards for the highest-quality wine (made with grapes from a defined area whose quality is "guaranteed"). These wines can be identified by the pink or green label on the neck...and the scary price tag on the shelf. Only a limited number of wines in Italy can be called DOCG. They're generally a good bet if you want a quality wine, but you don't know anything else about the winemaker. (*Riserva* indicates a DOC or DOCG wine matured for a longer, more specific time.)

Indicazione Geographica Tipica (IGT) is a broad group of wines that range from basic to some of Italy's best. These wines don't follow the strict "recipe" required for DOC or DOCG status, but give local vintners creative license. This category includes the Super Tuscans—wines made from a mix of international grapes (such as cabernet sauvignon) grown in Tuscany and aged in small oak barrels for only two years. The result is a lively full-bodied wine that dances all over your head...and is worth the steep price for aficionados.

Staying Connected

One of the most common questions I hear from travelers is, "How can I stay connected in Europe?" The short answer is: more easily and cheaply than you might think. For a very practical one-hour lecture covering tech issues for travelers, see www.ricksteves.com/travel-talks.

The simplest solution is to bring your own device—mobile phone, tablet, or laptop—and use it just as you would at home (following the tips below, such as connecting to free Wi-Fi whenever possible). Another option is to buy a European SIM card for your mobile phone—either your US phone or one you buy in Europe. Or you can travel without a mobile device and use European landlines and computers to connect. Each of these options is described below, and you'll find even more details at www.ricksteves.com/phoning.

USING YOUR OWN MOBILE DEVICE IN EUROPE

Without an international plan, typical rates from major service providers (AT&T, Verizon, etc.) for using your device abroad are about $1.70/minute for voice calls, 50 cents to send text messages, 5 cents to receive them, and $10 to download one megabyte of data. At these rates, costs can add up quickly. Here are some budget tips and options.

Use free Wi-Fi whenever possible. Unless you have an unlimited-data plan, you're best off saving most of your online tasks for Wi-Fi. You can access the Internet, send texts, and make voice calls over Wi-Fi.

Many cafés (including McDonald's) have free hotspots for customers; look for signs offering it and ask for the Wi-Fi password when you buy something. You'll also often find Wi-Fi at TIs, city squares, major museums, public-transit hubs, airports, highway rest stops (Autogrills), and aboard trains and buses.

Sign up for an international plan. Most providers offer a global calling plan that cuts the per-minute cost of phone calls and texts, and a flat-fee data plan. Your normal plan may already include international coverage (T-Mobile's does).

Before your trip, call your provider or check online to confirm that your phone will work in Europe, and research your provider's

How to Dial

International Calls

Whether phoning from a US landline or mobile phone, or from a number in another European country, here's how to make an international call. I've used one of my recommended Florence hotels as an example (tel. 055-213-154).

Initial Zero: Drop the initial zero from international phone numbers—except when calling Italy.

Mobile Tip: If using a mobile phone, the "+" sign can replace the international access code (for a "+" sign, press and hold "0").

US/Canada to Europe

Dial 011 (US/Canada international access code), country code (39 for Italy), and phone number.

▸ To call the Florence hotel from home, dial 011-39-055-213-154.

Country to Country Within Europe

Dial 00 (Europe international access code), country code, and phone number.

▸ To call the Florence hotel from Germany, dial 00-39-055-213-154.

Europe to the US/Canada

Dial 00, country code (1 for US/Canada), and phone number.

▸ To call from Europe to my office in Edmonds, Washington, dial 00-1-425-771-8303.

Domestic Calls

To call within Italy (from one Italian landline or mobile phone to another), simply dial the phone number, including the initial 0 if there is one.

▸ To call the Florence hotel from Rome, dial 055-213-154.

More Dialing Tips

Italian Phone Numbers: Italian phone numbers vary in length; a hotel can have, say, an eight-digit phone number

---

international rates. Activate the plan a day or two before you leave, then remember to cancel it when your trip's over.

Minimize the use of your cellular network. When you can't find Wi-Fi, you can use your cellular network to connect to the Internet, text, or make voice calls. When you're done, avoid further charges by manually switching off "data roaming" or "cellular data" (in your device's Settings menu; for help, ask your service provider or Google it). Another way to make sure you're not accidentally using data roaming is to put your device in "airplane" or "flight" mode (which also disables phone calls and texts), and then connect to Wi-Fi as needed.

Don't use your cellular network for bandwidth-gobbling tasks,

and a nine-digit fax number. Italy's landlines start with 0; mobile lines start with 3 and cost substantially more to dial.

Toll and Toll-Free Calls: Italy's toll-free lines, called *numero verde* (green number), begin with 800 or 803. They can be dialed free from Italian phones without using a phone card but don't work from the US. Any Italian phone number that starts with 8 but isn't followed by a 0 is a toll call (generally costing €0.10-0.50/minute). International rates apply to US toll-free numbers dialed from Italy—they're not free.

More Phoning Help: See www.howtocallabroad.com.

European Country Codes			
Austria	43	Italy	39
Belgium	32	Latvia	371
Bosnia-Herzegovina	387	Montenegro	382
Croatia	385	Morocco	212
Czech Republic	420	Netherlands	31
Denmark	45	Norway	47
Estonia	372	Poland	48
Finland	358	Portugal	351
France	33	Russia	7
Germany	49	Slovakia	421
Gibraltar	350	Slovenia	386
Great Britain	44	Spain	34
Greece	30	Sweden	46
Hungary	36	Switzerland	41
Ireland & N. Ireland	353 / 44	Turkey	90

such as Skyping, downloading apps, and watching YouTube. Save these for when you're on Wi-Fi. Using a navigation app such as Google Maps over a cellular network can take lots of data, so do this sparingly or use it offline.

Limit automatic updates. By default, your device constantly checks for a data connection and updates apps. It's smart to disable these features so your apps will only update when you're on Wi-Fi, and to change your device's email settings from "auto-retrieve" to "manual" (or from "push" to "fetch").

It's also a good idea to keep track of your data usage. On your device's menu, look for "cellular data usage" or "mobile data" and reset the counter at the start of your trip.

Hurdling the Language Barrier

Many Italians—especially those in the tourist trade and in big cities—speak English. Still, you'll get better treatment if you learn and use Italian pleasantries. In smaller, non-touristy towns, Italian is the norm. Italians have an endearing habit of talking to you even if they know you don't speak their language—and yet, thanks to gestures and thoughtfully simplified words, it somehow works. Don't stop them to tell them you don't understand every word—just go along for the ride. For a list of survival phrases, see page 571.

Note that Italian is pronounced much like English, with a few exceptions, such as: *c* followed by *e* or *i* is pronounced ch (to ask, *"Per centro?"*—To the center?—you say, pehr CHEHN-troh). In Italian, *ch* is pronounced like the hard c in Chianti (*chiesa*—church—is pronounced kee-AY-zah). Adding a vowel to the English word often gets you close to the Italian one. Give it your best shot. Italians appreciate your efforts.

Use Skype or other calling/messaging apps for cheaper calls and texts. Certain apps let you make voice or video calls or send texts over the Internet for free or cheap. If you're bringing a tablet or laptop, you can also use it for voice calls and texts. All you have to do is log on to a Wi-Fi network, then contact any of your friends or family members who are also online and signed into the same service.

You can make voice and video calls using Skype, Viber, FaceTime, and Google+ Hangouts. If the connection is bad, try making an audio-only call. You can also make voice calls from your device to telephones worldwide for just a few cents per minute using Skype, Viber, or Hangouts if you buy credit first.

To text for free over Wi-Fi, try apps like Google+ Hangouts, Whats App, Viber, Facebook Messenger, and iMessage. Make sure you're on Wi-Fi to avoid data charges.

USING A EUROPEAN SIM CARD IN A MOBILE PHONE

This option works well for those who want to make a lot of voice calls at cheap local rates, and those who need faster connection speeds than their US carrier provides. Either buy a basic cell phone in Europe (as little as $40 from mobile-phone shops anywhere), or bring an "unlocked" US phone (check with your carrier about unlocking it). With an unlocked phone, you can replace the original SIM card (the microchip that stores info about the phone) with one that will work with a European provider.

In Europe, buy a European SIM card. Inserted into your phone, this card gives you a European phone number—and Euro-

PRACTICALITIES

pean rates. SIM cards are sold at mobile-phone shops, department-store electronics counters, newsstands, and vending machines. Costing about $5-10, they usually include about that much prepaid calling credit, with no contract and no commitment. A SIM card that also includes data costs (including roaming) will cost $20-40 more for one month of data within the country where you bought it. This can be faster than data roaming through your home provider. To get the best rates, buy a new SIM card whenever you arrive in a new country.

I like to buy SIM cards at a mobile-phone shop where there's a clerk to help explain the options and brands. In Italy, the major mobile phone providers are Wind, TIM, Vodafone, and 3 ("Tre"). Certain SIM-card brands—including Lebara and Lycamobile, both of which operate in multiple European countries—are reliable and economical. Ask the clerk to help you insert your SIM card, set it up, and show you how to use it. In some countries—including Italy—you'll be required to register the SIM card with your passport as an antiterrorism measure (which may mean you can't use the phone for the first hour or two).

Find out how to check your credit balance. When you run out of credit, you can top it up at newsstands, tobacco shops, mobile-phone stores, or many other businesses (look for your SIM card's logo in the window), or online.

UNTETHERED TRAVEL: PUBLIC PHONES AND COMPUTERS

It's possible to travel in Europe without a mobile device. You can check email or browse websites using public computers and Internet cafés, and make calls from your hotel room and/or public phones.

Phones in your **hotel room** generally have a fee for placing local and "toll-free" calls, as well as long-distance or international calls—ask for the rates before you dial. Since you're never charged for receiving calls, it's better to have someone from the US call you in your room.

If these fees are low, hotel phones can be used inexpensively for calls made with cheap international phone cards (*carta telefonica prepagata internazionale,* KAR-tah teh-leh-FOHN-ee-kah pray-pah-GAH-tah in-ter-naht-zee-oh-NAH lay—sold at many post offices, newsstands, street kiosks, tobacco shops, and train stations). You'll either get a prepaid card with a toll-free number and a scratch-to-reveal PIN code, or a code printed on a receipt.

You'll see **public pay phones** in a few post offices and train stations. The phones generally come with multilingual instructions, and most work with insertable Telecom Italia phone cards (sold at post offices, newsstands, etc.). With the exception of Great Britain,

Tips on Internet Security

Using the Internet while traveling brings added security risks, whether you're getting online with your own device or at a public terminal using a shared network. Here are some tips for securing your data:

First, make sure that your device is running the latest version of its operating system and security software, and that your apps are up-to-date. Next, ensure that your device is password- or passcode-protected so thieves can't access it if your device is stolen. For extra security, set passwords on apps that access key info (such as email or Facebook).

On the road, use only legitimate Wi-Fi hotspots. Ask the hotel or café staff for the specific name of their Wi-Fi network, and make sure you log on to that exact one. Hackers sometimes create a bogus hotspot with a similar or vague name (such as "Hotel Europa Free Wi-Fi"). The best Wi-Fi networks require a password. If you're not actively using a hotspot, turn off your device's Wi-Fi connection so it's not visible to others.

Be especially cautious when accessing financial information online. Experts say it's best to use a banking app rather than sign in to your bank's website via a browser (the app is less likely to get hacked). Refrain from logging in to any personal finance sites on a public computer. Even if you're using your own mobile device at a password-protected hotspot, there's a remote chance that a hacker who's logged on to the same network could see what you're doing.

Never share your credit-card number (or any other sensitive information) online unless you know that the site is secure. A secure site displays a little padlock icon, and the URL begins with *https* (instead of the usual *http*).

each European country has its own insertable phone card—so your Spanish card won't work in an Italian phone.

Public computers are easy to find. Many hotels have one in their lobby for guests to use; otherwise you can find them at Internet cafés and public libraries (ask your hotelier or the TI for the nearest location). If typing on a European keyboard, use the "Alt Gr" key to the right of the space bar to insert the extra symbol that appears on some keys. Italian keyboards are a little different from ours; to type an @ symbol, press the "Alt Gr" key and the key that shows the @ symbol. If you can't locate a special character, simply copy it from a Web page and paste it into your email message.

MAIL

You can mail one package per day to yourself worth up to $200 duty-free from Europe to the US (mark it "personal purchases"). If you're sending a gift to someone, mark it "unsolicited gift." For details, visit www.cbp.gov, select "Travel," and search for "Know Before You Go."

The Italian postal service works fine, but for quick transatlantic delivery (in either direction), consider services such as DHL (www.dhl.com).

Transportation

If your trip will cover more of Italy than just Rome, you may need to take a long-distance train or bus, rent a car, or fly. Buses are an alternative to trains (and may be your only option for reaching some small Italian towns), but they are generally slower and less efficient. Renting a car is great for touring the small hill towns of Umbria and Tuscany north of Rome, but you'll have to drive on narrow Italian roads. I give some specifics on trains and flights here. For more detailed information on transportation throughout Europe, including trains, flying, buses, renting a car, and driving, see www.ricksteves.com/transportation.

TRAINS

To travel by train affordably in Italy, you can simply buy tickets as you go. For travelers ready to lock in dates and times weeks or

months in advance, buying nonrefundable tickets online can cut costs in half. Note that the Italy rail pass is generally not a good value; but if your travel extends beyond Italy, there are various multicountry rail passes that might be worth checking into. For advice on figuring out the smartest train-ticket or rail-pass options for your trip, visit the Trains & Rail Passes section of my website at www.ricksteves.com/rail.

Types of Trains

Most trains in Italy are operated by the state-run **Trenitalia** company (www.trenitalia.com, a.k.a. Ferrovie dello Stato Italiane, abbreviated FS or FSI). Since ticket prices depend on the speed of the train, it helps to know the different types of trains: pokey R or REG *(regionali)*; medium-speed RV *(regionali veloce)*, IR (InterRegio), D *(diretto)*, and E *(espresso)*; fast IC (InterCity) and EC (EuroCity); and super-fast Frecce trains: Frecciabianca ("White Arrow"), faster Frecciargento ("Silver Arrow"), Frecciarossa ("Red Arrow"), and the newest Frecciarossa 1000 or Freccemille (up to 225 mph). You may also see the Frecce trains marked on schedules as ES, AV, or EAV. If you're traveling with a rail pass, note that reservations are required for IC, EC, and international trains (€5) and for Frecce trains (€10). You can't make reservations for regional trains, such as most Rome-Civitavecchia connections.

A private train company called **Italo** runs fast trains on major routes in Italy. Italo is focused on two corridors: Venice-Padua-Bologna-Florence-Rome and Turin-Milan-Bologna-Florence-Rome-Naples. Their high-speed trains have fewer departures than Trenitalia, but they do offer discounts for tickets booked well in advance. In some cities, such as Milan, their trains use secondary stations—if taking an Italo train, pay attention to which station you need. Italo does not accept rail passes, but they're a worthy alternative for point-to-point tickets. You can book in person (look for Italo ticket offices or their red machines), by phone (tel. 06-0708), or on their user-friendly website (www.italotreno.it).

Schedules

At the train station, the easiest way to check schedules is at a handy ticket machine (described later, under "Buying Tickets"). Enter the desired date, time, and destination to see all your options. Printed schedules are also posted at the station (departure—*partenzi*—posters are always yellow).

Newsstands sell up-to-date regional and all-Italy timetables (€5, ask for the *orario ferroviario*). You can also check www.trenitalia.it and www.italotreno.it (domestic journeys only); for international trips, use www.bahn.com (Germany's excellent all-Europe schedule website). Trenitalia offers a single all-Italy telephone number for train information (24 hours daily, toll tel. 892-021, in Italian only, consider having your hotelier call for you). For Italo trains, call tel. 06-0708.

Be aware that Trenitalia and Italo don't cooperate at all. If you buy a ticket for one train line, it's not valid on the other. Even if you're just looking for schedule information, the company you ask will most likely ignore the other's options.

Point-to-Point Tickets

Train tickets are a good value in Italy. Fares are shown on the map

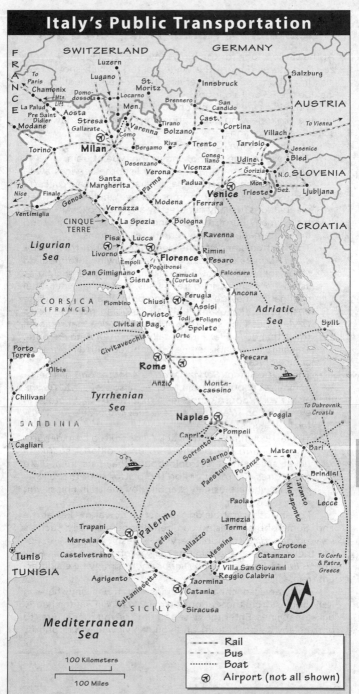

Italy's Public Transportation

FRANCE

SWITZERLAND

GERMANY

Luzern
To Paris
Chamonix (Mtn. Lift)
Lugano
Locarno
St. Moritz
Innsbruck
Salzburg
Domodossola
Men.
Brennero
San Candido
To Vienna
AUSTRIA
La Palud
Pre Saint Didier
Modane
Aosta
Stresa
Gallarate
Varenna
Tirano
Cast.
Cortina
Villach
Torino
Como
Bergamo
Bolzano
Trento
Tarvisio
Jesenice
Bled
Milan
Riva
Conegliano
Udine
SLOVENIA
Desenzano
Vicenza
Gorizia
N.G.
Santa Margherita
Verona
Padua
Mon.
Trieste
Sez.
Ljubljana
To Nice
Finale
Parma
Venice
To Nice
Ventimiglia
Genoa
Modena
Ferrara
Vernazza
CINQUE TERRE
La Spezia
Bologna
CROATIA
Pisa
Lucca
Ravenna
Ligurian Sea
Livorno
Florence
Rimini
Pesaro
Empoli
Poggibonsi
Falconara
San Gimignano
Camucia (Cortona)
Siena
Perugia
Ancona
CORSICA (FRANCE)
Piombino
Chiusi
Assisi
Adriatic Sea
Orvieto
Todi
Foligno
Spoleto
Civita di Bag.
Orte
Split
Civitavecchia
Porto Torres
Olbia
Rome
Pescara
Chilivani
Anzio
Montecassino
Tyrrhenian Sea
To Dubrovnik, Croatia
SARDINIA
Naples
Foggia
Cagliari
Capri
Pompeii
Sorrento
Matera
Bari
Salerno
Paestum
Potenza
Brindisi
Taranto
Metaponto
Lecce
Paola
Lamezia Terme
Crotone
Trapani
Palermo
Cefalù
Milazzo
Messina
Catanzaro
To Corfu & Patra, Greece
Marsala
Castelvetrano
Villa San Giovanni
Reggio Calabria
Tunis
TUNISIA
Agrigento
Caltanissetta
Taormina
Catania
SICILY
Siracusa
Mediterranean Sea

100 Kilometers

100 Miles

	Rail
	Bus
	Boat
✈	Airport (not all shown)

Deciphering Italian Train Schedules

At the station, look for the big yellow posters labeled *Partenze—Departures* (ignore the white posters, which show arrivals). In stations with Italo service, the posted schedules also include the FS or Italo logos.

Schedules are listed chronologically, hour by hour, showing the trains leaving the station throughout the day. Each schedule has columns:

- The first column *(Ora)* lists the time of departure.
- The next column *(Treno)* shows the type of train.
- The third column *(Classi Servizi)* lists the services available (first- and second-class cars, dining car, *cuccetta* berths, etc.) and, more importantly, whether you need reservations (usually denoted by an R in a box). All Frecce trains, many EuroCity (EC) and InterCity (IC) trains, and most international trains require reservations.
- The next column lists the destination of the train *(Principali Fermate Destinazioni)*, often showing intermediate stops, followed by the final destination, with arrival times listed throughout in parentheses. Note that your final destination may be listed in fine print as an intermediate destination. For example, if you're going from Rome to Orvieto, scan the schedule and you'll notice that regional trains that go to Florence usually stop in Orvieto en route. Travelers who read the fine print end up with a far greater choice of trains.
- The next column *(Servizi Diretti e Annotazioni)* has pertinent notes about the train, such as "also stops in..." *(ferma anche a...)*, "doesn't stop in..." *(non ferma a...)*, "stops in every station" *(ferma in tutte le stazioni)*, "delayed..." *(ritardo...)*, and so on.
- The last column lists the track *(Binario)* the train departs from. Confirm the *binario* with an additional source: a ticket seller, the electronic board that lists immediate departures, TV monitors on the platform, or the railway officials who are usually standing by the train unless you really need them.

For any odd symbols on the poster, look at the key at the end. Some of the phrasing can be deciphered easily, such as *servizio periodico* (periodic service—doesn't always run). For the trickier ones, ask a local or railway official, try your *Rick Steves Italian Phrase Book & Dictionary*, or simply take a different train.

You can also check schedules—for trains anywhere in Italy, not just from the station you're currently in—at the handy ticket machines. Enter the date and time of your departure (to or from any Italian station), and you can view all your options.

on page 553, though fares can vary for the same journey, mainly depending on the time of day, the speed of the train, and advance discounts. **First-class** tickets cost up to 50 percent more than **second-class.**

Frecce and Italo trains each offer several classes of service where all seats are reserved: Standard, Premium, Business, or Executive on Frecciarossa; Smart, Prima, or Club on Italo; and standard first and second class on other trains. Buying up gives you a little more elbow room, or perhaps a better chance at seating a group together, if you're buying on short notice. Ticket price levels for both companies are Base (full fare, easily changeable or partly refundable before scheduled departure), Economy (one schedule change allowed before departure, for a fee), and Super Economy or Low Cost (sells out quickly, no refund or exchange). Discounted fares typically sell out several days before departure. Fares labeled *servizi abbonati* are available only for locals with monthly passes—not tourists.

Speed vs. Savings: For point-to-point tickets, you'll pay more the faster you go. Spending a modest amount of extra time in transit can save money. On longer, mainline routes, fast trains save more time and provide most of the service. For example, a round-trip ticket between Rome and Civitavecchia costs €15 on a Frecce train (45 minutes each way), but €5 on a regional train (1.25 hours each way). Super-fast Rome-Venice trains run hourly, cost €76 in second class, and make the trip in 4 hours, while infrequent Inter-City trains (only 1-2/day) cost €50 and take 6 hours.

Discounts: Families with young children can get price breaks—kids ages 4 and under travel free; ages 4-11 at half-price. Ask for the "Offerta Familia" deal when buying tickets at a counter (or, at a ticket machine, choose "Yes" at the "Do you want ticket issue?" prompt, then choose "Familia"). With the discount, families of three to five people with at least one kid (under 12) get 50 percent off the child fare and 20 percent off the adult fare. The deal doesn't apply to all trains at all times, but it's worth checking out.

Discounts for youths and seniors require purchase of a separate card (Carta Verde for ages 12-26 costs €40; Carta Argento for ages 60 and over is €30), but the discount on tickets is so minor (10-15 percent respectively for domestic travel), it's not worth it for most.

Buying Tickets: Avoid train station ticket lines whenever possible by using the ticket machines in station halls. Pay all ticket costs in the station before you board, or you'll pay a penalty on the train. You'll be able to easily purchase tickets for travel within Italy (not international trains), make seat reservations, and even book a *cuccetta* (koo-CHEH-tah; overnight berth). If you do use the ticket windows, be sure you're in the correct line. Key terms: *biglietti*

PRACTICALITIES

Open or Non-Reserved Ticket—Need to Validate

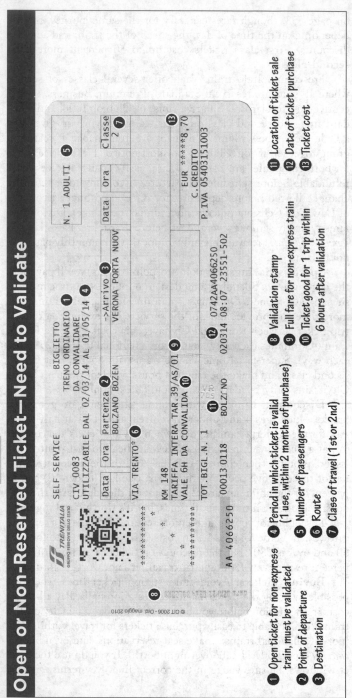

1 Open ticket for non-express train, must be validated

2 Point of departure

3 Destination

4 Period in which ticket is valid (1 use, within 2 months of purchase)

5 Number of passengers

6 Route

7 Class of travel (1st or 2nd)

8 Validation stamp

9 Full fare for non-express train

10 Ticket good for 1 trip within 6 hours after validation

11 Location of ticket sale

12 Date of ticket purchase

13 Ticket cost

Reserved Ticket (Fast Train)—Need Not Validate

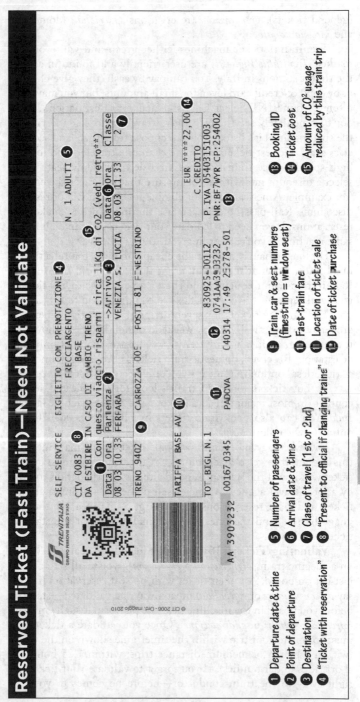

1 Departure date & time
2 Point of departure
3 Destination
4 "Ticket with reservation"
5 Number of passengers
6 Arrival date & time
7 Class of travel (1st or 2nd)
8 "Present to official if changing trains"
9 Train, car & seat numbers (finestrino = window seat)
10 Fast-train fare
11 Location of ticket sale
12 Date of ticket purchase
13 Booking ID
14 Ticket cost
15 Amount of CO_2 usage reduced by this train trip

PRACTICALITIES

(general tickets), *prenotazioni* (reservations), *nazionali* (domestic), and *internazionali*.

Trenitalia's ticket machines (either green-and-white or red; marked *Trenitalia/Biglietti*) are user-friendly and found in all but the tiniest stations in Italy. You can pay by cash (they give change) or by debit or credit card (even for small amounts, but you may need to enter your PIN). Select English, then your destination. If you don't immediately see the city you're traveling to, keep keying in the spelling until it's listed. You can choose from first- and second-class seats, request tickets for more than one traveler, and (on the high-speed Frecce trains) choose an aisle or window seat. Don't select a discount rate without being sure that you meet the criteria (for example, Americans are not eligible for certain EU or resident discounts). Rail-pass holders can use the machines to make seat reservations. If you need to validate your ticket, you can do it in the same machine if you're boarding your train right away.

For longer-haul runs, it can be cheaper to buy Trenitalia tickets in advance, either at the station or on their website. Because most Italian trains run frequently and there's no deadline to buy tickets, you can keep your travel plans flexible by purchasing tickets as you go. (You can buy tickets for several trips at one station when you are ready to commit.) For busy weekend or holiday travel, however, it can be a good idea to buy tickets in advance, whether online or at a station. Reserved, domestic train tickets purchased online offer a "ticketless" option that means you only need the booking code.

To buy tickets for **Italo** trains, look for a dedicated service counter (in most major rail stations) or a red ticket machine labeled *Italo*. You can also book Italo tickets by phone (tel. 06-0708) or online (www.italotreno.it).

You can't buy most international tickets from machines; for this and anything else that requires a real person, you must go to a ticket window at the station. A good alternative, though, is to drop by a local travel agency. Agencies sell domestic and international tickets and make reservations. They charge a small fee, but the language barrier (and the lines) can be smaller than at the station's ticket windows.

Validating Tickets: If your ticket includes a seat reservation on a specific train *(biglietto con prenotazione)*, you're all set and can just get on board. An open ticket with no seat reservation (it may say *da convalidare* or *convalida*) must always be validated—stamp it before you board in the machine near the platform (usually marked *convalida biglietti* or *vidimazione*). Once you validate a ticket, you must complete your trip within the timeframe shown on the ticket (within 6 hours for medium-distance trips; within 1.25 hours for short rides under 6 miles). If you forget to validate your ticket, go right away to the train conductor—before he comes to you—or

Train Costs in Italy

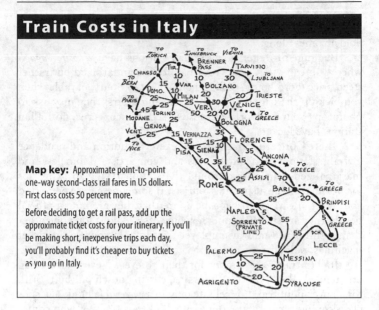

Map key: Approximate point-to-point one-way second-class rail fares in US dollars. First class costs 50 percent more.

Before deciding to get a rail pass, add up the approximate ticket costs for your itinerary. If you'll be making short, inexpensive trips each day, you'll probably find it's cheaper to buy tickets as you go in Italy.

you'll pay a fine. Note that you don't need to validate a rail pass each time you board (just make sure you've validated it before its first use).

Train Tips
Seat Reservations: Trains can fill up, even in first class. If you're on a tight schedule, you'll want to reserve a few days ahead for fast trains (see "Types of Trains," earlier). Purchasing tickets or pass holder reservations onboard a train comes with a nasty penalty. Buying them at the station can be a time waster unless you use the ticket machines.

If you don't need a reservation, and if your train originates at your departure point (e.g., you're catching the Rome-Assisi train in Rome), arriving at least 15 minutes before the departure time will help you snare a seat.

On the platforms of some major stations, posters showing the train composition *(composizione principali treni)* indicate where first- and second-class cars will line up when the trains arrive (letters on the poster are supposed to correspond to letters posted over the platform—but they don't always). Other stations may post the order of the cars on video screens along the track shortly before the train arrives. Since most trains now allow you to make reservations up to the time of departure, conductors post a list of the reservable and nonreservable seat rows (sometimes in English) in each train car's vestibule. This means that if you board a crowded train and get one of the last seats, you may be ousted when the reservation holder comes along.

Baggage Storage: Many Italian stations have *deposito bagagli* where you can safely leave your bag for a standardized but rather steep price (€6/5 hours, €12/12 hours, €17/24 hours, payable when you pick up the bag, double-check closing hours; they may ask to photocopy your passport). Because of security concerns, no Italian stations have lockers.

Theft Concerns: In big cities, exercise caution and prudence at train stations to avoid thieves and con artists. Homeless and marginalized people lurk around the station trying to skim tips (or worse) from unsuspecting tourists. If someone helps you to find your train or carry your bags, be aware that they are not an official porter; they are simply hoping for some cash. And if someone other than a uniformed railway employee tries to help you use the ticket machines, politely refuse.

Italian trains are famous for their thieves. Never leave a bag unattended. Police do ride the trains, cutting down on theft. Still, for an overnight trip, I'd feel safe only in a *cuccetta* (a bunk in a special sleeping car with an attendant who keeps track of who comes and goes while you sleep—approximately €20 in a six-bed compartment, €25 in a less-cramped four-bed compartment, €50 in a more private, double compartment).

Strikes: Strikes, which are common, generally last a day (often a Friday). Train employees will simply explain, *"Sciopero"* (strike). But in actuality, a minimum amount of "essential" mainline service is maintained (by law) during strikes. When a strike is pending, travel agencies (and hoteliers) can check to see when the strike goes into effect and which trains will continue to run. Revised schedules may be posted in Italian at stations, and station personnel still working can often tell you what trains are expected to run. If I need to get somewhere and know a strike is imminent, I leave early (before the strike, which often begins at 9:00), or I just go to the station with extra patience in tow and hop on anything rolling in the direction I want to go.

FLIGHTS

The best comparison search engine for both international and intra-European flights is www.kayak.com. For inexpensive flights within Europe, try www.skyscanner.com.

Flying to Europe: Start looking for international flights at least four to six months before your trip, especially for peak-season travel. Off-season tickets can usually be purchased a month or so in advance. Depending on your itinerary, it can be efficient to fly into one city and out of another. If your flight requires a connection in Europe, see my hints on navigating Europe's top hub airports at www.ricksteves.com/hub-airports.

Flying Within Europe: If you're considering a train ride that's more than five hours long, a flight may save you both time and money. When comparing your options, factor in the time it takes to get to the airport and how early you'll need to arrive to check in.

Well-known cheapo airlines include easyJet (www.easyjet. com) and Ryanair (www.ryanair.com), which both serve Rome. But be aware of the potential drawbacks of flying with a discount airline: nonrefundable and nonchangeable tickets, minimal or nonexistent customer service, pricey and time-consuming treks to secondary airports, and stingy baggage allowances with steep over-age fees. If you're traveling with lots of luggage, a cheap flight can quickly become a bad deal. To avoid unpleasant surprises, read the small print before you book.

These days you can also fly within Europe on major airlines affordably—and without all the aggressive restrictions—for around $100 a flight.

Flying to the US and Canada: Because security is extra tight for flights to the US, be sure to give yourself plenty of time at the airport. It's also important to charge your electronic devices before you board because security checks may require you to turn them on (see www.tsa.gov for the latest rules).

Resources from Rick Steves

Begin your trip at www.ricksteves.com: My mobile-friendly **web-site** is *the* place to explore Europe. You'll find thousands of fun articles, videos, photos, and radio interviews organized by country; a wealth of money-saving tips for planning your dream trip; monthly travel news dispatches; a collection of over 30 hours of practical travel talks; my travel blog; my latest guidebook updates (www. ricksteves.com/update); and my free Rick Steves Audio Europe app. You can also find links to follow me on Facebook and Twitter.

Our **Travel Forum** is an immense, yet well-groomed collection of message boards, where our travel-savvy community answers questions and shares their personal travel experiences—and our well-traveled staff chimes in when they can be helpful (www.rick-steves.com/forums).

Our **online Travel Store** offers travel bags and accessories that I've designed specifically to help you travel smarter and lighter. These include my popular bags (rolling carry-on and backpack versions, which I helped design...and live out of four months a year), money belts, totes, toiletries kits, adapters, other accessories, and a wide selection of guidebooks and planning maps.

Choosing the right **rail pass** for your trip—amid hundreds of options—can drive you nutty. Our website will help you find the perfect fit for your itinerary and your budget: We offer easy, one-stop shopping for rail passes, seat reservations, and point-to-point tickets.

Tours: Want to travel with greater efficiency and less stress? We organize **tours** with more than three dozen itineraries and more than 900 departures reaching the best destinations in this book...and beyond. Our Italy tours include "the best of" in 17 days, Village Italy in 14 days, South Italy in 13 days, Sicily in 11 days, Venice-Florence-Rome in 10 days, the Heart of Italy in 9 days, a My Way: Italy "unguided" tour in 13 days, and a week-long Rome tour. You'll enjoy great guides, a fun bunch of travel partners (with small groups of 24 to 28 travelers), and plenty of room to spread out in a big, comfy bus when touring between towns. You'll find European adventures to fit every vacation length. For all the details, and to get our Tour Catalog and a free Rick Steves Tour Experience DVD (filmed on location during an actual tour), visit www.ricksteves.com/tour or call us at 425/608-4217.

Books: *Rick Steves Rome 2017* is one of many books in my series on European travel, which includes country guidebooks, city guidebooks (Venice, Florence, Paris, London, etc.), Snapshot guidebooks (excerpted chapters from my country guides), Pocket guidebooks (full-color little books on big cities, including Rome), "Best Of" guidebooks (condensed country guides in a full-color, easy-to-scan format), and my budget-travel skills handbook, *Rick Steves Europe Through the Back Door.* Most of my titles are available as ebooks.

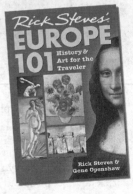

My phrase books—for Italian, French, German, Spanish, and Portuguese—are practical and budget-oriented. My other books include *Europe 101* (a crash course on art and history designed for travelers); *Mediterranean Cruise Ports* and *Northern European Cruise Ports* (how to make the most of your time in port); and *Travel as a Political Act* (a travelogue sprinkled with tips for bringing home a global perspective). A more complete list of my titles appears near the end of this book.

TV Shows: My public television series, *Rick Steves' Europe,* covers Europe from top to bottom with over 100 half-hour episodes. To watch full episodes online for free, visit www.ricksteves.com/tv.

Travel Talks on Video: You can raise your travel I.Q. with video versions of our popular classes (including talks on travel skills, packing smart, cruising, tech for travelers, European art for travelers, travel as a political act, and individual talks covering most European countries), see www.ricksteves.com/travel-talks.

Audio: My weekly public radio show, *Travel with Rick Steves,* features interviews with travel experts from around the world. A

complete archive of 10 years of programs (over 400 in all) is available at www.ricksteves.com/radio. I've also produced free, self-guided audio tours of the top sights in Rome. Most of this audio content is available for free through my **Rick Steves Audio Europe app,** an extensive online library organized by destination. For more on my app, see page 8.

APPENDIX

Useful Contacts 559
Holidays and Festivals 560
Recommended Books and Films 561
Conversions and Climate 564
Packing Checklist 567
Italian Survival Phrases 569

Useful Contacts

Emergency Needs
Police: 113
Ambulance: 118
Road Service: 116

Embassies
US Embassy: 24-hour emergency line—tel. 06 46741, nonemergency—tel. 06-4674-2420 (by appointment only, Via Vittorio Veneto 121, http://italy.usembassy.gov)
Canadian Embassy: Tel. 06-854-442-911 (Via Zara 30, www.italy.gc.ca)

Directory Assistance
Telephone Help (in English; free directory assistance): 170
Directory Assistance (for €0.50, an Italian-speaking robot gives the number twice, very clearly): 12

Holidays and Festivals

In Italy, holidays seem to strike without warning. For instance, every town has a festival honoring its patron saint. The Vatican Museums close for a multitude of Catholic holidays; check the schedule at http://mv.vatican.va.

This list includes selected festivals in Rome, plus national holidays observed throughout Italy. Many sights and banks close on national holidays—keep this in mind when planning your itinerary. Before planning a trip around a festival, verify its dates by checking the festival's website or TI sites (www.italia.it and www.turismoroma.it).

In Rome, hotels get booked up on Easter weekend (Good Friday through Monday), April 25 (Liberation Day), May 1 (Labor Day), June 29 (Sts. Peter and Paul), November 1 (All Saints' Day), and on Fridays and Saturdays year-round. Some hotels require you to book the full three-day weekend around a holiday.

Jan 1	New Year's Day
Jan 6	Epiphany
April 2	Rome Marathon (www.maratonadiroma.it)
April 16-17	Easter weekend (Good Friday-Easter Monday)
April 21	City Birthday
April 25	Italian Liberation Day
May 1	Labor Day
June 2	Anniversary of the Republic
June 15	Feast Day of Corpus Christi
June 24	St. John the Baptist Day
June 29	Sts. Peter and Paul Day
Mid-July	Trastevere's Noantri Festival
Aug 10	St. Lawrence's Day
Aug 15	Feast of the Assumption (Ferragosto)
Nov 1	All Saints' Day
Dec 8	Feast of the Immaculate Conception
Dec 25	Christmas
Dec 26	St. Stephen's Day

Recommended Books and Films

To learn more about Italy past and present, and specifically Rome, check out a few of these books and films. For kids' recommendations, see page 391.

NONFICTION

Absolute Monarchs (John Julius Norwich, 2011). This warts-and-all illustrated guide to the most significant popes in history is a readable best seller.

Ancient Rome: The Rise and Fall of an Empire (Simon Baker, 2007). Baker chronicles the rise and demise of the great Roman Empire and its powerful leaders.

City: A Story of Roman Planning and Construction (David Macaulay, 1974). Macaulay's illustrated book about the Eternal City will please both kids and adults.

A Day in the Life of Ancient Rome (Alberto Angela, 2007). Travel back to the world of gladiators and grand banquets in this 24-hour journey through the ancient city.

Eat, Pray, Love (Elizabeth Gilbert, 2006). Gilbert undertakes a stirring journey of self-discovery through Italy, India, and Indonesia (also a 2010 movie with Julia Roberts).

A Literary Companion to Rome (John Varriano, 1992). In these 10 self-guided walking tours, Roman sites associated with Ibsen, Dickens, Woolf, Wilde, and other great writers are explained in detail.

Michelangelo and the Pope's Ceiling (Ross King, 2003). The story behind the Sistine Chapel includes Michelangelo's technical difficulties, personality conflicts, and money troubles.

The Pope's Elephant (Silvio A. Bedini, 1997). Pope Leo X's favorite pet was an albino elephant named Hanno, and his story is also an account of the end of Rome's Golden Age.

Rome and a Villa (Eleanor Clark, 1952). This masterful collection of vignettes by the wife of Robert Penn Warren touches such diverse topics as Rome's Protestant Cemetery and Hadrian's Villa.

Saints & Sinners (Eamon Duffy, 1997). Everything you always wanted to know about the popes, but were afraid to ask.

The Seasons of Rome (Paul Hofmann, 1997). A former *New York Times* bureau chief reveals the eccentricities of Rome often overlooked by tourists.

The Secrets of Rome: Love and Death in the Eternal City (Corrado Augias, 2005). Augias takes readers back through 27 centuries of Roman history, secrets, and conspiracies.

APPENDIX

When in Rome (Robert Hutchinson, 1998). A lapsed (sometimes irreverent) Catholic discovers the roots of Christianity in Vatican City.

FICTION

The Agony and the Ecstasy (Irving Stone, 1958). Stone fictionalizes Michelangelo's struggle to paint the Sistine Chapel (also a 1965 movie starring Charlton Heston).

Angels & Demons (Dan Brown, 2000). *The Da Vinci Code* author's page-turner about a secret society and a time bomb in the Vatican (also a 2009 movie starring Tom Hanks).

Clash of Civilizations Over an Elevator in Piazza Vittorio (Amara Lakhous, 2006). The multicultural community of a Roman apartment building confronts the death of one of its members.

The Decameron (Giovanni Boccaccio, 1348). Boccaccio's collection of 100 hilarious, often bawdy tales is a masterpiece of Italian literature and inspired Chaucer, Keats, and Shakespeare.

The First Man in Rome (Colleen McCullough, 1990). The author of *The Thorn Birds* describes the early days of the Roman Republic, in the first of a best-selling series of historical fiction.

I, Claudius (Robert Graves, 1934). This brilliant history of ancient Rome is told by Claudius, the family's laughingstock who becomes emperor himself. The sequel is *Claudius the God* (1935).

Italian Journey (Johann Wolfgang von Goethe, 1786). In his 18th-century collection of writings, Goethe describes his travels to Rome, Sicily, and Naples.

Lucrezia Borgia (Maria Bellonci, 1939). In this historically based tale of court intrigue, a daughter of Pope Alexander VI navigates passions, plots, and controversy in Renaissance Rome.

My Brilliant Friend (Elena Ferrante, 2012). The first of four titles in the Neopolitan Novels series traces two girls' coming of age in mid-20th-century Naples.

Pompeii (Robert Harris, 2003). The engineer responsible for Pompeii's aqueducts has a bad feeling about Mount Vesuvius in this historical novel.

The Roman Spring of Ms. Stone (Tennessee Williams, 1950). A wealthy American widow and former stage actress haunts the Eternal City in the years after World War II, seeking purpose amid its grandeur.

A Soldier of the Great War (Mark Helprin, 1991). A young Roman lawyer falls in love with an art student, but World War I rips them apart.

That Awful Mess on the Via Merulana (Carlo Emilio Gadda, 1957). This detective story about a murder and a burglary in an apartment building in central Rome shines a harsh light on fascist Italy.

The Woman of Rome (Alberto Moravia, 1949). This classic tale of obsession and betrayal set against the backdrop of Mussolini's fascist regime follows a young model who attracts destructive passions.

FILM AND TV

Ben-Hur (1959). At the height of the Roman Empire, a Jewish prince is enslaved by a friend, and later seeks revenge in a stunning chariot race (the film won a record 11 Oscars).

Bicycle Thieves (1948). A poor man looks for his stolen bicycle in busy Rome in this inspirational classic of Italian Neorealism.

Caterina in the Big City (2003). A teenager whose family moves to Rome from a small town is the focus of this bitter comedy about the crisis of contemporary Italian society.

La Dolce Vita (1961). Director Federico Fellini tells a series of stories that capture the hedonistic days of early 1960s Rome.

Gladiator (2000). An enslaved Roman general (Russell Crowe) fights his way back to freedom in Ridley Scott's Oscar winner.

The Great Beauty (2013). This thoughtful movie, named best foreign film at the 2014 Academy Awards, showcases Rome in all of its decadence and splendor.

Massacre in Rome (1973). Richard Burton and Marcello Mastroianni star in this historical drama, which recounts one of the bloodiest events during the Nazi occupation of Rome.

Mid-August Lunch (2008). A broke Roman bachelor gets more than he bargained for when he agrees to take care of an elderly lady during a summer holiday to pay off a debt.

Quo Vadis (1951). A Roman general falls in love with a Christian hostage in this epic that includes the burning of Rome, the crucifixion of St. Peter, and the madness of Nero.

Rome, Open City (1945). Roberto Rossellini's war drama is set in the Eternal City during the WWII Nazi occupation.

Roman Holiday (1953). Audrey Hepburn plays a princess who escapes her royal minders, falls for an American newspaperman (Gregory Peck), and discovers Rome on the back of his scooter.

Spartacus (1960). In this epic directed by Stanley Kubrick, a gladiator (Kirk Douglas) leads a slave revolt in the last days of the Roman Republic.

A Special Day (1977). On the day of Hitler's visit to Rome, the wife (Sophia Loren) of a militant fascist has a fateful meeting with a persecuted journalist (Marcello Mastroianni).

Conversions and Climate

NUMBERS AND STUMBLERS

- Europeans write a few of their numbers differently than we do. 1 = 1, 4 = 4, 7 = 7.
- In Europe, dates appear as day/month/year, so Christmas 2017 is 25/12/17.
- Commas are decimal points and decimals are commas. A dollar and a half is $1,50, one thousand is 1.000, and there are 5.280 feet in a mile.
- When counting with fingers, start with your thumb. If you hold up your first finger to request one item, you'll probably get two.
- What Americans call the second floor of a building is the first floor in Europe.
- On escalators and moving sidewalks, Europeans keep the left "lane" open for passing. Keep to the right.

METRIC CONVERSIONS

A kilogram is 2.2 pounds, and 1 liter is about a quart, or almost four to a gallon. A kilometer is six-tenths of a mile. I figure kilometers to miles by cutting them in half and adding back 10 percent of the original (120 km: 60 + 12=72 miles, 300 km: 150 + 30=180 miles).

1 foot = 0.3 meter	1 square yard = 0.8 square meter
1 yard = 0.9 meter	1 square mile = 2.6 square kilometers
1 mile = 1.6 kilometers	1 ounce = 28 grams
1 centimeter = 0.4 inch	1 quart = 0.95 liter
1 meter = 39.4 inches	1 kilogram = 2.2 pounds
1 kilometer = 0.62 mile	32°F = 0°C

ROMAN NUMERALS

In the US, you'll see Roman numerals—which originated in ancient Rome—used for copyright dates, clocks, and the Super Bowl. In Italy, you're likely to observe these numbers chiseled on statues and buildings. If you want to do some numeric detective work, here's how: In Roman numerals, as in ours, the highest numbers (thousands, hundreds) come first, followed by smaller numbers. Many numbers are made by combining numerals into sets: V=5, so VIII=8 (5 plus 3). Roman numerals follow a subtraction principle for multiples of fours (4, 40, 400, etc.) and nines (9, 90, 900, etc.). The number four, for example, is written as IV (1 subtracted from 5), rather than IIII. The number nine is IX (1 subtracted from 10).

Rick Steves Rome 2017 would translate as *Rick Steves Rome MMXVII*. Big numbers such as dates can look daunting at first. The easiest way to handle them is to read the numbers in discrete chunks. For example, Michelangelo was born in MCDLXXV. Break it down: M (1,000) + CD (100 subtracted from 500, or 400) + LXX (50 + 10 + 10, or 70) + V (5)=1475. It was a very good year.

M = 1000	XL = 40
CM = 900	X = 10
D = 500	IX = 9
CD = 400	V = 5
C = 100	IV = 4
XC = 90	I = duh
L = 50	

CLOTHING SIZES

When shopping for clothing, use these US-to-European comparisons as general guidelines (but note that no conversion is perfect).

Women: For clothing or shoe sizes, add 30 (US shirt size 10 = European size 40; US shoe size 8 = European size 38-39).

Men: For shirts, multiply by 2 and add about 8 (US size 15 = European size 38). For jackets and suits, add 10. For shoes, add 32-34.

Children: For clothing, subtract 1-2 sizes for small children and subtract 4 for juniors. For shoes up to size 13, add 16-18, and for sizes 1 and up, add 30-32.

ROME'S CLIMATE

First line—average daily high; second line—average daily low; third line—average days without rain. For more detailed weather statistics for Rome (as well as the rest of the world), check www. wunderground.com.

J	F	M	A	M	J	J	A	S	O	N
52°	55°	59°	66°	74°	82°	87°	86°	79°	71°	61°
40°	42°	45°	50°	56°	63°	67°	67°	62°	55°	49°
13	19	23	24	26	26	30	29	25	23	19

FAHRENHEIT AND CELSIUS CONVERSION

Europe takes its temperature using the Celsius scale, while we opt for Fahrenheit. For a rough conversion from Celsius to Fahrenheit, double the number and add 30. For weather, remember that 28°C is 82°F—perfect. For health, 37°C is just right. At a launderette, 30°C is cold, 40°C is warm (usually the default setting), 60°C is hot, and 95°C is boiling. Your air-conditioner should be set at about 20°C.

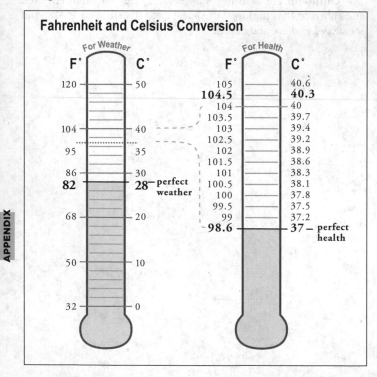

Fahrenheit and Celsius Conversion

APPENDIX

Packing Checklist

Whether you're traveling for five days or five weeks, you won't need more than this. Pack light to enjoy the sweet freedom of true mobility.

Clothing

- ☐ 5 shirts: long- & short-sleeve
- ☐ 2 pairs pants (or skirts/capris)
- ☐ 1 pair shorts
- ☐ 5 pairs underwear & socks
- ☐ 1 pair walking shoes
- ☐ Sweater or warm layer
- ☐ Rainproof jacket with hood
- ☐ Tie, scarf, belt, and/or hat
- ☐ Swimsuit
- ☐ Sleepwear/loungewear

Money

- ☐ Debit card(s)
- ☐ Credit card(s)
- ☐ Hard cash ($100-200 in US dollars)
- ☐ Money belt

Documents

- ☐ Passport
- ☐ Tickets & confirmations: flights, hotels, trains, rail pass, car rental, sight entries
- ☐ Driver's license
- ☐ Student ID, hostel card, etc.
- ☐ Photocopies of important documents
- ☐ Insurance details
- ☐ Guidebooks & maps
- ☐ Notepad & pen
- ☐ Journal

Toiletries Kit

- ☐ Basics: soap, shampoo, toothbrush, toothpaste, floss, deodorant, sunscreen, brush/comb, etc.
- ☐ Medicines & vitamins
- ☐ First-aid kit
- ☐ Glasses/contacts/sunglasses

- ☐ Sewing kit
- ☐ Packet of tissues (for WC)
- ☐ Earplugs

Electronics

- ☐ Mobile phone
- ☐ Camera & related gear
- ☐ Tablet/ebook reader/media player
- ☐ Laptop & flash drive
- ☐ Headphones
- ☐ Chargers & batteries
- ☐ Smartphone car charger & mount (or GPS device)
- ☐ Plug adapters

Miscellaneous

- ☐ Daypack
- ☐ Sealable plastic baggies
- ☐ Laundry supplies: soap, laundry bag, clothesline, spot remover
- ☐ Small umbrella
- ☐ Travel alarm/watch

Optional Extras

- ☐ Second pair of shoes (flip-flops, sandals, tennis shoes, boots)
- ☐ Travel hairdryer
- ☐ Picnic supplies
- ☐ Water bottle
- ☐ Fold-up tote bag
- ☐ Small flashlight
- ☐ Mini binoculars
- ☐ Small towel or washcloth
- ☐ Inflatable pillow/neck rest
- ☐ Tiny lock
- ☐ Address list (to mail postcards)
- ☐ Extra passport photos

Italian Survival Phrases

English	Italian	Pronunciation
Good day.	*Buon giorno.*	bwohn **jor**-noh
Do you speak English?	*Parla inglese?*	**par**-lah een-**gleh**-zay
Yes. / No.	*Sì. / No.*	see / noh
I (don't) understand.	*(Non) capisco.*	(nohn) kah-**pees**-koh
Please.	*Per favore.*	pehr fah-**voh**-ray
Thank you.	*Grazie.*	**graht**-see-ay
You're welcome.	*Prego.*	**preh**-go
I'm sorry.	*Mi dispiace.*	mee dee-spee-**ah**-chay
Excuse me.	*Mi scusi.*	mee **skoo**-zee
(No) problem.	*(Non) c'è un problema.*	(nohn) cheh oon proh-**bleh**-mah
Good.	*Va bene.*	vah **beh**-nay
Goodbye.	*Arrivederci.*	ah-ree-veh-**dehr**-chee
one / two	*uno / due*	**oo**-noh / **doo**-ay
three / four	*tre / quattro*	tray / **kwah**-troh
five / six	*cinque / sei*	**cheeng**-kway / **seh**-ee
seven / eight	*sette / otto*	**seh**-tay / **oh**-toh
nine / ten	*nove / dieci*	**noh**-vay / dee-**ay**-chee
How much is it?	*Quanto costa?*	**kwahn**-toh **koh**-stah
Write it?	*Me lo scrive?*	may loh **skree**-vay
Is it free?	*È gratis?*	eh **grah**-tees
Is it included?	*È incluso?*	eh een-**kloo**-zoh
Where can I buy / find...?	*Dove posso comprare / trovare...?*	**doh**-vay **poh**-soh kohm-**prah**-ray / troh-**vah**-ray
I'd like / We'd like...	*Vorrei / Vorremmo...*	voh-**reh**-ee / voh-**reh**-moh
...a room.	*...una camera.*	oo-nah **kah**-moh-rah
...a ticket to ____.	*...un biglietto per ____.*	oon beel-**yeh**-toh pehr ____
Is it possible?	*È possibile?*	eh poh-**see**-bee-lay
Where is...?	*Dov'è...?*	doh-**veh**
...the train station	*...la stazione*	lah staht-see-**oh**-nay
...the bus station	*...la stazione degli autobus*	lah staht-see-**oh**-nay **dehl**-yee ow-toh-boos
...tourist information	*...informazioni per turisti*	een-for-maht-see-**oh**-nee pehr too-**ree**-stee
...the toilet	*...la toilette*	lah twah-**leh**-tay
men	*uomini / signori*	**woh**-mee-nee / seen-**yoh**-ree
women	*donne / signore*	**doh**-nay / seen-**yoh**-ray
left / right	*sinistra / destra*	see-**nee**-strah / **deh**-strah
straight	*sempre dritto*	**sehm**-pray **dree**-toh
What time does this open / close?	*A che ora apre / chiude?*	ah kay **oh**-rah ah-**pray** / kee-**oo**-day
At what time?	*A che ora?*	ah kay **oh**-rah
Just a moment.	*Un momento.*	oon moh-**mehn**-toh
now / soon / later	*adesso / presto / tardi*	ah-**deh**-soh / **preh**-stoh / **tar**-dee
today / tomorrow	*oggi / domani*	**oh**-jee / doh-**mah**-nee

In an Italian Restaurant

English	Italian	Pronunciation
I'd like...	*Vorrei...*	voh-**reh**-ee
We'd like...	*Vorremmo...*	vor-**reh**-moh
...to reserve...	*...prenotare...*	preh-noh-**tah**-ray
...a table for one / two.	*...un tavolo per uno / due.*	oon **tah**-voh-loh pehr **oo**-noh / **doo**-ay
Is this seat free?	*È libero questo posto?*	eh **lee**-beh-roh **kweh**-stoh **poh**-stoh
The menu (in English), please.	*Il menù (in inglese), per favore.*	eel meh-**noo** (een een-**gleh**-zay) pehr fah-**voh**-ray
service (not) included	*servizio (non) incluso*	sehr-**veet**-see-oh (nohn) een-**kloo**-zoh
cover charge	*pane e coperto*	**pah**-nay ay koh-**pehr**-toh
to go	*da portar via*	dah **por**-tar **vee**-ah
with / without	*con / senza*	kohn / **sehnt**-sah
and / or	*e / o*	ay / oh
menu (of the day)	*menù (del giorno)*	meh-**noo** (dehl **jor**-noh)
specialty of the house	*specialità della casa*	speh-chah-lee-**tah** **deh**-lah **kah**-zah
first course (pasta, soup)	*primo piatto*	**pree**-moh pee-**ah**-toh
main course (meat, fish)	*secondo piatto*	seh-**kohn**-doh pee-**ah**-toh
side dishes	*contorni*	kohn-**tor**-nee
bread	*pane*	**pah**-nay
cheese	*formaggio*	for-**mah**-joh
sandwich	*panino*	pah-**nee**-noh
soup	*zuppa*	**tsoo**-pah
salad	*insalata*	een-sah-**lah**-tah
meat	*carne*	**kar**-nay
chicken	*pollo*	**poh**-loh
fish	*pesce*	**peh**-shay
seafood	*frutti di mare*	**froo**-tee dee **mah**-ray
fruit / vegetables	*frutta / legumi*	**froo**-tah / lay-**goo**-mee
dessert	*dolce*	**dohl**-chay
tap water	*acqua del rubinetto*	ah-kwah dehl roo-bee-**neh**-toh
mineral water	*acqua minerale*	ah-kwah mee-neh-**rah**-lay
milk	*latte*	**lah**-tay
(orange) juice	*succo (d'arancia)*	**soo**-koh (dah-**rahn**-chah)
coffee / tea	*caffè / tè*	kah-**feh** / teh
wine	*vino*	**vee**-noh
red / white	*rosso / bianco*	**roh**-soh / bee-**ahn**-koh
glass / bottle	*bicchiere / bottiglia*	bee-kee-**eh**-ray / boh-**teel**-yah
beer	*birra*	**bee**-rah
Cheers!	*Cin cin!*	cheen cheen
More. / Another.	*Di più. / Un altro.*	dee pew / oon **ahl**-troh
The same.	*Lo stesso.*	loh **steh**-soh
The bill, please.	*Il conto, per favore.*	eel **kohn**-toh pehr fah-**voh**-ray
Do you accept credit cards?	*Accettate carte di credito?*	ah-cheh-**tah**-tay **kar**-tay dee **kreh**-dee-toh
tip	*mancia*	**mahn**-chah
Delicious!	*Delizioso!*	day-leet-see-**oh**-zoh

For more user-friendly Italian phrases, check out *Rick Steves' Italian Phrase Book & Dictionary* or *Rick Steves' French, Italian, & German Phrase Book.*

INDEX

A

Accommodations: *See* Sleeping

Acqua Paola: 95

Aeneas, Anchises, and Ascanius (Bernini): 278

Air-conditioning, in hotels: 516

Airports: 421–423; customs regulations, 510; souvenir shopping, 409; VAT refunds, 509

Air travel: 554–555; budgeting, 5

Alexanderplatz: 411–412

Alexander the Great: 291–292, 318, 462, 492

Almanac, Rome: 6

Almost Corner Bookshop: 18

Altar of Peace: *See* Ara Pacis

Ambulance: 20, 504, 559

American Catholic Church: 85, 86

Americans, as "temporary locals": 9

Amphitheaters: Ostia Antica, 434–435; Pompeii, 494. *See also* Colosseum

Ancient Appian Way: *See* Appian Way

Ancient Rome: 11, 35–58; books about, 561–562; with children, 392; eating, 378–382; gelato, 381; guided tours, 30–33; history of, 162, 169, 171, 495–498; maps, 39, 153, 352–353; modern amenities, 152–153; nightlife, 413; religion in, 169, 301; sights, 35–58; sleeping near, 350–351; tourist information, 152; transportation, 152–153; walking tours, 142–185; Colosseum, 142–156; Palatine Hill, 174–185; Roman Forum, 157–173. *See also* Appian Way; Capitoline Hill; Colosseum

Andrew, Saint: 88

Anglo-American Bookshop: 18

Anthony, Saint: 331

Antinous: 296

Antipasti (appetizers): 366, 525. *See also* Eating

Antiques, shopping for: 399, 400, 408

Antoninus Pius and Faustina, Temple of: 164

Apartment rentals: 518–520

Aperitivo buffets: 364, 380, 529

Aphrodite Crouching: 296

Apollo and Daphne (Bernini): 276–277

Apollo Belvedere: 243–244

Apollo del Tevere: 297

Appian Way: 108, 332–342; biking, 335, 395; eating, 335; map, 337; transportation, 333–334; walking tour, 336–342

Apps: 18, 511–512; for foodies, 375; journey planners, 21; mapping, 510

Aqueduct (Pompeii): 491

Aqueduct Park: 341–342

Aracoeli Church: 44–45

Ara di Cesare: 167–168

Ara Pacis (Altar of Peace): 47, 75–77, 416; eating near, 377–378

Archaeological museums: Etruscan Museum, 68–69; Museum of Roman Civilization, 107; Museum of the Walls, 342; Naples Archaeological Museum, 458–464; Ostia Museum, 439–440; Palazzo Nuovo, 193–195. *See also* Art museums; Capitoline Museums; National Museum of Rome; Vatican Museums

Architecture: churches, 499. *See also* Churches and cathedrals; *and specific buildings*

Arch of Constantine: 38, 47, 151–152

Arch of Septimius Severus: 171–172

Arch of Titus (Arco di Tito): 159–162

Art: books about, 561–562; Sketching Rome Tours, 32. *See also* Archaeological museums; Art museums; Churches and cathedrals; Mosaics; *and specific artists and artworks*

Art museums: at night, 412; daily reminder, 17; free Sundays, 35; general tips and hours, 17, 43, 511–512; price hike alert, 34–35; reservations, 8, 43; Roma Pass, 17, 42–43; Etruscan Museum, 68–69; Galleria d'Italia Palazzo Zevallos Stigliano (Naples), 468; Galleria Doria Pamphilj, 60; MAXXI, 69–70, 501; Montemartini

Museum, 101–102, 394; Museo dell'Ara Pacis, 47, 75–77, 416; Museo della Via Ostiense, 98–99; Museo Palatino (Imperial Palace), 180–181; Museum of the Imperial Forums, 55–56; Palazzo dei Conservatori, 187–193; Scuderie del Quirinale, 89, 412; Villa Farnesina, 92–95, 299, 331. *See also* Borghese Gallery; Capitoline Museums; Vatican Museums

Asclepius: 320

ATMs: 505–506

Audio Europe, Rick Steves: 8, 9, 30, 557

Auditorium Parco della Musica: 70, 410–411

Augustus: 45, 50, 54, 55, 75, 76–77, 162, 289–290, 300, 497; House of, 183; Mausoleum of, 414, 416

Aurelian Wall: 96, 98, 99, 342

Autostazione Tiburtina: 420–421

B

Back Door travel philosophy: 10

Banca Intesa Sanpaolo (Naples): 468

Banco di Napoli (Naples): 468

Baroque period and sights: overview, 498, 500. *See also specific artists and sights*

Bars and cafés: 412–414, 527–528; *aperitivo* buffets, 364, 380, 529; Naples, 466, 470. *See also* Wine bars

Bar Toto: 209

Basilica (Pompeii): 487

Basilica Aemilia: 168–169

Basilica Maxentius: 162–163

Basilica of Constantine: 162–163

Basilica San Pietro: *See* St. Peter's Basilica

Baths of Caracalla: 107–108, 342

Baths of Diocletian: 79–84; map, 79; orientation, 47, 79–80; self-guided tour, 81–84

Baths of Neptune (Ostia Antica): 434

Baths of the Forum (Pompeii): 488–489

Battle of Alexander: 461–462

Beaches: 396, 430

Bed-and-breakfasts (B&Bs): overview, 518. *See also* Sleeping

Beer: 536. *See also* Bars and cafés

Beggars: 19

Bellini, Vincenzo: 465

Belvedere Torso: 245

Benedict XVI, Pope: 228, 251, 501–502

Bernini, Gian Lorenzo: 60, 74, 87, 190, 209; biographical sketch, 280; Borghese Gallery, 275–277, 278; Four Rivers Fountain, 116; St. Peter's Basilica, 217, 219, 227–230, 231, 234; *St. Teresa in Ecstasy,* 84–85; Sant'Andrea al Quirinale, 88; scavenger hunt, 231; Sinking Boat Fountain, 124; tomb, 308

Beverages: 535–539

Biking: 29–30; Appian Way, 335, 395

Biscottificio Artigiano Innocenti: 327

BNL Bank (Naples): 468

Bocca della Verità: 40, 394

Bones, in Capuchin Crypt: 70–71, 392

Books, recommended: 561–563; for children, 391

Bookstores: 18

Borghese Gallery: 67–68, 271–285; guided tours, 272; maps, 275, 282; orientation, 46, 67–68, 271–273; reservations, 271–272; self-guided tour, 273–285

Borgo Pio: eating, 386; shopping, 407–408

Borri Books: 18

Borromini, Francesco: 87–88, 116–117, 312

Boxer at Rest, The: 293

Boy Extracting a Thorn: 189–190

Boy with a Fruit Basket (Caravaggio): 279

Bramante, Donato: 95, 216, 223, 255

Breakfast: about, 522–523

Brothel (Pompeii): 492

Brown, Dan: 85, 563

Bruno, Giordano: 111, 114

Brutus: 168, 189, 289

Budgeting: 5–7

Buses: 22–28, 420–421; to/from airports, 422, 423; Appian Way, 333–334; journey planners, 21; major routes, 23, 26, 28; map, 24–25, 547; Naples, 456, 457; reading the signs, 27; tickets, 21–22; Tivoli, 442–443; tours, 32, 458

Business hours: 398, 504

C

Cabs: *See* Taxis

Cafés: *See* Bars and cafés

Caffè Greco: 124

Caffè Mexico (Naples): 466

Caffè Tazza d'Oro: 118–119

Caligula: 166, 184, 217–218, 290, 291, 300, 497; Palace, 166

Call center: 16, 144

Calling of St. Matthew (Caravaggio): 133

Cameras: *See* Photography policy

Campidoglio: *See* Capitoline Hill

Campo de' Fiori: 11, 111, 114; eating, 369, 372; market, 111, 115, 369, 409; nightlife, 413; shopping, 400–401; sleeping near, 354–355

Canova, Antonio: 274–275

Capanne Romulee: 184–185

Capitoline Hill: 40–41, 186; map, 41

Capitoline Museums: 44, 186–195; eating, 186–187; map, 188; orientation, 44, 46, 186–187; self-guided tour, 187–195

Capitoline She-Wolf: 190

Capitoline Venus: 195

Capitolium (Ostia Antica): 438

Cappella Sansevero (Naples): 471, 475–476

Capuchin Crypt: 70–71, 392

Caracalla: 194, 298; Baths of, 107–108, 342

Car and drivers: 32–33, 442

Caravaggio: 60, 269–270; Borghese Gallery, 279–280; in Naples, 468, 473, 476–477; San Luigi dei Francesi, 59, 117, 132–134; Santa Maria del Popolo, 73–74, 414

Carcere Mamertino: 39–40

Car travel (driving): 423–424; Pompeii, 480

Casa del Fauno (Pompeii): 491–492

Casa del Poeta Tragico (Pompeii): 490

Casa di Augusto: 183

Casa di Livia: 183–184

Casa di Menandro (Pompeii): 493

Castel Nuovo (Naples): 470

Castel Sant'Angelo: 47, 63–66, 393

Catacombs: 47, 340–341; of Priscilla, 77–78, 334, 392; of San Callisto, 109, 334, 339; of San Sebastiano, 108–109, 334, 338

Cathedrals: *See* Churches and cathedrals; St. Peter's Basilica

Catherine of Alexandria, Saint: 315–316

Catherine of Siena, Saint: 139

Cecilia, Saint: 325–326

Cecilia Metella, Tomb of: 336–337

Cell (mobile) phones: 8–9, 539–543

Cerasi Chapel: 74, 414

"Chapel of Maradona" (Naples): 472

Chigi Chapel: 73–74, 414

Children: 389–397; best sights and activities, 392–397; books and films, 391; travel tips, 389–392

Children's museum, Explora: 394–395

Christ Bearing the Cross (Michelangelo): 59, 139–140

Churches and cathedrals: architecture, 499; general tips and hours, 17, 43, 512; with children, 392–393; Domine Quo Vadis, 339; Gesù Church, 59, 134–138; Gesù Nuovo (Naples), 471, 474–475; Naples Duomo, 473, 476; Pio Monte della Misericordia (Naples), 473, 476–477; St. Paul's Outside the Walls, 102–104; St. Peter-in-Chains, 58, 196–200; San Bernardo, 86; San Carlo alle Quattro Fontane, 87–88; San Clemente, 91, 303, 314–318; San Francesco di Paola (Naples), 469; San Giovanni in Laterano, 47, 89–90, 310–314; San Luigi dei Francesi, 59, 117, 132–134; San Paolo Fuori le Mura, 102–104; San Pietro in Montorio, 95; Santa Cecilia, 324–326; Santa Chiara (Naples), 471, 475; Sant'Agnese, 116–117; Santa Maria degli Angeli, 79–80; Santa Maria della Immacolata Concezione, 70–71; Santa Maria della Pietà, 205; Santa Maria della Vittoria, 84–85; Santa Maria del Popolo, 73–74, 414; Santa Maria in Aquiro, 119; Santa Maria in Aracoeli, 44–45; Santa Maria in Cosmedin, 40, 394; Santa Maria in Trastevere, 92, 328–331; Santa Maria Maggiore, 91, 303–308; Santa Maria sopra Minerva, 59, 138–140; Sant'Andrea al Quirinale, 88; Santa Prassede, 309–310; Santa Susanna, 85, 86; Sant'Ignazio, 59, 118, 140–141, 393; walking tour, of Pilgrim's

Rome, 301–318. *See also* St. Peter's Basilica
Ciampino Airport: 423
Cimitero Acattolico per gli Stranieri al Testaccio: 99–100
Circumvesuviana train: 454, 480
Circus Maxentius: 337–338
Circus Maximus: 179–180, 342
Civitavecchia: 424–425
Classical music: 411
Claudian Aqueduct: 314
Cleopatra: 98, 119, 289
Climate: 7, 566
Clothing sizes: 565
Coffee: 535–536. *See also* Bars and cafés
Coin collection, at National Museum of Rome: 300
Colosseum: 35, 142–156; with children, 392; eating near, 381–382; legacy of, 155–156; map, 146; nightlife near, 413; orientation, 35, 46, 142–145; tours, 144–145; walking tour, 145–155
Column of Phocas: 172
Column of the Immaculate Conception: 123
Commodus: 189, 191
Constantine: 187–188, 312, 337, 340, 497; Arch of, 38, 47, 151–152; Basilica of, 162–163
Constantine Room (Vatican Museum): 252–254
Convents, sleeping at: 343, 349, 351, 354–355, 361, 521
Conversion of St. Paul (Caravaggio): 74
Correggio: 284
Corsia Agonale: 117
Corso Umberto I: 474
Corso Vittorio Emanuele II: 115
Costs of trip: 5–7
Creation of Adam (Michelangelo): 259, 262
Credit cards: 7, 505–508; lost or stolen, 19–20, 508
Crime: *See* Theft alerts
Cripta dei Frati Cappuccini: 70–71, 392
Crucifixion of St. Peter (Caravaggio): 74
Cruise ships: 424–425
Cryptoporticus: 184
Cuisine, Roman: 366–367, 524–525, 530–535. *See also* Eating

Curia (Senate House): 169–170; Pompeii, 486
Currency and exchange: 505–506
Customs regulations: 510
Cyril, Saint: 317

D
Daily reminder: 17
Danae (Correggio): 284
Dancing Faun: 461
David (Bernini): 275–276
David with the Head of Goliath (Caravaggio): 279
Da Vinci, Leonardo: 268–269
Da Vinci Airport: *See* Fiumicino Airport
Day trips: 427–494; map, 427; Naples, 449–479; Ostia Antica, 429–440; Pompeii, 479–494; Tivoli, 441–448
Debit cards: 7, 505–508; lost or stolen, 19–20, 508
Della Rovere Chapel: 73
Department stores: 407
Deposition (Caravaggio): 269–270
Deposition (Raphael): 283
Desserts *(dolci):* 367. *See also* Gelato
Diana the Huntress: 249
Dining: *See* Eating
Diocletian: 79, 80, 300, 497. *See also* Baths of Diocletian
Directory assistance: 559
Discounts: 505; Roma Pass, 17, 42–43; train tickets, 549. *See also* Money-saving tips
Discus Thrower, The: 296–297
Disputa (Raphael): 256–257
Doctors: 20–21
Dolce Vita stroll: 47, 74, 414–416; eating, 377–378; map, 415
Domenichino: 284
Domine Quo Vadis Church: 339
Domitia: 295
Domitian: 115, 176, 294
Domus Augustana: 178–179
Doria Pamphilj Gallery: 60
Doriforo: 464
Drinking water: 20, 535
Drinks: 535–539
Driving: *See* Car travel
Drugstores: 20, 504
Dying Gaul: 194
Dying Niobid: 292–293
Dynamic currency conversion (DCC): 508

E

East Rome: 12; eating, 382–383; map, 80–81; sights, 78–91; sleeping, 344–350

Eataly: 387–388

Eating: 362–388, 521–539; ancient Rome, 378–382; Appian Way, 335; budgeting, 5–6; Campo de' Fiori, 369, 372; Capitoline Museums, 186–187; with children, 389–390; courses, 366–367, 524–525; fixed-price meals, 526; food tours, 375; general tips, 363–364; Jewish Ghetto, 368–369, 373; money-saving tips, 526; Naples, 477–479; North Rome, 377–378; ordering tips, 525–526; Pantheon neighborhood, 369–377; near Piazza Navona, 372–373; Pompeii, 483; pricing, 521–522; restaurant phrases, 570; seasonal produce, 531; near Spanish Steps, 377–378; near Termini Train Station, 382–383; Testaccio, 386–388; tipping, 508, 523–524; Tivoli, 447–448; Trastevere, 365, 368; near Trevi Fountain, 374; near Vatican City, 383–386. *See also* Bars and cafés; Food; Gelato; Markets; Pizzerias; *Tavola calda;* Wine bars

Eating Italy Food Tours: 101, 375

Egyptian art, at Vatican Museums: 240–243

Egyptian obelisks: 72, 117–118, 119, 122, 217–218

Electricity: 504–505

E-mail: *See* Internet access

Embassies: 559

Emergencies: 20, 504, 559

Enotecas: See Wine bars

Entertainment: 410–416; budgeting, 6; current schedule, 16

Esquilino market: 409

Etruscan art, at Vatican Museums: 247–248

Etruscan Museum: 68–69

E.U.R.: 104–107; map, 105

Euro currency: 505–506

Exchange rate: 505

Excursion areas: *See* Day trips

Explora children's museum: 394–395

F

Families: *See* Children

Farnese Collection (Naples): 460–461

Farnese Gardens: 185

Farnese Hercules: 461

Fascist architecture: 76–77

Fatamorgana: 381, 405

Feltrinelli International: 18, 121

Fermi, Enrico: 404

Festivals: 560

Fish market, in Naples: 477

Fiumicino Airport: 421–423; souvenir shopping, 409

Flea markets: 408

Food: foodie resources, 375; Roman cuisine, 366–367, 524–525, 530–535; seasonal produce, 531; tours, 375. *See also* Eating; Gelato; Markets; Pizzerias

Formaggio (cheese): 533–534

Forno Campo de' Fiori: 111, 369

Foro Romano: *See* Roman Forum

Forum Baths (Ostia Antica): 439

Forums: Ostia Antica, 438–439; Pompeii, 486–487. *See also* Roman Forum; Trajan's Forum

Forums of Augustus and Nerva: 54

Fosse Ardeatine: 501

Fountains: 44, 57, 73, 86, 95, 117, 209, 445; drinking from, 20, 152; Four Rivers, 116; Sinking Boat, 124; Trevi, 47, 121–122, 395; Via delle Quattro, 86–87

Four Rivers Fountain: 116

Fra Angelico: 140

Francis I, Pope: 228–229, 502

Francis Xavier, Saint: 138

Funiculars, in Naples: 457, 469

G

Galleria Alberto Sordi: 121, 407

Galleria Borghese: *See* Borghese Gallery

Galleria d'Italia Palazzo Zevallos Stigliano (Naples): 468

Galleria Doria Pamphilj: 60

Galleria Principe di Napoli (Naples): 465

Galleria Umberto I (Naples): 451, 471

Gallery of the Candelabra (Vatican Museums): 249–250

Gardens: *See* Parks and gardens

Gelato: 534–535; ancient Rome, 381;

heart of Rome, 117, 395; Naples, 474; Pantheon neighborhood, 120, 377; near Vatican City, 385

Gesù Church: 59, 134–138; map, 135

Gesù Nuovo Church (Naples): 471, 474–475

"Ghetto," use of term: 202

Gianicolo Hill: 95–96

Giolitti: 120, 377

Gladiators: 46, 144, 147, 149–151, 155, 274

Golden House: 154

Gold shops, in Naples: 473

Gordiano: 194

Gran Caffè Gambrinus (Naples): 470

Graves: *See* Catacombs

Greek sculpture: at National Museum of Rome, 291–293; at Vatican Museums, 243–247

Groceries: *See* Supermarkets

Guidebooks, Rick Steves: 556; updates, 3

Guided tours: *See* Tours

Guides: *See* Tour guides

H

Hadrian: 63–66, 154–155, 295–296, 445–447

Hadrian's Villa (Tivoli): 442, 445–447

Hard Rock Café: 71

Health concerns: 20–21

Heart of Rome: 11, 110–124; map, 112–113; nightlife, 413; shopping, 399–401; walking tour, 111–124

Hermaphrodite Sleeping: 297

History: 495–500; ancient Rome, 162, 169, 171, 495–498; Jewish Ghetto, 202–204; Ostia Antica, 430–431; Pompeii, 483–484

Holidays: 560

Holy Door (St. Peter's Basilica): 220

Holy Stairs: 89–90, 303–304, 314

Hospitals: 21

Hostels: 350, 520–521

Hotels: 514, 516–518; rates and deals, 513–514; reservations, 7, 343–344, 515. *See also* Sleeping

House of Augustus: 183

House of Livia: 183–184

House of Menander (Pompeii): 493

House of the Faun (Pompeii): 491–492

House of the Tragic Poet (Pompeii): 490

House of the Vestal Virgins: 165

Hunt of Diana, The (Domenichino): 284

Huts of Romulus: 184–185

Hydromania Water Park: 396–397

I

Ice cream: *See* Gelato

Ignatius of Loyola, Saint: 134, 136–137, 140–141

Il Capanno: 396

Il Pentagrappolo: 381, 412

Il Sodoma: 94–95

Imperial Forums: 46, 50–54; map, 51

Imperial Palace: 176, 178–179, 181–183

Information: *See* Tourist information

Innocent X, Pope: 60, 116, 312

Inspiration of St. Matthew (Caravaggio): 133

Internet access: 17, 517, 539, 542

Internet security: 544

Isola Tiberina: 320–321

Italian Center for American Studies: 209

Italian Independence War Memorial: 95

Italian language: *See* Language

Italian Parliament: 119–120

Italian restaurant phrases: 570

Italian survival phrases: 569

Itineraries: 12, 14–16; Naples, 450

J

Jazz music: 411–412

Jesuits: 138; Gesù Church, 59, 134–138

Jewelry stores, in Naples: 473

Jewish Ghetto: 61–62, 201–210; eating, 368–369; history of, 202–204; map, 203; orientation, 201–202; shopping, 401; tours, 30, 202; walking tour, 205–210

Jewish Museum: 61–62, 206–207

John Paul II, Pope: 61, 104, 204, 220, 226, 502; tomb, 232–233

John XXIII, Pope: 226

Julius Caesar: 50, 53–54, 59, 76, 111, 162, 170, 288–289, 300, 496; Temple of, 167–168

Julius II, Pope: 58, 197–199, 254

K

Keats, John: 99–100, 123

L

La Disputa (Raphael): 256–257
La Meridiana: 83
Language: online translation tips, 505; restaurant phrases, 570; survival phrases, 569
Language barrier: 542
Laocoön: 244–245
Largo Argentina: 59–60; gelato, 377; sleeping, 354–355
Largo Garibaldi (Tivoli): 443, 447
Largo 16 Ottobre 1943: 207
La Rinascente: 407
Last Judgment, The (Michelangelo): 263–267
Laundry: 18
Leonardo da Vinci Airport: *See* Fiumicino Airport
Leonardo Express train: 418, 421
Liberation of St. Peter (Raphael): 253–254
Live music: *See* Music
Livia: 76, 175, 290, 299; House of, 183–184
Local guides: *See* Tour guides
Loggia of Galatea (Villa Farnesina): 93
Loggia of Psyche (Villa Farnesina): 93–94

M

Maderno, Carlo: 86, 216, 217
Maderno, Stefano: 325–326, 339
Madonna of Palafrenieri (Caravaggio): 279
Mail: 544–545. *See also* Post offices
Mamertine Prison: 39–40
Manfredi Lighthouse: 96
Map Gallery (Vatican Museums): 250–251
Maps: apps, 510; legend, 2. *See also* Map Index
Maradona (Diego) Chapel (Naples): 472
Marcus Aurelius: 41, 44, 120, 189, 191–192
Mark Antony: 98, 119, 168, 170, 289
Markets: 408–409; Campo de' Fiori, 111, 115, 369, 409; Naples, 467, 477; Porta Portese, 408; seasonal produce, 531; Testaccio, 101, 386,

409; Trionfale, 386, 409; Via Sannio, 310, 408
Martyrdom of St. Matthew (Caravaggio): 133–134
Martyrdom of Saint Ursula (Caravaggio): 468
Masolino: 315–316
Mausoleo di Cecilia Metella: 336–337
Mausoleum of Augustus: 414, 416
Maxentius: 38, 151, 163, 312, 315, 316; Circus and Villa of, 337–338
MAXXI (National Museum of Art of the 21st Century): 69–70, 501
Medical help: 20–21, 504, 559
Mercato di Testaccio: 101, 386, 409
Mercato Esquilino: 409
MercatoMonti market: 404, 408
Mercato Trionfale: 386, 409
Metric system: 564–565
Metro (subway): 22; journey planners, 21; map, 24–25; Naples, 451, 455–457; Ostia Antica, 429; tickets, 21–22; Tivoli, 442
Michelangelo: 41, 44, 48, 83, 114, 128–129, 190; *Christ Bearing the Cross*, 59, 139–140; *Moses*, 58, 197; *Pietà*, 230–232; St. Peter-in-Chains Church, 58, 197–199; St. Peter's Basilica, 216, 217, 219, 220, 222–224, 230–232; Sistine Chapel (Vatican), 257–267
Milan vs. Rome: 56–57
Mill (Ostia Antica): 436
Minibus tours: 32–33
Mobile phones: 8–9, 539–543
Mondo Guide: 457, 458, 481
Money: 505–510; budgeting, 5–7
Money belts: 5, 19, 391, 506
Money-saving tips: 505; eating, 526; free Sundays, 35; Roma Pass, 17, 42–43; sleeping, 513–514; train tickets, 549
Montecitorio: 119–120
Montemartini Museum: 101–102, 394
Monte Palatino: *See* Palatine Hill
Monte Testaccio: 100–101; eating, 387; nightlife, 413–414
Monti: 11, 56–58, 379; eating, 379–381; market, 404, 408; nightlife, 413; shopping, 401, 404–405; sleeping, 348, 351

Mosaics: 91, 102, 104, 107, 195, 230, 246, 274, 278–279, 306–308, 309–310, 313, 325, 330–331, 491–492

Moscati, Giuseppe: 474–475

Moses (Michelangelo): 58, 197

Moses, Fountain of: 86

Mount Vesuvius: 480, 487, 489

"Mouth of Truth": 40, 394

Movies, recommended: 563; for children, 391

Movie theaters: 412

Multisala Barberini: 412

Mummies, at Vatican Museums: 241

Musei Capitolini: *See* Capitoline Museums

Musei Capitolini Centrale Montemartini: 101–102, 394

Musei Vaticani: *See* Vatican Museums

Museo Archeologico (Naples): 458–464

Museo dei Fori Imperiali: 55–56

Museo della Civiltà Romana: 107

Museo dell'Ara Pacis: 47, 75–77, 416

Museo della Via Ostiense: 98–99

Museo Ebraico: 61–62, 206–207

Museo e Galleria Borghese: *See* Borghese Gallery

Museo Nazionale Etrusco di Villa Giulia: 68–69

Museo Nazionale Romano Palazzo Massimo alle Terme: *See* National Museum of Rome

Museo Palatino (Imperial Palace): 180–181

Museo Storico della Liberazione: 90–91, 314

Museum of Roman Civilization: 107

Museum of the Altar of Peace: 47, 75–77, 416

Museum of the Imperial Forums: 55–56

Museum of the Liberation of Rome: 90–91, 314

Museum of the Risorgimento: 49

Museum of the Walls: 342

Museums: with children, 394–395; daily reminder, 17; free Sundays, 35; general tips and hours, 17, 43, 511–512; at night, 412; price hike alert, 34–35; reservations, 8, 43; Roma Pass, 17, 42–43. *See also* Archaeological museums; Art museums; *and specific museums*

Music: 410–412; Naples, 470

Musician Angels (Vatican Pinacoteca): 268

Mussolini, Benito: 45, 48, 50, 53, 75, 104–106, 204, 217, 323, 500

N

Naples: 449–479; eating, 477–479; helpful hints, 454–455; maps, 452–453, 456; orientation, 451; planning tips, 450; sights, 458–477; tourist information, 451; tours, 457–458; transportation, 428, 451, 454, 455–457; walking tours, 464–474

Naples Archaeological Museum: 458–464; eating near, 479

Naples Civic Museum: 470

Naples Duomo: 473, 476

National Museum of Art of the 21st Century (MAXXI): 69–70, 501

National Museum of Italian Emigration: 49

National Museum of Rome: 78, 286–300; maps, 288, 294; orientation, 46, 78, 286–287; self-guided tour, 287–300

Necropolis (Ostia Antica): 432

Neighborhoods: 11–12; maps, 13, 14; shopping by, 398–407. *See also specific neighborhoods*

Nero: 145, 154, 226, 230, 293, 300, 339, 497

Nerva: 50, 54, 295

Nightlife: 410–416; budgeting, 6; current schedule, 16

North Rome: 11; eating, 377–378; map, 68; sights, 67–78

Numbers: *See* Roman numerals

Nuovo Olimpia: 412

O

Obelisks: *See* Egyptian obelisks

Open Door Bookshop: 18

Opera: 411; Naples, 470

Organized tours: *See* Tours

Ostia, beaches: 396

Ostia Antica: 429–440; history of, 430–431; map, 431; orientation, 430; self-guided tour, 431–440; transportation, 427, 429–430

Ostia Museum: 439–440

Oviesse/OVS: 407

P

Packing checklist: 567

Palace of the Civilization of Labor: 107

Palace of Tiberius: 166

Palaestra: 494

Palatine Hill: 38–39, 174–185; map, 177; orientation, 38–39, 46, 174–175; tours, 175; walking tour, 176–185

Palazzo Capranica: 119

Palazzo dei Conservatori (Capitoline Museums): 187–193

Palazzo della Civiltà del Lavoro: 107

Palazzo delle Esposizioni: 89, 412

Palazzo del Quirinale: 88–89

Palazzo Madama: 117

Palazzo Massimo alle Terme: *See* National Museum of Rome

Palazzo Mattei: 209

Palazzo Nuovo (Capitoline Museums): 193–195

Palazzo Pamphilj: 116

Palazzo Reale (Naples): 469–470

Pantheon: 58, 117–118, 125–131; churches near, 58–59, 131–141; eating near, 374–376; gelato, 377; maps, 128, 129; orientation, 46, 58, 125–126; picnicking near, 376; self-guided tour, 126–131; sleeping near, 355–357

Pantheon neighborhood: 11, 117–119, 125–141, 352–353; eating, 369–377; gelato, 120, 377; maps, 59, 354, 370–371; nightlife, 413; sights, 58–62; sleeping, 352–358; supermarkets, 353–354; transportation, 352–353; walking tour, 125–141

Parco degli Acquedotti: 341–342

Parking: 423–424; Pompeii, 480

Parks and gardens: Aqueduct Park, 341–342; Farnese Gardens, 185; Gianicolo Hill, 95–96; Quirinale Gardens, 88; Vatican Gardens, 212; Villa Borghese Gardens, 67, 395

Parliament building: 119–120

Pasquino: 115

Passeggiata: 47, 74, 411. *See also* Dolce Vita Stroll

Passports: 7, 504

Pasta: overview, 531–533. *See also* Eating

Paul, Saint: 102, 104

Pauline Borghese as Venus (Canova): 274–275

Paul V, Pope: 95, 282

Pedestrian safety: 20; Naples, 455

Performing arts: *See* Music; Opera

Peter, Saint: 199–200, 215–216, 224–226, 230, 339. *See also* St. Peter's Basilica

Pharmacies: 20, 504

Phone numbers, useful: 559

Phones: 539–544

Photography policy: 126, 196, 238, 273, 287, 304, 459, 511

Piano, Renzo: 70, 410

Piazza Bellini (Naples): 465–466

Piazza Borghese, shopping: 406

Piazza Capranica: 119

Piazza Carità (Naples): 467–468

Piazza Colonna: 120

Piazza Costaguti: 209, 368

Piazza Dante (Naples): 466

Piazza del Campidoglio: 41, 44, 47

Piazza della Madonna dei Monti: 57, 401, 413

Piazza della Repubblica: 84

Piazza della Rotonda: 126, 131

Piazza delle Coppelle, market: 409

Piazza del Plebiscito (Naples): 469

Piazza del Popolo: 72–73, 414

Piazza del Quirinale: 89

Piazza di Montecitorio: 119–120

Piazza di Pietra: 60–61, 119

Piazza di San Bernardo: 86

Piazza di San Giovanni in Laterano: 314

Piazza di Santa Maria in Trastevere: 92, 328; eating, 365

Piazza di Spagna: 123–124. *See also* Spanish Steps

Piazza Farnese: 114; eating, 400

Piazza Garibaldi (Naples): 474

Piazza Gesù Nuovo (Naples): 471

Piazza in Piscinula: 321

Piazzale delle Corporazioni (Ostia Antica): 435–436

Piazzale Giuseppe Garibaldi: 96

Piazza Marconi: 105

Piazza Mattei: 209

Piazza Navona: 11, 115–117, 395; eating near, 372–373; gelato, 117, 395; shopping near, 399–400

Piazza Risorgimento, eating: 383–385

Piazza San Domenico Maggiore (Naples): 471

Piazza Sette Settembre (Naples): 466–467

Piazza Venezia: 45, 48; map, 41

Piazza Vittorio Emanuele II, shopping: 399

Pickpockets: 18–19, 23, 144, 506; Naples, 454–455

Picnics (picnicking): 364, 529–530; with children, 390. *See also* Markets

Pietà (Michelangelo): 230–232

Pilgrim's Rome: 89–91, 301–318; maps, 90, 302; walking tour, 304–318

Pinacoteca (Borghese Gallery): 281–285; map, 282

Pinacoteca (Vatican): 267–270; map, 269

Pintauro (Naples): 469

Pinturicchio: 45, 73

Pio Monte della Misericordia Church (Naples): 473, 476–477

Pius IX, Pope: 123, 306

Pizzerias (pizza): 367, 477, 526–527, 530–531; ancient Rome, 379, 380, 381; Naples, 477–479; North Rome, 378; Pantheon neighborhood, 369, 372, 373, 374; near Termini Train Station, 382–383; Testaccio, 387; Trastevere, 365, 368; near Vatican City, 385–386

Police: 20, 504, 559

Police reports: 19–20

Politics: 500–502

Pollaiuolo, Antonio: 233

Polo Nord Gelateria (Naples): 474

Pompeii: 479–494; helpful hints, 480–482; history of, 483–484; maps, 481, 482–483, 485; self-guided tour, 484–494; tours, 481–482; transportation, 480

Ponte Cestio: 320–321

Ponte Fabricio: 205

Ponte Sant'Angelo: 66–67

Pope: death and succession, 223; seeing the, 212–213. *See also specific popes*

Porta del Popolo: 72

Porta Marina (Pompeii): 484

Porta Nolana Open-Air Fish Market (Naples): 477

Porta Portese flea market: 408

Porta Romana (Ostia Antica): 432–433

Porta San Pancrazio: 96

Porta San Paolo: 98–99

Porta San Paolo Station: 420, 429

Porta San Sebastiano: 342

Portico d'Ottavia: 207

Post offices: 99, 544–545; Vatican City, 212

Presepe: 472

Primo piatto: 366, 525. *See also* Eating

Priscilla, Catacombs of: 77–78, 334, 392

Produce markets: *See* Markets

Protestant Cemetery: 99–100

Public transportation: *See* Transportation

Pubs: *See* Bars and cafés

Puppet shows: 395

Pyramid of Gaius Cestius: 98, 394

Q

Quirinale Gardens: 88

Quirinale Hill: 88–89

Quirinale Palace: 88–89

R

Rail passes: 545, 550–551, 555–556

Rail travel: *See* Train travel

Raimondo de Sangro: 475–476

Rape of Proserpina (Bernini): 277

Raphael: 130; biographical sketch, 254; Borghese Gallery, 283–284; Chigi Chapel, 73–74, 414; Vatican Museums, 252–257, 268; Villa Farnesina, 93–94

Raphael Rooms (Vatican Museums): 252–257; map, 253

Reader feedback: 9

Religious souvenirs, shopping for: 407–408

Remus: 166–167, 184–185, 190, 495–496

Renaissance: 498, 500; art at Vatican Museums, 251–257. *See also specific artists and artworks*

Rental apartments: 518–520

Republican Warehouses (Ostia Antica): 433

Resources from Rick Steves: 555–557

Restaurants: *See* Eating

Rest on the Flight to Egypt (Caravaggio): 60

Rickshaws: 67

Roman cuisine: 366–367, 524–525, 530–535

Roman Forum: 38, 157–173; guided tours, 158; map, 161; orientation, 38, 46, 157–159; shopping near, 401, 404; tourist information, 158; walking tour, 159–173

Roman Holiday (movie): 40, 416, 563

Roman numerals: 564–565

Roma Pass: 17, 42–43

Rome, ancient: *See* Ancient Rome

Rome Auditorium: 70, 410–411

Rome from the Sky Elevator: 6, 50

Rome vs. Milan: 56–57

Romulus: 166–167, 184–185, 190, 495–496; Huts of, 184–185

Room and board: *See* Eating; Sleeping

Room of the Perspectives (Villa Farnesina): 94

Rosticcerie: 364, 528, 530

Rostrum: 170–171

Royal family, Italian: 131

Royal Palace (Naples): 469–470

S

Sacred and Profane Love (Titian): 285

Safety concerns: 18–20; Naples, 454–455

St. Catherine Chapel (San Clemente): 315–316

St. Jerome (da Vinci): 268–269

St. Paul's Outside the Walls: 102–104

St. Paul's Within the Walls: 411

St. Peter-in-Chains Church: 58, 196–200; orientation, 47, 58, 196–197; self-guided tour, 197–200

St. Peter's Basilica: 62, 211–235; background of, 215–217; church services, 214; climbing the dome, 215, 234, 393; dress code, 62, 214; guided tours, 214–215; maps, 216, 221; orientation, 46, 62, 211, 214–215; self-guided tour, 220–234

St. Peter's Square: 217–219; map, 218

St. Restituta Chapel (Naples): 476

St. Teresa in Ecstasy (Bernini): 84–85

St. Zeno Chapel (Santa Prassede): 310

Salumi: 533

San Bernardo Church: 86

San Callisto, Catacombs of: 109, 334, 339

San Carlo alle Quattro Fontane Church: 87–88

San Clemente Church: 91, 303, 314–318

San Crisogono Basilica: 327

San Francesco di Paola Church (Naples): 469

San Gennaro Chapel (Naples): 476

San Giovanni in Laterano: 47, 89–90, 310–314; map, 311

San Gregorio: *See* Santa Maria della Pietà

San Ignazio Church: *See* Sant'Ignazio Church

San Luigi dei Francesi Church: 59, 117, 132–134

San Martino (Naples): 457, 469

San Paolo Fuori le Mura: 102–104

San Pietro Basilica: *See* St. Peter's Basilica

San Pietro in Montorio Church: 95

San Pietro in Vincoli: *See* St. Peter-in-Chains Church

San Sebastiano, Catacombs of: 108–109, 334, 338

Santa Cecilia Church: 324–326

Santa Chiara Church (Naples): 471, 475

Sant'Agnese Church: 116–117

Santa Maria degli Angeli Church: 79–80

Santa Maria della Immacolata Concezione Church: 70–71

Santa Maria della Pietà: 205

Santa Maria della Vittoria Church: 84–85

Santa Maria del Popolo Church: 73–74, 414

Santa Maria in Aquiro Church: 119

Santa Maria in Aracoeli Church: 44–45

Santa Maria in Cosmedin Church: 40, 394

Santa Maria in Trastevere Church: 92, 328–331

Santa Maria Maggiore Church: 91, 303–308; map, 305

Santa Maria sopra Minerva Church: 59, 138–140

Sant'Andrea al Quirinale Church: 88

Santa Prassede Church: 309–310

Santa Susanna Church: 85, 86

Sant'Ignazio Church: 59, 118, 140–141, 393

Scala Santa (Holy Stairs): 89–90, 314

School of Athens (Raphael): 255–256

Scuderie del Quirinale: 89, 412

Seasonal produce: 531

Seasons: 7

Secondo piatto: 366, 525. *See also* Eating

Secret Room (Naples): 462–463

Self-guided tours: *See* Walking tours

Senate House: *See* Curia

Septimius Severus: 298; Arch of, 171–172

Sfogliatella: 469, 470

Shelley, Percy Bysshe: 99, 100

Shopping: 398–409; budgeting, 6–7; clothing sizes, 565; hours, 398, 504; map, 402–403; Naples, 465, 467, 471, 473; neighborhoods, 398–407; VAT refunds, 509. *See also* Markets

Sienkiewicz, Henryk: 339

Sightseeing (sights): 34–342; at a glance, 46–47; best viewpoints, 6; budgeting, 6; with children, 390–395; daily reminder, 17; free Sundays, 35; general tips and hours, 17, 43, 510–512; itineraries, 12, 14–16; maps and navigation tools, 510; Naples, 458–477; at night, 412; Ostia Antica, 431–440; price hike alert, 34–35; Roma Pass, 17, 42–43; Tivoli, 443–447. *See also* Walking tours; *and specific sights*

Silver shops, in Naples: 473

SIM cards: 542–543

Sinking Boat Fountain: 124

Sistine Chapel (Vatican): 257–267; maps, 258, 259, 260–261; reservations, 236

Sixtus IV, Pope: 233

Sixtus V, Pope: 85, 86, 89, 301; tomb, 308

Sketching Rome Tours: 32

Sleep code: 344, 514

Sleeping: 343–361, 513–521; air-conditioning, 516; near ancient Rome, 350–351; budgeting, 5–6; online reviews, 520; Pantheon neighborhood, 352–358; rates and deals, 513–514; reservations, 7, 343–344, 515; near Spanish Steps, 357–358; near Termini Station, 344–350; Trastevere, 358–360; types of accommodations, 514–521; near Vatican City, 360–361

Smartphones: 8–9, 539–543

Soccer: 328–329, 406, 472

Socrates: 292

Sora Margherita: 209, 368

South Rome: 12; maps, 97, 103; sights, 96–109. *See also* Testaccio

Spaccanapoli (Naples): 467, 471–472

Spanish Quarter (Naples): 468–469

Spanish Steps: 74, 123–124, 416; eating near, 377–378; nightlife near, 413; sleeping near, 357–358

Spanish Synagogue: 207

Special events: 560

Stadium (Imperial Palace): 178

Stairs: at Capitoline Hill, 40–41, 44. *See also* Holy Stairs; Spanish Steps

Steves, Andy: 33

Students, weekend tour packages: 33

Subway: *See* Metro

Supermarkets: 345, 353, 364, 376, 529; Eataly, 387–388

Swiss Guards: 213, 219

Synagogues: 61–62, 206–207, 324

T

Tabularium (Capitoline Museums): 193

Tavola calda: 387, 479, 523, 528

Taxes, VAT refunds: 509

Taxis: 28–29; to/from airports, 422–423; Naples, 451, 457; tipping, 508; Tivoli, 442

Teatro dell'Opera: 411

Teatro di Marcello: 207

Teatro di San Carlo (Naples): 470

Telephone numbers, useful: 559

Telephones: 539–544

Temperatures, average monthly: 566

Tempietto: 95

Tempio del Divo Giulio: 167–168

Temple of Antoninus Pius and Faustina: 164

Temple of Castor and Pollux: 166

Temple of Isis (Pompeii): 492–493

Temple of Julius Caesar: 167–168

Temple of Jupiter (Pompeii): 486

Temple of Jupiter (Rome): 192–193

Temple of Mithras: 317–318

Temple of Saturn: 172

Temple of Venus and Rome: 154–155

Temple of Vesta: 165

Terme del Foro (Ostia Antica): 439

Terme del Foro (Pompeii): 488–489

Terme di Caracalla: 107–108, 342

Terme di Diocleziano: *See* Baths of Diocletian

Terme di Nettuno (Ostia Antica): 434

Termini Train Station: 417–419; eating near, 382–383; maps, 80–81, 346–347, 384–385; nightlife near, 413; pharmacy, 20, 418; services, 418–419; shopping, 407; sights near, 78–91; sleeping near, 344–350; tourist information, 16

Testaccio: 12, 96–101; eating, 386–388; map, 97; markets, 101, 386, 409; nightlife, 413–414; sights, 98–101

Testaccio Market: 101, 386, 409

Testaccio Village: 101, 413

Theater (Ostia Antica), 434–435; (Pompeii), 493

"Theater of the Universe" (Borghese Gallery): 278–279

Theft alerts: 18–19, 504; hotel rooms, 517–518; Naples, 454–455; train travel, 554

Throne Room (Imperial Palace): 181–182

Tiberius: 76, 184, 290, 291, 300; Palace of, 166

Tiber River: 11, 66, 97, 320–321

Tiburtina Bus Station: 420–421

Tiburtina Train Station: 417, 419–420

Time zones: 504

Tipping: 508–509, 523–524

Titian: 285

Titus, Arch of (Arco di Tito): 159–162

Tivoli: 441–448; map, 444; transportation, 427–428

Tomb of Cecilia Metella: 336–337

Tomb of the Unknown Soldier: 48–49

Toro Farnese: 460–461

Tour guides: 8, 30; Colosseum, 145; Jewish Ghetto, 202; Naples, 457; Pompeii, 481–482; tipping, 508–509

Tourist information: 16, 503–504; Naples, 451; Pompeii, 480–481; Tivoli, 443

Tours: 30–33; Borghese Gallery, 272; Colosseum, 144–145; Jewish Ghetto, 30, 202; Naples, 457–458; Palatine Hill, 175; Pompeii, 481; Rick Steves, 556; Roman Forum, 158; St. Peter's Basilica, 214–215; Tivoli, 442; Vatican Museums, 238. *See also* Walking tours

Traffic safety: 20; Naples, 455

Train stations: 417–420. *See also* Termini Train Station

Train travel: 417–420, 428, 545–554; to/from airports, 421–422; budgeting, 5; Circumvesuviana, 454, 480; general tips, 553–554; maps, 547, 553; Naples, 451, 454; Ostia Antica, 429–430; overnight train, 7–8; Pompeii, 480; schedules, 545–546, 548; tickets, 546, 549–553

Trajan: 50–53, 152, 181, 295

Trajan's Column: 46, 50–52; eating, 380

Trajan's Forum: 46, 52; map, 51

Trajan's Market: 46, 52–53

TramJazz: 412

Transfiguration, The (Raphael): 268

Transportation: 21–30, 417–425, 545–555; to/from airports, 421–423; budgeting, 5; with children, 392; journey planners, 21; maps, 24–25, 547; Naples, 451, 454, 455–457; Ostia Antica, 429–430; Pompeii, 480; tickets, 21–22; Tivoli, 442–443. *See also* Buses; Car travel; Metro; Taxis; Train travel

Trastevere: 12, 91–92, 319–331; bookstore, 18; eating, 365, 368; maps, 322–323, 356–357; nightlife, 413; sleeping, 358–360; tourist information, 16; transportation, 26, 319–320, 358–359; walking tour, 320–331

Travel agencies: 18

Travel insurance: 7

Travel smarts: 4–5

Travel tips: 504–505

Treasury Museum (St. Peter's Square): 233

Tre Scalini: 117, 395

Trevi Fountain: 47, 61, 121–122, 395; eating near, 374

Trionfale market: 386, 409

Trip costs: 5–7

TV shows, recommended: 563

U

Umberto I: 130

UPIM: 407

V

Vatican City: 11, 62–63, 212–213; dress code, 62, 214, 512; eating near, 383–386; guided tours, 30–32; maps, 64–65, 358–359; post office, 212; seeing the pope, 212–213; shopping, 407–408; sleeping near, 360–361; tourist information, 62; walking tours, 211–270. *See also* St. Peter's Basilica; St. Peter's Square; Vatican Museums

Vatican Gardens: 212

Vatican Museums: 63, 235–270; with children, 393; eating, 238–239; guided tours, 238; maps, 239, 240, 242, 249, 253; orientation, 46, 63, 235–239; reservations, 236; self-guided tour, 239–270; Sistine Chapel, 257–267

Vatican Pinacoteca: 267–270; map, 269

VAT refunds: 509

Vespasian: 50, 293, 294

Vestal Virgins: 149, 165; House of the, 165

Vesuvius: 480, 487, 489

Via Abbondanza (Pompeii): 488

Via Appia Antica: *See* Appian Way

Via Baccina: shopping, 405

Via Balbo, market: 409

Via Caio Cestio: 99

Via Candia, eating: 385–386

Via Casa di Diana (Ostia Antica): 437–438

Via Cavour: 54, 57

Via Cola di Rienzo, shopping: 399

Via Condotti: 124, 406, 416

Via de' Funari: 209

Via dei Banchi, shopping: 400

Via dei Baullari: 115

Via dei Coronari, shopping: 399–400

Via dei Fori Imperiali: 48, 50, 52, 54, 55

Via dei Genovesi: 324, 326–327

Via dei Salumi: 323–324

Via dei Serpenti, shopping: 404

Via dei Tribunali (Naples), eating: 478–479

Via del Babuino, shopping: 405

Via del Boschetto, shopping: 401, 404

Via del Corso: 120–121, 414, 416; nightlife, 413, 416; shopping, 405–406

Via del Governo Vecchio, shopping: 400

Via del Greci, shopping: 406

Via della Croce: eating, 378, 390; shopping, 406

Via della Lungaretta: 327

Via della Madonna dei Monti, shopping: 405

Via della Pace, market: 409

Via dell'Arco de' Tolomei: 321–322

Via della Reginella: 208; shopping near, 401

Via della Stamperia: 122

Via delle Carrozze, shopping: 406

Via delle Muratte: 119

Via delle Quattro Fontane: 86–87

Via del Nazareno: 122–123

Via del Portico d'Ottavia: 208–210; eating, 369; shopping near, 401

Via del Quirinale: 88

Via del Salvatore: 117

Via del Tempio: 205

Via di Gesù e Maria, shopping: 406

Via di Panico, shopping: 400

Via di Pasquino: 115

Via di Propaganda: 123

Via di San Giacomo, shopping: 406

Via di Santa Maria del Pianto, eating: 369

Via di Sant'Ambrogio: 208

Via Firenze, eating: 383

Via Flavia, eating: 382–383

Via Fontanella, shopping: 405

Via Forcella (Naples): 473

Via Giubbonari, shopping near: 401

Via Giulia, shopping: 400

Via Laurina, shopping: 405–406

Viale di Trastevere: 327

Viale Giulio Cesare, eating: 385–386

Via Leonina, shopping: 404

Via Margutta, shopping: 406–407

Via Mario de' Fiori, shopping: 406

Via Monserrato, shopping: 400

Via Nazionale, shopping: 399, 401

Via Orfani: 118, 119

Via Panisperna, shopping: 404

Via Pignasecca Market (Naples): 467

Via Sacra: 159, 162, 163–164

Via Sannio market: 310, 408

Via Toledo (Naples): 466

Via Urbana, shopping: 404–405

Via Veneto: 70

Via Vicaria Vecchia (Naples): 473

Via Vittoria, shopping: 406

Via XX Settembre: 85–89
Vicolo dell'Atleta: 324
Victor Emmanuel II: 467, 470, 500; tomb, 130
Victor Emmanuel Monument: 47, 48–50
Viewpoints, best: 6
Villa Borghese Gardens: 67, 395
Villa d'Este (Tivoli): 443–445
Villa di Livia frescoes: 299
Villa Farnesina: 92–95, 299, 331
Villa Giulia: 68–69
Villa Gregoriana Park (Tivoli): 447
Visitor information: *See* Tourist information

W

Walking tours: guided, 30, 31–32, 457; Appian Way, 332–342; Borghese Gallery, 271–285; Capitoline Museums, 186–195; Colosseum, 142–156; Dolce Vita stroll, 47, 74, 414–416; heart of Rome, 110–124; Imperial Forums, 50–54; Jewish Ghetto, 201–210; Naples, 464–474; National Museum of Rome, 286–300; Ostia Antica, 431–440; Palatine Hill, 174–185; Pantheon neighborhood, 125–141; Pilgrim's Rome, 301–318; Pompeii, 484–494; Roman Forum, 157–173; St. Peter-in-Chains Church, 196–200; St. Peter's Basilica, 211–235; Trastevere, 319–331; Vatican Museums, 235–270
Water parks: 396–397
Weather: 7, 566
Weekend Student Adventures (WSA Europe): 33
Wi-Fi: 17, 517, 539, 542
Wine: 367, 375, 537–539; labels and lingo, 538; resources and school, 375
Wine bars *(enoteche)*: 412–414, 528; ancient Rome, 380, 381, 412, 413; North Rome, 378, 413; Pantheon neighborhood, 369–370, 375; near Termini Station, 383, 413
World War II: 207, 501; Fosse Ardeatine, 501; Museum of the Liberation of Rome, 90–91, 314

Z

Zeno, Saint: 310
Zoo: 395

MAP INDEX

Color Maps
West Rome: IV
East Rome: VII
South Rome: VIII
Italy: X

Introduction
Map Legend: 2

Orientation to Rome
Overview of Maps: 13
Rome's Neighborhoods: 14
Greater Rome: 15
Rome's Public Transportation: 24

Sights in Rome
Rome: 36
Ancient Rome: 39
Capitoline Hill & Piazza
     Venezia: 41
The Imperial Forums: 51
Pantheon Neighborhood: 59
Vatican City & Nearby: 64
North Rome: 68
Baths of Diocletian: 79
Near Termini Station: 80
Pilgrim's Rome: 90
Testaccio: 97
South of Testaccio: 103
E.U.R.: 105

Heart of Rome Walk
Heart of Rome Walk: 112

Pantheon Tour
Pantheon Cross-Section: 128
Pantheon: 129
Churches near the Pantheon: 132
Gesù Church: 135

Colosseum Tour
Colosseum: 146
Modern Amenities in the Ancient
     World: 153

Roman Forum Tour
Roman Forum: 161
The Roman Empire at Its Peak: Pax
     Romana A.D. 120: 163

Palatine Hill Tour
Palatine Hill: 177

Capitoline Museums Tour
Capitoline Museums Overview: 188

Jewish Ghetto Walk
Jewish Ghetto Walk: 203

St. Peter's Basilica Tour
Old & New St. Peter's: 216
St. Peter's Square: 218
St. Peter's Basilica: 221

Vatican Museums Tour
Vatican Museums Schematic: 239
Vatican Museums Overview: 240
The Ancient World: 242
The Long March: 249
Raphael Rooms: 253
Sistine Chapel: 258
The Sistine Schematic: 259
The Sistine Ceiling: 260
The Last Judgement: 265
Pinacoteca: 269

Borghese Gallery Tour
Borghese Gallery—
     Ground Floor: 275
Borghese Gallery—Pinacoteca: 282

National Museum of Rome
National Museum—
     Ground Floor: 288
National Museum—First Floor: 294

Pilgrim's Rome Tour
Pilgrim's Rome: 302
Santa Maria Maggiore: 305
San Giovanni in Laterano: 311

Trastevere Walk
Trastevere Walk: 323

Ancient Appian Way Tour
Ancient Appian Way: 337

Sleeping in Rome
Hotels near Termini Station: 346
Hotels & Restaurants near Ancient
  Rome: 352
Hotels in the Pantheon
  Neighborhood: 354
Hotels & Restaurants
  in Trastevere: 357
Hotels and Restaurants
  near Vatican City: 358

Eating in Rome
Restaurants in the Pantheon
  Neighborhood: 370
Restaurants near Termini Station:
  384

Shopping in Rome
Shopping in Rome: 402

Nightlife in Rome
Dolce Vita Stroll: 415

Day Trips
Day Trips from Rome: 427

Ostia Antica
Ostia Antica: 431

Tivoli
Tivoli Area: 444

Naples & Pompeii
Naples: 452
Naples Transportation: 456
Pompeii & Nearby: 481
Pompeii: 482
Pompeii Tour: 485

Practicalities
Italy's Public Transportation: 547
Train Costs in Italy: 553

Our website enhances this book and turns

Explore Europe

At ricksteves.com you can browse through thousands of articles, videos, photos and radio interviews, plus find a wealth of money-saving travel tips for planning your dream trip. And with our mobile-friendly website, you can easily access all this great travel information anywhere you go.

TV Shows

Preview the places you'll visit by watching entire half-hour episodes of Rick Steves' Europe (choose from all 100 shows) on-demand, for free.

ricksteves.com

your travel dreams into affordable reality

Radio Interviews

Enjoy ready access to Rick's vast library of radio interviews covering travel

tips and cultural insights that relate specifically to your Europe travel plans.

Travel Forums

Learn, ask, share! Our online community of savvy travelers is a great resource

for first-time travelers to Europe, as well as seasoned pros. You'll find forums on each country, plus travel tips and restaurant/hotel reviews. You can even ask one of our well-traveled staff to chime in with an opinion.

Travel News

Subscribe to our free Travel News e-newsletter, and get monthly updates from Rick on what's happening in Europe.

Audio Europe™

Rick's Free Travel App

Get your FREE **Rick Steves Audio Europe**™ app to enjoy…

- Dozens of self-guided tours of Europe's top museums, sights and historic walks
- Hundreds of tracks filled with cultural insights and sightseeing tips from Rick's radio interviews
- All organized into handy geographic playlists
- For iPhone, iPad, iPod Touch, Android

With Rick whispering in your ear, Europe gets even better.

Find out more at ricksteves.com

Pack Light and Right

Gear up for your next adventure at ricksteves.com

Light Luggage

Pack light and right with Rick Steves' affordable, custom-designed rolling carry-on bags, backpacks, day packs and shoulder bags.

Accessories

From packing cubes to moneybelts and beyond, Rick has personally selected the travel goodies that will help your trip go smoother.

Shop at ricksteves.com

Experience maximum Europe

Save time and energy

This guidebook is your independent-travel toolkit. But for all it delivers, it's still up to you to devote the time and energy it takes to manage the preparation and logistics that are essential for a happy trip. If that's a hassle, there's a solution.

Rick Steves Tours

A Rick Steves tour takes you to Europe's most interesting places with great

great tours, too!

with minimum stress

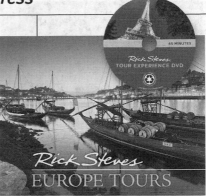

guides and small groups of 28 or less. We follow Rick's favorite itineraries, ride in comfy buses, stay in family-run hotels, and bring you intimately close to the Europe you've traveled so far to see. Most importantly, we take away the logistical headaches so you can focus on the fun.

Join the fun

This year we'll take 18,000 free-spirited travelers— nearly half of them repeat customers—along with us on 40 different itineraries, from Ireland to Italy to Istanbul. Is a Rick Steves tour the right fit for your travel dreams? Find out at ricksteves.com, where you can also get Rick's latest tour catalog and free Tour Experience DVD.

Europe is best experienced with happy travel partners. We hope you can join us.

See our itineraries at ricksteves.com

A Guide for Every Trip

BEST OF GUIDES

Full color easy-to-scan format, focusing on Europe's most popular destinations and sights.

Best of France
Best of Germany
Best of England
Best of Europe
Best of Ireland
Best of Italy
Best of Spain

COMPREHENSIVE GUIDES

City, country, and regional guides with detailed coverage for a multi-week trip exploring the most iconic sights and venturing off the beaten track.

Amsterdam & the Netherlands
Barcelona
Belgium: Bruges, Brussels, Antwerp & Ghent
Berlin
Budapest
Croatia & Slovenia
Eastern Europe
England
Florence & Tuscany
France
Germany
Great Britain
Greece: Athens & the Peloponnese
Iceland
Ireland
Istanbul
Italy
London
Paris
Portugal
Prague & the Czech Republic
Provence & the French Riviera
Rome
Scandinavia
Scotland
Spain
Switzerland
Venice
Vienna, Salzburg & Tirol

THE BEST OF ROME

me, Italy's capital, is studded with
nan remnants and floodlit-fountain
res. From the Vatican to the Colos-
, with crazy traffic in between, Rome
nderful, huge, and exhausting. The
ds, the heat, and the weighty history

of the Eternal City where Caesars walked
can make tourists wilt. Recharge by taking siestas, gelato breaks, and after-dark
wafts, strolling from one atmospheric
square to another in the refreshing evening air.

ed *Pantheon*--which
st dome until the
ly 2,000 years old
y over 1,500).

of Athens in the *Vat-*
dies the humanistic
ce.

ladiators fought
nother, entertaining

Rome *ristorante.*
ds at St. Peter's
seriously.

, toss in

Rick Steves guidebooks are published by Avalon Travel,
an imprint of Perseus Books, a Hachette Book Group company.

POCKET GUIDES

*Compact, full color city guides with
the essentials for shorter trips.*

Amsterdam	Paris
Athens	Prague
Barcelona	Rome
Florence	Venice
Italy's Cinque Terre	Vienna
London	
Munich & Salzburg	

SNAPSHOT GUIDES

Focused single-destination coverage.

Basque Country: Spain & France
Copenhagen & the Best of Denmark
Dublin
Dubrovnik
Edinburgh
Hill Towns of Central Italy
Krakow, Warsaw & Gdansk
Lisbon
Loire Valley
Madrid & Toledo
Milan & the Italian Lakes District
Naples & the Amalfi Coast
Northern Ireland
Normandy
Norway
Reykjavik
Sevilla, Granada & Southern Spain
St. Petersburg, Helsinki & Tallinn
Stockholm

CRUISE PORTS GUIDES

Reference for cruise ports of call.

Mediterranean Cruise Ports
Northern European Cruise Ports

Complete your library with...

TRAVEL SKILLS & CULTURE

*Study up on travel skills and gain
insight on history and culture.*

Europe 101
European Christmas
European Easter
European Festivals
Europe Through the Back Door
Postcards from Europe
Travel as a Political Act

PHRASE BOOKS & DICTIONARIES

French
French, Italian & German
German
Italian
Portuguese
Spanish

PLANNING MAPS

Britain, Ireland & London
Europe
France & Paris
Germany, Austria & Switzerland
Ireland
Italy
Spain & Portugal

Credits

RESEARCHER

To help update this book, Rick relied on...

IAN WATSON

Ian has worked with Rick's guidebooks since 1993, after starting out with Let's Go and Frommer's guides. Originally from upstate New York, Ian speaks several European languages, including Italian, and lives with his family in Germany.

Avalon Travel
An imprint of Perseus Books
A Hachette Book Group company
1700 Fourth Street
Berkeley, CA 94710, U.S.A.

Printed in Canada by Friesens
Third printing August 2017

ISBN 978-1-63121-449-3
ISSN 1527-4780
For the latest on Rick's lectures, guidebooks, tours, public radio show, and public television series, contact Rick Steves' Europe, Inc., 130 Fourth Avenue North, Edmonds, WA 98020, 425/771-8303, www.ricksteves.com, rick@ricksteves.com.

Rick Steves' Europe

Managing Editor: Jennifer Madison Davis
Special Publications Manager: Risa Laib
Editors: Glenn Eriksen, Tom Griffin, Katherine Gustafson, Suzanne Kotz, Cathy Lu, John Pierce, Carrie Shepherd
Editorial & Production Assistant: Jessica Shaw
Editorial Intern: Megan Simms
Researcher: Ian Watson
Graphic Content Director: Sandra Hundacker
Maps & Graphics: David C. Hoerlein, Lauren Mills, Mary Rostad

Avalon Travel

Senior Editor and Series Manager: Madhu Prasher
Editor: Jamie Andrade
Associate Editor: Sierra Machado
Copy Editor: Patrick Collins
Proofreader: Suzie Nasol
Indexer: Stephen Callahan
Production & Typesetting: Rue Flaherty
Cover Design: Kimberly Glyder Design
Maps & Graphics: Lohnes and Wright, Kat Bennett, Mike Morgenfeld

More for your trip!
Maximize the experience with Rick Steves as your guide

Guidebooks
Florence, Venice, and Italy guides make side-trips smooth and affordable

Phrase Books
Rely on Rick's Italian Phrase Book & Dictionary

Rick's TV Shows
Preview where you're going with 18 shows on Italy

Free! Rick's Audio Europe™ App
Get free audio tours for Rome's top sights

Small Group Tours
Rick offers several great itineraries through Italy

For all the details, visit ricksteves.com